D1707624

We dedicate this book to the musicians, both the living and the dead, no matter from whence they came; for their perseverance and devotion to the making of good, *puro, musica Afro-Cubana.*

This is a very special book and I could never have accomplished it without the love, patience and support from my wife Linda, and always and above to my sons Joey, Jr., Eric and Vincent LoBianco. I also want to thank my co-writer's wife Mildred Perez for her insight and patience.

In addition, David and I could not have reached this landmark event without thanking an amazing friend, Robert Sancho. A Special thanks to Pete Hamill, Joe Madera and New York Supreme Court Justice Edwin Torres, and to my beloved friend of many years Margie Puente.

Joe Conzo

MAMBO DIABLO

My Journey With TITO PUENTE

JOE CONZO

With

DAVID A. PÉREZ

An Imprint of Hal Leonard Corporation

Backbeat Books
An Imprint of Hal Leonard Corporation
7777 West Bluemound Road
Milwaukee, WI 53213

Trade Book Division Editorial Offices
33 Plymouth St., Montclair, NJ 07042

Published by Backbeat Books in 2012

Originally published by Author House™ in 2011

Printed in the United States of America

Book design by Author House™

Library of Congress Cataloging-in-Publication Data is available upon request.

ISBN 978-1-61713-029-8

www.backbeatbooks.com

Moved by the clave
La Mancha sings through your rhythms
Branding your sound with the language of
Our ancestors
Dancing with darkness
Even in the light
"Afro-Cuban music is what I play"
And we are both instrument
And audience
Giving and taking
A collection of Souls
For our *Diablo*

Rachel Kara Pérez
(Singer/actor; Tito Puente Scholarship Fund recipient, 1994-2000)

Contents

Foreword

Pete Hamill on Tito Puente

One evening in the mid-1960s, I climbed the stairs of the Palladium on Broadway and entered the greatest dance hall in New York. The place was packed, the floor trembling with dancing, the music filling the vast room. I was a kid then, fresh out of the U.S. Navy, and had no clear notion of what I wanted to do with my life. But I was starting to seek out what I loved. One thing I loved was Latin music.

I heard the music before I ever saw the bands. The entrance to the sound was a disk jockey named Symphony Sid, who started his radio show at midnight on WEVD, and kept going until 3 a.m. He gave us the latest in modern jazz, Bird and Max and Dizzy, Monk and Miles. But Sid started adding Latin music to his usual menu. I used to listen to Sid before I went off to the Navy. When I returned, he was playing more Latin jazz.

And so I walked into the Palladium, where the guys were all dressed a lot better than I was, and the women were the most beautiful I had ever seen. I was too frozen to ask any of the women to dance. I was sure I would look like another disjointed gringo, an occasion of laughter or pity. But I stayed for hours that night, as three separate bands alternated on the stage of the Palladium.

Machito and his Afro-Cubans.

Tito Rodríguez.

Tito Puente.

On the same night.

I was drawn most of all to Tito Puente. The word salsa was not yet invented to describe this music. But it was clear that, in their different ways, all three bands were creating a music that was charged with sound of cities. That is, the sound of what American cities were becoming after World War II, when the great Puerto Rican migration was gathering strength. Tito Puente was a product of New York City, of East Harlem, of the U.S. Navy, of Juilliard. He was listening to the new music coming up from Cuba, mambo, cha cha, but he was listening with the musical mind of a born New Yorker. His arrangements were full of power *and* subtlety, of celebration *and* defiance of hard times. His work on timbales sparkled and surprised, at once drove the music and embellished it. Above all, he provided an emotion that was desperately needed by his primarily poor Puerto Rican fans in that difficult era: he gave them joy.

The music seemed to say: *Mira,* we are *here,* 'mano. This is *our* town, too. We have our piece of New York, earned through sweat and sacrifice. We ain't going *no*where. And, hey what's the name of that guapa in the red dress? *Oye, como va*?

Joe Conzo and David A. Pérez tell the full story of Tito Puente and his times in this rich, invaluable book. On one level, it's a story about the evolution of American music. But it's also about the gathering strength of the Latino presence as part of the larger American alloy. Specifically the New York alloy. At the same time Conzo and Pérez tell the story of an extraordinary individual.

It was my good fortune, several decades after my first visit to the Palladium, to know Tito Puente. He was usually a joy to be with, smart, restless, full of that special New York laughter based on absurdity. He was also complicated. He was open about many things (as this book shows). At the same time, there were places where even a friend could not go. For those of us who once shared his company, Tito is gone, but not forgotten. The music will live forever.

New York. 2010

Acknowledgments

I have wanted to write a book about my very best friend Tito Puente, ever since he passed away on May 31, 2000. Dozens of books have been written about him over the years. This one is a little different. I try to focus on Tito as a person, as a musician and as my friend. One of my goals is to clear up some of those stories that have been inflated with each retelling. My intention is to present a realistic picture of a grand performer, composer, arranger, instrumentalist, a great artist who was a dear friend and mentor to me. I just want to say that there are many people who encouraged me to write this book and they know who they are. I thank you all for your support. Some of you, I am sure, will make it a point to let me know that I did not include information that you deem crucial or important to the life of my friend. Some of you may even criticize me for not mentioning your name. For any omission you think I made, I offer my humble apologies. This book is about Tito Puente. I hope you enjoy it.

"Afro-Cuban music is what I play," Tito frequently told me in an energized and exasperated pitch. "This 'salsa' shit is nothing." One of his last tirades on the word salsa happened when we were in Puerto Rico. A lifelong dream to perform with the Puerto Rican Symphony Orchestra was about to be realized. Tito was excited. He was pacing. I'm sure the nervousness was what brought on his outburst. Nevertheless, he insisted, "Don't forget that, Joe – Afro-Cuban music is what I play," I nodded in agreement. I looked at my best friend, smiled and told him: "Don't worry Pops, when we get back to New York we'll start writing down all of this history." He smiled. It was time for him to go on stage.

"Yeah! Joe, you put all this history on the record. There is so much history," he said. "So much that needs to be told, and things that need to be cleared up. Yeah! Joe, just get it right," he sighed as he approached the concert hall stage. His swagger intensified. He laughed. "Here we go." The applause was loud and clear. They loved him. Tito gleamed.

The Tito Puente I knew was consumed by his music. This was the most important thing in his life. He was a tense and energetic person. He was forgetful about things he considered unimportant. His personal life, outside of the world of music, was, to use his words "a chaos and tangled." He was a perfectionist when it came to making music and he had an ego that was unbelievable. When it came to making business decisions they were usually based on impulse. He was the first to admit that he was a terrible businessman. He did not like to tell people "no," which I think is one of the reasons he kept to himself. Maintaining his band took up most of his time from the moment he struck out on his own in 1949. He shared this task with his close friend and partner Jimmy Frisaura. Jimmy kept the books, the schedules, did the payroll and handled all the administrative duties, in addition to playing a solid horn. Jimmy and I became close, and I have him to thank for the history about the orchestra during the 1950s. Jimmy's memories helped to fill in many gaps of missing information.

Pops, as I called him in later years, was generous, giving, caring and thoughtful about things around him. With his family affairs, it was the opposite. While he provided all the basic necessities for his family, he failed miserably as a family man. The word "family," and "love" was not something he knew how to handle. Late night performances, rehearsals, and travel were his reasons for not being a more involved parent. Sometimes, he acted uneven when confronted with tough decisions. Other times he just turned his back on them and hoped that the problems would go away. Tito liked to laugh, joke and kid around. He could be one hell of a prankster. He could tell a tale, man, could he make up stories!

When he was asked questions about his life and career – depending on whom he was talking to – he would just make up random stories. Whatever he thought the listener or interviewer wanted to hear is what he would tell them. This is why there are so many conflicting accounts of his life. He loved to tell whoppers. Tito could look you straight in the eye and tell you one thing about his childhood and in the same breath turn to another person and relay the same event but with a different set of facts. It was his way of being funny and even mischievous, I guess. He was most comfortable in his environment – the world of music, the world of entertainment. Tito was driven, obsessed. He wanted to be better than others. He was happiest in the limelight. When his orchestra played great he smiled. However, he was intolerant of any miscue in a performance, and he would not hide the fact that he was irritated. He was unforgiving in this respect. Everyone knew a musician was going to get a verbal flogging if there was a goof or a bad note. This was Tito's way.

There were difficulties in his life. When the era of the big bands began to fade he was unsure how he would proceed in order to maintain his popularity, keep his orchestra working, and counter the new hybrid sounds of Afro-Cuban music. To Tito it was always about Afro-Cuban music. His romantic interludes are legendary but rarely talked about. He drank too much and used cocaine when it was the preferred illegal substance of the rich and famous. There were always friends, fans, and musicians with a ready supply of the powder for his indulgence. In the early 1960s he focused on change and staying on top.

My friendship with him lasted over 39 years. We grew closer through the years and I think it was based mostly on mutual trust. Tito was 19 years older than me so I was like a kid brother, I guess. He had a brother who passed away at the age of four in a tragic accident when he fell from a fire escape. Tito did not live an exemplary life you could say, but who does? His music helped him overcome many of those shortcomings. He was a person of *"El Barrio."* He never forgot his roots. He was a New Yorker and he walked with that swagger and cockiness that is so recognizable to people from New York.

Tito's list of intimate and cherished friends was very short. Tito did not trust many people. His closest friends were Jimmy "Vincent" Frisaura and myself. Tito and Jimmy were like peas in a pod – they covered for each other. They were both womanizers. There were countless acquaintances, associates, and people who said they were his friends. However, Tito only referred to Mario Bauzá, Frank "Machito" Grillo, Charlie Palmieri, Joe Loco, Miguelito Valdés and Federico Pagani – as friends in his inner circle. Much of what is set down in this book is due in no small part to Jimmy Frisaura and Charlie Palmieri. Almost at the same time that I became friends with Tito, I got close to Jimmy and Charlie. Jimmy was a terrific trumpet player – part of what Tito called his "mob connected trumpet section." The core of his horns was Italian. Tito and Jimmy had been friends forever. Jimmy had more stories about Pops than one could imagine. When he wasn't playing, recording, paying bills or attending to band problems, more than likely Jimmy could be found at the racetrack. He loved the horses. "If he wasn't so big," Tito liked to brag, "Jimmy would be riding the horses."

Tito often described Charlie as "the scholar." He told me a lot about my friend that was key to this story. He was Tito's favorite piano player.

There have been countless articles written about Tito. Various writers have attempted to get into his head and explore his music. Josephine Powell, who worked with Tito on a number of projects and worked on his behalf to get a much-deserved Star on Hollywood's Walk of Fame in 1990, wrote a book that overflows with enthusiasm about Tito. The book, When the Drums are Dreaming, published in 2007, follows Tito's life from before his birth. It is full of anecdotes but only begins to tell the story of the man and his music. I suspect Tito was into his storytelling when Ms. Powell was interviewing him. For example, Tito never recorded or played Arsenio Rodríguez's *"Bruca Manigua,"* as he told her. However, she does give a West Coast perspective about Tito.

Mambo Kingdom, published in 2002, and written by musicologist Max Salazar (April 17, 1932- September 19, 2010), delves into the people who made it possible for the success of the mambo in New York. Here too is a lot of conflicting information. For example Mr. Salazar concludes that Tito and Willie Bobo did not get along. "Percussionist Willie Bobo also became Puente's antagonist; a rivalry had existed even before they were introduced," the book states. This is not true. Also, according to Salazar, in 1952 the friendship of Tito Rodríguez and Tito Puente "began to deteriorate because of the custom of top billing on marquees." They remained friends as long as both Titos were alive. My book will give you a different take on the friendship of the two bandleaders. On the other hand, Salazar's volume is important because it provides a wealth of information about the people who made the music.

Steven Loza wrote Tito Puente and the Making of Latin Music, published in 1999. The historical researcher and musician from the West Coast attempts to provide a chronology of Tito's musical compositions and examines many of his early works. Loza makes an effort to find out from Tito why Puerto Ricans embraced Afro-Cuban music in New York and how Tito Puente, Tito Rodríguez and Machito fit in. Tito is rather vague in the long interview. He usually avoided answering questions about subjects that were distasteful to him or that did not interest him. He did this by offering a lot of gibberish or as he would say: "I would talk a lot of shit!" Tito did not like "salsa." He was vehement about that. In fact, the masters (Tito's inner circle of friends), as I call them (See: Chapter 11, A Gathering of Masters) were not enamored with the word or the music genre either. When the subject was politics Tito avoided it like the plague. This was not something he enjoyed discussing.

I want to make this book about Tito just a little different. He was my friend; my very best friend and I think he would want me to tell people who he was – with no holds barred. He'd want me to tell it like it is.

My co-writer David A. Pérez is an author and writer by profession. He has spent much time and effort researching Afro-Cuban music. He has a passion for the Cuban charangas and the classical music history of the Caribbean and the United States – the habanera with all its relatives – danza, danzón, tango and American ragtime. For more hours than I care to remember, David kept me on the telephone probing my mind, tapping my thoughts to clarify a point or clear up an inconsistency, asking question after question. He was relentless and untiring in helping me bring this project to life. He researched and reviewed what had been written and documented about Tito. He questioned me on every aspect of the man, his music and his inclination for living. We spent hours, talking, listening to the music, studio recordings and countless live sessions that both David and I had collected over the years. Many of these unpublished sessions are masterpieces – like Tito taking a more than 10-minute piano solo, the Tito Puente Orchestra backing up Sammy Davis, Jr. and Billy Eckstine, and the combined bands of Tito and Machito live and in concert. There were hundreds of live sessions David and I reviewed, talked about and documented. The story evolves around the music Tito played. We interfaced the historical facts that were parallel to Tito's world. He lived in a turbulent world that was constantly changing. There was racism, world war, migration and social unrest. He lived and achieved success, although not without injury. Here is a picture of Tito growing up that goes back to when his parents arrived in New York– his environment, musical training and interests – right up to the time when we were in Puerto Rico in 2000. Tito told a lot of this to me. David helped me fill in the historical reference points. Tito left me a lot of information. He had a sense of history and always reminded me that if his story were to be told he wanted it told honestly and accurately.

David and I worked daily nearly two years, and for hours on end each day. David often called – at the strangest hours – to get me to clarify a particular incident, to have me scratch my head for a detail that Tito and I talked about when we were together. He made me search my records, my notes and my documents for anything that might be worthy. We spent long hours in the music room of his home in Highland Mills, just talking. There was always some kind of music in the background; I think it was designed to jar my memory. Tito was rather blunt. I recorded a lot of his statements on pieces of paper; so we set it down in a way that is more narrative, more personal and more intimate.

I also want to express my profound thanks for the invaluable work that Marcos F. Pérez (a.k.a. Sonny) did in reading the manuscript over and over as he filled in the historical gaps. He lived those early days at the Palladium. I am grateful to him for giving life to that crucial period in Tito's life. Sonny befriended Antonio Arcaño in Cuba, and was able to spend considerable time talking to the maestro. That information about the mambo and its development from the Cuban perspective has been invaluable.

The Pérez brothers were so supportive in helping me piece together this work. Sonny often sat at the piano, plucking out the notes that sprang from hundreds of recordings and live music sessions that I provided him with so he could help me to relate the essence of Tito's music. He learned to play percussion with Federico "Popi" Pagani in the early 1950s. David is an amateur flautist who learned how to play the Cuban flute – unadorned five key-six hole wooden flute – with his friend Joaquin Oliveros of Cuba. The brothers were cousins of Federico Pagani, and still maintain close family ties in Puerto Rico.

José Madera, Jr. was the musical director of the Tito Puente Orchestra for many years. His assistance was invaluable. He worked with Tito for nearly 30 years and was the musical director for a long stretch. His musical pedigree reaches back to when his father, José "Pin" Madera played saxophone in the Machito Orchestra. He also helped to fill in many gaps in Tito's life.

I want to thank my wife Linda for her patience. David and I sat down with Roberto Sancho, a long time music enthusiast and friend. Judge Edwin Torres provided important information about the Palladium Ballroom hey days. He was a dancer, and knew Tito. Tito listed Bob and the judge as among the few people he could always count on. Finally, heartfelt thanks go to Mildred Pérez, David's wife, who provided much of the proofreading and editing. A special thank you to "DUBI" from Joe and Bob.

Tito enjoyed life; he enjoyed being at the center of things. The spotlight gave him energy. He had an untiring ability to make music. If people were dancing he was keyed up and ready to go on. He was a perfectionist about his music. Everything else was secondary. I always knew this about him.

It took a lot of courage to walk up to Tito the first time. I never imagined that we would become so close – like brothers. Tito was cagey. I knew this because Machito told me that his former timbalero liked to keep to himself. I know what he was talking about. In 1959, Puerto Ricans were still migrating from the island, jobs were hard to find and people were just struggling to keep their heads above water. Nevertheless, we had the music, and Tito Puente was already an icon in the neighborhood.

The night I met him was unforgettable. The orchestra had just finished its set when I walked into the Palladium, one flight up from Broadway and 53rd Street, in New York City. It was crammed. Just a half a block away the Birdland was also packed. When I walked by with a few friends we could feel the vibrations of the music filtering into the busy street. It was Saturday night and it was New York. In those days the bands looked sharp. Tito's band was always stylish. He had a reputation for being demanding. Saturday night at the Palladium was usually a mixed crowd, but mostly Latinos from the five boroughs. Sundays were usually busy at the Palladium as well.

Tito did not hang around El Barrio, around 110th Street, during this time. I usually saw Machito. He was active, walking around, meeting people, and talking to friends. Machito always had a few words for me when we met around the neighborhood. In a way I was more an admirer of the Machito Orchestra than the other two – Tito Rodríguez and Tito Puente.

The romantic one was Tito Rodríguez. I used to see him at the Park Palace in El Barrio. His orchestra was just as tight in delivering music as the others. Some claim he was the best of the three. He certainly was the most "tipico" or tropical in terms of his style. He had a very special sound and he generated a romantic feeling. And, the women loved him. Machito's reputation for innovation, experimentation and originality was already legendary. Machito was powerful and had that Cuban drive. The orchestra could play anything, play it well and play it like no other orchestra. Machito was the leader, but Mario Bauzá was the man who created the musical dynamics. They all knew each other – Puente, Rodríguez and Machito and Mario. Machito was the mentor – he had been around the longest. Mario was extremely instrumental in helping to mold Tito. Mario could be abrasive but he enjoyed passing on his musical knowledge to Tito. The bandleaders had something in common – they sought excellence and they were fierce competitors.

There are new details that have emerged about Tito, about his life and about how he went about the business of making music and entertaining. I anticipate this view will give a fresh perspective. We forget he was more than a drummer. He composed, arranged, and played several instruments, and played them well. He paved the way the world over for others to follow, and never forgot his roots. He was a proud Spanish Harlem born Puerto Rican, who took great pride in that fact. In some ways he was flawed and troubled, making his accomplishments all the more remarkable.

Joe Conzo

Editor's Notes

Every book has a start – something that prompts a writer or a scholar to seek out materials on a particular theme or person to pursue a new angle of revelation on a recognizable subject, and to tell a story. This tome arose from two seemingly unrelated sources – one very personal and the other more traditionally educational. I have been obsessed with Afro-Cuban music, its roots and origins and how it intertwined with the Cuban charangas – the ensembles that use violins, wooden flute or flutes and percussion. My family says that I am secretly a mixture of Afro-Cuban and Puerto Rican… in my heart and soul I guess this may be true. But I also have a profound love of the real music of Puerto Rico –the danza. My interest in the life and music of Tito Puente has been from a peripheral point of view.

My personal interest in the subject arises from my childhood in which I was treated to listening to music that my father's Cuban friends often played. He also had a extraordinary collection of records with music from just about every corner of the world. I took lessons on the piano for what seemed forever, and the first chance I got switched off to the flute. When Joaquin Oliveros visited New York for concerts, I began my study of the unadorned flute. One of those visits he made was to play with the Tito Puente Orchestra in 2000. That occasion was the annual Tito Puente Scholarship Fund Dinner. Both my children received scholarships to pursue their arts studies. According to Joaquin, the music of Tito Puente was still quite popular in Cuba.

My interest in Tito Puente's music has existed since my youth. He led one of the three big bands. I always enjoyed listening to his softer side – his use of flutes in many arrangements gave his orchestra a unique quality. He was always ahead of the curve following the changing interests in his fans, and observing them long before new dances turned into obsessive fads. He had to be in those days. There was fierce competition among all the bands – big and small.

One can draw some parallels with historical situations. More than 100 years before, America's first authentic musician and composer, Louis Moreau Gottschalk, sought to unify European musical foundations with the Afro-Cuban. He was born in New Orleans. He lived in Cuba and Puerto Rico, and influenced many young Cuban and Puerto Rican musicians. He had a penchant for beautiful women. He often had to make a quick get away when an amorous encounter came to public attention. Tito Puente's adventures are celebrated – some true, some enhanced. But he inspired and encouraged many young musicians to follow in his footsteps.

So my interest in working with Joe was certainly piqued. No one knew Tito Puente the way Joe did. He has countless stories about his friend that provide the clues to a complex man. Some stories are humorous and some are on the dark side.

I was acquainted with Joe Conzo for a number of years; we said hello whenever our paths crossed. I knew that he was a very close friend of Tito Puente. He and Bobby Rodríguez (Tito Puente Scholarship Fund) helped me schedule an interview with Mr. Puente for a magazine article I was researching. On several occasions Joe indicated that he wanted to take all the notes he kept of conversations with Puente, organize the materials collected that referenced in one way or another the life of this prolific musician, recordings that existed and any other information and write a book. Simply stated, he wanted it to be about his very best friend, Tito Puente. Joe wanted it to be accurate, informative and intimate. He wanted to demonstrate that some legends and stories about Tito were just untrue. In short Joe wanted to present an honest account of what he believed was a story of a man – Tito Puente – a musical genius. When Tito died we continued to stay in touch. I agreed with Joe that the story was worth telling.

Over a period of several weeks Joe and I continued to converse and plan a path for the book that he envisioned. What has emerged is based on Joe's personal experience up close and personal with Mr. Puente. I don't think there is anyone else that knew Tito Puente like Joe Conzo. There was a passion between them that surpassed friendship… they were more like brothers. My interest is wholly historical and biographical. My objective has been to give depth and life to the Tito Puente that Joe knew. Joe Conzo wanted this book to be more than just "Tito was the king of the timbales," or "Tito recorded more than 100 albums." The actual number of album releases was 138 when we started the project two years ago. It is still growing as researchers, aficionados and various types of canvassers discover additional Puente treasures. In fact one afternoon while doing our research Joe discovered a tape that featured the Tito Puente Orchestra in a live session. Playing by his side – the timbales – was Miguelito Valdés. Certainly this item will one day make it to a studio and finally to a store for purchase. Chalk up another album for Maestro Puente. Joe discovered a live session with Tito Puente leading the band while Sammy Davis, Jr. was holding the microphone. Billy Eckstine and the Tito Puente Orchestra is an example of another gem in Joe's collection. Joe hopes that some day the legal issues and controversies surrounding the last live performance of Tito Puente with the Puerto Rico Symphony Orchestra, will be resolved. That would be yet another album. The search for the music continues.

Meanwhile, our principal aim was to present as much insight and understanding of Tito Puente and his music making by describing him in a narrative style – that is to tell his story in the words that he left for Joe, and filling in the gaps with historical reference. A big part of this effort is also possible because of Joe's relationship with Vincent "Jimmy" Frisaura, the right hand of the Puente organization. He shared with Joe a lot of intimate information. There were many others that provided Joe Conzo information about personal encounters with Tito Puente along the way. The few close friends in Tito Puente's inner circle also shared their experiences.

The book follows a simple path, starting with the crowning achievement Tito Puente sought – performing with the prestigious Puerto Rico Symphony Orchestra, molded by the great Pablo Casals, and then looks back to the arrival of Tito's parents in a cold New York City in the early 1920s. There were many Puerto Ricans living in New York. My mother came over on the same converted freighter SS Coamo, that Tito Puente's mother and father boarded in Puerto Rico to travel to New York. In those days the transplanted islanders were searching for a better life, struggling and like everybody else trying to make ends meet. By today's standards El Barrio was very small, the Puerto Ricans and Cubans that lived in New York at that time were scattered in every part of the City. Throughout the narrative the information that Joe provides was extracted from many sources. Tito liked to use expletive words often, especially in a private setting or when interacting with his orchestra. Jimmy Frisaura's tales form a crucial part of Tito's story. As Joe always reminded me "Jimmy was with Tito forever. They were close." In a way, this is also a story about Jimmy, Charlie and Joe Loco – these were Tito's confidants. They were formidable musicians. Joe Conzo brings them to life too in his journey with Tito Puente.

To provide an accurate picture both of us – Joe and I – decided to blend together historical events with many of the personal events of Tito's life. I realize that this is something of an unorthodox approach but we believe it would provide a better picture of Tito Puente moving about in his environment.

In each chapter we attempt to explore particular salient themes – Tito's youthful apprenticeship, his musical interests that spanned a wide spectrum, the things that interested him and influenced his early years as a bandleader, the Palladium, and the golden period. Of interest are the lengthy and detailed, and unedited conversations that Tito, Charlie Palmieri and Joe Loco shared in their 1674 Broadway office during the years 1970-

1979. Joe also provides records of various gatherings of Tito, Machito, Mario, Miguelito, Charlie and Federico as they drank and dined at the Asia Restaurant in midtown Manhattan. When Miguelito passed away in 1978, the group moved to Lord Jim's Restaurant downstairs from the office on Broadway. Eddie and Sonia Rodríguez owned the conveniently located restaurant and watering hole. In the new location Joe continued to document the conversations.

Joe Conzo, like me, is a New York Puerto Rican through and through. He met Ernesto "Tito" Puente in 1959, at the legendary home of Latin music – the New York Palladium Ballroom. It was probably in the fall, according to Joe. And it was probably a Saturday night. He went to see Puente's orchestra with a few friends. He had always liked the music but he was more of a Machito follower. After all Frank Grillo –(Machito) was a neighbor in El Barrio and Joe went to the same school that son, Frank Grillo, Jr. attended. He followed the big three bands, as they were known, from an early age. His uncles, cousins and neighbors always talked about Machito y sus Afro-Cubanos, the Tito Puente Orchestra and the Tito Rodríguez Orchestra.

The Park Palace was where Joe would see the big bands, the conjuntos and the ensembles that mostly played Afro-Cuban music in the 1950s and early 1960s. He had been to the Palladium often, but never to see the Tito Puente Orchestra. *"Abaniquito,"* was one of my favorite recordings. *"Cuban Carnaval"* was the first long play album I ever bought," according to Joe. "In the 1950s we were still listening to 78-rpm records." The first meeting was brief and cordial. More than a year would go by before Joe and Tito would fortuitously meet again – in Tokyo, Japan. Conzo was in the Army, stationed in the Far East – actually he was on his way to Korea. The Tito Puente Orchestra was spreading the seeds of Afro-Cuban music. Machito had been to Japan as well.

The second meeting was as brief as the first. Conzo and Puente bumped into each other at a club where the orchestra was performing, at the bar. The conversation, like the first time, was brief and hazy. Puente could not remember Conzo's name, only that he had seen him before. The bandleader smiled when he saw Joe standing at the bar of the nightclub. "'What are you doing here?' he says to me," Joe tells the story. From this point on and over many years the two men would form a friendship and a bond that would last until Tito's death in 2000.

Joe Conzo's mother arrived in New York aboard the SS Borinquen – a converted merchant vessel – in 1939. He was born in 1942. He is the son of an Italian father and a Puerto Rican mother. He lived in an apartment on 118th Street and Third Avenue. His mother, Olga, and his father divorced in 1947. He and his younger sister, Emma were raised by his mother's aunt, Consuelo Pérez. She spoke very little English but while mom was out working, Doña Consuelo ran a very tight and strict home. Joe's mother remarried later and moved to the Bronx. Joe is not shy about his six marriages. He shrugs off his disappointments and maintains "I think I got it right now." He is the father of three boys – Joseph Jr., Eric and Vincent LoBianco.

"My mother listened to Martin Block and the Make Believe Ballroom, and just about every kind of music there was. The radio in the 1940s and 1950s was still for music. We did not watch too much television. I remember we had one – a tiny screen. It was not used that much." There was a lot of Puerto Rican music – bomba, plena and danza. There was a lot of international Latin music played on the radio. Carlos Gardel sang tangos. The Mexican mariachis were popular.

He attended Public Schools 57 and 83, just as Tito had years earlier. By the way the late actor Burt Lancaster also attended P.S. 83. And, just like Tito the actor did not finish high school. For nearly 10 years Joe battled the demons of heroin addiction. Joe spent time in Puerto Rico, serving in the National Guard. His mother tried to keep him out of harm's way, but it seemed futile. He returned to New York, was drafted and shipped out to Korea. Boredom in an overseas outpost led to drug use; and it would take 10 years to finally shed the dependence, but not all of it. His description of those years is rather vivid and through his struggle – sleeping in the streets, telling lies to get money for his habit, and struggling in a shadow world, he began to listen to the advice of community activist, popular bandleader and friend Machito, and Tito. There was also Dr. Arnoldo Mora, a psychiatrist, who provided him with years of continuous support through a methadone drug treatment program he administered as well as providing employment. Joe and Tito became close friends during this period. The two were inseparable.

The story that Joe relates on these pages gives the reader a picture of a complex man – not just the "Music Man" that was conjured up by Meredith Wilson. Tito Puente claimed to have no taste for political things or issues. Yet he was acutely aware that all was not well with the Cuban people in 1957, when he spent a number of days in Havana being honored and feted by his Cuban hosts. He understood racism. He did not want to deal with it, but he did because his band was so diverse. Joe relates how he balanced his friendship with the Cuban singer Celia Cruz, who despised to her dying day Cubans who remained in Cuba. Tito enjoyed dealing with both Cubans in or out of Cuba. Tito may not have liked politics but he knew how to deal with it in his way.

As the life of Tito unfolds, several other portraits of him are revealed – his enjoyment of classical music, jazz and how he used these elements, mixed them into his own world of Spanish Harlem, and what emerged is the seeds of a new culture. Tito Puente played Afro-Cuban music but with his own style – it included his world. For a guy who said he did not like politics here again we find Tito Puente playing Cuban music with a Cuban drive and a very New York style.

He was one of the pioneers that opened the doors for many others to follow. In many ways, he was in the eye of the storm of the 1950s, that started a new culture in the United States – New York Puerto Ricans. Where the evolution will end up is anyone's guess. Nevertheless, in the midst of this swirl of change was Mr. Puente, serving up his unique style of Afro-Cuban music. Tito Puente loved women, loved history, loved being recognized and loved life. Yet, his passion was music.

There is no one that knows Tito Puente better than Joe. Over the years Tito came to rely on him for many things. Tito shared his personal life with him, kept him informed about his plans, his dreams, and his aspirations. Tito often told him about his life in El Barrio, growing up in New York, learning his trade, and getting close to the things he loved. Tito's idols included Jimmy Cagney and George Raft. "Tito walked like those two guys. Sometimes he talked like them," quipped Joe. Tito venerated Gene Krupa. He loved classical music. "People don't realize that Tito was much more than a percussionist and a showman."

Joe Conzo tells the story… I inserted a lot of technical information and history, but it is Joe's records, notes and memory, his voice, that gives us a unique picture of an American icon – Tito Puente, the man and his music.

David A. Pérez

Mambo with Me

The music started softly. First the violin section introduced the melody. The violas and cellos honed in on the music. The Puerto Rico Symphony Orchestra[1], under the baton of Josélin Pabón[2], sounded inspirational. I stood with Tito behind the large stage of the Puerto Rico Bellas Artes Centro Luis A. Ferré.

Pops was decked out in his slick black tuxedo with all the modern frills. He was focused on the music, on the large orchestra, and on his musicians in the center of the symphony. He was excited. After all, the Puerto Rico Symphony Orchestra was setting the stage for him. This was his moment of great achievement. To him, right now, everything that had happened before was what had led him to this point. Tito had worked hard throughout his career. This was his crowning glory. This was a dream come true.

A half hour before the start of the concert, workers and technicians were busy setting up the stage. Musicians of the symphony were backstage, already warming up. In the wings Tito gathered up some of his musicians. No one was paying attention to the small huddle backstage. Beyond where he stood there were shouts and commands coming from every direction as stagehands set up the microphones, seating for the orchestra. It was busy.

"I need a taste, some blow," he growled. "Does someone have some fucking candy?" Someone handed him a small bag of the white stuff. He slipped out a back door and disappeared for a few minutes. By the time he returned to the dark corner behind the stage everything was in place. Pabón tapped the music stand in front of him. Everything was ready.

The conductor turned his head slightly downward. This was the unspoken and rehearsed signal to the small group of musicians that sat in the center of the symphony orchestra. Tito's musical director and percussionist José Madera, Jr. was ready. He was a veteran of the Tito Puente organization. His father, José "Pin" Madera was something of a legend – as a saxophonist he had been one of the original members of Machito y sus Afro-Cubanos. The younger Madera had played and recorded for many orchestras, but he had been with Tito for nearly 30 years. He was ready. Madera looked to the other members of Tito's band – Sonny Bravo seated at the grand piano; Mitch Frohman, saxophone and flute; Mario Rivera, saxophone; Bernardo Minoso, bass; Ray Vega, trumpet;

Lewis Kahn, trombone/violin; and John "Dandy" Rodríguez, percussion. They were eager. They were ready.

Madera and the men that were Tito's core musicians also sensed that this was important to Tito. Strangely, Tito and his musicians, during the last decade, had grown closer. Tito had a rule, always keep them at a distance. Throughout his life he had trusted few people and that included those that worked for him. It was his way. But all that changed. Madera could not explain it, nor could any of the others. "It was a different Tito. We knew he wasn't feeling good but he seemed to have gotten a blast of energy. He was pumped up for this," recalled Madera.

"You're getting old Pops, I ribbed him as we watched the warm up of the orchestras.

"Kiss my ass," he retorted.

Whatever the reason, Tito now had a different view of his musicians. Even when he was the stern taskmaster, aloof and cool, he always looked out for his musicians, and they knew it. "Musicians are a dime a dozen," he told me. "But, good musicians have to be coddled and taken care of, even if you don't like them."

The introductory crescendos of the symphony orchestra exploded and then softened from one song into another. The horns, reeds and the Puente percussive unit graced the audience with a medley of tunes composed by Pedro Flores and other Puerto Rican composers. The mood changed. The orchestra shifted and played Rafael Hernández's *"El Jibarito,"* in an upbeat tempo. Tito smiled. The orchestra followed with his *"Preciosa"* that symbolizes the passionate patriotism of Puerto Ricans. These were hometown favorites. The audience was enchanted.

The entire orchestra, including Tito's ensemble was playing now. The audience was taking it all in. Tito never stopped smiling as the music came to a climax. There was utter silence; you could hear a pin drop.

The voice broke the quiet. "Ha grabado mas de 120 discos. Sé ha presentado en las más importantes salas. Ha ganado cinco Grammys. Es reconocido por su aportación a la música y cultura del planeta. Señoras y señores esta noche se presenta a Tito Puente y la Orquesta Sinfónica de Puerto Rico." In a concise somber phrase the announcement described Tito's successes –winner of five Grammy awards, and recognized for his contributions in music and culture around the world. The audience erupted into a furious and emotional outburst of applause.

The percussive rumble starts to build as Tito Puente slowly walks out to center stage. He smiles as he passes Sonny Bravo sitting at the grand piano. Tito salutes the conductor. He reaches the timbal array, lifts his sticks and then the combined Puerto Rico Symphony Orchestra and the Tito Puente Orchestra soar easily into a rip roaring full bodied *"Mambo Adonis,"* – that Tito re-titled *"Machito Forever,"* as a memorial to his friend and mentor, Frank "Machito" Grillo. More than that, the tune composed by Tito is a stark reminder to all present that Afro-Cuban big band jazz, big band sophistication and precision is alive and well. The tempo, the intricate interwoven syncopated variations of horns, reeds, percussion and an enlarged classical string section were indicative of how Tito was forever linked to his roots. He was masterful, energized. His orchestra and the symphony bonded easily. The harmonies of the brass glided over the strings of the symphony orchestra. The piano and the percussion tied the two elements –classical and Afro-Cuban jazz-together.

The conductor follows the path provided by the percussion – Tito, Madera and Dandy. The crescendo builds. This is Tito's moment. His jaw twitches, his mouth opens. The sticks rise above his head. The break by the smaller unit does not falter. Sonny wails on the keys of the piano keeping the two distinct orchestras together – functioning as one large orchestra. Tito smiles, almost laughs. This is the best, so far, of all the Tito Puente Orchestra performances with more than a half dozen symphony orchestras throughout the United States. Tito was smiling and his eyes sparkled. It seemed hard to believe that this was the same Tito that had trouble walking a few hours earlier.

One at a time his men get their licks in, Mario on saxophone, Ray on trumpet weaved improvised cadenzas over the montuno laid down by the orchestral assemblage. The two units – one classical and the other jazz and Afro-Cuban melded easily. It was a powerful exhibition of two genres coming together. There were breaks, typical in Afro-Cuban music, followed by choruses that included Madera, Bravo, along with Lewis who doubled on trombone and violin. Several others in the Tito Puente Orchestra also added their punctuated scales. The band played a series of riffs with an almost Asian harmony – Tito liked this feeling. His voyages throughout Asia after World War II, had sparked an interest in the oriental flavors. The entire orchestra, more than 40 pieces, explodes with bugle style riffs, haunting string guajeos. Then it comes to a halt. The audience erupts into boisterous applause. Tito is beaming.

When the ovation died down Tito, as he customarily did, walked a few steps to an open microphone. "Para mí es un orgullo estar aquí. Humildemente yo le doy las gracias. Puerto Rico es el pueblo de mi madre - ella fue instrumental en mi exitosa carrera. Gracias." His voiced trembled with emotion.

Then he spoke in English. "Hi, I'm Tito Puente. I was born in New York. I'm Puerto Rican and I play Afro-Cuban music," he always reminded his admirers and detractors. In his memoirs of the Cuban farándula (entertainers) *"La Ultima Noche,"* Bobby Collazo mentions Tito as "Un puertorriqueño con alma de cubano," (a Puerto Rican with a Cuban soul). This indeed was Tito.

Tito arrived in Puerto Rico a few days after he and his orchestra performed in a concert setting with the Dallas Symphony Orchestra. It was a George Gershwin medley that opened that concert on April 22, 2000. Tito felt an attachment to Gershwin's style. Both Gershwin and Tito had studied the Schillinger System of Music – a unique 12-tone method of composing and arranging used in the 1930s. Tito had always maintained that Gershwin, like Maurice Ravel, Claude Debussy and Manuel de Falla were among the most influential musicians in his long career. Ravel and Debussy provide an extraordinary impressionistic and full sound orchestration, he maintained, while de Falla captured the flavor of Spain.

My friend looked weary and frail as he came through the San Juan, Puerto Rico Luis Muñoz Marin International Airport. He walked slowly, it seemed as he was almost measuring each step so as not to lose his breath. I sensed that he was not well and when I asked him how he felt he laughed off my concern. He had been suffering a shortness of breath for some time. In New York, when he played at Town Hall, I had to help him walk to his car. The next morning we were on the flight to San Juan. We talked a lot about music. At one point he said in a low voice: "I'm all that is left, Joe. They are all gone. I'm probably not long for the world either." Quickly he recovered. "Oh shit! We are going to have a great show in Puerto Rico."

Pops was not going to let anyone know how he really felt.

The Puerto Rico Symphony Orchestra is the island's foremost musical ensemble, and one of the most eminent orchestras of the Americas. The Commonwealth of Puerto Rico Government sponsors it. Its 76 regular musicians perform a 48-week season that includes symphonic concerts, operas, ballets, pops, educational and children's concerts. It also offers outdoor concerts throughout the island. In addition, the orchestra has educational outreach programs in public and private schools. The history of the the symphony orchestra dates back to 1956, when famed cellist Pablo Casals visited the island to see his family and to discover the land where his mother was born. Soon after, he dedicated most of his work to foster classical music in Puerto Rico. In 1957, he organized the first annual Casals Festival, where he invited internationally renowned classical musicians to perform in a concert format. It was during this multi-week festival that Commonwealth lawmaker Ernesto Ramos Antonini presented a bill which would create the Puerto Rico Symphony Orchestra. The first live concert was performed on November 6, 1958 in Mayagüez, hometown of Pablo Casals' mother.

The symphony orchestra has hosted various internationally renowned artists, including Plácido Domingo, Luciano Pavarotti, Justino Díaz, Kiri Te Kanawa, and Alicia de Larrocha, among others, and it has performed in various Central and South American countries as well as on the U.S. mainland. Like so many symphony orchestras around the world it is constantly searching for new music to add to its evolving repertoire and to expand its audience base. Tito Puente and his Orchestra were a perfect fit.

Since the mid 1960s, Tito was considering how to best blend the two distinct types of music – classical and Afro-Cuban big band. Classical composers had long worked on incorporating Afro-Cuban rhythms and harmonies into classical works – Gershwin, Copland are among the many. But Tito did not want to lose the essence of pure or authentic Afro-Cuban sounds. He often recalled how Duke Ellington was featured with classic orchestras around the world. He sought the same for the music he played.

As the Puerto Rico Symphony Orchestra and Tito's band performed, the energy inside the performing arts theater increased. After the opening mambo, *"Machito Forever"* the orchestras played *"Maria Dolores,"* composed by A. Alguerod. Mario Rivera's saxophone solo was gently inspiring. *"Noche de Ronda"* represented the music of Agustín Lara. It reminded me of his 1957 RCA Victor recording when Tito arranged the classic for a string chamber ensemble and included Hugo Montenegro on glockenspiel. The vibe solo was placid and measured. Tito's tribute to the Cuban Orquesta Aragón started with Abelardo Valdés' *"Almendra"* – the haunting 1940 melody that had become a standard.

"El Bodeguero," composed by flautist Richard Egües that put the Cuban charanga on the world map, followed it and continued with several other cha cha chás. *"I'm Going to go Fishing"* was one of Duke Ellington's favorites. Ellington and Peggy Lee composed the tune.

"Cumbanchero," composed by Rafael Hernández, had the audience on its feet. It may not have been one of the preferred tunes of the Puerto Rican composer but it was a favorite of many Latin American performers.

The violins, the horns, the Tito Puente Orchestra delighted the audience. Tito's sustained timbal solo was fiery and one that gripped all present. He was at his best. "It was like he was a young man again," recalled Madera. But when it was over, Pops walked a few steps to his left, just in front of Madera's tumbadoras. He sat down on a stool that was provided. It was the first time in his career, the first time during a performance that Tito sat while on stage. I knew something was wrong; we all guessed he was not well. He smiled and stood up again. He was ready.

Ellington's *"I'm going to go Fishing"* was extended. Lewis Kahn on trombone, Mitch Frohman and Mario Rivera on saxophones and Ray Vega on the trumpet each produced improvised cadences that were supported by the percussion and the Puerto Rico Symphony. *"Oye Como Va,"* was a crowd pleaser but once again *"Fofi,"* Tito's Afro-Cuban inspiration that produces a driving rhythm and reaches a tempestuous final ignited the audience. They rose to their feet clapping the 3-2 clave beat that is the basic element of Latin music. Mitch played his flute over the more than 20 strings – violins, violas, cellos and contrabasses, and keeping time with Bernardo – a newcomer from the Mongo Santamaría band – laying down the montuno bass lines while Sonny banged out piano riffs. Frohman was stirring. Even Tito had caught a second wind and was moving his feet while he kept strict tempo on the cowbell. The coda was spontaneous and uproarious. Tito had conquered his audience.

He was lustrous. Briefly, he felt young again.

The promoter of the event was Rafael "Rafo" Muñiz, one of eight sons of television producer and comedian Tommy Muñiz. However, from the start it was obvious to all of us, Tito, José, and the other musicians, that the promoter was "something of an odd ball." The three-day event was not well promoted. The main theater of the performing arts complex seats 1,200 patrons. Despite the poor promotion of the event more than 95% of the seats were filled over the three day period. Tito sensed there existed turmoil between the promoter and the performing arts center administration. Tito could never get a straight answer any of his questions from Muñiz or from the executives at the Bellas Artes Performing Arts Center. In the old days he would have exploded, but he was not feeling well. We sensed something was wrong.

Tito was also aware that Ralph Mercado had booked many of the former Fañia All Stars into Híram Bithorn Stadium for a reunion concert. Among the headliners was his friend Celia Cruz, Willie Colón, Johnny

Pacheco, Larry Harlow, Papo Lucca and Ray Barretto. Tito believed that he had more drawing power than the Funny All Stars."

I had read the newspapers and found a few ads referencing the Fañia All Stars concert. "I guess Ralph is not pushing too hard – especially after what happened with Celia," I said.

Tito shrugged. "The ones worth a shit in the Funny All Stars is Ray Barretto and Larry Harlow, maybe the other piano player, Papo Lucca. Celia would have been a draw had she not pissed off the Puerto Ricans by lashing out at Andy Montañez. But she is pig headed – she has always been like that." He shrugged

We walked the streets of San Juan – Santurce, the Condado, and Old San Juan. George Rivera, the public television documentary film producer and director, followed Tito and I around as we toured the city. People waved to us. This was not like Hollywood where the paparazzi were constantly stalking celebrities. The people knew who Tito was. They were friendly. When he stopped to talk to the children in Old San Juan's Plaza de Armas, you could see the excitement in their eyes.

The conversations were in Spanish. "Hi. Do you know who I am?" Tito asked.

There were smiles and cheers from the youngsters. "You're Tito Puente," they chimed loudly in unison.

"Do you know what I do!"

Again the chorus sang out: "You play music."

"Salsa!" one voice yelled with energy.

Tito was not going to ruin it. He smiled. He hated the word salsa. So be it.

He smiled and continued greeting the young and old. He clasped hands with everyone. He even embraced some of the youthful admirers – not something he did very often. I recalled at this moment that I could count the times he showed any emotion. Tito relished this brief time with the young people in the historic plaza. But alas we had to move on.

Next we went to the Commonwealth of Puerto Rico Capitol Building in Puerta de Tierra, on the fringe of the old historic city that overlooks the Atlantic Ocean. Tito had trouble climbing the steps. "Are you all right Pops?" I said concerned.

He grumbled: "Fuck you. I'm fine."

Tito was eloquent when he received Puerto Rico's acclamations and more honors were bestowed on him. He spoke only a few words to the legislators who were gathered in the Senate chamber of the Commonwealth of Puerto Rico. He was glad it was a brief ceremony. "Puerto Rican ceremonies have a tendency of continuing for hours, and hours..." He laughed as we walked slowly from the building. On the steps leading out, down to the parking area we bumped into Charlie Hernández, a University of Puerto Rico professor and son of Puerto Rico's immortal composer Rafael Hernández. The conversation was brief but in the few minutes we talked Tito recalled his piano teacher – long ago – Victoria Hernández[3]. Charlie smiled warmly when Tito told him about his aunt.

She was his first piano teacher, Señora Hernández. The sister of one of Puerto Rico's greatest composers had often spoken to him about the wonders of the small Caribbean Island (the largest island of the Lesser Antilles or the smallest island of the Greater Antilles). She was stern, Tito often recalled. "I think she even used to strike my fingers with her small pointing stick." But he had fond memories of her. She was a strong and positive influence on Tito.

Victoria Hernández had been his piano teacher for many years in his youth, starting when he was about eight-years-old. She provided him with dozens of Habaneras – the foundation of Puerto Rico's danza, the Cuban danzón, the tango and even American ragtime. His piano teacher had taught him many of the pieces he was hearing. It must have been racing through his mind as he listened, walking with his mother Ercilia Puente the eight blocks from 110th Street and Fifth Avenue in El Barrio, to 117th Street for a weekly piano lesson. Sometimes Tito had to be dragged, screaming and crying. He would rather be hanging out with his friends, playing stickball, or shooting marbles, anything was better than listening to the demanding piano teacher.

"She was tough!"

Soon after we were back in Santurce meeting with the members of the symphony orchestra, discussing with orchestra director Pabón and Madera the program that would be presented over the next three nights. The music had been sent early on so it was just a matter of routine. Tito wanted everything just right. Talking to Madera and me, he recalled the first concert that the orchestra staged in California, at the Hollywood Bowl. "It was not the smoothest shit we ever did. But we got it out and even with the bumps, goofs and mistakes it sounded good. We did not have enough time to rehearse. The musicians in the Hollywood Bowl Orchestra were good, damn good, but you know they did not know clave." We laughed.

After that near fiasco Tito took it upon himself to copy the music, label the scores and get it to the appropriate people with sufficient time. When

Madera took over the leadership of the band it became his responsibility. Tito liked José because he reminded him of Jimmy Frisaura, the late trumpet player and partner. Tito and Jimmy had been together for nearly 50 years. The Tito Puente Orchestra was in good hands. Tito returned to the Caribe Hilton to get ready for the Thursday night opening concert. When he came down to the lobby, decked out in his tuxedo it seemed to us that he had managed to re-energize himself. He was beaming, almost glowing. "Let's go," he yelled to us. We followed.

The musicians were a little anxious the morning following the second night's success when Tito did not come down for breakfast. "He is not answering our calls," one of them told me.

"He is probably doing something he should not be doing and doesn't want us to bother him," I said.

"Look, even if it was that, he would answer the telephone," Dandy Rodríguez said.

I went up to his room and knocked on his door. "Yeah, yeah, who is it?" a gruff voice said.

"Tito, Tito, its me – Joe. Are you all right?"

"Fuck you. I'm fine. I'll be right out." A few minutes later he came out of the room dressed casually. "What's all the fucking commotion?" he asked.

"We were worried," I responded.

Tito forced a smile. "I'm fine. You are all pussies. Leave me alone."

"You look like shit," I said as we approached the group of musicians.

Tito was unyielding, even mad. "Kiss my ass."

The performance Thursday and Friday nights were remarkable accomplishments for Tito and the orchestra. I missed Saturday night because Tito had asked me to scurry cross-town to see how the "Funny All-Stars" were doing. It was raining when I got there so many of the patrons at the baseball park had already left. Just before the rain started to fall Celia came out and was booed because of her critical remarks about hometown idol, Andy Montañéz. She knocked him in the newspapers for working in Havana and for teaming up to perform in a number of concerts with Cuban performers who still lived in Cuba. On Sunday morning I got a call that Tito had suffered a heart attack. I was shocked. He had collapsed after the Saturday night performance and was taken to Pavía Hospital in Santurce. I spoke to Margie – Tito's wife - in New York, who reassured me that Tito was okay – it was not a heart attack. "I'm on my way to Puerto

Rico," she said. He collapsed from exhaustion. I hustled over to Santurce. Audrey, Tito's daughter, was already at the hospital.

"It's all bullshit," Tito cried out when I walked into his room. "I just felt faint, that's all. What about Ralph's Funny All-Stars concert," he inquired.

"The fans booed the shit out of Celia."

"I told her to stay clear of the concert, especially after she opened up on Andy. Man, she is pig headed."

"Celia told me you should see a doctor."

He was exasperated. "Oh shit, tell her to leave me alone."

"Hey I'm just passing on the message."

He growled. "It's all bullshit."

Audrey Puente came into the room. "How is the band? Is everybody okay? Make sure they are taken care of," he said in a firm voice.

I nodded.

"Make sure the band is okay. They're like my sons." He was looking straight at me. He repeated his words, slower. "They're like my sons."

"Just rest."

"I'll have plenty of time to rest when I'm dead," he fumed. "It's all bullshit."

I left him with Audrey.

When I returned that afternoon Margie Puente was with him. He was in good spirits. "It was a great concert. I can't wait for the next one. But I'm not sure what can top this – you know being in the land of your heritage, doing all the shit you planned… Well I have more fish to fry. How are the boys – the band?" He continued to insist that he was fine. "Its all bullshit." Once again he gazed at me and then shifted his eyes to his wife. "Make sure the band is taken care of."

I smiled at him. But I could not help but wonder if deep down inside he felt that his time was running out. I nodded to him. "I'll see you in New York."

La Vida Es Un Sueño

At 11:00 p.m., Tuesday, May 31, 2000, I was lying in bed at home in the Bronx. Suddenly I felt a chill. It got damn cold. I yelled out: "Oh God! No!" As suddenly as I got that chill it went away. I was glad I was alone. Ronnie Puente promised that he would keep me informed about Tito's condition following his open-heart surgery at New York Medical College Hospital. He did not call but I knew Tito had died. Ronnie called at 11:10 p.m.

The telephone rang at 11:07 p.m. I picked it up on the first ring. "Joe, is that you?" It was Ralph Mercado.

"I know why you are calling. Tito is dead," I said nervously.

"How the fuck did you know? It just happened."

"Tito told me. He came and said goodbye."

There was silence. I hung up.

Tito was officially declared dead at 11:05 p.m.

I lay there, in the dark just thinking. The last time I saw Tito was on the 29th of May. I drove to his house in Tappan, New York, where he was being kept in isolation. Margie was surprised to see me. "What are you doing here?"

"Tito called me. He wanted me to bring him some music."

From the kitchen Tito shouted. "Who is that?" He came to the door and greeted me. Tito had returned to New York. Upon his return, he had been in seclusion for nearly a month – no one was allowed to call him or see him, only the immediate family. We were only able to talk on the telephone late at night. When everybody was sleeping Tito would call me. He often talked in whispers. "Hi Joe," he would whisper. "They don't let me see anyone. What a bunch of bullshit." On the last call on Saturday night, May 28, 2000, I told him that I had obtained a copy of the recording by the Puerto Rico All Stars of *"Ti Mon Bo."* He insisted I bring it to him the next day. So I drove up to Tappan.

We went into the kitchen. Tito slipped the recording into the radio/ CD player. Tito had already been to the hospital once but because of the Memorial Day holiday, the surgery had been postponed. He still was not sure that he wanted to go through with the operation. And as we listened to the music I think I was able to convince him once and for all that it was the best thing, that he had to have the surgery. The music soothed him.

"It is pretty good, eh," he said.

I smiled. "Oh yes, almost as good as the original."

He rolled his eyes. I figured he remembered that the original featured two of the best sidemen that ever played for him – Mongo Santamaría and Willie Bobo. It was recorded in 1957.

After about an hour it was time to say goodbye. As I turned to leave he called out to me. He walked over to where I was standing. "I'll be seeing you in a few days," he said. He flung his arms around me. We both clutched one another. It was the first time in all the years we were friends he had hugged me like that. We had been friends from the early 1960s. We traveled together and did all kinds of shenanigans. We spent long hours talking and listening to music. We fought and argued – sometimes ferociously, we made up and fought again. We were very close. He was more than my best friend. I had only seen him break down once, and that was when Machito died. Publicly anyway he never allowed himself to be emotionally expressive. I smiled when we pulled apart. He smiled. We said nothing. After a moment I turned and left.

Tito had lived life to the fullest. He was a genius of music. I know this. Tito lived for his music. He was consumed with it. Nothing else mattered.

Dancing Under Latin Skies

Harlem Nocturne

Hitting a rubber ball with a broomstick came naturally to Tito. In fact, he claimed that playing stickball in front of his apartment building on 110th Street, in El Barrio was preferred over practicing piano. By his own admission he was pretty good at it – playing this New York game. Nevertheless, he had to balance his sports activities with music. His mother insisted on it. Tito began his music training early. By the time he was eight-years-old his mom was dragging him a half dozen blocks up to 117th Street, to sit in front of the piano in Victoria Hernández's living room.

Tito said that the room where he received his music lessons was not very big. He sat quietly in front of the piano while the sister of the man who would become Puerto Rico's most beloved composer, Rafael Hernández, counted. "Uno, dos, tres, cuatro." Over and over she counted until Tito was dizzy. She held a small wand and lightly banged the top of the old piano. There was nothing but scales, and more scales. "In those days it was that way. You learned the basics –until you had it memorized," Tito remembered. She was a strict teacher. She taught music as if she was sure you were going to succeed. There were a variety of books – all with scales in every key signature and fingering exercises. It was more than a year before Tito recalled seeing the most basic of melodies – a simple tune.

He was born in New York and raised in Spanish Harlem – El Barrio. His parents came from Puerto Rico. New York had always been an ideal location for both Cubans and Puerto Ricans either to migrate for political reasons or just to find work. It was in New York that Cuban and Puerto Rican patriots first gathered in the late 1800s, to seek assistance from the United States to oust the Spaniards from their respective islands.

The apartment where Tito lived was on the fourth floor. It was a five-story walk up. There had been other apartments. The Puente family moved to wherever the father, Ernesto Sr., could get to work easily, or even take advantage of a cheaper rent. In those days families moved around to get the best rent possible. At one point the Puente family lived in Brooklyn. It was a short-lived stay in Brooklyn. Tito's memory was vague. "My father probably lost his job so we moved."

Tito used to trek up and down four flights of stairs in the building in East Harlem. "People were always coming and going and when no one was looking I was out the door to play stickball." He loved playing stickball. The neighborhood in those days was still a kaleidoscope of diverse ethnic groups – Jewish, Italian, some Irish, and of course the Puerto Ricans and Cubans. Spanish was not spoken in the streets, at least not when they were playing stickball. At home it was the opposite. His parents spoke no English.

As a young boy there was little money to go around and even the subway was beyond the tight budget. You had to walk to the grocery store, walk to school, walk to church, walk to get a haircut, walk to get anywhere. The subway was a luxury, and besides you did not have to take it unless you were heading downtown – and who went downtown – the bustling midsection of Manhattan. "No, the subway was not as important as you would think," he reflected.

"My father had all sorts of jobs and he liked to play cards. He was not home a lot," Tito remembered. "He came home late, sometimes very late. My mother was always figuring out how to make ends meet. But we never went hungry." Tito often had to walk 12 to 20 blocks a day. He walked by the Park Palace over on 110th Street and Fifth Avenue. He enjoyed listening to the music that came from the building. At home there was always music on the radio. The neighborhood, in the late 1920s, was constantly changing.

Doña Ercilia Puente was the backbone of the family. She scrimped and saved. She quietly looked for what money Tito's father did not squander with his frivolous gambling and other bad habits. She must have suspected that his lack of presence in the Puente household was because of other interests. She did not complain. What money she managed to get she used to pay the rent, buy groceries, buy clothing, take care of the basic needs of the household, and pay for music lessons,. "My father did not realize how she was keeping us above water." This was not a subject Tito talked about much. When he did broach the subject his eyes darkened – there were a lot of sad memories hidden away. Tito recognized that there was something of his father in him. "You know what they say, the fruit does not fall far from the tree!"

Tito was not a good student. He admitted that he hated to sit and listen to the teacher. He much preferred to be on the street playing – shooting marbles, playing stickball, or just hanging out with the guys. He was not a much better music student, at least not initially. His mom literally had to drag him down the street for piano lessons and then for dance lessons. Somewhere along the line he began to enjoy it. Dancing became fun. Eventually he even began to enjoy the piano. He remembered that there were cylinders of music in the apartment. The cylinder was the early form of recorded music. The 78-rpm record followed and was in use by 1912. Music, sports and the Boy Scouts were Tito's interests in the late 1920s and early 1930s, in a New York City that was forever on the move, ever changing, and always challenging. Tito and his family were in the midst of the Great Depression[4].

Puerto Ricans, as well as Puerto Rican organizations, have been in New York City since the early 1800s. It was only after 1900, however, that significant numbers of Puerto Ricans arrived, and the bulk of the migration occurred in the 1950s and early1960s. The migration of Puerto Ricans after the American takeover has been classified into three major periods. During the first period, 1900–1945, the pioneers arrived and established themselves in New York City in the Atlantic Avenue area of Brooklyn, in East Harlem and such other sections of Manhattan as the Lower East Side, the Upper West Side, Chelsea and the Lincoln Center area. Some began to populate sections of the South Bronx. In those days the Spanish speaking families – mostly Puerto Ricans and Cubans - moved around, always looking for bargains in the apartment rental market.

The world Tito Puente was born into was shaped long before. Migration from Puerto Rico to the mainland was as a result of surplus labor – lack of jobs, and a need for labor on the mainland. Many economic factors were at work – no jobs on the island, overpopulation, poverty and a search for a better life were part of the migration at the start of the 20th century that continued right up until the start of World War II. American companies played an active role in recruiting Puerto Ricans and Cubans to work in the United States. During the early 1900s and even before, farm recruiters from Hawaii convinced many Puerto Ricans to settle on the Pacific islands. The Commonwealth government, formed in 1948 when the island's status changed, has denied it pushed for migration but it certainly did not discourage it, at least prior to 1960.

By the 19th century, Puerto Rico had become a bustling trade center and host to thousands of immigrants. The population grew from 70,250 in 1775, to 330,051 in 1832. During this period, the population of the island multiplied more than 13 times. As the population grew it became increasingly diverse. Although most of the 19th century immigrants to

Puerto Rico mostly came from Spain and its possessions, a great many came from other European countries. Common Puerto Rican surnames, for example, Colberg, Wiscovitch, Petrovich, Franqui, Adams, Bonini and Solivan, reflect ethnic diversity. Cuba's migration was from the same European sources. However, the Spanish needed slaves for the large plantations. The African population swelled. Both Cuba and Puerto Rico joined forces and their political leaders, many of them based in New York City, sought means and ways to have the United States assist the two islands in ousting the Spanish[5]. The Spanish American War in 1898 accomplished this, but the patriots did not get all the results they wanted.

From the very start of independence Cuba was troubled by corrupt leadership, prejudiced U.S. government and business interests and less than desirable economic conditions. Puerto Rico did not have any autonomy such as it had achieved under the Spanish rule. Its economic condition deteriorated over the 50 years following the war. Between the 1920s and the early 1940s, the combined pressures of mass mobilization, revolution, economic crisis, and the threat of foreign intervention from the United States compelled Cuban politicians from across the ideological spectrum to come to terms with the struggling working class and the poor as a factor in national and international politics.

In 1920, a large group of wealthy landowners, professional politicians, merchants, bankers, and plantation owners had a tight grip over national politics, and the idea that the state should be "popular" was abhorrent to the ruling groups. By the early 1930s, however, social protest from the underclass became so widespread that the established mechanisms of social and political control no longer functioned. Yet, at the time, it was by no means clear how "the masses" or people were to be incorporated into the political process. It was one thing for political elites to recognize that the popular sectors were a force to be reckoned with; it was another matter to create new political institutions and dialogue to harness their energy. Before anyone could accustom themselves to the idea of the people as political actors, in the summer of 1933 Cuba exploded in social revolution.

For the eight years prior to 1933, Cuba had been ruled by Gerardo Machado y Morales. Between 1925 and 1930, Machado's rule faced no serious opposition. By 1929, however, the economic crisis sparked by the world depression threw the established political and economic order into chaos. Social forces that were outside the traditional political circles increasingly besieged all factions of the Cuban elite. Prior to 1933, the police or the rural guard violently and sometimes easily suppressed the occasional student march or worker's strike. From the late 1890s to the 1920s, the Cuban population was too fragmented, socially and economically to present a sustained threat to the ruling elite. By early 1933, the intensity of popular protest had reached unprecedented levels. Machado was increasingly isolated from the political elite, and economic crisis and labor unrest challenged the political and social order.

With the revolution of 1933, the young and relatively inexperienced revolutionaries found themselves pushed into the halls of state power by worker and peasant mobilizations. Between September 1933 and January 1934, a loose coalition of radical activists, students, middle-class intellectuals, and disgruntled lower-rank soldiers formed a provisional Revolutionary Government. University professor, Dr. Ramón Grau San Martín, directed this coalition. The Grau government promised a "new Cuba" with social justice for all classes and the abrogation of the Platt Amendment. While the revolutionary leaders certainly wanted diplomatic recognition by Washington, they believed their legality stemmed from the popular revolt that brought them to power and not from the approval of the U.S. Department of State. Throughout the fall of 1933 the government decreed a dramatic series of reforms.

The Platt Amendment was unilaterally abolished, and the political parties of the machadato were dissolved. The Provisional Government granted autonomy to the university, women obtained the right to vote, the eight-hour workday was decreed, a minimum wage was established for cane cutters, and compulsory arbitration was promoted. The government created a Ministry of Labor, and a law was passed establishing that 50 percent of all workers in agriculture, commerce, and industry had to be Cuban citizens. The Grau regime set agrarian reform as a priority, promising peasants legal title to their lands. For the first time in Cuban history, the country was governed by people who did not negotiate the terms of political power with Spain (before 1898) or with the United States (after 1898).

The Provisional Government survived until January 1934, when it was overthrown by an equally loose antigovernment coalition of right-wing civilian and military elements. Led by a young sergeant, Fulgencio Batista y Zaldavar, this movement was supported by the United States. At the time, it appeared that Cuba would revert to traditional methods of state domination. Previously, whenever the struggle for state power got out of hand, U.S. diplomats brokered a compromise among competing factions: there was no indication that anything would be different this time around.

Nonetheless, Cuba after 1933 was a very different country from what it had been only a few years earlier. The experiences of revolutionary struggle and mass mobilization became a part of the Cuban political landscape. The revolution of 1933 politicized Cuban society in fundamentally new ways.

Between 1934 and 1940, a new political and economic consensus based on authoritarian and reformist principles emerged. After the revolution of 1933, most political groups in Cuba--from the far right to the communists--drew the conclusion that a new and modern state should intervene in society to modernize the country's political and economic structures. This reformist impulse concluded in 1940, when a new constitution proclaimed political democracy, the rights of urban and rural laborers, limitations on the size of sugar plantations and the need for methodical state intervention in the economy. It also attempted to protect the role of private property. Although Cuba had several civilian presidents from 1935 to 1940, it was clear to all that the strong man (Batista) was the ruler of Cuba. Following seven years of controlling Cuban politics from behind the scenes, Batista became president of Cuba in 1940.

Because of turmoil in Cuba, thousands of Cubans migrated to the United States seeking better opportunities. The same reasons pushed many Puerto Ricans to move north – a chance for a new start and a chance for improvement. The two ethnic groups, who in the words of Puerto Rican patriot & poet Lola Rodríguez de Tió and often echoed by Cuban patriot José Marti are "one bird with two wings," met in New York. With this migration the artisans and musicians followed.

Rafael Hernández was the first musician to sound a Latin music note in 1919, when he sang and played guitar at an East 99th Street house party. Hernández was one of several Puerto Ricans who played in the James Reese Europe Army band that toured the European continent during World War I. During the first two decades of the 20th century, James Reese Europe emerged as the most renowned bandleader of New York's entertainment world. Famed for his syncopated orchestral accompaniment of the dancing team of Irene and Vernon Castle, Reese Europe became a major figure in promoting the popularity of public dancing and stimulated a ragtime-based music that contributed to the emergence of jazz. During World War I, his 369th Infantry Band the "Hell Fighters," was hailed by French and American troops as the finest ensemble in the Allied Army[6].

Hernández, one of Puerto Rico's most cherished composers, and his sister Victoria, were among the first Puerto Ricans who settled in Manhattan in 1919, and then after spending several years in Cuba, returned in1925 to the United States. He rented an apartment at 102nd Street and Second Avenue. At this time he formed Trio Borinquen. In 1926, Cuban trumpeter-bandleader Vicente Sigler became the first to play Latin music with a big band in New York City. His orchestra was also one of the first to be recorded. In April 1927, Cuban Alberto Socarras relocated to New York.

In 1930 two events gave Latin music prominence - the first was a dance held at the Park Palace Jewish Caterers at 110th Street and Fifth Avenue, which resulted in the opening of dance halls, after-hour clubs, Spanish-speaking movie theaters and music stores. The second event was in April 1930, when the Cuban band of Don Azpiazu overwhelmed the audience during its two week appearances with a rousing version of *"El Manisero,"* The Peanut Vendor. (Vocalist Antonio Machin walked out of a stage wing throwing peanuts to the audience singing "Mani...Mani.")

Latin music was more than entertainment; it was a reminder of the two Caribbean islands – Cuba and Puerto Rico and its traditions. Music was also a means to earn a few more dollars to supplement the primary income. Almost every Puerto Rican and Cuban family had at least one musician, a self-taught vocalist, maracas player or guitarist. Poor families who could not rent a hall for a wedding, a baptism or a birthday party, held it in their apartment.

During the 1930s, a house party was a happy event. The apartment and hallways were perfumed with spicy aromas of garlic and oregano emanating from pernil (pork) in the oven. Trios or quartets that consisted of a lead vocalist, a maracas player who doubled as a second voice, a guitarist, sometimes a pianist (if the apartment had a piano), and a trumpeter, provided the live music in the living room, Tito said. At one particular party, Trio Matamoros' *"Echale Candela"* was played to give the student musicians an idea of how music of the 1930s sounded. Some historians claim that during the decade of the 1930s, the Puerto Rican and Cuban relationships were strained[7]. The conflict was about who was a better dancer, and was instigated by ruthless dance promoters.

The fact that Cubans and Puerto Ricans spoke Spanish more than anything helped to unite them even though their countries, after ending hundreds of years of Spanish colonialism, were headed in two very different directions. José Marti was still a hero to both groups, the flags of the two islands were similar, and the history of their fight for "libertad" from Spain was still fresh on people's minds.

Tito often recalled that there were parties in apartments. "In my little place there were Cubans, Puerto Ricans and a lot of Italians and Jews. Don't kid yourself, there were rivalries, there was mistrust, but somehow we all managed to get along." In the 1920s, there was still a substantial Italian population that mixed together with the arriving Puerto Ricans. "The only wars we had were over who was a better dancer," he laughed.

Puerto Ricans became U.S. citizens as a result of the Congress approving the Jones Act in 1917, and could travel without problems to the mainland. Cuban tourists, unlike Puerto Ricans, could not remain in the United States after 29 days for fear of being arrested and deported. A small percentage of Cubans who were citizens or permanent residents did compete for menial jobs and housing in New York City but it never became an issue. While many Cuban and Puerto Rican families lived in Brooklyn's downtown area, mostly Puerto Ricans moved into the Bronx in the 1920s and 1930s. El Barrio was the focal point of the majority of Puerto Ricans.

The granting of citizenship status in 1917 induced Puerto Ricans to migrate north. It was in this context that Antonio Puente and his 16-year-old son, Ernesto, boarded the SS Coamo on March 5, 1920, for the three-day voyage to New York. The vessel initially was built for State Line – a British company – in Scotland in 1891. It was christened the State of California. In 1901 it was renamed SS Coamo – thousands of Puerto Ricans made the voyage to New York on this old ship. Tito's grandfather was born in 1880. Ernesto was born in San German. The first residence in New York was listed as 111 West 134th Street on the Upper West Side of Manhattan. What would become known as El Barrio boundaries ran northward from 96th Street to 125th Street, and from Fifth Avenue to the East River.

New York City was teeming with new arrivals mostly from Europe. Puerto Ricans initially were spread out but slowly congregated into East Harlem. There was a lot of construction, bridges, streets, buildings, installation of electricity and gas conduits. Nightlife was booming and entertainers from around the globe made it a point to visit New York City.

Rafael Hernández, Rafael Duchesne and Juan Tizol passed through the teeming city en-route to join the 369th Infantry Regiment band. Tizol later joined Duke Ellington's orchestra; Hernández continued his travels and settled for a while in Havana, then New York, and Duchesne returned to Puerto Rico after working with the Noble Sissle Orchestra[8] in 1921. It is hard to imagine Duchesne playing Charleston and swing. He is most noted for his classical style offerings of danza music.

In 1923, Ernesto Puente had been in New York about three years. His young wife, Ercilia Ortiz, who was born in Ponce, Puerto Rico gave birth to Ernesto Anthony Puente, Jr. at Harlem Hospital, located at125th Street and Lenox Avenue. "I was listed as a black baby," Tito recalled. On the other hand, life was not easy. "My father was always struggling to make a buck and we never had enough to make the rent – not easily anyway. He was not home much." His eyes darkened and his voice sharpened whenever the subject came up. I learned early in our friendship that he did not like to talk about his father. Tito was deliberately vague about their relationship. He would make up stories about anything to do with his father. It depended on his mood. Pleasant memories were always inflated for the public. Dark memories were recalled with vagueness. The relationship with Ernesto Sr. was one of those mysteries that Tito was never specific about. Tito's father was a workingman and in this environment, it meant he was never around. His mother was the disciplinarian.

Anna Puente, the younger sister and also his dancing partner, was born in 1928. Ercilia also gave birth to Alberto, who died tragically in a fall from their tenement firescape at age four. Tito Puente watched his brother in horror as he slipped and accidentally tumbled from the firescape where they were playing. Firescapes were the outdoor areas that parents from the tropics used for recreation. They tried to keep a watchful eye on their children but accidents were not uncommon.

Throughout his life I think that the death of his brother haunted him. Maybe he felt he could have helped, or maybe it was the horror of witnessing this tragedy. I don't think Tito ever dealt with the loss of his brother. He told me that he drew closer to his sister after the accident. I always suspected that our friendship made up in a small part for that loss.

His mother was dark skinned. His father was fair skinned. The family had just moved from Brooklyn and settled into the apartment at 110th Street, between Park and Madison Avenues. Tito liked to say that maybe his knack for rhythm came from the Silver Jubilee Exposition – it was the 25th Anniversary celebration of New York's union – the five boroughs coming together. Before the union the five boroughs were separate cities and jurisdictions.

El Barrio was just starting to feel the influx of islanders. It was still white on the East Side, and across Lenox Avenue was where the blacks lived. Before he was a year old he was in Puerto Rico. By the time he was three, he returned to New York. Ernesto returned to the island hoping to settle there once and for all, but the economy was in very bad shape. Upon returning to New York, Ernesto went from job to job. He became a distant figure in the family. There is no clear picture about Tito's father. Tito referred to him occasionally, but whatever transpired in the Puente household on 110th Street, he kept to himself. Ernesto Sr. apparently shared very little in the way of a family life. It was up to Doña Ercilia to look after the family.

By the time Tito was 10-years-old he was enrolled in a dance class. His mother still walked him to Doña Victoria's studio several blocks away. Tito still cried, screamed, and even lied to his mother about not being able to practice, hurting his leg, his hand, whatever occurred to him. Once he told his mother the music books were forever lost. "I don't think she bought the story," Tito recalled wryly. In tears he explained this to Victoria one day. She had substitutes ready for his lesson. A week later Tito located the lost music books.

Victoria opened Almacenes Hernández in 1927, possibly the first Puerto Rican-owned music store in New York City. Located on 1724 Madison Avenue between 113th and 114th Streets. The store supported her family and gave Rafael time to write music while he lived in New York. In mid 1928, she opened the Hernández Record Store on Madison Avenue between 113 and 114 Streets. She sold 78s, pianola rolls, maracas and guitars. In a room at the back of the store there was a piano that was utilized to teach students. One summer day in 1929, Victoria urged her brother to leave the room so she could instruct one of several students. Rafael took his guitar and a tin can of black coffee out onto the sidewalk, sat down near the edge of the curb, feet in gutter, tuned his guitar and began to sing and write lyrics on a piece of paper. The lyrics to the tune he composed that afternoon about an island in the Caribbean, its scenery, its folkways and all the abstract and intangibles of Puerto Rico – *"Lamento Borincano."* Perhaps the most popular of all his compositions, was written on the sidewalk in front of the Hernández Record Store in 1929. In 1929 Tito was in his second year of taking piano lessons with Doña Victoria. His mother purchased many of the records of the Puerto Rican bands at the shop.

By 1933, Tito had stopped fighting his mother's aspirations. In fact, he was now interested in dance classes, still taking piano lessons and intrigued with percussion. "Man, she was tough," he often reminded me when he recalled Victoria Hernández. It had been struggle between him and his mother to see if he would have to practice tap dance, practice the piano or play stickball. "I remember I used to put my old shoes in the trash bag. 'Mom,' I yelled to her as I grabbed the bag with the garbage, 'I'm going to take the garbage out.' I ran out the door and headed straight for where the guys were playing stickball." He smiled. "She caught onto me pretty quickly – my mother was smart that way."

He often described the small apartment as he remembered the "pianola" that took up a large part of the living room. This is where he worked on his music studies. Even though money was in short supply he had to study music. While Tito was studying piano and learning various forms of dancing, he was tapping on things – boxes, tables, and chairs. He liked to listen to music. The Xavier Cugat Orchestra was heard on the radio almost daily. Cuban orchestras were streaming in and out of the New York to perform and record. The radio was popular and it played music. The radio stations played music from everywhere.

Recording companies were pursuing just about every type of music from around the world, pushing out records and releasing them to radio stations. On any summer afternoon blaring out of the fourth floor window of the Puente apartment you could hear the latest music from Puerto Rico, Cuba and points further south. Mrs. Puente loved music – it seemed she loved all kinds of music, Tito recalled. "The bands from Puerto Rico were among her favorite – mostly danzas. She adored Carlos Gardel. He was the big name in those days." Gardel died in 1935 in an airplane crash in Medellín, Colombia. Millions of his fans throughout South America mourned his death. His body was taken from Colombia through New York and back to Brazil.

At the Puente home, however, there was little mourning. Paying the rent and eating was more important, according to Tito. "Mom applied her wits – you know common sense." By the time the stock market crashed in 1929, Puerto Ricans living in what would become El Barrio, were adapting to the new environment, and even blending their cultural heritage to everyday life. The rent party was a purely black Harlem custom. In an apartment set aside for a party, there would be soul food and plenty to drink. A prominent pianist would be invited to play, the neighbors got the word and squeezed into the small apartment for a nominal fee that was used to pay for the entertainment and the rest set aside to help pay the coming month's rent. The Puerto Ricans that settled into El Barrio used the same method, but when there was no piano the music of tropical strumming guitars, a few voices singing the songs popular in Puerto Rico, Cuba, or some other far off place south of the border, had the same result – paying the rent. Sometimes Tito performed on the piano in the living room; sometimes he danced with his sister for the enjoyment of neighbors and guests. "Mom always had something up her sleeve," according to Tito.

"By the time we were in our early teens," he recalled, "Joe (Loco) would join in either at the piano or try to make me look like a bad dancer." Joe Loco was none other than Joe Estévez, who was Tito's neighborhood pal. He also studied piano and was quite a dancer.

Mrs. Puente pressed Tito into the New York School of Music where once a week he studied formal music – the piano, the saxophone and solfege (solfeo). It did not matter how bad things were economically; Tito had to keep up with his music. The years before World War II were a time in which El Barrio changed. Blacks populated west of Fifth Avenue. It was all mixed up on the East Side – Jews, Italians and a steady stream of Puerto Ricans mixing in. The civic associations sprang up too. This was the way the islanders maintained their connections to Puerto Rico. There were civic associations that dotted the neighborhood – Cuban, Puerto Rican and Spanish – all a great way for immigrants to stay connected to their roots.

The Spanish speaking population grew. The people fought to maintain their culture – food, banding together in the neighborhood, joining local organizations that were formed by islanders from a particular rural community, or just participating in recreational church activities. The central theme of the organizations, neighbor gatherings, and maintaining a link to one's ancestry – beyond helping to pay the rent – was entertainment. Opportunities in entertainment business improved as the population grew. Ercilia Puente helped organize a social club, or "civica" with her best friend, Mercedes San Juan – the mother of one of Tito's first loves, Olga San Juan.

"Our mothers were friends and we were enrolled in a Puerto Rican children's club that was called 'Infancia Hispana.' The president was my mother and Tito and I danced and sang together. We sat around the campfire when we went to camp, and he would imitate Mickey Rooney. Tito was always the clown and made us laugh. I was nine or 10." Olga San Juan recalled in an interview in 1997[9].

Olga San Juan[10] went on to become known as the "Puerto Rican Pepper Pot," and was the girl all the boys chased at dances in the church. Tito had a childhood crush on Olga San Juan. He never denied it – so did everyone else - Bobby Capó (1922-1989), Joe Loco and Tito Rodríguez, later were also in love with the actress. She was born in Coamo and came to the United States around 1940. Capó had worked for the orchestra of Rafael Hernández in Puerto Rico as a vocalist. His break as a singer in the United States would come with Xavier Cugat. He moved around New York and eventually made a name for himself as a songwriter. Some of his unforgettable melodies are: *"Piel Canela," "El Negro Bembón," "El Bardo," "Luna de Miel en Puerto Rico," "Sin Fe," "Triángulo,"* and *"María Luisa," "Llorando Me Dormí,"* and *"Sale el Sol."* The song *"Jacqueline,"* dedicated to former first lady Jacqueline Kennedy was composed in 1960.

The moms – Tito and Olga's - had their children attend dance school together. Tito and Olga studied Spanish Flamenco dancing, and then Tito took up dancing on his own. Other dances that were popular in the period were tango and gaucho. This was the era of Rudolph Valentino and Fred Astaire. "It was no big deal. In fact a man that danced was a very macho thing," Tito liked to remind me. Gaucho music, of course, comes from Argentina – sort of cowboy music of the Pampas. The tango – one of those music forms that has its roots in the habanera rhythm - was also popular.

The habanera, the soul of the Puerto Rican danza, is also the origin of what became known as the mambo. Gardel replaced Valentino, who died suddenly in 1926, as the international Latin idol. The Argentine made the tango global. He was popular with Puerto Ricans. The women, young and old, loved him. He died in1935, but his popularity does not seem to have diminished - more than 70 years after his death.

"We had a lot of barriers to break on the streets of New York. It was not always rosy. There were Blacks, Italians, Jews, and Irish all around us. We did not speak English and we had little exposure to the outside world. We sort of had to incorporate our music into the neighborhood. I guess looking back, the neighborhoods of the different ethnic groups were close and tight structures that offered each of us a sense of security. But our music drove us. It was not exposed like jazz, until after the war (World War II). We used to move around a lot but within the same few blocks. I remember my closest friend was Joe Loco, and later Tito Rodríguez – we lived either on the same block or within a few blocks of each other. We were close. Charlie Palmieri became a close friend when his family moved into El Barrio. We all loved Cuban music. We did not know much about it then, but looking back – well! Wow! It was dancing music. We all danced." Tito and I would talk for hours and hours about his "old days" in the neighborhood.

"At first, when I used to practice piano I never gave it much thought – you know, about how to make the music. It was always there. The music of the black bands like Cab Calloway, Ellington and Chick Webb was quite visible in Harlem. The radio blasted music from New Orleans. At home we listened to Carlos Gardel. I never gave it much thought – that is that the tango was a relative of the danzón. We listened to a lot of Cuban music. The conjuntos and trios were becoming popular. In the 1930s, the record companies were running around recording everything and anything. There were many stores selling records and they were cheap. There were many record companies." Cuba had developed a powerful network of radio stations that transmitted music around the island, and in turn, as had been the custom in the 1900s, Cuban music was listened to and played in Puerto Rico. The Puerto Rican danza was a staple of the orquesta tipica. In Cuba the orquesta tipica would eventually evolve into conjuntos, charangas and influence the styles of the local society orchestras. Tito had the music of two cultures, only thing was he did not know for sure which one was which, nor would he care for a long while.

Walking across to Harlem and taking in the sounds and sites was breathtaking, according to Tito. "Stand at the crossroads of 135th Street and Fifth Avenue in Harlem and you will be at the center of what was a vibrant area –on the south by Central Park, on the north by 155th Street, and stretching across from St. Nicholas Avenue over to the East River. There were opera houses, nightclubs and exclusive restaurants. There was the Cotton Club, the Lafayette, the Lincoln and the Alhambra Theater. There were plenty of whorehouses too." All this was accessible to Tito, and he maintained that the sights and sounds had a profound influence on him.

When you are raised in this type of environment it has to rub off on you. Of course seeing the Machito band, and sitting in with him during 1940 and 1941, would have a profound impact on him. "Maybe I was 13-years-old or younger when I played for Machito in the neighborhood. He was a nice guy – always had a smile. On weekends he would be at 110th Street and Fifth Avenue – near the Park Plaza. I played on Sundays. I would sit in with the group. I guess he saw I was talented and could handle what they were playing. The rumba was in vogue – not the Cuban rumba, but something the Americans came up with – light and bouncy. They taught me a lot about what street musicians do, it was important because this was how you learned to jam – to improvise. It was not easy. There are great musicians that can't improvise. And, there are a lot of musicians that can improvise that can't play in a band – you know a formal band. I liked jammin' with these guys but I was still going to school."

Between jamming with the Cuban and Puerto Rican musicians at the Park Plaza on weekends, Tito was also a Boy Scout, attended weekly meetings, and continued to play stickball in the neighborhood schoolyard. These activities were fitted in between his music lessons. He was enrolled at Public School 83, and his recollection was that "it was horrible." In addition to lessons with Doña Victoria, his mother found the money to enroll him in a branch of the New York School of Music that was located on 125th Street and Lenox Avenue.

Tito continued to try to outfox his mother and spend more time on the street. "It seemed with each new plan I thought up she had one to outsmart me. I swear she used to inspect the garbage even when I was in high school." His father, Ernesto Sr,. was aloof and distant but Tito and his younger sister never suspected that there was anything wrong. "He was never around. I figured he was working. That is what a father does," he shrugged.

In the late 1930s, Mario Bauzá sent for his brother-in-law Frank "Machito" Grillo from Cuba. Mario was married to Machito's sister, Estella. Machito was one of the nicest guys in the music business. By the way, not only could he sing, but he was an incredible dancer too. He set out to be a singer, and music was his life from an early age. He was the son of a cigar maker. He acquired the nickname Machito, as a youngster. He sang in many Havana groups, and also became a very proficient clave and maraca player, essential instruments in Cuban music. He finally relocated to New York in 1937, where he immediately found work singing, and landed in Conjunto Moderno, with whom he made his first recordings. He moved on to the Conjunto Caney, and recorded with them until 1939. He became lead singer for pianist Noro Morales, and did a short stint with Xavier Cugat, recording with both.

Noro Morales[11] moved to New York City in 1935, and within two years was leading his own rumba band. Installed as the house band at the legendary club El Morocco, Morales was at the center of the rise of Latin jazz in the early 1940s. Xavier Cugat took Morales' composition, *"Bim, Bam, Bum"* and recorded it for one of his earliest hits. Many of the great names in Latin music drifted through Morales' orchestra during this time: a young Machito, Tito Rodríguez, and Tito Puente. Morales was a major influence on Charlie Palmieri, and to a lesser extent his younger brother Eddie Palmieri. All of them lived within a few blocks of each other in Spanish Harlem.

Noro remained a popular and successful act on the New York scene for more than 20 years, appearing annually at the Daily News Harvest Moon Ball, and working clubs such as the Copacabana and the China Doll. After more than 25 years in New York, he was homesick for his island of Puerto Rico. In the late 1950s the music business in the United States was on a downward turn. The big bands or the swing era were being replaced by small conjuntos, ensembles, and venues such as the Palladium Ballroom were no longer profitable. Noro suffered from glaucoma brought on by diabetes and was beginning to lose his eyesight. All this contributed to his decision to go back home. In 1960, he did just that. His sister Alicia, through some business connections in Puerto Rico, negotiated a contract for him to play with his big band at La Concha Hotel in San Juan for six months. He performed at La Concha for nearly four years. Noro actually organized a new band in Puerto Rico. He chose the best local musicians he could find and brought others from New York with him.

Accompanied by the distinguished group of musicians he had brought together in Puerto Rico, Noro Morales continued his recording career. He made at least two albums for the Marvela and Fragoso labels. Accompanied by a small rhythm group he re-recorded some of his old hits such as: *"Perfume de Gardenias," "Silencio," "Arráncame La Vida,"* and *"Malditos Celos."*

Although he did cater to popular tastes, Morales usually stayed true to his Puerto Rican roots, using a traditional line-up featuring a rhythm section that included bass, bongos, conga, timbales, and claves, with himself on piano. In spite of his indomitable spirit, besieged by diabetes, glaucoma, and kidney problems, Noro Morales died on January 14, 1964, at the relatively young age of 53. He is buried in Puerto Rico, where he is recognized as a musical legend. He was a strong influence on musicians like Tito, who were just teenagers in the 1930s.

Noro's younger brother, Esy Morales (1917-1950) was considered one of the great flautists in American jazz. He appeared in a number of film noir with his jazz ensemble in the 1950s; and it is reported his masterful fluttering and his exotic style of playing intrigued Cuban flautist, Richard Egües, a young Cuban piano teacher who would join Orquesta Aragón in 1954 as its flautist. Unfortunately, Esy passed away at a young age, a victim of drug abuse. Humberto was the other brother who was considered a top percussionist and in later years gravitated toward Afro-Cuban jazz. In 1939 he joined with Noro and Esy to form an orchestra. Esy Morales was one of several flautists that Tito held in high esteem. "His style was exotic. It was his own style and I always believe that many guys picked up that way of playing – minor notes, rolling chromatic scales –very striking. He did not blow hard, and he had, it seems to me, a unique understanding of blending the black note and the white note – African and European harmonies."

El Barrio and neighboring Harlem was a kaleidoscope of musical convergence. The influence of the different cultures meeting within the designated boundaries – sometimes blending, but usually clashing was the atmosphere in which Tito grew up. The music he heard was on one side of the cultural flux a mixture of the remnants of ragtime, sophisticated big band as performed by black orchestras, European music and the beginnings of big band jazz. On the other side he was fed the music of his mother's homeland – danzas, the music of the tango, and the music of Cuba. Here too things were in a constant state of flux as the Puerto Rican and Cuban bands on their respective islands battled to contain or blend with the influences of the North American continent. Tito took it all in – the music. Formal education was another matter. He was not a good student. Tito did not like school. He did not want to go to school.

However, he had stopped challenging his mother about music. He enjoyed playing piano. Tito liked to listen to classical music and liked most music genres of the day. Tito liked banging on boxes, playing his trap drums and listening to not only Humberto Morales play timbales – the Cuban style timpani used in some Latin orchestras, he enjoyed sitting in with the Cuban percussionists at the Park Palace, a few blocks from where he lived. He became a disciple of Cuban timbalero Montesino.

Carnaval In Harlem

Tito and I used to chew the fat a lot about how he got to know Machito and all the other great Afro-Cuban music pioneers. Machito came from Cuba as a young man. His brother-in-law, Mario Bauzá had plans for him. Machito and Mario would become important in the development of Tito's music interests. Moreover, Machito grew to be one of two men whom he considered "like a father."

Machito and Mario became mentors to Tito. In his early teens Tito was still playing piano, practicing drums and observing first hand just how the Cuban percussionists played – congas, timbales and bongos. Tito was also playing the saxophone with local pick up street groups. Whenever he could he sat in with any group that let him at the Park Palace. Usually Machito waved him up on stage to let him take a turn at playing basic rhythms.

Whenever a group played at the church, the neighborhood teenagers were there for the dance. Olga San Juan was one of many young beauties that Tito and his pal, fellow dancer and piano player Joe Loco liked to chase. "It was all show – I would do my thing, Joe and the other guys would show off – it was all to get the ladies to look at us. We probably looked dumb," Tito recalled. "Joe was the best dancer. But I had the better lines – I had the gift of gab."

By the mid 1930s, Tito was starting to become serious about his music. "We all lived on the same few blocks; Joe Loco, Tito Rodríguez and Olga San Juan. We hung out at the civica, or I was playing with Machito whenever I could. Tito was singing somewhere. Joe Loco was already on his way to being a great pianist. Joe was the oldest, I think. He started playing the violin. I think Olga was already thinking about being an actress." Joe's real name was José Estevez. Tito, who was the jokester of the gang, gave him the name "Loco" – crazy after Joe was involved in an accident – he was hit by a bus while crossing the street. "Who knew then that it would stick," Tito reflected in later years.

In 1936, the Duke Ellington Orchestra played at the Savoy Ballroom. The Ellington sound Tito said was one of elegance and sophistication. But while Harlem was experiencing a rebirth on the East Side, the Puerto Ricans were clinging to their music – the romantic boleros, the son that was increasing in popularity in the central mountains of Cuba and pushing into the urban places like Havana. In a historic framework what was happening was that the son was perceived as "white" music and was embraced by Cuban urban whites. The danzón was being pushed from popularity. In New York we did not really understand this and when Tito was a teenager it was not a concern.

"We liked Cuban music. It did not matter how or where it came together. It just sounds right. It was great for dancing. It gave Latins – Puerto Ricans a sense of ownership – this is my opinion. Later, I learned you could do just about anything you wanted to the basic concept of Afro-Cuban music - play it straight and romantic or design the same piece as a jam session – you know a descarga. There is so much you could do with it," was one of the many ways Tito described it.

From his mother, Ercilia, Tito learned much about music too. She did not read a note of music and had no formal education. But she loved pretty much all Latin music, favored the tango and Carlos Gardel, and the Puerto Rican danzas of Juan Morel Campos[12]. However, one of her favorite danzas was "*Mis Amores*"-my love, composed by Simon Madera (great grand father of José Madera). I have been told that Morel Campos was something of a ladies' man. Most of his music was dedicated to the beauty of women. Like the tango, the danza and the danzón come from the habanera. It is also the rhythm of American ragtime.

There were many things going on in Tito's life in the late 1920s and 1930s. He reminded me often about the "Great Depression." This was an awful time for most Americans. It was even worse for Puerto Ricans and other Latins that lived in the United States. "When I tell you things were bad," he said in one of his more serious moments – almost like when he was directing his orchestra, "it was not a good time."

Joe Loco was nine and dancing in a vaudeville show. Tito was looking for a dance partner. It turned out to be Gracie Barro, according to what I have been told. She had been Joe's partner and he left her standing in the backstage shadows when he was hired to dance in a vaudeville show.

"Joe was a great dancer. Sometimes we practiced together in one of our apartments. There were always new complicated dance steps to learn. Shit we were smart-ass kids. Joe twisted and turned and we would come crashing down over the furniture. I think that is why our mothers pushed us to learn piano – in the long run it was cheaper. The furniture lasted longer," Tito laughed.

Rumba Timbales

"There was Gene Krupa and Benny Goodman and Harry James. These guys could really play."

He listened to all the bands of the period. But his favorites were Benny Goodman, Count Basie and Duke Ellington. On his list was also the orchestra of Chick Webb, Stan Kenton (later), and even Charlie Spivak and Artie Shaw. These bands always seemed to be playing in and around New York. There may have been no work, and many businesses were boarded up, and people in El Barrio were struggling, but there were dozens of theaters and nightclubs not far from where he lived. He could get to the place by walking or on the subway. Tito worked on his music studies and found time to listen and see the bands. At an early age he was already an opportunist and he made sure that he was always in a position to sit in wherever he could with other musicians, between school and music lessons. It was not easy. "Those were great bands," he liked to remind me.

Tito talked often about Krupa and how much he impacted his approach to playing percussion. Sometimes when I hear Tito playing I can't help think that so much of his style came from Gene Krupa. Tito integrated it to the Afro-Cuban format and it became his own. There were a lot of drummers and percussionists that Tito favored, but he maintained that Krupa was the most exceptional. "His style was incomparable, in your face. His thumping on the bass drum, the rolls and time cuts and strikes lifted the band and gave it incredible depth." Tito often explained to me that Krupa was a unique person in the music world. It was obvious he had a profound impact on Tito.

Gene Krupa[13] was born in Chicago; Illinois on January 15, 1909, His father died when Gene was a child and his mother labored as a milliner to support the family. All of the children had to start working while very young. Gene began at age 11. His brother Pete worked at Brown Music Company, and got Gene a job as errand boy. Gene started out playing sax in grade school but took up drums at age 11, since it was the cheapest item in the music store where he and his brother worked. "I used to look in their wholesale catalog for a musical instrument - piano, trombone, cornet - I didn't care what it was as long as it was an instrument. The cheapest item was the drums, 16 beans, I think, for a set of Japanese drums; a great high, wide bass drum, with a brass cymbal on it, a wood block and a snare drum." Gene's drive to drum was too strong, and his mother's expectation of him becoming a priest evaporated. In 1925, Gene began his percussion studies with Roy Knapp, Al Silverman and Ed Straight. Krupa started playing with Joe Kayser, Thelma Terry and the Benson Orchestra. A popular hangout for musicians when Krupa was embarking on his musical career was "The Three Deuces." All the guys playing in small bands would gravitate here after hours and jam till early in the morning. Gene was able to sharpen and develop his style playing with other jazz players such as Mezz Mezzrow, Tommy Dorsey, Bix Beiderbecke and Benny Goodman in these saloons. Krupa's big influences during this time were Tubby Hall and Zutty Singleton. The drummer who probably had the greatest influence on Gene during this period was the great Baby Dodds. Dodds' use of press rolls was reflected in the way Krupa played, especially during his time with the Benny Goodman Orchestra. Tito often talked about the drummers that influenced Krupa. "Many of these guys were self-taught, and came into their own after having to play for pennies, if they ever got paid at all."

Krupa has often been considered the first drum "soloist." Drummers usually had been strictly timekeepers or noisemakers, but Krupa interacted with the other musicians and introduced the extended drum solo into jazz. His goal was to support the other musicians while creating his own role within the group. He is also considered the father of the modern drum set since he convinced H.H. Slingerland, of Slingerland Drums, to make tuneable tom-toms. Tom-toms up to that point had "tacked" heads, which left little ability to change the sound. The new drum design was introduced in 1936 and was termed "Separate Tension Tunable Tom-Toms."

Krupa was a loyal endorser of Slingerland Drums from 1936 until his death. Krupa was called on by Avedis Zildjian to help with developing the modern hi-hat cymbals. The original hi-hat was called a "low-boy" which was a floor level cymbal setup that was played with the foot. This arrangement made it nearly impossible for stick playing. His first recording session was a historical one. It occurred in December of 1927 (Tito was four-years-old) when he is noted to be the first drummer to record with a bass drum. Krupa, along with the rest of the McKenzie-Condon Chicagoans were scheduled to record at Okeh Records in Chicago. OKeh's Tommy Rockwell was apprehensive to record Gene's drums but gave in. Rockwell said "Alright, but I'm afraid the bass drum and those tom-toms will knock the needle off the wax and into the street."

Red Nichols recruited the percussionist when he moved to New York in 1929. Krupa, along with Benny Goodman and Glenn Miller, performed in the pit band of the new George Gershwin play *"Strike Up the Band."* Gene had never learned to read music and "faked" his parts during rehearsals. Glenn Miller assisted him by humming the drum parts until Krupa got them down. After *"Strike Up the Band*" completed in January 1930, Hoagy Carmichael gathered several great musicians together for many historical sessions. Gene played on some legendary "jazz" recordings with Bix Beiderbecke, Adrian Rollini and Joe Venuti. Krupa played in one more pit band with Red Nichols for Gershwin's *"Girl Crazy."* He then joined Russ Columbo's band that indirectly led to his joining Benny Goodman's group. Goodman urged Krupa to join his orchestra with the promise that it would be a real jazz band. After joining, Goodman, Krupa became disheartened because the band was relegated to playing dance music and Benny Goodman[14] was considering packing it in. When the band was contracted at the Palomar, Goodman decided to go for broke and play their arrangements. The audience went wild and the band took off. The Goodman group featured his drummer prominently in the full orchestra and with the groundbreaking Goodman Trio and Quartet.

The Trio is possibly the first working small group that featured black and white musicians. On January 16, 1938, the band was the first "jazz" act to play New York's Carnegie Hall. Gene's classic performance on *"Sing Sing Sing"* (composed by Louie Prima) has been heralded as the first extended drum solo in jazz. After the Carnegie Hall performance, tension began to surface between Goodman and Krupa. Audiences were demanding that Krupa be featured in every number and the bandleader didn't want to lose the spotlight to a sideman.

The sound of the big orchestras fascinated Tito, and Krupa was his idol. The sophistication with which the orchestra delivered swinging dance music and then almost in the same breath take you on a romantic voyage that lifted you off your feet made Tito light up. Anytime we reminisced his eyes sparkled and gleamed when he thought about the days when the big bands were popular. I did not live through the depression. I was born in 1942. But when we talked about it the music was what helped Tito overcome some of those tough times.

Jazz music was an important part of Tito's life as a teenager. Louis Armstrong, Fats Waller and so many others were heard on radio, and in 78-rpm record grooves. Tito was always turned on by good music. It may amaze younger people today that 60 years ago it was easy to find exciting jazz on the radio. In Harlem, Tito recalled, "you could hear live music coming out of the whorehouses – piano, a bass, and sometimes a muted horn. You not only could get laid, but you could listen to good music."

It was a little harder to spot the Spanish language music, but it was there too. There were so many good bands, large and small, to be heard and Tito liked to say that he was "all ears" when it came to listening to them. Mutual, CBS, and two NBC (red and blue) radio networks were just part of the mix of radio stations – there was no television. Radio "remotes" – described like this because they were not from broadcast studios but from a remote place, made some bands famous. Many orchestras and ensembles were willing to work for less than their usual wage if their place of employment had a network radio remote. These were hard times for all. It was a struggle for musicians too.

Some of the hits that came from remote sessions include: Artie Shaw's *"Begin the Beguine,"* Charlie Barnet's *"Cherokee,"* Woody Herman's *"Woodchopper's Ball"* and Glenn Miller's *"In the Mood."* This last one was written by Joe Garland, a veteran saxophonist with a prominent black band, who began to earn substantial royalties on these big hit years later, only after joining ASCAP. This hit really caught Tito's attention. "The sax is deep and weighty," he said.

The swing era[15] that was about to be ushered in had a profound impact on Tito and scores of his peers. To hear Tito talk, this was what was happening and "we were right there – we just didn't realize it, at least not right away. Still, we were being fed this great music and like most young people – we loved it. We were in the front seat." During the swing era you could get into a ballroom and see a live band for a dollar or less. There you could dance a simple box step or something similar to the fox trot of the 1920s that moved you around the entire floor and let you dream you were gliding as gracefully as Fred Astaire. This was Tito's world. The difference was he had a wider choice, as he liked to point out. "We had jazz and swing, and we had Latin. It was progressing too."

Cuban y Puerto Rico Son...

Even though Xavier Cugat had a light Latin sound, tailored to the commercial market he had a substantial influence on Afro-Cuban music being accepted in New York. "He was a shrewd businessman who had common sense," explained Tito. "It was almost like a sixth sense – he knew when to shift gears and modify his sound."

Xavier Cugat was born in Barcelona, Spain, in 1900, and spent his childhood in Havana. Until the mid 1920s, he played for the Vincent López Orchestra in New York City. In 1927 he dashed off to Hollywood and by 1931 he took hold of the rumba or rhumba as it became known. By 1934, he was the house band of New York's Waldorf-Astoria Hotel. "These were top bands, smooth and easy to listen to." Tito said. "I guess they appealed to the older and more sophisticated crowds of that era. People my age were looking for something else. I guess every generation wants to leave a mark, make an impact, leave something behind."

Modesto Azpiazu[16] was a popular band that came from Cuba in 1932.

He was known as Don Azpiazu. Around the corner from where Tito lived, on 111th Street, was the theater where Myrta Silva appeared and Noro Morales played piano. You could hear it on the street. Alberto Socarras started an orchestra in 1934, to play in the Savoy Ballroom and the Cotton Club, among the places in Harlem. For Tito this was just more music to absorb. His interest at the time was the swing bands and dancing. But he continued to study the piano and tap on anything that he could. Throughout the period of the 1930s, phonograph companies recorded anything and everything they could lay their hands on. Some recordings have become classics, some have been lost forever, but Tito liked to remind me that "all the old stuff is not good – it should stay lost." However, there was a lot of good stuff.

The music of Don Azpiazu is one of many forgotten treasures in Afro-Cuban music lore or what is now called "salsa." His was the band whose 1930 "Manisero" not only became a huge national hit, launching a decade of rumba-mania, it was also the first U.S. recording of an authentic national Afro-Cuban style (in other words, Latin music, not U.S. music to a Latin rhythm, like the 1920s tangos). Equally important, Azpiazu's *"Peanut Vendor"* introduced to the Americans all those Cuban percussion instruments we now take for granted. His second recording, *"Aquellos Ojos Verde,"* or *"Green Eyes"* was the first example of true crossover with a North American vocalist.

More important yet, this was simply a very fine band indeed, by the standards of its peers. Alberto Socarras (b. Sept. 18, 1908, Manzanillo, Cuba, d. Aug. 26, 1987, New York, N.Y.) is a forgotten musician of the 1930s. A mulatto, he played saxophone and flute for Chick Webb's orchestra and was part of the Harlem scene. Socarras was the other flute player that captivated Tito. "He could play very fast, but he was always cautious because he was focused, he had a solid tone and a clean sound. He played the standard flute mostly, but occasionally would pick up the wooden flute with five keys. I used to see him play saxophone with Webb's orchestra. He was good." Before reaching New York he played in a family band that accompanied silent films in Cuba. He came to the United States in 1927, played with Vincent Sigler and Nilo Melendez and then got a job working with Lew Leslie's Blackbirds Orchestra (1928-33). He played an exciting flute that places him with many of the jazz greats. His final years were dedicated to composing classical music.

By 1939, hundreds of releases were in record company catalogs. Brunswick produced *"Masabi," "África," "El Diablo,"* and *"Porqué Lo Dices,"* in 1935. The RCA Victor catalog was extensive and included some of the earliest recordings of Cuban music (on cylinders) from 1906. Orquesta

Antonio Ma. Romeu, the father of the modern Charanga Orchestra (violins, wooden flute, piano, güiro and timbales or cavalry timpani) were on the list. In one of his early recordings, around 1927, a clarinetist by the name of Mario Bauzá was included in most of the selections. A few years later after playing trumpet for Chick Webb, he organized the Machito y sus Afro-Cubanos Orchestra.

In addition to working on his percussion proficiency with trap drums, Tito continued to study piano and saxophone. The piano lessons were classically structured. "Music lessons were focused on classical music, learning scales, practicing arpeggios, and a lot of repetition. There were no short cuts. Sight reading was something that came naturally as a result of practicing scales, chords, etudes and harmonic variations." He played some pop but mostly it was the danzas of Puerto Rico that were placed before him. "I probably learned more about Puerto Rican music during my piano lessons than even I imagined possible," he revealed. "There are terrific music traditions on the island." Puerto Rico developed a big band tradition, perhaps not as trendy as the Cuban orchestras became when their sound reached New York, but just as sophisticated.

The Puerto Rican orchestras[17] were as proficient in musicianship and ability as any other orchestras and bands of the swing era. Military musicians from Puerto Rico were among the best instrumentalists of their time. These men were drawn to the Army by its offer of employment, musical training, advance training and abundance of time for practice. The influential swing era of the big bands was looming. Many of the towns maintained municipal bands or "orquesta tipicas." These played marches, classical music and the popular danzas.

The 1920s and 1930s saw the emergence of the jazz-type bands with their trumpets, saxophones and trombones and a change in musical style. One of the earliest was the Jolly Kings Orchestra, organized in 1923 in Mayagüez. Its first leader was trumpet player Julio "Yuyo" Martínez. The Happy Hills Orchestra followed claiming the distinction of being the band with the longest continuous operation in Puerto Rico. The Happy Hills Orchestra was also the first dance band in Puerto Rico to have been led by a woman, Joséfa "Pepita" Nazario. In 1929, the Cuervos de la Noche Orchestra was a local favorite in the town of Quebradillas. Its leader was Angel García and among its members was Rafael Muñoz, who went on to lead one of Puerto Rico's most celebrated orchestras.

It was always surprising to me that Tito had considerable knowledge of these orchestras that were popular in Puerto Rico. "Mom used to listen to this music. I don't know where she got it from, but she got it and I listened to," he explained. "You also had to live on the fourth floor of 110th Street. The record player was always playing this stuff. When the record player was broke or turned off then mom had it coming out of the radio. I mean really, this is what the young people listened to and danced to."

The compositions and arrangements may sound a little subdued, even corny, he noted, but musically speaking "these musicians were ahead of their time. Too bad the recording industry was not able to capture the essence of these orchestras. I loved them."

Among the Puerto Rican big bands are Carmelo Díaz Soler Orchestra, Rafael Muñoz and his Orchestra, Pepito Torres Orchestra and César Concepción and his Orchestra. The Carmelo Díaz Soler Orchestra was founded in the 1920s. It was organized in Ciales. Díaz Soler was a military bandmaster. He studied classical music and played cornet, bass, the bombardino and piano in school and through private music lessons. He served his apprenticeship playing with the Police Band of San Juan, and the San Juan Firemen's Band. In 1914, he organized his first ensemble; a small group called "*Sombras de la Noche"* that provided musical background for the silent movies at the Teatro Tres Banderas. In the 1920s, he changed the name of the band to Orquesta Euterpe, which eventually was expanded to Orquesta de Carmelo Díaz Soler. The instrumentation was formatted along the lines of an "orquesta tipica" that played Puerto Rican danzas in their traditional style. It included: violins, bombardino, trumpets, saxophones, guitar, bass, piano, rhythm and vocalists. Euterpe was one of the most popular orchestras during the 1920s and 1930s. Its repertoire included: danza, danzón, bolero, waltz and foxtrot. Its recordings were played over the radio and in Tito's home in New York City. In 1927, the Carmelo Díaz Soler Orchestra traveled to Camden, New Jersey, to record 52 songs for Columbia Records. The majority of the songs were danzas, but the session also included some danzónes and other popular rhythms[18].

Carmelo Díaz attracted some of the best musicians and composers of the period. Among them are: Rafael Alers, Jesús María Escobar, Francisco López Cruz, Juanchín Ramírez and Carmelo's own two children, Angel Luis Díaz and Miguel Angel Díaz. The orchestra was one of the first in Puerto Rico to use vocalists and one of the first bands to play on the radio broadcasts. It became a fixture in the noon program of the West Indies Advertising Company on station WKAQ. Each Sunday the Carmelo Díaz Soler Orchestra playing danzas, danzónes and even swing characterized afternoons in Puerto Rico. The orchestra remained active and popular until its leader died, June 21, 1942.

Rafael Muñoz became the leader of what is considered one of Puerto

Rico's most historical orchestra. He was born in Quebradillas. His teacher was Don Concho Piña, a master musician who taught him to play instruments such as the trumpet, bass and flute. Muñoz honed his skills as a musician in Quebradillas, first with the Municipal Band and then with the Cuervos de la Noche Orchestra. He excelled as a flutist. The young musician moved to San Juan seeking to further develop his skills. In San Juan he continued his musical studies with composers Luis R. Miranda, Rafael Márquez and Jesús Figueroa. He played trumpet with the Mario Dumont Orchestra. In 1925, Muñoz joined the Midnight Serenaders Orchestra led by Augusto Rodríguez. That orchestra performed nightly at the Condado Vanderbilt Hotel.

When the Escambron Beach Club was inaugurated in 1932, Rivero was asked to organize an orchestra to play in the ballroom. Rafael Muñoz was one of the musicians he selected to join his band. Two years later, Rivero departed for New York, and Rafael Muñoz was selected to take his place. On May 12, 1934, at the Escambron Beach Club in San Juan, Rafael Muñoz gave the downbeat and the Rafael Muñoz Orchestra was born. This orchestra became one of Puerto Rico's most popular big bands.

Muñoz had the stature reminiscent of the great bandleader Paul Whiteman, who was known as "The King of Jazz" in the 1920s before the introduction of swing bands. Muñoz carefully chose the members of his band based not only on their musicianship, but also on their behavior on and off the bandstand. The original Rafael Muñoz Orchestra included: Pepito Torres, Jossie Henríquez and Alfredito Hirsch, saxophones; Miguelito Miranda and Arcadio Ruiz, trumpets; Samuel Rivera, trombone; Rufo Oben and Luis Cardona, violin; Rafael Petitón Guzmán, piano; Juan Pratts, drums; Rafael Muñoz, bass. The vocalist was Deogracias Vélez. At various periods in the band's history it featured pianist Noro Morales, Miguelito Miranda, César Concepción, the González Peña Brothers, the Elvira Brothers, Pepito Torres and Roberto Cole. Every one of these musicians would eventually become respected bandleaders. Muñoz carefully selected his vocalists to complement the sweet, romantic sound of his orchestra. The crooning voices of José Luis Moneró, Victor Luis Miranda and Victor Garay fit into the support function the bandleader wanted. The pair were capable of singing romantic lyrics of such boleros as: *"Olvídame, Pétalos de Rosa," " Di Corazón," " Esperanza," "Enojo"* and *"No Podré Olvidarte."*

The Rafael Muñoz Orchestra remained at the Escambron Beach Club until 1942. Afterward, the band moved to the Condado Hotel and then to the Normandy Hotel. In 1944, unexpectedly, Rafael Muñoz left for New York City, and that marked the end of the orchestra that has been called "The orchestra of yesterday, today, and forever." The orchestra recorded more than 300 selections for the RCA Victor, Decca and Verne labels. Rafael Muñoz died on September 2, 1961.

New York and Havana were not the only venues where band competition was fierce. It was just as furious among the Puerto Rican bands. At the peak of popularity the Rafael Muñoz Orchestra had to face challenges from up-and-coming orchestras that had an array of exceptional musicians. One of those was Pepito Torres from Vega Baja, who at one time played saxophone with the Muñoz Orchestra. He worked in New York, where he absorbed the new sounds and techniques of swing music. He returned to Puerto Rico in 1940, and incorporated his ideas into his own band. He was influenced by the black bands of Harlem and by the swing era bands. He particularly wanted to have a strong saxophone section that would be featured in all the arrangements. In order to get the special sound he wanted, Torres brought together a group of gifted, young saxophonists. At different times, the sax section included Pepito Torres, Rafael Torres, José "Pepin" Trujillo, Chino Acevedo, and Luisito Benjamin, who also played piano. Featured on trumpet were Pete Rivera, Miguelito Miranda, Alberto Torres and Pedrito Romero.

During its brief existence the Pepito Torres Siboney Orchestra made noteworthy contributions to Puerto Rican popular music. Vocalists Joe Valle and Manolín Mena performed the romantic boleros, backed by spicy rhythms of the orchestra. Torres passed away in his native town of Vega Baja, on June 17, 1997.

The César Concepción Orchestra has been Puerto Rico's finest and most popular orchestras. Concepción had a complete musical education and experience with swing bands in the United States. When Concepción returned to the island he established his orchestra that some claim mirrored the excellence of the Glenn Miller, Benny Goodman, and Harry James orchestras. He wanted the best musicians he could find. His blueprint for this objective was with a front line of five saxophones, backed by a three-piece trumpet section. He visualized that his own trumpet playing would give the orchestra a distinctive sound. "Cesar Concepción was a strong trumpet player, subdued and a lot like Charlie Spivak," according to Tito. The Concepción band was one of Tito's favorites.

"At home the bands of Puerto Rico were part of the musical diet. To me they played an important role in what was happening to music. The musicians were studious and serious. A lot of Puerto Rican musicians were recruited in the United States for both white and black bands of that period. You know – the give and take. We were always learning from each other, only a lot of us did not realize it," my friend explained. "The Cubans learned from the Americans, the Puerto Ricans learned from the Cubans and the Americans, well you know, they picked up from both the Cubans and Puerto Ricans – makes for a heck of a mix, eh! The funny thing is that growing up in El Barrio I had no idea what nationalities most of these bands were. It was all music to me – just good music."

Tito listened and absorbed the music the bands of Puerto Rico played. But Benny Goodman and his orchestra was the magnet. This was his focus. Tito followed the orchestra on radio. For Tito, drummer Gene Krupa was sensational. He heard the November 6, 1935 session from the Congress Hotel in Chicago. He was intrigued by the aggressive arrangements for percussion and learned them all just by listening to the music being piped over the airwaves. Krupa was an incredible showman that reminded Tito in later years of New Orleans percussion styles – a rambunctious technique that was a by-product of the Dixieland jazz era that overwhelmed ragtime music. This is one of the things that influenced the Ukrainian-American Krupa.

The style these bands played sprang from military ensembles. In the Caribbean they were called "tipicas." The percussion was mostly in the hands of the tympani or timbal player. The timbales are two drums of distinct size. The larger drum is 14 inches from side to side and the smaller one is 13 inches across. The larger drum is placed on the left and the smaller drum to the right of the musician. They are played with a 12-inch wand. The timbales are a rhythmic instrument and extremely important in Afro-Cuban and Latin American music. In Cuban music, they give life to rumbas, guarachas and all other rhythms marked by a Cuban style. In its early days (1879-1916), the danzón was interpreted by the orquesta tipica, which included woodwind and brass instruments, violins, acoustic bass, güiro (gourd scraper believed to be of indigenous Caribbean origin), and the creole timpani, a smaller version of the European timpani. During the first two decades of the 1900s, the orquesta tipica was gradually replaced by the charanga francesa, or simply charanga, which features five key, six hole wooden flute along with piano, bass, violins, güiro and creole timpani which were eventually replaced by the timbales. The tipica format was also the stepping-stone that led to the Cuban conjuntos.

The percussive instrument was one of the many ways that Cuban composers – white, black and mulatto – were able to introduce African rhythm into their music. African drumming was prohibited in Cuban white gatherings. The timbales/pailas (pails) or tympani were acceptable.

In the late 1930s, the small cowbell was permanently added to the timbales setup; this innovation is generally credited to Ulpiano Díaz, timbalero with the charanga Arcaño y sus Maravillas[19]. The orchestra was led by flautist Antonio Arcaño and included Israel "Cachao" López on bass, and his brother Orestes López on cello and piano. The cowbell was a device that had been used by the Yorubá, who were Africans brought to Cuba as slaves. The cowbell was first introduced to the tipicas in the early 1900s, at the peak of their popularity in order to help make them more exciting during the extended version of the classic danzón. The timbales were invented in order to provide a more portable, less booming replacement for the timpani. In the early days of the charanga, timbaleros (timbal players) would tune their drums to specific notes (usually a fourth or a fifth apart), often changing to a new key between songs as a concert timpanist would.

As in New Orleans, competition among Havana bands was fierce, and the louder the better. This was what Tito liked listening to. Krupa's style called for a long booming sound from the large bass drum, plenty of rattling in the snares to carry for distance over a lot of strong brandishing brass. This engrossed and intrigued Tito. He liked the other bands too, but he revered Benny Goodman and Gene Krupa. When Goodman appeared in the Manhattan Room at the Pennsylvania Hotel, he enlarged the band with Harry James and Ziggy Elman. The two trumpeters added a subliminal range to the music that Goodman played. When the band opened at the Paramount Theater in Times Square, Tito timed it exactly so that he could be there.

Missing school would not be a problem. He would have a story for his mother. He was attending Central Commercial High School. He was a few days shy of becoming 15-years-old. He cut class, rode the subway down to Midtown Manhattan and waited on line for hours to get into the theater. It was what kids did in those days.

Tito told me with a gleam in his eyes, "My heart just pounded and I trembled with excitement as they played. I got up and danced in the aisles with all the other people. I knew right there what I wanted to do. I wanted to play just like Gene Krupa."

People went crazy in those days for big band music. Tito loved jazz. Tito confirmed this on more than one occasion. Tito told me about how Benny Goodman could really swing. "Let's Dance," he says to me in a loud voice that echoes through the restaurant where we are having lunch one afternoon. Whenever he reminisced about swing era his voice vibrated. "Let's Dance, rang through the large room as the stage came up. We were all dancing wildly - I mean it. You had to be there to see it, to feel it. Gene Krupa was incredible. I could not take my eyes off him. The way he handled the percussion. It fit right in. If he played loud it was because he was supposed to. He could lay back and coast along, allow the brass to swing, back up the soloist. He was smooth."

Krupa started out with Goodman in 1933. He set a drum percussive standard that few could master. Sitting to the left of Harry James, the two were a duet and worked out sparkling routines. Harry would play, and Krupa would rattle off the same thing on the snare drum. This is something that Tito would incorporate into his own orchestral styles. In many ways Tito absorbed much of what he heard and saw from Gene Krupa. The ways that Krupa kept time fired up the musicians. He could be overbearing at times – even loud – but he knew how to step back and just mark time. Krupa played behind soloists and ensembles using both sticks on the snare drum, playing 1-2-3-4 with the right stick on the snare and accenting on the two and four with the left stick. This was interspersed with rim shots, accents on the tom-toms or small crash on cymbals, and every so often a spirited riff.

There was nothing that the Benny Goodman Orchestra couldn't do. Krupa would kick off with *"Sing, Sing Sing,"* and it drove Tito crazy. "Then came *'One O'clock Jump,'* followed by *'and the Angels Sing,'* - kind of easy going." Tito practiced everything he heard – day in and day out, and even signed up for a contest at the Paramount that included Krupa and Goodman as judges. He was still playing the piano; learning the saxophone, and learning how to be a dancer. Yet his immediate attention was to learn every roll, every strike and beat that Krupa performed.

"When I got to the Paramount that day, it was just after school. I was dressed very sharp. I got my number. There were loads of contestants my age, 14 and 15. We had to play with Goodman's band, and then do our solo. I practiced every day before sitting up there with those musicians. I played '*Sing, Sing, Sing.'* I did the Gene Krupa's spotlight ad-lib almost note for note! It was something I did right from the beginning and I won. There was a little syncopation too – Latin shit, Wow! I never forgot that day." The prize was $10 – a lot of money in 1937. The important event escalated Tito's interest in the big bands – American big bands and the Latin bands. In retrospect, he often reflected "it was my mother who started me on a steady diet of Puerto Rican music – all those bands that existed in Puerto Rico, and other places."

But the swing bands drew him, and Benny Goodman was now an inspiration. He wanted to learn all he could about the clarinet player and bandleader. Goodman[20] was born into a large, poverty stricken family, and began playing the clarinet at an early age. He was associated with the Austin High School Gang, having gone to school with drummer Dave Tough. By the time he was 12, Goodman appeared onstage imitating famous bandleader/clarinetist Ted Lewis. It was at this concert that Ben Pollack heard the young clarinetist and Goodman was soon playing in Pollack's band. His first recordings were made with the Pollack group in 1926. From these early recordings one gets a strong example of the influences at the time including Jimmie Noone, who was then with Doc Cook and His Dreamland Orchestra, and Leon Roppolo of the New Orleans Rhythm Kings. During this period Goodman recorded his first 78 rpm records as a leader with members of the Pollack band including one 1928 date, which features the only known recording of Goodman on alto and baritone saxophones. Following the musical migration out of Chicago and into New York, Goodman became a very successful and popular free-lancer, joining the likes of Tommy and Jimmy Dorsey in New York studios. In 1934, Benny put together his first big band, featuring Bunny Berigan on trumpet, Jess Stacey on piano and Gene Krupa on drums. With the addition of some excellent, sophisticated arrangements by Fletcher Henderson, the "swing era" was born. Goodman spent the next 50 years recording and touring with various groups big and small, including some very successful trips to Russia and the Far East. He also played many concerts on a classical format that received mixed reviews. Known by musicians for his standoffish and "stingy" nature, many sidemen had a love/hate relationship with Goodman. That aside, its clear that without Goodman the "swing era" would have been nowhere near as strong when it came, if it came at all, Tito and many others believed.

The Swing Era or Rhumba Craze

When I look back to all the talks and moments I shared with Tito, I can't help but think about how confusing it must have been growing up in New York. Latinos, even though there was a substantial population, were relatively confined to the neighborhood. There was racial bigotry to deal with. The blacks were doing their own thing. The swing era was just starting. Cuban music was relegated to a secondary role, toned down to suit the Anglo population – it was called rhumba or rumba[21]. There had been a Depression. The gangsters were selling and bootlegging booze, and willing and able to kill for their territory. Tito maintained many links to these people, just to survive.

Likewise, on the horizon World War II was looming. Tito always looked at this time as one in which he obtained his knowledge and tools to pursue his career in music. "There was so much music. The swing era produced so many successful bands with so many great musicians.

Internationally, there were bands, also with great musicians, all trying out new things. It was a hell of a time to be involved in music. It was live, for the most part."

In 1935, the United States was starting to climb out of the Great Depression that followed the stock market crash of 1929, and to hear Tito talk it was a great time. Times were hard but the swing era - golden age of the big bands - was in its initial phase. In 1935, President Franklin D. Roosevelt was creating large federal agencies, and Social Security legislation was approved in Congress. The Republican Party complained about the President's "New Deal" and Democrats enjoyed President Roosevelt's "fireside" chats over the radio.

Composer George Gershwin's *"Porgy and Bess"* opened in New York. Fred Astaire sang about being in heaven while dancing *"Cheek to Cheek"* with Ginger Rogers in the smash movie *"Top Hat."* The music was by Irving Berlin. In 1935, Elvis Presley was born in Tupelo, Mississippi. The birth of the swing era is usually dated August 21, 1935. The Benny Goodman Orchestra opened this night at the large Palomar Ballroom in Los Angeles. After years of struggling, the orchestra opened with young fans standing and cheering wildly around the bandstand. Before Goodman's success, white jazz fans were a small yet devoted group. The Latino support for this music, according to Tito, "was mostly located in East Harlem."

Most white people knew little about the music of people like Fletcher Henderson, Duke Ellington or most jazz musicians. If they had heard of Ellington it was as one who played "jungle music for "copper colored" dancers at the Cotton Club in Harlem, where blacks performed before white audiences, and possibly as the composer of *"Sophisticated Lady."* There were those who did know about Paul Whiteman's orchestra and singers Bing Crosby (a vocalist of the Paul Whiteman establishment), Al Jolson, and Gene Austin. These entertainers quietly crossed back and forth between the color barriers. White people had heard of Louis Armstrong. But Goodman changed the public thinking about dance band music, popular music, and jazz and orchestra leaders. He put jazz musicians up front where they had seldom been before. Years later it was Tito's view this was a crucial opening – a breakthrough for struggling Latin musicians, because behind jazz came Afro-Cuban music, authentic and exciting. Goodman and Krupa were his idols. As a teenager, he admitted often he did not have a clue about racial injustice. "Look where I come from – who really knew these things? I guess we were living them and it wasn't until much later that you begin to look at the world a little differently – more closely."

's Wonderful

There were dances all around El Barrio on Friday and Saturday. Every civica had live music. La Milagrosa Catholic Church was also a place that hosted dances - something many people in the neighborhood looked forward to – summer, fall, winter and spring. Another local club was "Casita Maria," located at 110th Street and Lexington Avenue. Everybody got dressed up for the gatherings and there was always live music. The parish in East Harlem had dances to raise money for the congregation. One weekend in 1935, Noro Morales and his brothers came in with the orchestra - younger brother Esy – the flautist, and Humberto, the percussionist. In the audience were 15-year-old José Estevez (Joe Loco), 13-year-old Tito, and Johnny Rodríguez, who was 20-years-old, and the sole supporter of 10 siblings. One of the younger brothers was Tito Rodríguez, a future bandleader, singer and dancer.

Tito enjoyed the music, but at this time in his young life his interests in music gravitated to the swing bands. Noro Morales was not a fan of the swinging jazz movement. He preferred to play the tempered music of his homeland, mixed with a few guarachas, some ballads and even soft American music with a "rhumba" beat. He was laid back and liked the easygoing sounds of Puerto Rico – like the danza, bomba and plena. Tito often reflected that this was a time of emotional conflict for him. The Benny Goodman Orchestra was much on his mind.

"Looking back at this time, I don't think any of us – people my age, you know, the teenagers like me and Joe understood what was happening. We were Puerto Ricans, with distinct cultural traditions. Our parents were dealing with incredible changes. Most of them did not speak English. It was difficult. Also, Noro was there. He played smooth and soothing music. But we liked Benny Goodman – you know jazz." By this time, as much as Tito enjoyed hoofing he had to take it easy. A bicycle accident a few years earlier curtailed his maneuvers on the dance floor. His Achilles heel was severely damaged.

He could still move, but with a subdued motion as he described it. "Joe and the others really had no pity on me. They were interested in conquering the beauties."

Soon he would be drawn to the Cuban sound of Orquesta Casino de la Playa. The majority of the musicians that formed this band were playing with Los Hermanos Castro Orchestra. Among these were Miguelito Valdés, Walfredo de los Reyes, Sr., Anselmo Sacasas and Guillermo Pórtela. But now his main attention was drawn to the swing bands that were battling over the airways, in ballrooms and on records. The way people danced was changed forever, Tito recalled. These bands responded to dancers – young dancers. It was exciting.

In those days many of the big bands used two or three dancing acts that they secured through booking agencies[22]. Cab Calloway's orchestra, for example, might see an act he liked and he would have the manager of the band track it down and book it for a future engagement. In the 1930s, the most well-known African-American theater circuits was called 'Round the World. Its tour comprised such independent theaters as the Howard in Washington, D.C., the Lafayette in Harlem and the Royal in Baltimore. There were others. These dance acts coincided with the big band era. By the mid 1930s, many dancers had modified their routines to perform with the big bands on stage. Without warning or apparent preparation, they would insert a variety of floor and air steps, a spin or a flip, or syncopated pauses, other types of hesitations and twists, and then easily return to the routine. "One of my favorite things to watch was tap dancers."

Tito had his own tap routine as a dancer. He liked the snappy way dancers tapped and moved. I used to see him – every so often – do one of those steps. "Does it remind you of something," he exclaimed - The Palladium, of course. That also brought a gleam and a smile. "I thought once that I would either be a dancer or a stickball player," he laughed.

It always impressed Tito to see the hoofers perform with the big bands. Honi Coles worked as a single with Count Basie, Claude Hopkins, Jimmy Lunceford, Fats Waller, Duke Ellington, Lucky Millinder, Louis Armstrong and Cab Calloway. Buster Brown toured with Count Basie and Dizzy Gillespie; Bunny Briggs worked in front of the Ellington Orchestra; Jeni LeGon danced with Fats Waller's orchestra – there were so many and Tito enjoyed watching many of them more than once. The premier stage and number one testing ground in America was Harlem's Apollo Theater. Beginning in 1934, stage shows were built around such well known jazz bands as those led by Duke Ellington, Count Basie, Don Redman, Chick Webb, Fletcher Henderson and others. There were four or five shows daily. Each one started with a short film followed by a seven-act revue. "We forget that the dancing bands or swing era bands were tied to the dancing. It was all connected."

Tito also used trained front line dancers with his band. Even though he was limited in movement because of his accident as a teenager, he would get in with the dancers and do a few steps. The dancers were often contracted by the Puente orchestra, by either Machito and Tito Rodríguez, or any big band that was playing at the Palladium. Some of these included: Cuban Pete and Millie Donay; Augie and Margo; The Mambo Aces and the Cha Cha Taps. These were all popular in the 1950s but Tito used them much like the swing era bands did. He was a showman.

"There were not only band battles going on, but dance battles as well and the Lindy or Lindy Hop as it was called changed. The dancers did it all. The music was pulsating and the dancing was rocking." Between music lessons, going to school, and studying piano, Tito found time to visit the clubs in Harlem and in other parts of the city where the big bands were bruising each other. The Savoy's success in no small part is due to the famous "battle of the bands" staged there with the dancers, creating visualizations of the music. You can imagine a young Tito Puente right in the middle of all this. He was not shy, and liked to brag about his ability to move around the floor.

For most of the 1930s, the all time favorite at the Savoy was the hard-driving band of Chick Webb. By the way, Mario Bauzá, who formed Machito and his Afro-Cubans, and was instrumental with Webb in discovering Ella Fitzgerald, was Webb's musical director. When a band battle was scheduled, Webb's musicians trained like prizefighters and had special section rehearsals to prepare for the "kill." The 1930s was setting the stage for what was to transpire after World War II, according to Tito. The swing bands were setting the stage for Tito Puente and his orchestra, and for all the other great bands that would be popular in the 1950s.

One of the most famous battles at the Savoy was the night the Benny Goodman Band faced Chick Webb and his Little Chicks. This was one of Tito's favorite episodes. He had read and listened to the tales from historians, critics and participants. The Savoy was packed and many more people waited outside. For blocks, traffic was backed up in every direction – with about 25,000 people trying to attend. Goodman pulled out all his guns, but could not win the crowd. When Webb ended the session with a drum solo, the dancers exploded in a thunderous ovation. Goodman and Gene Krupa, it has been reported, just stood by quietly. Even Tito agrees. The Savoy was Webb's home base, he played on and off at the ballroom for 10 years until 1939. "He had a phenomenal dance band," Tito declared.

The Savoy was one of those places that Tito often referred to in the framework of it being an incredible place where culture and music progressed. "It had a lot to do with American jazz and it had a lot to do with how we as Latinos composed, performed and exported our music – at least in the United States."

In 1935, Tito was beginning to understand that the soft, lush tropical melodies of Puerto Rico were not what he wanted to play. He often practiced danzas and bombas on the piano, even tried some melodies on his sax. There was no stirring. "It was tropical and exotic, but it did not move me." Standing in the church with Joe Loco and listening to the music of Noro Morales probably inspired him to somehow bring the old and the new together- but just how remained a task that had to be accomplished. There was a lot happening in the mid to late 1930s. Joe Loco was very much a dancer but with a strong leaning to the American jazz genre.

Tito was slowly steering toward his Latin roots but while the music of Noro Morales was plush, exotic and tropical, he was not interested in the bombas, plenas and danzas his mother loved so much. It was the percussion. You have to remember that as a youngster he was already jamming with the Cubans and other percussionists that lived in the neighborhood. "Noro's brother Humberto was so good. I used see him. He was one of Noro Morales' percussion men. I played with Noro one night at the El Morocco, I think in 1937. It was nice. We were all dressed. They played society Latin – some rumbas – soft. It was not for me. In the neighborhood it was a little more pungent – you know – African."

"The "rhumba" craze was in full throttle during the swing era. Yet the rumba bands were always second fiddle to the American bands. They were fillers or came in when the top billed orchestra took a break. "We used to see them in Harlem all the time – some big names, some not so big - Noro Morales, Alberto Socarras, and a lot of others," described Tito.

Desi Arnaz led a band in a Manhattan nightclub. Arnaz began his career as singer with Xavier Cugat's band in 1935-36; he formed his own band at The Conga Club in Miami in1938, at the height of the "conga craze." His Broadway musical debut in *"Too Many Girls,"* was in 1939 and was followed by the RKO film version of the musical, in 1940. Arnaz worked with the Lecuona Cuban Boys in Cuba, directed by none other than Ernesto Lecuona, and toured the United States during the 1930s and became a huge success. Lecuona composed several scores for four MGM films during the early 1930s, and earned an Academy Award nomination for the title song to 1942's *"Always in My Heart"* (Estas Siempre En Mi Corazon). Lecuona was named the cultural attaché to the Cuban embassy in Washington, D.C., in 1943.

The real rumba was Cuban and African in origin. It had nothing in common with the American version. Rumba arose in Havana in the 1890s. As a sexually charged Afro-Cuban dance, rumba was often suppressed and restricted because it was viewed as lewd. In the 1920s, the prohibition in the United States caused a flourishing of the relatively tolerated cabaret rumba as American tourists flocked to see crude short plays or shows in small Havana theaters that featured racial stereotypes and generally incorporated the main three Afro-Cuban percussive genres. This form is completely African in origin.

The rumba developed among the different African ethnic groups, primarily from Central and West Africa, who were brought to Cuba as slaves. Its development in Cuba dates back to the mid-19th century during the Spanish Colonial period. The authentic rumba was played for solemn and religious services and occasions. It was also party and dance music in which everyone participated. At first, it was performed outdoors in patios, backyards and empty lots. Eventually it moved indoors into small rooms and clubs. Following the African tradition, those present must play, scrape, rattle or beat something. It could be a drum, a wooden box, a chair, sticks, spoons, or maracas. It is formal music in terms of specific beats, rhythms and timing. The audience is in a participatory ritual. The parties went on for days. In Cuba the parties are called "rumbones" or "rumba" festivals. The "rumbones" spring up for a variety of occasions such as: holidays, birthdays, baptisms, weddings, or whenever a group of people gets together for a good time.

There are three main variants of the rumba developed in the middle 1800s, the guaguancó, the colombia, and the yambú. The tempo of the guaguancó is slightly slower than that of the Colombia and faster than the yambú. The American version of rumba that was popular when Tito was growing up was not even close to the real thing. "It had nothing to do with the real thing," he pointed out.

There is also a strong Spanish and even French influence on Afro-Cuban music. The root of this is the habanera that is heard in many musical genres. It is the origin of the Argentine tango, the Puerto Rican danza, the Cuban danzón and American ragtime. The phenomenal richness of European folklore, mixed with the vigor of African music, created an explosive and exuberant musical tapestry in the new world. The habanera, which has impacted every music genre since it beginnings in the Caribbean, has proven to be one of the most versatile and stimulating rhythms. The English Country Dance or the contradanza that was brought to Hispanola (Haiti) by the French is one of the principal parents, the other being West African slaves that were transported to the Caribbean. The contradanzas in 2/4 time have shown a remarkable resiliency, for their descendants are still flourishing. Although the melodies of the early contradanzas are obviously

European, their composers soon began to use rhythmic patterns of African origin in their accompaniments.

The basic and ever-present tresillo (a 16th note, an eighth note and another 16th note, followed by two eighth notes) appeared when popular musicians rhythmically misinterpreted the European triplet-formula of two versus three in equal counting. The 19th century witnessed the quick evolution of dance music rhythmically different from European models, which rapidly influenced the sophisticated piano compositions of Manuel Saumell and of Ignacio Cervantes (1847-1905), as wcll as the heavily romantic works of Nicolás Ruiz Espadero (1832-1890). In Puerto Rico, Manuel Gregorio Tavárez and Juan Morel Campos were the two key composers that shaped the new music. The New Orleans born composer-pianist Louis Moreau Gottschalk spent several years in Cuba and Puerto Rico and was a close friend of Saumell and Espadero. He mostly likely influenced a young Tavarez during one of his San Juan piano concerts.[23]

The danzón, another direct descendant of the habanera was born in the late 1870s - the official year is 1879 and composer Miguel Failde introduced it. He led an orchestra known as a tipica – wind and brass instruments and violins. These ensembles were the hybrids of military bands. The ensembles were the same in New Orleans and in Puerto Rico. Around the end of the 19th century the charanga francesas began to appear – three to six musicians in tuxedos playing background music at the high scale brothels that dotted the Havana area.

Classical pianist Antonio María Romeu incorporated the piano to the sextet while playing at an after hours pub before 1912. The charangas (ad hoc) francesas (named because it was in the French style brothels that they played) gained in popularity eliminating the noisy brash tipicas from competition by the end of the teens. Louis Moreau Gottschalk[24] (1829-1869) - was born in New Orleans. Gottschalk was attracted to the pre-jazz Creole music of his native city and the Afro-Caribbean tunes of the islands he explored for five years. Gottschalk's father, a stockbroker, was born in England. His strikingly beautiful mother was related to the French aristocracy and was born in Haiti.

The young Gottschalk began to play the piano at the age of three. He was only 12 when his parents sent him more than 3,000 miles away to Paris, then the center of the music world, to study piano and composition. There he was refused admission to the Paris Conservatory. The director claimed that America "could produce nothing but steam engines." He took private lessons, and rapidly became the artistic and social rage of the continent. He spent more than a decade in Europe, where he "hobnobbed with the socially high and mighty, but also earned the admiration of artists of the caliber of Chopin, Liszt and Berlioz."

Gottschalk toured constantly, from Cuba and Puerto Rico to Canada, from New York to California. However, from 1857 to 1862, he dropped out of the concert scene entirely and traveled in South America and the Antilles, Haiti, Puerto Rico, Jamaica, Martinique and Guadeloupe. Gottschalk spent three years in Argentina, Peru, Chile and Uruguay, and arrived in Rio de Janeiro, Brazil, in May 1869. Six months later he collapsed during a recital while playing his own composition, Morte. He died before the end of the year, at age 40. He traveled the islands of the Caribbean with Cuban composer José White (*La Bella Cubana*). His piano works stimulated "the cultural ragbag" of New Orleans - a mixture of "French quadrille and vaudeville, Italian romantic opera, what was called the Cuban tango and contradanzas and sundry Creole hybrids between the elitist and the populist." Much of his music for the piano is the basis of what would become American ragtime. The popular rumba of the 1930s was a mixture of all these influences.

That was one thing that there was a lot of – nightclubs and places to listen to dance music or just listen to music. It was all live," Tito explained in one of those moments of reflection. "Can you imagine the word 'rhumba' spelled with an h – it was an American fad," he continued.

Tito first heard Orquesta Casino de la Playa[25] in 1937. It was the new rage of Cuban orchestras. It had the same impact on him that Benny Goodman and Gene Krupa had. He maintained that this Cuban ensemble was probably the single biggest influence on him in terms of musical direction. Miguelito Valdés was the singer. "It was different from everything Cuban that came before," he said. At the time Gene Krupa was his hero, but Casino de la Playa hooked him for the rest of his life on Afro-Cuban music. From this point in his life his musical sensibilities were focused on incorporating Afro-Cuban music into mainstream swing, jazz and popular music. His classical music training would help him achieve some of those objectives. He had no idea he would become an American musical force or that his name would be mentioned alongside many of the pioneers he admired. He always reminded me of how good these legendary musicians were. "They did a lot of testing, trying out new things. It is not always easy to change what is popular – these guys did." As far as Tito was concerned this was the beginning of the end for the Rumba Era.

Miguelito Valdés and Tito would eventually form a close and lasting friendship. "Miguelito always reminded me that the Casino de la Playa group was not big, but they had terrific orchestration – a big sound. The

Afro sound was vibrantly present. This was something that was prohibited – you know – the racial thing. These musicians understood how to blend the complicated structure and at the same time made it exciting and danceable. Classical composers like Debussy could do that – give a feeling, get a big sound with just the right notes being played at certain times," is how Tito explained his being lured to the Afro-Cuban sound.

Valdés[26] started singing in 1927 with a few amateur ensembles and groups, then decided music was his career while he was working in Panama during the early 1930s. In June 1937, Valdés became the vocalist for the Orquesta Casino de la Playa, which was among Cuba's five most popular orchestras. He left Cuba for New York City in April 1940, and joined Xavier Cugat at the Waldorf Astoria. The spot earned him much fame, enough so that he started his solo career in 1942. He recorded for several recording companies, appeared in 12 movies, and went into semi-retirement in 1955. He resumed work in 1963, and hosted a television show for 10 years. He died in 1978 of a heart attack while performing on stage in Bogotá, Colombia. As a young man he was indoctrinated in the Santería culture. His mother, America, was a priest in the religion. Valdés provided much of Tito's education relevant to the Santería. As I said before the two became inseparable friends.

Many Afro-Cubans are practitioners of Yorubá Santería. The spirits or deities of the lucumí pantheon are called orisha. The ensembles of the lucumí rites include three percussion instruments and a large rattle or shaker. The African deities were super-imposed on the Christian saints because the Spaniards did not permit the African slaves to worship their Gods. This was one way to get around the problem. In Haiti, the Dahomeans spread voodoo, another name for Santería. In Cuba, the Yorubás brought lucumí or abakua (also known as ñáñigos). When the slaves and their French masters fled Haiti in the late 1780s, a number of "tumba francesas" were organized. These drum societies also follow many of the traditions of Santería. In these complex societies are found the ingredients that melded with European music. Valdés was a white Cuban who learned many of the complex songs and was able to popularize them through, among others, Orquesta Casino de la Playa.

From the start the orchestra was in high demand. It was heard daily over the CMQ national Cuban radio station. It toured Central and South America. Its performances were seen on stage in Puerto Rico, Dominican Republic, Venezuela and many other places. Its RCA Victor recordings were among the most popular in the late 1930s. It played the compositions of Arsenio Rodríguez that became instant hits among the South, Central and Caribbean listeners and it had a huge following in the United States.

"Babalu," composed by Margarita Lecuona, *and "Bruca Manigua,"* composed by Arsenio Rodríguez are still hugely popular. "But no one has done them the way Miguelito and Casino de la Playa did them," according to Tito. "The melodies and the performances are unique." Among the hits of the Casino de la Playa that Valdés composed is *"La Rumba Soy Yo."* He composed many selections for the orchestra before departing in 1940 for New York.

Josie Powell (When The Drums are Dreaming -2007) writes that Tito claimed he recorded the Arsenio Rodríguez composition in 1952. with Vicentico Valdés on vocals. "'I did it note for note,' Tito boasted."' The fact is that Tito never recorded it and never included it in his large repertoire of music. As I have said several times, when being interviewed Tito loved to enhance events, tell stories and depending on his audience might even change facts. This was Tito. He was a prankster. Maybe that day he felt like telling one of his whoppers. The fact remains that he never recorded it nor did he play it – it just did not happen.

The bolero *"Dolor Cobarde"* inspired him. Valdés composed it. It was romantic, soft, and made up his mind. I was always curious as to why this particular bolero, more than anything, piqued his interest in Afro-Cuban music. Knowing Tito the way I did, it surprised me that he was awestruck by a bolero. It was a side of him that not many people knew. He was a romantic. I would say you mean you went crazy over a bolero and not something like *"Bruca Manigua?"* He responded: "Hey, this stuff was groovy, and swinging in a strange way. These guys had a big band sound, just like the big bands of the swing era – maybe not as big. Obviously Casino de la Playa was influenced by American sounds." Tito still played traps when he first heard this tune, but as soon he could afford it, he bought a set of timbales.

Tito did not forsake the big bands. With money he made from playing with different groups in the neighborhood, he jumped on the subway and headed to Midtown to see the bands, or just walked over to the Harlem ballrooms wherever there was music. "We struggled but things were cheap. The subway was about a nickel, admission to dances and concerts were not that expensive," he always reminded me. He started playing for the Ramón Oliverio Orchestra in 1935, and stayed with him until the late 1930s. The band featured trumpets and saxophones, which was organized in El Barrio. Tito always managed to make some money, no matter how tough things were.

One can begin to see a picture emerging of Tito Puente developing into the personality he became. He worked hard and long to mimic the style of Orquesta Casino de la Playa, and at the same time he had a profound interest in swing music. He was, without realizing it, tying together the two musical genres – swing and Afro-Cuban - melding them, shaping them to his taste. "I was always blown away by the sharpness and crispness of Casino's musicians. This was a new sound that they came out with, swinging, sharp and percussive. It was nothing like the rumba."

Johnny Rodríguez – the older brother of Tito, like Machito, became like a father to him. Rodríguez and Tito struck up a friendship one evening at a La Milagrosa Church dance. Born Juan de Capadocia Rodríguez Lozada in 1912, in Camuy, Puerto Rico, Johnny, as he was known, was a vocalist, guitarist, composer and bandleader. In the 1930s he traveled back and forth from Puerto Rico to New York. His younger brother Pablo 'Tito' Rodríguez was born in 1923, in Barrio Obrero (Santurce), Puerto Rico. Tito moved to New York in 1940. He lived a few blocks from the Puente family, who lived at 53 East 110th Street. Like Tito Puente, both Johnny and his younger brother, Tito, were outstanding dancers. Tito Rodríguez was also a composer, and an exceptional vocalist. The two Titos would become good friends. In life they were fierce competitors and much would be written about their rivalry, but their friendship endured. The older Johnny's interest in Tito Puente was based on his musical abilities that were talked about throughout the neighborhood. "He had a progressive quality. Tito was always looking to improve the music that was presented to him. He was something of a rebel," according to Johnny Rodríguez.

In 1937 and into 1938 numerous events were transpiring. In Cuba Antonio Arcaño with bassist Israel 'Cachao' López and brother Orestes López was trying to stem the tide of American music flowing into Havana – The swing era was having its impact beyond the United States. "We were fighting to keep our music on an even keel – interesting, energetic and popular to the young dancers who were drifting to the American big band sounds," Arcaño related[27].

Arcaño y sus Maravillas would go on to devise a "New Rhythm" (Nuevo Ritmo) that would become known as the Mambo. Arcaño was born on December 29, 1911. He was the son of Rita María Betancourt de Arcaño, a pianist. His adolescent years were spent in the barrios of Regla and Guanabacoa, where Armando Romeu tutored him on solfege, clarinet and cornet. Arcaño's cousin, José Antonio Díaz, taught him the flute – the ancient version that was still popular in Cuba – a wooden conical instrument with six holes and five keys. It was a difficult instrument to play because it required fork fingering. Arcaño debuted at La Bombilla cabaret at Marianao's Beach Resort when he was 16-years-old in 1927.

For nine years he was the flutist for the orchestras of Armando Valdéspí, Orquesta Corman, Habana de Servia, Antonio María Romeu, Belasario López, Orquesta Gris de Armando Valdés-Torres, and in 1936 he joined vocalist Fernando Collazo's La Maravilla del Siglo. The other members of this ensemble included Cachao and pianist Jesús López (no relation). Arcaño played at cabarets and ballrooms that were filled with dancers who purchased tickets for five cents a dance. The dance hostesses earned three cents while the cabaret claimed two cents. The musicians were paid $1.75 for work from 9 p.m. to 2 a.m. Some cabarets paid more. Nonetheless, musicians had to eke out a living somehow.

The Cuban flautist leaned to the far left in terms of his politics. There were prohibitions on playing music with African percussion. The musicians were paid poorly. In 1937, he split with Collazo and formed a "cooperative" in which each musician would receive an equal share. Arcaño became the musical director and changed the orchestra's name to "La Primera Maravilla Del Siglo" (The First Wonder of the Century). He debuted in Matanzas' El Salón Central. During this period, one of Cachao's first compositions and arrangements for Arcaño was *"Resa del Meletón,"* which Arcaño recorded for Gema Records in 1957 as "*Chanchullo*." In 1938 Arcaño y sus Maravillas introduced the public to the Orestes López composition *"Mambo."* For the most part, and in the words of Arcaño "it was not well received by the general public. In actuality, there was an outcry by the public. The young dancers however liked it."

Up until 1937, the Cuban danzón had three parts: 1) introduction 2) paseo (the walk) 3) la comparsa (main theme). This was the classical format introduced in 1879 by Miguel Failde. It underwent several changes in the 1920s when the danzonete was introduced to include the Cuban son. The third part was replaced in 1938, when Orestes' mambo was heard over the Mil Diez radio station[28].

The orchestra introduced the selection: *"Africa Viva,"* in 1939. The melody was a variation on *"Somewhere Over The Rainbow,"* from the movie *"The Wizard of Oz."* According to Arcaño it was agreed to incorporate many popular American melodies into the new danzón de nuevo ritmo format – this practice had been popular in the genre that used the habanera rhythm as its base. The reason for this approach was to stem the flow of American pop music that was becoming popular in Cuba. In 1940, Arcaño heard the sound of conga drum and added it to his rhythm section. He got the idea from Arsenio Rodríguez, who was the first to introduce the conga drum in popular Cuban dance music.

Almost at the same time Arsenio Rodríguez[29] devised what would become known as the son montuno. Rodríguez was a prolific composer and lyricist, and a superb tresero. He elevated the trio and sextet aggregations that were popular into the conjunto format – that included from three to five trumpets, the tres and a full Afro percussion complement. It is impossible to overstate the importance of Arsenio Rodríguez in Cuban music. Arsenio, like Arcaño started to redefine the sound of Cuban music in the 1930s. He is considered a founder of what would be called "mambo" in the 1950s.

Despite all this, Arsenio remains on the margins of the official musical pantheon and is a largely forgotten figure. Very little is known about his life. Sources disagree about his date of birth, the year and even the place of his death, even his name. It's believed that Arsenio was born on August 30, 1911, in Güira de Macurijes, a small village in Matanzas. Arsenio was descended from Congolese tribesmen. His grandfather, who had been transported to Cuba from the Congo as a slave, proudly passed on his knowledge and traditions to all 18 of his grandchildren. Throughout his life Arsenio proudly celebrated his African heritage that permeates all his music in stark contrast to the bands playing to predominately white audiences in Havana's sophisticated nightclubs and casinos[30].

Arsenio was blinded when kicked in the head by a mule. This tragedy would not prevent him from becoming an outstanding musician. At the age of 15, Arsenio met Victor Feliciano, a carpenter who also made instruments, from whom he learned to play guitar, bass, maracas and bongos. Feliciano also taught Rodríguez how to play tres until he became too ill to tutor him. However, it was the tres that would become identified with him. Listening to the treseros Nene Malfugas, Eliseo Silvera and Isaac Oviedo inspired him. Arsenio created his own very personal style. Such was his mastery that he earned the nickname "El Ciego Maravilloso" (The Blind Marvel). During the early 1930s Arsenio formed his first group, Sexteto Boston, performing his own compositions almost exclusively, a characteristic that would come to be a defining one.

The sextet was disbanded in 1937, and Arsenio joined José Interian's Septeto Bellamar. He was fired soon afterward. However, it was a good year for the blind musician. Miguelito Valdés recorded his composition and sang *"Bruca Manigua," "Ven Acá Tomas"* and *"Fuñfuñando* with Orquesta Casino de la Playa. Miguelito recorded many more Arsenio compositions with the Casino de la Playa until his departure for the United States in 1940. Arsenio plays tres on one of the recordings, *"Se Va El Caramelero."*

Pride in each of their respective styles created circumstances that would have a profound impact on the music played during the period in

Cuba and outside of Cuba. Arcaño would enlarge the charanga orchestra size to that of a small chamber orchestra and he would incorporate the African percussion. The wooden flute would dance over the complicated string ostinatos or guajeos and the piano would improvise on the theme. Arsenio Rodríguez added a tumbadora (conga), piano and a second (and later third) trumpet in a completely new formation that became referred to as a conjunto. It was an extraordinary innovation, completely transforming the whole sound and definition of Cuban music.

Sexteto Miquito, the precursor of Conjunto Casino, as far back as 1935 had experimented with a piano. What was different was the way Arsenio used the piano. The piano was added to many sextets to replace the tres. Rodríguez used both thus giving his ensemble depth. Arsenio's trumpet player Benetín Bustillo, who joined the band in 1943, started copying Antonio Arcaño 's flute riffs on the trumpet and this in turn inspired Arcaño to extend the "nuevo ritmo" of the danzón to give his flute and piano more freedom to improvise.

The montuno was nothing more than a field yell, a simple repeated vocal refrain - sung by the peasants from the mountainous east (Oriente) of the island. Incorporated into the son, it was the perfect backdrop both for vocal improvisations (soneos) sung by the lead singer (sonero) and for instrumental improvisations by the lead musicians - tres and trumpet. Arsenio also mixed in many elements from guaguancó - a rumba form played only with percussion and vocals. These several innovations caused nothing less than a revolution in Cuban music. All the essential innovations of the mambo were already in place and indeed many elderly Cubans maintain that the mambo is nothing but the son montuno by another name.

Jimmy Cagney and George Raft

While Cuba was immersed in revising its musical landscape, Tito was busy playing traps, soaking in everything he could learn about the music of the big bands, buying 78-rpm records with the music of Casino de la Playa, and keeping up his musical studies – piano and saxophone. Even though he could not dance as intensely as he once could because of his injury in 1933, Tito was still drawn to the ballrooms and shows that featured music and dance. Two of his favorite dancers, believe it or not, were not performers with the big swing bands. They were not even Latinos. He loved to watch James Cagney[31] and George Raft[32]. "Those fellows made it look easy," Tito used to say whenever he talked about these old timers. In fact not only did he like the way they moved on the floor but Tito walked like them – a swagger of self-confidence, smooth and soft self-assured steps – that was where Tito got it from – from Raft and Cagney.

Everything that there was to know about the two actors/hoofers, Tito knew. George Raft was born in New York in 1895. He spent his childhood in the tough Hell's Kitchen area of New York, and then left home at 13. He went on to be a prizefighter, an extraordinary ballroom dancer, as well as a taxi-driver, meanwhile maintaining close contacts with New York's gangster underworld. He eventually made it to Broadway, and then went to Hollywood in the late 1920s. At first considered a Valentino-like romantic lead, Raft soon discovered his forte in gangster roles. He was the actor most responsible for creating the 1930s cinema image of gangster-as-hero, particularly after his portrayal of coin-flipping Guido Rinaldo in *"Scarface"* (1932). This was one of Tito's favorite movies – especially the "Bolero" dance scene.

Raft was a close friend of notorious gangster Benjamin "Bugsy" Siegel since they were boys together in New York. Siegel actually lived at Raft's home in Hollywood for a time while trying to make inroads for organized crime within the movie colony. Raft was highly successful for almost two decades.

By the early 1950s he was acting in European films in a vain attempt to regain critical respect, but was unsuccessful. He starred in the mid 1950s television series *"I Am the Law,"* a failure that seriously hurt his financial status. In 1959, the Castro government, further damaging his revenues, closed a Havana casino he owned. Meanwhile, he owed a great deal of money to the U.S. government. In the mid 1960s he was denied entry into England, where he managed a high-class gambling club, because of his underworld associations. Most of his film appearances after 1960 were cameos. He died of leukemia on November 24,1980, in Los Angeles, California. He is interred at Forest Lawn (Hollywood Hills), Los Angeles, in the Court of Remembrance. The actor was married to Grace Mulrooney from 1923 to her death in 1970, and though they split up soon after the marriage she would never let him divorce her. He was involved with many women, most notably Betty Grable, with whom he carried on an extraordinarily public courtship in the early 1940s.

Tito was gripped in Jimmy Cagney's portrayals and movements both on stage and on the screen. "His New York style seeps through to the character," Tito claimed. However superficial, violent, brutal or downright nasty, it had an underlying insightful and considerate side. He was the boy-gone bad, who, with the right breaks, could have made good. One of Tito's favorite movies with Cagney was *"Angels With Dirty Faces."* It is an excellent example of Cagney, the gangster and murderer, who is hero worshipped by the "Dead End Kids."

Cagney was a master of improvisation too. How can anyone who's seen it, forget the grapefruit in Mea Clarke's face (*Public Enemy*). It was originally scripted as "Slaps her with an omelet." In addition, when he danced – he was free, easy and even light. "Yeah! I guess Fred Astaire was the best, but who could ever imitate the Cagney style," Tito said.

James Cagney was born in the Yorkville section of Manhattan. His father was a bartender and amateur boxer. It was something the young Cagney developed a life long passion for - boxing. As a youth, he had a terrific reputation as a fighter. He entered show business after World War I. A fellow employee at Wanamaker's told him a troupe of vaudevillians were auditioning singers and dancers, and paying $35 a week. Cagney auditioned, and although he could neither sing nor was he trained to dance, he got the job. Cagney stayed in vaudeville until 1929, when he moved to Broadway to star with Joan Blondell in *"Penny Arcade."* This got him and Blondell an offer to go to Hollywood for screen tests, winning him the role in the 1930 film '*"Sinners Holiday."* Cagney attributed his dancing style to the instruction he received from Johnny Boyle and Harland Dixon.

It was Dixon who taught Cagney how to swagger, look masculine while performing such things as shoulder twists and knee snaps. "These things were picked up by many of the dancers during the days when the Palladium was in full bloom," was Tito's belief. "Jimmy Cagney was something of a perfectionist. You could see that in his moves." Boyle was more of the traditional dance instructor and taught Cagney such things as Irish jigs, reels plus every conceivable kind of buck dance, hard shoe dance, and just about any dance.

Cagney is usually remembered as the tough guy and gangster. In 1942 he had the chance to change his image. He made the movie *"Yankee Doodle,"* in which he starred as American icon song and dance man George M. Cohan. This enabled him to show off his dancing skills and won him an academy award. Tito liked to see and talk about this film more than any other. He first saw it while serving in the South Pacific.

Jimmy Cagney and his brother Bill formed their own production company once *"Yankee Doodle"* was completed. Cagney made four films under its umbrella between 1943-1946, when he returned to Warner Bros. Cagney retired from the movies in 1961. He moved to his 800-acre ranch in Duchess County, New York with his wife, Frances (Billy) Willard Cagney. They were married in 1921, and remained together until his death. Cagney enjoyed his retirement, he was able to relax, read, play tennis, swim, paint, and write poetry - very different from his gangster image. He did come out of retirement in 1980, to make *"Ragtime"* with his old friend Pat O'Brien.

Tito was able to get a job as a percussionist with Cuban pianist José Curbelo. The pianist had heard of Tito and had seen him play with other rumba bands. The job Tito got was for a three-month stint in Miami Beach at the prestigious Brook Club.

Curbelo was born in Havana in 1921, of a Cuban father and an American mother. The family was musically inclined – his father, Faustino, was a pianist and bassist with Xavier Cugat. Curbelo was a founding member of the Cuban big band Orquesta Riverside in 1938. This was the new rival to Casino de la Playa. In those days you did not jump on an airplane. Curbelo and Tito drove down to Miami, stayed in a motel that cost $5 weekly and was told that the orchestra had to play everything – foxtrot, waltz and tango. Tito was in Miami three months. He felt it was an eternity. "There really was not much happening in this place. It was very quiet. I felt I was missing out on what was happening in New York." Tito took long walks on the lonely beach and did a lot of reading. "It was beautiful but isolated."

He did like the fact that the orchestra was polished and well dressed – bolero jackets (short tight fit jackets). Curbelo's orchestra was the second band behind Nat Brandwyn, who had top billing. Tito was well aware that Brandwyn was connected to a crime organization. "If you want to work in show business you had to deal with the fact that many of the clubs were operated by organized crime. It was that way in those days – from one end of the country to the other." The Brook Club was a sprawling one-story Spanish hacienda surrounded by palm trees and tropical foliage. It featured a gambling casino and the entertainment was top notch – Joe E. Lewis, the comedian and the Xavier Cugat Orchestra were among the many big names that played the club. A young Desi Arnaz auditioned for Cugat at the Brook Club. At the time he had a five-piece quintet that included the son of Al Capone.

Tito realized soon enough that New York City had changed. He was not sorry he had been away so long, only that he was not able to be part of what was happening. "You know you can't do it all, but you want to be around when it is happening," Tito said when describing New York and its constant state of change. Noro Morales and his orchestra were no longer at the Conga Club. José Curbelo organized a permanent orchestra and became the second band at the Manhattan Club. Desi Arnaz went off to Hollywood. Diosa Costello[33] and[34] helped Tito get his job with the Pupi Campo Orchestra. She was a close friend of Campo. She first met Tito when he was rehearsing at the club with Machito's orchestra.

Costello became well known and popular in the 1930s-50s for her fiery performances on Broadway stage and screen, She began her career in New York City singing and dancing in the Puerto Rican clubs of Spanish Harlem. As audiences began to seek out the first wave of Latin music in the United States, Costello began performing at the major midtown Manhattan clubs, often partnering with the then unknown Cuban conga-player Desi Arnaz. Arnaz was just one of the many Latin performers whose careers Costello helped to launch and encourage. She was born in Guayama, Puerto Rico, and lived for a time in an orphanage in San Juan before moving to New York as a young girl in the 1920s. There she worked briefly in candy and shoe factories before her first success onstage.

Costello first appeared on the Broadway stage in 1939s hit musical *"Too Many Girls,"* with Arnaz. She stayed in New York when Arnaz went to Hollywood for the movie version of the show, where he met Lucille Ball. Soon after she co-starred with Buddy Ebsen and Maureen O'Hara in *"They Met in Argentina"* (1941), and performed with Laurel and Hardy in their last Hollywood film, *"The Bullfighters"* (1945). Costello was best known as a nightclub performer, but returned to Broadway in 1951 as Bloody Mary in the hit musical *"South Pacific,"* after touring with the show's first road company for the previous year. She also returned to Hollywood to appear with fellow Puerto Rican actor José Ferrer and Rita Hayworth in "*Miss Sadie Thompson*" (1953); interestingly, none of them were portraying Latino characters in the film.

Costello is believed to have been the first Latina to front an orchestra in the major nightclubs of New York City, in the 1940s, and she ran her own nightclub in Miami in the late 1950s. Costello later moved to Las Vegas, where she still lives. Her involvement with Tito was brief but to him she was quite a lady.

One of the important crossroads in young Tito's life came when Johnny Rodríguez took him under his wing. Johnny spoke about his association with Tito a few years before his death with music collector Henry Medina. Tito was still honing in on his musical studies, following the big bands of the swing era and practicing the drums.

Johnny recalled in an interview: "I have known Tito since he was a young teenager. I knew his mother and his father. When Tito was 13, I was in New York looking for new opportunities. I had some success in Puerto Rico. I was walking one day around 110th Street and Park Avenue. I heard music coming from a first floor apartment. He was probably rehearsing with friends. I approached the building, walked to where the music was coming from and the sound of the percussion was strong and distinct. I met Tito and the teenagers he was practicing with. He told me his name and that he lived two blocks from where we were standing."

"We went to his home. I told them I wanted to help Tito with his music. His mother, of course, was concerned about his schooling but was agreeable to my helping Tito." Johnny Rodríguez knew that Tito had a solid sense of rhythm from the dances at La Milagrosa Church and several of the other clubs in El Barrio. He heard him play on a number of occasions at various rehearsals. "One night I brought him to the Stork Club in Manhattan. I had planned to introduce my brother Tito (Rodríguez) as a bongocero. I wanted to have Tito play the timbales in the group. This was a club where mostly American music was played. There was a Mexican singer in the show. I organized a small floorshow for late one night. Tito Puente was on timbales and Tito Rodríguez was the bongocero."

The next event was to have Tito included in a recording. "We got together for a recording date, May 1940 and it featured Tito Rodríguez." Tito Rodríguez had been living in New York with his older brother for two years – on and off. He lived a few blocks from where Tito Puente lived. We used the Rafael Hernández guaracha composition - *"Los Hijos de Buda."* In this recording Tito played timbales in the opening throughout the recording, and at the end. There are strains of Cuban syncopated percussion, but more than this Tito introduced a freewheeling approach – strains of Gene Krupa are evident throughout – in the context of the rumba. The success of the recording was due to Tito Puente's exhibition on the timbales. It was a departure from what percussionists using this instrument had done before. "Johnny let me do my thing. I wasn't sure how it would turn out. I call it something like a mixing of the old and new. Whew! It worked," was Tito's take.

Tito made 18 recordings with Johnny Rodríguez's Stork Club Orchestra, his conjunto and the Conjunto Siboney, also led by Johnny. Among those recordings is a selection: *"No Quiero Que Vuelvas,"* composed by Tito with vocals by Tito Rodríguez. During this period, Tito left school to pursue a music career. Occasionally he played stickball with the guys in the neighborhood, but he was consumed with his music. He kept playing the piano and practicing on the saxophone, but the timbales were now his focus, his passion. Leaving school did not end his education; in fact he became a profuse reader. Tito enjoyed reading about history, fiction, anything he could get his hands on.

Tito Rodríguez became a close friend to Tito over the years, and the two of them frequented the Park Plaza on the second floor. On the first floor was the Park Palace. Both of the dancehalls catered to Puerto Rican and Cuban dancers. It was here that the two aspiring musicians started in earnest to pursue their music interests. Rodríguez was the same age as Tito. He became one of the pursuers, along with Bobby Capó and Tito Puente of the actress Olga San Juan. According to Tito, he fell for her head over heels. Before coming to New York Tito Rodríguez was a vocalist for the Conjunto Tipica Ladi.

Ladislao Martínez Otero[35], a composer, a cuatro player with immense stature in Puerto Rican music throughout his life promoted Puerto Rican typical music. Ladi composed more than 500 melodies, many of them danzas. In 1934 he organized a string ensemble that briefly featured the teenager Tito Rodríguez.

Older brother Johnny Rodríguez was always someone who Tito looked up to. He had taken time out from his professional career and provided Tito with opportunities that were important to his growth as a musician. "I enjoyed talking with him about Puerto Rico. You know he was always going back and forth. It was not easy. I think he always got edgy being in New York and wanted to be in the tropics. But he was always there for me."

It was no secret that Johnny was gay. Tito mentioned to me how difficult it must have been in the 1930s to be gay. "There really was not an understanding about what must have been going on in his head and body." Duke Ellington's pianist and arranger, and composer of *"Take The A Train,"* Billy Strayhorn was gay[36]. "Most others in the jazz and Latin music genres in those years kept quiet. Not only did you have to deal with being a minority – Latino or black – but also then you had to deal with being a gay person. I think people have a different perspective now. We understand more that not everybody is the same – every single person is different." Tito observed in later years.

In 1930, while in Puerto Rico, Johnny Rodríguez organized the Estrellas Boricuas quartet. In 1932 he was one of the entertainers that helped to inaugurate the Escambron Beach Club in Puerta de Tierra, Old San Juan. He recorded with the Rafael Muñoz Orchestra. He was busy in New York and Puerto Rico during the 1940s and was contracted by NBC and CBS for several television appearances – making him the first Puerto

Rican to appear on network television. In 1967 he opened his "Cotorrito" nightclub – sort of a "Cage Au Faux" club. Johnny's "Santurce Club" closed in 1987. He passed away in 1997.

Soon after his induction into the recording business, thanks to Johnny Rodríguez, young Tito played drums for the Tommy Dorsey band – as a result of a fisticuff between a youthful Frank Sinatra[37] and a cocky Buddy Rich. It was a bizarre situation at the Hotel Astor in New York. Tito knew the Dorsey repertoire from listening to the recordings in his home. He was playing with the back-up rhumba orchestra led by Puerto Rican Ralph Rogers the night of the incident. Tito watched it all from the sidelines. To say the least Tito was flabbergasted by the public spectacle.

Frank became a star within a few months of starting with Dorsey when he recorded *"I'll Never Smile Again."* The song launched him and became number one on the hit parade for weeks. Dorsey placed Frank Sinatra's name above everyone – above Connie Haines and Jo Stafford and the Pied Pipers and above the other musicians, including Buddy Rich, who by now had taken a serious disliking to the cocky vocalist. Buddy Rich was a terrific percussionist, brilliant and dynamic. "He was certainly powerful," was Tito's description. He was probably as famous in the Swing Band circuit as Gene Krupa. Rich did not like the new singer. He felt that he was in his own way as talented as the young singer. Rich was equally arrogant, and like Sinatra had a violent temper.

That night Frank sang his slow ballads, and soon he was complaining that Buddy Rich was messing up on the drums on purpose. Tommy Dorsey tried to keep the peace. "Buddy called Frank a fuck. Sinatra then grabbed a heavy glass pitcher filled with water and ice and threw it – aiming at Rich's head. He ducked and the pitcher splattered spraying his clothes with water. Rich was pissed and cursing. Shit was he pissed." Tito looked on shocked, but he loved being around famous people. He was a Frank Sinatra fan; he listened to Dorsey on records, or heard the remotes on radio. That is the way it was. Also watching the ruckus was Jo Stafford. "All she did was shrug. She had seen the two guys duke it out before." A few minutes after the uproar Rich walked out of the club.

Now Dorsey needed a percussionist and it was late and there was no one else available. "It took a lot of convincing to let Dorsey let me sit in," according to Tito. There was no one around that late at night and thanks to Roy Eldridge encouraging the bandleader Tito sat in. As he put it, "I sat in timidly. There was Frank Sinatra. I backed him up on one song, maybe two. I just played background music. I was a little bit overwhelmed, but it was exciting. No kidding, shit, I was scared of messing up. Sinatra was a stickler for perfection. I had just seen him and Buddy Rich nearly crash to the floor. But the band played, Frank sang and even threw a smile of approval my way. What the hell did I know? Later on I pinched myself to make sure I was not dreaming." From this point on Tito and Frank Sinatra did have a relationship, albeit professional, but nonetheless they did talk when occasionally their paths crossed.

The episode, as Tito referred to the Rich-Sinatra confrontation, left Tito in something of a predicament. He was a drummer, struggling to make it, Sinatra was a young singer struggling to make it, and Rich already had some fame. Tito was 18-years-old and his inclination was to side with Sinatra. "We were both young and up and coming. I guess Rich may have been right. He was cocky, but so was I."

Miguelito Valdés and Tito met in 1940 while he was rehearsing with the Machito Orchestra at La Conga Club. Valdés arrived in New York with Anselmo Sacasas and there was Tito looking up at his idol – the singer from Casino de la Playa. Remember, Tito knew how to play the entire Casino de la Play repertoire. That day Tito and Miguelito became friends for life. The Machito Orchestra was making a reputation for itself and Tito was along for the ride.

Machito's father operated a restaurant but he was first and foremost a cigar maker. But it was also a musical family, and Machito grew up singing and playing with many of the leading musicians of Cuba. After playing with a few groups in Havana, he moved to New York City in 1937. His friend (and brother-in-law), Mario Bauzá sent for him to provide the vocals in his new musical endeavor. It was a gamble, Machito often recalled, but he wanted to try it out, and Bauzá was convincing.

Bauzá, a classical musician by training, and Machito were life-long collaborators. Machito scraped around for a few years, working mostly as a singer, with Noro Morales and Xavier Cugat, while Bauzá served as musical director for the Cab Calloway and Chick Webb orchestras. With Machito at his side, Bauzá decided to form a group and try out a style that combined Cuban rhythms and melodies and orchestrations derived from swing. The timing was fortuitous, since there was a temporary shortage of new songs due to a strike by members of ASCAP. Bauzá and Machito were members of the new syndicate, BMI. Advertised and promoted as the Afro-Cubans, the group was soon signed to Decca Records. The new band had a few inconsequential hits with numbers like *"Sopa de Pichon"* (Pigeon Soup) and Bauzá 's composition, *"Tanga."* It was recorded for Clef

Records in 1948. Neither Machito nor Bauzá expected that *"Tanga,"* which became the theme song of the orchestra, or for that matter the orchestra would have such an impact on the way Afro-Cuban music would be played in the United States[38].

Machito's sister, Graciela, came to the U.S. to sing with the band after he was drafted into the Army in the first months of 1943. Polito Galindez, a Puerto Rican, took over vocals with the orchestra while Machito was in the service. He would be discharged due to an injury in late1943. He resumed performing and became a regular act featured in weekly radio broadcasts from La Conga Club. The Bauzá -Machito band began to influence many of New York's jazz musicians, most notably Dizzy Gillespie, who had worked with Bauzá in Cab Calloway's band and was now pioneering a new style that would eventually be called "bebop."

Another jazz performer influenced by Machito and his Afro-Cubans was Stan Kenton, whose band would enjoy huge popularity soon after World War II. Kenton called the Machito orchestra the "greatest exponent of Afro-Cuban jazz" and even recorded a Latin-flavored number titled, "Machito." He and Machito shared the bill in a historic concert at Manhattan's Town Hall on January 24,1947.

The first model of the Machito Orchestra was unveiled on December 3, 1940, at the Park Palace Ballroom in El Barrio. Among the Bauzá featured musicians were: pianist, Gilberto Ayala; timbalero, Tony Escoiles; saxophonist, Johnny Nieto, and Machito as the vocalist. Tony Escoiles, alias "El Cojito" (The Lame One), was a bongó player who switched to timbal. He had played with several local groups in the Spanish Harlem area. The Cuban-born Escoiles joined the Machito Orchestra in 1940. Tito Puente replaced him in 1941.

Johnny Nieto was a Puerto Rican clarinetist and saxophonist who first played with Alberto Iznaga's Siboney Orchestra and, in 1940, became a member of the Machito Orchestra. He was called for military service in 1943, and did not rejoin the band upon his discharge. His brother, Ubaldo "Uba" Nieto, a piano player was recruited by Machito as a percussionist. He was unique, according to Tito. "No one else could play the way he played timbales – it was Cuban, but it was his own style. He was strong and in your face – nothing fancy- just driving." Tito, the energetic teenager, joined the Machito Orchestra when he was only 18-years-old. He sat in with the orchestra on and off during 1941.

"This was a very tight and structured organization. There were not that many Cubans in it that is why we always laughed when they announced 'the Afro-Cubans,'" laughed Tito. Machito, who now lived a few blocks from the Puente family, was an enthusiastic supporter of the young New

York Puerto Rican musician. "Like Johnny (Rodríguez) before, Machito sort of became another parent," Tito said. In his youth he looked to both Machito and the older Rodríguez as mentors. In a way they replaced his father, who was rarely around. "Tito has his father's character," Machito often concluded. Johnny Rodríguez concurred. Tito played with the band until 1942, when he was drafted into the U.S. Navy.

Mario Bauzá was the grand designer of Machito's "Music engine." He realized his dream of developing a Latin band that played authentic Cuban music as well as jazz pieces backed by a rhythm section composed of genuine Afro-Cuban instruments. In addition to his responsibilities as musical director, Mario played trumpet with the band. On May 29, 1943, the Machito Orchestra played *"Tanga,"* in a non-rumba style and with the new driving sound that would become the essence of the Machito y sus Afro-Cubans orchestra. Many music historians consider this tune as the first Latin jazz tune ever written.

Trumpet player Bobby Woodlen was one of Mario's early recruits. The African-American musician had a long experience with big jazz orchestras and contributed significantly to the development of the group with his arrangements. He was also a composer, and the band recorded some of his numbers. One of the best remembered is his bolero *"Inolvidable"* (Unforgettable). This number should not be confused with the Julio Gutiérrez classic sharing the same title. Freddie Skerritt was an alto saxophone player, also recruited by Mario. He was a mainstay of the saxophone frontline of the Machito Band, from1941 until his retirement in 1955.

Gene Johnson's smooth tone, as the lead alto player of the sax ensemble, gave the Machito Orchestra its distinctive sound. Even though Gene was not of Latin descent, he picked up all the nuances of the music's syncopation. Using Johnson as the leader, Bauzá had the sax section working as a well-polished machine by rehearsing it separately from the rest of the band. According to Tito, Mario worked his musicians with a "drive for perfection." As a young man Tito was impressed by his work ethic. "Sure, other bands worked their asses off, but this was incredible. Mario was a driven man. He wanted it right. He knew from the start that if he was going to succeed he had to be better than everyone else – no shit!"

Tito was very busy and very much in demand in 1940. He introduced a whole new way of playing Afro-Cuban percussion into the scene. Before him the Cubans that played the Park Palace really did not have musician status and were considered "street" drummers. They also were a little more conservative in terms of taking jobs wherever possible and simply supplying subtle background percussion. Influenced by Gene Krupa, Tito was not going to sit back, even if he was nervous. His first real timbales or "pailas cubanas" were probably purchased in 1940. In the recording he made with Johnny Rodríguez, he was still using modified traps.

In 1941, Tito recorded with the sophisticated and smooth Vincent López Orchestra and then, later that same year he played for the Noro Morales Orchestra. Morales with Tito recorded for Decca Records, and appeared in four music film shorts - *"The Gay Ranchero," "Cuban Pete," "Ella,"* and *"Mexican Jumping Bean."* These were not Tito's favorites. These were forgettable and even regrettable, he moaned when the subject came up. These films depicted a stereotype Latin to a naïve American public.

Japan Mambo

Blowing a bugle call on a ship that was in the midst of a sea battle was not something Tito could ever imagine. It changed him forever – it made him older than he was, and more rigid in his beliefs. If asked about his war experiences he would frown. If pressed to speak about it he would get loud-mouthed and insensitive.

On December 7, 1941, the Japanese bombed Pearl Harbor, "a day that will live in infamy," President Roosevelt declared, and a day that brought the United States into World War II. The Jimmy Lunceford Swing Orchestra was two beating with style and grace at the Strand Theater in Brooklyn. The Duke Ellington Orchestra was touring the West Coast. Jazz violinist and storyteller Joe Venuti was at the Paramount Theater in Toledo. The Cab Calloway Orchestra was in Albany.

Pianist Jay McCann's band, with Charlie Parker in the reed section was playing in the Blue Room of the Streets Hotel in Kansas City. A new band led by pianist Stan Kenton was in Los Angeles. The Nat King Cole Trio was in Philadelphia. Machito and his Afro-Cubans were at the Conga Club. In almost every major city the swing bands, the filler or rumba bands, ensembles and combos played live music. The quality of these bands was about to change. After Pearl Harbor, big bands lost more key players to the Army, thus making Nat King Cole Trio's *"Gone With the Draft"* more meaningful. Tito was just 18-years-old and the full impact of how the war would change his life was still to come.

The world conflict had started in 1938, when Germany expanded its borders, marched into Poland and carved it up with the Soviet Union, attacked France and Greece; drawing Great Britain into the conflict. As the European war exploded and expanded the organized crime syndicates or as they were known, the Mob, got involved in new business ventures – supper clubs, restaurants, jukeboxes that were placed by the thousands in bars and dancehalls, and gambling. The Mafia turned its interest to Havana as well.

Nearly two million young people were coming of age into a job market reeling from the aftermath of the Great Depression. There were more than four million unemployed Americans. Tito was working with Machito and his Afro-Cubans. By this time he had given up the trap drums and playing the Cuban style timbales. "I always practiced with both." He learned the Cuban percussive techniques when he frequented the Park Palace just by listening to the many types of Afro-Cuban street drummers. Much of his Cuban style was learned with Carlos Montesino, an Afro-Cuban percussionist who frequently played at the Park Palace. He had learned the fundamentals of the complex danzón, how to use the cowbell, play the sides or cascara. The cowbell was introduced into the Cuban orquesta tipicas, the forerunners of the charanga orchestras (violins, unadorned five key wooden flute and percussion). The cowbell is used in Yorubá music. "The danzón is complex. You have to feel your way through it," he explained. "One of the most difficult things to accomplish on the timbales is the roll, because of the way you have to hold the sticks."

Tito always had an insatiable appetite for learning new things. Music was his passion. He studied and practiced the piano all the time. He played the saxophone, learning much of the technique from watching Mario Bauzá and his musicians. He listened to every kind of music. He enjoyed George Gershwin, Claude Debussy, and Maurice Ravel. These composers had a way of arranging that gave the orchestra a unique quality – fullness and a contemporary feeling. Playing for the Machito Orchestra would require a deeper understanding of Afro-Cuban rhythms. The orchestra still favored the "Rhumba" music that was popular, but Mario was about to change all that. "I had it in me. I was ready to do it." Machito featured Tito as a soloist allowing him to move the timbales to the front of the orchestra where he played standing – this was a first, according to Tito. He was the first to play in this fashion, but a percussionist named Mano López, while playing for the Xavier Cugat Orchestra did the same thing in a musical segment of a film *"Go West, Young Man,"* in 1936. But it had never been done in a dance band.

Machito and his Afro-Cubans completed half of the album that was signed with Decca Record by June of 1941. There were several tunes included in the album composed by Cuban musician/composer Gilberto Valdés. He played piano and the unadorned flute. He would be featured with Machito's Orchestra and Dizzy Gillespie in 1948, playing the wooden flute for the first time in a large orchestra setting.

Tito did not finish work on the Machito album. He was drafted into the U.S. Navy and soon found himself aboard the U.S.S. Santee[39], an escort aircraft carrier used to protect merchant convoys. The converted oil tanker had a complement of 1,500 officers and sailors. It had been constructed in 1939 at the Sun Shipbuilding Company, in Chester, Pennsylvania.

"The U.S.S. Santee had only five experienced aviators on board, and very few of her officers and men had previously smelled salt water,"[40]. Tito and his ship participated in the first American military assault on German-occupied territories in North Africa – Operation Torch. The Santee was part of the Southern Command of the Task Force. For the most, part the 34,000 American soldiers and the naval support were inexperienced and seeing action for the first time. The controversial Major General George S. Patton, who would later command the U.S. 3rd Army, led the assault. Leading up to the assault the escort vessel gathered up the troop transports in the Caribbean. The U.S.S. Santee and hundreds of naval ships headed out of the Caribbean Sea bound for the Mediterranean Sea and the unknown.

"All cloak and dagger," Tito groaned. During the voyage from the Caribbean basin to the Mediterranean, the Santee performed escort duty, spotting and seeking German U-boats and keeping the sea-lanes clear. "Everyone on board was scared shit," Tito recalled. "I was never sure about anything except that we were all scared." Tito volunteered for bugle duty, helped to organize a small band aboard the ship and shifted from percussion to piano to saxophone and back. "It was a way of keeping cool. My music helped me stay calm."

As the small escort carrier slid into the Pacific Theater of Operations, Tito worked on his bugle calls. One quiet evening he placed the bugle to his lips and blew several of the calls used to raise the crew. "All hell broke loose," he moaned. "Everyone was running all over the place. The fucking intercom that we used was on. The captain was furious; everyone wanted to kill the little Puerto Rican. I made myself scarce for several days. But eventually I was called in by my commanding officer that... well he had me tracked down. It was ugly, he was pissed." During his tour of duty he composed and arranged music for the small ensemble of 12 men. Rehearsals were tricky. They had to accommodate the schedules of the men, the periods of "silent running," and call to general quarters – these were frequent and nerve wracking. "We had five saxes, trumpets, trombones, bass, drums and piano. I was the drummer. Then I played sax and then piano. It all depended on who was available. Some guys were flying planes, some were on deck, some were seasick and some left the ship for reasons I would never know – it was the Navy and we were at war. We played all the big-band music – Glenn Miller, Tommy Dorsey." Latin music was limited to Xavier Cugat rhumba selections like *"Lady in Red,"* and maybe *"Brazil,"* made popular by Carmen Miranda.

Laughing and very drunk one night he told me "the guys liked things like *'The Beer Barrel Polka'* and *'Der Fuehrer's Face.'* Spike Jones recorded them. We could never play them the way Spike Jones did. We played a lot of hokey stuff – mid west and south. Coming from New York I guess made me something of a celebrity. The guys liked hearing my stories about Manhattan nightlife. We were all so innocent then – even home sick. I remembered when I said goodbye to mom at Pennsylvania Station. 'Just have the rice and beans ready when I get home,' I told her. God! How she cried."

The first American invasion of the conflict was a success - but not before the Germans countered and caused severe problems. The Santee lost nearly half of the aircraft it carried. It was Tito's first test under fire. Like thousands of other Americans the experience would prove to be valuable for what was to follow. After Morocco was secured the Santee was ordered to convoy ships in the area of the Panama Canal, and down the South American coast. Merchant ships carrying classified war material was all that was told to the Santee. The workload aboard ship was heavy but Tito found time to rehearse and even compose some of his music. He forwarded to Machito and Mario a composition titled *"Bajo de Chapotin."* According to Tito they also received an arrangement of *"Cuando te Vea,"* he would record later. On January 24, 1944, the Santee returned to Norfolk and Tito was excited to visit his mother, father and sister Anna, and spend time with Milta Sanchez, his girlfriend.

Tito always believed that he missed something during the years he was in the Navy. It was his usual nervousness. A month later Tito was aboard the Santee once again, this time bound to the Panama Canal and then to San Diego assigned to the Pacific Fleet. If nothing else, the pocket carrier had the best orchestra. Many of the sailors on his ship made the claim to him and to others.

During this tour of duty Tito learned a great deal about arranging techniques and composition from a pilot who played tenor saxophone and served as arranger for the big band of Charlie Spivak.[41] Tito called him Sweeney. He could never remember his first name. Tito had no idea what happened to Sweeney. But for a few months the aviator and Tito worked together – on music composition, studying harmony, and arranging techniques. Sweeney was part of the ship's band. His recollection was that he had a smooth sound. "I don't know what happened to him, but he was smooth and very clued-up about organizing good charts." "He showed me the foundation of writing a good chart, how to lay out voicing and get colors out of the brass and reeds. I began writing at this time."[42] According to Tito, the members of the Santee ensemble often taught each other how to get certain sounds, a feeling by changing a simple note or chord. When the sailors and airmen of the band were not working they liked to play all sorts of music.

Spivak's music always interested Tito. "it was smooth and laid back in its precise delivery," he said. But then – he liked pretty much all kinds of music. He was always learning, teaching himself. "In a strange way the Navy served me as a learning tool – at least when we were not being shot at." Sources differ on bandleader Charlie Spivak's[43] birth. Some say that he was born in the Ukraine in 1907, and that he immigrated to the United States with his parents while still a child, settling in Connecticut. Another source says that he was actually born in New Haven, Connecticut, in 1905. Whichever the case, Spivak studied trumpet as a youth and played in his high school band. He worked with local groups before joining Don Cavallaro's orchestra. In 1924 he became part of Phil Sprecht's band, remaining with Sprecht until 1930.

He left Ben Pollack band in late 1934 after three years and joined the Dorsey Brothers and then signed up with Ray Noble the following spring. During 1936 and 1937, Spivak worked mainly as a studio musician, including stints with Gus Arnheim, Glenn Miller, and Raymond Scott's radio orchestra. He joined Bob Crosby in January of 1938, staying until August, when he went to work for Tommy Dorsey. He left Dorsey in June of 1939 for Jack Teagarden. In late 1939 Spivak was encouraged by Miller to form his own orchestra, which Miller backed financially. Spivak's new band debuted in November of 1939. Within a year, however, Spivak was forced to disband due to internal conflicts. Not letting his initial failure deter him, he then took over Bill Downer's orchestra. Spivak's new band emerged as one of the top commercial outfits in the country, surviving the post-war band bust and continuing until the late 1950s.

Despite Spivak's past employment with some of the top jazz groups of the day his orchestra played it straight, focusing on ballads and popular numbers. Featured in the band during its formative years were drummer Davey Tough, bassist Jimmy Middleton, and trumpeter Les Elgart. Nelson Riddle played trombone and shared arranging duties with Sonny Burke.

Early vocalists were Garry Stevens and the Stardusters quartet, which featured June Hutton. When Hutton left in 1944 to join the Pied Pipers, where she replaced Jo Stafford, Spivak brought in former Gene Krupa vocalist Irene Daye. Daye and Spivak were married in 1950. Other vocalists during the 1940s included Tommy Mercer and Jimmy Saunders.

In the beginning days of his orchestra Spivak, known as ''Cheery, Chubby Charlie,'' played his trumpet with a mute, trying to project a softer tone. He later switched to playing open trumpet, for which he received great critical acclaim. He was one of the better trumpet players of the era, though Harry James undoubtedly overshadowed him. He never completely gave up his mute, however, until later in his career. In the late 1950s Spivak moved to Florida, where he continued to lead a band until 1963, when illness forced him to briefly retire. After recovering he led bands in Las Vegas and Miami. In 1967 he organized a small outfit that played regularly at the Ye Olde Fireplace restaurant in Greenville, South Carolina, with Daye as vocalist. Daye fought cancer during the last years of her life, finally losing that battle in 1971. Spivak remained at the restaurant up until his death in 1982. In his last few years he led a new 17-piece orchestra. Tito often listened to this music when he returned to New York after the war. His interest was in the softness of the horn section.

While serving aboard the U.S.S. Santee, Tito was informed of his sister's death from spinal meningitis. It was a stinging blow to him. He was severely saddened by the loss of his sister. He was given emergency leave and via military transport flew to New York.

During his one week at home, he escorted his parents to La Perla del Sur Civica (social club) on 116th Street and Madison Avenue. He sat down at the piano and performed dedications to his mother or *"Mis Amores"* – a Puerto Rican danza composed by Juan Morel Campos and *"Clair de Lune"* composed by Claude Debussy in memory of his late sister[44]. He was grief stricken for a long time. He rarely, if ever spoke about his sister. He left that for others to do.

Soon he was back on board his escort carrier. He was happy to get a break from the long tedious voyages funneling supplies, war material and troops to and from Pacific area combat zones. On board the ship there was little information coming from home – every bit of information was filtered and there was little opportunity to get letters to loved ones. During one of his brief furloughs in the San Diego area, he renewed his friendship with Olga San Juan, whose family had moved west so that she could pursue a career in Hollywood. There were dozens of "Latin style bands in the area," according to Tito. With Olga at his side they tried to see them all. Briefly, he was reacquainted with Desi Arnaz who was with Lucille Ball, he recalled. Soon his ship pulled out once again headed toward the combat zone of the South Pacific.

Tito served in nine battles while in the Navy, in both the Atlantic and the Pacific Oceans. While in the Pacific his shipped was attacked. The Japanese fleet moved into the area of the American fleet undetected through the San Bernardino Strait between Luzon and Samar and into Leyte Gulf. By this time the American beachhead with its unloading ships would be caught in between thus causing the destruction of Admiral Kincaid's Seventh Fleet. The Santee was part of the combat sea group. It was waiting for the Japanese attack. The entire squadron from the Santee was airborne when the Japanese struck. It seemed like hours to Tito. His commanding officer yelled at him to blow the bugle call to abandon ship. The Santee had been hit several times.

When a torpedo hit, the explosion impacted the bridge. Tito went down. His duty uniform was in tatters; his helmet was bent and twisted from the impact of the tremendous explosion. Outside the two naval fleets were engaged in a fight to the finish. There was noise everywhere. Men yelling! Bombs exploding! There were cries of anguish (U.S. Naval Report - 1947). When he arose with the help of other shipmates he was bleeding.

As they struggled to get him to the sickbay the repair crew was able to contain the fires on the ship. The flight deck was cleaned up and the squadron was able to land on the damaged deck. Tito had been hit with shrapnel. He had the scar on his face for the rest of his life. Though bandaged up Tito blew taps for the dead as the ship floated in the combat zone. This was one of the last sea battles of the war. Somehow, he had endured. He did not think he would.

"Joe, there were so many dead, all around me. I just wanted to go home." Others tell most of the stories about Tito's combat service. He was fine with that. The war was something that made him feel sick, gave him the chills and even made him shake. I never brought up the subject with him.

His ship had achieved nine honorable citations: Presidential Unit Citation; American Defense Service Medal; American Campaign Medal; European-African-Middle Eastern Campaign Medal with two stars; Asiatic-Pacific Campaign Medal (seven stars); Philippine Presidential Unit Citation and Philippines Liberation Medal. His mother got his ribbons and he put the war behind him.[45]

Tito opted for an extended voyage home. Rather than fly he boarded several naval transport vessels that slowly made its way across the Pacific stopping in more than a half dozen ports-Burma, Thailand, the Fiji Islands and others. Here he took in the cultures, the exotic sounds of the orient. The sounds he heard, the people he met and saw influenced his way of playing music more than he realized.

Mucho Puente

The Late, Late Scene

Tito's reaction to what was in the large manila envelope should not have surprised me, but it did. After glancing inside at the contents, he threw it across the room and nearly sliced my head off. "I don't want this shit," he said angrily. "It's bullshit. I don't want to see that stuff."

We were in my apartment, up most of the night reminiscing, unwinding after a long night. The day before had been a busy one. Tito and Charlie (Palmieri) had been at the office early working on new music, arrangements. Joe Loco was there too. I got to the midtown office around noon. Tito was in the back, listening to music with Charlie. The radio was blaring. Joe was playing the piano. Charlie was huffing and puffing. The room was cloudy. But then again, it was always like that. We went for lunch, drinks and whatever. In the evening we went to the Bronx. The band was performing at one of the local clubs. In the wee hours Tito and I slipped into an after hours joint somewhere in Manhattan.

"Man" groaned Tito, "too much candy! Too much juice – just too much shit." We arrived at my apartment, back in the Bronx. Tito threw himself on the sofa and I managed to make it to the kitchen to brew coffee. It was still dark outside. We just sat and talked for a long while.

The sun had been up for sometime. The doorbell rang out. "Shit!" I gasped, moving to the door in an uneven manner. It was a special delivery of an envelope sent by Ralph Mercado. Inside the delivery envelope was a document with official Navy identification addressed to Tito. He opened it. He looked at the contents, only briefly and than angrily threw it at me.

"I don't want this stuff. I don't even want to see it," he said angrily. I picked up the envelope and the photo. The photo was of someone being buried at sea and Tito was standing at attention, holding his helmet. "I never want to see that shit again," he shouted and stood up. I picked up the picture and filed it in a cabinet where I kept Tito Puente memorabilia. I never brought it up again. More than 25 years had gone by since the end of World War II, it was still a bad memory.

More than anything Tito wanted to forget the horrors of World War II.

He was no different than the thousands upon thousands of veterans who returned home in 1945 and 1946. Tito wanted to return to his old job. He wanted to return to the New York City he had left three years earlier. He wanted to play his music. He did not realize, at least not right away, that the city he left had changed. The rhumba was just about dead and buried, the big bands were slipping away and Afro-Cuban music was gaining a foothold – thanks to his mentor, Machito.

Returning World War II veterans and immigrants from Europe created a postwar economic boom and the development of huge housing tracts. New York emerged from the war unscathed and the leading city of the world, with Wall Street leading America's ascendance as the world's dominant economic power; the United Nations headquarters (built in 1952) emphasizing New York's global influence; and the rise of new artistic endeavors and expressions in jazz in the city precipitating New York's displacement of Paris as the center of the world.

World War II was the most widespread war in history, and countries involved mobilized more than 100 million military personnel. Total war erased the distinction between civil and military resources and saw the complete activation of a nation's economic, industrial, and scientific capabilities for the purposes of the war effort; nearly two-thirds of those killed in the war were civilians - nearly 11 million of the civilian casualties were victims of the Holocaust, which was largely conducted in Eastern Europe, and the Soviet Union. The conflict ended in an Allied victory. As a result, the United States and Soviet Union emerged as the world's two leading superpowers, setting the stage for the Cold War that would last nearly 50 years. Colonialism gave way to self-determination and independence movements in Asia and Africa, while Europe itself began traveling the road leading to integration.

The Mafia turned its attention to developing Las Vegas and taking control of a corrupt Cuba. The United States turned a blind eye on Cuba, supporting the regime of dictator Batista. In Puerto Rico the poverty expanded and grew, and the migration of thousands of Puerto Ricans seeking work began. El Barrio was overflowing with the islanders. The economy of the United States was shifting from one that was primarily manufacturing to one that was service oriented. This made jobs harder to find for the untrained unemployed. The shipyards along the Hudson River were disappearing. New York City was changing.

Tito expected to get his old job back as the percussionist for the Machito Orchestra after the war. But there was no place to put percussionist Uba Nieto, who needed the job. Everyone was struggling. While he was trying to figure out what to do next, Tito married Milta, and soon after she got pregnant. He also had access to the GI Bill. He began his study of arranging and additional musical theory when he enrolled at the Juilliard School of Music in Manhattan. The stint with Marti, a Brazilian, was not what Tito was looking for. But he did need to work. "He was a nice guy and played easy to dance music." Tito played traps and was able to once again view the stars and personalities that frequented the Copacabana – Marlene Dietrich, Lana Turner, Humphrey Bogart, and even his childhood idol, George Raft. Miguelito Valdés sang there occasionally.

While studying at the Juilliard School of Music – in 1946 it was located on West 122nd Street where the Manhattan School of Music stands now - the striking thing to Tito was how progressive Machito and the Afro-Cubans had become. "They were really into another stratosphere," Tito often reminded me. "They changed the music. They got into the real Cuban stuff."

And still, he used to remember, besides the Machito organization that was under the musical direction of Mario Bauzá there were other musical forces coming down the pike – some he knew of and some he would learn about as he started thinking about how someday he would like to direct his own band.

Antonio Arcaño was now the most popular Cuban orchestra. It was a charanga that included six violins, two cellos, a full percussion section (including a tumbadora or conga), güiro (gourd), piano and the unadorned flute. With Arcaño played the López brothers – Cachao, bass, and Orestes, cello, Jesús López (no relation), piano, and Ulpiano Díaz, píala or timbales. Every night this orchestra could be heard on radio playing the new style danzón mambo. The flute player during this period was José Antonio Fajardo.

He became universally known as the King of the Mambo; Damaso Pérez Prado[46] was one of the most important musicians involved in the hugely popular Afro-Cuban dance craze. Whether he actually created the rhythm is disputed, but it's abundantly clear that Prado developed it into a bright, swinging style with massive appeal for dancers of all backgrounds and classes. To Tito the Cuban pianist was "a legend in his own mind." Tito was not the only one with this opinion. Prado's mambo was filled with piercing high-register trumpets, undulating saxophone counterpoint, and harmonic ideas borrowed from jazz. While his tight percussion arrangements allowed for little improvisation, they were dense and sharply focused, keeping the underlying syncopations easy for dancers to follow.

Pérez Prado was born in the heavily Afro-Cuban area of Matanzas, Cuba, on December 11, 1916 (though he habitually gave his birth date as five years later). According to Spanish custom, he carried both his father and mother's last name. Starting in childhood, Prado studied classical piano, and by the time he finished school, he was good enough to play piano and organ professionally in local clubs and movie theaters. His earliest job was with a local charanga. He moved to Havana around 1942, and freelanced for a number of smaller orchestras over the next year or so. Chiefly a pianist at this point, he also landed an arranging job with Gapar Roca de la Peer, which sometimes supplied material to the highly popular Orquesta Casino de la Playa.

The orchestra's lead vocalist, Cascarita, liked Prado's work, and soon he was hired as arranger and pianist. This was the early platform Prado needed to develop his own arranging style, and after-hours jam sessions around Havana were already influencing his rhythmic concepts. Seeking to bring more excitement into the well-established rumba rhythm, Prado began to experiment with the hard swing of American jazz, influenced especially by the harmonically sophisticated big-band music of Stan Kenton. He also sought to build new Afro-Cuban-derived rhythms, including a pattern that was dubbed the mambo, whose early forms were traced back to Arsenio Rodríguez and Arcaño. He spent time in the Havana Radio Progreso studio observing Arsenio Rodríguez, and also listened to Arcaño who was at the CMQ studio. Some historians believe that he was intrigued with the music of Stan Kenton, who had assumed the spotlight in the United States as one of the most progressive orchestras.

While he was at sea, Tito heard Kenton's orchestra. He found it frontline and driving. Kenton introduced new methods for playing jazz in a large orchestra. The use of his brass was "enticing and provocative."

Prado's innovations were greeted with outright hostility from Cuba's conservative musical establishment, similar to the reaction it displayed to the new style of music introduced by Arcaño and Rodríguez. No longer able to find arranging work, he left Cuba in 1947, to try his luck in Puerto Rico. He eventually joined a touring group that swung through Argentina, Venezuela, Panama, and Mexico, and emerged as their star attraction. In 1948, he relocated to Mexico City and set about putting together his own orchestra, which featured a core membership of Cuban expatriates. One of those was singer Beny Moré, who performed and recorded with Prado (among several other bandleaders) through 1950; the association helped make Prado's orchestra a top draw in Mexico City, and set Moré on a path to becoming one of Cuba's best-loved singers. RCA's Mexican division signed Prado as an artist in his own right in 1949, and his first 78-rpm record, *"Que Rico el Mambo."*

Pérez Prado, who showed Bauzá several of his arrangements, visited the Conga Club. "I looked through them. I saw they were guarachas. We had plenty of those and we were starting to get away from this type of music. This was in 1943. He never used the word mambo," Mario told Tito on one occasion that they were recalling the old days. This conversation took place in 1974, at the Asia Restaurant in Manhattan where Tito, Charlie, Federico, and others used to hang out. The restaurant served Cuban-Chinese food and was located at West 55th Street and Ninth Avenue. More about what we talked about later. Tito had me record some of those informal gatherings. Before returning to Havana, Pérez Prado did spend time with Pupi Campo and Diosa Costello. He was the guest of the couple in their Manhattan apartment for several weeks.

By the end of World War II conjuntos – two or three trumpets – with a percussion section of bongos, tumbadora and güiro were becoming quite popular and along with the large Cuban jazz orchestras such as the Riverside, were taking over the spotlight from the smoother charanga orchestras.

Tito returned to New York to seek his position with Machito, according to a federal law that required that all returning servicemen be offered their prewar jobs. But Uba Nieto, who had taken Puente's job as percussionist with Machito, had a family to support. His brother, a sax player in the band had been killed in action, so Machito and Tito agreed it would be best if Nieto kept the job. Puente was offered a contract with Frank Marti's Copacabana band. But he considered these placements as temporary. He was nervous and looking into the future.

Machito, Kenton and Curbelo

In Tito's view two of the most progressive musical organizations around the mid 1940s was Machito y sus Afro-Cubanos, and the Stan Kenton Orchestra. He felt an urge to go in the progressive direction but as yet was not sure just how to do it. He was going to be a father, he needed to work, and he wanted to study more music. He enjoyed rubbing shoulders with the stars and he loved the attention he got for his showmanship. If anything Tito was not shy.

There have been few jazz musicians as consistently controversial as

Stan Kenton[47]. Dismissed by purists of various genres while loved by many others, Kenton ranks up there with Chet Baker and Sun Ra as one of jazz's top cult figures. He led a succession of highly original bands that often emphasized passion, power and difficult harmonies over swing, and this upset listeners who felt that all big bands should aim to sound like Count Basie. Kenton always had a different vision. Tito wanted to do something like this.

Kenton played in the 1930s in the dance bands of Vido Musso and Gus Arnheim but he was born to be a leader. In 1941, he formed his first orchestra, which later was named after his theme song *"Artistry in Rhythm."* Earl Hines-influenced Kenton was more important in the early days as an arranger and inspiration for his loyal musicians. Although there were no major names in his first band (bassist Howard Rumsey and trumpeter Chico Alvarez come the closest), Kenton spent the summer of 1941 playing regularly before a very appreciative audience at the Rendezvous Ballroom in Balboa Beach, California. Influenced by Jimmie Lunceford, who, like Kenton, enjoyed high-note trumpeters and thick-toned tenors, the Stan Kenton Orchestra struggled a bit after its initial success. Its Decca recordings were not big sellers and a stint as Bob Hope's backup radio band was an unhappy experience; Les Brown took Kenton's place.

By late 1943 with a Capitol Records contract, a popular release in *"Eager Beaver"* and growing recognition, the Stan Kenton Orchestra was gradually catching on. Its soloists during the war years included Art Pepper, briefly Stan Getz, alto saxophonists Boots Mussulli and singer Anita O'Day. By 1945 the band had evolved quite a bit. Pete Rugolo became the chief arranger. He expanded on Kenton's chief ideas of arranging and improvisation in a big band. Bob Cooper and Vido Musso offered very different tenor styles and June Christy was Kenton's new singer; her popular hits (including *"Tampico"* and *"Across the Alley from the Alamo"*) made it possible for Kenton to finance his more ambitious ventures. Calling his music "Progressive Jazz," Kenton sought to lead a concert orchestra as opposed to a dance band at a time when most big bands were starting to break up. By 1947, Kai Winding was greatly influencing the sound of Kenton's trombonists. The trumpet section included such screamers as Buddy Childers, Ray Wetzel and Al Porcino. Jack Costanzo's bongos were bringing Latin rhythms into Kenton's sound and a riotous version of *"The Peanut Vendor"* contrasted with the somber *"Elegy for Alto."* Kenton had succeeded in forming a radical and very original band that gained its own audience.

As a student attending Juilliard, the experimental sounds coming from Kenton and his sidemen caught Tito's attention. He liked the way Kenton and Rugolo balanced the brass – steady saxophones carrying one harmony, the trumpets and trombones sliding aggressively over the reeds. "It was strong and firm sounding," is the way Tito described Kenton's music of the late 1940s. "He was never satisfied. He was always looking for something new." Kenton was one of the bandleaders that would continue to impact Tito's thinking – always looking to the future.

Tito considered that the Machito and Kenton styles struck a unique balance between arranged music and improvisation. "An improvised jazz chorus stands in danger of losing its authenticity and of becoming dishonest and untrue when it is copied by someone who did not create it. Kenton seemed to understand something of what Afro-Cuban music was about. Bauzá understood the elements of American jazz so that they could be incorporated easily and without shock into an Afro-Cuban big band format. The hard part for the two orchestras, in the 1940s, was getting people to like the sound. Everything was changing so fast," Tito reflected.

In 1949 Stan Kenton took a year off. In 1950 he put together his most advanced band, the 39-piece Innovations in Modern Music Orchestra that included 16 strings, a woodwind section and two French horns. Its music ranged from the unique and very dense modern classical charts of Bob Graettinger, to works that somehow swung despite the weight. Such major players as Maynard Ferguson (whose high-note acrobatics set new standards), Shorty Rogers, Milt Bernhart, John Graas, Art Pepper, Bud Shank, Bob Cooper, Laurindo Almeida, Shelly Manne and June Christy were part of this remarkable project but, from a commercial standpoint, it was really impossible. Kenton managed two tours during 1950-51 but soon reverted to his usual 19-piece lineup.

The Machito orchestra was rather distinctive in 1946-47. Tito spent a lot of time following the orchestra, looking at the new arrangements and now listening to one of the new additions, a fellow by the name of René Hernández, a Cuban pianist who had been playing for the orchestra of Julio Cuevas in Cuba. Mario Bauzá recruited him. It was obvious that he had a sense of the Afro-Cuban syncopation or off beat timing as it came to be described that was so important to the music. René Hernández arrived in November 1945 to take over the piano work for Joe Loco, who had been drafted. Poor eyesight had kept Joe safe from being drafted early but by the fourth year of total war many of the previous restrictions were being lifted.

Quickly, Hernández orchestrated a new book consisting of varied tempos, many of which were in the time measure of 4/4 or what came to be called the "four beat mambo" similar to what Antonio Arcaño y sus Maravillas had been playing in Cuba, but without the danzón introduction, and similar to the open ended montunos that had been introduced years earlier by Arsenio Rodríguez. The Machito orchestra was ready for the opening of the Christmas season at the Caribbean Club in downtown Miami and then for a 12-week appearance at the Brazil Club – arranged by Miguelito Valdés. The Brazil Club catered to such dancers as Mickey Rooney, Ann Sheridan, John Carrol, Virginia Hill and many others. Miguelito also frequented it. Tito recalled that Rooney was also a terrific hoofer and on the ballroom floor he was capable of incredible moves. But there was concern about the band's opening.

"There was a lot of tension among the musicians," Bauzá recalled (Asia Restaurant, 1976). "We had black musicians, white musicians and brown musicians and Miami was very restricted. When we were rehearsing one afternoon the promoter was shocked to see the members of the band. He wanted us to stop. Miguelito yelled at him. I was ready to pull out, if they paid me, but Miguelito convinced the promoter that if we did not open it would be an ugly situation." The day that Mario told the story Miguelito, Tito, Federico, Charlie and Machito were sitting at the table. Eventually, Miguelito won the argument and the Machito orchestra opened.

"Miguelito had a convincing way about him," according to Tito. "He could be cool as a cucumber, but he could be quite the opposite."

"Yeah," smiled Mario. "He was getting hot about half way through the discussion."

Miguelito chimed in, "All I said was that if Machito and the Afro-Cubans walked, that everyone would lose money…"

"Bullshit. It got a little more intense than that," inserted Mario. The remark was followed by laughter.

In 1945 Beny Moré arrived in Mexico City. He was the singer for the Conjunto Matamoros that had been contracted to appear at the legendary cabaret Río Rosa. When they were just at the point of returning to Cuba, Beny asked Miguel Matamoros for permission to remain in Mexico because he was now engaged to a Mexican girl. He also wanted to move away from the popular conjunto because he felt restrained by the strict way in which Matamoros arranged the ensemble's music. He married Juana Bocanegra Duran in Mexico City in 1946. After a long and difficult search for work, he began performances at the Río Rosa Club. He was the featured soloist with some of the best Mexican orchestras – Mariano Merceron, Rafael de Pas, and Chucho Rodríguez to mention a few. In 1948 he connected with Pérez

Prado, who by now was one of Mexico's biggest celebrities. The mambo as introduced by Pérez Prado was the craze of the Mexican capital. The danzón had national status and was not going to go away as was hoped by Pérez Prado and his promoters.

Meanwhile, the José Curbelo Orchestra was playing Miami Beach and the Borscht Belt, the New York Catskill Mountains resorts. Curbelo was becoming more popular than Noro Morales. He was even considered by his followers as more swinging than Anselmo Sacasas, Bartolo Hernández, Carlos Valero and Marcelino Guerra. These bands appeared nightly at the midtown Manhattan clubs. Curbelo was still mild mannered and conservative, according to Tito, but he was changing, and changing rapidly. The 15-piece outfit that Curbelo put together featured Curbelo senior – bass; Francisco "Chino" Pozo – bongo; Carlos Vidal – tumbadora; Tito Puente – timbales; and, Tito Rodríguez – vocalist. Puente was also paid an additional $10 for arranging much of the band's repertoire. The extra money was used to further his studies at the Juilliard School of Music.

Working with Curbelo the two Titos established a closer friendship and a rivalry as well as a reputation for chasing beautiful women. "Some of it was true," Tito laughed. But his eyes gleamed. "We always had a eye for the pretty ladies, but most of the stories are bullshit," Tito maintained.

Gene Krupa had just served three months in jail for a bogus drug charge in the early 1940s. When he completed his sentence he decided to reorganize his orchestra and introduce the new sounds of bebop into his music. While many big bands could not remain financially afloat as bebop grew in popularity, Krupa managed to keep his full big band together up until 1950 and then toured with a smaller group. His chief competitor on percussion was Buddy Rich.

Buddy Rich[48] was perhaps unmatched when it came to the combination of playing solos with speed and power. His innovation did not match his ability as say, compared to Tony Williams or Elvin Jones, but his raw speed was incredible! He was born in 1917 and was a prodigy. He was born into a show business family and began playing vaudeville at the age of 18 months as "Traps, the Drum Wonder" and was playing on Broadway at the age of four under the name "Infant Taps." He was completely self-taught. He played with many of the major swing bands in the 1930s and early 1940s, such as Harry James, Tommy Dorsey, Artie Shaw, Bunny Berigan, and Benny Carter. By the mid 1940s he had easily dethroned his friend Gene Krupa as the "King of Drummers." However, Tito still idolized Krupa and could take or leave Rich. He felt Rich was more of a showman than a musician. This was kind of funny since Tito liked to think of himself as a showman. “But music is first.”

Rich also played in smaller settings, such as on the trio recording with Lionel Hampton and Art Tatum, where he more than held his own, and with Charlie Parker, Lester Young, and Dizzy Gillespie, though he was more of a swing drummer than a bebop drummer. In the 1950s, he led his own small group and also displayed his singing. There are several rare recordings of Buddy Rich, Ella Fitzgerald and Charlie Parker playing with the Machito orchestra. Tito thought these to be “incredible.’ But he remained adamant about Krupa - it was all about delivery and style he used to say.

“I don’t know if he remembered me from his flare up with Frank, but Buddy was always friendly and I never brought up the incident. I’m pretty sure someone told Buddy that I sat in for him that night,” Tito laughed.

Simply put, Tony Williams was another great percussionist. Williams made his mark on jazz when he joined Miles Davis’ quintet at the age of 17. Technique-wise, he was far ahead of his time. He was the most admired and imitated drummer of the 1960s. His advanced polyrhythms and his whiplash beats propelled Miles Davis’ group forward and pushed the limits of freedom for the soloists. Funny thing was, Miles couldn’t play in some clubs because Williams’ youth prevented him from being in certain clubs. Williams’ rhythmic drive and innovation was one of the primary reasons that Miles Davis’ music was rejuvenated during the 1960s, according to Tito.

Tito used to say that Elvin Jones was one of the most influential drummers around. He was born in Pontiac, Michigan in 1927 and had two brothers, Thad and Hank, who were also jazz musicians. He developed an original style based on parts of bebop, but he used advanced, complex polyrhythms (playing different rhythms with each hand and foot). “Playing two rhythms – at the same time – is a difficult thing to do. Many of the Cuban timbaleros going way back mastered this type of arrangement,” Tito said.

After a stint in the army from 1946-49, Jones moved to Detroit and was part of the jazz scene before moving to New York in 1955. He worked with Teddy Charles and the Bud Powell trio and recorded with many players, such as Miles Davis, Donald Byrd, and Sonny Rollins at a famous Village Vanguard session.

Bebop

Tito kept playing the saxophone on and off. He never gave it up but he realized early that there was only one Charlie "Bird" Parker[49]. "There was no one quite like him," the Old Man said often when talking about how he wanted to arrange a piece for his orchestra. Parker was one of the most important figures in jazz history and also one of its greatest tragic heroes.

The Bird got his nickname (also known as "Yardbird") from his love of chicken. He came from Kansas City and was a self-taught alto saxophonist who did not realize that many jazz songs of the day were only played in a few keys, so he learned them all. Parker quit school at the age of 15 to become a musician. His early days as a musician were not easy. On one occasion he tried playing *"Body and Soul*" in double-time and was laughed off the stage. Another time, he was playing in a jam session with the Count Basie Orchestra. They were playing "*I Got Rhythm*" and Bird lost the key and couldn't find it. Basie's drummer, Jo Jones completed his humiliation by throwing his cymbal at Bird's feet. Bird continued practicing and got to the point where he could play Lester Young's solos in double time. Parker then joined Jay McShann's band and the Billy Eckstine Orchestra, and during this period he finally figured out how to play the music he had been hearing in his head. He joined Dizzy Gillespie, Charlie Christian, Kenny Clarke and Thelonious Monk at the after-hours jam sessions at Minton's Uptown House in Harlem, and there Bebop was born. Parker's style revolutionized jazz and he became the messiah of modern jazz. Parker and Gillespie formed a legendary small group during this time that played some of the greatest jazz ever. The two musicians made frequent excursions into Afro-Cuban music playing their solos with the Machito orchestra. It almost seemed like divine forces brought all these people to the same place at the same time in history. However, Parker had a self-destructive streak and would do anything for a thrill. He lived an amoral life, and any "high" he could get. His heroin habit caused him to miss many gigs, which led Dizzy to leave the group. Eventually the drug was the cause of a nervous breakdown that landed Bird in a mental hospital. He came back and reformed his quintet with Miles Davis taking Gillespie's place and continued making great music. In one of his more unique ventures, Bird made the first "with strings" album, in which he was backed by a stringed orchestra. It was the first of a popular series of recordings of this type that many other artists made. Bird's self-destructive life style finally caught up with him in 1955, when he died at the age of 34. He had so badly abused his body that the doctor who examined him estimated his age at 60. Besides his often imitated, but never matched style, he left behind a terrible legacy with other jazz musicians, who also did drugs, thinking if they used like Bird, they could play like Bird. His playing was fast, perky, and very bluesy, all wrapped up into one. He could make you bounce around one moment and feel his pain the next. His music is rooted in the Kansas City blues and every song he played had a blues twist to it.

Thelonious Monk[50] was a favorite of Tito. He was certainly one of the most unique pianists and composers in jazz. He could be called "eccentric." Tito usually referred to him as "shrewd and insightful." He was the house pianist at Minton's Uptown House jazz club in Harlem and along with Charlie Parker, Dizzy Gillespie, Kenny Clarke, and Charlie Christian, helped to invent the style of bebop. Monk was known as "the high priest of bop." However, he didn't catch on in popularity as quickly as the others. His style was far different. He used unconventional chords in his music. He also played sparsely, had a unique sense of rhythm, and used empty spaces effectively in his music. His composing reflected this as well. It is hard to describe his music to someone who has never heard it. The music was "like missing the bottom step in the dark." Missing a chord change, according to Tito "is like falling into an empty elevator shaft." His music is very unique and very cool, though. It's unlike anything you've ever heard. "It's like being so laid back that you could fall off a chair," was Tito's view. While his peers recognized his genius, it took the public about a dozen years to do so.

He did not compose a large body of work, about 60-70 songs, but many of his compositions have become jazz standards, which include, but are certainly not limited to, *"Ruby my dear,"* "Well you needn't*,"* *"Round Midnight*" (one of Tito's all-time favorite songs!), "*Mysterioso*," "*Monk's Dream*," *"Blue Monk," "Trinkle, Tinkle,"* "*Pannonica*," and *"Straight, No Chaser."* Even when he did a conventional popular song, such as "April in "*Paris*," or "*Body and Soul*," he would re-write the chords, and put his own unique fingerprint on it. Monk has been called "the first great jazz composer after Duke Ellington." When asked why he didn't write more, he said that he was going to keep playing his songs until people heard them. Besides his compositions, Monk also influenced the bebop revolution through his look; his Bohemian appearance and affection for shades and eccentric hats did much to define the postwar hipster.

After playing at Minton's in 1943, he joined Coleman Hawkins. He was falsely imprisoned on a drug offense, and was subsequently banned

New York, he recorded with his own group. In the early 1940s he left the Goodman organization to form his own touring band.

Hampton's band advanced the talents of Illinois Jacquet, Dexter Gordon, Ernie Royal, Jack McVea, Charlie Mingus, Monk Montgomery, Wes Montgomery, Quincy Jones, Benny Golson, Fats Navarro, Kenny Dorham, Clifford Brown, Dinah Washington, Betty Carter, Joe Williams, Arnett Cobb, and Earl Bostic, among many others. His wife, Gladys Hampton, was his manager throughout much of his career. Many musicians recall that Lionel took care of the music and Gladys ran the business. Hampton's recording of *"Flying Home"* (1939) with the famous honking tenor sax solo by Jacquet, later refined and expanded by Cobb (1946), is considered by some to be the first rock and roll record.

Tito described Hampton as a "fully equipped and capable musician who was exciting to watch and listen to. He could make you freak out." He was known for his tireless energy and his skill on the vibes, drums, and lightning speed two-fingered piano. The bars on the vibraphone are laid out like the piano; Hampton played both instruments the same way. Tito and Lionel were drawn together during the early 1950s. Tito would sit in with the Hampton ensemble when he played down the street from the Palladium Ballroom, and Hampton would join in with the Tito Puente Orchestra unannounced at the Latin dancehall. Lionel Hampton died of cardiac arrest in New York City on August 31, 2002. He was interred in the Woodlawn Cemetery, Bronx, New York.

There are a number of vibraphonists that Tito enjoyed listening to in addition to Hampton. Terry Gibbs was his contemporary but had been playing professionally in the jazz environment since the early 1940s. He was a native of Brooklyn, New York, and was born Julius Gubenko on October 13, 1924, discovered the bebop jazz style when he heard legends Dizzy Gillespie and Charlie Parker play in Manhattan's 52nd Street jazz clubs during the 1940s.

He claimed to have had a nervous breakdown when he heard the music. Gibbs's career accomplishments include membership in the Woody Herman Four Brothers Band, leadership of his own Dream Band, and appearances on television shows with Steve Allen, Regis Philbin, and Mel Tormé. His more notable collaborations include work with clarinetists Bud Powell and Buddy DeFranco. Terry practiced secretly on his brother's vibes whenever he could.

Gibbs's first big break came when he was 12 years old. One of the most popular radio programs of the era was Major Bowes Amateur Hour, a weekly talent contest that was broadcast nationwide from a studio in New York City. His confidence in his xylophone-playing skills bolstered by his weekly sessions with Albright, Terry appeared in one of these weekly radio contests and won. Almost immediately, he began making professional appearances in the city and beyond. The name change from Julius Gubenko to Terry Gibbs came in two distinct steps. A boxing enthusiast, the young Brooklyn resident particularly admired a fighter named Terry Young, whose boxing style he sought to emulate. Close friends began calling him Terry, and Julius was largely forgotten. A few years later, when he was about 16 years old, Terry hit the road on tour with a bandleader named Judy Kayne.

When he turned 18, shortly after the United States entered World War II, Gibbs joined the Army and was trained as a tank driver. However, he never got to see any action at the front, because he was assigned to the 8th Service Command in Dallas, Texas, a unit that produced movies and radio programs for the Army. They needed a drummer, and Gibbs fit the bill. During a furlough from the Army, Gibbs returned to New York, where he continued to focus on bebop and to its popular proponents, Charlie Parker and Dizzy Gillespie. After his discharge from military service, Gibbs left the drums behind and concentrated almost solely on the vibraphone. Among the bands for which he played in the years following the Army were those of Tommy Dorsey, Chubby Jackson, and Buddy Rich. In the late 1940s he worked with Woody Herman. In 1950, Gibbs formed his own band and worked for Mel Tormé on television. Although the band dissolved after the Tormé television show was dropped, Gibbs re-formed it at the end of the decade and took it to the prestigious Monterey Jazz Festival in 1961. In 1951, Gibbs joined the Benny Goodman Sextet.

Both Down Beat and Metronome polls declared him "the number one vibraphonist in the world" from 1950 through 1955. Gibbs was in New York in 1957 – he was not sure if he should move, but a lot of jazzmen were moving west. On the West Coast, he formed the Dream Band, whose members included Conte Candoli, Richie Kamuca, Mel Lewis, Joe Maini, and Frank Rosolino. The Down Beat Critic's Poll in 1962 declared Gibbs's group "the best band in the world." One of the most fruitful collaborations of Gibbs's career has been with clarinetist Buddy DeFranco. He is still working today and is still considered a rather fast player – it seems he plays everything in double time.

Cal Tjader[53] (July 16, 1925–May 4, 1982) has been called the greatest Anglo Latin jazz musician. Interestingly, both Tito and Cal were learning the vibraphone at about the same time – Tjader on the West Coast and Tito on the East Coast. Unlike other American musicians who experimented with the music from Cuba, the Caribbean, and Latin America, he never abandoned it, performing it until his death. Tjader primarily played the vibes. He was also accomplished with the drums, bongos, congas, timpani, and the piano. He worked with numerous musicians from several cultures. Tjader is often linked to the development of Latin rock and acid jazz. Although fusing jazz with Latin music is often categorized as "Latin jazz" (or, earlier, "Afro-Cuban"), Tjader's output swung freely between both styles. Like Tito, he too was learning the vibes after World War II.

Callen Radcliffe Tjader, Jr. was born in St. Louis, Missouri to traveling Swedish immigrant vaudevillians. His father was a tap dancer and his mother played piano, a husband-wife team going from city to city with their troupe to earn a living. At the age of two, Tjader's parents settled in San Mateo, California and opened a dance studio. His mother instructed him in classical piano and his father taught him to tap dance. He performed around the Bay Area as "Tjader Junior," a tap-dancing wunderkind. He performed a brief non-speaking role dancing alongside Bill "Bojangles" Robinson in the film "The White of the Dark Cloud of Joy."

Tjader taught himself the drums. Like Tito, Tjader was a fan of Gene Krupa and the Benny Goodman Orchestra. When they met years later they would talk about some of the things that impacted the way each approached music. Tjader also taught himself bongos overnight in order to record with Nick Esposito. He joined a Dixieland band and played around the Bay Area. At age 16, he entered a Gene Krupa drum solo contest, making it to the finals but ultimately losing. The loss was overshadowed by that morning's event; Japanese planes had bombed Pearl Harbor.

Tjader served in the Army from 1943 until 1946. Upon his return he enrolled at San Jose State College under the GI Bill majoring in education. (He hoped to become a schoolteacher.) Later he transferred to San Francisco State College, still intending to teach. It was there he took timpani lessons, his only formal music training. At San Francisco State he met Dave Brubeck, a young pianist also fresh from a stint in the Army. Brubeck introduced Tjader to Paul Desmond. The three connected with more players and formed the Dave Brubeck Octet with Tjader on drums. The Octet experimented with jazz, employing odd time signatures and non-Western keys. Although the group only recorded one album (and had an abysmal time finding work), the recording is regarded as important due to its early glimpse at these soon-to-be-legendary jazz greats. After the Octet disbanded, Tjader and Brubeck formed a trio, performing jazz standards in the hope of finding more work. The Dave Brubeck Trio succeeded and became a fixture in the San Francisco jazz scene. Tjader taught himself the vibraphone in this period, alternating between it and the drums depending on the song.

Jazz pianist George Shearing recruited Tjader in 1953, hoping the vibes would add sparkle to his group's sound. When Shearing later decided to go Latin, Tjader thought himself a conga player. Tjader played them as well as the vibes. The Down Beat 1953 Critics Poll nominated him as best New Star on the drums. While in New York City, bassist Al McKibbon took Tjader to see the Afro-Cuban big bands led by Machito and Chico O'Farrill, both at the forefront of the budding Latin jazz sound. In New York City he also met Mongo Santamaría and Willie Bobo, who at the time were an integral part of Tito's orchestra.

Tjader is often wrongly credited as the musician who brought the vibraphones to Latin jazz. Tito Puente, and probably Tito Rodríguez deserve the honors, as they performed Afro-Cuban tunes on the vibraphone in the late 1940s and early 1950s – a few years before Tjader made the transition. But Tjader certainly molded and expanded the sound of vibes in Afro-Cuban music.

Changing New York

New York was changing. The outbreak of World War II opened the doors to many of the migrants who were searching for jobs. Since a large portion of the male population was sent to war, there was a sudden need of manpower to fulfill the jobs left behind. Puerto Ricans, both male and female, found themselves employed in factories and ship docks, producing both domestic and warfare goods. Thousands of islanders and Puerto Ricans living on the mainland either joined or were drafted to serve in the battlefields just as Tito Puente was doing.

The advent of air travel provided Puerto Ricans with an affordable and faster way of travel to New York. The one thing that all of the migrants had in common was that they wanted a better way of life than was available in Puerto Rico, and although each held personal reasons for migrating, their decision generally was rooted in the island's impoverished conditions as well as the public policies that sanctioned migration. It was not long before the Puerto Rican "Barrios" in the South Bronx, Spanish Harlem, Manhattan's Lower East Side and Brooklyn's Atlantic Avenue, began to resemble "Little Puerto Ricos" with their "bodegas" (small grocery stores) and "piragueros" (shaved ice cone vendors) on every corner.

Puerto Ricans arriving in New York embraced the relatively new mambo that was being introduced by Machito, and as of 1947, Tito Rodríguez and his Lobos Del Mambo, a conjunto. Pupi Campo, Noro Morales and José Curbelo were now convinced that this was the way to go. It is estimated that from 1946 to 1950 nearly 40,000 Puerto Ricans migrated to New York

Most of the newly arrived Puerto Ricans settled in New York City. An additional 58,500 islanders arrived between 1952 and 1953. Many soldiers who returned after World War II made use of the GI Bill and went to college. Puerto Rican women confronted economic exploitation, discrimination, racism, and the insecurities inherent in the migration process on a daily basis, however they fared better than did men in the job market. The women left their homes for the factories in record numbers. By 1953, Puerto Rican migration to New York reached its peak when 75,000 people left the island. Operation Bootstrap ("Operación Manos a la Obra") the name given to the ambitious projects which industrialized Puerto Rico after1948, was engineered by Teodoro Moscoso[54] who was the island's Economic Development Administrator for the first Puerto Rican elected governor, Luis Muñoz Marin.

Muñoz Marin, who had lived in New York as a bohemian and wrote poetry, won the 1948 election by defeating the Statehood Republican Party, and the Nationalist Party that favored independence. The Popular Democratic Party that Muñoz organized favored the Commonwealth – common citizenship, common defense and common money. He obtained from President Harry S. Truman and the U.S. Congress commitments to improve economic support as well as provide tax breaks for businesses on the island. His goal was to reduce poverty, eliminate abject poverty and bring Puerto Rico into the 20th century. Most agreed he was successful, but he does have his detractors.

New York Mayor Robert F. Wagner, Jr. began a campaign to recruit Puerto Rican laborers to work in the city's factories. Wagner calculated that the city would benefit greatly by the attracting what was considered "cheap labor." Discrimination was rampant in the United States and it was no different in New York. There were signs in restaurants that read "No dogs or Puerto Ricans allowed."

The Puerto Rican Nationalist Party leaders conceived a plan to attack the Blair House with the intention of assassinating the President, and at the same time attack the House of Representatives. Pedro Albizu Campos, a nephew of Puerto Rican composer Juan Morel Campos, led the Nationalist uprising on the island. Muñoz Marin called out the National Guard – many of whom were World War II veterans, and quickly crushed the uprising. These events had a negative impact on the Puerto Rican residents of New York. Americans viewed Puerto Ricans as anti-Americans and the discrimination against them became even more widespread.

The islanders continued to pour into New York. In this tumultuous setting the recent arrivals from Puerto Rico embraced Cuban music and lifted the Palladium Ballroom in midtown Manhattan into the Mecca of Afro-Cuban dance music. The Palladium was one of many nightclubs that dotted midtown Manhattan that hosted or presented a menu of Latin dance music and cool bebop jazz. In 1947 it was propelled into historical prominence.

In Step With Pupi

On a recommendation from his friend Charlie Palmieri, who was featured on the piano for Brazilian bandleader Fernando Alvarez, Tito landed in the Pupi Campo Orchestra.

Like Tito, so did Campo idolize Stan Kenton. He also held Pérez Prado in high esteem. Tito figured that his tenure with the Campo band would be a move in the right direction. "He was a showman, flamboyant and colorful," Tito surmised. There was a certain jazz influence that even Campo acknowledged." Campo did not believe Latin musicians could fit in with the new harmonies that were being developed. But Tito disagreed with his premise that "most Cuban musicians just can't play that kind of harmony because they are classically trained and are not into jazz fundamentals. He just did not get it."

"Cuban and Puerto Rican musicians were forever being influenced by American jazz. Jesus Christ! I swear he (Campo) was a great guy, but he had blinders," recalled Tito. During the 1950s, the orchestra was featured on Jack Paar's television show. During one of the shows Campo met and married Betty Clooney, the sister of pop and jazz vocalist Rosemary Clooney. Campo later settled into Las Vegas, where he remained a featured performer for several years. Prior to his marriage he romanced Diosa Costello, whom Tito believed helped him get his job in the Campo orchestra.

Campo was a dapper man about town, according to Tito. When Tito joined his orchestra he got to test his own organizational skills in terms of giving Campo's band a more "Afro-Cuban sound." Yes, the band played rumba and other Latin flavor music but with Tito in the mix suddenly the Campo Orchestra was revealing its propensity to play authentic Cuban music such as was being played by Curbelo and Machito. Tito revealed himself to be a harsh taskmaster when it came to music.

The band always had great musicians. Charlie Palmieri was his musical director. He was an extraordinary pianist when he was playing for Jack Paar in 1953, according to Tito. Joe Loco was the original piano player and added a lot of jazzy intonations. Also on piano was Al Escobar. But as far as Tito was concerned it was a show band, nothing like Machito or even Curbelo had. "But the pay was good." Among the musicians that played for Campo between 1948 and 1951 (probably for recording sessions) was trumpets: Paul Cohen, Chubby Kuesten, Al Porcino, Jimmy Frisaura and Tony Russo; saxes: Joe Herde, Sol Rabinowitz, Joe "Pin" Madera, Nat Cappi, Frank Socolow and Irving Butler; trombone: Johnny Mandel; piano: Joe Loco or Al Escobar; percussion: Chino Pozo, Johnny "La Vaca" Rodríguez, Alex Campo, Tito Puente, Jimmy Nevada; vocal: Vitin Avilés; and, bass Amadito Vizoso.

Trumpeter Jimmy Frisaura and Tito formed a friendship at this juncture that would last nearly 50 years. Jimmy became Tito's musical director and band manager until his death in 1998. Jimmy was an invaluable member of Tito's orchestra. Not only was he a solid musician, but he kept the band focused, managed the accounts payable, and made sure that everyone got to wherever they were supposed to be on time. "He did all the things that I needed done. He was an exceptional musician, and a good friend. We fought, and he got pissed at me, but that is what happens in a family," quipped Tito. "It's Jimmy's job to get us all to the right place, and on time. It is also his job to make sure he doesn't forget how to play the trumpet."

Frisaura was an excellent trumpet player, who like Tito was a fan of Stan Kenton and his progressive big band style of orchestration. He was also intrigued by the Machito Orchestra's new approach to playing "Latin music." Before joining up with the Pupi Campo's orchestra Jimmy worked in an array of bands, mostly one-night stands. At birth he was named Vincent James Frisaura, October 2, 1924, of Italian parents. Like Tito he was intrigued by the music of the swing era, and he enjoyed listening to Harry James and Charles Spivak play their trumpets.

"He was a great trumpet man," Tito said to me one day as Jimmy listened. "But I used to yell at him to keep him in line," he added with a grin.

"Bullshit," responded Jimmy. "I kept it all together for you." Silence for a moment and then the two of them were laughing and embracing. They drank together, chased women, fought and screamed profanities at each other for more than 30 years. Tito and Jimmy were close – closer than most people ever get. Jimmy was perhaps just one of a handful of friends that Tito would make in his lifetime. According to Tito, Jimmy had a unique sense of timing that some musicians have difficulty achieving in Afro-Cuban music. "Jimmy was always on clave," according to Tito. "He never missed a beat. Imagine that."

Al Escobar was born on March 8, 1930, in Barranquilla, Colombia. His family moved to New York in 1936 where his father, a classical musician, tutored him in music theory, composition and playing the piano. Like Tito, he was floored by the sound of Casino de la Playa's music. He learned all of the piano solos that Anselmo Sacasas played in the recordings and when he met Tito for the first time while playing for Campo, he demonstrated some of those improvisational chords that Sacasas used. "I liked him right away. He had a strong sense of what I was looking for. You know, clave."

The early rehearsals with Tito at the helm of the Campo Orchestra were tedious, according to Escobar and Frisaura. "Tito always had lots of breaks because he used the Schillinger system of mathematics. Escobar studied with Tom Timothy who was familiar with the 12-tone system. "Absolutely true," exclaimed Tito. "I wanted to use the syncopated pauses and breaks that the Cubans used in their music. Machito was doing it. Antonio Arcaño was a master of the syncopated break – it was almost out of time. "You have to feel it," Tito often said. To him the new rhythm or mambo had nothing to do with tempo – it conveyed many different feelings, depending on how it was played.

"Many jazz lovers and almost all music fans are of the opinion that there is a contradiction between improvisation and arrangement. Because, in their view, improvisation is decisive, the presence of an arrangement must automatically indicate a state of decadence since the more arrangement, the less improvisation," Tito said. "The swing era bands started using improvisation with heavy orchestration. The Afro-Cuban rhythms as tight and rigid as they are give us more expressive liberty."

Tito realized early on that there was a huge American market for Afro-Cuban music. The rumba had been popular with the mainstream market, albeit even if it was not authentic, but the potential was huge. He composed the *"Earl Wilson Mambo"* for the Campo band and on it Joe Loco displays his virtuosity on the piano. Arrangements of *"How High the Moon"* (Hamilton-Lewis) and *"What Is This Thing Called Love?"* (Cole Porter) display Tito's progressive nature and his ability to delve into the American standards. This would become a standard of the mambo era. These were recorded by Campo in 1948.

The Pupi Campo Orchestra opened for an engagement at the Chelsea Hotel in Atlantic City, New Jersey, in the summer of 1948. This was the seaside resort that catered to a mostly Jewish clientele. Every season from July through Labor Day, local residents braced themselves for the onslaught of noisy tourists who flooded to the boardwalk and the beaches. Atlantic City had been used to house military personnel during World War II, and had not been a beneficiary of the robust post war economy. But the city had been at the center of dance crazes that dated back to the turn of the 20th century – ragtime, jitterbug, tango, rumba and lindy hop. In 1948 Tito with Pupi Campo's Orchestra was going to introduce it to the mambo.

It was a busy summer for Tito. He had his wife Milta and their baby, Ronnie with him. Joe Loco was also on hand. He would leave the band soon to pursue his artistic endeavors in a jazz oriented environment. "He was an incredible piano player. He could play anything but he was always drawn to jazz. Sometimes he reminded me of Art Tatum – cool, relaxed, and elegant. He could also do a Fats Waller – furious and intricate." Joe was his boyhood pal and he enjoyed working with him. He also enjoyed working with Charlie Palmieri, a few years younger than Tito, but with an acute ability to interweave Afro-Cuban and American standards. "They could play in clave." This was the key to the new sound.

The hard work with Campo's orchestra would be useful to Tito. Legend has it that Campo died of a heart attack while leading his band on the west coast. Tito smiled and rolled his eyes whenever Pupi Campo's name came up. "He definitely was something of an acrobat. The maracas fit into his antics. He was always jumping around on the stage. I think he was a little nuts – in a happy way." Lightheartedly Tito recalled, "Pupi may have been the only Cuban I ever knew who had no inclination of how to maintain clave." Another big laugh.

The Schillinger Method

An important part of Tito's education in music was the Schillinger System. He felt it would allow him to expand his range of musical scoring. Before World War II broke out Tito had decided to pursue a career in musical film scoring. He talked to musicians that recommended he investigate the Schillinger method. "I was not sure how it would fit into what I had as my dream, but the idea of working with an expanded tonal range – 12 instead of the usual eight intrigued me. While in the Navy, the idea stuck in my head. I read about guys like Gershwin working with this system. I liked his music, his style, so I decided to give it my best shot." Tito dropped out of high school after his third year. His education did not stop. He studied music in the Navy. When he returned to civilian life he entered Juilliard from 1946 until 1949.

The following excerpt written by Harry Lyden describes the Schillinger System of Musical composition that Tito Puente studied for nearly two years. He maintained that this approach broadened his understanding of music in general and often said that it helped him in his field of endeavor – incorporating his sense of Afro-Cuban music into big band themes.

> "The cornerstone of the Schillinger System is his Theory of Rhythm. Once the process of generating rhythm patterns is understood, Schillinger's Encyclopedia of Rhythms proves to be an invaluable aid. It is easy to read and comprehend and affords a wealth of information. The two-volume Schillinger System of Musical Composition is very difficult and requires years of study, but with the coordinated simultaneous study of the Encyclopedia of Rhythms and cross-reference to his Mathematical Basis of the Arts it begins to make sense. The manifolds are as critical to understanding Schillinger as are the rhythm generators. From these comes quadrant rotation, composition from geometric projection and infinite series. Step by step, this system is interesting and most valuable.
>
> "The fundamental components of music – visuals, scales, cadences, triads and sevenths - are transformed into their coherent natural geometric form, in color and in third dimension in the system developed by Schillinger. This enables the musician to visually analyze these musical structures as well as their mirror images, thus dissolving the inherent bewilderment people encounter in music studies. It also accelerates the learning process by a thousand fold by enabling us to see the general overall mechanics of music.
>
> "Currently a music student is precluded and forbidden from expressing geometries because of the manner in which music is read, written down and described. For example if a dozen composers were asked to compose a horizontal or vertical

line, a specific triangle, a tetrahedron, a square, a pyramid, a sea shell or a pine cone we would get a dozen different compositions for each of these simple forms. Not so with visual music because it enables these blind architects to see these forms and compose the structures accordingly.

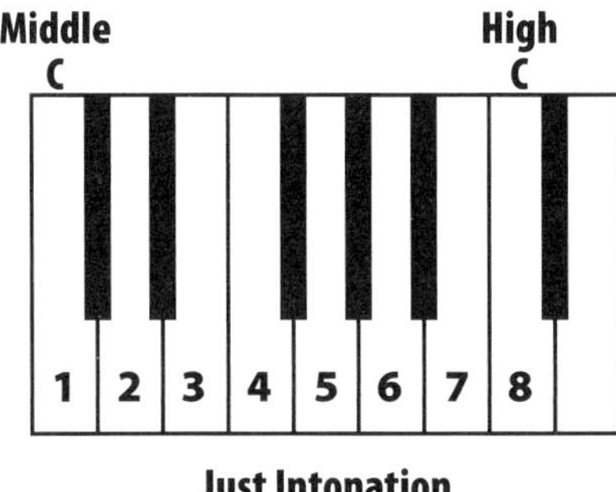

Just Intonation

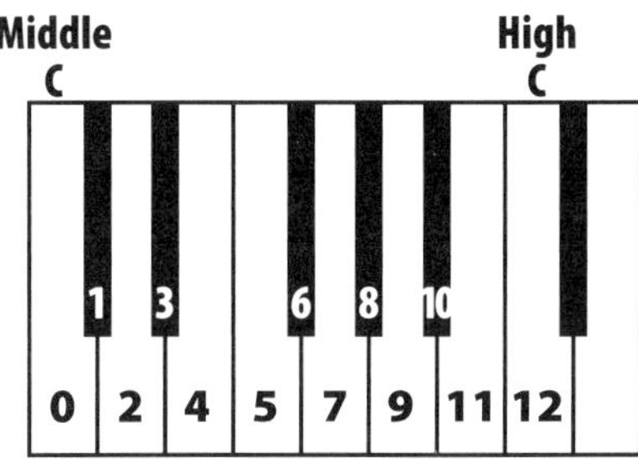

Equal Temperment

"Tradition from the days of the Just Intonation tuning system still has us counting to 8; C being 1, D being 2, E, 3, etc. Since the 1700s, however, musicians have been using the Equal Temperament system where C is zero; C sharp is 1, D is 2, E flat is 3, etc. B is 11 and C octave is 12 and not 8. Music has remained in the dark, without geometric form, because we still refer to C as 1 instead of zero. Geometry begins with 0, not 1. With C as 0, coherent visual form ensues.

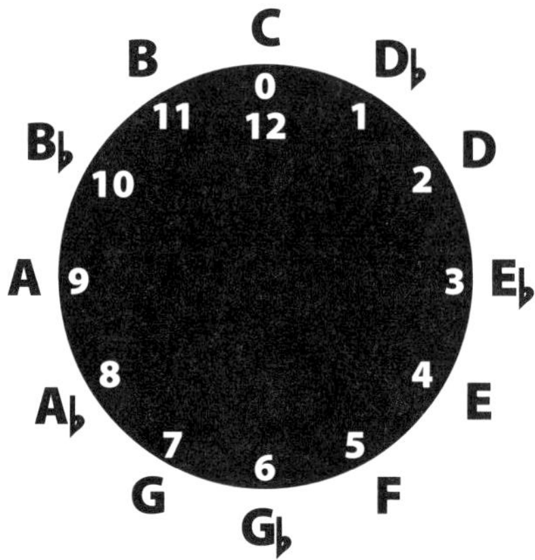

The twelve notes in our primary selective system are used because 12 is the most versatile number; 12 is the smallest number with the most divisors.

"The 12 notes in the primary selective system are placed on the 12 numbers on the clock: middle C is zero (midnight), C sharp (D flat) is 1 o'clock, etc. The C octave in the treble is +12, high noon, or 360 degrees. The C octave in the bass is -12, or yesterday noon!

"With C as zero, Schillinger categorizes music into two general forms: symmetric and diatonic.

Symmetric

The Symmetric category therefore is 12/1 or one 12-note chromatic scale. 12/2 is two six-note whole tone scales. 12/3 yields three four note diminished scales. 12/4 yields four three note augmented scales. 12/6 gives us six two note flat fifth scales.

The Symmetric category therefore may visually express a circle or the spokes of a wagon wheel, a hexagon, chicken wire, snowflakes, the benzene ring, squares, and equilateral triangles. The flat 5th scale may represent a satellite circling the earth or an electron orbital, vertical lines, horizontal lines, 30 degree and 60 degree lines, hemispheres, orange slices, a baton (stationery or thrown into the air as a majorette would during a parade). The mirror images or manifolds as Schillinger calls them are alike in this category. A later correspondence will describe the wave mechanics of these polar, non-polar and planar enantiomeres geared towards science from fact learned in music.

Diatonic

"In the remaining general category, the Diatonic, we find these manifolds radically different than in the Symmetric category. This is where the real essence of music is. Most of us know our diatonic scales, cadences and 7ths, but their manifolds are least understood if ever thought of at all. The enclosed diagrams illustrate the principles of the manifolds. Simply, if we place both thumbs on 0 (middle C) and play the C diatonic Ionian scale with the right hand, and using the same intervals in the left hand, it will reflect C's Phrygian mode. In this case the intervals are 0 2 2 1 2 2 2 1. C's Phrygian is thus in the key of A flat, starting at C.

"In music, navigation is currently in the meets and bounds system. Since Schillinger was a scientist and navigated his music theories by grid coordinates, permit me to offer a comparative example.

"In 1948 an invention appeared which revolutionized navigation. It ranks second only to the invention of the compass and is known as the Visual Omni Range. Its concept is similar to Schillinger's manifolds. The principle is simple: two beacons or discs rotating in opposite directions, each emitting a radio signal at a certain frequency. When both beacons start at 0 or North they are "in phase".

As they rotate in opposite directions they become out of phase by 30 degrees, 60 degrees, ...180 degrees, etc., until the cycle is complete. The receiver in the aircraft measures the phase displacement and registers what magnetic direction the aircraft is in relation to the VOR. Two such devices permit triangulation and will pinpoint the exact location. Virtually all the navigation used today uses the

VOR. Schillinger developed this same principle to navigate in music some 30 years before it was formulated for the VOR. Once this general principle is grasped more complex manifold signals readily fall into place.

"The logic of this for scales, diads, triads and sevenths is clear. Cadences are no exception. Cadence is fundamental to music and there are two general forms: Classic and Modern. We also find two general forms of mathematics that deal with mechanics: classical mechanics and quantum mechanics. Until about 1900 classic cadences predominated in music, as did classical mechanics in mathematics. Each era is confined within the limits of its mathematical or musical systems.

In the classical mechanics, Euclidian and Newtonian systems prevail, triangular measurement dominating this system. In classical music, harmonic triads prevail. After 1900 quantum theory envelops all science with a 4th dimensional parameter being added to the classical system. In music the RE SOL DO LA (D-, G7, CM, A-) 4th dimensional cadence tones appeared in music; particularly in Scriabin, Youmans, Gershwin. As in science from that time on (1900-1925) all things entered the quantum era.

"Once the mechanics of music is seen as a whole we see and grasp this overview as we would view a plastic model of an internal combustion engine or a clock. Once the concept of the component parts is understood it makes things easier to comprehend. Perhaps all of us agree that our knowledge of the 7ths is proportional to our understanding of music. "Sevenths are where it's at" is a truism. As pianists we review our scales, cadences and 7ths, but when the manifolds are included with each of them in turn, they cause a profound intellectual and physical improvement. Each entity has its unique shape and position; each is special, so much more so now that visual perception is the new parameter."

Joseph Schillinger[55] was called a "Renaissance Man," a mathematician and pianist of the first rank who established music as a natural science. Schillinger was a true genius whose intellect germinated a magnificent system to explain how music works, what it is and how to make it. And make it they did. George Gershwin and Glenn Miller were two of the many fortunate ones who personally studied with him. Using patterns given to them by Schillinger, these artists gained fresh new ideas for their particular style. All exhibited their best work after studying with Schillinger.

What was this magic? What was it that brought out the classic beauty of *"Summertime"* or the jazz classic *"Pennsylvania 6-5000?"* Considering the results of his students' work, clearly Schillinger's methods are far superior to any others known.

Schillinger's credentials are so rich that it takes time to mentally digest them. Born in Kharkov, Russia on September 1, 1895, Joseph Schillinger was destined for greatness. From the time he was five until he entered the University at St. Petersburg, he studied design, music, and mathematics and developed his theories by teaching himself the piano. He always took time to help others and devoted his life to the study of music and art. His formal academic years included intensive study of mathematics and physics under the best minds at the University - along with drama, art, dance, history, language and electrical engineering, and four years of classical music studies and composition.

His knowledge of how music works on a natural scientific basis enabled him to understand other complex sciences such as math and physics as well. He obviously held a unique and very special concept that permitted this enlightenment. The early proof of this was after graduating from the University, Schillinger was appointed professor of music at the Kharkov Institute of Music. In addition, he served as a member of various boards of education on a national scale. He was professor of the history of the arts at St. Petersburg, and organized the first jazz band in Russia. His contemporary and friend Dimitri Shostakovich compared Schillinger to Beethoven. Vladimir Horowitz agreed. He was very special indeed.

When he came to the United States in 1928 there was no television, no stereo, no color photography; just half the population of today, and prohibition was the law of the land. America was a rural, not urban society. Silent movies and radio unified the people - it was their media. During this period, sound motion pictures were gradually replacing the silent film in theaters. Schillinger helped solve the problems of the coordination of sound track with the film track, a formidable obstacle at that time. New music was essential for this new invention. Background music had to be of certain rhythmic duration and freshly composed to fit the time, mood, excitement, etc., of the picture. It certainly had to be pleasing to the audience. Schillinger taught correct set design for scenes and the method for finding the best angle for the camera. Such knowledge was essential if this movie business was to be elevated to an art form.

Musicians like Leith Stevens, Franklin Marks and Carmine Coppola attest to Schillinger's teachings. Schillinger collaborated with Leon Theremin, a Russian inventor and physicist, and developed the first electronic music synthesizer that RCA Victor manufactured. During this time radio was in its halcyon days and Schillinger was the first to introduce his methods to this media - high drama, exciting adventures, comical as well as sad programs benefited enormously from his tailor-made compositions that were fitting to the story.

Schillinger taught at Columbia University - music, fine arts and mathematics. He lectured and traveled widely and the list of people who studied with him is impressive. What is more impressive is the result of the lessons. For 25 years Schillinger devoted his time to developing a master text entitled, <u>The Mathematical Basis of the Arts</u>. In this masterwork he applies the same fundamental principles to spatial form as he does to tonal form with his first work. Many awaited the publication of Schillinger's master text. This new work promised to reveal the secrets of writing music in the style of Mozart, Joplin, and Gershwin. It also would enable a composer to construct entirely new forms of his or her own, of like magnificence.

Devotees and disciples of Schillinger and those who love music labored long and hard, piecing each pattern together and struggling with large globs of unfamiliar numbers. The patterns Schillinger taught his students are especially important. Those who have learned these patterns even without knowing about Joseph Schillinger have a much better command of the instrument, thus rapidly catapulting themselves into advanced structures. And it is important to realize these patterns are universal in form and shape and in no way resemble the incoherent hodgepodge of an oscilloscope. In other words they are geometric.

As old attitudes changed so did the tools, music and mathematics. Thanks to technology, seemingly undecipherable formulae and mysterious numbers in the pages of Schillinger suddenly were transformed into electrifying geometric coherence, in color and in third dimension. Sophisticated computers now produce visual and accurate number maps through previously uncharted areas of music. Visual color, three dimensional geometric displays of notes, chords, scales, cadences and manifolds enable the student to grasp and learn music 1,000 times faster. Schillinger's manifolds or mirror image patterns enable the facile and correct modal transposition that all composers and players desire. His rhythm book enables us to find or generate any and all rhythms, past, present, even future.

Schillinger's legacy is remarkable. Since music is a natural science, it must follow the same fundamental laws, as do other sciences. This fact gives us a superior tool to reveal new secrets of science. As the talkies in 1928 heralded the coda of the silent film, a decade later dawned the realization that the movies were a true art form. Television would wait in the wings for 20 years before it would attain like status and "they'll never have color" was a statement forgotten. Amazing technology within the grasp of average people more than a 100 years after the birth of Schillinger - enabling them to compose any or all of these art forms: television, movies, art and music of any kind including symphonies. Schillinger saw and predicted this. Synthesizers, video recorders, computers, as well as the piano itself, are the tools of the 21st century.

Schillinger was a professor at The New School in New York City and taught celebrated composers like Benny Goodman, and a host of Hollywood and Broadway composers. His books were published after his death and his system enjoys a cult following, although it is still considered controversial in traditional circles. There are a limited number of Certified Schillinger Teachers of this system in the world.

In New York, Schillinger flourished, becoming famous as the advisor to many of America's leading popular musicians and concert music composers. These include George Gershwin, Benny Goodman, Glenn Miller, Paul Lavalle, Oscar Levant, Tommy Dorsey, and Carmine Coppola among others. Gershwin spent four years studying with Schillinger.

He died early from lung cancer. The Schillinger estate resisted efforts by others to interpret and explain his theory, and by the 1960s it was generally forgotten. His pupils had included distinguished jazz musicians, interested in immediate practical use. The reasons for the decline in awareness of Schillinger's work are several. During his life, the concert music establishment criticized him as being a promoter of mechanized creativity. His work was radical, speaking directly to musicians involved in popular music, which fed largely on jazz, and was in conflict with an *avant-garde* who looked to Europe, and to certain ascendant figures, such as Schaeffer and Stockhausen, for its theory.

Tito was always intrigued by the method that Schillinger developed as he was by the man's genius. In the realm of Afro-Cuban music he was not sure where it would fit in. "It is just another mechanism that helps to expand horizons, and look for new ways to make good music," he smiled.

On the Way to Broadway

Tito decided to leave Pupi Campo in 1948. He admitted he was a little apprehensive, but nonetheless Tito wanted to strike out on his own. Actually, the way he explained it to me it was Joe Loco who instigated Tito into becoming a bandleader. When Tito told Joe that he was going to do it, his childhood pal smiled. The final move was made in July of 1949. By this time all was not well with his family. His marriage to Mirta seemed to be on the rocks. He was busy. He was away a lot from home and music had become his mistress. At this point in his life he could not share, and as he later thought about it, music was always his priority.

Joe Loco was sitting at the piano at the Manhattan Embassy Club. Tito was standing a few feet away looking at several music scores. He and Joe were busy getting ready for the evening show that the Pupi Campo Orchestra would present. Federico Pagani walked into the large room and stood quietly as the orchestra ran through several tunes. One of the selections was *"Picadillo."* Tito nodded over to Federico. Joe smiled. The music kept going.

New York in 1948 was a city of contrasts. The United Nations building was under construction. New York Governor Dewey seemed headed for the White House. Midtown Manhattan was teeming with nightlife. There were supper clubs, nightclubs, jazz clubs and all them featured live music. There were dancehalls that had hostesses for patrons to dance with, and dancehalls like the Savoy that showcased the best music available. Every kind of music was available – country music, popular music, jazz and Latin for the pleasure of the consumer. The Palladium was located at West 53rd Street and Broadway.

Private clubs throughout the five boroughs sponsored dances often matching an American dance band with one that played the new kind of music. Churches and synagogues hosted dances to raise money. Civic clubs were doing the same thing. New York was truly a city that did not sleep. Hotel ballrooms and supper clubs were used after hours for dancing to live music. There were before-theater clubs and after-hours clubs that were scattered throughout the city's five boroughs and accessible via taxi or subway. El Barrio was jumping with Afro-Cuban rhythms and Harlem was still home to dozens of nightclubs where big bands played and mixed it with the Afro-Cuban bands.

The new word that was in use was "mambo." The rhumba vogue seemed to have slid into a void. The China Doll, the Havana Madrid, the Copacabana, and just about every club on or near the Great White Way was into the Mambo craze. But no one seemed able to pinpoint what exactly "the mambo was," explained Tito as he recalled the era. "Pérez Prado was playing it in Mexico City. Machito was playing a combination of new style music that was a cross between Afro-Cuban and jazz. Tito Rodríguez was into the new sound with his conjunto. José Curbelo and Pupi Campo had recorded tunes using the word mambo. But it was still being defined here and in Cuba."

In 1948, the orchestras, bands; ensembles and trios dressed elegantly to perform. The dancing public dressed stylishly too. The women wore the latest fashions to the clubs that dotted Manhattan and the outer boroughs. This was the way it was in New York City – elegance and splendor. The gentlemen matched the ladies in attire. The Palladium was entering its age of elegance and this was not lost on Tito. He felt history was in the making and he was going to be part of it. By this time he had visited Havana on numerous occasions. He knew what was happening in Cuba. He listened and he learned.

Pérez Prado was doing in Mexico City what he had failed to do in Havana – popularize his big band approach to the mambo. *"Que Rico El Mambo,"* Pérez Prado's third recording became a national success in Mexico. Vocalist Beny Moré was touring with him. In 1948, the American Federation of Musicians went on strike, banning all recorded music, permitting RCA Victor International to take advantage of the situation and flood its Latin division into the American market. When Pérez Prado went into the RCA recording studio in Mexico City in March 1949, he was on the stage set for his success. Internal business decisions to stay with the 45rpm record rather than use the 12-inch long play album designed by Columbia Records, had nearly cost the company the Cuban market a few years later.

Antonio Arcaño y sus Maravillas[56] was now known as La Radiofonica (a charanga that was the size of a mini chamber orchestra), and José A. Fajardo was playing the unadorned flute. Orquesta Riverside was competing with Casino de la Playa for top billing in Havana's posh nightclubs. Conjuntos were taking over the landscape in the musical confrontations with the more subtle sounding charangas. The mob was pressing to take over the gambling and entertainment industry in Havana. In 1948 Arsenio Rodríguez, with his pianist Lili Martínez, vocalist Rene Scull and Carlos Ramírez, trumpet players Rafael Corbacho, Felix Chapotin and Ruben Calzado, percussionists Felix Alonso and Antolin Suárez, and bassist Lazaro Prieto were playing in the Havana nightspots. Rodríguez would leave Havana in 1953 never to return. His musical booking agent was Antonio Arcaño – these were the two founding fathers of modern Cuban music.

In January 1947 Luciano Pozo González, known as Chano Pozo[57*] (born Cuba, 1915-died New York 1948), moved to New York at the urging of Miguelito Valdés, and by February he was at the studios of Coda Records to begin a series of historic sessions. This was to be an all star Cuban lineup that featured Arsenio Rodríguez, Miguelito Valdés, Carlos Vidal, and Chano Pozo on congas, with José Mangual on bongos. They proceeded to record the first authentic rumba ever; doing four tunes in the barrio style they all came from, even one dedicated to "El Africa," the old neighborhood. Chano did a tribute to the Abakuá god "Abas." These are milestones in that they were just done with percussion, going back to the African traditional drumming, unheard of at the time. Chano did more recordings in the days to come with Machito and his Afro-Cubans, and also some sessions with Arsenio Rodríguez. These were more mambo numbers with vocalist arrangements, and he was the percussionist.

Dizzy Gillespie had his hand on the pulse of the Afro-Cuban beat since his days with Mario Bauzá back in 1938. By 1945 he was hot, and famous for his bebop band. In that same summer he had a Cuban conga player named Diego Iborra sitting in with his band. He had a feeling to go more in that direction and his old friend Bauzá recommended the conga player, Chano Pozo. Chano was Cuban and his sense of timing, and was a challenge for Dizzy's band, which were not all receptive to his joining the band. There was a fusing of the clave beat into swing time, and vice versa. Tito was constantly experimenting with the same elements, as were Joe Loco, Charlie Palmieri and Tito Rodríguez – and many others from that area of 110th Street and 5th Avenue. Chano traveled to Europe in January of 1948 with Dizzy and his band, which was a very successful tour with the band hitting on all cylinders. Chano's drums were stolen and he went back to New York to get a replacement set. He stayed on in New York longer than he should have, and as fate would have it his life ended tragically on December 2, 1948. He was shot in a bar over a shady dope deal gone sour. He was 33 years old.

Federico Pagani watched quietly as Tito and Joe Loco with a few members of the Campo orchestra ran through *"Picadillo."* He smiled over to Tito and then said "¿Algo nuevo, Tito? ¿Que es esa mierda?" Pagani was a musician and a director of the Los Happy Boys that played at the Park Palace in the 1930s. They all new each other, and had their own way of communicating.

Tito laughed. "Es una mierda con picadillo." (Its shit with chopped meat). There was laughter.

Tito looked up, smiled and huddled with Joe. Joe played the base line a few times and Tito hummed the melody. Bass player Manuel Patot picked up the music. Chino González followed on the trumpet. It was all spontaneous and improvised, according to Tito. When they stopped playing Tito looked over to Federico. "Well!"

Joe Loco added with a wide grin: "Tu sabes – picadillo con…" They all laughed. The montuno with the strong bass lines had been something that Tito had been working on for a long time. "There is a little of everything in it and you can add and take away as you go along. There is something haunting about it," Tito said. Similar pieces like *"Chanchullo,"* composed by Israel "Cachao" López in 1938, and the danzón *"Almendra"* composed by Abelardo Valdés in 1940, with the simple repetitive phrasing was what Tito compared his framework piece. "Think about Ravel's Bolero," he explained. "You can play on and on and it will always have something new to listen to."

It was a few minutes later when Pagani urged Tito to provide him with a pick up group for Sunday's matinee at the Palladium. "De ahora en adelante son Los Piccadilly Boys," Pagani announced to those gathered around him. "You know, like Piccadilly Square in London." More laughter. Tito believed that this was the defining moment – he was ready to pursue organizing his own orchestra. In a way it was Federico Pagani who pushed him in this direction, probably sooner than later.

Tito did not have many close friends but he considered Federico one of them. He was one of the major contributors to improving and expanding the Latin American music market in New York. In a city filled with subtle and not so subtle ethnic and racial barriers, Pagani was a force in helping to tear them away. Throughout his life he worked to help find employment opportunities for young aspiring entertainers and musicians. Though only five feet, six inches tall in the eyes of many of his peers he was a giant. "He never said no," according to Tito. "Anyone who had a problem he would try to help. Anyone who had an idea – bad or good – he listened to, and he was always looking out for new opportunities for guys like me."

Pagani was born January 12, 1907, to parents Andrea and Federico Pagani in San Juan, Puerto Rico. He had little or no relationship with his father, a musician who played the bombardino (the horn-like instrument used to play Puerto Rican danza) and composer. The senior Pagani served in the Army during World War I, and had a large family with another wife – four sons and two daughters. Federico moved to New York in 1925, and lived with family friends at 99th Street and 3rd Avenue. He bantered about doing various jobs and eventually landed a job as a band boy with Puerto Rican trumpeter Augusto Coen. He learned to read and understand contracts while at the same time learned the rudiments of "clave" playing the bongos from Coen's pianist Noro Morales. After joining the American Federation of Musicians (Local 802), he formed the band Los Happy Boys. His rivals in the 110th and Park Avenue area were Coen, and Alberto Socarras.

In 1938 Pagani gave up Los Happy Boys and organized La Guerilla where he played bongos, sang a little, Moncho Usera conducted and a young Joe Loco played the piano. During World War II he turned his attention to promoting. His shows at the Triborough Theater on 125th Street were always sold out. He brought in acts from Mexico, Cuba and Puerto Rico. He promoted dances that featured the music of Alberto Socarras, Alberto Iznaga, Noro Morales, Machito, Miguelito Valdés and Marcelino Guerra. He was successful in most of his promotional efforts.

Federico was married to Carmen for more than 50 years; they had three children. His son, Pagani, Jr., Federico "Popi" played timbales for Charlie Palmieri in 1952 and then for the Tito Rodríguez Orchestra. His style of playing, according to Tito, was rather unique – a mixture of Cuban and New York. "Popi had a strong sense of clave and understood the Cuban foundations." He learned his trade well with the musicians at 110th Street and Park Avenue. Popi passed away in 1970 – victim of drug abuse. The senior Pagani died of Parkinson's disease on December 21, 1987. His daughter – Ana – lives in Florida.

In 1948, with the help of Mario Bauzá, Federico Pagani was working as a promoter and ticket collector at the Alma Dance Studios at 53rd Street and Broadway. Tito and Federico always enjoyed talking about the Palladium's golden period and how Tito had made his decision to start a new orchestra in a very competitive and tenuous atmosphere.

"Federico was influential in my making the move," he recalled. "I knew I was going to make it. I knew what I wanted to do. I just did not know when. Federico nudged me to do it sooner rather than later," he said. (Asia Restaurant – 1978)

During the week before he gathered up his makeshift band for the matinee at the Palladium, Tito went to the movies to see George Raft play the role of a bookie in "Race Street." And in "Time of Your Life," he watched Jimmy Cagney play Joe 'T' in a whimsical film version of William Saroyan's Pulitzer Prize-winning play about a rundown San Francisco waterfront bar, populated by a group of lovable characters. Both films also starred William Bendix. Tito usually did not like to be alone, but occasionally he would dash off to see a movie on the sly to see his heroes and to do a little thinking.

The Piccadilly Italians

Tito always laughed whenever we talked about the "Piccadilly Boys." According to him the pick up group that first appeared at the New York Palladium or the Alma Dance studios as it was known, could have been called "The Mafia Boys." The trumpets were hand picked by Jimmy Frisaura were Italian. Pagani introduced Tito Puente's trumpet and Afro-Cuban percussion ensemble as the "Picadilly Boys." Tito knew they would sound good. Jimmy had assured him that the horn section would sound strong and fresh. Although he did not mention it by name, Tito Rodríguez had been working with a trumpet conjunto for about a year. Tito was one of one of the primary arrangers for Tito Rodríguez

Playing with an ad hoc ensemble or "piquete" was nothing new for Tito. He had been doing it for some time. Whenever he had a day off from working with the Pupi Campo Orchestra, he was playing somewhere to make some money, to get his name out there, to gain acceptance. He was driven and ready to move on. He just wanted it to be different. The ensemble that was introduced by Federico Pagani featured Jimmy Frisaura, Al DeRisi, and Tony DeRisi on trumpets; Manuel Patot, bass; Charlie Palmieri, Al Escobar and Luis Varona alternating on piano; Angel Rosa, vocals; Chino Pozo, bongo; Frankie Colón, conga, and Tito on timbales and vibes.

Everyone was talking about the mambo in 1948. To Tito there were several different versions. One of the mambo rhythms was that of Arcaño and his orchestra who was obviously the most successful of the mambo fad, at least in Cuba. He had heard it first hand, and up front, he often claimed. His visits to Havana began around 1947. He was never specific about how many visits he made to Havana. "Just know that I saw all of what they (the Cuban musicians) were doing and I took in all of it," he stated emphatically.

Arcaño's style was simple and straightforward. He described it as follows: "I followed the feet of the dancers thinking up new phrases on my flute. It excited the dancers. Macho (Orestes) López played a montuno on the violin and Cachao punctuated the rhythm with his offbeat phrasing."This was the mambo or the new rhythm that Arcaño y Sus Maravillas developed. By today's standard it was still very classical, very structured.

The mambo as described by Arcaño is "a type of syncopated montuno (monotonous or repetitious) that has a certain savory rhythmic flavor. It is informal yet eloquent. The piano player advances on the mambo theme, the flute hears it and is inspired, the violin plays and repeats double chord phrases while the bass adapts and delivers accentuated rhythmic patterns. The timbalero maintains a steady beat on the bell, the güiro follows a similar pattern and the tumbadora ties it together." In a classic sense what Arcaño described is a Bach style fugue, a form of jazz —one instrument improvising off another. However, the design was controlled. Tito considered this and how he would make it work in his ensemble.

At the core of the "Nuevo Ritmo" or mambo is the ostinato or guajeos – as Cuban musicians call it. In the background, there is also the fugue sometimes called a canon. The fugue is the most fully developed procedure of copied counterpoint, in which the theme is stated successively in all voices of the polyphonic texture, tonally established, continuously expanded, opposed, and reestablished; also a work employing the procedure. Before Johann Sebastian Bach explored the depths of this procedure the fugue was known as a canon. The fugue or counterpoint is prevalent in Afro-Cuban – European blueprint of music.

The guajeo is the "rhythmic process in which the Afro-Cuban musicians, but especially the pianist or violinist, invents swinging melodic phrases of two or four bars length. Gilberto Valdés, considered the "George Gershwin of Cuba in the 1940s and 1950s, explained that the taste of the guajeo is derived from the son montuno, the rural form which took Havana by storm with its primitive instruments or largely West African design in 1916, and which has since come to serve as the perennial font for improvisation, an acid test for apprentices, like the 12-bar blues in jazz. Tito would use a combination of trumpets, saxophones and reeds to accomplish this. Machito was already doing it.

How do the guajeos work in Latin music? It is not enough to call them "riffs' or mini cadenzas; the swing band riff for example, often is no more than punctuation, a few notes repeated here and there, but frequently at either end of the bridge. The Cuban ostinato is open-ended, repeating itself seemingly endlessly, sometimes at the same pitch. By way of contrast the melodic line of jazz improvisation is like a mural, the Western symphony like an art gallery. But Afro-Cuban jazz and "classical" (i.e. symphonic) music are not "higher" or "better" in relation to each other, they are simply different, each with its own aims and intentions, and the production of guajeos of quality is a formal goal of the Afro-Cuban just as the building of a musical architecture is an aim, often of symphonic composition.

Tito's arsenal of musical study also included the classical genre. It is surprising how few of his fans realize the extent of his musical study and knowledge. It went far beyond the Schillinger System. One of his quiet passions was classical music from the Romantic period and especially Claude Debussy, whom he considered an important composer in terms of "modern movement and orchestration." Debussy could make two instruments sound like three, and he could make a trio sound like a six piece ensemble. He was a superb director and arranger of sound, among other things." He loved the masters – Beethoven, Mozart, Bach, to name a few. But he studied Bach's approach. Ravel intrigued him and some of Igor Stravinsky's works captivated him. Manuel de Falla was a favorite in terms of feeling and explosive sound.

Tito was acutely conscious of how Arsenio Rodríguez and his conjunto had incorporated the trumpets and even added the tres to support the working piano. "He may not have studied the classics," quipped Tito, but Arsenio and so many of them Cubans had a knack for effect and drive." The work of Arsenio Rodríguez and the innovations of the Casino de la Playa orchestra were crucial steps that Afro-Cuban music was taking. "The doors were flung wide open with all these innovations," he maintained. :All of these guys, perhaps knowing what the other ones were doing, but probably not knowing it, took gigantic steps in making Afro-Cuban music not only popular but danceable around the world.:

Was it fusion? In a recorded conversation this is what Tito had to say: "In some way you could say it was fusion " a mixture that had been going on for centuries. But it was very Cuban " all the elements of good music were in the mix. Did they (Cubans) borrow from say the United States? Of course they did. We are all influenced by what the other guy is doing – for better or for worse. In the 1930s when the Conga and the Rumba were popular it was the Americans that were borrowing and mixing Cuban music – a lot of it was junk, but then came guys like Machito and others, and a course correction was made. In Cuba I guess Arcaño took what he needed from the Americans and followed a very Cuban direction. At the center of all this change are dedicated and educated musicians with an objective – making good music. That is the way it has been."

In Mexico, Pérez Prado was already considered the father of the new mambo. He successfully incorporated the brass – trumpets and saxes with a prolific percussion section. It seemed to Tito that his rhythm was bouncy, like what is played in Cuba's Oriente province – Santiago, Cuba. Tito wanted his "rhythm to be more powerful, more driving, more Kentonish – more New York."

Every jazz ensemble – large or small – consists of a melody section and a rhythm section. Tito considered this in piecing together his ensemble's repertoire. There is always tension between the two. He was leading a dance band, but he wanted it to be progressive. "Borrow a little bit from everyone and come up with your own sound," he moaned one day thinking back. "I wanted it to be just right so that I could cultivate it into my dream."

Tito did a lot of soul searching to come up with the sound and he kept talking to me about how he would listen to Ravel's Bolero or go to the movie to view his boyhood heroes –Cagney and Raft. The Frenchman in Paris composed the Spanish dance in ¾ time accompanied by clicking castanets in 1928. When Arturo Toscanini directed the American premiere in 1929 it created a sensation, and set into motion a wave of popularity. In a short period it was performed by every major American orchestra, was heard in theaters and radio, was reproduced simultaneously on six different recordings and was transcribed for every possible combination of instruments – including a jazz band. Bolero was the theme song in one of George Raft's movies. Bolero seemed to haunt my friend. Whenever he discussed the formation of his orchestra he inevitably mentioned Bolero. "One haunting melody and it just builds up," he exclaimed. "Fascinating! No!"

"Tito was remarkable. He brought a whole new concept into play. It was different and it was new. Christ, it was just what we had been waiting for," exclaimed Federico Pagani "It was Afro-Cuban and it was jazz."(Asia Restaurant –1976).

Years later in a conversation with Jimmy Frisaura, he recalled that the Italian horn section that he recruited for that session and those that followed while Tito pondered breaking away from Pupi Campo were "exactly what he (Tito) was looking for – powerful instrumentalists who had an understanding of clave. The guys were very familiar with Afro-Cuban music and they knew Tito was something of an obsessive leader. It worked out well – here we are 30 years later..."

Tito was very careful to maintain an excellent rapport with the people that operated and or owned New York City nightclubs that featured live music. He wanted to perform and showcase his band. The Palladium had a reputation that it was connected to dubious business interests. The Copacabana, the China Doll, and even the Havana Madrid (later also know as the Chateau Madrid) restaurants were among the many. The owners respected Tito, and he was ever so cautious as to how he dealt with each and every nightclub owner.

In 1931, John Perona, an Italian immigrant, opened El Morocco[58] as a speakeasy at 154 East 54th Street, where the Citigroup Center now stands. Part of what made the club famous was the photographs taken by Jerome Zerbe that were always in the newspaper the next day. People knew from the background zebra stripes on the banquettes where the celebrities had been. In 1961, it moved to a four-story townhouse at 307 East 54th Street. Tito would play and record an album in the club in the 1950s.

The Copacabana (referred to as The Copa) was famous for its entertainers. Tito would be among the many headliners that took the stage at the club. He was keenly aware that he was one of a scant few Latinos to reach the stage of the original Copacabana. The club opened November 10, 1940, at 10 East 60th Street in New York City. Although Monte Proser's name was on the lease, he had a powerful partner: mob boss Frank Costello. However, Jules Podell looked after his interests, and within a few years Proser was out and Podell was the official owner. In 1944, Harry Belafonte was denied entry to the Copacabana because he was black. He was in the U.S. Navy at the time. Eventually Podell was persuaded to change his policy, and Belafonte returned in the 1950s as a headliner at the club. The nightclub was the venue for the launch of Dean Martin and Jerry Lewis as a duo. They were frequent performers at the club. In any event Tito was prepared to play a prominent role in New York City nightlife. At one point or another he would headline each and every one of the midtown Manhattan clubs.

Jimmy Frisaura never forgot his Italian heritage. He came from the Bronx, and even though he immersed himself into Afro-Cuban music and the people that made it, he maintained his connections. "You know that everywhere we played people would always ask me and some of the other boys how it was that we played in a band that played 'Spanish music.' I laughed. Then I would say, 'Just look around. Who owns the club?" In those days nearly all the places we played were mob connected. I guess Tito kept me around just in case," Jimmy explained.

Tito's take on Jimmy's explanation: "He's right. We had to walk a fine line. We wanted to make sure that we did not step on anybody's toes.

Jimmy knew all these guys when we were starting out – at least it seemed that way."

Jimmy was a big Harry James fan. At a young age Jimmy was being referred to as the "Harry James of the Bronx."

Cuban Connections

Even though Tito did not have a formal education he had an insatiable appetite for learning. And when it came to learning about music he was obsessed. He loved jazz. Tito listened to classical music, and often expressed the inner workings and approaches that the "Great Composers" provided in specific pieces. He loved the big symphonic sound, the way an orchestra could change mood and feeling. He paid close attention to the intricate sound of small ensembles and solo instruments. Music was his vice, he said. "More than anything else, I love music."

There are a number of historical references that claim Tito started visiting Cuba around 1946. One day he told me that he first went to Havana around 1950. Then in another conversation he recalled an earlier visit while he was still playing with the Pupi Campo Orchestra. And yet, on another occasion he said that he met several Cuban musicians while visiting Cuba a few weeks after returning from the Navy, in 1946. One has to keep in mind that Tito, when not in the public eye, was very private. He did not like too many people to know what he was up to. He did not like politics, he did not speak about religion, and when it came to music he gave his listeners what he thought they wanted to hear him say. The fact remains he knew Havana well. He talked about people he had met and had seen in cabarets, on the streets, and in places that were not frequented by tourists. New York City was Tito's first love. Havana was next on his list.

The principal objective of his sojourns to Havana was to see first hand what was happening in the world of music. He used his contacts from 110th Street and Park Avenue – Mario, Machito and others. Federico Pagani had considerable knowledge of places, people and events that were going on in Cuba. During one of his visits in 1955, he met Celia Cruz.

On each visit he made new discoveries. In 1944 Batista[59] was ousted as president and moved to his mansion in Daytona Beach, Florida. In 1948 he was not eligible to run for president, but was able to win a position in the Cuban Senate even though he was still living in Florida. He decided to run for president and was given permission by then president Grau San Martin, another favorite of the Cuban people. There were early indications that showed Batista was going to get crushed in the elections so he started to plot another coup, as he still had strong ties to the military. Batista forcibly took power over Cuba and eliminated the process of democracy in 1952.

During the next several months Batista became partners with the Sicilian Mafia through his connection with Jewish boss Meyer Lansky. There was a reason for Batista's long stay in the world famous Waldorf Astoria in New York in the late 1940s, that is where he made the final plans with Lansky on how the revenues from casinos would be distributed. "There were dozens of casinos throughout Havana," Tito confirmed.

"The Mob" had carte blanche to casino licenses and permission to run their operation in Cuba. Along with the casinos came all the negative influences like prostitution, drugs and corruption. Havana became the "Latin Las Vegas" and the working people of Cuba were stuck in the middle with no place to go. Batista's dictatorship was tough and totally corrupted as his special police, comprised of high-ranking military personnel, roamed the island enforcing Batista's laws.

In the early 1950s, Havana was a major drug distribution port for Lucky Luciano's heroin ring, The Cuban government and the crime syndicate led by Luciano made all the major decisions in the penthouses of the Hotel Nacional. Batista never had in mind to protect the Cuban people as he fled Cuba with his family like rats when Fidel Castro entered Havana on December 31, 1958. In this period of time Havana was a city of contrasts. "There was segregation and it was ruthlessly enforced. On the streets you could see the poor, begging, looking for anything to help them through the day. The people that took me around tried to keep me from noticing these things, but it was hard to avoid," Tito said during a rare conversation about his visits to Havana.

Tito went to Havana accompanied or alone, perhaps two nights, sometimes just overnight. He never was open about whom he hung out with, what he did and or who he was with. It was cheap to fly in from Miami. It took a little longer coming down from New York. But one has to remember that Havana was the Mecca of Afro-Cuban music. Tito wanted to explore every facet of it. He visited the large clubs like the Tropicana. He listened to music at the clubs in the main hotels and visited every music store and publishing source he could find. The music scores were cheap - $1. He would buy several copies and simply pass them out to his musicians.

You can just imagine what he got to see. Orquesta Riverside was popular. Conjunto Casino was renowned. There were so many ensembles that were playing in the many nightclubs of the sprawling tropical city. Facundo Rivero, a composer and pianist, was popular, Conjunto Matamoros, Los Guaracheros de Oriente, Celia Cruz was singing with Sonora Matancera.

The Sonora Matancera also featured among others Puerto Rican Daniel Santos and Mario Muñoz (Papaíto) and pianist Javier Vázquez; Conjunto Modelo featured a conga player known as Félix "Chocolate" Alfonso and tres player Niño Rivera. Elena Burke and Omara Portuondo were starting their careers singing in local nightclubs. Senen Suarez featured flautist Gonzálo Fernández at the Tropicana; Celina y Reutilio provided the folksy feeling; and every hotel had a full orchestra. Dozens of charanga orchestras played at major nightspots throughout Havana – Orquesta Neno González, Orquesta Belisario López, Orquesta Sensación, Arcaño y sus Maravillas, and Orquesta Melodías del 40, that also fronted for the radio and later TV clowns Pototo Y Felomeno.

He saw the earliest versions of the cha cha chá. This was the latest music trend in Havana that was introduced by Enrique Jorrín[60] in 1949. Jorrín was a violinist / composer with the Arcaño orchestra and was wooed away in 1945 by bread baker/singer Ninón Mondéjar, who had just organized Orquesta América to play at his Socialist Party Club. Between 1953 and 1954 the orchestra recorded more than 50 cha cha chás, and some mambos, most of which have become classics. Tito obtained the charts to many of these. He never said how and he never said when. Make no mistake he had them.

If Tito could not find it he also had his friend Miguelito Valdés who would provide him with names of musicians and directions to the place. Tito was never specific about how many times he visited Cuba for the "purpose of finding facts." But he claimed that it was a vital part of his musical education "seeing it first hand, in its raw state." He made many friends in Cuba and he cherished all of the time he spent mixing it up with the Cuban people and getting to better understand the complexities of the music he had become so involved with.

He told me: "Learning about the intricacies of Afro-Cuban music is a rather complex process. African music in Cuba has many different variations, different shapes. When you study Afro-Cuban music you have to distinguish between music descended from Dahomey, or the Yorubá, or the Carabali and Conga. It requires scientific study and a lot of work."

Afro-Cuban drums compose an entire arsenal – ñáñigos, tensed with strings and wedges, one-side and played with two hands is one way. Then you have okónkolo (small), itótele (medium) and iyá (large) – this is huge. There is the tumba and tahona. The drums are used for different functions. To this array are added, although not a rule, the cajon, the marimbula, the güiro, the econes, or the cowbells of the Yorubá, and claves. Afro-Cuban music incorporates many tunes and many different music-making instruments. They are rituals and non-rituals. Some of the music is for

Santería – very solemn and serious. “You really have to study all this to get even a limited understanding,” Tito explained. If I did not have it recorded I would have failed to really grasp what he was saying. Suffice to say that Cuban music was complex and detailed and he wanted to learn all he could.

What struck Tito during his visits were the number of street percussion groups, the singers and the dancers. “It was all so spontaneous and vibrant,” he pointed out. “In the clubs the dancers were smooth and easy. They did not move like we did in New York – I guess the influence of the swing bands made us more prone to movement. But the dancers – especially those in the cabarets – had a way to excite the musicians who for the most part punctuated their rhythm to the movement of the feet. It was awesome. I mean we did this too, but in Havana it was so unrestrained and unrehearsed.”

Bebo Valdés harnessed the influences of American jazz, Cuban melodies and African rhythms when he became the principal pianist and arranger for the house orchestra of Havana’s Tropicana nightclub. Pedro “Peruchin” Justig was doing the same thing with Orquesta Riverside. A 24-year-old trumpet player Alfredo “Chocolate” Armenteros was working for the Julio Gutierrez Orchestra. Vocalist Olga Guilot was already famous in the United States. The Lecuona Cuban Boys were popular and at the Club Montmartre there was a new show every week. The San Souci Cabaret was keeping pace. Working orchestras in and around Havana included Orquesta Cosmopolita, which featured Vicentico Valdés on vocals, Humberto Suarez, piano and Alejandro “El Negro” Vivar, trumpet; Julio Cueva y su Orquesta with René Hernández on piano (until 1948) and Rolando Laserie, vocalist; Orquesta Almendra that featured flautist Miguel O’Farrill and popular female vocalist Dominica Verges. There were so many that Tito mentioned.

The conjuntos, orchestras, charangas, trios, duos and every sort of entertainment rolled into and out of Havana almost daily. The entertainers and musicians traveled around the country and visited the United States, Canada, Europe, the Caribbean and South America. It was a busy time. Tito took all of this in. Each visit to Havana brought new knowledge, expanded his curiosity, and provided him with new insight.

The Golden Period of Cuban music probably commenced soon after World War II, and continued through the 1950s, until January 1, 1959. Up until this moment and for more than a century, the impact of Cuban music on North, South, Central America and the Caribbean has been formidable.

Tito Puente's Melody

In March 1949, or there about, Tito quietly discussed his intention to depart the Pupi Campo Orchestra with three people. First he told Frisaura, while they were sharing a hotel room during an engagement with the Pupi Campo Orchestra. Soon after he disclosed his intention to depart with Joe Loco and Charlie Palmieri. They thought it was a great idea. Tito explained that he wanted to organize an orchestra that was going to be taking the mambo dance into areas never imagined. He did not invent it. That was for Antonio Arcaño, Arsenio Rodríguez, Pérez Prado and anyone else who thought they might have a hand in the new rhythm to figure out. Tito wanted his music to be danceable, exciting, energetic, groovy and progressive.

"That is one of the best ideas you ever had," the trumpet player blurted out in an excited tone. "Damn, it's about time." Frisaura had been urging Tito to make the break ever since they began playing matinees at the Palladium on Sundays a few months earlier. Jimmy was going to be his administrator and manage the band. "Tito was brooding over this move for a long time," Jimmy said.

According to Jimmy, "Tito was real serious, very unlike him. It was something that he wanted to do. I wanted him to do it and when he told me he wanted me as his partner I told him not to wait too long. I was teasing him. I finally got him to smile."

Next was Joe Loco. "Why not," exclaimed Joe? "I have been thinking about this for a long time. You know, getting the jazz feeling into it." At the time the pianist was a few years from setting out on his own. He would become one of Afro-Cuban jazz music's most respected musicians. He believed most music could be arranged for jazz and that jazz had its roots in both classical and African traditions. In developing a jazz format for Afro-Cuban music he was right behind Mario Bauzá and Machito y sus Afro-Cubanos.

Loco had been the pianist with Fernando Alvarez's Copacabana Samba Band, decided to leave it to form his own orchestra but in the interim joined up with Pupi Campo's orchestra. One night in October 1948, he sat in for pianist Al Escobar. With Tito on timbales and Joe on piano they played *"Earl Wilson Mambo," " Mambo Rhapsody," "Capullito de Aleli"* and several others. The improvising on the keyboard and the timbal solos highlighted the night at the club. The room trembled with the punctuated rolling solos of Tito's percussion. The eloquence of the piano improvised cadences made one think of Fats Waller strutting through the keys, or the cool elegance of Art Tatum - the Campo Orchestra had never sounded like this. It was one of those things that you have to be there to see, Tito said. "It all fell into place. The crowd was into it, the band got into it and Joe and me – well we were always into it."

It surprised Tito that the crowd, which he considered to be somewhat standoffish, got so into it. "A few months before we would have been bouncing along with a few foxtrots, and then for excitement a few rumbas. Things were changing even faster than I realized." Whenever he recaptured his music events, his body seemed to lift and his eyebrows stretched.

The Pupi Campo Orchestra recorded the selections a few months later, although without the extensive Loco-Puente improvisations.

Tito agreed. "I know I'm ready."

Joe knew he was ready and that he had been ready for some time. He was about to leave the Campo organization too, but decided to wait just a little longer.

Although he did not have to explain his reasons for wanting to start his own orchestra he detailed them for his friends separately. "I guess I was convincing myself that this was what I wanted to do. Jimmy was always pushing me to make the move. He was a real pain in the ass. I guess he was looking for work for his Italian buddies," laughed Tito, whenever he retold the story.

"Both Joe and Charlie were as excited as I was, although I did not show it. I really was scared as shit," Tito laughed.

In explaining his intention he noted carefully his experience as a percussionist, as an arranger and as a leader. The years with José Curbelo and the time spent with Pupi Campo encouraged him to move on. He worked for Noro Morales and Frank Marti, and other rumba bands. He had experienced the thrilling Machito Orchestra. But Tito was cautious. He learned what really makes a band work – how it must be organized, how it travels, and how it should sound. For years he followed closely the big bands – Benny Goodman, Stan Kenton, Duke Ellington and Charlie Spivak. There were many more, perhaps as good, maybe even better, but those were the bands he felt had influenced his thinking.

Learning to be a skillful percussionist had taken him a while. But his idol Gene Krupa had provided him with the styles and showmanship he required. The Cuban influence was apparent from his early years at the Park Palace where he listened and learned from the old-timers. This was the spiel he provided to Joe, Charlie and Jimmy. And they all agreed that the time was now.

Before notifying Pupi Campo about his departure he had one more person to tell – Federico Pagani. The promoter was as excited as the others in his intimate circle. A few days later Tito informed Pupi Campo. The news did not sit well with the flamboyant bandleader.

"I pissed him off even more when he found out who was in my new band," shrugged Tito.

Tito's first band included most of the Picadilly Boys. It included Jimmy Frisaura (lead trumpet/band administrator) Chino González (trumpet), Luis Varona (piano), Angel Rosa (vocals), Manuel Patot (bass), Manny Oquendo (bongos), and Frankie Colón (tumbadora). Tito was on timbales, vibraphones and when needed American drums.

When the news of Tito's departure became public Pupi Campo's nephew, Bobby Navarro revealed that his "…uncle was distraught. He was so mad. He and Tito were so close."[61] Campo it seems was mostly annoyed by the fact that several members of his orchestra went with Tito.

However, Tito maintained that Pupi had sort of come to suspect he might bolt at any moment. "It was the business we were in," Tito said. "I did not take away his band. Jimmy came with me. He was my friend and it was not a surprise to anyone that we left together. Luis Varona also came along. Pupi still had Joe and Charlie as back ups."

The Campo Orchestra soon recovered and became the NBC Tonight Show Orchestra for Jack Parr, and Charlie Palmieri ably assumed the role of musical director. Joe Loco finally jumped too and struck out on his own.

The nervous Tito gathered up his small conjunto and quickly assembled them at the Luis Varona Music Studios, located at 116th Street between Park and Madison Avenues. This was going to be the first rehearsal and both Tito and Jimmy were anxious with anticipation. So was everyone else in the studio. The bulk of the selections were pop standards. It was a grueling process to get everything down and play it the way Tito wanted it played. He anticipated he would have to be conservative, at least until the band was able to get contracts that were lucrative. "I was worried and so was Jimmy, but we knew we were good," Tito shrugged.

Jimmy was of the same frame of mind. "With anything new you are always taking a chance. I felt good about it."

Tito still had some income from composing and arrangements for the Spanish Music Center (SMC). He composed and arranged *"El Mambo de Broadway," "Enchanted Cubano," "Afro-Cuban Serenade,"* and *"Picadillo"* which was re-titled: *"The Arthur Murray Rhumba."* The session was recorded by Tito Puente and his Mambo Devils (Los Diablos del Mambo). During this transition period he was also approached by his old friend Tito Rodríguez and was contracted to arrange several selections. Additionally, Tito signed up trumpeter, Tony DeRisi and bongocero Chino Pozo.

Tito Puente and his Orchestra debuted at El Patio Club, in Long Island, July 4, 1949. Anthony Benedetto was also on the bill. Today he is known as Tony Bennett. They remained friends until Tito passed away. The private club does not exist today. It was a few miles from the Hamptons. He continued to call the conjunto style ensemble the Picadilly Boys, the name that Federico Pagani had baptized them with and unlike the Sunday matinee performance at the Palladium, he was now playing for a mostly Jewish crowd. He was playing mostly subdued American tunes, and in between, some Afro-Cuban melodies – not exactly what Tito had in mind.

Mambo Diablo

From the moment in 1949 that Tito Puente formed his orchestra until 1953 it was a roller coaster ride. His every fiber was focused on making his orchestra the most successful in offering good music. He had competitors but he was not at all concerned about them, not in the least.

We often talked about this period. His body language was energized; his smile as he spoke was steady and genuine. It was apparent to me that this period in his life had a special meaning. "I was the best!" he laughed. Then in a more serious tone he explained: "This was a time when New York was quaking with music. And I was in the middle of it."

I asked him one day: "Weren't you worried about Machito and Tito Rodríguez?"

The gleam and the smile emerged. "Hell no! I wasn't competing with them. They did their thing and I was going to do mine. Those were two of the best damn orchestras that ever existed," he said forcefully. "Machito and Mario Bauzá were masterminds. They were so ahead of their time. Don't let anyone tell you that Machito and the Afro-Cubans was not the best damn orchestra of all time. Tito and I were the kids on the block. We did our thing and we beat each other over the head." He laughed. "And, as kids on the block what better goal or prize than to catch and surpass the best (more laughter). We never did. But shit, we tried..."

Again I asked – already knowing to some extent his response – what about the other Tito?

"He was terrific. He was almost as good a dancer as me (*laughter*), and his orchestra was sensational. The ladies loved him. Everybody thinks we stopped being friends but that is not true. With us it was about the top billing – you know – whose name goes on top. But musically speaking his orchestra had its own unique style. You know, Joe, that's the way it was in those days – you did not want to sound like the other guy, and you were always looking to be better than the other guy."

Flamboyant Singers and Sidemen

Contrary to what many musicologists have concluded that Tito's musical inclinations leaned toward Machito and Bauzá traditions, and his early work reflects the more classical Afro-Cuban traditions, Tito believed the mambo was something that could be played in different styles and in different tempos. Tito believed he could invoke different moods by changing a simple harmonic phrase, establishing a melody in a certain key or tone. His early recordings represent this. His mambo was somewhere between what Arcaño, the López brothers – Israel "Cachao" and Orestes' syncopated rhythm emulated, and the more aggressive montuno developed by Arsenio Rodríguez. Whatever it was, it was driving music. He took all of this in and added his own flavors and his own ideas. He mixed in those that came from Goodman, Krupa, Kenton and a host of others.

"We forget just how intertwined all our music is," he reflected. From his visits to Cuba he observed how the Cubans were adapting to the forceful American music and rather than fight it off "they took it on and made it their own. We do the same thing with their music. We have been doing this for 100 years – New Orleans, Havana, New York."

The rhythmic syncopated *"Abaniquito,"* composed by José Curbelo and Bobby Escoto, is a prime example of the classic Cuban influence on Tito. It featured his new singer Vicentico Valdés. The piano strings it all together with a steady Cuban style guajeo or ostinato while the trumpets perform the Arsenio Rodríguez approach with short three and four note riffs. The percussion section led by Tito is driving – not too fast nor too slow – just driving. It is a dance piece and the percussion – Manny Oquendo on bongo, Frankie Colón on congas and Tito's timbales seem to interject the dancers' excitement. The piano takes a long solo - typical of those that Arcaño's piano player Jesus López interjected in the danzón mambo. All this music is fitted into 2:46 minutes. It was one of Tito's first big hits in 1949. The popularity of *"Abaniquito*" made it to Havana where it was recorded and re-recorded by local orchestras. One of the best examples this was made by the charanga Orquesta Sensación. Tito's Tico recording was on Side B. On the lead side Tito recorded *"Mambo Macoco,"* a more traditional piece that still has rumba intonations, but includes flaring trumpets and percussion. Side A and B of this Tico 78-rpm give us a glimpse of how Tito was evolving. This recording featured Mario Bauzá on trumpet, and Graciela on chorus.

The November 23, 1949 recording of *"Ran Kan Kan"* that was released on RCA Victor, has become the classic example of Tito's transition from a purely Cuban oriented musician to the one that made the mambo synonymous with New York. The musicians are: Vitin Avilés on lead vocals, Vicentico Valdés, chorus; Jimmy Frisaura, Al DeRisi, Tony DeRisi and Bernie Glow, trumpets, Luis Varona, piano, A.D. Jimenez, conga; Chino Pozo, bongo and Manuel Patot, bass. An irony of this release is that Vicentico did not want to sing lead because he was still not sure if he wanted to be associated with the Tito Puente Orchestra. "He wasn't sure that we were going to make it," Tito said. The rest is history.

Dapper Vicentico Valdés met Tito at a cafeteria in midtown Manhattan in September 1948, courtesy of percussionist Chino Pozo. Valdés was wearing a black pinstripe suit. At first Tito was not overly impressed by the singer, who at the time had a Cuban cigar dangling from his mouth. But Tito had heard him sing. He wanted to hear more. After a brief conversation Valdés was invited to a recording session for the Verne Record label. He sang his song the ballad *"Tus Ojos"* while Tito played the vibes. Tito liked what he heard and Vicentico enjoyed working with the flamboyant Tito. Verne Records released the tune that listed Tito Puente and the Mambo Boys as the ensemble. The other tunes that were recorded at the session were *"Camaguey,"* composed by Israel "Cachao" López, *"Cal Miller Mambo,"* by Tito Puente and *"Dame Un Mambo,"* composed by Pepe Delgado.

Valdés was born into a musical family. His older brother Alfredito Valdés had been a lead singer for the legendary Sexteto Habanero. Alfredito was a strong influence on his style and had gotten him a job with the popular charanga Orquesta Cheo Belén Puig. He then moved to Orquesta Cosmopolita until 1942 when he went to Mexico City. He was popular throughout Mexico City singing with the bands of Arturo Nuñez, Rafael de Paz and Chucho Rodríguez, with whom he recorded *"Tumbaito"* and *"Obsesion."* He returned to Cuba's nightlife for a while before heading out to Los Angeles and then decided to return to New York City.

Vocalist bandleader Marcelino Guerra, who still maintained his own band, gave Vicentico a job. Soon afterward he went to work for Tito, not sure that the young Puerto Rican bandleader was going to be successful. He had miscalculated the success of *"Ran Kan Kan."* He soon decided to join with Tito. There was a certain give and take between Tito and Vicentico, according to Jimmy who watched the two men work together over the next few years. "What you had was two guys with egos the size of a truck," laughed the trumpet player and manager of Tito's band. "They did not fight, but everybody got a sense that they were always trying to out do the other – you know, like walking into a room first. If Tito got recognition, applause and accolades, then Vicentico did his damnedest to get the same attention. They were two hams. That's show business!"

Tito and Vicentico had a flare up over top billing during a sojourn to California in 1953. However, by that time Vicentico had pretty much decided he wanted to try out leading his own band. Tito was dismayed and maybe even hurt. Vicentico was one of his favorite singers – always. But Tito was the leader of the orchestra – it was that simple. There could only be one boss and one top billing – The Tito Puente Orchestra. But they remained friends throughout their lives.

The lead voice on "*Ran Kan Kan,*" Vitin Avilés[62] was know as "El Cantante Del Amor" (the singer of love) was born in Mayaguez, September 30, 1930. He passed away January 1, 2004 at a New York hospital. He had a long and successful career as a vocalist and was already well known when Tito met him while working for Pupi Campo. Avilés probably recorded what is considered the most popular merengue album with the Xavier Cugat Orchestra in 1955. His voice is heard on hundreds of recordings for different popular Latin orchestras. His smooth voice always kept him in demand. Two Cuban songwriters, Tony Fergo and José Carbó Menéndez, composed his first recording in 1947, *"La Televisión,"* which announces the arrival of the latest invention to Latin America – the television. He worked with Noro Morales, Miguelito Miranda, Mon Rivera, Charlie Palmieri and many others.

He was a favorite of Tito. Vitin was easy going, had a great sense of humor and more importantly could fill in wherever needed – he was that kind of musician. He was always proud of his work on *"Ran Kan Kan,"* and helping Tito to get off on the right track. Whenever Vitin and Tito were together it was laughter, jokes, a lot of storytelling and great music.

In the early formation of the Tito Puente Orchestra, two solid percussionists joined him – one from Cuba and the other from El Barrio. Ramón "Mongo" Santamaría[63] originally took up the violin but then switched to drums – bongos and timbales - before dropping out of school to become a professional musician. A performer at the Tropicana Club in Havana, Mongo traveled to Mexico City with a dance team in 1948. He played briefly for the Pérez Prado Orchestra. He moved to New York City in 1950, where he made his American debut with Tito, and spent six years trading percussive barrages with him and performing and recording some of the great classics of Afro-Cuban music. He died on February 1, 2003, at Baptist Hospital in Miami, following a stroke.

The number two punch was Willie Bobo[64]. He was one of the great Latin percussionists of his time, a relentless swinger on the congas and timbales, a flamboyant showman onstage, and an engaging singer. He also made serious inroads into the pop, R&B and straight jazz worlds. Growing up in Spanish Harlem, Bobo began on the bongos at age 14, only to find himself performing with Pérez Prado for a very short while. He served as Mongo Santamaría's translator, and joined Tito Puente for a four-year stint at age 19. He learned to play timbales in the streets of Harlem and while with Tito developed his own unique style, so too did Willie Bobo. Tito was a little taken aback by his "audaciousness and aggressiveness." However, the two rivals managed to string together a series of historic recordings. With Mongo and Willie at his side it was Tito's belief that this was his greatest percussive unit. "There was never anything like them before, and nothing to equal their ability and performance on stage or in a studio. When Willie passed away in 1983 after a long battle with cancer, Tito displayed a rare moment of sadness.

The replacement of a vocalist after Vicentico Valdés departed did not seem to be a problem. Tito recruited Gilberto Monroig who at the time was working for his old boss José Curbelo. Tito noted that at the time, Curbelo did mention that Monroig was somewhat problematic and careless. He had a lackadaisical work ethic. Despite this Tito felt sure he could work with the vocalist. Monroig had a terrific voice, and at first it seemed that it would be a smooth transition from Valdés, who had recorded more than 50 tunes with the Puente Orchestra. Monroig's voice was considered smoother and more versatile. His voice is heard on *"Picao y Tostao,"* which was well received by the New York Puerto Rican fans. In a period of 12 months between 1953 and 1954, Monroig recorded 14 selections with Tito and for the Tico label. But it was not a smooth ride for the new singer.

Monroig had fallen victim to drug abuse and was often late for recording dates or did not show up at all. When the Puente Orchestra played the Catskill circuit he was often late. Monroig's last recording with Tito *was "Malcriada,"* a bolero that was said to have been one of his most successful. He was born in 1930, in Santurce, Puerto Rico. Upon arrival in New York in 1950 he was signed by Alfredito Levy, and by 1952 was with José Curbelo. He fought his drug demons for a major part of his life and was highly regarded on the island where he passed away in 1996. For the time being Tito decided he would do without a permanent vocalist. He wanted to experiment.

The Not So Latino Fans

Through 1953 Tito was busy recording and shaping his style, and playing his brand of mambo and other Afro-Cuban music in Long Island, matinees at the Palladium and in the Catskill mountains. Borscht Belt is an informal term for the summer resorts of the Catskill Mountains[65] in Sullivan and

Ulster Counties in upstate New York which were a popular holiday spot for New York Jews. (Borscht is a kind of beet soup popular with people of Eastern European origin.) The term Borscht Belt can also refer to the Catskill region itself. Borscht Belt hotels, bungalow colonies, summer camps, and kuchaleyns (a Yiddish name for self-catered boarding houses) were frequented by Jewish New Yorkers, particularly in the 1940s, 1950s and into the1960s.

As a result, the Catskills was also nicknamed the Jewish Alps and Solomon County (a modification of Sullivan County), by many people who visited there. Well-known resorts of the area included Brickman's, Brown's, The Concord, Grossinger's, The Granit, Kutsher's Hotel and Country Club, the Nevele, Friar Tuck Inn, The Pines, Raleigh and The Windsor.

The tradition of Borscht Belt entertainment started in the early 20th century with the indoor and outdoor theaters constructed on a 40 acre tract in Hunter, New York, by Yiddish theater star Boris Thomashefsky. Comedians who regularly performed in the Catskill Mountains resorts include: Morey Amsterdam, Woody Allen, Milton Berle, Shelley Berman, Mel Brooks, Lenny Bruce, George Burns, Red Buttons, Sid Caesar, Jack Carter, Myron Cohen, Bill Dana, Rodney Dangerfield, Phyllis Diller, Betty Garrett, George Gobel, Shecky Greene, Buddy Hackett, Danny Kaye, Alan King, Robert Klein, Jack E. Leonard, Jerry Lewis, Jackie Mason, Jan Murray, Carl Reiner, Don Rickles, Joan Rivers, Freddie Roman, Jackie Vernon, Jackie Wakefield, Jonathan Winters, and Henny Youngman. The entertainment also included the New York based Latin bands. One of the most popular starting around 1950, was the Tito Puente Orchestra.

Tito was well known on the summer circuit. He enjoyed the Catskill Mountains. Many of the dancers that vacationed in the mountain resorts were clients of the Palladium Ballroom. When he was not playing he was mixing it with celebrities. Tito was not shy, not at all. But even Tito noticed that as the 1950s closed out and 1960 approached, the crowds were getting smaller, and older. Things were changing.

The changes in demographic and travel patterns resulted in the decline of the area as a major vacation destination. A major factor was the decline of discrimination or "restriction" in the hotel and travel industry by the 1960s. Prior to that time, many resorts and hotels, implicitly or otherwise, did not welcome Jews. Also, the end of rail service to the Catskill resorts added to the dip in numbers of vacationers. The post WWII slump of the area also coincides with the increase of air travel. When families could go to more far off destinations for the same money spent going to the Catskills, new venues began to win out.

There was difficulty in playing the Catskill Mountains summer circuit.

The fair skin musicians were permitted to stay in the bungalows while the darker skin musicians were restricted. "We never were comfortable up there. There were a lot of people who gasped when they looked at us, at least until they heard us perform," recalled Tito.

"I remember the racism. Vicentico and Mongo had to stay in the black cabin area at the Concord. The rest of the band stayed at the main hotel. I stayed with Vicentico and Mongo," recalled Jimmy. It went up Tito's rear and irritated the shit out of him." On the light side Jimmy added, "I confused the shit out of the tourists to see me and Willie parading around together. Overall, I found a lot of these people a little bizarre – like unaware, after all the shit they had gone through you would think they would be more understanding." Willie Bobo told me one day in recalling the Catskill excursions "It was really difficult for Tito." He remembered Tito throwing a temper tantrum because one of the musicians was asked to carry luggage to a guest's room. "Man did he blow up. You dumb mother fuckers, Tito yelled," Willie said. "The people in the lobby were scared shit. Jimmy had to calm him."

He got over it. At night he enjoyed mingling with the stars but he still fumed over the stupidity of segregation, especially from people who had suffered through the holocaust. The young people loved him, though. "They raised the roof when we played," explained Tito.

During this period of time Tito's fame was growing by leaps and bounds one could say. He was recording for Tico and it was during this period that the war of egos between the two Titos began to unfold. In a number of interviews after he disbanded his orchestra Tito Rodríguez claimed that he never had any problem with Tito. "We were fierce competitors and we both wanted our bands to have top billing," he said.

Tito reflected: "It was strictly media hype. Maybe we were not as close as we used to be, but we were never mad at each other. He probably ran the best organization of all of us. No, the media went with it and we went along for the ride.

"Mambo La Roca," "Lo Dicen Todo," "El Timbal," "Mambo En Blues" "Vibe Mambo," and *Mambo Diablo,"* are just some of the hits recorded by Tito during his early years as a bandleader. The mambos give an early glimpse of Tito's musical inclinations –strong blaring trumpets are curt, tight and unifying, pounding proficient Afro-Cuban percussion all managed by the leader. His sound was driving and organized.

The Korean War (1950-53) forced changes in his orchestra. Charlie Palmieri replaced pianist Gilberto López in 1952 and Mongo Santamaría replaced Frankie Colón. The battle for top billing at the Palladium Ballroom started in earnest in 1951–1952 between the two Titos. It was a controversy and a feud that would consume the historians of Afro-Cuban music, writers and media throughout the lives of both Titos. Machito was generally the one with top billing at the historical ballroom. In 1952, the Tito Puente and Tito Rodríguez orchestras were neck and neck in Tico recordings. These were 78-rpm releases. Both bandleaders were getting new material from Havana. Tito was mixing his music – jazz with vibes, romantic and the Cuban mambo. His numerous visits to Havana were paying off. He did not say much to his competitors about how and where, or even when he was in Havana. Tito was this way. He kept a lot to himself.

"We were going back and forth between the studio a few times a week," Jimmy recalled. "It was like a roller coaster. The dances ran late. We had rehearsals early in the morning. There was a lot of drinking and other things as well. Even when Tito was distracted he managed to nudge himself to the recording studio, bash all of us and we just kept on going."

Tito often recalled the late nights at the clubs –"in Brooklyn, the Bronx and in Manhattan. There were nightclubs everywhere. The economy of the city was bursting." There were usually two orchestras, sometimes three. If a Latin club hosted the dance the two bands played the latest mambos. Other clubs hosted a Latin band and an American music ensemble. "It was funny to hear them play Afro-Cuban music. Well, at least they tried. Everybody was into the mambo."

The Catskill Mountains gigs gave him the opportunity to expand his fan base. "There were few Latinos around the Catskills. But from a music perspective we got to try out a lot of things before taking them into the Palladium. The Jewish people loved me. The Italians loved me. The music of the era was more accepted than we ever imagined."

The years starting from his first formal appearance at a club not far from the Hamptons in 1949, the excursions up to the Catskill mountains, the more than four recording sessions each week for Tico and other record labels, daily appearances at radio stations and crisscrossing the City of New York provided the Tito Puente Orchestra with the means to gauge its public, a process to understand what and who the fan base was, and in return Tito Puente delivered his version of the New York mambo.

Precision was crucial to Tito in playing his style of big band dance music, and delivery of the syncopated Afro-Cuban jazz method. He tried out trombones but didn't like the sound and got rid of them. He brought in saxes and developed their place in his band. He had several models, but foremost on his mind was the Stan Kenton Orchestra model. Kenton had many gifted soloists, as did Machito. Zoot Sims on tenor played for both orchestras, Lee Konitz on alto, Gerry Mulligan wrote arrangements such as *"Swinghouse"* and *"Young Blood."* The two organizations furnished artfully simple examples of sections used in contrapuntal ensemble play. Tito incorporated this into his orchestra. The sounds of Afro Cuban music that he introduced during his early years were progressive beyond his expectations.

Scoring for brass in unison was something Tito liked. He probably first heard it in a Stan Kenton orchestra or possibly in the Woody Herman Band. Machito did it too. But his approach was slightly different. Tito built up the sound, slowly and deliberately. It became his trademark. He worked his sax sections to achieve a flutelike transparency and lightness through his use of the lead instrument. Then while the trumpets were riffing with combinations of four and five notes – sometimes just two notes – the saxes rolled in. He could be rather majestic. The classical effect was sometimes apparent. He was always listening to classical music, and he especially enjoyed Wagner and Beethoven. The two composers had a big sound. Tito turned to Mozart for light airy feelings. Manuel de Falla was another favorite from which Tito drew inspiration.

Tito sought a strong sound that could at the same time be mellow. In 1950 he recorded *"Take The A Train,"* composed by Billy Strayhorn. This is an example of Tito's vision as early as 1950. Using a robust steady driving percussion he has the winds instruments roll along while the "Italian" trumpets led by Jimmy, bustle in and out. Joseph Herde, Irving Butler, H. Berge and Sol Rabinowitz comprise the sax section. This is a 1950 recording and one of Tito's early endeavors to enlarge and incorporate the saxophones to expand the conjunto sound. It was released on RCA Victor. Tito liked the smoothness of it and always hoped that he did justice to the Duke Ellington Orchestra classic. Billy Strayhorn, the Ellington pianist and arranger, composed the piece in the 1930s while he rode on the subway up to Harlem to interview for the job. He was a smooth and gentle kind of arranger, in Tito's opinion. "He was a rare individual."

Fierce Competition

Tito was busy – busier beyond his wildest dreams. From 1950 until 1955 he was rehearsing and recording dozens of 78-rpm releases for RCA Victor and Tico Records. Tito became unquestionably a Tico Records star, both in the label's earliest years and much later, near the end of its existence. Tito participated in 164 different recording sessions for Tico during this period. There were others, including Tito Rodríguez and Machito, but Tito churned out recording after recording. In 1955 he switched back to RCA Victor when he recorded some of his greatest classics. But it was not all roses, as Tito often reminded me and stated to others in the music business. Tico was terrific, but it had limited exposure and distribution so RCA Victor seemed the way to go, but almost from the start the executives at RCA had a love affair with Pérez Prado and the mambo style he was promoting. "RCA was notorious for limiting Tito's releases while they promoted what they thought would be popular," Jimmy maintained all through his career and to his death.

In the fall of 1949, Puente gave Tico its first big New York area hit, *"Abaniquito."* Dick "Ricardo" Sugar began giving the single regular airplay on his show. Among Tito's other early hits were the *"Mambo Macoco,"* the groundbreaking *"Vibe Mambo"* and his version of the Cuban tune *"Lo Dicen Todos"* that was composed by Arsenio Rodríguez. George Goldner found himself supervising a landmark recording after Tito convinced him to schedule a session for a first-of-its-kind all-percussion album. There was nothing in the studio but Latin percussion instruments. His band consisted of Mongo Santamaría, Patato Valdéz and Willie Bobo, and a big bottle of rum that they passed among them. When the night was over, they had recorded *"Puente In Percussion,"* the classic first long play album that became the benchmark for hundreds of subsequent Afro-Cuban recordings in the United States. Other highly regarded albums, originally released as 78rpms for Tico included *"Mamborama," " Puente In Love," " Tito Puente Swings, Vicentico Valdés Sings,"* and *"Mambo With Me"* – recorded in the early 1950s[67].

His rival Tito Rodríguez was also a Tico star. He decided to expand The Mambo Wolves from a conjunto to a ten-piece orchestra, and scored bestsellers with such sides as *"Mambo Gee Gee"* (otherwise known as the *"George Goldner Mambo"*), *"Mambo Mona (Mama Guela)," "La Renta"* and the risqué *"Chiqui Bop."* Tito Rodríguez also recorded for Tico and RCA Victor between 1949 and 1958. In 1960 he went to United Artists group of labels.

Meanwhile, the Pérez Prado orchestra was top draw in Mexico City. RCA's Mexican division signed Prado as an artist in his own right in 1949, and his first 78 rpm record, *"Que Rico el Mambo"* and *"Mambo No. 5,"* was a hit across much of Latin America, reaching the United States.

The recordings made by Tito between 1949 and 1951 for RCA Victor[68] were mainly marketed and distributed regionally. The company was in the throws of a marketing fiasco until nearly the mid-1950s deciding if it should use the 45-rpm record or switch to the long play 12-inch record developed at Columbia Records. RCA Victor made the wrong decision staying with the 45-rpm seven-inch record and suffered considerable loss of the music market. Tito was not important to the corporate executives. In 1950, RCA reissued it in this country with the A-side's title changed to *"Mambo Jambo."* It had moderate success. During 1950, Prado released numerous singles in Mexico; most of them were titled in tribute to a broad range of social classes and occupations, which helped make them wildly popular. Moreover, Prado appeared in several Mexican films, generally playing himself and spotlighting his stage act and directing his orchestra.

The early 1950s were a busy time for Prado, who staged a number of international tours as the mambo sound spread like wildfire. Prado's first U.S. tour was in 1951, with Beny Moré accompanying him; because of musicians' union rules, he was often forced to hire local musicians in place of his Mexican crew, and train them rigorously in a very short period of time with little knowledge of English. The tour was a tremendous success, however, especially on the West Coast, and RCA started releasing his records on their main RCA Victor imprint, rather than consigning them to a specialty subsidiary. In late 1953, Prado caused a stir when Mexican officials abruptly deported him to Havana; his sudden disappearance (he was arrested in a backstage dressing room) sparked rumors of kidnapping before he finally resurfaced to explain that he had forgotten to renew his visa.

In 1953, Tito's star was rising. He was successful and his creative energies were still focused on giving him uniqueness and success in terms of his musical contributions. He was busy playing, moving his orchestra from event to event, and making sure that he and Jimmy gathered up the musicians for rehearsals and recordings. One of his successes caused something of stir, albeit not at the moment, but later. He fumed over the insinuation.

"There was Tito Puente's twenty-ninth birthday celebration in 1953 when Noro Morales performed *'Serenata Ritmica'* and Puente ad-libbed on vibes; those ad-libs became the *'Philadelphia M*ambo'.'" (Mambo Kingdom, Page 93, Salazar – 2002)

The melody that is known as *"Philadelphia Mambo"* is crisp and based on a thumping bass line. It was never fully scored. According to Tito *"Philadelphia Mambo"* was pounded out one day by the bass, piano and percussion. "I sat in a room, wrote the basic concept of the montuno on the piano. I arranged the music for the trumpets – there was not a hell of a lot to do – Jimmy and the boys mostly improvised the riffs and off we went."

"Tito gave me the idea of what he wanted the trumpets to do," Jimmy explained. "We practiced it a few times and then off he (Tito) went to work out the details on the piano. There weren't a lot of details on the chart," Jimmy laughed. Tico Records gathered up a dozen sessions and released *"Puente In Love,"* which includes the 1953 *"Philadelphia Mambo."* In later years Tito told me he "did not have a clue as to where the *'Serenata Ritmica'* bullshit came from." There is also a rare recorded version with Afro-Cuban lyrics played by Noro Morales and his Orchestra. Tito said "Noro's version was very unusual at the time."

In a long play Tico album titled *"Mambo Caravan"* the riveting *"Mambo Diablo*" is heard. It is a spellbinding piece of music that Tito composed as an instrumental. The vibes blend into the percussion. The trumpets provide fireworks. The piano and bass work in a contrapuntal approach. The result is intoxicating. "It is open ended. By that I mean you can play it with just about any instrument. The montuno – tumbao with minor adjustments was a showpiece for the orchestra. On any Wednesday night at the Palladium this was a showstopper. There was nothing like it - I always told him I could almost see the damn little devils all dressed up, holding pitch forks and dancing. He laughed.

Pérez Prado returned to the U.S. in 1954, embarking on another hugely successful tour of the West Coast. He then made his way to New York, where his orchestra played several upscale venues that helped make mambo all the rage among upper class. Spurred by mambo nights in clubs across the city, mambo was pushing its way into the pop mainstream, as traditional pop crooners and R&B/blues artists alike recorded Latin-flavored novelty items paying tribute to the emerging fad.

But Pérez Prado was never booked at the Palladium, nor did he play in the New York City clubs that were fans of Afro-Cuban music spawned by Tito and a host of other bands. "He was not in the same league with Puente, Machito and Rodríguez," was the conclusion of promoter Federico Pagani. "We were in a Afro-Cuban music frame of mind."

Seeing that Pérez Prado's mambo music could cross over to the lucrative white market, RCA Victor pushed aside the stronger and more authentic Cuban mambo played by Tito and his orchestra and others in the New York area, and began to modify it for mainstream consumption, scoring minor hits with covers of the theme from the Italian film "Anna" and the South African tune *"Skokiaan,"* which signaled the beginning of a more polished studio sound. Pérez Prado and RCA Victor scored a breakout pop hit in early 1955 with *"Cherry Pink and Apple Blossom White,"* which was used as the theme to the Jane Russell film "Underwater!" Ironically for the Cuban-born El Rey del Mambo, his first major hit was an adaptation of a French song *"Cerisier Rose et Pommier Blanc."* and its underlying rhythm was a cha cha. The original issue was titled *"Cerezo Rosa."* Powered by a dramatic, swooping trumpet lead by Billy Regis, *"Cherry Pink and Apple Blossom White"* spent an astounding ten weeks at number one on the pop charts, making it one of the biggest instrumental hits of all time. The accompanying album, *"Mambo Mania,"* was Prado's first full-length 12-inch long play album, and mostly featured material he had recorded while he was in Mexico.

Tito did not sit idly while RCA Victor was pushing the Pérez Prado brand. He arranged his own version of *"Cherry Pink and Apple Blossom White,"* with a softer sound yet using the strong percussion supplied by Mongo and Willie. The 78-rpm recording features Tito, of all places, in the saxophone section, and includes him taking a subdued – Lawrence Spivak style – solo. Later, the tune was included in the Tico LP compilation album: *"Dance Cha Cha Chá."*

"We wanted to give it a smoother sound while keeping the sturdiness of the Afro-Cuban percussion," Tito said about the piece years later. Jimmy recalled on a number of occasions that in the 1950s "Tito liked to play his saxophone. He played it on several recordings." However, Tito's version never got the play that the Pérez Prado version did.

"But he (Pérez Prado) never made it in New York. He had the musicians, but not the style to excite or even please New York Latinos," Tito said. Tico Record, in those days, did not have the resources to push the Tito Puente Orchestra beyond the region. Nonetheless, he always felt his version of the popular song was better.

Prado took advantage of his success to attempt more ambitious compositions during this period. His first effort in this vein was 1954's *"The Voodoo Suite,"* an impressionistic tone poem for Afro-Cuban big band that incorporated elements of jazz and exotica. West Coast trumpeter Shorty Rogers helped out on the arrangements, and the results often recalled Stan Kenton's progressive big-band mood music, albeit with a Latin sound. The 1956 album *"Havana 3 A.M."* was a wilder jaunt that ranked as probably the purest, most authentically Latin record of Prado's commercial period. There were many commercial projects; the biggest was 1958's *"Prez,"* which fell just short of the Top 20 on the pop LP charts. That same year, Prado scored his second number one single with the self-composed *"Patricia,"* a slinky if passive instrumental spotlighting his organ playing. The tune was later used in a steamy, controversial sequence in director Federico Fellini's classic "La Dolce Vita."

RCA continued to record Tito, albeit not with the enthusiasm that it showed for Pérez Prado. Despite this the Tito Puente Orchestra recorded dozens of regional hits between 1949 and 1951 that included: *"Ran Kan Kan," "Arinanara"* (rumba version), *"Timbal y Bongo," "Candido,"* (composed by Israel "Cachao" López), *"Take The A Train,"* and *"Guayaba."* Between 1955 and 1956 Tito gathered what many consider his greatest orchestra – he was focused and ready to work on and record *"Cuban Carnaval,"* a long play album that was popular in the New York region and at the time not elsewhere. Tito was always disappointed that RCA did not push and promote this album. Some consider this to be his greatest album.

Tito had an eye on his mentor's band-the highly energetic and progressive Machito y sus Afro-Cubanos, who continued on a steady path of success from 1949 through the mid 1950s and even beyond. The orchestra featured Flip Phillips and Charlie Parker in the "Afro-Cuban Jazz Suite," recorded in 1948. Composer Chico O'Farrill was featured on the "Second Afro-Cuban Jazz Suite," released in 1951. Machito and his orchestra recorded on Decca, Mercury and for Tico. It played the Palladium and performed in the Catskills resorts. The success of his mentor's band did not concern Tito in the least, as long as he got top billing.

"The 10 Magic Fingers of Latin Music," as José Curbelo was known also continued to be successful. In 1952 he was recording for Tico Records, featuring Sabu Martínez on percussion and Al Cohn on tenor saxophone. His singers included Gilberto Monroig, Santitos Colón, Mon Rivera, Willie Torres and Tony Molina. He was a fierce competitor but Tito and José also remained good friends.

The orchestra that Tito gathered for this recording of *"Cuban Carnaval"* and that played at Palladium Ballroom into 1956 included the following musicians: Tito - vibes, timbales and chorus; Nick Travis, Frank Lo Pinto, Jimmy Frisaura, Gene Rapeati, Bernie Glow, Andres Forda and Sam Seavors – trumpets; Alvin Gellers – piano; Bobby Rodríguez – bass; Mongo Santamaría, Willie Bobo, Carlos "Patato" Valdéz, Candido Camero and John Rodríguez, Sr. – Afro-Cuban percussion; Santo Ruso, Eddie Bert, Robert Ascher, Sam Takvorian – trombones; Jerry Sanfino, Marty Holmes, Ed Caine, Sol Schlinger, Allen Fields, José 'Pin' Madera, Sr. and

Dave Kutzer – saxophones and flutes; El Viejo Macucho, Yayo El Indio and Tony Molina –vocals. This recording, according to Tito, was popular in Havana. He heard selections from it while visiting and was also approached by local musicians who had nothing but praise for it. Tito always felt good about it – the way it turned out.

"They (RCA Victor executives) always played down the New York market. They were having a love affair with Pérez Prado. He always sounded like he was in a hurry to get to the bathroom – go figure," he moaned when he thought of the competition. He told me once that RCA Victor nearly lost the Cuban market by delaying signing on talent from the island in the early 1950s. "By the time they got down there the majority of entertainers worth anything were under contract. I think they signed Orquesta Aragón in 1953, but it took them a while to figure out how to distribute their music. There was Enrique Jorrín, who made a number of great recordings for them while he was in Mexico. They never released those recordings in the United States – you know they were all chasing after Augh! (The sound that Pérez Prado made in his recordings.)" Tito laughed.

It irritated Tito to no end, but he pressed on. His was the *"Mambo Diablo."* – the devil's mambo and no one was going to catch him, especially not Pérez Prado.

Palladium Nights

It was midnight and the dancers had been cleared from the dance floor. Three sets of timbales were placed in the middle of the floor. The packed dancehall quieted. All the patrons were waiting with anticipation for what was to come! The Tito Puente Orchestra members sat in their places on the stage. The musicians were immaculately dressed in their dark blue-gray tuxedo jackets, black pants and black patent leather shoes. They sat quietly holding their instruments. Additional percussionists, some from other bands, came out and sat directly in front of the orchestra. There were four congeros, a campanero, a bongocero and a maraquero. The voice rang out: "Ladies and Gentlemen – Mr. Tito Puente, Mongo Santamaría and Willie Bobo."[69]

The applause lifted over a drum roll. The orchestra struck up its fanfare as the three men walked onto the center of the dance floor. It was Wednesday night and the ballroom was packed. Everyone waited in anticipation – three sets of timbales. The three men walked quickly to their instruments. Tito's tuxedo jacket was black-blue. Mongo and Willie were dressed like the rest of the orchestra. Willie and Mongo stood on either side of Tito. The bass struck the montuno beat. A few bars later the bongocero began a steady rhythm, striking each head with proficiency. He was followed by the piano and güiro playing together. Alvin Gellers wasn't playing anything fancy, just chords that fit easily into the firm rhythmic pattern that had been established.

Tito struck a roll from one head to the other. Mongo followed with his roll, a slightly higher pitch. Willie joined in. Tito continued the drum roll as both sidemen began striking the basic mambo beat on the cowbells. The fans and dancers crowded together, nudging closer and closer, ever more tightly. The three drummers were striking the bell while keeping time. The tempo was driving. The crowd applauded. Between his rapid rolls, his syncopated smacks, Tito would look back at his orchestra. There was a faint smile. He turned back to gaze at the large crowd. He could see the crowd was swaying, clapping, even cheering.

Each musician took solos as the other two percussionists kept precise time. Then they played intricate beats on the bells and double heads, never faltering from the strict Afro-Cuban beats. They anticipated one another. Willie performed another solo while Mongo and Tito kept the steady beat. Willie and Tito traded barrages. Mongo and Willie traded licks, Tito and Mongo demonstrated their virtuosity. The rhythm men behind them maintained the torrid locomotion. The montuno was strong, deliberate.

Tito, Willie and Mongo were now discharging a driving beat on the large bells. Willie was damn good, and Tito always knew this. There was a little bit of a rivalry between the two, but right now it was the music they were playing that drove them. The crowd screamed. Tito jumped in front of the stage and began dancing. Mongo and Willie were keeping fierce time. The clave from the other percussionists - tumbadoras, bongocero – was thumping. This was the Tito Puente Orchestra at its best. This was the New York Palladium Ballroom. This was the best Afro-Cuban music to be found outside of Cuba. There was no doubt about that.

You could sense the thrill, you could feel the excitement. It became obvious to everyone that this was one of those moments that would become Palladium lore. Tito looked from Mongo to Willie, and then salted the heads of his timbales. The orchestra kept up with ease and polish. It seemed the trumpets knew what Tito was going to do and anticipating it, laid down a barrage of blaring syncopated horn blasts that caused incredible exhilaration. Mongo came in on cue – a brief nod from Tito. Then Willie followed. They went back and forth.

Tito relived the excitement of that moment often. It was a culmination of what became a routine yet exciting night of dancing at the Palladium located in the heart of midtown Manhattan. Starting around 1949, and extending until 1966 when the ballroom closed, the Palladium was the Mecca for dancing to live music in New York. There were hundreds of nightclubs, ballrooms, dancehalls, and after-hour clubs in and around New York City during these years but nothing will ever equal or surpass the Palladium. It became the cultural location of thousands of Puerto Ricans who were establishing their roots in the churning city. The kind of Latin music these people embraced was nothing like what they had left behind in Puerto Rico – it was piercing, boisterous and almost uncouth to some ears – but is was Latin and authentic. And historically, Puerto Rico and Cuba had been coupled for hundreds of years so this music was not so unfamiliar or strange.

Puerto Ricans were not the only ones that embraced the fiery Afro-Cuban music. New York Jews, Italians and blacks loved the hot tropical music that had evolved in New York City. And in the middle of it was Tito with his relatively new orchestra. He was enjoying every minute of it.

Everyone danced at the Palladium young and old, white and black,

Latino, Jewish, Italian and Irish – just about everyone. There were other popular clubs for New Yorkers that wanted to dance mambo - the Manhattan Center, the Riviera Terrace to name a few.

But the Palladium Ballroom, located at 53rd Street and Broadway, ballyhooed itself as "Home of the Mambo." Any New Yorker, from the average working person to celebrities like James Dean, Marlon Brando and Eartha Kitt might be seen there and that's just for starters, brushing up on the latest mambo variations. It was more expensive than the average ballroom of the period. The $1.75 admission entitled the adventurous fan to mambo instructions early in the evening, plus an amateur contest for mambo dancers, plus a professional mambo show from 11 to midnight including dancing – they preferred this to anything else.

History's Dancehall

The Palladium Ballroom,[70] a second-floor dancehall, became famous for its excellent Latin music. At the end of World War II, people began moving from Puerto Rico to New York City in large numbers, all this while the popularity of swing, foxtrot, and big band music was slowly fading.

Sometime in 1947, music promoter Federico Pagani approached Palladium owner Maxwell Hyman, about booking Latin music into the club that was losing its luster from the wartime period and losing customers because of the demise of the big bands. There were other owners, but Federico dealt with Mr. Hyman. The first of the Latin bands to play the ballroom was Machito, on a one-shot Sunday afternoon deal. It was an overwhelming success. Pagani continued to push the owners and a second Latin Matinee was approved. It featured José Curbelo and his Orchestra, Marcelino Guerra and his Orchestra, Noro Morales Orchestra and Joséito Mateo's merengue ensemble. It was a resounding success that Pagani followed up with seeking out his old friend Tito Puente who was just starting out.

From this point the reputation of the ballroom grew. Machito, Tito and Tito Rodríguez were the principal draws at the start. There were often problems with the legal authorities over a number of issues. The problems of selling liquor to minors, transportation of drugs, illegal drugs on the premises, you name it, the police and New York City officials kept a close watch on the ballroom and its landlords who were suspected of being involved in organized crime. This did not concern the dancers. It did not concern the orchestras.

Tito, Machito, Federico, Mario, Charlie and Miguelito had long and hard talks about why the authorities pressured the Palladium Ballroom proprietors. "The ownership was not straight forward and clean in the eyes of the law," quipped Tito during one of their meetings at the Asia Restaurant that were held almost on a weekly basis in the 1970s.

"It had more to do with the success of the place," responded Mario. "They (the establishment) had a problem with minorities being so successful. It was not so much that they were after the owners. They just did not like Latinos being successful."

Miguelito chimed: "Just like in Cuba, before Fidel. Not that he is any better…"

"Well we always got along with Hyman," Machito said.

"There were too many people with their hands in the pot – too many people that we did not know about. But in those days there was still a lot of prejudice. I don't care what you say," recalled Mario.

Miguelito, Charlie and Tito laughed. "Like I said, just like in Cuba when Batista was running things," Miguelito re-emphasized.

They paused to sip their drinks. Mario took a deep puff on his Cuban cigar. "You know you are breaking the law smoking those damn things," quipped Tito.

"Do you want one?"

Tito nodded. "There will never be anything like it. You can't plan something like what happened during those years. It just happened. We were just there to take it all in," offered Charlie with a grin.

The conversation would continue for hours while the group had lunch, drinks, dinner, and more drinks and a few cigars. It was generally this way when these guys got together.

Since the mid-1930s, the living heart of jazz in New York had been two blocks of old brownstones on the West Side — 52nd Street, between Fifth and Seventh Avenues. Never, not even in New Orleans at the turn of the century or along the brightly lit Chicago Stroll in the 1920s, had so much great jazz been concentrated in so small a space. Seven jazz clubs still flourished there in the early 1940s. The Spotlite, the Yacht Club, and the Three Deuces were on the south side of the block between Fifth and Sixth; Jimmy Ryan's, the Onyx, and Tondelayo's were right across the street. And there were two more clubs a block further west — Kelly's Stable and the Hickory House. The street's unofficial queen was Billie Holiday. It had seemed like "a plantation" to her when she and Teddy Wilson were working there in the mid-1930s, she remembered, but now black musicians were everywhere, black and white customers mingled with greater frequency, and the quality of musicianship that surrounded her was simply astonishing. Her very first engagement at Kelly's Stables included on the same bill, a quartet led by Coleman Hawkins; the hardest-swinging violinist in the history of the music, Stuff Smith and at intermission, the pianist Nat "King" Cole and his trio. And competing clubs up and down the street featured attractions only slightly less stellar.

Jazz musicians went from being featured attractions to poorly paid accompanists. The Royal Roost was one of a few clubs that established itself a few blocks southwest of 52nd Street, but with the exception of the legendary Birdland (named for Charlie Parker), most of them vanished by the time Elvis Presley came north. Birdland opened in late 1949, with a bill that included its namesake, Lester Young, Max Kaminsky and Tristano. The years between 1949 and 1959 when the Palladium and Birdland were popular were also years in which the New York Police Department and various drug enforcement authorities spent considerable resources in targeting what was known as Jazz Alley or Bop City. It was always Tito's belief that a lot of the police activity had to do with the fact that Latinos, like blacks, were achieving too much success.

But the Palladium Ballroom went on to be successful. The dancehall in the middle of the Great White Way underwent a number of renovations to spruce it up. Upon entering the location and walking up the flight of stairs the large dance floor was in full view. The right side had a long wooden rail and people stood behind it to watch the dancers or the band. The bar was long and located at the back of the large room. It was not graceful. But it had a inexplicable magnetism. It helped launch many careers and new ventures.

There were other ballrooms that dotted the City. El Club Caborrojeño far north on Broadway at 145th Street was one of the most popular. Others included the Broadway Casino in Washington Heights, El Cubanacán (114th and Lenox Avenue), the Park Palace and Park Plaza on 110th Street and 5th Avenue, and Gloria Palace on 86th Street and Third Avenue, as well as Bronx night spots the Tropicana (on Westchester Avenue and 163rd Street), The Tritons, located next to the Hunt's Point Palace (Southern Boulevard and 163rd Street) La Campana (149th Street and Third Avenue), the Manhattan Center (on 34th Street and Seventh Avenue). The Taft Hotel hosted, through private clubs, Saturday night dances that featured the best orchestras including Tito Puente. Many of the midtown hotels also hosted dances from time to time. But the highly visible Palladium in the heart of midtown was the most popular – the most famous.

By 1951 the Palladium had helped to launch the recording company Tico that promoted the big three New York Bands. Soon other orchestras, quintets, ensembles and dance acts were being booked into the Palladium. Federico Pagani was traveling to and from Cuba searching out the most popular bands to have them perform alongside to one of the big three.

There certainly were many historic moments during the almost 20 years the Palladium Ballroom was open. It was not a smooth ride for the owners. There were legal conflicts, run-ins with the police. One night in 1961, as a packed ballroom was swaying to the music of Rolando Laserie to the pulsating rhythm, someone announced on a loudspeaker: "This is a raid!"

The police found marijuana, several handguns, knives and heroin. Detectives Sonny Grosso and Eddie Egan of "The French Connection" fame coordinated the raid. It was staged in response to a woman who worked for the Manhattan District Attorney's office who claimed she was offered marijuana while she was at the Palladium. Officer Grosso told this to Tito and me one evening when we attended New York State Supreme Court Judge Edwin Torres' birthday party. A number of news reports from the period indicated that the move to shutdown the dancehall had more to do with the keeping the minorities – Latinos and blacks – from frequenting the midtown section. Other accounts indicate that the raid was the work of an over-zealous assistant district attorney. Judge Torres has suggested the latter was true.

In all 25 people were arrested. Hyman was served with several summonses and was accused of operating a house of prostitution. He denied all charges. The Palladium continued to function, albeit without a liquor license until May 1, 1966 when the orchestras of Eddie Palmieri and Ricardo Ray, and Orquesta Broadway were on hand to see the lights go out forever.

The dance floor and bandstand of the New York Palladium was recreated in the feature film "Mambo Kings" that starred Armand Assante and Antonio Banderas. In it Tito played himself and Desi Arnaz, Jr. played Desi Arnaz, Sr. The orchestra, the Mambo Kings Band, was designed to give a feeling of the era of the Broadway ballroom. While we were filming on the west coast Tito often noted "it would have made more sense to recreate the Palladium in New York. The ambiance is missing out here. The dancers… Well, they don't know the moves." He was right.

Elegance and Grace

There were restrictions to being admitted to the Palladium – the men had to be appropriately attired - jacket and tie was required. If they did not have one they were made available for a fee. The women were elegant and fashionably dressed – it was that period in New York. The dancers came from every point in the city and even farther away. They spoke many languages – not just English and Spanish. The ethnic mix was for the most part Puerto Rican, Cuban and other Latinos. The blacks came from Harlem; the Jews came from their neighborhoods in the five boroughs. Italians and Irish and others were present. They all came to dance and hear the music – the music made popular by the Tito Puente Orchestra, Tito Rodríguez and his Orchestra, Machito y sus Afro-Cubanos. A lot of others played the Palladium. The requirement to get booked is that you had to be good. You also had to audition, Tito said.

The women were provocatively dressed in style. Casual dress was not acceptable for men or women. The latest fashions were sported by most of the patrons.[71] Soft but wide shoulders, corseted waist, and full hips were hallmarks of period wear, but silhouettes were more varied. On these outlines, women wore a trim bodice and very full knee-length skirt, or a fitted short, boxy jacket or blouse with a pencil-straight skirt. Both solids and classic floral brocades were common; the effect of overlaying contrasting sheer chiffon or net on a flesh-colored under-dress was daringly popular.

Colors for the evening were both subtle and bold, as peacock blues and hot pinks. Flutter hems, which were curved evenly up and down, and scalloped edges appeared occasionally in full-skirted evening dresses. The women, young and old, slender and robust spared no effort to present themselves on the Palladium dance floor. Most evening detail appeared in sculpted pleats and necklines, or toned-down rhinestones and corde`, which added style without being cumbersome or uncomfortable. Hems fell to the knee or a little below it – it was the style of the 1950s.

In this attire the men and women gathered at the Palladium to dance mambo and many other types of music that the big bands poured out, and the smaller conjuntos and sextets dispensed. The men tried out their latest steps, the women followed, gently or in time and occasionally surprised their partner with a new, even more intricate set of moves. The couples moved across the dance floor with ease and agility, efficiency and grace. Each couple was in a strange way trying to out do the others, but all within the framework of the music.

The live music was well played. The promoters would not hire an orchestra or ensemble without an audition. The orchestras played everything, fast mambos, slow groovy mambos, boleros, merengues, and guarachas. They even played pasodobles; foxtrots, tango and you name it. But the mambo drove the dancers, and later the cha cha chá became a dance of interest. The dancers excited the bands and made them play better. The soloist improvised off the moving bodies. The better the dancer, the more intricate moves they made; the better the solo of the musicians - the more pulsating the riffs, the more punctuated the percussion breaks," Tito said. This was Tito's world.

The Palladium rocked, as Tito liked to say. Club-goers of the era reported seeing stars of the period such as José Ferrer and his wife Rosemary Clooney, Marlon Brando, George Hamilton, Ava Gardner, Bob Hope, Sammy Davis Jr., Louie Prima, James Dean, Tony Martin and his wife Cyd Charise, Eartha Kitt and others. Celebrities entered discretely. If it was Wednesday you could say with absolute certainty that the stars were dancing at the Palladium. Each Wednesday night[72] the dancers glided onto the floor, dressed to kill and ready to show off the latest intricate steps that had been practiced during the previous week. The flashier the step, the more complicated the moves of each couple – the more oohs and ahs were heard. "You just did not go to the Palladium to stand around and drink," Tito related. "You had to have a new move every week. Everybody was into it – from the Barrio to upper stardom – I mean everybody grooved."

The Palladium was known not only for its music but for the exceptionally high quality and innovation of its dancers, fueled by weekly dance competitions. Ability to dance, not class or color, was the social currency inside the club. Tito's favorites were the Mambo Aces - José Centeno and Anibal Vásquez were Puerto Ricans who started dancing as a team at the Havana Madrid, and Augie and Margo. Augie Rodríguez was a New York-Dominican and Margo was Tito's cousin. The dance team appeared in a live broadcast from the Havana Riviera Hotel for the Steve Allen Tonight show in 1958, shortly before the Batista Regime collapsed and Fidel Castro took control.

Pagani introduced the Mambo Aces to Tito in 1949 and soon after they were working at the Palladium as part of the Puente orchestra floorshow. Tito had a preconceived idea of what these two dancers needed to accomplish in order to be successful. He was a dancer. Tito wanted them to be "Latino and New York at the same time." He never forgot Jimmy Cagney and George Raft moving about and being suave, smooth and still looking tough. He conveyed this to the two dance teams. Tito was as tough on the dancers, as demanding as he was on his orchestra.

Augie and Margo were also on a short leash during rehearsals. Tito never let up on them. Everything had to be just right and the Mambo Aces, and Augie and Margo lived up to his expectations. They were also busy giving mambo and later cha cha chá lessons to the ladies. They also worked the Borscht Belt in the summer with Tito.

I remember making the movie *"Mambo Kings"* with Tito. He stopped the dance sequence in the ballroom scene, shouted that "everyone is out of clave – time..." The director of the movie, Arnie Glimsher, gazed in surprise. Tito stopped the music. "Everyone is out of time," he repeated as Michael Peters (the choreographer of Michael Jackson's video –"Thriller") walked toward him. Tito then apologized but held his ground. The dance number was reshaped and the entire scene had to be restaged. The number that the dancers were unable to complete before Tito taught them some moves was *"Pa' Los Rumberos,"* which he had composed. He was always a perfectionist about music or dancing.

Many others teams followed in the footsteps of the Mambo Aces, some good, some very good and some exceptional - but for Tito The Mambo Aces had a "Cagney – Raft feel – very New York. Augie and Margo were smooth and easy." Tito often watched the dancers. It was once his passion, and he never forgot how to dance even though restricted in movement because of his injury. Sometimes, late at night while his band was on break he would have no trouble finding a suitable partner to dance with on the Palladium Ballroom floor.

One of the most popular bands to perform at the Palladium was that of Arsenio Rodríguez, whose band members included Arsenio's bassist Alfonso "El Panameño" Joseph and others. Singer Celia Cruz and the Sonora Matancera, Beny Moré and his orchestra, Orquesta Aragón and José A. Fajardo y sus Estrellas Cubanas and others came from Cuba to play there, Miguelito Valdés appeared often with Tito and Machito. The list of entertainers included Cesar Concepción y su Orquesta from Puerto Rico, Cortijo y su Combo, also from Puerto Rico, Bebo Valdés from Cuba. The list goes on and on.

The Big Three

Marcos "Sonny" Pérez who was at the Palladium one wintry night in 1954, recounted the following event for me. It provides an exciting portrait of the interaction of the three greatest bands of Afro-Cuban music ever in New

York. Tito often talked about how the three bands would gather in a jam session whenever they crossed paths, usually at the Palladium.

"It was starting to snow hard outside on Broadway. It was cold. Machito and his orchestra was playing and it was an hour before closing. The Palladium was packed. It was Wednesday night in the winter of 1954. The stars were out, the women were beautiful and the music was exhilarating. The dance floor was jam-packed and no one was making any moves to leave because of the weather. Along the side where the bar was located people stood shoulder-to-shoulder, holding drinks, just watching the band perform.

"The trumpets rose over the steady sax harmonic triads. Machito was improvising shaking the maracas with Graciela leading the chorus of vocalists. The large room was pulsating. This was straight improvisation – a chorus from one selection, a set of harmonies from another standard in the Machito repertoire, and then a change in tone and yet another popular melody. The orchestra seemed to sense the excitement of the moment. Tito Rodríguez walked out and stood a few feet from Machito. Now the two of them were singing and the dancers were stomping even harder. His dark tuxedo jacket contrasted with Machito's suit. The trumpets roared. The percussion was pounding and driving steadily. There were more dancers flowing onto the large floor.

"Now the Machito orchestra was joined by members of the Puente orchestra and from Tito Rodríguez's orchestra. The two singers – Tito and Machito smiled as Tito Puente strolled out and stood next to Monchito Muñoz. He picked up the sticks and began smacking the bell in unison with Monchito. The rest of the musicians filled the bandstand. It was René Hernández now taking an embellished and syncopated piano interlude. 'Juega' some of the band members yelled. His solo was a mixture of pure Cuban harmonies and American jazz riffs that were so familiar to him. Puente and Monchito were joined by Uba Neito, who played for Machito – was the third timbalero. The three bass players were playing in unison, every so often one would dig into a deep tumbao and the dancers would respond.

"Gradually the piano solo came to a close as the saxes – there were seven, eight – the crowded bandstand made it hard to tell, engaged with tight haunting riffs. The music built up. The trumpets slid into *'El Manisero,'* then changed to *'Lindas Cubanas,'* and several other familiar choruses. The percussion was building up. Crash! Tito was taking a solo. The room was shaking, the people were gasping with satisfaction. Tito was rolling.

Some people stopped dancing to watch him. Most continued dancing – the music was too good to stop.

"There were three men playing tumbadoras – two of them were the old style without keys for tuning – they never lost a beat. As the timbal solo ended and Tito slid back into a timekeeper mode, Patato elevated his playing. The saxophones were keeping steady time with a mixture of four and five note modulations. It seemed that the three orchestras were hell bent on keeping the lights of the Palladium on until the storm dispersed, and this was alright for the multitude of people gathered in the ballroom. Now the three drummers were conversing – soloing off of one another. No one wanted it to end.

The music continued after the percussionists slid back into a steady beat. The trumpets flared with several riffs led by Jimmy Frisaura. The saxes took over, sliding gently under the trumpets, then with a robust haunting ostinato. The dancers did not want it to end. The music began to diminish. The dancers applauded, even before the coda. Machito, and the two Titos stood together, smiling, clasped hands. It was obvious they were the kings of New York's mambo. "One more time," yelled Machito. The tempo picked up, the orchestras were rolling again. The dancers were sweating, but the moves of the couples were precise, well coordinated and even extravagant. The crowd around the bandstand was packed tight and could hardly move.

The two Titos and Machito were smiling. They were gazing into the audience with satisfaction as the music faded. It was over.

When it was over the people drifted to the coatroom. The musicians of the three bands were packing. Mario Bauzá came to the front and after a few words with Machito and the two Titos, he turned and shouted to the members of his orchestra: "Remember rehearsal at 7:00 this morning." Some rolled their eyes, other shrugged.

"Yeah," exclaimed Tito. "My guys have until 7:30 a.m. to show up."

This was typical of so many nights as Tito often pointed out. Charlie Palmieri told me that one night while he was playing his last set with his Duboney Charanga Orchestra he was joined on the bandstand by Pepe Palma of Orquesta Aragón. Between sipping Scotch whiskey drinks they played the piano, and Arsenio Rodríguez sat in with his tres. By the time they finished the members of Orquesta Aragón and Arsenio Rodríguez and his Conjunto were all on the bandstand. "The jam session lasted about 20 minutes and the people wanted us to keep on going," Charlie recalled. "It was something else."

On another occasion, as Tito was about to leave the ballroom he noticed the musicians of Orquesta Nueva Ritmo de Cuba teamed with the Tito Rodríguez Orchestra and a few minutes later were joined by some of the musicians of La Playa Sextet.

Tito had seen the flute player, José "Rolando" Lozano playing with Orquesta Aragón in Havana years earlier on one of his many visits. Orquesta Nuevo Ritmo de Cuba was not Cuban in origin. Cuban percussionist Armando Sanchez around 1958 organized it in Chicago. It featured Puerto Rican vocalist Pellin Rodríguez, who would later join Andy Montañéz in Puerto Rico as the vocalist for El Gran Combo. Lozano left Orquesta Aragón in 1955. He was contracted by Ninón Mondéjar along with his brother, Clemente (also a flautist) to play with the new Orquesta América in Mexico City. The brothers played the unadorned six-hole, five-key wooden flute. Rolando achieved fame playing for Cal Tjader and Mongo Santamaría who took over Orquesta Nuevo Ritmo, and then with George Shearing and with his own ensemble.

In 1961 he recorded with Tito's orchestra. "He was one sensational flute player. He had a knack for the Cuban music and understood the nuances of playing American jazz. He reminded me a lot of Gilberto Valdés[73] who had organized a charanga a few years earlier." I have only seen a few cats like him – Alberto Socarras who was a pioneer could do it all too. There are one or two others that could give you an almost sensual feeling." Lozano lived in California. Tito Rodríguez had experimented with several charanga recordings in 1957, while good he was unsuccessful. In 1961 he used a full charanga orchestra for his recording of "Charanga – Pachanga," on the United Artists label.

As conceited and high and mighty as the three bandleaders were, they were first and foremost showmen. They knew and understood what the public wanted. "Don't kid yourself we all wanted top billing. But if we were crossing paths, and in those days at the Palladium, we crossed paths often, we knew that the public wanted to see us perform – alone, and together. We gave them what they wanted," Tito said.

Tito's Cha Cha Cha

There are countless historical reports as to when the cha cha chá was introduced, at least in New York City. Tito visited Cuba often before it became popular. On one of those visits he saw Orquesta América probably as early as 1950. He had musical scores with compositions by Enrique Jorrín; he knew that as early as 1952 the radio stations in Havana were playing what he called "new music."

During 1954 he recorded a slew of cha cha chás that he quietly introduced to the Palladium dancers, even as Orquesta América in Havana was recording dozens of cha cha chás that would soon become the new dance craze. The members of this orchestra included Jorrín and Antonio Sanchez on violins, and Alex Sosa on piano. Sosa went to Mexico with Mondéjar, and the reconfigured Orquesta América, and finally settled in California by 1960.

Jorrín introduced his new cha cha chá to Cuban dance floors while playing with Orquesta América in1949, with his new song: *"La Engañadora."* It was not an immediate success and since it resembled the mambo there was not much to get excited about. According to Jorrín, the sound made by the shoes of the dancers on the floor sounded like "cha-cha-chá," while they tried to follow the new rhythm that, at the beginning, was simply called "mambo-rumba." The word rumba that he used should in no way be confused with the popular American style rumba of the 1930s. Jorrín was referring to the Afro-Cuban/Yorubá rumba. In 1952 he introduced his latest cha cha chá: *"Silver Star."* He continued composing new music for Orquesta América but his feud with bandleader Ninón Mondéjar was on the verge of exploding into all out war. Mondéjar, a vocalist claimed to have invented the new music that was quickly becoming popular. The new dance and its music were both known as "triple mambo" or "mambo with güiro rhythm." By 1952 the new dance had been more defined.

The Cuban composer made the new cha cha chá more distinguishable by eliminating the introduction or danzón and adding two to three voices singing in unison with little or no vibrato. The güiro and quijada (jawbone) became an integral part of the new dance. The Cuban dancers quickly adapted to the slower paced rhythm. What Tito observed was that the new Jorrín cha cha chá required very small steps because of its tempo. The rhythm is almost a series of small gliding steps that touch the floor. It is danced to 4/4 time, meaning that there are four beats to a measure. The count is slow-slow-quick-quick-slow, and dancers turn while executing the steps. Like the mambo or any other Cuban dance genre, clave is crucial. Tito enjoyed doing spins and dips, and he observed that new ones could be added, as well as a huge variety of fancy footwork.

Lock steps, turns and sideways motions are also part of the new dance, with breaks, or places where dancing stops entirely for a moment – very Cuban, according to Tito. Weight must be shifted carefully to make motions appear seamless. The cha cha chá requires a lot of hip motion, which is how dancers make it expressive. The pelvis is held in one position and left free for this motion. Although the cha-cha uses smaller steps, dancers in competition often elongate their movement slightly to travel across the floor. Alternating between long and short steps remains the key to winning a cha-cha competition.

"By the end of the summer of 1954, two out of three recordings in New York were cha cha chás and that "disc jockeys Dick "Ricardo" Sugar and Bob "Pedro" Harris plugged La Playa Sextet's *"El Jamaiquino,"* and it became the first recognized cha cha chá hit in New York City." (Mambo Kingdom, Max Salazar – 2000)

Tito heard the tune *"El Jamaiquino,"* composed by Niño Rivera, played by Arcaño y sus Maravillas around 1950, only then it was scored as a 4-beat mambo, not more rhythmically punctuated than the new cha cha chá, and with a certain bebop quality. This was one of Arcaño's favorites and he introduced it about the time that Jorrín was developing his "mambo rumba."

Arcaño expressed his own opinion of his former violin player's new dance music. "It resembled the mambo in a lot of ways. The musicians could still express themselves – improvise. It is very smooth but with extended guajeos Jorrín's montuno can be carried out to levels of sound." (Talk With Arcaño, 1989 – Marcos F. Pérez) José A. Fajardo, who was now leading his own orchestra, composed several cha cha chás in 1951 – *"Carolina,"* and *"Los Tamalitos de Olga."* Tito Rodríguez and his Orchestra recorded *"El Jamaiquino"* in 1953. Machito and his Afro-Cubans recorded the same tune for the Seeco label in 1952. Tito's version was released in 1953 on Tico.

Tito had obtained original scores and transcriptions for the new cha cha chás. He had bigger fish to fry. Working late at night in his apartment in Manhattan Tito selected 12 tunes that had been arranged for charangas. He lived alone at the time, separated from his wife now for several years. As much as he relished the pulsating nights leading his orchestra, rubbing shoulders with the rich and famous, and participating in the activities of a single man, Tito had trained himself early on to be alone so that he could integrate his music into a growing repertoire of the Tito Puente Orchestra.

He did not want to do anything fancy, just get the music recorded. He knew Pérez Prado and RCA Victor were pushing *"Cherry Pink and Apple Blossom White."* Tito's arrangement has him playing the saxophone and taking a solo in contrast to the Pérez Prado version. It was in the public domain so he included it on his list. His adaptations were simple and yet striking. There was nothing fancy about this music. He wanted to convert what Cuban rhythm, violin and flute orchestras played to a brass format – one that would be acceptable to the demanding New York Latino public.

He understood that unlike Cuba where one could be subtle, easy going and almost laid back in approaching driving rhythms – a unique contrast that did not escape him – he had to be bold and forceful with Jorrín's cha cha chá. The saxophone section would assume the role of violins, backed up by occasional trumpet riffs that Jimmy Frisaura was developing. Frisaura was aware of Tito's need for speed. Tito contracted saxophonist flautist Jerry Sanfino to do the flute work. For the two voices that were needed to give the tunes the Cuban feeling Tito decided that he and Willie Bobo would do all the singing.

He began recording the tunes between 1953 and 1954. Tito Rodríguez had already recorded *"El Jamaiquino,"* with the innovation of using the "quijada." This percussion instrument was used with the güiro or gourd in many of the Cuban charangas during the 1950s. Machito y sus Afro-Cubanos introduced the same melody with a completely different approach. Tito was determined that his version would be "completely different." The 12 songs: *"Me Lo Dijo Adela"* (Odilio Portal), *" Cero Codazos, Cero Cabezazos"* (Rafael Lay), *"El Jamaiquino"* (Niño Rivera), *"Oigan Mi Cha Cha Chá," "Cherry Pink and Apple Blossom White," "Los Tamalitos de Olga"* (José A. Fajardo), *"Vacilon*" (Rosendo Ruiz, Jr.) *"Espinita,*" (Tito Puente), *"Cógele Bien el Compás"* (Ninón Mondéjar), *"Cha Cha Chá for Lovers"* (Nick Jiménez), *"Carolina"* (José A. Fajardo) and *"Mango Mangue*" (Francisco Fellové). The selections were originally released on 78-rpm records and released in LP form on Tico in 1954.

Tito was already trying out a few new things with his two compositions. *"Espinita"* provided him a vehicle to introduce new concepts with the vibes. He was never satisfied and wanted to try out new things. A young pianist who played for the up-and-coming Joe Cuba Sextet composed the selection *"Cha Cha Chá for Lovers."* Tito, Willie and Mongo provided the vocals. "There was a lot of give and take and since it was all new we had a chance to shift gears a little – a little bit of Cuban, some New York and a lot of drive," Tito described the new rhythm. A lot of people did not realize that he was doing the vocals with his two sidemen. "We sounded very good, eh!" There was a lot of flute work on the recordings, played by Jerry Sanfino. At the Palladium the flute was played by any one of his reedmen. Tito did not want to be fancy. He wanted authenticity and sweetness. As he went along he adjusted the tempo to be more in tune with this style.

The vibes were taking hold in Afro-Cuban music, at least in the New

York region. Tito often showcased them at the Palladium. Cal Tjader and George Shearing[74] stopped by one night to see Tito and his orchestra. Jazz pianist George Shearing had recruited Tjader, hoping the vibes would add sparkle to his ensemble sound. When Shearing later decided to include Afro-Cuban music in his repertoire, Tjader played congas and played them as well as the vibes. While in New York City, bassist Al McKibbon took Tjader to see the Afro-Cuban orchestra led by Machito and Mario at the forefront of the blossoming Latin jazz sound.

Tjader also visited the Palladium with Shearing where he saw Tito playing and also met Mongo Santamaría and Willie Bobo. It was a turning point in Tjader's musical career. From that point he began moving in the direction of Afro-Cuban jazz-fusion. Shearing had experimented with Afro-Cuban music but after his visit to the Palladium he made the genre more prominent in his repertoire. Followers of Tjader maintain that once Tjader moved into the Afro-Cuban genre jazz critics dismissed him.

Tjader left Shearing in 1955 and began playing the vibes almost exclusively, and performing authentic Afro-Cuban music. He made dozens of recordings for Fantasy Records, while presenting his style of Afro-Cuban jazz on the West Coast. Tjader's approach to the mambo, according to Tito was distinctive and bold. He approached the West Coast market with a mixture of pop classic arrangements scored for the mambo, and added his own music and some from the East Coast – all in his tasteful style. In the spring of 1956, his quintet included the Duran brothers, Manuel and Carlos (bass and piano), who handled both jazz and Afro-Cuban pleasingly. Luis Miranda, a veteran of the Machito organization, teamed with Bayard Velarde to produce authentic Afro-Cuban percussive foundation.

Tito's composition *"Philadelphia Mambo,"* was among the earliest recordings made by Tjader. Basically a simple number that Tito made up on the spur of the moment, with only two chord changes in a minor key, produces a peculiar hypnotic effect, so typical of the mambo. The Tjader style of playing vibes was almost opposite of Tito's, soft and rolling. But in *"Philadelphia Mambo"* he uses the long piano montuno played by Carlos to provide a nifty improvisation and then falls back to support Duran's piano solo.

Joe Loco, Tito's childhood friend from El Barrio had formed a quintet that featured his piano and Pete Terrace on vibes in 1953. Leading the quintet Joe Afro-Cubanized versions of American standards that became popular and as a result became a regular in the jazz club circuit. He would go on to record for Tico Records, Columbia and Ansonia (an album titled

"The Music of Rafael Hernández"). Because of contractual conflicts at one point in the mid 1950s, Loco's quintet assumed the name The Pete Terrace Quintet. Joe often asked Tito to help him out and on many of the Columbia recordings Tito is heard playing the vibes. "Our contracts often meant that we could not receive credit. It was the way it was."

Louie Ramírez made his pro debut by replacing Pete Terrace in 1956. His first recording was with Joe Loco for Ansonia Records in 1957. In 1956 Pete Terrace gathered up pianist Charlie Palmieri, conga player Freddie Aguirre, bassist Julio Andino and bongocero Bobby Flash to record a classic album for Tico: *"A Night In Mambo Jazzland."* Tito referred to it as one of the best studies of the mambo and how well it was suited to jazz. "What is there not to like about it? Joe also made a lot of inroads into this fusion of jazz and mambo," Tito articulated.

The vibes and the new cha cha excited Tito – something new to incorporate into his music. After the initial Cuban style releases he began turning his attention to reshaping the cha cha chá to fit into the more progressive and percussive New York scene. He wanted the big band sound to be felt, but he did not want it to be overdone. Tito decided on making it, perhaps a little more driving than Jorrín had contemplated. The Stan Kenton approach would suffice but with considerable means to keep everything under control. He wanted to include vibes and have the saxophone voices deliver with measured softness. You have to remember that he was still looking for his sound, and while this was going on he also understood just how competitive it was – working every day, rehearsals for shows, rehearsals for recordings, scoring new music, and keeping one step up on the rivals. He never lacked energy.

Occasionally, you could walk up the stairs to the Palladium dance floor listening to the Tito Puente Orchestra and clearly hear the masterful strokes of Tito on vibes. Then suddenly see Tito playing the saxophone, playing the timbales or just standing on the side while Lionel Hampton delivered the vibe improvisation. Sometimes during a break Tito would dash up the street to Birdland, and join in with Hampton's ensemble. It was a extraordinary thing to see, according to Tito.

Teach Me Tonight

The DeCastro Sisters were a female singing group: consisting of Peggy, Cherie and Babette DeCastro. (When Babette retired in 1958, a cousin, Olgita DeCastro Marino replaced her.) In 1945, the DeCastro family moved to the United States from Cuba. The sisters became protégées of

Carmen Miranda, and formed a singing trio in Miami, Florida. They had a style something like the then-popular Andrew Sisters, but with a Latin flavor. The biggest hit for the group was *"Teach Me Tonight,"* in 1954. Tito met the sisters at La Conga Club where they were appearing as the opening act for his friend Miguelito Valdés. He introduced the three sisters to Tito.

After the introduction the young ladies made the Palladium one of their hangouts. "They loved my music," was how Tito described the relationship. Peggy, Cherie and Babette always brought a gleam to his eyes. What he remembered about his crossover recordings with the DeCastro Sisters was: "I don't know how successful the recordings I made with them were, but it sure was fun."

Band manager Jimmy recalled how Tito liked to scare them with his pranks. "He had that serious look about him – all business you know. Then when they least expected it he would crack a joke or do something silly. Sometimes he would complain to them about their being so lighthearted and dizzy. Then he would laugh. But they would roll along and sometimes even give him some of his own medicine. Tito liked them, for a while, anyway. But in those days we were very busy, trying out new things all the time. He was always restless."

The sisters worked at the Palladium for several engagements with the Tito Puente Orchestra. This was at the height of the mambo craze in 1954, and they also appeared with him at the New York Apollo Theater. To get them ready for each show he worked them hard. "Tito walked around during rehearsals with score in hand, pencil in his ear and looking damn serious. No one messed with him. When one of the girls missed a step on the floor, his look was even more severe. He would stop everything and everyone was tense. Then he would smile. He would start the music up again, walk over to the nearest sister and show her the steps and moves. Tito was light on his feet, you know."

The DeCastro Sisters began a decade earlier as a Latin act that was dropped when they were signed by the otherwise hillbilly-oriented Abbott Record label. The sisters made 31 big band accompanied recordings that were pop oriented. From Miami to Hollywood to New York City they traveled after working with Tito's band. Walt Disney invited the sisters to Hollywood to sing background vocals on *"Zip-A-Dee-Doo-Dah."* On the flip side of the 45 rpm record was *"It's Love,"* which the producers had projected to be the hit.

A Cleveland disc jockey turned it over, played it and got bags of mail. The evocative tune became the sisters' biggest hit. Novelty and pop tunes like *"Boom Boom Boomerang," "Cuckoo In The Clock," "Rockin' and*

Rollin' In Hawaii," "Cowboys Don't Cry," "Don't Call Me Sweetie," "Old Timer's Tune" the upbeat *"Biddle-Dee Bop"* and *"You Take Care Of Me* (I'll Take Care of You), torch songs like *"No One to Blame But You," "Give Me Time," "If I Ever Fall In Love," "It's Yours,"* and the country tune *"That Little Word Called Love"* were part of their repertoire "They are as full of energy, spirit and innocence as the 1950s, and very un-Cuban!" was how Tito recalled them. He felt strongly that it was his interest and involvement however briefly with the sisters' career that provided the spark to their success.

The DeCastro* sisters grew up in Cuba, though each was born in a different country - Margarita Dolores, known as Peggy, was born in the Dominican Republic, Cherie - the United States, and Babette - in Cuba. They were singing and dancing by the early 1040s and used several different variations of names as performers, including The Americanitas, The Marvel Sisters, The Fernando DeCastro Sisters, and finally they shortened it to their family name DeCastro Sisters. Their act included comedy, both intended and unintended, singing, dancing and apparent acting on stage. They appeared in the 1947 film Copacabana, and several others including The Helen Morgan Story. For nearly 40 years the DeCastro Sisters were regular performers at Las Vegas casinos and later were inducted into the Casino Legends Hall of Fame.

Stylistically, the DeCastro Sisters were a husky voiced vocal trio patterned after the Andrews Sisters, with a similar variety of romantic ballads and novelties in their songbook. Toward the late '50s, the group experimented with that era's equivalent of bubblegum music bouncy, fluffy pop/rock loaded with nonsense words.

Their recordings as the DeCastro Sisters on the Tico label with Tito's orchestra *were "Cuban Nightingale"* (Sun Sun Babae*),"I Do" and Jumbalato"* and *"Tonight I Am In Heaven."* For Tito is was a fun recording where he got to get his orchestra to support a trio of female singers – in English and Spanish. He was the only one of the three big bands to do this. Tito Rodríguez released his own version of *"Sun Sun Babae,"* that same year. It was much more successful than Tito's. "It was much more swinging than the one I did," he said. Tito played the tune at Birdland in 1952.[75]

One afternoon at the Asia eatery, Federico Pagani recalled the other "Palladium." The Club TropiCaliente[76] opened in the mid 1940s, according to Federico. "It was nothing like the Palladium, but a lot of famous people from the Boston area went there to dance, and there was always a big crowd from New York City." Club TropiCaliente was the idea of Luis

Cuevas, founder of Verne Records, and Sidney Siegel, founder of Seeco Records, the two labels of Latin music in the early 1940s. In late 1941 Cuevas and Siegel supposedly met at the Park Palace in El Barrio, and began to talk about ways to expand the market for Afro-Cuban music north of Manhattan. They recruited Federico. The three secured the financial backing from Michael Redstone, father of Sumner Redstone (of Viacom fame) and then owner of Bay Village's Latin Quarter, a Moulin-Rouge style nightclub founded by Lou Walters, father of Barbara Walters. Club TropiCaliente opened at a location on West Newton Street.

Just as celebrities flew from Miami to Havana for a single night of revelry at the Tropicana, New York region celebrities and entertainers hopped on an evening train to Boston for a night at the Boston's Afro-Cuban music hotspot. On the early morning return train, New Yorkers would catch just enough shut-eye to be able to stagger back to their offices in midtown and Wall Street. By 1952 Amtrak offered express service from Penn Station to Boston's Back Bay Station. The express train was called "The Caliente Line," while the express return trip affectionately nicknamed "The Boston Hangover." Amtrak continued the express service until 1964, and has never since managed to match the inter-city speed of those earlier trips, the fastest of which, according to legend, was 2 hours and 37 minutes, set on August 17, 1956. The club opened on New Year's Eve, to tremendous success, catapulting the club to the top of everyone's social list. Pagani contracted Xavier Cugat Orchestra, for the sets up to midnight, and for the sets after midnight, Augusto Coén y Sus Boricuas. Pagani, who used Cugat's name to attract wealthy customers, and Coén's name to attract Latino, African-American, and Jewish fans. Coén was Afro-Puerto Rican and Jewish. The "Club TropiCaliente closed its doors for good on September 28th, 1968.

"One New Year's Eve I convinced Tito and Tito Rodriguez to play at the club. I told them they would have equal billing."

Tito laughed. "Oh yeah. He did it in a smart way." Tito explained, "We were billed as 'Tito and Tito bands."

"So if you liked Tito Puente, you would say his name first. If the dancers liked Tito Rodríguez, his name would be said first. These guys had egos – very big ones," Federico said.

"Shit!" Tito laughed.

"The funny things is that some of the musicians played for both bands that night. Charlie Palmieri had two jackets, one for each band."

Between his performances at the Palladium Ballroom, playing at dances in and around New York City and traveling around the country, Tito was invited to Cuba in1957 to be honored along with dozens of Cuban musicians and entertainers that had contributed to the island's musical heritage in foreign lands. "It was an honor," Tito said, "to be standing there with all the great artists." Mario Bauzá had helped get Tito placed on the list of those to be honored, Tito became the only Puerto Rican to achieve such a distinction. The New York Palladium was on everyone's lips in the streets of Havana. It was world famous, he recalled.

"Some of the best Afro-Cuban music ever played in the United States was played at the Palladium," exclaimed Tito. He often recalled the excitement of the place, the glitter, the beautiful women, and the magical moments that he spent playing his music there. "The battles were fierce – I mean between the three of us (the two Titos and Machito). And it was not always over the music."

One night on Thanksgiving eve 1958, Tito stopped by the Palladium after finishing a performance at a nearby location, he recalled. "Arsenio was playing with José Fajardo. Wow! It was exciting. You could hear the music from the street – violins, Fajardo's high-pitched wooden flute. It was incredible. I walked into the place, it was packed. There in the middle of Fajardo's orchestra was sitting Arsenio. I understand that he knew Fajardo from Cuba – you know Fajardo played for Arcaño. The two musicians -Arcaño and Arsenio - were very close. A lot of history there that night." He smiled.

"There was so much excitement and I was not part of it," he said with a laugh. "But that was the Palladium. Federico Pagani and Catalino Rolan brought this band in from Cuba. I had seen Fajardo play in Cuba. He was very modern, dashing – willing to try anything new in music. He had two trumpets with him that night. Amandito Armenteros took a long trumpet solo and then Fajardo came in. They were good." The other trumpet player in Fajardo's charanga orchestra was Chocolate Armenteros. Fajardo's Cuban All Stars – as they were known – also featured Tata Guines on conga, Alberto Valdés (a nephew of Vicentico) on pailas cubanas (timbales) and René "Latigo" Hernández on piano.

The Saturday and Sunday following Thanksgiving Day the Tito Puente Orchestra and Fajardo y sus Estrellas Cubanas went head to head. The music that the two orchestras played was pulsating and driving. Fajardo used his five violins to provide the strong guajeos that consistently changed and shifted adding more excitement to the music. The two trumpets filled in gaps and Fajardo's powerful flute solos left people breathless. Tito was on fire too.

Tito's saxes provided the steady resounding repetitive ostinatos, and like his Cuban counterpart Fajardo, he too manipulated his horns-varying the riffs, cutting in with off-beat breaks, exploding the brass - the sounds of music were resonating, shaking the floor, driving the dancers to perform incredible acrobatic feats. Tito's ringing and resounding striking of the cowbell and the build up of his orchestra was unforgettable to those in attendance.

"It was a helluva weekend," Tito said. "Fajardo had an incredible orchestra. To look at these types of groups (charangas) you would think they were soft. But the drive of the percussion and those damn violins – it was terrific. I had to really push my guys. But we all loved it." From the confrontation so to speak, Tito got more ideas as to what he wanted to do. "Fajardo built up and drove his group. I wanted to do this too. I thought of him and of how Stan Kenton gets that build up." Fajardo and most Cuban ensembles take measured breaks. This is so especially in the Arcaño mambo style. "I liked this. It provided the listeners and dancers with juice and inspiration. You know you build up the drive of the orchestra with your saxes and then – Bang! The percussion takes a break, usually off beat, while the orchestra continues to play. Then you bring it all together and drive it home."

Many of these ideas and observations had already been incorporated into the Tito Puente style. That night merely served to inspire him and continue to move in this direction.

"Looking back – less than a month and a half later Fidel Castro would march into Havana, oust Batista and everything would change.

One of those Wednesday nights at the Palladium, Marlon Brando and Quincy Jones were waving goodbye to Tito as his orchestra filled the room with music. Brando yelled, Tito recalled, "We're are going up the street to the Birdland." He smiled and then shrugged. Quincy Jones enjoyed both genres – jazz and Afro-Cuban, but he has openly admitted that his first love was jazz. He and Brando frequented both Jazz Alley and the Palladium. Brando preferred the Palladium. As they departed down the stairs the band began playing *"That Old Black Magic.* Usually, trumpet player Gene Santori provided the vocals and was joined by Tito for the scat.

As Santori approached the microphone into the room walked Sammy Davis, Jr. The son of a black vaudeville star and a Puerto Rican dancer, Davis had not yet become the world-class actor, singer and dancer that was an integral part of the Rat Pack. He was still working with the Will Mastin Gang, but would soon be venturing out on his own. He waved at Tito and before Santori could begin the song, Davis jumped onto the state.

"Oh no you don't," he gasped. "This is my song." Santori slid back into the trumpet section and away went Sammy with the Tito Puente Orchestra backing him.[77]

Cuban baseball player Mini Minoso played for the Cleveland Indians. Whenever the team came to town he could be found after hours on the dance floor of the Palladium. On one occasion Tito and vocalist Santos Colón decided to honor him. Enrique Jorrín had already composed the popular cha cha chá *"Minoso Al Bate,"* in 1954. Tito and Santitos came up with their own rhyme during a break and applied it to Tito's melody of *"Guancona."* This is what Minoso heard that night in 1960:

"Oye Minoso ven pa'ca
Que yo te quiero ver bailar
Yo se que tu sabes jugar
Y a la pelota tu le das, ja ja.

"Oye Minoso ven pa'ca
Que yo te quiero ver bailar
Yo se que tu sabes jugar
Y a la pelota tu le das, ja ja.

"Orestes Minoso, Orestes Minoso
Eres una estrella de cubita bella.
Tierra singular
Minoso caminando de verdad!

"Oye Minoso ven pa'ca
Que yo te quiero ver bailar
Yo se que tu sabes jugar
Y a la pelota tu le das, ja ja.

"Oye Minoso ven pa'ca
Que yo te quiero ver bailar
Yo se que tu sabes jugar
Y a la pelota tu le das, ja ja."

"In a strange way I guess the Palladium was tied to Cuba, at least where music is concerned," was another of Tito's reflections. In the many years we were friends he always reminded me that we should keep close tabs on history. I tried to jot down, and make notes of our talks – "Joe make a note"

– he would say, followed by the word "history." The following is a collection of many of his different thoughts about the New York Palladium:

"The New York Palladium was a place where people came to dance to good music. All of us that played there over the years – and I am talking about me, Machito and Tito (Rodríguez) provided the best music we could. I don't mean by this that the others that played there were not good – they were. You had to be good, very good to play at the Palladium.

"Every band, ensemble, conjunto, dance act, you name it was a reflection of the best music that Latinos in New York City had to offer. It was great music. It was Afro-Cuban music with a New York twist. And when others came from the outside they understood that they had to live up to the quality the Palladium had come to demand. The orchestra members were dressed to kill, the leaders made sure everyone was on time, the music was exceptional. The dancers were beautiful. The ladies were gorgeous and their dance partners were tremendous.

"Like the musical that Lerner and Loewe composed: "Camelot," I remember when Richard Burton sings something like: 'for one fleeting moment there was… Camelot.' Well for a few years there was the New York Palladium where people – white, black, brown, Jewish, Puerto Ricans and Cubans, other Latinos, Italians, and just about everyone came through the doors of the New York Palladium, forgot their problems and just listened to the best music and danced away their problems, for a few hours anyway."

Tito's Cuban Carnaval

Occasionally Tito expressed his annoyance about the departure of Vicentico Valdés. It caused him to rethink about what he was doing in terms of his own music. Did he need a strong singer with his band? Always looming in the shadows, so to speak, were the orchestras of his mentor Machito y sus Afro-Cubanos and his childhood friend Tito Rodríguez. Both orchestras were known for their consistently strong vocalization – Machito and Tito. They had sensational voices. But each one kept the singing to a limited role – support for the orchestra. Tito believed that it was the whole rather than the single star or singer that made the orchestra. The orchestra was everything, it was the showpiece.

Stories and official reports that Tito and Vicentico had a falling out over top billing during a performance in Los Angeles spread quickly. Vicentico had a big following on the West Coast among the Mexican American fans, so his name was placed above Tito's. Fact is that Tito did not fire his favorite singer. Vicentico went off to try being a bandleader. "He was one of the best," Tito often affirmed. However, this said there is no denying that Tito was something of an egomaniac when it came to whose name appeared on the top of a marquee. He always battled for his name to be on top. Years later Tito and Vicentico would share the stage, travel to Cuba together, and remain friendly.

Vicentico quickly started his own orchestra that included Manny Oquendo as one of the prominent sidemen. Interestingly, the departure of Oquendo, who had been with Tito's ensemble from the start, bothered my friend more than the exodus of Vicentico. They had been friends as youths in El Barrio. They rarely spoke after Manny joined the Valdés band. Mongo was already with Tito. He had replaced Frankie Colón, who was drafted as a result of the Korean conflict and Willie Bobo came on to replace Oquendo. Willie also served as Mongo's translator. The abrupt departure of Vicentico was followed by Tito's next misstep, taking on Gilberto Monroig. He was a great singer. But he had more demons in his closet than could be contained. "He was the most unreliable guy I every had the misfortune to deal with. He had a terrific voice, but he caused us a lot of grief," Tito said, and Frisaura agreed.

"So the question became what do we do?" Jimmy said. "Tito pondered the situation for a few days. He wanted to wait and see if this guy would turn around. He did not. He was always late, and sometimes he did not even show up. I wanted to dump him but Tito held out hope. Well, it did not work out."

When he made his decision it was firm and final. Tito did fire Monroig and at the same time decided he would not look for a new singer. He decided he wanted to explore the many aspects of Afro-Cuban music. He had seen much during his visits to Cuba. He felt that he could connect his vision of American jazz with Cuban harmonies and rhythms – not like had been done before and in a way that would capture the interest of a wide public. The mambo was king and the cha cha chá was taking hold.

There was the new rhythm of the cha cha chá that he had heard while on one of his "in and out" visits to Havana. "The two voices, sometimes three voices, all singing in unison," had sparked his interest. "I wanted to try something like it and with Gilberto gone, I got the idea to do this – the chorus – with me, Willie and Mongo."

Everybody Does Mambo and Cha Cha Cha

One night Tito, Jimmy and Willie were having coffee around the corner from the Brooklyn Paramount. "Tito and Willie got into it after a young woman exclaimed that Willie was really good tonight. Back and forth they went and when Mongo came in they tried to get him into the discussion – it was getting loud and ugly."

"Tito turned to Mongo. 'Who is a better drummer?' Mongo looked at me. He shrugged. In a mixture of Spanish and English he finally said 'You are like a married couple and if I get into it you will both put me down as the reason for a divorce.' Thank God for Mongo's sense of humor! It was always like that with Tito and Willie. They loved each other. But then it got serious. We started talking about the future and Tito was already there." The Tito Puente Orchestra was probably at its busiest during this period, and would befor the next few years. Some say that this was the beginning of Tito's golden period. It may well have been.

By 1954 there were two kinds of mambos that people danced in the United States. There was the mambo inspired by the so-called "Rey del Mambo" Damaso Pérez Prado and his Orchestra. People stood on lines in Los Angeles and other points on the West Coast to see his brand of mambo and Afro-Cuban music. The other type of mambo was the strong percussive Afro-Cuban style that was the rage in New York. Several "Mambo USA" shows were planned, promoted and conducted in the early 1950s, none with any significant success. In 1954 one got underway at New York's Apollo Theater with Tito 's *"Mambo Birdland"* the opening number. The list of bands included Joe Loco Quintet, Pupi Campo Orchestra with Candido Camero, Cuban vocalist Mercedes Valdés, Puerto Rican singer Myrta Silva, and Gilberto Valdés and his charanga orchestra. The sparkling lineup did little to promote the stronger New York styles. In fact it was a dismal flop. There were other tours between concerts and dances around New York.

A mambo show traveled to Boston, Philadelphia, Cleveland, Chicago, San Francisco, and St. Louis and finally into Miami. Tito said, "We had to opt out of going to the southern parts because most of our guys were black. Maybe this had some impact on our ability to expand our popularity. But I think it had to do more with our type of music. It remained truer to the roots – Afro-Cuban. Most Americans liked the rumba so it was obvious they would take to the lighter mambos played on the West Coast. It was the style introduced by Pérez Prado and pushed by RCA Victor. I don't think any of us – bandleaders and musicians - were going to change our format. Remember we were much closer to the original mambos that were coming out of Cuba. I guess our heritage being so closely knotted also helped, you know Cuban and Puerto Rican."

The mambo show journey as far as Jimmy was concerned was anything but fun. The musicians had to stay in pretty dismal hotels. "They were flop houses," according to Jimmy. "The food was not too good either." There were frequent nights the artists of the Mambo Show played for 20 or 30 people in some of those cities. It was not the Palladium, Tito remembered.

Although disappointed by the lack of national acceptance, Tito felt good about the pathway he was taking. He was happy to get back to New York, playing for a public that revered him and his orchestra. The Palladium never looked better.

Everybody was recording the mambo during those days. Vaughn Monroe recorded *"They Were Doing The Mambo."* This was followed by Perry Como's *"Papa Loves Mambo,"* and then with Rosemary Clooney's *"Mambo Italiano."* In December as Tito prepared to move to RCA Victor, a slew of Christmas mambos were released, including Pete Rugelo's *"Jingle Bell Mambo."* Popular bands like Xavier Cugat's played mambo. There was an *"Arthur Murray Mambo"* – originally Tito's *"Picadillo."* It was recorded for SMC.

Arthur and Kathryn Murray[78] visited the Palladium frequently. They were huge fans of Tito Puente, the mambo and the craze permitted them to expand their network of dance studios. "They were nice people. They danced smoothly, although I don't think that their style was up to what the dancers were doing in the Palladium. Still, they were nice people," Tito observed. Tito often partnered with Kathryn Murray on the dance floor of the Palladium. "It was good for business," Tito laughed.

During 1955 Tito and his orchestra continued to ascend in popularity. His mambo was fiery and experimental. *"Puente In Percussion,"* was released by Tico Records in 1955 and featured only three percussionists, Mongo Santamaría, Willie Bobo and guest artist Carlos Patato Valdéz. Bobby Rodríguez was on bass. It was a reluctant George Goldner that gave Tito the okay to proceed, not expecting the album to produce much in the way of revenues. Tito was satisfied with the results, the sales and the achievement of his excursion into the African roots of Cuban music.

He was living in Manhattan so it was easy to get to and from work. He rode the subway, which suited him since he did not have to cope with rush hour crowds. If the subway was too crowded he would walk – he enjoyed walking the streets of New York. He indulged in numerous romantic interludes some more serious than others and some considerably problematic. In 1953 he met Aida Pereira with whom he had a son, Richard Puente. The romance was not long lasting, and one of many during this time. But it was contentious. Richard, who became a successful musician with the disco group Foxy, died in his sleep July 19, 2004, as a result of injuries sustained in a mugging 10 years earlier.[79] Although not inclined to the Afro-Cuban music his father pursued, he had a successful career that included two Grammy nominations and two gold records. He was 51-years-old.

Aida traveled to Havana with Tito, according to her younger son, Ari Carlini. "My mother was very friendly with a great many stars, including Sammy Davis, Jr., Shirley McLain, George Raft, Shelly Winters, Buddy Hackett, Warren Beatty, Buck Henry and Morgana King. 'I even met gangster Meyer Lansky twice as a kid! My mother used to dance in Havana, Cuba at one of his hotels; that was before Fidel Castro came to power,'"[80] Tito met Aida at the Palladium while he was performing. The affair soured before Aida gave birth. Tito's quixotic affairs were many throughout his life. Some have been documented, some were tempestuous, and some were troublesome. Legends about his promiscuity have arisen. He was always looking beyond the horizon, and adventure and romance intrigued him, excited him and even drove him. Tito acknowledged some of his favorite women through designation as composers of some of his recordings: *"Guayaba"* (Ercilia Ortiz – Tito's mother); *"Ah Ha"* (1962), Aida Pereira), *"Mambolero"* (Milta Sanchez – first wife), and *"Margie's Mood"* (Margie Puente – his widow).

In 1955 he refined his technique of cha cha chá and expanded the orchestra's repertoire. The orchestra he would showcase for the next decade was solidly shaped – it was quite a band. It was as big as the Stan Kenton Orchestra and as talented, skilled and experienced in the jazz venue as any existing orchestra of the period. At this juncture he did not miss any of his vocalists. "In fact, Willie and I did the choruses just fine. Mongo chipped in and when we needed someone it was just for that particular occasion," was Tito's view.

"Mongo liked to kid Tito and Willie about their relationship. 'Maybe you two guys could become a famous singing duet like they have in Cuba.' I thought it was funny," Jimmy said.

Tito was satisfied that in terms of experience he had the right group of people. There would be changes along the way but with Jimmy by his side, Tito felt that with this orchestra he would be able to indulge in innovative forages, explore jazz, Afro-Cuban rituals, orchestrate techniques for the American standards, and introduce Afro-Cuban big band music to places where it had not been heard before.

Tito Moves to RCA Victor

When Morris Levy offered Tito an opportunity to return to RCA Victor he considered it carefully. RCA Victor was a complex corporate structure that was not particularly suited to the aspirations of a New York Puerto Rican bandleader, nor was it attempting to reach the growing U.S. Latino market. But RCA Victor gave Tito the break he was seeking to expand his musical interests and to produce some of the ideas that had been spinning in his head since he organized his first orchestra. Tico Records was maintaining a narrow point of view as far as permitting Tito to experiment. Tito's vocalists – Vicentico and Monroig – were gone. He had developed a special relationship over the years with Levy, who now was in charge of the RCA Victor Birdland Series. It was time to move on.

"RCA was a big company. I knew they were pushing a more toned down version of the mambo. They liked Pérez Prado's style – it fit into their picture of Afro-Cuban music. I don't think they were sure just what to make of violin orchestras like Orquesta Aragón. These guys were successful, but they did not fit in somehow. They (RCA Victor) had had a lot of problems in introducing the long play albums – it cost them dearly to favor the 45-rpm records. I would be a small fish in a big ocean. But in the jazz division of RCA Victor I would be able to try some new things. My music would have a wider market, even if they (executives) were not sure how to market the music. I took the shot," Tito said during one of our talks about his work at the large record company.

The RCA Victor Company[81] throughout the 1940s and leading into the 1950s, made a series of technological and marketing blunders that cost the record label substantial revenues and limited its ability to contract Latin entertainers. In 1949, RCA Victor developed and released the first 45-rpm record to the public, answering CBS/Columbia's 33⅓ rpm "Long Play" record.[82] The 45-rpm record became the standard for pop singles with running times similar to 10-inch 78-rpm discs (less than four minutes per side). However, RCA also released some extended play (EP) discs with running times up to 10 minutes, primarily for classical recordings. (One of the first of the extended 45-rpm recordings was a disc by Arthur Fiedler and the Boston Pops Orchestra featuring Tchaikovsky's *"Marche Slave"* and Ketelbey's *"In a Persian Market."* A number of Tito Puente Orchestra recordings from 1949-51 were packaged into 45-rpm extended play albums. These were later re-packaged into long play albums. The 45-rpm did not catch on and in 1950, realizing that Columbia's LP format had become successful and fearful that RCA was losing market share, RCA Victor began issuing long plays.

But by this time much of its Latin American market and a large market share of the United States had diminished. The executives countered by signing Damaso Pérez Prado and his orchestra to push his version of Afro-Cuban music that had become popular in Mexico. It also sought to place under contract popular Cuban orchestras like Orquesta Almendra in 1955, Orquesta América (Mexico) 1955-57, and the father of the cha cha chá, Orquesta Enrique Jorrín (Mexico) 1954-57. Later it added Beny Moré and his Orchestra (Cuba). The company never marketed these in the United States leaving a clear field for Pérez Prado and Orquesta Aragón, which were contracted in 1953 in Havana. Pérez Prado was clearly RCA Victor's darling.

Early Tito Puente Orchestra recordings, 1949-1951, were issued on 78-rpm and then converted to 45-rpm extended play and 10-inch 33 1/3-rpm albums. But despite the popularity of his orchestra on the East Coast, the company limited the marketing. The promotional function did not consider that the Puente style of music, or for that matter, his chief competitor, Tito

Rodríguez and his Orchestra, would catch on elsewhere in the United States.

While Tito was recording for Tico, RCA concentrated on the classics and trying to figure out how to sell long play albums. Among the first RCA LPs released was a performance of *"Gaite Parisienne"* by Jacques Offenbach with Arthur Fiedler and the Boston Pops Orchestra, which had actually been taped in Boston's Symphony Hall on June 20, 1947; it was given the catalogue number LM-1001. Popular albums were issued with the prefix "LPM." When RCA later issued classical stereo albums (in 1958), they used the prefix "LSC." Popular stereo albums were issued with the prefix "LSP." In the 1950s, RCA had three subsidiary or specialty labels: Groove, Vik and "X". Label "X" was founded in 1953 and renamed Vik in 1955. Groove was an R&B specialty label founded in 1954.

Through the 1940s and 1950s, RCA was in competition with Columbia Records. A number of recordings were made with the NBC Symphony Orchestra, usually conducted by Arturo Toscanini; sometimes RCA utilized recordings of broadcast concerts. When the NBC Symphony was reorganized in the fall of 1954 as the Symphony of the Air, it continued to record for RCA, as well as other labels, usually with Leopold Stokowski. RCA also released a number of recordings with the Victor Symphony Orchestra, later renamed the RCA Victor Symphony Orchestra, which was usually drawn from either Philadelphia or New York musicians, as well as members of the Symphony of the Air. By the late 1950s RCA had fewer high prestige orchestras under contract than Columbia: RCA recorded the Chicago Symphony Orchestra and the Boston Symphony Orchestra, whereas Columbia had the Cleveland Orchestra, the Philadelphia Orchestra, and the New York Philharmonic Orchestra.

On October 6, 1953, RCA conducted experimental stereophonic sessions in New York's Manhattan Center with Leopold Stokowski conducting a group of New York musicians in performances of Enesco's *"Rumanian Rhapsody No. 1"* and the waltz from Tchaikovsky's opera *"Eugene Onegin."* There were additional stereo tests. Initially, RCA used RT-21 ¼ inch tape recorders (which ran at 30 inches per second), wired to mono mixers, with Neumann U-47 cardioid and M-49/50 omni-directional microphones. Then they switched to an Ampex 300-3 ½ inch machine, running at 15 inches per second (which was later increased to 30 inches per second). These recordings were initially issued in 1955 on special stereophonic reel-to-reel tapes and then, beginning in 1958, on vinyl LPs with the logo "Living Stereo." Sony BMG has continued to reissue these recordings on CD.

In September 1954, RCA introduced 'Gruve-Gard' where the center and edge of a disc are thicker than the playing area, reducing scuffmarks during handling and when used on a turntable with a record changer. Most of RCA Victor Records' competitors quickly adopted the raised label and edges. The Toscanini stereo albums, however, were never issued by RCA (they were the last two concerts he conducted with the NBC Symphony Orchestra). They were not issued until 1987 and 2007 respectively, when they appeared on compact disc on the Music and Arts label, and betrayed no sign whatsoever of the Maestro's apparent memory loss in the last concert, probably because the rehearsals had also been taped in stereo and portions of them were included in the final edit.

Tito Rodríguez had signed with RCA Victor in 1953 thus stoking the fires that the two friends – the two Titos – were really feeling ill will toward each other. The fact is that there was a fierce competition between the two bandleaders, but the two boyhood friends were still on speaking terms, and Tito was even arranging music for his friend. "We let it fester," claimed Tito. "It was good for business. Maybe we were not as close as we used to be. We were busy trying to earn a living. But we were not archenemies. But we kept it to ourselves." It was well known in musical circles that Rodríguez was not happy with Tico Records or RCA Victor Records and that he disliked bandleader and booking agent José Curbelo. So he opted to book his own band. "I can't speak for Tito (Rodríguez) but he was sitting in the middle of a company that was big and constantly changing its mind. Like me Tito (Rodríguez) knew that RCA Victor was pushing Pérez Prado. He took a chance early. I followed later. I guess it worked out for him even though the record company tended to shove us aside," Tito recalled. Rodríguez had mixed success while he was with RCA Victor. He returned to Tico in 1958 shortly after the long play album *"Senor Tito"* was released.

In 1955, RCA purchased the recording contract of Elvis Presley from Sun Records for the then astronomical sum of $35,000. Elvis would become RCA's biggest selling recording artist. His first gold record was "Heartbreak Hotel," recorded in January 1956. In 1955 Damaso Pérez Prado received a Gold Record from RCA for the success of *"Cerezo Rosa,"* (re-titled – *Cherry Pink and Apple Blossom White*). In 1956 the Tito Puente Orchestra was wooed back to RCA Victor. Tito knew that he would have to work hard to convince the powers that be to market his music to a wider audience. He was ready to do this. There were other dynamics at work and Tito was well aware that he would have to fight to get his music properly promoted – it was worth it, he thought.

In 1957, RCA ended its 55-year association with EMI and signed a distribution deal with Decca Records, which caused EMI to purchase Capitol Records. Capitol then became the main distributor for EMI recordings in North and South America with RCA distributing its recordings through Decca in the United Kingdom on the RCA and RCA Victor labels with the lightning bolt logo instead of the His Master's Voice Nipper logo RCA set up its own British distribution in 1971.

In the Afro-Cuban market (that later was designated Latin American and now salsa) sale of 50,000 units or albums would constitute a Gold Record. Pérez Prado's *"Cherry Pink and Apple Blossom White"* sold as a single, reached the plateau of one million, unheard of in the American music market. Tito's *"Dance Mania"* album sold close to 50,000 units. No other bandleader in the Afro-Cuban music genre ever came that close – not even Machito and the Afro-Cubans. American pop standards for Gold designation were much higher.

Morris Levy (August 27, 1927 - May 21, 1990) became an American music industry executive, who is best known as the owner of the record label Roulette Records. Levy and Tito would become good friends with Levy being dubbed by many as "Tito's Godfather." He was born Moishe Levy in the Bronx. Levy is also frequently referred to as "The Godfather of the American music business" because of his alleged links with the Mafia (specifically the Genovese family).[83] His detractors claim that he cheated many of his black artists out of royalties and it is reputed that he was in the habit of falsely claiming authorship of songs. After leaving the Navy he became the proprietor of numerous night clubs in New York at the dawn of the bebop movement in the late 1940's -- the most famous of which was Birdland, which Levy supposedly took over from mobster Joseph "Joe the Wop" Catalano in 1949.

During this period Levy learned the value of owning the publishing rights of a piece of music - as each time a song he owned was performed or played he was entitled to royalties. As a result he founded his first publishing company, Patricia Music, and commissioned George Shearing to compose a signature piece for the club -- the celebrated *"Lullaby of Birdland."* He founded Roulette Records in 1956, where he began his supposed practice of claiming authorship on many early songs of the rock-and-roll era that he did not have a hand in composing. A notable case is the song *"Why Do Fools Fall In Love."* originally recorded by Frankie Lymon and the Teenagers, which is presumed to have been wholly written by lead singer Frankie Lymon.

In the mid-1970s Levy filed a much-publicized lawsuit against John Lennon for appropriating a line from the Chuck Berry song, *"You Can't Catch Me*" (Levy owned the publishing rights) in The Beatles' song *"Come Together."* Lennon ultimately settled with Levy by agreeing to record three songs from Levy's publishing catalogue during the sessions for his long play album *"Rock & Roll."* Levy sold Roulette Records and his publishing rights for an estimated $55 million.

Jimmy often related how he and Tito would sit in Levy's office and discuss "things." He would smile. I asked for details. Both Tito and Jimmy shrugged. Jimmy did say that Levy always got an earful from Tito about the industry.

"'They are always fucking us,' was Tito's opening line," according to Jimmy. "Morris would snarl and then groan, and then slide back in his big chair and calmly listen to Tito. 'We are treated like crap, shit. That fucking Pérez Prado… All the shit heads in this company are running around kissing his ass.' On and on went Tito," smiled Jimmy. "Then Morris would sit up, after a while and in his gruff voice tell Tito not to worry. "We will take care of the cock suckers, don't you worry." Then we would all laugh and talk about other things."

The rumors that Tito, and more likely Jimmy, had the blessing of Mafia bosses never subsided and as time went on even grew. Neither Tito nor Jimmy confirmed this, nor did they reject it. "Tito and Morris were both Navy guys," quipped Jimmy amusingly whenever the subject came up. Tito would shrug, role his eyes and smile. "Next!" he would growl.

Although investigations into his affairs began in the early 1950s, it was not until 1986 that law officials caught up with Levy. Levy was tried and convicted on charges of extortion but died in Ghent, New York before serving any time in prison. Over the years Tito and Levy developed a strong relationship and when Tito's mother passed away in 1978 he sent Tito a substantial amount of money-five figures. It was no wonder Tito decided to move over to RCA Victor at his friend's urging.

About the time Tito and his orchestra were preparing to begin recording the first RCA Victor Capitol Records released *"Stan Kenton And His Orchestra – Progressive Jazz."* The selection *"Cuban Carnival"* was recorded on side A. It was composed by Kenton protégé Pete Rugolo. The length of the selection was 2.45 and opened gingerly with the percussion that featured José Mangual, Carlos Vidal and of all people, Machito. The syncopated 3-4 Afro tempo slowly builds and builds and erupts into a frenzied 4-4 motif. Then with the Kenton panache it explodes and ends suddenly. "It was daring for its time," moaned Jimmy remembering the piece of music.

"Oh yes, yes! He (Kenton) was always out there. But what I had in mind for our album was lot different – a departure from what was being done," smiled Tito.

The recording sessions began in January 1956 and with each passing week and month the Tito Puente Orchestra produced history-making albums. One of the first sessions at Webster Hall in New York City was the 2.21-minute piece – *"Mama Inez"* (Moisés Simon). The melody went back to the early 1920s and had been done by orquesta tipicas, trios and conjuntos. It had been arranged as a danzón, a son and a rumba. Tito decided to open the piece as a very fast rumba that is introduced by the flashy trumpet section and then carried with the sax section playing a repeated riff or guajeo. The rhythm changes to a cha cha chá and Tito inserts his vibe solo while Alvin Gellers lays down a varied montuno. Finally, the orchestra closes out with a crisp merengue. The picture that emerges with the first recording is the beginnings of Tito's panoramic sense of Afro-Cuban music played by a big band.

On April 3, 1956 Tito Puente and his orchestra went into Webster Hall Studios to begin recording on the RCA Birdland label. As the orchestra set up "I told Tito, 'we have come a long way.' He looked at me, smiled and started barking out instructions of how he wanted things – you know, the taskmaster," Jimmy recalled.

Webster Hall[84] has a long history. Located in the heart of the East Village – East 11th Street, between Third and Fourth Avenues, it was originally built in 1886 by architect Charles Rentz and soon became the nation's first modern nightclub. It was a place where one could witness figures such as Emma Goldman (the outspoken exponent of Anarchist philosophy) herald the cause of free love and birth control on one night and, on the next night, see the refined atmosphere and grace of a society function celebrating New York's elite. Margaret Sanger led strikers to the building in 1912. Other patrons from the club's early years include painters Marcel Duchamp and Joseph Stella. During Prohibition, the theme of the balls held in the hall moved from the social and political trends to the pleasure-seeking manner of the speakeasy. Local politicians and police were said to turn a blind eye to the merrymakers who attended, despite, or perhaps because of, whispers that the venue was owned by the infamous mobster Al Capone. Appropriately, Prohibition's repeal was the cause for one of Webster Hall's biggest celebrations, "The Return of John Barleycorn."

In the 1950s, Webster Hall began featuring concerts from a diverse group of artists. The two Titos played at the club. So, too, did folk artists Pete

Seeger and Woody Guthrie. RCA Records recognized the extraordinary acoustical integrity of the building and converted it into their East Coast recording venue, Webster Hall Studios. "It was a perfect setting," according to Tito. "The acoustics was perfect for the mixture of brass and percussion we were going to be using." Others that used the studio included Carol Channing for the recording of *"Hello Dolly!"* and Harold Prince *recorded "Fiddler on the Roof."* Other luminaries such as Julie Andrews, Elvis Presley, Tony Bennett, Ray Charles, Harry Belafonte, and Frank Sinatra were in Webster Hall for recordings.

New York – Havana Influences

The orchestra that Tito assembled by 1956 was perhaps one of the most formidable and powerful in terms of musicians that he ever led. We often discussed this period and he usually agreed that from the mid point of the 1950s to the mid 1960s, the orchestra he led might have been incomparable to anything that came afterward. Tito and Jimmy had recruited the best musicians that they could find in and around New York.

Tito's 18-piece orchestra was full of life, skillful, persuasive and potent and had the sparkle that its leader desired. It included the likes of Bernie Glow, who began professionally in his early twenties, joining the popular Artie Shaw band for a stint that lasted several years. In 1947, he worked for two different and demanding big band leaders, the precise and unique Boyd Raeburn and the consistently high energy Woody Herman. In the 1950s he worked in New York studios on more than 100 sessions. He recorded on and off with Benny Goodman from 1955 to 1965, until a fight about a faulty music stand light ended their relationship. The trumpeter continued to perform and recorded with jazzman Bob Brookmeyer, taking part in Davis and Evans projects and teaming up with Dizzy Gillespie, the cream of the bop crop, in 1961.

A versatile trumpeter with a wide range, an appealing tone and strong technical skills, Nick Travis spent much of his abbreviated career as a studio musician although he was a terrific jazz improviser too. Travis picked up early experience playing professionally from the age of 15. He worked with Johnny McGhee, Vido Musso (1942), Mitch Ayres and Woody Herman between1942-44, before serving in the military. After his discharge, Travis played with many bands including Ray McKinley, Benny Goodman, Gene Krupa, Ina Ray Hutton, Tommy Dorsey, Tex Beneke, and Woody Herman again (1950-51), Jerry Gray, Bob Chester, Elliot Lawrence and Jimmy Dorsey (1952-53). Travis gained some recognition for his work as a key soloist with the Sauter-Finegan Orchestra (1953-56) but then he went into the anonymous world of the studios as a member of the NBC staff. Nick Travis emerged now and then, playing section parts with Gerry Mulligan's Concert Jazz Orchestra during 1960-62 and performing at Lincoln Center with Thelonious Monk's medium-size group in late 1963. He died unexpectedly in 1964 at the age of 38, from ulcers. Nick Travis led a record date of his own for RCA Victor in 1954, and he was also well featured on recordings with the small groups of Al Cohn (1953) and Zoot Sims (1956).

The trumpet section was rounded out with Frisaura and his friend Gene Rapeti. Frisaura was Tito's stalwart manager who had been a key to the success of the orchestra to date – his managerial ability served Tito well. And, in addition to paying the bills, following up on all the administrative tasks, his horn was strong and precise. "Even though we fought tooth and nail," Jimmy said, "we were inseparable. But I always had to be on my guard because Tito liked to play tricks – when you least expected it."

In the saxophone section was veteran Jerry Sanfino, who also frequently worked for the Tito Rodríguez Orchestra and was the featured flautist in his 1955 RCA Victor Rodríguez charanga recording endeavor; Marty Holmes; Ed Caine; Sol Schlinger, a veteran of the Benny Goodman Orchestra; Allen Fields; José "Pin" Madera and Dave Kutzer. Holmes was born in Brooklyn, and as a young man dabbled with violin and got into the reed family as a teenager. He picked up piano on his own and by the late ′40s had found employment in a series of dance bands. The Holmes surname was a stage name, probably changed from the original Hausman due to public distaste for all things German in this time period. The Puente connection would be long lasting and result in at least a dozen albums. He also did stints with Neil Hefti and Tommy Reynolds, among others. The sole Holmes solo effort was the festive Art Ford's *"Party for Marty,"* originally released in 1959.

The trombones were Santo Russo, Eddie Bert, Robert Ascher and Sam Takvorian. Russo was another Brooklyn native who also played the violin. In 1947 he played with Lee Castle and in 1949 joined the Artie Shaw Orchestra. Throughout the early 1950s he was busy playing with Art Mooney, Jerry Wald and Buddy Rich and with the Dorsey band. In addition to his big band and jazz affiliations he was also an active musician on Broadway.

Tito's percussion was one of the most powerful ever assembled at this time in the United States – and probably ever. Tito would always dispute this saying that Machito and the Afro-Cubans had the best percussion. Tito's percussion included Mongo Santamaría, who also played bongo;

Willie Bobo, who played just about every Afro-Cuban percussive instrument that was available and also American drums; Candido Camero, and Carlos "Patato" Valdéz. Patato's melodic conga playing made him a giant of Afro-Cuban jazz in Cuba and then for more than half a century in America. Patato died December 8, 2007 in Cleveland. He was 81 and lived in Manhattan.

Patato was born in Havana, played in the 1940s and early 1950s with such conjuntos as Sonora Matancera and Conjunto Casino. He became a star in the early days of Cuban television for his skillful playing and for his showmanship; his signature song was *"El Baile del Pingüino"* ("The Penguin Dance"), which was recorded with Conjunto Casino. He came to the United States in the early 1950s and settled in New York, where he quickly established himself as an indispensable player, performing and recording with the top names in jazz and Afro-Cuban music. He played with Dizzy Gillespie, Machito, Kenny Dorham, Art Blakely and Elvin Jones; he played with Herbie Mann from 1959 to 1972. The drums he played were tuned tightly to produce clear, precise tones, and he popularized the playing of multiple conga drums. He was known for his harmonious style and sharp precise playing. Candido Camero was born April 22, 1921, and is a Cuban percussionist who has backed many Afro-Cuban jazz and jazzmen since the 1950s. Early on he had recorded in his native Cuba with various ensembles. He moved to New York in 1952, and started recording with Dizzy Gillespie. During 1953-54 he was in the Billy Taylor quartet and in 1954 he performed and recorded with Stan Kenton. He has performed on numerous occasions with Tony Bennett. He was honored with the National Endowment for the Arts Jazz Masters Award.

John Rodríguez dubbed by Bauzá as "La Vaca" (the cow) rounded out the percussion unit. There was also Jimmy "La Vaca" Rodríguez, a percussionist (timbalero) who played for José Curbelo and La Playa Sextet. Up to the time John "Vaca" Rodríguez joined Puente for this particular recording, he had worked for nearly 50 different ensembles dating back to 1945. The list included Esy Morales, Miguelito Valdés, Noro Morales, Rene Touzet, Pete Terrace and Stan Kenton. On and off he also played for the Tito Rodríguez Orchestra. He was born in New York City to Puerto Rican parents. Federico Pagani got him a job with Tito's Picadilly Boys who were appearing at the Palladium on Labor Day in 1948. The "vente tu" or pickup group included Charlie Palmieri on piano, Luis Miranda and Frisaura among others. He provided a versatility and steadiness that made him a tremendous asset to the orchestra.

Tito called up jazz pianist Alvin Gellers at Charlie Palmieri's suggestion. Charlie was supposed to take over the piano slot but because of previous commitments – he had organized his own ensemble among other things – Gellers got the job. He was a New York Jew with exceptional musical abilities, including being able to sight-read and assist Tito in developing the intricate scores for the rest of the band. "Gellers' understanding of Afro-Cuban music made him a perfect fit," was how Tito described his piano player. When Gellers departed to pursue jazz music Tito recruited Ray Coen and then Gilberto López. Personal problems forced the departure of Coen.

Bobby Rodríguez was the bassist. He had been with Machito for several years and had participated in several historic sessions with Arsenio Rodríguez, René Hernández and Chano Pozo. He was a large man and his bass was just what Tito was looking for.

The uneasiness that Tito had as he prepared the music, rehearsed with his orchestra and continued with an active live performance schedule, was that his sound be authentic and distinct. Like most bandleaders of the period the one thing that Tito did not want was to sound anything like the orchestras of his chief competitors. He wanted to represent Afro-Cuban music in its purest form. His orchestra reflected the influences of the American big band swing era and the bebop period. Tito was drawn to the Kenton robust progressive style. But he knew that he was different. His percussion section was pure and deep. It was authentic and was an integral part of the orchestra. Kenton's format called for Afro-Cuban rhythms to support the brass.

His frequent excursions to Havana led him to discover that what was happening in New York in terms of the three top Afro-Cuban style orchestras that were popular along the East Coast was having a profound impact on the way Cuban music was being played. The charangas and conjuntos were the popular musical ensembles of the day. The large bands, and there were plenty, mainly played the hotels and large cabarets. "They did not swing like I did, or Tito (Rodríguez), or Machito did," was his opinion. "They played mostly for a white society type crowd – not much on swing. But it was changing."

Up to this point Cuban brass bands consisted of eight to 12 musicians and had limited or light percussion – this may have been due to prohibitions imposed by the government. The famous ensembles through the 1940s and into the early 1950s included Casino de la Playa, Hermanos Palau Orchestra, Havana-Riverside Orchestra, De O. Estivil Orchestra and Julio Cuevas to name a few. Aresenio Rodríguez and his giant conjunto included a full array of percussion. His friend Miguelito Valdés often confirmed

Tito's observations. "There was a lot of animosity to African music in the upper classes," Miguelito noted. "African percussion was kept out of the mainstream, at least until the 1950s."

American jazz was impacted in much the same way. Black musicians for the most part stayed away from deep African style percussion. "There were several reasons," Tito explained often. "The black musician wanted to break away from our roots and enter the mainstream. They (black jazz musicians) wanted to play for a larger base, expose the white population to 'cool jazz.' Dizzy and a few others did not care. Dizzy dove into the Afro-Cuban sounds headfirst, and so did Stan Kenton. They liked what we were doing. He worked with Arsenio, Machito and Chano."

By the 1950s Orquesta Riverside was formed, along with several others. Beny Moré returned to Cuba in 1953 and formed his "giant" orchestra. Chico O'Farrill began experimenting with large American style bands that included more percussion in the 1940s with the Machito band. For the next 50 years he would be one of the innovators who helped fuse the Afro-Cuban rhythms with the American jazz harmonies within the framework of the big band. O'Farrill was a true master of jazz compositions who was able to embrace his love of Latin rhythms with sweeping styles of such classical composers as Debussy, and Stravinsky.

He was born to an Irish-German-Cuban family and was expected to follow his father into the family law firm, after some training at an American military school. However, once in the United States he became influenced by the big bands of Benny Goodman, Artie Shaw, Glenn Miller, Tommy Dorsey and many others. His father did not object to his son pursuing a music career and arranged for Chico to study with Cuban composer Felix Guerrero. By 1945, the young trumpeter was already playing with the popular Cuban dance ensemble Orquesta Bellemar. He also played at the Tropicana Hotel in Havana as a member of Armando Romeu's orchestra.

He enjoyed all music and studied everything from Bela Bartok's *"String Quartets"* to Cuban sextets, trios and orquesta tipicas. He teamed up with Mario Bauzá to compose *"Carambola"* for Dizzy Gillespie, and some charts for Stan Getz's *"Cuban Episode."* In 1948, he moved to New York, where he worked as a ghostwriter for arranger Gil Fuller and composed for his hero, Benny Goodman's 1948 "bop" band. He composed the *"Afro-Cuban Jazz Suite"* for the Charlie Parker and Machito orchestras, as well as *"The Cuban Suite"* for Stan Kenton. Back in Cuba in 1950 he organized a studio all-star orchestra and recorded several 10" LPs for the Clef and Norgran labels. In the mid 1950s he contributed arrangements for a series of recordings that were not released until the 1990s. O'Farrill moved to Mexico City, where he worked as a bandleader. Tito considered that O'Farrill was a prime influence in the arrival of the big bands in Havana. But the bands of the two Titos and Machito certainly had an impact. Today, his son, Arturo O'Farrill leads an orchestra and is an educator, as well as composer.

In 1953 Moré returned to Cuba as a member of Bebo Valdés' Cuban big band. Accustomed to his days as a solo artist he decided to form his own band with trumpet player Alfredo "Chocolate" Armenteros as its first musical director. The orchestra included trumpeter Alejandro "El Negro" Vivar, José "Chombo" Silva on sax and trombonist Generoso "El Tojo" Jimenez. It was brash, multi-textured and dynamic.

"But unlike New York bands like mine, Tito Rodríguez and Machito, his (Bebo Valdés) was not pushing the boundaries of Afro-Cuban jazz, at least not early on. His music was more pop but it was anything but mechanical," in Tito's opinion. But Moré's band did go against the grain – it was the size of the American swing era bands and was structured along the lines of New York's big three Afro-Cuban style bands. It had four trumpets, five saxophones, one trombone, a piano, and a full percussion section." Tito had noticed his band on one of his visits to Havana. "It was a big band like the ones we are used to seeing here and Moré's own uniqueness – his voice and his dancing – gave it a particular style not seen before in Cuba."

Moré soon earned the nickname of "El babaro del ritmo." He and his band became internationally acclaimed and were revered throughout Cuba. Most important is what he conveyed in his singing: tenderness and direct emotional appeal in his boleros, a hip-shaking exuberance in his mambos. One of Moré's most popular songs was the result of the chemistry he shared with his band, and of his ability to improvise. In 1956, playing for a Venezuelan TV show, the band had 10 minutes to fill before their session ended. The band began improvising, and Moré started making up lyrics on the fly. The result was *"Que Bueno Baila Usted "* (How Well You Dance), which went on to become one of Moré's trademark songs.

Unfortunately, alcoholism presented a dark side to Moré's life, and it was one that would eventually kill him. Onstage he managed to out-perform many others and produce a captivating show, but behind the scenes it was not uncommon for Moré to be guzzling hard liquor right up to the moment he stepped on the stage.

Another important and innovative musician that was somewhat

popular in Havana was pianist, arranger and composer Bebo Valdés. Tito saw him play on a number of occasions. He was born in Quivican, Cuba. He started his career as a pianist in the nightclubs of Havana during the 1950s, and since then has achieved significant popularity. He is a former director of the famous Tropicana Club Orchestra in Havana during the pre-Castro days. Valdés played a major role in the development of the mambo that is rooted in the "ritmo nuevo" of Antonio Arcaño y sus Maravillas that combined syncopated son motifs and improvised flute variations. Valdés studied European and Cuban classical music at the Municipal Conservatory in Havana. After class he took in the music of the streets, the African-influenced rumba. Then in the early 1930s, he heard American jazz. His influences included Jelly Roll Morton, Tommy Dorsey and Dizzy Gillespie.

In 1948, Valdés exploited the influences of American jazz, Cuban melodies and African rhythms when he became the principal pianist and arranger for the house orchestra of Havana's Tropicana nightclub, the crown jewel of Cuban nightlife. The top singers and orchestras in Cuba soon went to Valdés for their arrangements. Valdés participated in many recordings with all-star orchestras during the mid 1950s and started his own orchestra 1960. Valdés left Cuba for Mexico in the early 1960s and briefly lived in the United States before moving to Sweden, where he resided until 2007. Nowadays he lives in Malaga, Spain. He is the father of the pianist Chucho Valdés.

"All of us had one thing in common. No! We had two things in common. We wanted to make good music that incorporated the best Afro-Cuban and jazz standards, and none of us wanted to sound like the other guy," exclaimed Tito one day while talking about how he went about preparing for his inaugural recording for RCA Victor. "We were influencing Cuba and vice versa." He always considered this to be a humorous aspect of the 1950s – Cuba had a strong influence on New York, and New York had a strong influence on Havana. "You know, Joe, not many people realize this – I guess we were sort of tied at the hip. You would have thought that the boys in the executive suite of RCA Victor, or for than matter any record company, would have been able to figure it out. No, shit… they wanted Augh!"

It was Tito's view that the most influential orchestra of the period was Machito and his Afro-Cubans. "These guys were on another planet." Mario, who recruited accomplished musicians with a jazz background, designed the orchestra's blueprint for success. Among them were saxophonists Freddie

Skerritt, Gene Johnson, and José "Pin" Madera; trumpeter Bobby Woodlen and percussionists like Patato Valdéz, Uba Nieto and Luis Miranda. He added John Bartee, Edgar Sampson and other arrangers with big band experience to arrange many of the band's charts. Despite its large size in terms of manpower the Machito Orchestra was subtle, powerful and in a strange way "very Cuban," was the way Tito put it. "It was laid back, you know… very syncopated, very modern. They could do everything. I loved them." It is interesting to note, "There were not too many Cubans in the band. Most of the musicians were either Puerto Rican or Anglo or Jewish."

The Afro-Cubans that Mario and Machito led had a high-powered brass identity. They promoted Afro-Cuban jazz around the world by marrying traditional rhythms with inspired jazz soloists. From the late 1940s and into the 1960s stars of the jazz world appeared in featured roles and contributed outstanding performances. Personnel circa the 1950s included: Machito – leader and vocals; Joe Livramento, Joe Newman, Mario Bauzá (musical director), Francis Williams, Doc Cheatham, Paul Cohen, Paquito Dávila- trumpet; Santo Russo, Jimmy Russo, Eddie Bert, Bart Varsalona, Rex Peer- trombone; Cannonball Adderley- alto saxophone; José Madera, Ray Santos, Jr.- tenor saxophone; Leslie Johnakins- baritone saxophone; René Hernández- piano; Roberto Rodríguez- bass; José Mangual- bongos; Uba Nieto- timbales; Candido Camero, Carlos "Patato" Valdéz- congas. In the opinion of most, and including Tito, this lineup had no rival in the realm of Afro-Cuban music. "There was nothing quite like this before and there will probably not be anything like it in the future – take my word on this," Tito said.

Machito and his Afro-Cubans would go on through the 1950s, and 1960s, to record more than 30 albums for a number labels - Decca, Mercury, CBS, Seeco, Tico/Roulette, RCA Victor, Cotique and Gene Norman Presents (GNP). They would perform steady through this period, though by the end of the 1960s the engagements were drying up, as they would be for all the live music venues.

Tito Rodríguez had an orchestra that was as powerful as that of Machito's but with a definite leaning toward the tropical. "Tito had a terrific voice. He was a great dancer and his band played up those points," Tito explained. "He could turn it on to a full Afro-Cuban jazz mode and he could be the opposite. He ran a very tight organization. He could be flamboyant."

Many of the musicians that played for Tito Rodríguez also played on and off with Tito Puente. Rodríguez's band sported a powerful percussion section that included Ramón "Monchito" Muñoz on timbales, Wilfredo

"Chonguito" Vicente on conga and Johnny Rodríguez, Sr. or Little Ray Romero on bongo. In 1955 Tito Rodríguez made several recordings with a charanga style orchestra that included Jerry Sanfino's timid flute work. This occurred nearly five years before the charanga sound caught on in New York City. In 1961 Alberto Socarras provided the Cuban style improvisation for flute and support when Tito tried again with his *"Charanga – Pachanga"* for United Artists. He was not afraid to take chances.

For long hours Tito toiled at the piano in his home and in the studio in preparation for the crucial recording sessions. He admitted much later he never imagined, not even remotely, that the recordings would achieve such historic thresholds. In between getting ready for the *"Cuban Carnaval"* album he found time to compose his only bolero: *"Sin Amor."* It was released as a 45-rpm recording. On the other side was his tune, *"No Me Obligues."* The vocals were by Hilda Nieves, the girlfriend of a friend of Tito, who owned a dry cleaning shop in Manhattan. When I asked him about her he shrugged. "I did a favor for a friend, so what!"

One afternoon while Tito and Alvin Gellers were revising several scores they heard clapping coming from the studio. "It sounded like clave, but it was all mixed up. I walked to the studio and there was Jimmy standing with the guys from the reed and horn sections (about 10 musicians). He shouted to them as he clapped. 'Now count 1, 2, 3, pause, 1,2." He kept repeating it. Some of the guys got it and some were lost. 'Jesus Christ,' Jimmy shouted, 'its clave. If you don't understand it you know he is going to be pissed.' I looked at Alvin and we both laughed." Obviously, Tito said, the orchestra put it all together.

The following excerpt offers a view of the Cinquillo and Africa blending – or clave[85]:

> "The building block of Afro-Cuban or Afro Latin music is clave, a 3/2 (occasionally reversed) rhythmic pattern that covers two measures that are treated as if only one. This is so fundamental that, as Cuban musicologist Emilio Grenet points out, to play out of clave "produces such a notorious discrepancy between the melody and the rhythm that it becomes unbearable to ears accustomed to our music." Clave has a strong first part and an answering second part. It is like a call and response

structure common in African music. It is the method that African rhythm patterns or eight notes and rests, usually built up of combinations of two and three beats, is incorporated into European music. It is what the slaves in Saint Domingue contrived, maintained and fomented.

"The complex rhythms that the Africans brought to Haiti were vast. In addition, unlike European traditions the beats, melodies, songs, rhythms were not written down – they were passed on father to son, etc. The disruption caused by the slave trade was not fatal in terms of the music. Over a period, some of these rhythmic patterns were woven into the European. There are a number of theories as to how the clave beat arrived in the Caribbean, survived and was incorporated into Afro-Cuban music via the habanera and beyond:

When the 700,000 African slaves arrived in Cuba during the 1770s, these, for the most part, did not forget the bell patterns from the traditional music of their homeland and history but rather incorporated them into music making in the new surroundings.

The pan-West African bell pattern shown in Example 1, or something similar, existed during the 1700s.

Ex. 1. West African bell pattern

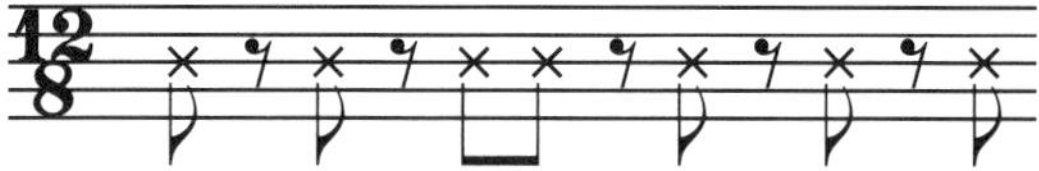

This assumption is based on the pattern's prevalence today among many different African peoples covering an expansive area.

"As new practices emerged from the combining of various African peoples in the New Worlds, new performance styles arose "As the Clave inscription suggests, the performance of clave is a living and breathing tradition shaped by the performance practice of individuals. Each musician contributes to the proliferation and evolution of the tradition by his or her own subtle variations of feel and nuance. Over time, a subtle peculiarity or feel may become the standard, replacing an older practice. Rumba is a style of music originating from African slaves and their descendants living in Cuba. Some of the oldest recorded Cuban rumba styles, such as rumba Columbia originating from the small towns of the island's interior, are performed with a 12/8 feel, similar to music where the bell pattern in Example 1 is performed. However, in rumba Columbia the bell pattern or clave is slightly different from the West African bell pattern. Instead of consisting of seven strokes, the rumba Columbia clave contains only five. (See example 2)

Ex. 2. Rumba clave pattern

"In some Haitian musical styles, the rumba Columbia pattern started on the third stroke instead. The reason for this reduction from seven strokes to five may never be known since it occurred hundreds of years before recording technology was available before the first Africans arrived in Hispanola. It may have started with an individual variation or was the result of the fusing of two or more African styles.

"Another later style of rumba, Guaguanco, emerged from urban areas in a quasi-4/4 feel instead of 12/8. The duple meter feel may have been the result of the influence of marching bands and other Spanish styles often heard in the larger cities throughout the 1700s. The clave used in Guaguanco appears to be an adaptation of the clave rhythm found in rumba Columbia to fit the new metric feel (see example 3.) This pattern is most often referred to as rumba clave. The next step of the evolution came from a simplification of styles. The son clave, used in salsa, displaces the final stroke of the three-stroke measure of the rumba clave by one eight note.

"'San Pascual Bailón,' is the oldest existing example

> of a contradanza. It was issued in Havana in 1803, as a work for solo piano, but there is controversy on this point. Some sources maintain that the music was scored for a military type brass band. The "habanera" developed in Cuba in around the late 1830's and formed the basis of the Cuban and Puerto Rican danzas – much more sophisticated than the folksy more rambunctious contradanza that was popular at the time. The influence of clave is noticeable in this piece of music.
>
> "'El Sungambelo,' written in 1813 is the first stage of the danza. It was written in a rapid 2/4 time signature and is identical to the contradanza. The piece is a four-section scheme and it is repeated twice (A B A B). In listening closely to the selection it is easy to detect that the music is already taking on a tropical flavor.
>
> The extraordinary melodic, rhythmic, and choreographic richness was beginning to take hold. In his book "La Habana Artistica," published in Havana, in 1891, Serafin Ramirez states that this contradanza and "San Pascual Bailón" originally was an orchestral piece and it was eventually published between 1881 and 1891. There are no other formal records of this – this is a further indication of how unreliable musicians are as a resource or for historical documentation." (Carpentier, Alejo. *Music in Cuba* (English translation by Brennan, Timothy), Regents of the University of Minnesota Press, 2001)

Jimmy kept at it until most of the musicians got it down. Tito and Alvin went back to the piano, Jimmy told me.

Drawing on his knowledge, education of the big bands of the swing era, the Afro-Cuban experience and his experience, he focused on striking a balance. There are three kinds of melodic improvisation in a big band that Tito considered vital. The first is the simplest, the original written melody is respected completely; the only change lies in the lengthening or shortening of some notes, repetition of others, use of tonal variations and dynamics to bring out its values in conformity with the personality of the interpreter. Tito believed that this was the motif that was most common in the Pérez Prado style of playing.

The second method of improvisation, the melody remains completely recognizable but its phrases are subject to slight additions and changes; here and there a note is added or subtracted and perhaps a whole phrase is transmuted, but to the layman listener the original melody remains perceptible throughout, either in the actual statement or by in-direction. This was a gimmick that was common with the charangas and the Cuban style so called jazz bands. The charangas, led by Arcaño, modified this and expanded the "montuno" so that the piano and flute could improvise.

Finally, the third type of improvisation, the soloist in a big band departs entirely from the melody; in fact rather than using it as a point of departure, he uses instead the chord patterns of the tune. To the trained ear of the jazz musician it will still be apparent on what basis he is improvising. There are three-sub divisions in this category. There are the notes that are decided upon completely impromptu; the notes that are predetermined to the degree that they follow a natural sequence (possibly as part of an arpeggio, chromatic sequence or scalar run), and third, the notes that are played automatically, without real cerebration because they happen to lie under the fingers and perhaps because they are part of a previously used sequence at the back of the performer's mind. Often these notes may constitute a musical cliché or they will be a direct quotation from some other and completely unrelated work. Tito enjoyed using the three forms in his orchestrations. This third method was most prevalent in the arrangement of Machito and Stan Kenton. The two orchestras in Tito's view were more progressive in terms of their music. Tito wanted to strike a balance. "We are a dance band but with sufficient depth to include progressive and innovative styles."

> "The 'oriental' flavor which Puente has often characterized the composition (Picadillo) set itself immediately into motion with an opening brass theme following an eight-bar tumbao-patterned solo for bass and piano left hand." (Tito Puente and the Making of Latin Music – Steven Loza –2000)

"There is a lot of the Moorish influence on Spain. This influence has been transported from Spain into the Caribbean," was Tito's take on this. As a young student Tito listened to Manuel de Falla* along with the other classical composers. He felt that in classical music terms de Falla was able to convey the mood of our heritage in terms of the Spanish influences.

> "Manuel de Falla met Claude Debussy in 1905 and fell under the magic charm of the French composer, absorbing the ideas of Impressionism that were to influence all his major works. The most immediate effect of this new influence was the composition of the three Nocturnes for orchestra and piano "Nights in the Gardens of Spain." Then followed what is probably Falla's masterpiece, the ballet *"El Amor Brujo,"* In these pieces he captures the essence of the Spanish expression. So completely is he the master of his materials that he is able to give them variety instead of monotony, and a universal rather then narrow provincial appeal." (Concert Companion – 1947)

Tito liked to quote this and then follow up in his own words by saying "Falla understood the Andalus or Moorish flavors and was able to develop a oriental feeling. I think that many Latino composers, and I like to include myself, transposed some of this into the mambo and into Afro-Cuban jazz."

De Falla was one of those classical composers that really excited Tito. Falla's two lavishly Iberian ballet scores: *"El Amor Brujo"* (Love, the Magician), from which is drawn the Ritual Fire Dance (often heard in piano or guitar transcriptions), and the flamboyant *"El Sombrero de Tres Picos"* (The Three-Cornered Hat). He also gained a permanent place in the concert repertory with his evocative piano concerto, "Nights in the Gardens of Spain." Born in 1876, de Falla first took piano lessons from his mother in Cádiz, and later moved to Madrid to continue piano and composition study with Felipe Pedrell, the musical scholar who had earlier pointed Isaac Albéniz toward Spanish folk music as a source for his compositions. Pedrell interested Falla in Renaissance Spanish church music, folk music, and native opera. The latter two influences are strongly felt in *"La Vida Breve"* (Life is Short), an opera for which Falla won a prize in 1905, although the work was not premiered until 1913. A second significant influence resulted from de Falla's 1907 move to Paris, where he met and fell under the Impressionist spell of Claude Debussy, Paul Dukas and Maurice Ravel. It was in Paris that he published his first piano pieces and songs. In 1914 Falla was back in Madrid, working on the application of a quasi-Impressionistic idiom to intensely Spanish subjects; *"El Amor Brujo"* drew on Andalusian and Moorish folk music.

Falla wrote another ballet in 1917, *"El Corregidor y la Molinera"* (The Magistrate and the Miller Girl). He was persuaded to expand the score for a ballet by Léonide Massine to be called *"El Sombrero de Tres Picos,"* and excerpts from the full score have become a staple of the concert repertory. In between the two ballets came *"Nights in the Gardens of Spain,"* a suite of three richly scored impressions for piano and orchestra, again evoking Andalusia – a source of flavors that would pepper the Caribbean. In the 1920s, de Falla altered his stylistic direction, coming under the influence of Stravinsky's Neo-Classicism. He composed a harpsichord concerto, with the folk inspiration now Castilian rather than Andalusian. After 1926 he essentially retired, living first in Mallorca and, from 1939, in Argentina. He was essentially apolitical, but the rise of fascism in Spain contributed to his decision to remain in Latin America after traveling there for a conducting engagement. He spent his final years in the Argentine desert, at work on a giant cantata, *"Atlántida,"* which remained unfinished at his death in 1946.

There was a cross section of musical influences on Tito that included classical composers like de Falla, Debussy and Ravel. He also felt that in Cuba there was a strong calling to the Asia flavors as heard in Abelardo Valdés' 1940 danzón – mambo *"Una Taza de Arroz,"* (A Cup of Rice) that pays tribute to the large Cuban Chinese population. There were many others that fell into this category. His basic calling was rhythmic, syncopated, percussive and controlled. The brass and reeds are used to interact with the percussion. Finally, the oriental influences that filtered into Tito's musical approach stemmed from his travels through Asia, on his way home from World War II. "The sounds, the atmosphere, and everything there was fascinating."

The saxophone section provides the steady riffs or guajeos (as they are called in Cuba). These play off the montuno that is established by the bass and piano, and the trumpets perform a measured counterpoint action with the sax section. The trombones are used in mid tone to low register to provide additional power or to support the trumpets a little further up on the scale. Tito used the trombones to brighten and heighten his sound. Critical to the motif is that the piano ostinato or montuno is constantly shifting and changing to enliven and excite. The riffs coming from the brass and reeds also change.

Adding to all this, the orchestra is rehearsed to take what in Cuban music is known as "off-beat" or "off-time" breaks. The saxophones maintain a steady humming ostinato, and then the percussion stops, performs a number of counted strikes and on the quarter beat resumes giving the dancer and listener the sensation that the music has been accelerated. "Of course it has not – it just sounds driving. Do this a few times during a performance and the dancers really get into it. There are many different Cuban style breaks that can be accomplished, but they have to be carefully scored and rehearsed."

Dizzy Gillespie referred to these breaks or pauses as a "crucial ingredient of Afro-Cuban music. It's like playing out of time..." Tito always thought of Dizzy's explanation as being simple, but "he got the point."

There is a gradual buildup of the horns and reeds and the percussion drives ahead. It is an Afro-Cuban pattern set within the framework of the American big band prototype. There are distinct flavors in this orchestra – oriental, African, American (more New York) and even classical. Tito drew on all his experiences, and as he pressed forward his sound became unique. Every aspect of what he produced was controlled and designed to intrigue and electrify. He could be subtle and romantic, and at the same time innovative. He was constantly searching for something different that fit into his frame of mind.

"Until the 1950s Latin arrangers were not trained to extend the opening of the voicing in the saxophone section, which gives it a real fat chord. But then we figured it out and went into major seventh chords. This had to be fit into the clave that is the key to Afro-Cuban music. The bass configuration and the correct piano syncopation have to be served up. Anyone can play this style, but it requires a lot of feeling," was Tito's view.

Prior to settling into the RCA Victor sessions, Tico Records released Tito's *"Puente in Percussion."* This was a hard sell to Tico and its sales were nothing to write home about. In fact, the Tico executives were disappointed. But the music in the long play album begins to give a glimpse of the direction Tito was taking. The initial recordings for RCA Victor reflect his approach to what he perceived was authentic and modern Afro-Cuban music. It was also especially very New York. It was his unique sound. It combined the best of the Yorubá traditions, Afro-Cuban dance music and American big band jazz influence. It sounded Cuban and it felt New York. The sound of the Tito Puente orchestra had a swagger and arrogance about it. It was as if Tito had incorporated the personalities that he enjoyed watching in his youth.

It was Tito Puente's sound. One could argue that the intensity, the steady buildup of the brass, the torrid pulse of the Afro-Cuban percussion in some ways resembled the Stan Kenton approach. On the other hand, Tito would tell you that this pattern was "straight forward and driving – a very

Cuban blueprint that is used to entice and excite the dancer and listener." It was also very much Tito's New York Afro-Cuban music style.

In his first offering on RCA, Tito put together what he often referred to as a tribute to the music of Cuba. The kaleidoscope of Afro-Cuban rhythms served up had something for everyone. The opening *"Eleguá Changó"* are the names of two African deities that are part of the Santería tradition. The powerful percussion easily carries the torrid 6/8-time beat, switching off to 4/4-time and back again. The full force of the brass and reeds effectively interact and even at times seem to challenge the drummers. Tito keeps everything under control and balanced and one is left almost breathless from the more than five-minute showpiece. The entire album was what Tito called "controlled Afro-Cuban jazz."

"Que Sera Mi China" was a spontaneous composition that Tito constructed almost as it was being recorded. Willie and Mongo came up with the phrases and title. Also in the chorus, but not listed in the RCA Victor contract, were singers Yayo El Indio and Tony Molina. On *"Cual Es La Idea,"* the sax section carries the montuno with the trumpets providing the riffs, straightforward. *"Pa'Los Rumberos"* is set up for Tito's timbal solo. It gives a picture of the influence of Gene Krupa's style. Tito displays controlled improvisational abilities. *"Happy Cha Cha Chá"* could be described as a fast cha cha chá or medium mambo. Jerry Sanfino takes the flute solo and Alvin Gellers displays his keyboard dexterity and his propensity for an authentic Afro-Cuban feeling.

The tight organization and structuring (less than two minutes of music) of Ray Bryant's *"Cuban Fantasy"* is the most open ended Afro-Cuban jazz jaunt and allows Tito to loosen his controls for a moment. But for the most part the selections on *" Cuban Carnaval"* are a study in tight orchestration that is strongly expressive. It is a big band extravaganza with authentic Afro-Cuban thumping. It opens from time to time, ever so briefly, to permit the instrumentalists some improvisational movement. It is Tito Puente at his most creative.

Between playing at the Catskill resorts, performing at the Palladium and appearing at numerous theater and dance venues the orchestra continued to record at Webster Hall at a mind boggling pace. In these days, Tito was keenly aware that he had to push hard. The competition was fierce. His imagination was in full throttle and his creative juices were flowing. He was looking for an edge, for a device and or attention-grabber that would keep him on the top. "If you want to have a chance to be successful," Tito often philosophized, "you need a gimmick, something to entice and create interest."

All That Jazz

Soon after the sessions Stan Kenton and his Orchestra were in New York City to record "*Cuban Fire*." When Tito heard it he smiled and noted the progressive style that the Kenton band took. "Strong and brash," he said. The difference between Tito and Kenton's approach was simply that Kenton permitted his men more room to improvise while Tito stood firm on making sure that the authentic Afro-Cuban rhythms were true to form – two approaches by two pros.

It also surprised Tito to hear from his friends including Miguelito, Mario and others that "*Cuban Carnaval*" was popular in Havana. The year 1956 was an exceptional one for Afro-Cuban music. It became very popular in Havana. This surprised RCA Victor. In September, Panart Record Company decided to record an album in which musicians would jam at a party. Ramón Sabat, the founder of the Cuban recording company, had signed most of Cuba's popular artists at this point. The Kenton achievements and the happenings at the New York Palladium were evident to him that he needed a gimmick to continue being a successful record producer. He spread the word throughout Havana about the event in which musicians and a selected group of friends were invited.

According to Tito, he and Mario spoke several times over the telephone. Mario informed him that Panart Records had just released the first of two long play albums. "It has to satisfy you, Tito, to know that your music is impacting musicians in Cuba." Mario and Tito spoke in Spanish for the most part. "He (Mario) had a knack for humbling me. I told him it was all of us who were responsible for what was happening in our small music world."

Mario was not happy about how little musicians were paid for such an outstanding set of recording sessions. "Things are going to change there," he told Tito, who shrugged it off. Tito did not like politics, not in the least. But he understood just where Mario was coming from. Miguelito had broached the subject of Cuba, poverty, and discrimination with Tito – often. But for now he was happy that his music was highly regarded.

The incentives to attend were free food, free liquor, and women that would be in attendance to dance with the musicians. The all-stars that showed up included Francisco Fellove, guitarist José Antonio Mendez, pianist Peruchín Justiz, trumpeter Alejandro "El Negro" Vivar, flutist Juan Pablo Miranda, tenor saxophonist José Chombo Silva, percussionists Marcelino Valdés and Walfredo De Los Reyes. There were others and as they played the music was recorded. Six months later Panart Records released "*Cuban Jam Session, Volume I.*" Its worldwide sales over a two-year period were estimated at more than one million dollars. The musicians that participated were paid only $20.00.

The New York influence continued - In 1956, Chico O'Farrill accepted offers to write music for hotel revues and a few RCA Victor albums. But Alvarez Guedes, who founded Gema Records in 1956, recorded selections of orchestrated jam sessions with the big bands of Chico O'Farrill and Bebo Valdés which were released as 78-rpm discs, then re-released on a 12" LP years later entitled *"Los Mejores Músicos De Cuba - Especial Del Bebo"* is clearly a mirror of what Tito Puente, Tito Rodríguez and Machito were doing in New York. It always pleased and satisfied Tito to know that his music was inspiring and having influence on other regions.

In the summer of 1956 Tito recorded *"Let's Cha Cha,"* which is lush with Alvin Gellers' piano, Tito's vibe work and flute work by Jerry Sanfino. Tito's approach is what he called "New York cha cha chá – a little bit faster than what the Cubans in Havana do, but just as groovy and tight. Dancers in New York like to show off, especially when they have a large ballroom. The Cubans move softly. Take your pick." There is plenty of interaction between Tito and Jerry's flute and Alvin takes off on several selections. Willie and Tito provide the Cuban voices in unison. The music is typical, tropical and driving.

It's A Puente!

Havana Nights

The band was in good hands. Jimmy Frisaura reassured Tito that everything would be fine and that his orchestra would be where it was supposed to be. "'You won't be missed,' I told him the day before he was leaving for Cuba. 'Shit, of course I will be missed, he replied in a pissed off voice. 'Willie and Mongo will handle the percussion. It will be all right.' He was like a little boy, excited, full of anticipation. This was big," recalled Jimmy to me. I had to laugh too. I could just see Tito.

Tito wanted to accomplish several things at the 1957 Havana Music Festival that was being staged to honor a long list of Cuban entertainers that had achieved various levels of success around the world. The event was the brainchild of promoter Gaspar Pumarejo who convinced the Cuban government to host the event. Dictator Fulgencio Batista was all for it. Havana was in effect the "Latin Las Vegas," a playground for gamblers and tourists eager to shed some of their wealth in the posh casinos that were operated by the mob. Tito was committed to several days of carefree debauchery, enjoying the entertainment at the Mecca of Afro-Cuban music, and gaining recognition for his contributions to Cuban music. He was 37 and his fame was growing.

Once again his long time friend Mario Bauzá provided the needed support and influence to get Tito added to the list of Cuban musicians and entertainers that would be making the trip to Havana to be honored over a period of several days. He flew out of New York with Mario, Machito, Graciela, Vicentico, Miguelito and several others. He was not sure what to expect during the next few days.

Mario and Miguelito were the most in tune with what was going on in Cuba. Looking back I realize now that they were concerned about where their homeland was heading – what was the future of Cuba, you know. Miguelito was always vocal about those things. Mario was a sensible businessman and musician who for years maintained, "Cuba is going down the toilet."

Havana in 1957 was at a crossroad[86]. The Mafia, led by crime boss

Meyer Lansky, and President Batista were reaping the benefits of the partnership. The United States government for the most part looked away from what was happening. In 1956, in the midst of the revolutionary upheaval, the 21-story, 383-room Hotel Riviera was built in Havana at a cost of $14 million. It was known as mobster Meyer Lansky's dream and crowning achievement. The hotel opened with a floorshow headlined by Ginger Rogers. Lansky's official title was "kitchen director," but he controlled every aspect of the hotel. Havana's hotels were packed year round with notable tourists that included Errol Flynn, Humphrey Bogart, Lauren Bacall, Frank Sinatra, and Ava Gardner.

In fact it was believed that Sinatra was in town in December 1946. Tito said that he made a quick visit to Havana about that time. "It was easy to get to Havana for an overnight," he said during one of our conversations. Sinatra's visit was related to a meeting of the main Mafia family bosses. The official reason that Sinatra was making the trip was that he was a guest of an Italian millionaire and he was going to receive a tribute in the National Hotel. A number of admirers of the famous singer were present. Lucky Luciano said that "if someone had asked if there was an apparent reason for such a meeting, it was to honor an Italian boy from New Jersey called Frank Sinatra" - the singer who had crossed paths with Tito in New York. Tito was going to stay at the National, but he did not expect to see Sinatra. The Mafia bosses meeting at the National Hotel ended in December 1946 with a huge celebration. The Casino Parisien was reserved with its good food and even better drinks that ranged from renowned brands of French champagne to Scotch whisky and Cuban rum. One of the most famous bands from Havana was hired, as well as dancers and members of the Tropicana, Sans Souci and Montmartre cabarets.

It was an unexpected surprise when close to midnight the lights went off, a small stage was lit up and before thunderous applauses came – there stood Frank Sinatra. Ernest Hemingway practically lived in Havana. Marlene Dietrich had a drink named after her. Other celebrities included Josephine Baker, Nat King Cole, Xavier Cugat, Carmen Miranda, Marlon Brando, Jimmy Durante and Edith Piaf. The list was endless.

Hundreds of nightspots and where other tourists do not venture were on the list of places Tito planned to visit. He might not get to them all, but still he had his list. He knew the city and he knew where to find what interested him. Havana had an ample number of these places. There was a row of spots in the area known as La Playita, including the Pennsylvania and Panchin Club. The dancing was basic and raw, although the liquor unprocessed –aguardiente is what the Cubans call it. As the Afro-Cuban rhythms got hot and heavy, the customers on the dance floor became more bawdy and loud. The outdoor cafes along Prado Boulevard are one of the reasons Havana was known as the "Paris of the Americas." El Dorado had an female orchestra, and you could listen to the music, sip a drink and watch the crowds go by. Scattered around town were several places with more or less authentic Spanish atmosphere (i.e., music and wine jugs). All of these were familiar to Tito, who soon after returning from the Orient and the Navy, began jumping over to Havana as time and money permitted. The bars and cocktail lounges, of which there were more than 100, not counting the 3,000 bodegas that also sold liquor by the glass or bottle, were open late. Nightlife extended throughout the city and into the suburbs.[87] Dozens of clubs were located in El Vedado. The nightlife extended throughout the coastal areas of Cuba, even into Santiago on the east coast. The better bars and cantinas provided live entertainment: singers, pianists or accordion players. Smaller nightclubs, like the Bambú and La Campana, had slot machines but no other gambling facilities. The music was genuine. Havana thus provided entertainment to suit all tastes. There was something for everyone in the nightlife of the "Pearl of the Antilles," the "Paris of the Americas." Tito knew this and expected it - dance, drink and dine, visits to the dives and the palaces – with no worry amidst the tropical grandeur and gaiety.

Terrorism was part of Havana too. The rebels dynamited a gas and electric distribution center. The impact affected the suburbs. A policeman, a woman and daughter, and a 78-year-old man were injured. Telephones throughout the business district in Havana were put out of commission. Havana was without service. Big department stores, such as El Encanto and Fin De Siglo, which depended on electric power for air conditioning and lights, could not open; automobile and pedestrian traffic ceased. All cafes, bars, and several nightclubs were affected. Powerful searchlights at the Cabana fortress across the bay from Havana were turned on the city to aid the police in maintaining order. In the Vedado residential area a bomb exploded at an intersection, damaging two automobiles parked nearby the home of Dr. Andres Morales del Castillo, Secretary to the President. In the central part of Cuba the Army was locked in battle with Fidel Castro's rebels. None of this escaped Tito, Mario, Machito, Vicentico, Miguelito or any of the other guests invited to Havana to be honored.

A few miles from Havana, Tito and Miguelito were able to track down a percussionist by the name of Chori. According to what Tito was told this was supposed to be the best "timbalero in Cuba." Silvano "El Chori" Shueg Hechevaría was from Santiago and even had a native fried food named after him – "La Chorisera." Chori was quite a showman who had been visited by such celebrities as Toña la Negra, Marlon Brando, Agustin Lara and Cab Calloway. After drinking for a while one night Tito and Chori crossed timbal sticks for a small wager. Tito won the bet, he told me. "The fellow was pretty good but he did not seem to have the ability to play smoothly – mark time. Good percussionists have to be able to keep steady time. Maybe it was because he was drunk. But so was I."

"It's funny, but in Cuba, the timbale players don't take solos, only conga players and the bongocero,' Tito noted." (When the Drums Are Dreaming, Josephine Powell – 2007)

Tito would not say something like that. One of his friends on the 1957 visit to Havana was Walfredo de los Reyes Jr., whose father was a member of the original Casino de la Playa orchestra, was a percussionist (drums and timbales) with considerable American jazz orientation and well known in jazz circles. Tito also knew Chuchu Esquinarrosa, who played timbales for Orquesta Sensación and Ulpiano Díaz, who worked for José A. Fajardo y sus Estrellas Cubanas and dozens of other orchestras. Díaz had the reputation as the best of the Cuban style timbaleros. There was also Guillermo Barreto, who was already making a name for himself with the new style of Cuban Jam sessions. In 1957 Barreto and Israel "Cachao" López would make history with the release of the *"Cuban Jam Sessions in Miniature,"* that featured Cuba's best. Several other albums would follow it. Cachao would also gather up many members of Arcaño's orchestra, who now played for Fajardo to record classic danzón mambos.

"I liked the way this Chori fellow played. But I don't think he could stand up in a long drawn out big band session or in any orchestra where the environment is controlled. I think of Willie Bobo, for example. He was a guy that could go toe to toe with me and not blink – endurance. Rhythm is time. If you can't keep it then everybody is off. This is why a lot of these Cuban drummers are so good. Time was part of their structure - some though were the opposite. Another guy I think about is Miguelito (Valdés). He had an incredible sense of rhythm and time. He could show off and together we would put on a show at the Palladium. In Afro-Cuban music the percussionist has to keep steady accurate time or tempo. Its only in shows that we get to take some liberties," Tito said. "Chori was great, but he drank a lot. I don't think he could make it in my band. He was a great guy, though."

The theme that Pumarejo concocted to honor Cuban entertainers living and working off the island revolved around "50 years of Cuban music," and featured a festival at the Cerro Stadium. From France came bandleader and pianist Marino Barreto, who is the person named in the famous danzón *"El Bombin de Barreto."* From Spain came Raul Zequeira and Leopoldo Junco; the honorees from Turkey included Antonio Machin, Raul del Castillo and Miguel Portillo. From France came Bandleader Marino Barreto. Everardo Ordaz, Gilberto Urquiza, Paco y Alfonso and Miguel Pazos traveled to Havana from Mexico. There were major problems encountered by Pumarejo. The majority of the musicians being honored were black. Many had left Cuba in protest and to make their fortune elsewhere. This did not sit well with the Batista Regime.

The ceremony honoring Cuban entertainers and Tito was held at City Hall in old Havana. But the most memorable parts of the trip were his participation with the local popular orchestras and ensembles, playing on the radio as an invited guest, rubbing shoulders with Cuba's best. "I was with Miguelito when we met up with Fajardo at the Montmartre Club. His orchestra was terrific. Cachao was playing for him and René "Latigo" Hernández was on the piano. He had one of the biggest most swinging orchestras. Fajardo had six violins, a cello, Tata Guines on conga, Ulpiano Díaz on timbales and Cachao on bass. He had a chorus line of dancing girls and him and another fellow were on each side playing the wooden flute. It was quite a sight," gasped Tito talking about his visit to Havana. The charangas were really popular in Cuba in 1957. The most popular charangas at the time were Orquesta Sensación, Orquesta Neno González, Orquesta Melodías Del 40, Orquesta Cheo Belén Puig and Orquesta América del 55, Chapotin and his Orchestra, and some musicians from the old Casino de la Playa Orchestra. There were many others. For example, Orquesta Aragón was up and coming and popular in the United States and Mexico, thanks to its recording contract with RCA Victor.

"Everybody and anybody that was in the music business were available. Everybody knew Miguelito. He took me around to many of his spots and introduced me to some of his old friends. Walfredo escorted me a few times," Tito said..

The event lasted a week. "I got to see and talk to a whole lot of musicians. I visited the Hotel Capri where George Raft operated one of the luxury casinos." Seeing Raft at the casino made Tito recall the 1935 film *"Rumba"* where Raft portrays a New Yorker, of Cuban descent hanging out in Havana because gangsters in the United States were out to get him. It was an okay movie," according to Tito. "He (Raft) does a few of those steps. He was smooth… Carole Lombard gets some strong dance lessons with him and looks lovely. She plays a bored rich girl in the movie, never too excited even when she's dancing. She gets some nice little bits of dialogue.

He was the fastest dancer in New York back in 1920s. In the first dance number in "Rumba" you get to see some of his moves. Ann Sheridan, an up and coming actress at the time is among the mass of dancers. "She was beautiful."

A story that Tito liked to recall about Raft was when "Castro marched into Havana (January 1, 1959) and hundreds of wild followers stormed the hotel and casino. Raft stood before them stared them down. He told him in his best New York accent to go somewhere else. The crowd departed." He shrugged. "I guess there is some truth to it," Tito smiled. "Raft was a tough guy, I mean a real tough guy and a great dancer."

Among the other celebrities that were in Havana during this period was singer Tony Martin and hoofer Donald O'Connor. They both had part ownership in Havana casinos. "Who knows, they may have been around. I was just excited to be in the middle of the Cuban music. George Raft was a bonus, I guess," he smiled. "We said hello at his club. Funny thing, he knew who I was and was surprised I knew who he was," Tito laughed.

Tito also got to see Conjunto Casino and spent time speaking with several of the musicians such as Roberto Espí who was one of the founders. He was a great singer and he even asked for Patato." Patato Valdéz played for the Casino ensemble in the early 1950s before going to New York where he joined the Machito Orchestra. He played on Tito's *"Cuban Carnaval."*

It turns out that Tito did not realize just how popular his *"Cuban Carnaval"* long play record was in Havana. He found out when he joined up with Jesús Goris, the owner of "Goris Record Shop" located on San Rafael and Escobar streets in the historic sector of Havana. Goris had been a representative of RCA Victor but decided to go it on his own. He also started the record label Puchito that included such names as Conjunto Jovenes del Cayo, Senen Suarez, Toña la Negra, Olga Guillot, Orquesta Sensación and many others. Colorful promotional material from Tito's latest LP was notably plastered over the walls of the shop. He spent all day signing records for customers. "I don't think I got this much attention when I rode the subway in New York," he reflected. Tito enjoyed the recognition of his fans. He valued privacy, but he loved to be recognized for his achievements.

While he was at the shop Gilberto Valdés stopped in to chat with Tito. They talked about the U.S.A. Mambo Show that flopped a few years earlier, and Valdés spoke of his project to record a danzón album that was going to feature more than 60 musicians including, Fajardo, Arcaño, Cachao, Cheo

Belen Puig, Pedro Hernandez and many others. Puchito released the album, *"Danzón Mambo,"* a few months later.

A dark side of the trip came the day that Tito and his group departed. There was police activity in various parts of the route – ominous signs that all was not well in Cuba. Castro and his men, who had been captured, tried, convicted -- and then released in a general amnesty in May 1955, were in control of the island's mountainous range. That amnesty turned out to be a major mistake of the ruthless Batista regime. Within two years, Castro returned from Mexico with his loyal followers on the history-making voyage of the vessel called the Gramma, landed on an isolated beach in Oriente Province, disappeared into the Sierra Maestra mountains and carried on hit-and-run guerrilla warfare. Pumarejo related these events to the departing group of musicians. However, he dismissed the eventuality of Castro taking control – but it was just a matter of time. For Tito the trip had been memorable, but it was time to go home, he had his orchestra to look after.

Even with all his success Tito knew the big band was a hazardous endeavor – a big gamble. This was especially so during the mid 1950s when it became apparent to Tito that the "live music market was shrinking." His reflections on the era were perceptive and accurate.

"I am an optimist," Tito often exclaimed. "The world of music is going well. Classical music is popular and every night the concert halls are filled with enthusiasts. I even like some of the new Rock n' Roll – not all of it, but some of it. As long as the young people like our music it will be all right. I don't know if I will ever get rich but as long as I can I want to put my music out there for people to enjoy. There is a lot of history in this music – Europe, Africa, the New World. I guess it represents the best of who we are. I love to see people dance, I love to hear them sing, and I love when they wave to me and recognize that I am the one giving them pleasure. I am an optimist."

Maybe he was!

Departures and Changes

The stories about the departure of Mongo Santamaría and Willie Bobo from the Tito Puente Orchestra at the end of 1957 are endless and it seems that with each telling gain negative and dark mystique. It was one of Tito's depressing moments. He was shaken to the core when they told him they were leaving. It caught him by surprise. "I was devastated," he said. The departure came in November 1957, after Tito had turned down yet another contract opportunity in Florida. For a number of years Willie and Mongo had given the Puente organization unique and unmatched Afro-Cuban percussive depth and perfection. The two musicians simply wanted to move on, to try new things. They also told Tito that it was time for him to get some of those jobs in the Deep South.

In 1954, the U.S. Supreme Court ruled segregation of public schools unconstitutional and Florida began integration in 1959; by the late 1960s, most public schools had integrated and several new universities were built. However, most of Miami's exclusive hotels and nightclubs remained off limits to blacks. The situation seemed to worsen after World War II when Florida's population began to grow rapidly as a result of migration from northern states.

Segregationists put in tighter restrictions for racial interaction. Machito and his orchestra had traveled south several times before the war, and while having to deal with racial issues, it managed. Tito had worked in Miami with José Curbelo. But by the 1950s things seemed to get worse. In 1956, two black women were arrested in Tallahassee for sitting in the front seats of a bus when they were expected to sit in the back. The entire African-American community began a boycott. This resulted in the revision of many laws and policies. Separate water fountains, bathrooms, restaurant seating, and hotel rooms disappeared. African-Americans began to see the changes that they had worked for all their lives. The turmoil made Tito cancel some of the tours with the band. "It was getting too dangerous. We were busy up north," he said.

After *"Cuban Carnaval"* came *"Top Percussion."* This is an album that explores the Afro-Cuban system of music – the lore of the Yorubá, who comprise the majority of the slaves that were transported from the African west coast. Morris Levy at first was skeptical, but he finally agreed to let Tito move forward with the project. "I wore his ass out," Tito claimed. Years later Levy told me that Tito certainly knew how to get his way. I doubted that Morris Levy was going to cave into Tito. He was probably thinking that this was one way to make money, if not immediately, later down the road. Levy and Tito had a unique relationship, and Tito and Jimmy were probably among the few that could ever knock heads with him.

The music that comes from Cuba is embedded in the religious beliefs of the descendants of former slaves.[88] Tito studied Santería and believed that it helped him to understand the complexities of the music, and more importantly, was able to play it properly. The Orisha are multi-dimensional beings that represent the forces of nature. The Orisha have characteristics and legends similar to those used to describe the ancient Greek and Roman pantheons. To the followers of Santería, however, the Orisha are not remote divinities; on the contrary, they are vibrant, living entities that take an active part in everyday life. The Orisha faith believes in an ultimate deity, Olorun or Olodumare, who is removed from the day-to-day affairs of human beings on Earth. Instead, adherents of the religion appeal to specific manifestations of Olodumare in the form of the various Orisha. Ancestors and heroes can also be enlisted for help with day-to-day problems.

Faithful believers will also generally consult a geomantic divination specialist, known as a babalao or Iyanifa, to mediate on their problems. Babalaos still exist in Cuba, Puerto Rico and many Spanish-speaking countries. This practice is known as Ifa, and is an important part of life throughout West Africa and the rest of the world. UNESCO, the cultural and scientific education arm of the United Nations, declared Ifa a "Masterpiece of the Oral and Intangible Heritage of Humanity" in 2005.

An important part of the traditional Yorubá faith is that the Yorubá believe was a son of the supreme god Olodumare or Olorun, and was sent by him from heaven to create the earth. Another version of this myth ascribes these episodes to Obatala, casting Oduduwa, as an usurper. Ori. Ori literally means the head, but in spiritual matters is taken to mean an inner portion of the soul, which determines personal destiny and success. Ase, which is also spelled "Axe," "Axé," "Ashe," or "Ache," is the life force that runs through all things, living and inanimate. Ase is the power to make things happen. It is an affirmation that is used in greetings and prayers, as well as a concept about spiritual growth. Orisha devotees strive to obtain Ase through Iwa-Pele or gentle and good character, in turn they experience alignment with the Ori or what others might call inner peace or satisfaction with life.

The Orisha pantheon includes Shango, Olokun, Ifá, Yemaya, Osun, Obatala, Oshun, Ogun, Ochosi, Oko, Soponna, Oya and Esu/Legba, among countless others. In the Lucumi tradition, Osun and Oshun or Ochun are different Orishas. Oshun is the beautiful and benevolent Orisha of love, life, marriage, sex and money while Osun is the protector of the Ori or our heads and inner Orisha. The Yorubá also venerate their Egungun, or Ancestors, Ibeji, god of Twins (which is no wonder since the Yorubá have the world's highest incidence of twin births of any group).

On the percussion sessions Tito added Evaristo Baró, bass; and Julio Collazo and Francisco Urutia on additional African percussion, join Willie Bobo, Mongo Santamaría and Tito in this daring percussive outing that was recorded in the summer of 1957.

"Night Beat" is Tito's excursion into the world of big band Afro-Cuban jazz. It is another effort by the master to try out new things. It features percussionists Mongo and Willie supporting rather than leading. For a

change of pace, Tito is heard leading a straight-ahead big band that includes soloists trumpeter Carl H. (Doc) Severinsen and tenor saxophonist Marty Holmes. From the opening stripper-style blues of *"Night Beat,"* through a variety of ensemble originals and an up-tempo *"Carioca,"* the music swings and is peppered with Tito on vibes. In this effort Tito generally avoids most of the expected Afro-Cuban influences. Howard Collins and Al Casamenti are added on guitar. This was a very interesting and musically satisfying departure for Tito.

"There was no big announcement. Mongo, Willie and Tito sat in the corner of the RCA Victor studio and talked," according to Jimmy. "All the musicians – those of us who had been around for a long time, knew something was up. Mongo used to get pissed at Tito for a lot of different reasons – mostly his distractions with women. But they always made up. But that day, well… Willie and Tito were stone faced. Mongo was quiet. They just sat in the corner talking. After a while they stood up. They started to shake hands but I guess emotions got the better of Willie and Tito. They embraced. Then Tito and Mongo embraced. We still did not know what the fuck was going on," Jimmy described the moment one night over several drinks. In fact, Jimmy always got tearful whenever he recalled the events.

Tito came over to where the band was gathered. He looked around, wiped his eyes and told his musicians what had just transpired. "I had never seen him so down," the trumpet player told me describing what went on. There would be many stories about how and why the two percussionists decided to leave – one might say at the height of the Tito Puente Orchestra's success. Jimmy went on, "'Mongo and Willie will be leaving the band after we find replacements. They want to try out some new things in California,' was what Tito uttered in a shaky voice. There was silence. 'Jesus, we have work to do,'" Tito said in an easy tone. Then Willie chimed in, 'Yeah, we're not married," Willie added in a somewhat jovial voice. Jimmy said everyone laughed.

As soon as it was learned that the two would be joining Cal Tjader the rumor mill started. Quickly the gossip spread that Tito had let them go so that he could hire "white percussionists" to take advantage of the opportunities in south Florida. The South was segregated and the restrictions applied to all. The three men – Tito, Willie, and Mongo refused to discuss such a ridiculous idea. Tito and Willie remained tight, often sitting in with each other whenever their paths crossed. Cal and Tito talked about it soon after and Tito said, "Cal was surprised that they were moving. When they approached Cal he insisted that he would talk to me. Cal was a straight shooter – very honest guy. He was happy to get them. They did some great things together. I had to consider the organization – the musicians. We had a reputation. I just moved on," he said.

Tito looked around for new rhythm men. He auditioned a handful of percussionists and finally decided on Ray Barretto, a jazz inclined all around percussionist who could read music. He had strong hands and pounded the tumbadora with a hard and deliberate stroke. He came strongly recommended by José Curbelo, who was disbanding his orchestra. Curbelo was settling into a career as a booking agent. Curbelo suggested to Tito that vocalist Santos Colón was available. Tito said that he would think about it.

Tito recruited Julio Collazo and Ray Rodríguez for the percussion, and he continued to use Patato, José Mangual, Sr. and Joe Rodríguez. Pianist Ray Coen replaced Alvin Gellers, who left to concentrate on jazz and other genres. Coen was an exceptional improviser. However, Coen was hindered by drug addiction. He was also not a sharp sight-reader, and stumbled on the complex scores that the orchestra used. Tito required a strong sight-reader and a more reliable pianist. Gilberto López slipped into the role.

The recording schedule was exhaustive – almost daily the orchestra was in the studio rehearsing while Tito continued to construct new melodies, score and arrange and impose his unique style. The band continued to work concerts, dances, weddings, special events – you name it the Tito Puente Orchestra was at its height of popularity. The travel schedule was demanding. On some occasions he traveled alone and recruited musicians at the location. His strict style and rigidity of expression was his to impose. Since Tito had no attachments, if he did not like what he heard he would find someone else – it was that simple.

Be Mine Tonight

In 1957 I purchased my first long play album – *"Cuban Carnaval"* even though I was a devoted follower of Machito and his Afro-Cubans. Machito was always in El Barrio, walking around during the day, talking with just about anybody. He and I attended the same church and we made our Confirmation at Our Lady Queen of Angels, between 113th and 114th Streets (between 2nd and 3rd Avenues). It was closed by the Archdiocese in 2007. Along the way he would be one of those few people that I always looked up to. He was a life long friend.

Tito and his orchestra was traveling and had appeared in Los Angeles'

Palladium. Also on the billboard was Rene Touzet and his Orchestra and Manny López, a popular West Coast attraction who played piano and led several types of Afro-Cuban music oriented orchestras. He recorded for RCA Victor too and had produced *"Cha Cha Chá If You Please,"* with a charanga style orchestra. Also appearing was Jack Costanzo and Tito Rodríguez. The show attracted 5,000 people. From there Tito headed to Arizona and worked his way back east.

As focused as Tito and his band was, there were moments that were memorable – but not because of the music. One night on the Arizona trip, Jimmy spent several hours trying to convince a hotel clerk that he was indeed "Jimmy Frisaura, the first trumpet on the Tito Puente Orchestra." The clerk had a different photo and conveniently neither the clerk or Jimmy could locate Tito to confirm his identity. "I did not suspect Tito of the mischief until years later," Jimmy recalled with a grin. "He was notorious for those damned pranks – especially when we were on the road." A trumpet player, whose name we will not reveal, was harassed throughout the night – telephone calls, knocks on the door. He was with his wife, so he said. One night several members of the orchestra were forced out of their beds because of a fire alert. They spent many hours outside in the cold until they realized there was no fire, it was a prank.

But when it was time for work, Tito walked out to lead his orchestra there was no kidding, no laughing, and no joking. He was the stern taskmaster, recalled Jimmy. "It was like that when he put together the music for Miss Abbe Lane."

It took a lot of doing for Tito to convince the powers that be at RCA Victor to let him do the album with Abbe Lane. Once again Morris Levy took the full brunt of Tito's arguments. Once Levy was on board, the executives at RCA Victor agreed but then did not release the album until 1959. In the late spring of 1957 the orchestra entered Webster Hall to record *"Abbe Lane with Tito Puente & his Orchestra."* It showcases a side of the Tito Puente Orchestra that many aficionados were not familiar with. His approach was simple - "keep it simple, keep it percussive and tight, and keep it smooth." Tito designed each of the selections to suit the frontline. "The orchestra will go where she (Abbe Lane) leads us. This is what good musicians do. I was not sure how good her Spanish was, but she said it was better than average. We agreed on a wide range of tunes – sort of international."

In this session Tito added Joe A. Mariani, who is heard on the French horn. It is a commercial effort but still very much in keeping with the unique Tito approach. Originally there was much speculation as to how the two got together. Tito and Xavier talked about having Abbe Lane sing with the orchestra for a few years. Xavier Cugat agreed that it would be a "good idea." At the time Ms. Lane, a fiery Brooklyn-born Jewish entertainer was better known for her photos on the covers of her husband Cugat's numerous long play record albums Everyone thought she was Latin. She was often seen at the Palladium alone, with friends and sometimes with her husband.

The sexy Latin-flavored songstress enjoyed some success with feature films while under contract to Universal-International in the early 1950s. She appeared on numerous television drama and game shows. Lane was born Abigail Francine Lassman in 1932. Her first husband, rumba king Cugat, heavily influenced her singing style. She was his third wife and was followed by Charo. Lane filmed quite a lot in Italy in the late 1950s and early 1960s but claimed that she was "too sexy for Italian television." Lane was divorced in 1964, and later remarried.

Cugat and Abbe Lane appeared regularly at the Coconut Grove in Los Angeles and he supplied the soundtracks for several musical shorts, but it was after moving to New York that Cugat had his greatest success after his orchestra became the house band for the Waldorf Astoria Hotel. Despite being criticized for his middle-of-the-road approach to Afro-Cuban music, Cugat remained committed to his commercial-minded sound in order to reach the widest audience. He later explained, "I would rather play 'Chiquita Banana' and have my swimming pool than play Bach and starve." Cugat and his orchestra remained at the hotel for 16 years. Whenever he saw Tito at the Palladium he liked to reminisce about how Tito (Puente), Miguelito Valdés, Tito Rodríguez and so many others had worked for him.

"He loved beautiful women who were always featured in Cugat's band," Tito said. He helped Rita Hayworth launch her career, and appeared in her film *"You Were Never Lovelier."* Cugat's recordings of the 1950s featured the singing of his third wife, Abbe Lane. It was not unusual to see Abbe Lane and Tito in the middle of the Palladium Ballroom. She was a terrific dancer. She had been an admirer of Tito and his orchestra for many years. "Yeah," quipped Jimmy, "we all talked about it, but all Tito did was laugh and said we were like old ladies – always gossiping. Who knows?"

"Noche de Ronda" or as it is titled for the long play album, *"Be Mine Tonight,"* is sung by Abbe in Spanish with the words composed by María Teresa Lara, and then switches to English. The orchestra follows her easily, almost gently and achieves a romantic mood or feeling that is very tropical. The first tune on the album is *"Pan, Amore Y Cha Cha Chá,"* a Cugat hit

that Puente keeps tight with the entire orchestra and the percussion led by Tito, Mongo and Willie. William Rodríguez was added for the drums.

Tito never forgot that when he was starting out many of his fans were Jewish. "They followed me around New York and showed up wherever I played. I guess Abbe Lane was part of that crowd too." The album is like a kaleidoscope of popular world music that was popular then. "Remember everyone was enjoying the Afro-Cuban beat so in a lot of cases we were able to slip in the clave," Tito said. The French bistro sound is heard on *"The River Seine*" (La Farge-Monrod-Robert-Holt), *"Arrivederci Roma,"* (Sigman-Rasel) is tastefully Cubanized a la Tito, and from the Broadway hit *"Damn Yankees"* Abbe and Tito perform the cha cha chá *"Whatever Lola Wants"* (Adler-Ross). In many of the tunes Tito scores his saxes to almost float and sound like violins, but the trumpet riffs give the music just enough punch. It was an album Tito enjoyed making. It was an album that RCA Victor did not promote, and that annoyed Tito.

A cult classic that was recorded during this hectic period was *"Mucho Puente."* It simply shows another, possibly elegant and softer side of Tito. In it he adds strings for such standards as *"Lullaby of the Leaves"* (Bernice Petkere and Joe Young); *"Noche de Ronda"* (María Teresa Lara); *"Duerme"* (Miguel Prado and Gabriel Luna); and, *"Poor Butterfly,"* (John L. Golden and Raymond Hubbell). Cuban standards such as *"La Ola Marina,"* (Virgilio González), *"Cuando Vuelva a Tu Lado*" (Maria Grever), *"Un Poquito de Tu Amor,"* (Julio Gutierrez and "

Almendra" (Abelardo Valdés) feature a quartet of guitars (no brass) headed by Al Caiola and Jerry Sanfino's flute. Tito handled *"Two For Tea"* (Vincent Youmans and Irving Caesar) as a straight cha cha chá. He uses his large orchestra in a series of guajeos that culminate in a double time ending and in which he uses the trumpets to echo the Cuban style ostinatos. The piano ties it all up together.

In Cuba, Arcaño and Cachao had taken the Youmans –Caesar classic and turned it into a slow four-beat mambo and re-titled it *"Camina Juan Pescado."* After the introduction of the melody Arcaño and his orchestra play off a lengthy guajeo pattern with the piano and unadorned flute improvising. Tito thought of doing it this way but he wanted the album to stay on keel – conservative so as to appeal to a wider audience. The album was mildly successful, and Tito always considered that it could have had more acceptance had RCA Victor taken more of an active effort to promote it. He never could understand just what "the executives that were supposed to market product did to earn their keep." He did have some choice descriptions of the way they conducted business.

Tito Puente, sitting, second from right, in the Boy Scouts, 1934.
(Joe Conzo Archive)

Tito Puente (rear/center) plays with Machito and his Rumba Kings, 1941.
A few months after this promotional photo was taken,
Tito was drafted into the U.S. Navy.
(Joe Conzo Archive)

Tito Puente, holding his helmet (left), looks on with ship sailors during burial at sea ceremony aboard the USS Santee, 1944. (Joe Conzo Archive)

Tito Puente (rear/center) performs with the Pupi Campo Orchestra, 1948. To his right is trumpet player Jimmy Frisaura. The bongocero is John "La Vaca" Rodríguez, father of percussionist John "Dandy" Rodríguez. Al Escobar is at the piano. (John "Dandy" Rodriguez Archive)

Tito Puente and Tito Rodríguez with friends at the beach, 1953. (Tito Puente Estate Archive)

Cal Tjader, Al McKibbon, Tito Puente, Miguelito Valdés, George Shearing and Luisito Benjamin at the New York Palladium Ballroom, 1954. (Joe Conzo Archive)

Tito Puente playing the saxophone with his orchestra at the New York Palladium Ballroom, 1955. (Joe Conzo Archive)

Miguelito Valdés (left) and Tito Puente duel on timbales while Gilberto Valdés (center) conducts orchestra during Mambo Show performance, 1955. (Joe Conzo Archive)

Tito Puente the dancer at the New York Palladium Ballroom, 1960. (Joe Conzo Archive)

Tito Puente playing vibes at the New York Palladium Ballroom, 1962. (Joe Conzo Archive)

Charlie Palmieri, Tito Puente and Kako work out on timbales during a Monday night show staged by the Alegre All-Stars at the Palladium Ballroom, 1963. (John "Dandy" Rodríguez Archive)

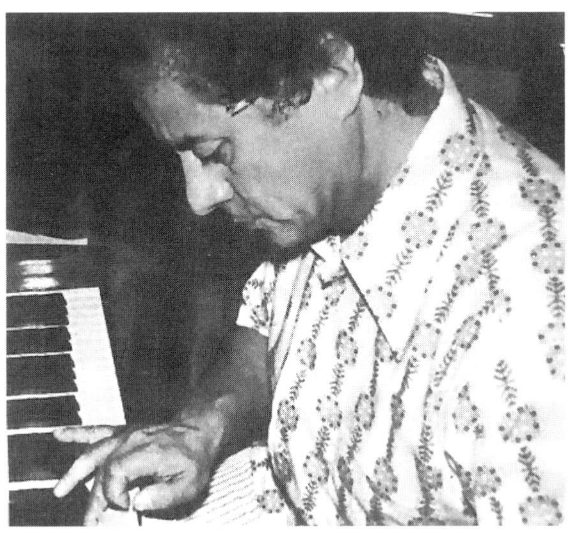

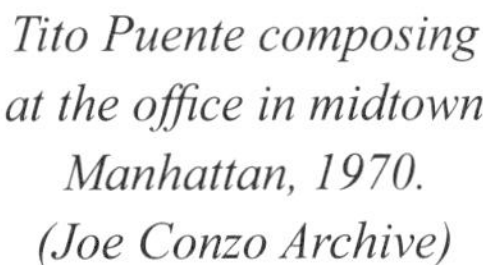

Tito Puente composing at the office in midtown Manhattan, 1970. (Joe Conzo Archive)

Top: Tito Puente, Miguelito Valdés and Israel "Cachao" López at the Tijuana Cat, West 54th Street, New York City, 1970. (Joe Conzo Archive)

Right: Sophy Hernández sings with Tito Puente Orchestra at Manhattan Center, New York City, 1971. She was the only female vocalist to be an official member of the band. (Sophy Hernández Photo Collection)

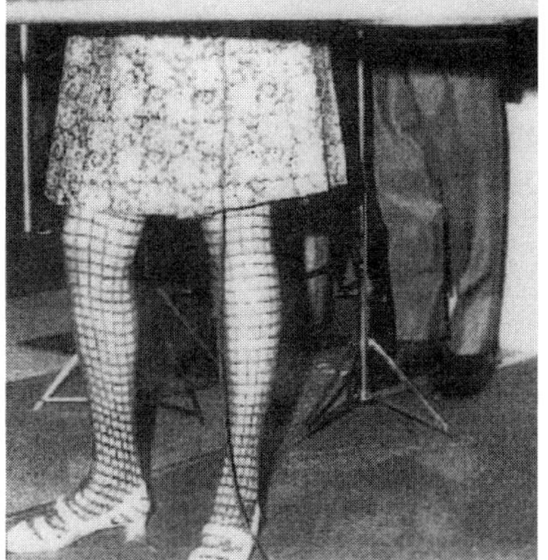

Tito Puente and his mentor, Machito, 1977. (Joe Conzo Archives)

Charlie Palmieri's departure for Puerto Rico – party at Beau's Restaurant in the Bronx, 1979. From left to right: Ray Barretto, Tito Puente, Machito, Charlie Palmieri, Johnny Pacheco and Joe Quijano. (Joe Conzo Jr. Archive)

Right: Tito Puente and Dizzy Gillespie at New York City Hall for a ceremony, 1981. (Courtesy of Carlos Ortiz, Nubia Music Society)

Bottom: Tito Puente and Billy Taylor, 1991. (Joe Conzo Archive)

Emma Conzo (author's sister), Al Pacino and Tito Puente celebrate their birthdays at Willie's Steakhouse in the Bronx, New York, 1992. (Joe Conzo Archive)

Tito Puente with Rita Moreno, 1995. (Joe Conzo Archive)

Bill Cosby, the author, and Tito Puente, 1995.
(Joe Conzo Jr. Archive)

Tito Puente at the White House – (left to right) President George Bush Sr. and First Lady Barbara Bush, 1991, and President Bill Clinton and First Lady Hillary Clinton, 1997. (White House Photos/Joe Conzo Archive)

Tito Puente with Tony Bennett, 1999.
(Joe Conzo Archive)

Grand opening – Willie's Steakhouse in the Bronx, New York. From left to right: Johnny Pacheco, Celia Cruz, Bronx Borough President Fernando Ferrer, Bill Cosby, Tito Puente and restaurant owner Kenny Giordano, 2000.
(Joe Conzo Archive)

Dance Mania

The discography for the period 1957 through 1960 is extensive and gives a view of the complex style of the Tito Puente Orchestra. He was always searching, looking to try new things, to present authentic Afro-Cuban music with the big band sound. His experimentation continued with the RCA Victor LP release of *"Tambo"* in 1960. At the time of release it had disappointing acceptance, even with the formidable line up of musicians that featured trumpeters Bernie Glow, Ernie Royal and Doc Severinsen, and Cuban flautist Alberto Socarras.

Tito remembers that he staged one of his patented temper outbursts. "I think I even cried," he told me. "I know I was gagging and having trouble breathing. They (RCA Victor executives) were such shit heads." As far as Tito was concerned the lack of popularity of *"Tambo"* at the time was due once again to the "short sightedness of media executives." But he was not going to give in or give up. In 1958 his rhythm section is added to Woody Herman's orchestra for *"Woody Herman's Heat, Puente's Beat"* that was released on Everest. There was a significant promotional effort Tito recalled. Sales were much better than expected by him and Woody Herman. "It was a good marriage and both of us worked to make it happen."

This was the direction Tito wanted to take his orchestra – explore the realms of jazz and swing with a strong challenging Afro-Cuban percussion contingent that did not hamper or hinder the swing of the orchestra. "This was something that all of us were trying out in one way or another – Machito, Rodríguez, Kenton and some of the other guys."

"Dance Mania" recorded in 1957 and released in 1958 was one of the most successful albums produced by any orchestra that played and recorded Afro-Cuban music. There was something in it for everyone. In it Tito introduces Santos Colón to vocalize in a prominent role. This was a major shift in the orchestra's approach during three previous years. Tito did not want a permanent lead vocalist. Tito wanted to try out new things and to experiment – instrumentalists, vocalists and percussion. Willie and Tito, for the most part, did the vocalization up until the arrival of Santos Colón. For years he had shared vocal responsibilities with Tony Molina. Colón was not Cuban and his voice had a little more range than many of the singers of the period. He understood the Cuban traditional poetic forms of improvising, but did not seem concerned with this conventional way of doing things.

Tito liked his voice, liked his approach and even if a little bit unorthodox in delivery, Santos had a good sound that fit into the orchestra. "The orchestra, the entity, the whole was what we are about. Santos was just what we needed," explained Tito. "I wanted to make sure that we could still play boleros and Santos was perfect. He had a sensual voice. I had not had his type of varied approach in a few years." Tito was also concerned with reliability. He had had bad luck with his last full time vocalist.

"El Cayuco" composed and arranged by Tito was an instant hit and highly popular whenever it was performed at the Palladium. The instrumental *"3-D Mambo"* was composed and arranged by Ray Santos, Jr.,[89] who appeared with the orchestra at various times, was inserted into the album for esoteric reasons. The instrumental piece is structured on the 4-beat mambo format and Tito wanted it just to keep everything on an even keel. "It had a New York Palladium feel to it," he maintained. It was Tito's formula of mixing Afro-Cuban and swing, the ingredients he had been nurtured on and the approach he wanted to maintain. Throughout, Tito manages to maintain his balance the typical Cuban call and response component and achieve a highly danceable and successful album. The basic elements are the Afro-Cuban, the guajeos and the contrapuntal riffs patterns are mambo. Santitos works his vocal inspirations neatly into the Puente model.

The 1950s was truly the battle of the big three Latin bands in New York City. Morris Levy contacted Machito and his orchestra. He wanted to do an album with the orchestra on his Roulette label. Jimmy and Charlie found out about it from Tito. "I was surprised that he was not pissed. In fact he welcomed the competition." Charlie laughed. "He always maintained that it was a logical move for Levy. He figured that Tito Rodríguez would not be far behind. Tito (Rodríguez) was always trying out new things."

Years later even Morris Levy told me that he was surprised by Tito's receptiveness to the Machito organization recording a big band Afro-Cuban jazz album. In his gruff voice he told me "Tito said 'shit that's a good idea.' I was expecting to have to kick his ass," groaned Levy to me.

In December 1957, Machito and is Afro-Cubans gathered at Metropolitan Studios in the Odd Fellows Temple at E. 106th Street and Park Avenue. The recording session was historic. The album *"Kenya"*[90] featured outstanding performances from alto saxophonist Cannonball Adderley and trumpeter Joe Newman, who were featured on *"Congo Mulence," "Oyeme," "Conversation," "Tururato," "Minor Rama"* and *"Frenzy."* Doc Cheatham was featured on *"Holiday,"* a cheerful cha cha chá that permits his pure trumpet tone to sweep the room with poise. Newman is featured on *"Blues a la Machito"* with a syrupy and brassy open tone that explores the common elements between the Afro-Cuban tradition and jazz. Adderley, Candido, Patato Valdéz, José Mangual, Jimmy Russo and Ray Santos, Jr. lift the session beyond expectation. *"Conversation" "Tin Tin Deo"* and *"Wild Jungle,"* are part of the menu. The album personnel included: Machito- leader and vocals; Joe Livramento, Joe Newman, Mario Bauzá (musical director), Francis Williams, Doc Cheatham, Paul Cohen, Paquito Dávila- trumpet; Santo Russo, Jimmy Russo, Eddie Bert, Bart Varsalona, Rex Peer- trombone; Cannonball Adderley- alto saxophone; José Madera, Sr., Ray Santos, Jr.- tenor saxophone; Leslie Johnakins-baritone saxophone; René Hernández- piano; Roberto Rodríguez- bass; José Mangual- bongos; Uba Nieto- timbales; Candido Camero, Carlos "Patato" Valdéz- congas. Several of these musicians played on and off with Tito, and are heard on *"Cuban Carnaval."* Machito and his Afro-Cubans, under the musical direction of Mario Bauzá would go on, through the 1950s and 1960s, to record over 30 albums under a variety of labels such as Decca, Mercury, CBS, Seeco, Tico, Roulette, and GNP. They would perform steady through this period, though by the end of the 1960s they would start to fade.

The ushering in of a new year, 1959 would change Afro-Cuban music the way no one could ever have imagined. Beny Moré was the headliner at the Delido Hotel on Miami Beach. Tito Rodríguez and his Orchestra were performing at the American Hotel. Other prominent entertainers that had crossed paths with Tito, such as Diosa Costello was presenting a tropical music and dance revue at the Lucerne, The DeCastro Sisters were the headliners at the posh Fontainebleau Hotel, and Anselmo Sacasas and his Orchestra were in the main ballroom. The Casino de la Playa Orchestra, for whom he had played, was a distant memory. In Havana, Fidel Castro was on the move and Fulgencio Batista was gathering his followers. He nervously advised his staff of how bad things were and that he would be departing Cuba – post haste. Batista formally resigned the presidency at 3:00 A.M. on January 1, 1959. He left from a military air base near Havana with an entourage of nearly 40 people, among them José Luis del Pozo, the Mayor of Havana – the man who had greeted Tito and the Cuban musicians nearly two years earlier. Beny Moré heard the news via lobby gossip while he was having drinks. He left the hotel and set a course for Havana.

Tito Puente and his Orchestra were appearing in New York City at the Palladium Ballroom. Tito rarely if ever spent family time during the holiday season. In a strange way his family was his orchestra, the people that accompanied him day in and day out. This is the way he wanted it. The world of Afro-Cuban dance music was about to change in ways, he admitted later, he could not have imagined. "None of us had a clue," he recalled. "It was good for Cuba, some said. Others were not sure. I had no idea how this was going to change things." Tito never traveled to Cuba after the arrival of Fidel Castro.

The orchestral craftsman followed his *"Dance Mania"* success with *"Dancing Under Latin Skies," "Mucho Cha Cha*" and *"Puente Live At Grossingers,"* in 1959. Once again in *"Mucho Cha Cha"* Tito leans to the experimental trying out several tunes with marimbas and using a young Johnny Pacheco's unadorned five key, six hole Cuban style flute. Tito considered that the unadorned flute gave his arrangements a "more tipico quality," while the modern or mechanical flute (as the Cuban musicians referred to it) provided an exotic jazz tone. He liked them both and used the two types to suit his particular requirements. Using the Cuban standard harmonies in implementation of his guajeos Tito switches constantly from one riff to another in much the way that the Arcaño Orchestra accomplished this in the 1940s and continued to do so into the 1950s.

However, Jimmy revealed to me on several occasions "Tito modified the scores that featured Pacheco. He was not as proficient as you would think, not like Gilberto Valdés, and Fajardo. But Tito wanted a certain feeling and tipico quality, and Pacheco was able to provide it with his style of playing."

"Guataca," a Puente composition spotlights Tito on marimbas and Pacheco on the Cuban flute. It builds up with Barretto displaying his improvisational skills. Cachao López composed *"Chanchullo"* while he was with Arcaño y sus Maravillas. The modern big band approach is typically Puente with the back and forth riffs, the saxes playing underneath and Pacheco fitting in his blend of tight improvisation. The Arcaño version featured a fellow by the name of Eulogio Ortiz on the unadorned flute. He was capable of taking one high F or G note and making it sound like three or four notes. His intonation and ability to hold certain notes was hard to believe," according to Arcaño (Interview with Arcaño - Marcos "Sonny" Pérez – 1993).

"Puente at Grossingers" was recorded live and for a mostly non-Latino audience in the Catskill resort. It is instrumental, with Santos Colón and Tito providing some timely catcalls during the breaks and when the orchestra pushed forward to driving conclusions. To me this album

underscores the brilliance of Tito. He understood his audience and played to their likes. Tito's approach was based on what he learned by watching the big bands and observing how they played to the audience. "Every crowd was different," he would recall. "Sometimes you think that the large crowd is going to swing and they turn out to be a total letdown. Then when you think you have to play soft because they are older, well they swing more and they want faster. You have to feel your way through it."

The album features several pop standards. *"How High The Moon"* (Nancy Hamilton & Morgan Lewis) is treated gently rather than in its usual brisk beat; *"That Old Devil Moon"* (E.Y. Harburg & Burton Lane) has a steady shifting cha cha chá swing; *"I Love Paris"* (Cole Porter) gets two treatments. The trumpets announce the selection, the saxes bring in the somber melody and using the short riffs throughout he maintains an intimate feeling.

"More Dance Mania," recorded in the summer of 1960, was not released in the United States. It pissed off Tito. He blew his stack, according to Jimmy. "When he learned that the record was only going to get limited exposure Tito became enraged." The album, according to the contracts was assigned a release date of 1968. Like the original it was vintage Tito Puente Orchestra danceable music.

Jimmy told me that it took a lot of drinks one night in a midtown Manhattan bar to calm Tito down. "He was not yelling or stomping on the floor," recalled Jimmy. "But his verbal description of the people that run the music industry – in general – was anything but endearing. All I can say is he had some choice words. And, I can't blame him. We really thought this second *"Dance Mania"* was going to be a winner. You know me, I would have bet on it."

Tito recalled that his reaction to the limited release was: "They fucked me again!"

The August 1960 gathering of two major orchestras that would face off in what some notable music authorities called a "cultural clash" followed the *"More Dance Mania."* To the contrary, it was the Tito Puente Orchestra and Buddy Morrow[91] and his Orchestra sitting in Webster Hall trading musical barrages. Something like this had never been accomplished. The arrangements were made by George Williams for the Morrow Orchestra and by Tito for his band. Later in life Tito felt that this was a significant achievement and quite possibly the end of an era.

Morrow was born Muni "Moe" Zudekoff, on February 8, 1919, in New Haven, Connecticut. He was known as "The "Night Train" man-

-or, more accurately, the white "Night Train" man. He studied music at Juilliard in the early 1930s, and then played with such big bands as Paul Whiteman, Artie Shaw, and Tommy Dorsey. After serving in the Army during World War II, he played with Jimmy Dorsey, and then formed his own band, which quickly folded. During the next few years he worked in studio ensembles on radio and movie soundtracks. His second attempt at forming a band, in 1951, was considerably more successful. Morrow was able to keep a steady flow of engagements at a time when many other big bands were folding.

He also won a recording contract with Mercury that produced a Top 10 hit in early 1952 with *"Night Train,"* a cover of a popular R&B hit by Jimmy Forrest. He moved to RCA in 1957, and participated in a few genre-stretching experiments, including the collaboration with Tito. He folded the band around 1960, soon after the historic session with Tito and returned to studio work, this time in television. He worked with Skitch Henderson and Doc Severinsen on the "Tonight Show" orchestra. In the early 1970s, he formed a jazz quartet that played in Vegas and the Los Angeles area.

Williams and Tito toiled for months to get the arrangements for the two orchestras as suited to their genres as possible, and more importantly to "meld rather than mix," Tito said. "I know that fusion had been going on between Afro-Cuban music and American jazz. Machito had introduced the fusion of the two as 'Cubop.' Stan Kenton incorporated Afro-Cuban percussion wonderfully into his large jazz orchestrations. This was not new. I wanted to do something a little different. Buddy was agreeable. He liked the idea that both orchestras would retain their style and also their personality."

Contrasting yet blending arrangements between the two orchestras is heard in the way that Tito arranged the song *"Autumn Leaves."* The vibraphone takes the lead and gently introduces this ballad. The brass and woodwinds blend in effectively a la Tito and it is all tied neatly together with a cha cha chá. The structured syncopated riffs bring it back to an easy sounding bolero. The Morrow band blasts onto the scene and then Tito joins in with his vibes - all in just about three minutes. *"The Continental"* is a mambo-cha. Tito Puente and his orchestra introduce it and there is an insertion of the Morrow brass before Tito returns to close it out. It is a short piece and gives the listener a glimpse at the versatility of Tito as an arranger. There is a lot more in this production. Tito and Morrow enjoyed working on this project.

The exchanges of the two full orchestras were something new and different. In it Tito manages to accomplish more than he first realized. It was a blending rather than an exchange. In the tune *"Harlem Nocturne"*

(Earl Hagen) the feeling is captivating. The feeling of Harlem is conveyed as not only a place where blacks and Puerto Ricans resided, but that once there were Italians, Jews and Irish that lived in the same area. The Morrow Orchestra swings gently in the opening. The Tito Puente Orchestra takes charge with a driving yet moderate cha cha chá with the saxophone section carrying the harmony. The Morrow orchestra returns with Buddy's trombone conveying a jazz feeling. Tito's percussion ensemble – Ray Barretto, José Mangual, Sr., Julito Collazo and Patato Valdéz bring us back to Spanish Harlem. Al Casamenti strums the guitar as the Morrow orchestra swings gently into motion. The guitar climbs an octave and Tito introduces the flutes as the two orchestras fade. The two bandleaders were extremely satisfied with their hard work. Both were very disappointed that the RCA Victor executives misplaced the unique and experimental sessions. "At least that is what they kept telling me," exclaimed Tito. More than 13 years would elapse before the album became commercially available.

"I believe that after this session the big structured bands started to fade. The swing era had long been over. The American big bands were gone. Now we were faced with the same thing," reflected Tito.

Times Are Changing

The pachanga dance craze had a tremendous impact on the sound of Latino New York. It was introduced in Cuba in 1958. Eduardo Davidson, a Cuban Jew, was a prolific composer in Havana. He composed a tune titled "Pancha Calma" for Fajardo and his orchestra and then *"La Pachanga"* for Orquesta Sublime. In 1955 Davidson introduced the Marencumbae, a Colombian/ Venezuelan type dance in Cuba with several of his compositions. The original music was called Pachanga with Marencumbae underneath it. Some spellings of the word have it as "Merecumbe."

As played by the Cuban ensembles the rhythm was a cross between a merengue and a fast driving montuno. Flute-and-violin charanga bands began to dominate. Charlie Palmieri recorded a violin, flute and rhythm album in 1960 for United Artists. It featured Johnny Pacheco, who soon after formed his own charanga. The two charangas introduced a driving new sound that was nothing like what was played in Cuba, but it caught on. Both Palmieri and Pacheco recorded for Al Santiago's Alegre label, which would later be bought out by Roulette.

However, for the time being, Alegre's artists were the big headliners– the Alegre All-Stars. Alegre recruited charangas led by Rosendo Rosell, Pupi Legarreta, and Alfredito Valdés, Jr. The big bands that were left were transformed. Machito, Pete Terrace, and Arsenio Rodríguez fit the pachanga into their repertoires. The playing of flautist Mauricio Smith was prominent on most if not all of the recordings Tico cut during this period. He got to strut his stuff under his own name in 1963 on an album called *"Machito Presents Flauta Nova."* By 1961 Ray Barretto had formed a Charanga and was recording for Riverside.

Cal Tjader, along with Mongo and Willie, issued a number of classic albums that also featured Cuban flautist Jose "Rolando" Lozano. Tjader enjoyed using the flute in many of his early sessions. He often used jazz flautist Paul Horn to insert the tropical flavors. The use of Lozano was a first for him. *"Manila"* (Mongo Santamaría) and *"The Continental"* (Herb Magidson and Con Conrad) are showcases for the former Orquesta Aragón and Orquesta América flautist. "I saw him work in Havana and I saw him at the Palladium. He had a powerful way of playing. He really understood jazz," was how Tito observed the Tjader effort. "Probably one of the best albums of the period," he concluded.

Tito Rodríguez and his Orchestra made changes. First he recorded a charanga album *"Charanga Pachanga*" with violins and flute. The Rodríguez album with a charanga style studio orchestra was successful and vindicated his first effort with violins, a flute and percussion ensemble. In the mid 1950s he tried producing several individual releases with a charanga. These were flops… not well received. Tito Rodríguez did not perform live with this studio orchestra but turned to his big band.

Keeping pace Tito released two Pachanga albums with his big band – *"Pachanga in New York, with Rolando Laserie,"* on Gema (1961) and *"Pachanga With Puente"* on the Tico label (1961). Even Mongo shifted his interest. He assumed the musicians from Orquesta Nuevo Ritmo and made a number of recordings while appearing around the city and on the West Coast.

As much as he enjoyed the sound of the charanga, Tito loved and preferred the sound of the big band even more. "It is in my blood and I was brought up on it. They were all out of their fucking minds. It was like a panic, a stampede. Every record label wanted to have someone recording with violins and flutes." During one of those gatherings at the Asia Restaurant indulging me, Charlie and Tito, there was a reference to the Pachanga era. Tito remembered: "It was crazy. All the record companies wanted us to add violins. Jesus!" he laughed. "Charlie tell Joe the story about your charanga."

Charlie recounted: "After we finished recording our album for United Artists in 1959, the executives at the company called me into the offices. Our recording was pre-pachanga era – we played mostly cha cha chás, a lot of American standards arranged for the Afro-Cuban style. Well, up the stairs I go wondering what they want with me. After a few minutes of conversation one of the bosses asks me: 'Do you think your orchestra is up to doing an album of just Hawaiian music?' I was speechless. I told my guys what happened. I made up my mind to move to another label."

Tito reinforced his point: "These guys were all shit heads making big bucks with no clue. I mean when the pachanga hit, Fidel was pissed at us, the young people were losing interest in our music and these guys (record company executives) in the big jobs got scared shitless. If they had a better idea of what was going on maybe the whole industry would not have gone to shit." He rolled his eyes. Charlie shrugged.

Music from Cuba continued to find its way into the United States even as the Castro Regime and United States government slipped further apart. Tito read the newspapers daily and thoroughly. He laughed when he recounted reading that U.S. State Department advisor William Wieland lamented, as the rift grew wider that "I know Batista is considered by many as a son of a bitch... but American interests come first... at least he was our son of a bitch."

President Dwight D. Eisenhower[92] officially recognized the new Cuban government after the 1959 Cuban Revolution that had overthrown the Batista government, but relations between the two governments deteriorated rapidly. Within days Earl T. Smith, U.S. Ambassador to Cuba, resigned his post to be replaced by Philip Bonsal. The U.S. government became increasingly concerned by Cuba's agrarian reforms and the nationalization of U.S. owned industries. Between April 15 and 26, 1959, Castro and a delegation of representatives visited the United States as guests of the Press Club. Many perceived this visit as a charm offensive on the part of Castro and his recently initiated government. His visit included laying a wreath at the Lincoln Memorial.

After a meeting between Castro and Vice-President Richard Nixon, where Castro outlined his reform plans for Cuba, the U.S. began to impose gradual trade restrictions on the island. On September 4 1959, Ambassador Bonsal met with Cuban Premier Fidel Castro to express "serious concern at the treatment being given to American private interests in Cuba, both agriculture and utilities." As the reforms continued, trade restrictions on Cuba increased. The U.S. stopped buying Cuban sugar and refused to supply its former trading partner with much needed oil, creating a devastating effect on the island's economy. In March 1960, tensions increased when the freighter La Coubre exploded in Havana Harbor, killing over 75 people.

Fidel Castro blamed the United States and compared the incident to the sinking of the Maine, though admitting he could provide no evidence for his accusation. That same month, President Eisenhower quietly authorized the Central Intelligence Agency (CIA) to organize, train, and equip Cuban refugees as a guerrilla force to overthrow Castro.

Each time the Cuban government nationalized American properties, the U.S. government took countermeasures, resulting in the prohibition of all exports to Cuba on October 19, 1960. Consequently, Cuba began to strengthen trade relations with the Soviet Union, leading the U.S. to break off all remaining official diplomatic relations. Later that year, U.S. diplomats Edwin L. Sweet and William G. Friedman, were arrested and expelled from the island having been charged with "encouraging terrorist acts, granting asylum, financing subversive publications and smuggling weapons." In 1961 Cuba resisted an armed invasion by about 1,500 CIA trained Cuban exiles at the Bay of Pigs. President John F Kennedy's complete assumption of responsibility for the venture, which provoked a popular reaction against the invaders, proved to be a further propaganda boost for the Cuban government. The U.S. began the formulation of new plans aimed at destabilizing the Cuban government. These activities were collectively known as the "The Cuban Project" (also known as Operation Mongoose). This was to be a coordinated program of political, psychological, and military sabotage, involving intelligence operations as well as assassination attempts on key political leaders. The Cuban project also proposed attacks on mainland U.S. targets, hijackings and assaults on Cuban refugee boats to generate U.S. public support for military action against the Cuban government, these proposals were known collectively as Operation Northwoods.

The takeover of Cuba by Castro also set in motion dismantling of the entertainment industry. The record companies soon disappeared and the recording studios were looted for many of the musical treasures that had been in the vaults. Fleeing Cubans took whatever they could carry. The militia mutilated, destroyed or stole what it deemed useful. Many entertainers, bandleaders, musicians and songwriters left the island. Some remained but it would be years before the Cuban government realized that much of its heritage had been lost. Of course, new musicians would surface, join with those that remained and slowly rebuild some of the lost treasures, continue exporting music – it would take time.

The pachanga would be the last Cuban oriented music fad, at least for the foreseeable future. New York's Latino population was twisting hips and waving red handkerchiefs to the rhythms of New York pachanga and was caught up in teenage dance crazes like the Twist, the Monkey, the Mashed Potatoes and The Watusi. During this time, the pop charts were bursting with dance records by artists like Little Eva, Chubby Checker, Major Lance and Joey Dee and the Starlighters. The trends and interests were changing. Tito was right! The youth spawned from the Puerto Ricans who had embraced Cuban music in New York were now taking a front seat and looking for something new to entice them, excite them and entertain them.

Morris Levy, who had convinced Tito to return to RCA Victor, was now the owner of Tico Records. It has been reported that Levy gained ownership of Tico via collection of a gambling debt from Goldner. The new owner was still a good friend of Tito, even though he had been the brunt of many of those wild verbal tirades against RCA Victor. Levy never held it against Tito; in fact he often sympathized with him. Goldner was still at Tico, although in a less prominent role. Levy talked Tito into returning to Tico.

Tito remembered a call from Morris. "'You know Tito, times are changing. Now that Cuba is closed and there is little left of it – I mean in the entertainment area. That motherfucker, Castro has really fucked up everything, you know. You are still an important vehicle to promote Afro-Cuban music. I'm here for you.'" Soon afterward Tito made the move.

Before settling in at Tico after five years at RCA Victor, Tito went to California for a series of performances. There was sufficient time for Tito and his orchestra to slip into a Hollywood studio and record an album for Gene Norman Presents (GNP) that featured José "Rolando" Lozano, the Cuban flautist who successfully incorporated his unadorned Cuban flute into the jazz framework. Lozano was working with Mongo and had settled in California. *"Tito Puente In Hollywood,"* was a strong offering during a time of musical turbulence and change – a little big band jazz and something "tipico" a la Tito. He adopted the Count Basie hit *"April In Paris"* but with an Afro-Cuban motif buried in the middle – rather exciting and even interesting. It is here where Lozano fits in his unadorned flute and the montuno is offered up in support. He returns to the original arrangement to close the number out. *"Guajira Flute"* composed by Tito is a showpiece for Lozano's skilled flute improvisations that are haunting and striking and leaning toward the American side of the jazz spectrum. In *"TP On The Strip,"* Tito provides stimulating scat vocals that perhaps were a little flat, but very effective. "It was a lot of fun to do this because we were able to mix in different things," Tito explained.

Tito Puente had other things to consider during the first few years of the 1960s decade. Latin music, as it was coming to be described, was, in his opinion starting to become somewhat diluted. "In a way it reminded me of when I was young and the rumba was popular. It was not really Afro-Cuban. It was nothing – light and bouncy shit. Now we are getting away from our roots again," he shrugged. In 1961 Tito was 38. The true sound of Afro-Cuban music was being pushed to the side and other influences were taking hold. I met Tito in 1959 at the New York Palladium. A few years later, soon after I returned from Korea we became close friends. He met Margie in 1963. It seemed Margie had a calming effect on him. She was a very patient person.

The music business was changing, especially the Cuban influences. He reminded me about that time: "Maybe you did not see it, but the signs of change were all around. At first I thought what was happening would be favorable for our music – you know the music we played was always explored. But now, looking back I am not so sure."

Performing in the Catskills, and Miami Beach and Hollywood provided the orchestra with a steady revenue flow. Tito was still in big demand and he was determined to keep it that way. But Tito had a feeling that this was not going to continue. For example, the Catskill contracts were shrinking. There were several reasons for this – the Jewish population was getting older and many were relocating to Florida; and, the small ad hoc non-Latino ensembles and bands were including a menu of mambo and cha cha chá in their repertoires. But Tito and Jimmy made sure that the bookings were scheduled so as to keep a steady financial flow. When Tito traveled to Spain, for example, he only took his core orchestra. This was in 1959. He traveled with most of his band to the Far East in the early 1960s.

The number of musicians scheduled to travel was based on the contract size, the length of time the orchestra would be on the road and the engagement requirements. Jimmy and Tito considered how the orchestra was to be moved carefully. "There were too many stories about promoters not coming up with the cash," Jimmy noted when recalling the planning logistics. "Too often the promoters ducked out and left the musicians stranded. We wanted to be as sure about anything as we could be."

"Take care of the boys (the musicians) first," was Tito's rule. "If we don't have them we have shit."

So far Tito had managed to negotiate a crossover of musical ideas, in his own way. His sound was also different. It was sharp, intoxicating and as he often stated it "was controlled." I believe more than anything it was "New York Latino," or as he would remind me in a sharp forceful tone "New York Afro-Cuban music." However you describe it was Tito's unique sound, admired by his peers, his friends and his rivals. No one else could sound like this. But as he reflected to me: "The 1960s presented new challenges."

Up until this moment Tito was firm in his commitment to good music. He refused to take what he perceived was second billing to Damaso Pérez Prado, the self-proclaimed king of the mambo, and he refused to give into a recording industry that he was convinced was clueless, and partly responsible for the problems that the music he loved was now having. He enjoyed the fact that RCA Victor executives referred to him as "Little Caesar." He often laughed about it. "They are lucky that they picked Edward G. Robinson's character and not the role that Jimmy Cagney played in 'The Public Enemy.' Sometimes I felt like going in to their offices and blowing up the fucks, really." His forehead narrowed, and his eyes glinted. I was not sure if he was kidding. Then he would relax and laugh.

The fights with the bosses at RCA Victor were often and loud. Tito stood his ground and had to remind them that his music was popular everywhere. "If you got off your fat asses you would see that," he shouted. Usually they did not listen. I imagine that most often when they saw him approaching they would run for cover. His temper was well known.

When Tito returned from Japan in the late summer of 1961, he was still thinking about how to get the upper hand musically speaking in the rapidly changing Latino music market. The Palladium was still going, but the signs were there too that all was not well. But Tito was an optimist and he new he would figure out his next move. Meanwhile, his orchestra opened the night at the Palladium on 53rd Street. Someone in the audience asked for *"Pare Cochero."*[93]

He looked around and saw Johnny Pacheco in the audience. He called out to him: "Johnny why don't you join us for this number." There was applause. Johnny jumped on the stage and put the four pieces of his wood flute together. Foot stumping Tito counted, "1, 2, 3." The orchestra opened. For the next 14 minutes the orchestra was pulsating and Pacheco would take what Tito later recalled as "one of his best flute solos."

"Tito just kept on going. He was that way," Johnny told me years later. "I don't think I ever played better. He (Tito) was driving. He was like a mad man."

Tito liked to use Pacheco on the wooden flute on occasion when he wanted to get a very "tipico" sound. Pacheco did not have the range of Tito's regular flute player, Jerry Sanfino, but he fit in nicely with many of those RCA Victor recordings in the late 1950s. Tito would eventually use Rolando Lozano in a GNP recording –*"Tito Puente In Hollywood."* This was a superb effort by Tito and his orchestra.

El Rey Bravo

Tito looked at Charlie Palmieri with sharp piercing eyes. The heavyset pianist had just completed his third album featuring a charanga. Charlie sipped his Scotch and soda and huffed and puffed on his cigarette as the two men sat in a bar a few blocks from the Palladium. Charlie had just told Tito that he was considering making a change, switching violins for trombones. "Everyone is interested in rock, the twist and that noisy shit," Charlie complained to Tito.

Charlie's younger brother, Eddie was leading the way with a new sound that was reaching craze proportions with the teenage Latinos of New York. It consisted of trombones, percussion, piano and the Cuban style flute that was used in charangas. The young up-and-coming musicians were flocking to the new brash sound. Eddie Palmieri was born in Spanish Harlem in 1936. Eddie joined his uncle's orchestra at age 13, where he played the timbales. But by the time he was 15 he was committed to the piano. Older brother Charlie was considered the more classically oriented of the two. His piano studies had commenced at seven and included attending the Juilliard School of Music – the same one that Tito attended. It was located 120 Claremont Avenue in Manhattan's Morningside Heights. The Manhattan School of Music currently occupies the building. He had been playing professionally since he was 16 years old.

In 1955 Eddie joined Johnny Segui's band. Charlie got him a job with the Tito Rodríguez Orchestra in 1959. He formed "Conjunto La Perfecta," in 1961. La Perfecta featured a trombone section (led by the late Barry Rogers) in place of trumpets, something that had been rarely done in Afro-Cuban music, and which demonstrated the early stages of Eddie Palmieri's unconventional means of orchestration. They were known as "the band with the crazy roaring elephants" for the configuration of two trombones, the unadorned wooden flute, percussion, bass and vocalist with a contagious and high-ceilinged sound.

"You should have kicked the shit out of Eddie tied up his hands and kept him in a closet and maybe all this crappy noise would not be taking hold," was Tito's initial response. Then he laughed. The two musicians had had quite a few drinks.

Charlie laughed too. "Shit, somebody else would have done it. The young people are not like us. Everyone is in a hurry."

"I know, these guys think they know everything, and just want to jump out there. I want to keep the band together, Charlie. I'm not ready to ditch it. We – you and me - have a lot of music left in us, you know."

Charlie laughed again. "You know me. I always gravitate to the sound of good music." Charlie Palmieri and his Duboney Orchestra's final recording as a charanga was in 1963, and was titled: *"Salsa Na'Ma."* Both Tito and Charlie realized many years later, that unwittingly this was the initiation into the prolonged "salsa" phase. As far as Tito and Charlie were concerned it was similar to the "rhumba era" of the 1930s. Tito was mentally prepared to cope with the new wave. He often admitted, mostly privately to his close friends, that he was disappointed with the direction Afro-Cuban music was taking. However, he was up to the challenge to continue to be as creative as possible, willing to try out new ideas, and even dabble in the contemporary sounds – even though he felt these were eroding authentic concepts.

I was discharged from the Army in September, 1963. Upon returning to New York, I rejoined my wife Lorraine Montenegro. Today she is the administrator of the United Bronx Parents. My son Joey was born in February. My son Eric was born the year Lorraine and I separated, 1965. I ended up in the hospital with a severe attack of anxiety, and I guess depression. Tito and Charlie visited me in the hospital frequently and offered encouragement. As much as I appreciated their help I started using drugs. My habit consumed me. To get money I sold my first record collection. After my divorce things went from bad to worse. José "Cheo" Feliciano[95] and Ismael Rivera shared my misery. We often shared the drugs we were able to score. On and off I worked in the garment district. My interest in music however, did not lessen. My mother was distraught with my addiction. She tried everything to get me to kick the habit. I moved up to the Bronx to live with her. It was a difficult time for my mother but she never gave up on me.

Machito's words of wisdom whenever he ran into me were simple and blunt: "Deja esa mierda ya!" He was always encouraging me to stop using drugs and straighten out my life. Dick Ricardo Sugar came into the music shop, Casa Alegre on Prospect Avenue in the Bronx and his words to me were direct: "That shit will kill you." Al Santiago, the owner of Casa Alegre, gave me a job at the record shop when I started my recovery program in 1968. Al knew me from the neighborhood and reached out to help. It was while I was working at the shop that I met Arsenio Rodríguez. Ray Barretto often dropped in to chat and a lot of the other musicians came by. Through my drug ordeal my friendship with Tito strengthened. Charlie and Jimmy and I became friendly. They confided their adventures with Tito to me and other musicians also met regularly at the record and book shop, Casa Latina in el Barrio, located at 116th Street near Lexington Avenue.

When I met up with Tito at the dances he echoed Dick Ricardo Sugar's words. "You're killing yourself, man!" It almost did. Tito often played at the Hunts Pont Palace. The billboard also promoted the Machito orchestra. I met Dr. Arnoldo Mora, a psychiatrist, during one of my hospital detoxification visits. He took an interest in helping me and at that this point things began to turn around. Dr. Mora was involved in the methadone treatment recovery program for drug addicts. My mind began to clear up. My friendship with Tito and his close circle of friends continued to grow.

I was able to keep in touch with him via telephone even though he constantly had to change his telephone number so that the women he flirted with could not call to harass him. Charlie used to always laugh about how often he had to copy down a new telephone number from Tito. "You can fill up an address book with Tito's telephone numbers," Charlie quipped.

Roulette and Tico Records

Tito felt that the big bands were suddenly old fashioned and the music of the last generation. The young dancers were into the new beats that combined various music forms and incorporated soul, boogie, and rock. The changes taking place impacted all forms of ballroom dancing. Dance studios, once popular were closing. Nightclubs that featured large orchestras were closing or refurbishing to fit in smaller, louder musical venues. Tito knew this and he understood that he would have to continue to push and be creative if he was going to survive.

The Tico Recording Company that Tito Puente returned to in 1961, in no way shape or form resembled the old Tico that he had been associated with. He was not sure what to make of all the changes. The world of Afro-Cuban music as he had known it, was disappearing. So with a shrug he confirmed with his old time business friend, Morris Levy that he was ready to record for Tico. Quickly, the orchestra recorded "*Pachanga con Puente*" followed by "*Vaya Puente*" in 1962. In Tito's view these were transitional albums. The music reflected for the most part well-orchestrated tunes that presented the full range of his orchestra. His goal was to make sure that his orchestra remained in the spotlight. He understood he needed to make some adjustments if he was going to keep up with changing times. Tito knew that the two Titos and Machito were no longer the big rivals. There were new bands and new music coming on the horizon. He wanted to be ready.

The years Tito had been with RCA Victor Tico Records, under the helm of George Goldner[96] had been a rocky ride. Goldner recorded in state-of-the-art studios with impeccable arrangements, and his Tico soundtracks were daring, lively, and tailored strictly to the tastes of big city consumers. The new Tico sounds were often bathed in a flowing echo, making them sound as if they were being played back in a subway station. Tico Records was about fancy, dressed-up Latin dance music, and the key word was sophistication. The swing and bebop influence was evident on nearly every recording date, and playbacks compared favorably to those of the best jazz bands working between 1957 and 1961. It was major label quality with small label ambiance; it drew so many artists through the doors of its busy offices at 220 West 42nd Street. It certainly was not Tico's royalty fee that by most accounts was scarcely competitive with that of the major music houses.

Unfortunately, Goldner spent money almost without thought. His passion for Latin music was dwarfed by his mania for gambling. Goldner lost thousands of dollars on horse races and casino games, and his dependence on loans from Joe Kolsky, who worked for Morris Levy, at the time the owner of the Birdland nightclub. Levy was well connected, and while Goldner was no pushover, he must have been more than a little discouraged. In 1955, Levy was influential in getting Tito signed with RCA Victor, Goldner could do little more than complain sullenly. By then, he was far too indebted to Levy to challenge his actions. On the other hand, Levy's seemingly inexhaustible sources of money gave Goldner the freedom to sign acts, record them and release product at a rate few other independent record label owners could afford. Goldner took advantage of the situation and began to branch out. He looked at the genre of rock n' roll and quickly realized that this was where there was real money. The Afro-Cuban or Latin market was miniscule by comparison.

In 1956 Goldner partnered with brothers Joe Kolsky and Phil Kahl in founding the Roulette Record label. Roulette was to be a vehicle for jazz and popular music releases. It wasn't long before Levy bought out Goldner's share, and installed himself as Roulette's chief executive officer. This left Tito at RCA Victor to fend for himself. Kolsky and Kahl sold their share of the business to Levy in 1961. The Roulette label went on to be one of the most important and longest running independent record companies in the recording business. It featured hits by Buddy Knox, Jimmie Rodgers, The Playmates, Joey Dee and The Starlighters and Tommy James and The Shondells.

Goldner was forced to sell his interests in Tico in April 1957. Rama, Gee and Mardi Gras also were sold off to Levy. As did all of his early labels, over time it became a subsidiary of Roulette Records. Yet, Goldner did not wash his hands of Tico - he still loved Latin music, and it was his first successful company, after all. He kept an active hand in its creative operations, and would occasionally supervise recording dates for the label until the end of his life.

To Tito there was nothing middle-of-the-road about Levy – he was either loved or loathed. Tito knew that the record entrepreneur was reputed to be in the employ of the Genovese crime family. Levy wasn't shy about throwing his weight around. Depending on the situation, Levy could come across as either warm, mellow and caring or very much a bully. "If you pissed him off he you could get into a hell of a lot of trouble," exclaimed Tito. When Levy was implicated in the "payola" scandal of 1959-60 and narrowly escaped indictment by a grand jury, Levy had already departed RCA Victor. He never mentioned or spoke of his business dealings with Tito. "This was probably why we got along so well. With him and me it was all music. I'm sure I pissed him off once or twice, but we always remained friends. He was always there for me," Tito reminded me.

Levy worked on the periphery of the jazz world for years, eventually becoming manager and then owner of several New York nightclubs. In 1949, he hit the big-time after opening Birdland. It became a Mecca for the cream of jazz talent: Count Basie, Dexter Gordon, Thelonious Monk, Miles Davis, Billie Holliday, and the club's namesake, Charlie "Yardbird" Parker, all headlined there. Celebrities like Frank Sinatra, Ava Gardner, Sammy Davis, Jr. and Marilyn Monroe flocked to Birdland, too. The atmosphere was very exciting, very glamorous, and very mob-connected. Levy got involved in the manufacturing side of the music business in order to record his Birdland acts, as well as claim a hefty chunk of their song income via Patricia Music, his publishing company. The standard *"Lullaby of Birdland",* composed by George Shearing was one of his earliest and most lucrative copyrights. After the Roulette takeover, several Tico artists decided to record for the label. Such conflicts-of-interest were typical of the way Levy did business: in addition to running Roulette and its sister labels, and publishing the songs his artists wrote, he had a hand in jukebox distribution!

Ethical slips notwithstanding, Levy did know how to promote and move inventory, and Tico Records certainly profited from his knowledge. Over the years he and Tito developed a relationship. Tito did not trust many people, but he confided in Morris Levy and vice versa.

"'There he goes again,' Levy would grumble," according to Jimmy. "'Fucking Tito is on a rampage again. Shit, what is it now?' I was sort of in the middle. Morris used to tell me his woes when we were out at the racetrack. But he liked Tito and he respected his knowledge of the business. Wherever Tito got something in his head he would run to see Morris. 'He (Tito) was relentless,' and usually got his way." Jimmy concluded it probably had to do with the fact that Tito and Morris were both Navy men.

The atmosphere at Tico Records began to look more professional after the business relocated to Roulette's office suite at 1631 Broadway. Photography for album sleeves looked more professional, informative liner notes (usually in both English and Spanish) replaced the catalogue list printed on the backs of early releases, and songwriter and publishing credits started appearing on albums for the first time. Many Tico albums got an extended life in the form of budget reissues.

Bandleader Rafael Seijo became Tico's head of A&R in 1960. During his brief tenure, Tico released albums by respected Puerto Rican pianist Noro Morales, Argentinean tango king Astor Piazzola, society bandleader Fernando "Caney" Storch, future *"Mission Impossible*" theme composer Lalo Schifrin, and pianist Marco Rizo, the music director for the *"I Love Lucy"* television show. More aggressively than Goldner, Seijo attempted to diversify and expand the music catalogue of the company beyond mambos and cha-chas, recording artists from international entertainers who performed in their traditional styles. Marco Rizo, Machito and Pete Terrace each contributed an album to a Seijo-conceived series that put a Latin-American spin on great North American standards by the likes of Cole Porter and Irving Berlin.

Tito felt that the Machito excursion into popular music was "an exceptional endeavor. This was an opportunity to explore new music and to expand interest in Afro-Cuban music." However, Tico failed to promote *"Machito Plays the Music of Irving Berlin."* As far as he was concerned it was another lost opportunity, one that he and Mario often discussed.

Tico artists kept Bell Sound Studio bustling with activity, and in the years just prior to Fidel Castro's takeover, a few recording sessions were also held in Cuba. Albums were issued in "dynamic stereo" for the first time. Pete Terrace expanded his quintet into a full orchestra, and possibly recorded some of his best dance music under Ralph Seijo's supervision, among them *"Chanchullo," "Broadway Mambo*" and *"Cha-Cha-Chá In New York"*. Seijo could also pull together a number of cha cha chá compilations such as "*In The Land of Cha-Cha-Chá,"* and "*I Dreamt I Danced the Cha-Cha-Chá*."

Tito was missed at Tico but Seijo masterfully began repackaging and reformatting the Tito Puente Orchestra hits of the 1950s. Ralph Seijo departed Tico in 1961 for the chance to record his own orchestra on the

Somerset label - just as the pachanga craze was beginning to take hold in the United States.[97] Teddy Rieg, who was the executive in charge of the jazz department at Roulette assumed the role of manager. To Tito's delight Tico issued such albums as *"Puente in Love"* - that highlighted his vibes and featured: *"My Funny Valentine," "Continental," "Autumn In Rome," "Philadelphia Mambo," "Cool Mambo,"* and *"Mambo Tipico;"* and *"Tito Puente Swings/Vicentico Valdés Sings"* with such hits as *"Gloria Eres Tu," "Si Me Dices Que Si," "Nueva Vida," "Luna Yumurina," "Soy Feliz,"* and *"Guaguanco en Tropicana."* These releases made Tito's transition to Tico a smooth one. "I think some of my fans thought that Vicentico was with me again," he noted.

Oye Como Va

Jimmy was at the track with of all people, Morris Levy. "He was always at the track when he was not working, shit!" Tito explained. "I had been looking for him and on impulse I called Morris' private line. I was told that he was with Jimmy. I was excited because a few days before Morris Levy had approved the latest set of recordings and I had this idea to use a violin and get into the fray with the charangas."

Three days later we were in the studio. "I think Jimmy lost his shirt taking Levy's tips on the damn horses. He did not say so, but when he was quiet it usually meant that he had taken a beating, and Morris told me 'go easy on the cock sucker, he is not feeling well.'"

It surprised everyone when Tito gasped in a loud sharp tone: "All right everybody. Just let it go. I want everyone to have fun with this crap," Jimmy related to me one afternoon. "We all looked at each other and then Tito stomped his foot. So we started to play." The tune was *"Oye Como Va,"* hastily composed by Tito and with little fanfare and or concern that it would ever be considered a melody that would become popular. To Tito this was a throw away song, or something to fill his latest long play album. It featured Johnny Pacheco on the Cuban style flute and a young violin virtuoso from Cuba by the name of Felix "Pupi" Legarreta. This was an open ended musical excursion into the realm of Cuban charanga music and by virtue of its rhythmic beat – a shot at the up and coming fusion of "Latin and black American rock."

"I don't know who was confused more, me, the musicians, or the people in the studio. I wasn't sure where this shit would lead us, but I wanted to try out something new. I wanted to stay ahead of the curve." At the time of the recording Tito conveyed to Jimmy that the big bands were renovating themselves. "Our time is passing, I guess, Jimmy. We have to change."

By the end of 1961 when Tito and his orchestra began rehearsing for the fourth Tico release much had happened. The 1961 Bay of Pigs incursion was an unsuccessful invasion by armed Cuban exiles in southwest Cuba, planned and funded by the United States, in an attempt to overthrow the government of Fidel Castro.[98] This action accelerated a rapid deterioration in Cuban-American relations. The Dwight D. Eisenhower Administration agreed to a recommendation from the Central Intelligence Agency, to equip and drill Cuban exiles for action against the Castro government. Eisenhower stated it was the policy of the U.S. government to aid anti-Castro guerilla forces. President John F. Kennedy continued to support the operation and followed through on the plan. By the end of April, more than 1,200 CIA trained Cuban invaders had been captured. The operation was a dismal failure. Cuban refugees continued to flee the island with most of them settling in the Miami area. The Cuban entertainment and music industry slowly fell apart. Many musicians departed the island, and by 1961 they were attempting to restart their shattered careers in Europe, Miami and New York.

By 1962 Machito and the Afro-Cubans were in a state of retooling, changing their style to suit the new types of rhythms that were becoming popular. The "*The New Sound of Machito (El Sonido Nuevo de Machito)*" was released in 1962, and a shadow of what the original orchestra had been. It featured the pachanga and incorporated the flute played by young Panama born jazz saxophonist/flautist Mauricio Smith. In 1963 Machito released: "*Machito Presents Flauta Nova - Mauricio Smith*" and "*Variedades.*" The Tito Rodríguez Orchestra released *"Back Home in Puerto Rico,"* and *"Latin Twist,"* in 1962, and followed up with *"Carnaval of the Americas"* in 1963. Keeping pace with changing times, working and recording was taking its toll on the big three. Tito decided, almost whimsically, that his principal adversaries of the Palladium Ballroom were no longer his concern. There were too many new bands and ensembles up-and-coming, too many types of music and he needed to focus on this fluid situation.

The album that the orchestra was working on was going to be titled: *"El Rey Bravo – Tito Puente."* Tito was trying something a little out of character for him. He had worked on the compositions and scored many of the tunes in a loose manner. "I was thinking of a descarga approach to some of the tunes. I was also thinking I wanted it to have some of that charanga flavor – violins and flute. I was also thinking about the new hybrid sounds – the new generation – all the funk and R&B shit." The charanga-pachanga craze was still in vogue but Tito was not sure if it was going to last too much longer. The wave of new music, Tito was inclined to think was headed to what he referred to as "a small sound."

He felt that the promoters of the assorted recording companies in their infinite wisdom had managed to confuse the consumer, he concluded. "Shit! You didn't know if you were listening or dancing to a pachanga. Was it a charanga that played the music – yes, but that's not the way the idiots in the executive suites were marketing the product – total confusion. I don't think that Joe Quijano was even sure and he tried to straighten everyone out with his successful tune *"La Pachanga Se Baila Asi."*

In the midst of the confusion the new wave of music was starting to hit the airwaves, Cuba was about to be isolated and if that was not enough the venues for big bands was shrinking. Tito had a plan. He told Charlie and Joe Loco and Jimmy what his plan was. Charlie was leading a successful charanga for the moment. "I will do an album that will really confuse the shit out of everyone," he proposed. It stands as one of his strongest recordings of the 1960s. One tune in particular on the long play 1962 album would eventually bring him tremendous recognition and unexpected financial rewards. They went and pitched to it George Goldner and Morris Levy. Goldner was more excited about the idea than Levy, according to Jimmy.

Jimmy recalled: "He (Levy) rolled his eyes and nodded to Tito. 'Sure, sure Tito. Do the fucking thing, do it.' We left and a few days later we went to work."

Tito composed *"Malanga Con Yuca"* and it features Legarreta playing the violin and Pacheco playing the Cuban flute. Tito had met Legarreta in Cuba during one of his visits. At the time the Cuban violinist was playing for Orquesta Sensación. "Pupi was a well trained musician who also played flute. All I had to do was point him in the general direction I wanted to go, and he easily introduced the mood I was seeking," according to Tito. At the time Pacheco was leading his own popular New York style charanga, which featured a combination of recent Cuban arrivals and Puerto Ricans. The way Tito introduced the violin gave his orchestra an interesting quality. Brass ensembles would introduce this style in the 1970s. The ever-restless Ray Barretto, who also had a charanga ensemble at the time, would start testing trombones, trumpets and flute with violins in the mid 1960s. Eventually he would form a conjunto of sorts.

"Tokyo de Noche," commemorates a visit to Japan and the Far East. *"Tombola," "Traigo El Coco Seco," "Africa Habla," "Batacumba"* (Brazilian Beat), *"Donde Vas"* and *"La Pase Gozando*" are typical powerful Tito cuts that once again display his versatility in mixing new and old rhythms. The timbal solo on *"Tito Suena El Timbal*" is crisp and resounding – something of Cuba and something of New York. *"Gato Miau Miau,"* was composed by Legarreta and is presented as a driving charanga style beat in which flute and violin take on the brass section. Once again Legarreta displays the Cuban freestyle of playing violin that was developed by Miguel "El Niño Prodigo" Borbon, who played for the popular charanga Orquesta Melodias del 40.

"Oye Como Va" (Listen to How it Goes) was composed by Tito on the run and he decided to let it flow at its own pace. Jimmy told me that Tito did not actually score it – put it on paper until years later. "It was a filler, you know Joe, to fill up the album," Jimmy explained. Tito literally had to order Santos Colón and several other musicians to be as playful and vocal as possible thus giving the piece a feeling of a miniature jam session. It's a medium paced cha cha chá that has something of bouncy boogie feeling. Black groups were playing new boogaloo tempo that was as yet unknown. Up-and-coming Latin ensembles that were popping up around New York were slowly modifying the bouncy funk black genre. You could say Tito was a little ahead of the curve on this one. It would be adopted and converted to suit Carlos Santana's rock style in 1972 and become a hit that Tito never imagined. Along the way it created some controversy as to its orgin. Here is what caused the commotion:

(1) "In 1957 the Arcaño orchestra recorded *'Resa del Meletón,'* for the Gema label under the title *"Chanchullo."* In 1963, Tito Puente built on the tune's introduction to compose *"Oye Como Va"*. (Mambo Kingdom, Max Salazar – 2002)

(2)"Oye Como Va" is a song written and composed by Latin jazz and mambo musician Tito Puente in 1963 and popularized by Santana's cover of the song in 1972 on their album *"Abraxas,"* helping to catapult Santana into stardom with the song reaching #13 on the Billboard Top 100. The song has the classic rhythm and tempo of cha cha chá. It has similarities with *"Chanchullo*" by Israel "Cachao" López. The Latin Beat Magazine writes, "Cachao's tumbaos for his 1937 composition of "*Resa Del Meletón"* (later changed to "*Chanchullo"*) inspired Tito Puente's signature tune *"Oye Como Va'."* On the original recording of the song the voice of

Santitos Colón, the Puente orchestra singer at the time, can be heard in the song along with those of Puente and other orchestra musicians. The song has numerous arrangements and remakes by numerous artists in various tempi. National Public Radio included the song in its "NPR 100: The most important American musical works of the 20th century.

Santana's arrangement is a "driving, cranked-up version in a new style of Latin rock (attributed to musicians like Santana), adding electric guitar, Hammond B-3 organ, and a rock drum kit to the instrumentation and dropping Puente's brass section. The electric guitar part takes on Puente's flute melody, and the organ provides accompaniment (with organist Greg Rolie's discretional use of the Leslie effect). There are several guitar solos and organ solos, all of which are rooted in rock and the blues but also contain licks similar to those of the original arrangement. (Wikiipedia, the free encyclopedia)

Tito was thrilled with the success of his song. However, whenever someone brought up the matter of his possibly using *"Chanchullo,"* his response was curt: "Bullshit!" When he calmed down he added: "All you have to do is listen to the fucking base line of the tune. Then listen to the base line of Cachao's piece. You have to be a fucking idiot not to hear the difference. One has nothing to do with the other. It was a simple piece of music that was not inspired or motivated by anything. I think Cachao would have said something to me if he thought I had lifted his music." Tito and Cachao played together over the years and the origin of *"Oye Como Va,"* or *"Chanchullo"* was never mentioned.

The 1957 version released on Gema was a 45-rpm. Cachao gathered up many of Arcaño's musicians and recorded *"Chanchullo,"* and *"El Que Sabe Sabe."* The two tunes are notable for the exhilarating flute improvisations of Eulogio Ortiz, who was one of Arcaño's principal flautists. He is also heard on a 1950 recording of *"Mambo,"* the 1938 Orestes López melody that is considered to have transitioned Afro-Cuban music. The two tunes were among Tito's favorites. "He just had a way of making you feel the music," exclaimed Tito. Also, Tito worked on the music for the original album toward the end of 1961, and finished recording it sometime in 1962. Santana released his Latin-Rock adaptation in 1972.

A technical error in the re-mastering process of the long play album *"Y Parece Bobo"* for Alegre Records resulted in the voice of Bobby Escoto being used. He was the original singer pegged by Tito for the 1962 album but his voice was shattered, so Chivirico Dávila replaced him. Years later a compact disc was released by Fañia and included the voice of Bobby Escoto. This is now a collector's item. The titles are: *"Dime Donde Vas," "Me Llevo Los Cueros," "En El Zorzal," "Llego el Frizao," "Eres Mi Reina," "En el Ambiente," "Yo Soy el Merenguero,"* and *"Guajeo Guajira." "Cuero Pa' Bailar,"* and *"Y Parece Bobo,"* is described as Oriza rhythms. Technically, an Oriza or Orisha is a force or spirit that reflects one of the manifestations of Olodumare (God) in the Yorubá religious system. These spiritual lineages are practiced regions of Brazil, Cuba, Dominican Republic, Puerto Rico, Jamaica, Guyana, Trinidad and Tobago, the United States, Mexico and Venezuela. Tito introduced the Afro-Cuban spiritual rhythms in albums that were recorded in the 1950s, including his successful and groundbreaking *"Cuban Carnaval."* Some considered that Tito's style mirrored that of Beny Moré. Tito had a different opinion. In the same year the Tito Puente Orchestra produced *"Bossa Nova With Puente"* for Roulette. In this set Tito presents a robust approach to the often softly toned and laid back bossa nova of Brazil. A few months before starting work on the Bossa Nova album Fajardo asked Tito and Charlie Palmieri to play with his charanga orchestra for a second Columbia album *"Sabor Guajiro."* Charlie plays on all selections and Tito plays vibes on the two bossa nova selections: *"Recado,"* and *"Murmurio"* (Luiz Antonio and Djalma Ferreira).

"It was an unimaginable recording schedule that we were keeping," explained Jimmy one day. "It was unheard of. Tito wanted to try out something new almost every day, it seemed." He laughed. "In between we were playing dances, traveling overseas, working dates in California, Puerto Rico. You name it we were there. Oh yeah we also had to rehearse." Tito was driven to keep up with the ever-changing music scene. The music he loved – Afro-Cuban and heavily syncopated – was evolving. He was determined that his band would evolve too.

During the mid 1960s on one of Tito's west coast swings – San Francisco, Los Angeles and Las Vegas, Mexican-American actor and friend Tony Martínez suggested to Tito that he add a trap drum to the percussion. The additional percussion would allow Tito to be less burdened with his having to play timbales at every performance. This had been the case, according to Jimmy, since the departure of Mongo and Willie. Willie was an exceptional trap drummer and so was Ray Barretto, who could fill in for Tito.

He added percussionist Mike Collazo to the band around 1966. It was a controversial move. There were a lot of fans that besieged him to "get rid of the American drums." I was one of those people. Charlie, Mario, Miguelito enjoyed annoying Tito about the use of American style or trap drums in a Latin band. Joe Loco was probably the most positive about the move, but even he told Tito that trap drums in an Afro-Cuban setting "gives the music a different feeling."

"Coño, Tito," Miguelito exclaimed, "el ritmo cambia con el timbre del el drum Americano."

He refused to listen and kept the trap drums in the band for a number of years.

Meanwhile, America's longest war was starting to heat up. The Vietnam War[99], also known as the Second Indochina War, and in Vietnam as the American War, occurred from 1959 to April 30, 1975. The war was fought between the Democratic Republic of Vietnam (North Vietnam) and the United States-supported Republic of Vietnam (South Vietnam). It concluded with the United States withdrawing under terms of the Paris Peace Accord of 1973, which preserved the division temporarily, and South Vietnam deciding to fight on, and which quickly fell without U.S. support. The country would be reunited in 1975, founding the current Vietnam.

During the controversial conflict, 15 million tons of munitions - as much as was employed in World War II, had a vast military superiority over their enemies by any standard one employs, and still they were unable to obtain victory. More than 1.4 million military personnel were killed in the war (only 6% were American soldiers. Estimates of civilian fatalities range from two to 5.1 million. The war was the result of U.S. support for France to retake its former Colony, Indochina, following the end of World War II. By 1954, the U.S. had supplied 300,000 small arms and spent $1 billion supporting the French military effort. The Eisenhower administration shouldered 80% of the cost of the war. The Viet Minh received crucial support from the Soviet Union and the People's Republic of China. Throughout the conflict, U.S. intelligence estimates remained skeptical of French chances of success. The Battle of Dien Bien Phu marked the end of French involvement in Indochina. The Viet Minh and their mercurial commander Vo Nguyen Giap, handed the French a stunning military defeat. On May 7, 1954, the French garrison surrendered. Independence was granted to Cambodia, Laos and Vietnam. Soon afterward the U.S. buildup commenced.

The Vietnam conflict fueled the racial turmoil of the 1960s. The Bronx was part of the racial crisis. The Bronx was not always synonymous with the image of a destroyed, drug and poverty riddled western city. There were several reasons for the decay of the South Bronx: white flight, landlord abandonment, changes in economic demographics and government indifference, as well as the construction of the Cross Bronx Expressway. The Cross Bronx Expressway, completed in 1963, was a part of renowned or infamous urban planner, Robert Moses' urban renewal project for New York City. But today many historians feel that the expressway was a main factor in the urban decay that was experienced by the borough in the 1970s and 1980s. Cutting straight through the heart of the South Bronx, the highway displaced thousands of residents from their homes, as well as dozens of local small businesses.

The somewhat already poor and working-class neighborhoods were at another disadvantage: the decreased property values brought on by their proximity to the Cross Bronx Expressway. The neighborhood of East Tremont, in particular, was destroyed by the inception of the expressway. The combination of increasing vacancy rates and decreased property values created some rather unappealing neighborhoods, places where previous residents and new homeowners would essentially not want to live. Construction of the roadway was not the only factor in the decay of South Bronx. In the late 1960s, population began decreasing as a result of new policies demanding that, for racial balance in schools, children be bussed into other districts. Parents who worried about their children attending school outside their district often relocated to the suburbs, where this was not a concern.

One of the many reasons for the decline of many middle class neighborhoods in the 1950s and 1960s, was the real estate policies enacted by New York City immediately after World War II, specifically rent control. Contributing to the decreasing population was the fact that New York City's outdated policies regarding rent control gave building owners no motivation to keep up their properties. Desirable housing options were scarce, and vacancies further increased. In the late 1960s,[100] by the time the city decided to consolidate welfare households in the South Bronx, the vacancy rate was already the highest of any place in the city. The phrase "The Bronx is burning" coined by Howard Cosell during a Yankees World Series game in the 1977, refers to the arson epidemic in the South Bronx during the 1970s. It was during this time that arson became popular because landlords could collect insurance money for the building. Sometimes, prior to being set on fire, the building would be stripped of wiring, plumbing, metal fixtures, and anything else of value so as to retain some of the owner's investments. Also, some fires in the South Bronx were simply caused because of deteriorating electrical systems or neglect on the landlord's part as they still are today. The presence of several of these vacant, burnt-down buildings contributed to the atmosphere similar to that of a war-devastated country.

In the midst of the 1960s upheaval in the Bronx, the Civil Rights movement was moving forward. Riots in numerous American cities took place during the 1960s, even as victories were won against legal segregation and disfranchisement in the South. The Civil Rights movement had raised hopes for further progress toward racial equality, but as blacks in Northern cities saw their hopes frustrated, the setting was established for large-scale disorder in cities such as Newark, New Jersey; Rochester, New York; Cleveland, Ohio; Cincinnati, Ohio; and Chicago, Illinois. Most significant was the Harlem Riot of 1964, the Watts Riot of 1965, and the Detroit Riot of 1967. Despite the recommendations of riot commissions about the social causes of these disturbances, local governments emphasized the use of force to contain the disorders.

Since the late 1980s, the South Bronx has been experiencing urban renewal in many of its neighborhoods with rehabilitated and brand new residential structures, including both subsidized multifamily town homes and apartment buildings. However, the steady growth of the real-estate market as well as the increasing population in some parts of the South Bronx cannot be contributed to traditional means of gentrification. Many of the newer residents are of the lower income strata having been displaced from other low-income sections of the city, born in the South Bronx (due to a higher birth rate), or from immigrants from Latin America and the Caribbean (primarily Dominican and Jamaican). This is because a significant percentage of New York City's affordable housing is being built in the South Bronx.

Celia Cruz and Other Friends

New York was benefiting from the Cuban migration north musically. José A. Fajardo left Cuba and his orchestra. Violinist Félix Reyna incorporated the band and called the charanga *"Orquesta Estrellas Cubanas."* Fajardo's flute was in demand. He was featured on one of two Hector Rivera's big band recordings produced by Epic Records. Rivera's all-star studio orchestra also featured vocalists Frank Souffront, Santos Colón, Rudy Calzado and Tito Rodríguez. Several reports allege that Vicentico Valdés was also available but it is unlikely because he was busy leading his own band. The two albums were favorites of Tito's and it amused him that some media writers included Valdés as one of the vocals. "All you have to do is listen to the Goddamn recording and you know who is on it. Besides, Vicentico would insist that the albums be titled: Vicentico Valdés features Hector Rivera."

For his part, Fajardo quickly organized two charangas – one in Miami and one in New York. The popular singer Rolando Laserie fled Cuba and teamed up with Tito and recorded *"Pachanga in New York, with Rolando La Serie,"* for the Gema record label. Featuring vocalists fit in nicely to Tito's plans. As the leader of a popular orchestra he knew he had to "continually reinvent himself to stay on top." Cachao left Cuba in 1961, and was recruited by Charlie Palmieri and then by Tito Rodríguez. Flautist Belisario López departed Havana in 1960 and formed his new orchestra that featured José 'Chombo' Silva as one of the violins. Olga Guillot, Fernando Albuerne, Xiomara Alfaro, Julio Gutierrez and Ernesto Lecuona. Los Guaracheros de Oriente, a trio that had worked many of the Havana nightclubs, were among the hundreds of musical entertainers that fled the island. Los Guaracheros de Oriente settled in Puerto Rico and continued working into the 1980s.

Composer and bandleader Mario Fernández, vocalist Javier Dulzaides (teamed with Belisario López), Pepe Delgado, Cascarita, Ernesto Duarte, Celio González, Alejandro 'El Negro' Vivar, Blanca Rosa Gil, La Lupe, Bebo Valdés, Javier Vázquez, Alejandro 'Chocolate' Armenteros and bandleader Rolando Valdés departed Cuba by the end of 1961. Also, among the departed was La Sonora Matancera and its lead singer Celia Cruz. The Cuban musicians and entertainers for the most part were drawn to New York and Miami with a handful settling either in Puerto Rico or in Europe. "My mother used to listen to these guys when Daniel Santos was with them," Tito recalled.

Celia Cruz, during the years following her hasty exodus from Cuba, frequented the Palladium. Tito had met her during one of his stopovers in Havana in 1951. Sonora Matancera was an octet that was popular in Havana. It was especially preferential with the white aristocratic sector. Notable vocalists of the trumpet ensemble included Puerto Ricans Daniel Santos (1948) and Myrta Silva (1950). Celia was one of several singers that were recruited to fill the gap left by Myrta, when she decided to return to Puerto Rico. "Celia had a powerful voice and incredible delivery," according to Tito. Bienvenido Granda and Celio González were the other vocalists of the Sonora Matancera.

Early specifics of her life are obscure. She refused to provide information about her birth date. It has been reported she born in Havana, on October 21, 1924. Growing up in the city's poor Santo Suárez neighborhood in a household of 14 children, including several cousins, Celia Cruz' early work was noticed because of her strong voice. One of her earliest achievements as a singer was winning a local contest –"La hora de te." Her mother was the chief reason she pursued a singing career in what was then a male dominated entertainment venue. But she observed the success of several famous Cuban songsters, mainly that of Paulina Alvarez, who was also the first woman from Cuba to lead her own orchestra. Sometimes Cruz traveled to the singing contests with a cousin named Nenita. "I was very skinny and tiny," she told Billboard Magazine in an interview conducted in 1980. "And since public transportation cost five cents each way and we didn't have enough money, I'd sit on Nenita's lap, because she was bigger. The drivers knew us and, sometimes, they'd let me sit on the seat beside her, if it was empty. One time, we had no money to return and we walked back. We arrived at 2 a.m."

The pursuit of a career in entertainment caused friction with her father who was hoping that his daughter would become a teacher. She enrolled at the National Teachers College, but quickly dropped out. Celia was able to find limited work as a singer for various groups. She enrolled at the Havana National Conservatory of Music, and was encouraged to seek a full-time singing career.

The step forward came in 1950, when she became the lead vocalist for La Sonora Matancera. Bandleader Rogelio Martínez showed confidence in Cruz when he continued to feature her despite the disapproval of fans. Puerto Rican vocalist Myrta Silva was still their idol. American record companies resisted the idea of making a La Sonora Matancera disc that featured the singer with the big voice, believing the rumba record with a female vocalist would not sell. Martínez assured Celia Cruz he would pay her himself if the recording was a dud. The record had favorable reviews and sold well in both Cuba and the United States, Cruz toured extensively through Central and North America with La Sonora Matancera in the 1950s.

When the Batista Regime was dumped in 1959, she and La Sonora Matancera were touring Mexico. Upon returning to Cuba, Celia Cruz quickly realized that the Castro government was not what she had envisioned and that life was becoming increasingly difficult. When she left Cuba on tour again she decided she would not return. The musicians, including Pedro Knight, the trumpet player she would wed, agreed that they would not return to Cuba. From Mexico the ensemble and Celia entered the United States and remained there. Cruz became a U.S. citizen in 1961. Cuban Communist leader Fidel Castro was furious and barred Cruz from returning to Cuba, enforcing the ban even after Cruz' parents' deaths. Cruz for her part vowed not to return to Cuba until such time as the Castro regime was deposed. In 1962 she married Pedro Knight.

Although Cruz had made numerous recordings with La Sonora Matancera, she experienced little success in the United States in the 1960s.

"Despite all she had been through Celia always had a smile whenever I saw her at the Palladium. I don't remember just how we decided to make a record together, but I wanted to do it," Tito said.

Tito recorded two albums with the energetic Cuban singer La Lupe. *"Puente Swings, La Lupe Sings,"* was followed by *"Tu y Yo – Tito Puente and La Lupe."* They were released in 1965 and commercially successful even though Tito guided the orchestra in maintaining the more traditional Afro-Cuban big band approach. However, the Tito Puente Orchestra nearly met its match working with Guadalupe Victoria Yoli Raymond. "She was a bitch," exclaimed Tito thinking about the turbulent recording sessions. The spitfire was born in Cuba to a poor family. She started out as a schoolteacher in Havana, but preferred the world of entertainment. She won a singing competition on the radio and then joined the "Trio Los Tropicales." Her performances in Havana nightclubs included rock 'n' roll songs in Spanish, combined with piercing erotic behavior that made her a hit in the Cuban music scene. She left Cuba for Mexico in 1962, and then came to New York, where she met Mongo Santamaría.

"Mongo Introduces La Lupe" was produced in 1963 and was one of her most successful albums. She appeared with Mongo at the various New York clubs, including the Palladium where Tito spotted her. He had heard and liked Mongo's recording. Tito saw an opportunity and approached his former percussionist and friend. Mongo was candid and described the singer as "wild, sometimes uncontrollable." Mongo was scheduled to depart for a tour in Puerto Rico and La Lupe was not going. "She says she is pregnant," Mongo informed his former boss. Eventually she would marry Puerto Rican singer Willy García.

"The last thing I remember Mongo telling me in his terrible English, mixed with Spanish," Tito recalled, "was 'don't say I didn't warn you.'" La Lupe signed up as a featured vocalist with Tito, and made seven albums with him. Tito never considered her as a member of his orchestra. "Every album was okay – some better than others, but it was like pulling an abscessed tooth. The woman was possessed. When people remind me that she was going to be a teacher, I think those kids in Cuba were saved by not having this crazy woman jumping up and down, invoking spirits, making strange sounds… Goddamn! She was something." But Tito felt she would fit in, somehow. "Just look around. Everyone was trying to figure out what was going on in the music business. The styles of bands were changing almost with every recording. I saw this as an opportunity."

"Tito Puente Swings – The Exciting La Lupe Sings," recorded in 1965

was a success. It took a toll on Tito and on the band. "We were exhausted," observed Jimmy. Tito's stout trumpet player and manager gasped, "Every number she sang she did something unexpected. I thought Tito was going to belt her. She could not follow a score. She was always gasping about something. I never saw anyone pee so much. I think Tito was exhausted after the sessions. What should have taken a day, took several days. She made us all a little nervous mostly because you could see Tito's anger build up to extreme rage. I don't think he really liked her. He liked her voice so he was willing to work with her. She had a knack for getting him pissed. " Jimmy added, "Tito was ready to toss the bitch out a window."

"'Look you fucking bitch, just do what I tell you. It is all written down. The fucking band will follow,' gasped Tito on more than one occasion," related Jimmy. "I have a vivid memory of those recording sessions. They were exhausting."

Tito's recollection was that he wanted to take her out behind the building and beat the crap out of her, but that would not have been appropriate. Eventually they got it done, and it was a success. Another successful album with La Lupe was *"The King and I/ El Rey y yo,"* which was released in 1967. La Lupe composed three tunes for the album – *"Cumba, Cumba," "Oriente,"* and *"Mi Gente."* Tito's arrangements fit La Lupe's boisterous style. Tito is both evolutionary and conventional in his delivery. *Homenaje a Rafael Hernández"* Tito considered to be highly successful, but was perhaps the most difficult to produce.

"The woman was always late. Then she would invoke some religious bullshit and start dancing around. It pissed me off," Tito said. "She simply could not follow instructions." The Puente Orchestra was under a self-imposed deadline to get this album recorded and turned over to Tico's marketing staff. Rafael Hernández was very ill at the time and Tito wanted to do something. "He was one of the great pioneers, here in New York, Puerto Rico, Cuba and around the world." The arrangements were by Tito. He worked on them late into the night.

"We would all be waiting and she would pop in flustered, muttering and talking gibberish. No one could understand her." On the 1966 recording that was released four months after Rafael Hernández passed away, she delivers a moving interpretation of *"Los Carreteros."* The album was one of Tito's favorites and it was an enormous success, especially in Puerto Rico.

La Lupe was voted the best singer by the Latin press in 1965 and 1966. It was during 1960s that she produced some of her greatest songs. In the 1970's La Lupe saw her career decline. She was banned from television in Puerto Rico after she tore her clothes off during an awards ceremony on national television. Tico Records, purchased by Fañia Records in the 1970s, renewed her contract but decided to focus their energies on the less controversial Celia Cruz. The Cuban firestorm retired, and found herself destitute and even homeless for a while. She became paralyzed following a domestic accident and was assisted in her recovery by an evangelical minister. After this, she converted to evangelicalism and recorded Christian orientated material until her death in 1992.

Everybody was moving closer to salsa. Joe Cuba and his sextet with the versatile bilingual singer Willie Torres jumped on the new boogaloo sound. His vibe sextet had been successful in the 1950s, generally backing up the big bands at the Palladium. Joe Cuba (Gilberto Miguel Calderón) was a Barrio bred Puerto Rican who played conga. He had assumed the leadership of the Joe Panama Quintet and maintained the group by playing mostly traditional music but with a tinge of jazz and English vocals. The ensemble also featured José "Cheo" Feliciano. Also in the mix was Johnny Colón, a trombone player whose 1967 *"Boogaloo Blues"* was a huge success with the so-called urban oriented Puerto Ricans that were just coming of age and searching for their roots. The fused doo-wop and R&B that had developed in the black communities was a logical step for the Puerto Ricans of East Harlem. Willie Colón with his Puerto Rican singer Hector Lavoe also became a focal point of the new music.

When the Palladium Ballroom closed in 1966 it was the end of an era. "The mambo was still played by us, but the excitement and anticipation of a night out dancing to a big band was dying a slow death," Tito concluded. "The elegance of seeing the dancers – men and women – dressed was passé. The bands were casual and noisy; the bands were now smaller and not as versatile. Everything was smaller, more casual, and in my view somewhat chaotic."

Jazz Alley in midtown was shrinking and the Palladium Ballroom was gone. Attorney Jerry Masucci became the central player with Johnny Pacheco, who was booking the small trombone conjuntos in clubs like the Cheetah, Casino 14, the Village Gate and the Corso. Larry Harlow and his orchestra was popular. After a disastrous visit to Los Angeles' Hollywood Palladium, Pacheco gave up his flute and charanga orchestra and switched to a traditional conjunto, modeling it after the Arsenio Rodríguez format. Promoter Chico Sesma managed to fill the ballroom but the dancers had difficulty with the pachanga dance, another reason the trend quickly faded. Ray Barretto was next to give up his charanga. But he often admitted to

Tito and Charlie that he did not like the direction Afro-Cuban music was going.

"Ray is a perfectionist," exclaimed Tito. "Like the rest of us 'old timers' he was perplexed about how the youth was jumping on anything and everything that was being played over the radio. He was ready to jump back into jazz but we told him to stay with it." Eventually Barretto developed the formidable disciplined conjunto style ensemble. It would evolve into Tipica 73, when the jumpy Barretto continued his musical explorations and decided to try new types of music. Ray Barretto's Charanga Moderna had become a fiery trumpet conjunto by 1967, along the way recording pop flavored fusion music, mixing trombones with violins (a format that would be adopted by the Cuban ensemble Los Van Van in the 1970s) and finally settling on more traditional Afro-Cuban concepts. Charlie was trying out something new with almost every recording. The Latin Boogaloo was in vogue and with it came Willie Colón and his Orchestra, Pete Rodríguez, Johnny Colón, the Lebron Brothers, and many others. "Some of these guys were good. Some were pretty bad," was Tito's sense of it. "It was a new generation of Latinos – the kids of those people that came here in the 1950s. I guess they were looking for something. That's what we all do."

Funk was in, soul was creeping in and Afro-Cuban was out. The Civil Rights movement was moving forward in full force – and segregation was collapsing, albeit not without a fight. Martin Luther King, Jr. led the inspired move and in 1968 was murdered. America and the Soviet Union had come to the brink of nuclear war over missiles in Cuba. There were race riots. The Bronx was on fire and El Barrio was changing. There was a war in Southeast Asia. Once known as French Indochina, American military advisors were sent by President Kennedy to help it contain communism. The French had been whipped and now it was split into two Vietnams. After Kennedy was assassinated in 1963, President Lyndon B. Johnson raised the stakes and increased the number of U.S. troops in the theater to 500,000.

The Spanish speaking youth was dancing to Latin R&B fusion.[101] Ricardo Ray, a Brooklyn born New York Puerto Rican and his friend, Bobby Cruz released *"Se Soltó"* LP in 1966. *"Danzón Bugalu"* combined the formal danzón line with the African-American R&B beat. The pianist was highly successful and the trend continued. The Shingaling followed. The new music and the accompanying dances were much looser, less intricate and easier to learn. "Everything was less formal. People came to dances in sports and casual wear. The younger bands did not use uniforms and were much smaller," was how Tito viewed it. "Eddie Palmieri had one of the better bands of the period. Ricardo Ray was a terrific piano player.

Joe Cuba was like the rest of us – he adapted and people thought that he was part of the new generation," Tito reflected.

Machito and his Orchestra tried to go a different direction and did a Latin Soul record in 1968 but things started to quiet down. Tito Rodríguez reinvented himself several times. But when the Palladium closed down in 1966, he decided to dismantle his band and go the solo route. "In a way he was smarter than the rest of us," Tito said when his friend informed him that the Tito Rodríguez Orchestra would be disbanded. Tito and I often bumped into him on Broadway and they would chat amicably for a while. His office was a block from where Tito, Charlie and Joe had their office.

Even Willie Bobo shifted into the new funk – soul sound. In 1963 he recorded *"Bobo Do That Thing Guajira"* for the Tico label. "Jesus Christ you too," Tito exclaimed one day when Willie visited the office on Broadway. "What the fuck is wrong with everyone in the world?" Joe Loco and Charlie were there that afternoon. "First Joe records something that is totally out of whack. Fucking Charlie is like Dr. Jekyll and Mr. Hyde and now you too."

"Hey leave me out of this. I got paid for that crap I recorded," quipped Joe.

Charlie shrugged and then smiled. "Tito is having one of his 'que pasa con la música' attacks today."

Willie laughed. "All I know is that my stuff sounds better than a lot of the shit that is out there. We can play it better. And, besides I have to eat."

"Well at least you and your guys played all the right notes," Tito chided. "If we can do anything we can play it right. The problem is that some of this shit is really bad, fucking bad. I mean really…"

"Shit, just awful shit," Willie added. "Even when we play all the right notes!"

"And with feeling," Charlie said rolling his eyes and puffed on his cigarette.

Tito kept to his program of featuring vocalists on recordings. It included a reunion with Puerto Rican singer Gilberto Monroig, former La Sonora Matancera vocalist Celio González, mixing it with the Puerto Rican vocal quartet, Los Hispanos, highlighting the Tito Puente Orchestra vocalist, Santos Colón. Tito and the orchestra recorded an album discovering Noraida Moré, widow of legendary Cuban sonero Beny Moré. She got an album deal and became the latest to benefit from Tito's arrangements and the ability of his orchestra to follow her style.

Tito produced her début, *"La Bárbara del Ritmo Latino,"* and the unswerving Charlie contributed arrangements. While it sold well enough to justify cutting a second album, *"Me Voy a Desquitar"* (I'll Get Revenge), Noraida never generated the kind of public attention Tico had hoped for.

There were flops too – big ones. Tito wished that he had not recorded *"Una Tarde de Julio,"* with 1960s popular singer Fabrizzo and *"What Now My Love,"* with Shawn Elliot. "Some ideas are just plain bad," he moaned. "Even I couldn't get excited about this shit." Another big bomb according to Tito was *"El Sol Brilla Para Todos,"* that featured La Lloroncita.

Tito teamed with Bobby Capó in *"Invitation to Love."* Most of the tunes were composed by Capó and arranged by Tito. He enjoyed working with Bobby. There were also strong albums that showcased the orchestra and displayed Tito's skillful arrangements. These were contemporary and yet still "tipico" *"Tito Puente in Puerto Rico," "Excitante Ritmo," Carnaval in Harlem,"* and *"Mucho Mucho Puente."*

Tito teamed up with Celia Cruz in the mid 1960s. His orchestra and Celia never appeared with Count Basie in 1962 at Carnegie Hall as declared by Josephine Powell in her biography of Tito (When the Drums Are Drumming –2007).[102] Celia continued working with La Sonora Matancera until 1964.

"It was always a pleasure to work with Celia," was Tito's take when he recollected his work with the Cuban vocalist. Somehow he managed to subdue La Lupe who was energetic if not down right rambunctious, rude and crude. Now he was working with Celia. She was articulate, powerful and her delivery fit right in. "Celia Cruz was a lady. She was the polar opposite of La Lupe," According Tito. She was punctual, prepared and cooperative. "Maestro," was how she referred to Tito during rehearsals, backstage during live performances and in public.

"Cuba y Puerto Rico Son," is the title of the first long play album and it borrows from a verse by the Cuban poet and patriot José Marti's about "Cuba and Puerto Rico, one bird with two wings." Tito conceptualized the album to incorporate various genres and compositions from several internationally acclaimed songwriters. One afternoon during rehearsals Tito looked at Celia and then at the band. He looked disconcerted. "Everybody take five." He left the area, stopping to fill his cup with old black coffee, picked up some pencils and several blank music sheets.

"Sorry it took me so long," he sighed as he handed out the reworked music to his musicians. "Jimmy do you need any time to go over the changes?" Jimmy looked at the rewritten arrangements and replied in the negative. Tito spoke with Celia and told her that in effect what he did was modify the octave on several of the pieces they were working on so that she would not have to dig down with her voice. "She was doing it and not complaining. But it did not sound right so I reworked the arrangements." Although it was not a huge success Tito was satisfied with the results. One of the most memorable selections on this long play album is "*Me Acuerdo de Ti*," composed by Gustavo Seclen M. It is a bolero-son in which Celia reminisces about the Cuba and Havana she was forced to abandon.

1
Como me acuerdo de ti
Mi linda Habana Querida
De Santiago y Camagüey
Cienfuegos y Santa Clara

2
De Matanzas no me olvido
De sus costumbres tampoco
Donde un día yo llegue
Para un toque de bembe

3
Tampoco olvidar quisiera
A esa tierra Pinareña
Donde se da el buen tabaco
Y sus mujeres: que buenas

4
Como me acuerdo de ti
Mi linda y querida Habana
De Monmartre y San Souci
De tu hermoso Tropicana

Coro

(Habana, Habana)
Si no es hoy será mañana

(Habana Habana)
Que yo cante el Tropicana

(Habana, Habana)
Mi linda Habana querida
(Habana Habana)
Yo no te olvido en la vida

(Habana mi cuba)
Quiero que tu nombre suba

(Habana mi Cuba)
Yo e de regresar a Cuba

Celia had tears rolling down her eyes. Tito and the musicians were quietly moved by the time it was over.

"Eso fue fantástico," exclaimed Tito to Celia. It was obvious to all of us that he too was taken by the poignant verses that Celia had sung. He normally would not say anything. Later he told me that Celia did indeed remind him of all the places she talked about in the song. Celia never performed the song again. In 1967, *"Tito and Celia in Spain,"* was recorded and it too proved to be a commercial success. In all Tito and Celia would collaborate on six albums and make dozens of appearances around the world.

But it was not always a smooth relationship. Celia Cruz despised anything and everything that was remotely associated with Cuba, Fidel Castro and those that still remained in Cuba. "It made for some very touchy situations," Tito recalled.

One night he was going to have cocktails with the members of Orquesta Aragón. It was during one of the rare visits the group made to the United States, around 1980. This is how Tito described it: "Shit! Someone came over to me and whispered as Celia and I and a few other people were having dinner that they had arrived at the restaurant. I tried to be nonchalant about the screw-up. I didn't want her to know that the guys from Aragón were nearby. I told someone to ask the group to wait – hidden away in another room. We finished eating – I mean really fast. Celia was smart. She knew I was trying to get her out of there. It was funny. A few people helped me escort her out of the restaurant through a rear door. There were several other "cat and mouse" maneuvers Tito had to make when Cuban musicians appeared on the scene. Tito shrugged it off.

"I got up and went to where the guys from Aragón were being kept. I apologized for their treatment and then I explained to Richard Egües what had just happened. As I told him he was laughing. I had to laugh too. We all laughed. Funny thing is that the Cubans that I knew, from Cuba, had the highest regard for Celia Cruz, and for her accomplishments."

My Fair Lady and Other Notables

Tito was not at all concerned by the departure from Tico, by Machito, Ray Barretto and Eddie Palmieri bands between 1967 and 1972. He continued pressing his intense performance and recording schedule. Pancho Cristal also left Tico, leaving Art Kapper, Miguel Estivíl, Fred "Paco" Weinberg and George Goldner to trade off production duties. Roulette produced the more jazz-oriented Tico sessions including Tito's excursion into the bossa nova and Machito's critically-acclaimed set "*Kenya*." To his credit, Levy preserved Tico's Latin orientation, and didn't try to hedge his bets by making it a jazz label. As always, jazz was a major influence, but danceable Latin sounds remained the order of the day for the owner.

Joe Cain was the A&R head of Alegre Records and agreed to double his workload and began overseeing Tico recording sessions. Cain brought Tito's featured vocalist of many years ago, Vicentico Valdés, back to Tico. In 1970 George Goldner passed away. He was in the process of starting yet another new record company when he died of a massive heart attack. "A part of music history went with him," according to Tito.

From 1962 through 1971 the Tito Puente Orchestra recorded more than 50 long play albums. There were dozens of concerts, hundreds of dances, and countless personal appearances. The moods of Afro-Cuban music had changed and Tito shifted his focus with each change. He continued to compose and arrange at a feverish pace. He was always exploring and attempting to find new ways to express his will through music. He was not disheartened by the changes. He embraced them, for better or worse. There were things that he did not like, people that annoyed him, but he dealt with failure by seeking and implementing new ideas. He even added Puerto Rican singer Sophy Hernández as a regular member of the orchestra. She remained with the organization for two years and then struck out on her own.

She told me "I loved working with Tito. It was a great experience. He worked you very hard, but it was worth the effort."

Playing pranks on the musicians was still one of Tito's pleasures and Jimmy confirmed this. One night out in Los Angeles bass player Bobby Rodríguez was the brunt of the playful Tito, who had someone contact a brothel. "Don't let him sleep," he told the madam.

All night long, Jimmy related, the telephone in Bobby Rodríguez's room rang – at 15-minute intervals. "The woman's voice was soft and erotic: 'Hello Bobby, I have some friends and we will be there to see you in a few minutes.' Bobby came down to the lobby several times, looked around. He saw a few of us in the bar but did not say anything. At one point he asked me: 'Where the fuck is Tito?' I shrugged." The prank went on until dawn.

On the way to the airport Tito asked Bobby, "You look tired… Did you sleep okay or were you out all night?"

Bobby Rodríguez shrugged, closed his eyes. "He was pissed!" Jimmy noted. Bobby always suspected it was Tito who kept him up all night. He had known Tito too many years not to know. It would be several months before he was told about the prank.

Sometimes Tito wanted to be alone so he could read, listen to classical music and visit Broadway. The Broadway musical *"My Fair Lady"* was a favorite of Tito. It played successfully on Broadway from March 15, 1956 to 1962. There was also a film version that turned out to be one of the top five most successful films in 1964 - The clever lyrics and easy to sing tunes were composed by Alan Jay Lerner and Frederick (Fritz) Loewe. Julie Andrews played the role on Broadway but was replaced by non-singing actress Audrey Hepburn in the film (whose voice was dubbed by Marnie Nixon). Ironically, that same year Julie Andrews was awarded a Best Actress Academy Award for her role in Disney's competing film, "*Mary Poppins*."

Tito pitched a Latin version of *"My Fair Lady"* to his friend Levy.

"Joe," he told me one day, "you know how bossy Tito could be. He pushed the concept of a big band Latin approach to the successful show and movie. He pushed and pushed until I was fucking tired of his fucking voice! He convinced me. Maybe he just wore me down. It is hard to say fucking no to Tito."

Soon after Levy agreed Tito was working late nights to arrange the music of Lerner and Loewe. He was looking for crossover acceptance and decided to include a range of national genres. *"Get Me to the Church on Time"* (mambo-rumba), *"Rain in Spain"* (montuno), *"Show Me*"(joropo); *"I've Grown Accustomed to Her Face," "Ascot Gavotte,"* (danzón); *"With a Little Bit of Luck"* (merengue); *"I Could Have Danced All Night"* (guaguancó), *"Embassy Waltz"* (joropo); and *"I'm an Ordinary Man*" (cha cha chá) are the tunes that Tito molded into a Latin format.

"Ascot-Gavotte" is a tasty danzón –mambo that features Tito playing the syncopated danzón beat before the orchestra slides gently into the

mambo-montuno with the entire orchestra driving the music. Santos Colón adds to the mood with his strong harmonizing. This album is another example of Tito's wide range of musical abilities. Most of the arrangements were worked on during the wee hours when he could be alone at the piano.

Whenever possible Tito joined in on jam sessions, sat in as a guest with other orchestras, battled with other percussionists and enjoyed the limelight and celebrity status he received. One of those moments occurred at the Chateau Madrid one afternoon in the mid 1960s. Fajardo, with several members of his charanga orchestra, was playing. In a sharp tone he called out: "Y ahora (and now)"... He proceeded to introduce the musicians who would participate in the next jam session. "El gran Tito Puente en los timbales... Charlie Palmieri al piano... El Gran Cachao en el bajo... Marcelino Valdés tocando la tumbadora... Aquí viene... Kako..." Fajardo went on to introduce Rolando Valdés on güiro, Osvaldo "Chihuahua" Martínez on percussion, and Pupi Legarreta on the violin. "Coño, Charlie dale un montuno," Fajardo commanded

Charlie Palmieri invented a textured and exciting guajeo. Cachao picked it up, Tito and the other percussion men followed in effortless fashion. They were off. For the next 40 minutes the group of all stars pounded away, playing around Charlie's guajeos and enjoying every moment. Tito was the first to solo. His hearty inventiveness served only to inspire those who followed. Charlie was next with one of his patented dazzling keyboard displays, ascending and descending arpeggios, octave slides and leaps – oh and a few strong poundings of all 88 keys. Fajardo announced each soloist throughout the impromptu session. About 20 minutes into the piece he announced: "Y ahora viene Mario Bauzá..." He had to be called twice and while he made his way to the small bandstand the all-stars wailed. Bauzá fit his saxophone into the music and then faded so that Kako followed by Chihuahua, followed by Tito, could exhibit their lively percussive skills.

"We will be here next week," Fajardo announced. "Tito nos vemos en el Palladium mañana." The music faded.

The next day, at the request of Morris Levy, Tito and Jimmy gathered up the musicians and went to A&R Studios in midtown Manhattan. The band was going to back the return of Rafael Cortijo and Ismael Rivera in an album *"Bienvenido Cortijo y Rivera."* Both had spent several years in jail for transportation and possession of drugs. Morris asked Tito to help him jump-start their careers. Tito agreed. The Puente orchestra is not mentioned in the liner notes of the Tico long play album. The 1966 LP got little publicity and little play over the radio.

One of Tito's most memorable percussion duels was shared with his pal Miguelito. Another was with Orlando Marin. Over the 10-year period that started in 1960, Tito faced off against many rival percussionists. Miguelito was one of the most versatile musicians you could ever find. He could do anything, was Tito's verdict. One night, at the Roseland Ballroom in midtown Manhattan, toward the end of the night Miguelito jumped on the bandstand as the orchestra was wrapping up a rendition of "*EL Cumbanchero.*" Miguelito picked up a pair of sticks that were nearby and joined Tito. The two men shared the one timbal. Patato was keeping time on the tumbadora and Chihuahua played the güiro while Tito boisterously blasted away. Then he stepped back for Miguelito to get his licks in. The crowd was going nuts.

Back and forth Tito and Miguelito went, provoking, tempting and inspiring one another with their syncopated percussive exhibition. The two masters went at each other with almost a vengeful pleasure. Miguelito would look over to Tito and smile. Tito stepped in and moved his drumsticks with rapid meticulousness. He looked at his friend and smiled. Back came Miguelito. And on it went. The fans in the dance hall had stopped dancing and looked in amazement at the two musicians.

Then unexpectedly the orchestra slid into the percussive fray. The saxophone section slipped with a steady five and six note guajeo. Tito and Miguelito were both sweating. The drum battle continued. The trumpets, with Jimmy leading the charge, came in over the reeds. The trombones followed. The entire orchestra rolled in with a tempestuous crescendo of horns and reeds. Tito and Miguelito played together – each musician anticipating the other. The conclusion was typical Tito Puente – driving powerful buildup and then crash. Right after this musical encounter, Tito introduced Chihuahua – a veteran percussionist who for many years played with Fajardo y sus Estrellas Cubanas. In typical Cuban fashion, somewhat laid back and extremely syncopated – concentrating his improvisation on strikes between the beats, the small percussion man was up to the task, and gave both Miguelito and Tito a run for their money. It was quite a show!

El Barrio bred percussionist Orlando was a few years younger than Tito. His favorite percussion men included Buddy Rich and Gene Krupa. He was friends with Eddie Palmieri, and Sabú Martínez among others. In June 1965 the Tito Puente Orchestra and the Orlando Marin Orchestra were contracted to appear at Virginia's in Los Angeles. Tito was invited to sit-in with Marin. A fierce timbal duel ensued with the two percussionists responding to one another's improvisations, always trying to go one better.

On February 12, 1965, Jazz at the Philharmonic matched Buddy Rich and Gene Krupa in an approximate three-minute drum duel that has become legendary in the annals of American jazz lore. Who won? Tito heard it and heard it again and again. He never tired of listening to it. "Rich was much more graceful. Gene was energetic and driving. I always lean toward Gene Krupa."

"Buddy Rich is the greatest drummer to have ever drawn a breath," exclaimed Gene Krupa in an interview soon after the drum battle. Buddy Rich responded in kind: "Gene is absolutely the first man when it comes to drums." Tito believed that Krupa and Rich, with there different styles, provided "rhythmic beauty," to the music they build. "They fit in with big bands, ensembles, trios, you name it. The key is they knew how to fit in, keep time, and lift it up a notch when the music called for it."

Tito's style was fully that of Gene Krupa. "Everything I learned – playing traps and drums – I learned from Gene Krupa. I just applied it to the timbales and mixed it in with the syncopated format used by Cuban drummers. Gene was incredible."

Norman Granz, producer and promoter of JATP said in an interview: "I'll never be able to say enough for him or about him. Frankly, I was worried at first about him (when he first joined the Jazz at the Philharmonic tour in 1952). Face it. Gene is a top cat to the public. He's like Louis and Benny. Tops. So I figured maybe he'd be a great attraction, yes, but you know, a little temperamental. Well, I'd play ball. I said, 'Gene, you want to take a plane or travel alone or anything, go ahead.' He laughed and said, 'What for Norm? I'm no better than anybody else.' What happened all through the tour was that Gene did anything I wanted him to do. And all the other cats are nuts about him. And I think, honestly, that they play better with his beat because they like him so much personally. As for Buddy Rich, finally, I reached the end of my patience with that guy. He was through, period. I wouldn't have him around, that's all."

The Other Tito

The feud between Tito and Tito Rodríguez continued to fester through the 1960s, and continued until Rodríguez passed away, February 28, 1973. The stories surrounding the dispute serve to make the rivalry legendary. One episode relates that Rodríguez demanded from United Artists that he be the only "Latin bandleader to record for UA.

"'He had a headache with Puente's competition,' Tobi (Tito Rodríguez's wife) remembered. 'He no longer would play second fiddle, and he was going to make sure that his recordings wouldn't be buried again. (Mambo Kingdom, Max Salazar – 2002)

Charlie Palmieri recorded his first albums with violins, flute and percussion in 1959 for UA. It was alleged that Charlie was hurt by Tito Rodríguez's insistence that he be the only Latino working for UA. Tito's tailored response to the allegation was "Bullshit. Charlie and I used to talk about it. He moved because he wanted to move. There was no conspiracy. I'm sure that Rodríguez knew that we were all under the gun. We had bigger concerns than pissing off each other. Times were changing."

"When Tito died an important part of our industry – those of us involved in making music that is based on the Afro-Cuban rhythms – ceased to exist. He was my friend, he was my rival, he was an inspiration to me, and he was an inspiration to those that followed in his footsteps," Tito expressed. Whenever he thought of the early days of the mambo, the band battles, the fierce competition among the big three bands, and the music that was produced, Tito would become somewhat melancholy.

He quickly registered a 180-degree mood swing when someone reminded him of the numerous reports, articles, essays and general news that the two Titos "endured a bitter rivalry."

"You know what I say to all that: bullshit!"

The items he most heard about were created in the media.

- *"Avísale A Mi Contrario,"* (Let my Rival Beware) was a popular mambo recorded by Tito Rodríguez and allegedly makes reference to Tito Puente. The song was composed in the 1930s by Cuban composer / musician Ignacio Piñiero.
- Justi Barreto composed *"Esa Bomba."* The selection was included in a popular long play album recorded by Rodríguez in the 1960s. Barreto was a close friend of the two Titos and Machito. It was reported that the title that in English means "flop," is supposed to refer to Tito Puente. It is unlikely this is what Barreto had in mind when he wrote the lyrics.
- The 1968 album by Rodríguez *"Estoy Como Nunca"* allegedly was supposed to remind Tito Puente that Tito Rodríguez is back and "Better than ever." This was strictly a media report with no substantiation.

- "Richard Nader, concert impresario, failed to do what many other promoters had been unsuccessful at since the Titos feud erupted in 1951: he could not get the two men on the same stage." (Mambo Kingdom, Max Salazar – 2002). In 1954 the two Titos jammed together on the same stage with Machito. This type of jam continued through the 1950s.
- Tito Rodríguez refused to allow his musicians to mingle with those of the Tito Puente Orchestra, according to an interview with musician Pat Rodríguez (no relation). (When the Drums Are Drumming, Josephine Powell – 2007). Interestingly, the band members often switched bands. For example, Jerry Sanfino (saxophone / flute); Monchito Muñoz (percussion); and Bernie Glow (saxophone), Willie Bobo (percussion), Charlie Palmieri (piano / arrange), Bobby Porcelli (saxophone) and Ray Santos, Jr. (saxophone) just to name a few played for the two Titos.
- Tito on several occasions expressed annoyance that Tito Rodríguez's photo appeared to the left of his. This is true since consumers generally read advertisement and look from left to right. Tito Rodríguez also complained about this on more than one occasion. The three bandleaders – Tito Rodríguez, Machito and Tito Puente – appear in a promotion photo taken in 1954, that is still used today. Machito once complained that he would retake the picture, but with him on the left. It was never retaken. Tito (Puente) and Tito (Rodríguez) expressed to me that this was "all bullshit." Tito Rodríguez used the photograph in his album "Palladium Memories" that was released in 1970. Tito had a copy of the photo hung prominently in his office in his home.

Finally, Tito Rodríguez, Jr.[103] in a video documentary honoring Tito Puente makes it a point to note, "My father and Tito Puente were life long friends. They were competitive – fiercely so. The feud was fueled by the media and the writers."[104]

Over the years Tito Rodríguez, Jr. and I have maintained a friendship. "Tito Puente was as my father put it, an accomplished musician. I had the utmost respect for Tito Puente. He always greeted me warmly and respectfully whenever we would cross paths. He always spoke highly of my father."

When Tito Rodríguez organized his recording company – TR Records – he established an office on the 12th floor at 1650 Broadway. A block away Tito, Joe Loco and Charlie Palmieri operated a music-arranging service –Bandaide – at 1674 Broadway. Birdland was located on the street level. Tito and Charlie worked on the musical scores that would be used on the TV show, "El Mundo de Tito Puente, which began in 1969 and aired over Channel 47. It was a bomb. Tito also used the location to keep the band's growing music book, at the time numbering more than 800 musical pieces, and manage his orchestra – although most of the managing, bookkeeping, filing, and payroll was maintained by Jimmy.

One afternoon Tito and I were walking on Broadway. We had just come out of the office building. Heading in our direction was Tito Rodríguez. The two bandleaders smiled and firmly clasped each other's hand. They spoke in Spanish. Whenever they ran into each other on Broadway they would stop and speak, in Spanish.

"Ola Tito," Tito Rodríguez said

"Como esta todo," responded Tito (Puente). "How is it going with your record company? I saw your record *"Inolvidable,"* is still high on the charts."

"It's a little hectic with the new company. But we'll get things into place."

Tito (Puente): "Someone was asking me the other day how it was when the bands used to battle. I told them that every time the three of us got together it was to the death."

The two musicians laughed. "Yeah. Those were great times. It is disappearing now."

"I know. I keep having to come up with new gimmicks just to keep going."

"Bueno, nos vemos pronto."

"Ciao."

Once I bumped into Tito Rodríguez and after a brief exchange he once again asked "If you are not working, I have a job for you. I need a distributor for my record company."

"Gracias Tito. But I'm working. But I appreciate the offer."

"If you need something let me know..."

I told him I would keep in touch. When I got up to the office I mentioned to Tito about our impromptu meeting downstairs and about the job offer. He smiled. "I hope he makes it with the record company. Shit. He has good business sense, but with the music business going to shit, I'm not sure..." He shrugged and then laughed. "I sort of miss him and his band. When we were going, we had to be good. When you see Machito, just ask him."

Tito Rodríguez disliked José Curbelo, with whom he worked. Curbelo was also a booking agent and Rodríguez often told Tito and me about his passionate hatred of these people. Curbelo was high on the list. In a radio interview shortly before his death, Tito reinforces his friendship with Pops and maintains that while they had gone their separate ways "we are still friends. I have the utmost respect for him because he is Puerto Rican." When Rodríguez passed away in 1973, Puente was the first to pay his respects at the Frank Campbell Funeral Home, on 81st Street and Madison Avenue.

The two Titos had the last laugh on the public. After the Palladium closed in 1966, the two Titos agreed quietly and privately that they would never share the same marquee billing because it would only benefit the "money hungry promoters and booking agents."

Puente smiled, even laughed and growled humorously. "Bullshit!"

Tito Rodríguez only laughed.

The Office

A few days after I had picked up Tito's collections of 78-rpm records from his mother I took the subway downtown to let Tito know that the several thousand discs were safely stored and not a single one was damaged in the transfer from one apartment to another. It was a warm summer day. Tito and the orchestra had been to Puerto Rico, swung back to New York and then across the United States to Los Angeles.

I was sipping my orange juice, when Tito looked up from what he was doing, threw his arms up in the air and looked at me. A little concerned I asked, "Well, what did I do?"

He smiled. "Joe, I was walking down the street the other day when a few teenagers walked up to me and said 'you look like somebody famous. Are you? No shit, it happened just a few blocks from here. I was about to tell them who I was and changed my mind. 'Who do you think you're talking too?' One of them asked me: 'Do you play trumpet for Joe Bataan?' I almost gagged."

Charlie was standing and gazing out to Broadway. Joe Loco was leaning back at his small cluttered desk. They were both listening intently.

"Who the fuck is Joe Bataan, is what I wanted to say, but I caught myself. I didn't curse them out. I was cool. Really! All of you would have been proud of me. With all the calm I could muster I explained to them who I was, and then told them about the music I play."

Charlie muttered with a grin: "Maybe you need to dye your hair."

"Shit no," laughed Joe (Loco). "He needs to focus and concentrate. As for me I'm getting ready to call it. This new shit the young people like is beyond me. I'm going to Puerto Rico."

Tito looked at him. "I was just there. It is warm. It is nice and it is fun, I'll admit, but shit I don't think I could stand to be on the island for too long. It's too damn small. I like Havana. It is big."

"You're still having illusions that that prick will get tossed and everything will be the way it was," Joe responded.

Tito shrugged. "No, that's never gonna happen. I just remember how I used to roam all over Havana – it was just big… Joe (Tito looked at me), so you got the records."

"All in great shape," I said. "I didn't break a single one in getting them out of your mom's apartment."

He smiled. "There is a lot of music there. I hope you take good care of them – I know you will."

Charlie walked back to his desk. "Last night I played at three different dances – one in Brooklyn and two in upper Manhattan – all for about $900 a piece. You can't get rich doing this – not the way things are."

"You know the promoter in Puerto Rico paid us $5,000 for three days, including travel and housing. Jimmy just finished paying off everyone and told me I should leave the country because the IRS will be after me. Shit! There is never enough, you know – damn taxes are a pain in the ass. I guess it could be worse. I heard someone went to California a few weeks ago and had to call New York because the promoter did not have enough to pay all the bills, including the band."

Charlie pushed on the desk and leaned back. "That was me. I was almost stranded out there. I called Joe (Loco) and he helped me get money for airfare. What a pain in the ass."

"You see why I'm getting the fuck out of this business. You can't trust anyone," Joe Loco responded. "I am going to find a quiet place to play tropical music and make sure I have a steady income."

Tito and Charlie started to laugh. "You'll be back," Tito countered. "You know that you can't stand to be away from me and Charlie."

"They just don't play my kind of music anymore. I'm getting too old for this shit…" (*Laughter*) "No, I'm going to Puerto Rico. You should consider it. Tito (Rodríguez) lives there and had a pretty good TV show."

Tito shrugged. "He is probably the smartest of us all. He saw the handwriting on the wall. Our time is over – you know, the big bands…" Tito shrugged again.

"Maybe you two should give in to the promoters and let them put you both on the same bill – a Tito and Tito Show," suggested Joe Loco with a sly grin.

"Bullshit! The only people that will make money on it will be the promoters… Bullshit! I don't think we ever will because in the long run both of us will be nothing but pawns, used, and exploited – no way. Let the promoters and media shit heads run around, and spin their wheels," Tito concluded.

I added my two cents: "The promoters and booking agents work for you. You don't work for them. That is why Rodríguez could not stand them and preferred to book himself and his orchestra. He was a shrewd businessman. "

"You're right," they all agreed. Charlie kept smoking. Joe sat at the piano and Tito was listening to the radio and scoring new music.

The office was an incredible place. Musicians came in and out. One afternoon I was waiting for the elevator. When the doors opened José Madera, Jr. and Willie Bobo came out.

"Hey man," said Willie. "What's happening? Your pal is out of control. The King is out of control."

Madera rolled his eyes. "Charlie is out of his fucking mind too."

I looked at them in surprise. "What the fuck is the King doing?"

Madera groaned: "Wait until you get up there and see for yourself. "

"The King (Tito) is hot wiring phone. Man! El esta tostado – fried…" laughed Willie.

I left them and took the elevator up. When I walked into the office, of course the radio was blasting, Joe Loco was at the piano, and Charlie was scoring music. He looked up, smiled and said: "I got to get this ready by tonight for the band."

"How many numbers?" I asked gently.

"Oh, about a dozen pieces. I'll get it done."

I looked around and did not see Tito. "Where is Tito…?"

Charlie looked toward the desk. I heard the noise. Tito was under the desk splicing wires, just like José and Willie said. "Shit, Tito are things that bad?"

"Fuck you," he growled and went about his business. He finally made the long distance call, without being charged for it because he switched the wires. It was just another day at the office.

A Meeting of Masters

The Asia Restaurant located on 10th Avenue in midtown Manhattan, in the vicinity of the Theater District, was not a fancy restaurant. It served Cuban-Chinese cuisine – nothing fancy, just plenty of food. The Chinese food was authentic but with a little Cuban flare. The *"Moros y Cristianos"* (white rice with black beans) was one of Tito and my favorites." The restaurant was neat, clean and the prices were reasonable. Tito, Charlie, and me started frequenting the Asia in the late 1960s.

By 1974 it was the hang out for the group to which I have come to refer to as the Masters[105] – Tito Puente, Charlie Palmieri, Miguelito Valdés, Machito, Mario Bauzá and Federico Pagani. Others that frequented the restaurant included, José Curbelo, Lou Pérez, Louie Ramirez, and Ray Barretto, and when they came into town, Willie Bobo and Mongo. It was the place where musicians could get the latest information about the industry, and the gossip.

As I have said previously Tito had a keen sense of history. He felt that somehow he was part of it – in terms of his small corner of the music world. "Joe, I want to record our conversations at the Asia. So bring along the tape recorder," he said one afternoon. I picked up the contraption and lugged it over to the restaurant. "I'll spring it on the guys that we are recording some of our conversations," he smiled as we walked from the office on Broadway over to 10th Avenue.

I laughed too. I wasn't so sure that the boys – Charlie, Miguelito, Federico, Mario and Machito would appreciate being recorded. Mario often moaned: "We talk a lot of shit." The conversations were often boisterous, down right blistering and rowdy. The musicians spoke in English, Spanish or both. They yelled at each other, they challenged each other's point of view; and often there were more than one and two conversations covering different topics going on at the same time. "Don't worry, I'm sure they'll get a kick out of it. It's history," Tito assured me.

"Shit!" I groaned borrowing from one of Mario's favorite words. "If they do agree who the fuck is going to want to listen to this?"

He swaggered across 9th Avenue with me and responded: "You'll figure that out… when we are all gone. Just think… You will have us – Mario, Miguelito, Charlie and me, and the others recorded for history." As we entered José Curbelo was leaving. "Hola Tito, Joe… Just stopped in for coffee."

"Why don't you join us?" Tito said after they embraced.

"No, tengo mucho que hacer…" He laughed. "Besides, you guys get too rowdy – Mario and Miguelito! Coño!" He departed. We entered and got the usual table. I got everything ready and surprisingly the group did not balk when told that the conversation this afternoon was going to be recorded. "I told you," Tito said nudging me. So here it is, a moment in history in 1974.

Miguelito was teasing me as I was figuring out how to connect the wires and microphone. "Oye, Joe ten cuidado que no te vaya a electrocutar." Everybody in the place laughed. He lit up a Cuban cigar.

Miguelito and Mario smoked Cuban cigars – big ones; Charlie and me smoked cigarettes. Macho and Federico did not smoke. Tito did not smoke. What follows is the transcription of this one particular day. The Masters were captured on tape debating, conversing, instigating, shouting, and challenging one another. It was a typical gathering.

Rembering Tito Rodríguez

Mario: "Hey Tito is it true that you are considering trimming down your band?"

Tito: It's been on my mind for a long time. I mentioned it to Joe and Charlie. It's getting hard to keep them busy. The clubs are closing up… You know. You have the same problem."

Mario: "Shit. So much has changed in the last 10 years. I never thought it was going to be like this."

Machito: "Its not all bad. There are some young musicians out there, making good music."

Tito: "Yeah, but most of them suck. They don't work hard at learning their trade. Everyone wants to be a star – you know, lay down a tumbao, get a singer, who can't sing, go into a studio and you have a hit. Jesus Christ! Half of these guys can't even read a note of music, and the other half struggle to read what is written."

Miguelito: "I think Macho is right, though, some of these young guys are good musicians. Siempre van haber buenos músicos, Tito. Que tu opinas, what do you think Charlie?"

Charlie: "Oh yeah! There is a lot of good stuff going on. But Tito is right – it's getting hard finding work for live groups.

Federico: "The bandstands are shrinking so you can't use all the musicians, and can you believe it there are less and less pianos. Everybody is starting to use the electric keyboard, or whatever they call it."

Charlie: "Some of them are not too bad."

Miguelito: "Shit! Some of them are awful. They sound like toys. Suenan como juguetes. I know you like to work out on them."

Charlie: "Its convenient when I practice."

Tito: "Well, at least the recording studios haven't gone berserk with that new shit. I really believe that Tito (Rodríguez) more than all of us here saw the handwriting on the wall. He closed down his band and just concentrated on being a romantic singer and a record entrepreneur."

Machito: "Where did you learn that word?"

Tito: "Hey, we use all kinds of words like that in El Barrio."

Miguelito: "Here, here, a toast to our compañero – el gran Tito Rodríguez."

Mario: "Tito siempre tenia un sonido muy especial, muy distinto ha el de Machito y la de ti (Tito)."

Habana and the Palladium

Tito: "I remember when I started – it seems like a hundred years ago. I wanted to play Afro-Cuban music. I got Jimmy and he got some of his Italian buddies. We put together a strong percussion section and we went to work.

Federico: "That was when the Palladium was making history. Coño, estábamos haciendo historia entonces."

Tito: "Yeah! They used to bring in the bands from all over. It was an incredible time."

Machito: "It is never going to happen again. But we were there – all of us. Recuerdo las competencias y como Federico se pasaba viajando a Cuba buscando nuevos grupos."

Federico: "Coño! One time I went Havana to try and get Arcaño to come and play at the Palladium. I looked all over the place for him. He was already retired but his charanga was still playing in some of the clubs. I think his cousin was running the band. I finally met him and we talked for a long time about the mambo, about the Palladium, about the big bands in New York. He was very interested. When I mentioned Pérez Prado he got very serious. Yo no sabia que Arcaño no le tenia mucha simpatía al Prado. Pero me lo expreso muy claramente. Si recuerdo bien hasta uso la palabra, maricón. He was not a fan of Sr. Pérez Prado."

Tito: "Augh! He sounded like he was taking a shit. I swear..."

Federico: "Anyway, Arcaño just had no interest in coming to the United States. I finally convinced him, but when I tried to make the arrangements, there was a problem with the money. Parece que los fondos para el viaje no existían. I never did find out what happened. I kept looking. I talked with Peruchin (Pedro Justig) who was playing for Orquesta Riverside. He was interested. But shit he was afraid to fly. I was anxious, I was thinking of trying to get Pérez Prado, but in Cuba he was not popular, at least not in the circles I was traveling in.

Mario: "I don't think he would have been a hit, not in those days."

Tito: "I went to see him at the Waldorf Astoria. He was okay. His sound was always bouncy, not energetic. That was my impression. He had a real big band too."

Mario: "Remember he is from Oriente – the east Coast of Cuba – the styles of music out in that part of Cuba are bouncy, influenced by the French, who came from Haiti. He was okay, but he reminded me a lot of Cugat – except he played more Afro-Cuban, but not strong enough."

Federico: "In 1958 I went back to Cuba and after missing Fajardo twice I caught up to him in el Montmartre. He really was excited about coming to New York. 'Coño, chico sabe que las cosas están difíciles aquí,' he said. I had no idea what he was talking about. All I wanted do was make sure he was ready and able. Yo le dije 'pues lo mejor será un viaje al Palladium de Nueva York.' We agreed. He came during the Thanksgiving Day holiday weekend. He knew he had to face off against you (Tito) so he added two trumpets."

Tito: "I played against him during the weekend. He did bring in a big charanga."

Miguelito: "Lo difícil que Fajardo se refería era que las milicias de Fidel estaban acercándose a la Habana ya para esa época. Everyone had high expectations that Fidel would make the right changes. I talked with family in Cuba almost every day. We all thought that at last he would make it possible for everyone in Cuba to have the same opportunities. Coño como lo cago. Fidel es un cabrón. Tumbo a un hijo de puta (Batista) y se elevo al mandato del país para joder con todos los cubanos."

Mario: "Coño, Miguelito pero le dio la libertad al negro."

Miguelito: "Si Mario, pero mira el precio que pagamos – digo, el que esta pagando esa supuesta libertad es el cubano que no se fugó."

Nervous Adolesence

Machito: "…I don't agree with you that it is the fault of the young people that our music is fading.

Mario: "Yo no dije eso, Macho, coño. Yo lo que digo es que cuando estábamos en nuestro florecimiento no nos dimo cuenta de como las cosas cambiarían en el futuro. Vivíamos para el momento. La juventud madura y se fue. Lo que digo es que los jóvenes no fueron traídos por los padres, ni por nosotros."

Machito: "No fue así. Nos tocaba a nosotros en asegurar el futuro. We had to teach the young people."

Mario: "¿Que tu opinas, Charlie? ¿No es correcto que los adolescentes hispanos en este país se le esta olvidando el idioma castellano?"

Charlie: "Yes and no."

Tito: "That's not the problem."

Mario: "Bullshit. That is the problem. Listen to the shit the young people like. Some of the singers can't even speak Spanish."

Tito: "Bullshit! Some of them can't speak English. But we are not teachers

Miguelito: "Parece que se fue pa'l carajo el romanticismo de la música, no. Todo ahora es apresurado y sin lentitud. You know – no ballads, no love and no poetry. La música en cuba – Coño – esta cagada también – todo es eléctrico. Me cago en Dios!"

Machito: "That is what I am telling Mario."

Charlie: "Part of it was Fidel – but not all. We lost our fans while we were getting older."

Tito: "I will go to my fucking grave and never quite understand how anybody with a fucking half of a brain can like that crap – boogaloo. Man that is shit."

Machito: "But if we want to make a living we have to play it, no…"

Charlie: "I have been trying to. I want to throw up sometimes. Its almost not even Latin…"

Tito: "Its not Afro-Cuban that's for sure."

Mario: "So what happened? Where did we lose our music?"

Machito: "Deja que Charlie te lo explique. 'Coño, no sea tan abusivo. Siempre tienes que tener la ultima palabra."

Mario: "¿Charlie tu no opina eso de mí?"

Charlie: "Claro que no. But the problem is that the music we play or played is no longer what the young people want to hear."

Tito: "You should have kicked the shit out of Eddie when he started that band."

Laughter

Mario: "Shit! Eso es un poco drástico. El no fue el que esta detrás del disturbio de nuestra música."

Federico: "El toca bastante bien – un poco alborotado, pero bien."

Machito: "Carajo, dejen que el hombre hable."

Tito: "I still think he should have kicked the shit out of his brother. After him came all the kiddy bands. Some of these guys can't even read music."

Mario: "They don't practice enough. Estos jóvenes músicos – y uso la palabra "músico" como una cortesía – no entienden un carajo de harmonía, teoría, ni como escribir una idea. Shit. Yes, Charlie you should have kicked the crap out of your baby brother, now that I think of it. Tito is right."

Laughter

Miguelito: "Dejen que Charlie hable, por favor señores. Ustedes están desconcertando y agitando demasiado. Charlie que es lo que tu ibas a decirnos?"

Laughter

Mario: "All I am saying is that everything that is going on with music today – nuestra musica – es culpa de los padres.

Tito:"So."

Miguelito: "Y que…"

Mario: "What I am saying is that we stopped looking out for one another. We were too worried about seeing our names in lights and we all forgot to take care of business… Nos olvidamos de nuestra juventud."

Tito: "Yo no estoy seguro… I'm not sure about that. I mean that we were not concerned about each other. I know we were competitors. Look at Tito (Rodríguez) and me – people think we hated each other. The stupid writers think there was an all out war. I swear some of those fucking media people even think I had a gun aimed at his fucking head. And, it doesn't matter what you tell them. No matter what you tell them – the writers or whatever shit they call themselves – they insist on reporting that I was gunning for Tito and he was gunning for me. What bullshit!"

Miguelito: "'Coño! A mí me lo dijo un joven en California los otros días que mi música – la música Afro-Cubana era aburrida y repetidora."

Charlie: "Maybe you should have kicked the shit out of him too."

Laughter

Miguelito: "Can you imagine the young people think our music is boring and repetitious. 'Coño! Carajo. Mira la mierda que están escuchando. Coño, ni se puede bailar. No me joda, coño."

Machito: "You know something American people don't think our music is boring or monotonous. You know why, because they are inquisitive and they take time to learn. They learn how to dance our music. They learn how to do the steps. Maybe they have trouble with clave, but they learn that too. Latinos are a dancing people so the young think that they know how to dance the music – this is not always true. Mario and I used to enjoy playing for American audiences. They were more responsive a lot of the times. Back in the 1940s and 1950s the young people – Latinos – were curious about our music. They took time out to hear it played, to learn about it. Today everyone is in a hurry and the young are not like their parents were…"

Federico: "Se creen que lo saben todo, no!

Mario: "Shit! Algo así…"

Machito: "The roots are not there anymore."

Charlie: "In the 1940s I used to hear the Machito band. They had something… Even those old Puerto Rican bands in Puerto Rico. Tito used play them in his house. His mother had tons of records."

Tito: "My mother loved the old bands. She loved the tangos, danzas – all that stuff. Come to think of it – I liked it too."

Charlie: "They were doing something different. Machito and Mario were directing the orchestra. They separated the two – jazz and American swing from Afro-Cuban. Mario in essence had two bands. He wanted to convey that the Machito band could play for an all Anglo – white crowd, and with the same musicians he could play an Afro-Cuban book. Now in New York, when the mambo came into play Afro-Cuban music was popular. We had José Curbelo and a lot of others. When Tito started with three trumpets he came with something fresh. He had jazz routes and three trumpets. Arsenio Rodríguez introduced this sound in Cuba. Tito Rodríguez had a same type of orchestra. But what was unique was that the two Titos was that they were completely different in the way they sounded. And, when they added saxophones it was entirely different. It was a crime to sound like the other band. These guys could play the same tune and make it sound different. It was the competition.

Tito: "And we always wanted to be fresh. We wanted to make sure our music was danceable and exciting."

Charlie: "And we were not afraid to borrow from the popular American music hits."

Machito: "We played for everybody. We played downtown for the white crowd. Uptown for the black crowd, in East Harlem for the Latin."

Mario: "What are you?"

Machito: "I'm not white and I'm not black…"

Mario: "Tú eres un negro. Un nigger, no…"

Laughter

Charlie: "Even the small combos, ensembles and back up bands that played the clubs in that time made sure their book or arrangements crossed over and were able to please mixed crowds. I remember Joe Cuba played a lot of American tunes – Stormy Weather, Donkey Serenade. But the most important thing was not to sound like the other guy. It was important to be different. And, if you listen to what was being played, especially among the big bands, the music they played was open and interactive. It relied a lot on the participation of the people – the dancers. The two were so interwoven that sometimes you couldn't tell where the performers – the band ended, the dancers took over.

Tito: "I think that the culture and the expressiveness of Afro-Cuban music had something to do with us – and I mean that to be authentic Afro-Cuban music – sort of separated the dancers from the music. Cultural – now we are very much aware that we are Puerto Rican, Cuban, Dominican, whatever, so that the band has to perform the politically correct music to pacify the people in the room. In the old days – shit listen to me…"

Laughter

Tito: "In the old days we were not worried about who and what to appease. We played good music whether it was from South America, Europe, the Caribbean, you name it and we played it. And if my orchestra came close to sounding like his (Machito) or like Tito's it was unacceptable."

Machito: "I am going to add something… Today the young musician is in a hurry. The musician wants everything to swing, to be fast. The musician is not interested in the harmony and the beauty part of the melody, like the bands of the past were interested in. The mambo we used to play had an introduction, a beginning, it had a body that could change and shift, and the coda was stimulating."

Charlie: "The mambo – the one that Arcaño and Cachao developed had a romantic introduction before they got into the swing. Arsenio and most of the conjuntos and orchestras all had introductions, a body or a place where harmonies and percussive accents could be highlighted."

Tito: "That is not repetition – it is swinging interaction inside the entire orchestra, or the orchestra and a soloist. In the Afro-Cuban music framework the sonero is a tool within the orchestra just like it was in the swing era. You wanted to hear the singer, but you also wanted to feel the soul of the instrumentalist, hear the give and take of the reeds and horns, experience the interacting riffs that were produced spontaneously by saxophones and horns while the entire band was in a driving mode. Somewhere it all changed – we lost it. Man, did we lose it."

Mario: "Shit! They all think that they can sing like Miguelito. All these young singers – some of them can't carry a note, coño! I sing better than some of them."

Tito: That is what has changed. The trouble is the young singers think they are some kind of stars – some kind of shit."

Mario: "Mierda, coño!"

Miguelito: "That Mario became a singer?"

Machito: "Sálvenos..."

Laughter

Tito: The sonero thinks he is the damn orchestra."

Mario: "Shit. And a lot of these singers should not give up their day jobs. Tito, Charlie, vamos a pedir otro round... ¿Quien quiere un tabaco cubano?"

Vicentico Valdés and his Hairpiece

Mario: "¿Oye Tito cuando fue que se le cayo la peluca a Vicentico?"

Extreme Laughter

Tito: "Shit! Don't look at me. I had nothing to do with that."

Federico: "Eso fue en el Palladium, creo, un miércoles."

Laughter

Tito: "What are you laughing at? Shit, you were there. For all I know tu fuiste el quien se lo tumbo de la cabeza."

Continued laughter

Miguelito: "Eso fue una noche que estaban las tres orquestas tocando y Mario empezó a relájalo... Que encojonamiento! Coño! Yo salí de ahí corriendo."

Tito: Yeah! He was pissed and it wasn't at me. It was you..."

Laughter

Mario: "Él estaba detrás del bandstand arreglándose el tupé. Yo lo vi y no pude aguantarme de risa. Coño! Entonces me dice que Miguelito estuvo jodiendo con él y que se patina su alfombra y se derrumbo al piso. 'Chico, té vez bien sin la peluca,' le dije. Shit! Me miro con un encojonamiento y me mando para el carajo. Me dijo: 'tú lo que eres es un maricón.' No pude controlarme la risa."

Machito: "Y por ahí vengo yo del break con los muchachos. Se puso rojo. Everybody was laughing.

Tito: "You see, everybody thought it was me. I wasn't even there. He must have been pissed. When he came out to sing he looked at me with a cold gaze. Shit was he fucking mad. It was you guys that pissed him off. I always thought that one of you knocked his tupé off his head…"

Machito: "It was Miguelito who started the commotion."

Miguelito: Oh no… All I did was tell him he looked fine without it. He must have bumped into something, or he did not have it on right."

Mario: "He never liked when we made fun of him with the rug.

Charlie: "He was very sensitive about his hairpiece."

Machito: "Chino Pozo told me that he paid $60 for the damn thing back when they were in Cuba."

Mario: "I think he used to wear it in Cuba and one night one of his girlfriends knocked it off his head in some club."

Machito: "Eso es lo que dijo Chino."

Miguelito: "Coño! Que relajo."

Charlie: "The funniest thing about the damn hairpiece was that one day he told me in a grim voice: 'everyone can laugh at me and my wig – behind my back. But don't you dare ever laugh at me about it.' I was just standing there, behind the bandstand, smoking during a break. He was fuming because I saw the wind blow his headpiece off his head as he walked to the back. He was very sensitive. I watched as he was straightening out the toupee. Then he walked away. I just kept quiet. He did not like anybody to kid him about his hairpiece."

Federico: "It really cost $60? Oye, eso fue costoso para esa época."

Charlie: "I think he had a few wigs. His hair always looked different."

Laughter

Tito: "I remember when we went to Cuba back in '57. He wouldn't get off the airplane until he could make sure that the damn thing was pinned down to his fucking head, and Mario started busting his balls."

Mario: "All I said was 'pídele a una de las azafatas si es que tienen pega para fijar la jodia peluca, coño!' Man! Did he get mad… It did not help that Graciela and Macho were laughing, and so was everybody else."

Miguelito: "Se le voló antes de llegar al terminal. You remember Tito."

Tito: "Man! He was running down the runway trying to grab it and all of us were watching and laughing. Damn, that was funny."

Loud lingering laughter

Afro-Cuban Music Renovation

Charlie: "Everyone is always asking these days what was so different about the big bands.

Tito: "We were good, eh!"

Miguelito: "We were incredible."

Machito: "You guys are all drunk..."

Mario: "Charlie es el que mira esto como se debe – es historia."

Charlie: "Well, in the late 1940s bebop was coming up. The Machito orchestras – Machito, Mario, Charlie Parker and even Dizzy Gillespie were trying out all kinds of things. Dizzy and Charlie Parker was trying to see how Afro-Cuban music fit in. Mario was focused on how to incorporate all he had learned with the black bands.

Mario: "The black bands were really good. They were always watching each other to see what was new. Then, one of them, maybe Chick Webb, would show up at a dance and introduce something a little different. 'Hey Mario, do you have something for tonight," Chick would ask me. Coño, siempre esperaba hasta él ultimo momento... But we would go to the ballroom and when the dancers least expected it he would signal for us to introduce a new tempo. No era nada de otro mundo, pero era diferente. Coño! Los negros se lo comían. Chick knew that someone would run and tell someone in another band. It was very competitive."

Charlie: "At the Palladium there was all kinds of people that came to see Machito, then Tito Rodríguez and then Tito. None of them had the same sound. None of them were trying to imitate the other. The Jewish dancers, probably more than the Latinos, really embraced the music. I guess they were weary of the rumba. There were all kinds of people dancing in the Palladium. And then in the 1950s the Puerto Ricans were starting to migrate from the island. Everything was in place. Then Mongo came from Cuba. I remember when Tito organized his conjunto. It was something new – four trumpets riffing with modern harmonies, usually heard in a jazz or big band orchestra. This was so different from the rumba, the guarachas that people were used to hearing. It was evolutionary. He had a full percussion section, as many guys as Machito had. But he sounded different. He was a success."

Tito: "I wanted to try different things. I just wanted to make sure that we didn't flop.

Charlie: "Well, if you did, Jimmy would have sent the Italian mob after you."

Tito: "He understood from the start what was going on. I guess it was his Bronx upbringing."

Laughter

Charlie: "The harmonies that were being arranged were interesting. Incredible stuff. By simply taking a major key, say like the key of C and then place a sharp before any note that half tone gives us a new picture. The same thing happens with the flat – a half tone lower. That was what we did when we played "Picadillo." It was a long time ago. What is happening today is that a lot of musicians don't study the classics; they don't learn the basic principles of making music. The orchestras of the 1940s were dynamic. Machito and the two Titos kept this going – they had a compelling sound that was like... you know, relaxed power."

Tito: "That was the way a lot of the Cuban orchestras played – very laid back."

Charlie: "Not only did we learn to be swinging, but we learned to subtly incorporate pulsating Afro-Cuban rhythms – not the rumba – into the unity and intonation of what we now call Cubop and mambo. Even the little groups were testing the limits of what the big three orchestras of the Palladium hey day were doing. Stan Kenton was always trying crossover jazz. And, Joe (Loco)... Well he was always taking the pop standards and shifting them around to fit his mambo jazz. I remember Hector Rivera made a couple of LPs with a big band during the pachanga era..."

Miguelito: "Recuerdo que era muy fuerte, pero mantuvo algo de lo suave..."

Federico: "Siempre me recuerdo que subiendo la escalera al ballroom del Palladium ya sé sabia quien estaba tocando - el estilo de los tres era muy distinto. Y había otras buenas orquestas. ¿Mario, te recuerdas de la orquesta de Marcelino Guerra?"

Mario: "Shit! Marcelino es un gran compositor y cantante. Su orquesta fue de las mejores, pero no pego. No sé porque. Hoy todos suenan igual... They all sound like shit."

Tito: "Yeah! The kiddy bands play everything in the key of C and figure that the faster it is the less likely is it that listeners will be able to detect errors."

Mario: "Shit! I studied six hours a day when I played for Romeu (Antonio Ma. Romeu). He was an incredible musician. Se sentaba y tocaba solo en el piano por horas. Él esperaba que todos los músicos en su orquesta ensayaban por igual que él. You have to study the classics. How the fuck can you play in a band if all you do is repeat everything over and over. Coño ya estoy viejo para esta jodienda."

Machito: "Coño! Creo que estas un poco tostado!"

Laughter

Miguelito: "Por eso es que tu hace que los músicos ensayan hasta los domingos."

Laughter

Mario: "If the band doesn't rehearse it sounds like shit."

Tito: "Charlie is like that. He plays the piano all day in the office and on Sundays too. Joe Loco is another one – practice, practice..."He even had me sitting in with him the other day. Charlie sees a piano or anything with white and black keys and he is drawn to it like a magnet."

Charlie: "You know me. Wherever there is a piano... but you practice a lot?"

Tito: "Every day."

Federico: "Tu sabes quien era así – René Hernández. Él miraba al piano como una mujer."

Miguelito: "More drinks. Ordena algo para picar..."

Tito Puente and Joe Loco

Mario: "Yo siempre recuerdo que Tito era un tremendo bailador... Before he became the King. Shit!"

Miguelito: "Siempre estaba detrás de las mujeres... Coño!"

Federico: "He was always on the prowl in the Palladium."

Tito: "Bullshit! The real good dancer was Joe Loco. I don't think I ever saw a guy put on moves like him, maybe Tito. Shit, I used to ask him to teach me his new steps. He would smile and tell me, 'if I teach you my secrets then I have you as competition.' Sometimes I think he felt sorry for me. Tito Rodríguez era un gran bailador. Shit! He was good."

Laughter

Mario: "That may be but only you used to think you could move around the Palladium like Cagney. You know... that swagger...Esos movimientos. Coño."

Machito: "I used to see you and Joe dancing all the time."

Tito: "You were pretty busy yourself."

Machito: "Yeah, but you were a better dancer than me."

Miguelito: "Ustedes están hablando mucha mierda. Yo acompañaba a Tito a los salones de bailes en la habana y veía sus movimientos de primera mano. El es una persona muy inquieta – muy inquieta."

Tito: "Look who is talking...Tu era el que conocías a todos los lugares donde tocaban buena música. Shit, you knew where all the good looking ladies were too."

Laughter

Mario: "I know Miguelito liked to chase anything with a skirt…"

Miguelito: "And I thought you were my friend."

Laughter

Tito: "Joe is the best dancer. He could put the moves on and he could be subtle. He moved on his feet like he played the piano. He used to watch those old movies – *'Singin' In the Rain'* – you know… He loved all that stuff."

Miguelito: "You were always dancing with Mrs. Murray from the dance studios."

Tito: "Business, you know. She and her husband were always after me to support their dance studios. They kept the interest in the music – at least for a while. She was a nice lady. Joe liked to dance with her too. Whenever they ran into each other in the Palladium they would dance. I'm telling you Joe was the killer on the dance floor."

Mario: "Shit! Me dijo Miguelito que tu levántate a Abbe Lane y esas hermanas de cuba. Shit!"

Tito: "Bullshit!"

Racism

Tito: "Half of our band in 1953 was black and the other half white. I used to get offers to go down to play in Miami but I turned them down because it was a pretty racist place – Miami. I worked there before with José (Curbelo) and you could see that things were not like they were up north."

Charlie: "I remember I met Mongo around 1952; he had played for Pérez Prado."

Tito: "Augh!"

Laughter

Miguelito: "Todavía el se cree que el es quien invento el mambo… Coño! Él es el único que pretende eso. Anyway, cuando Mongo y Willie lo dejaron perdió mucho de su sabor. No estaban con el mucho tiempo – muy poco, creo. Yo lo veía tocando en el Tropicana – detrás de una palma. Ahí es donde ponían los negros – eso era de blancos."

Tito: "They were two of the best guys I ever worked with... I really mean that."

Charlie: "Tito and I used to go into this place where he played. Tito was looking for a drummer because Frankie Colón was drafted and on his way to Korea. I told Tito that night up at the Tropicana – not the one in Havana - a club in the Bronx we used to go into for a nightcap, that he should hire him. It was tough in those days because there were all kinds of segregation, even up here. Black musicians couldn't hang out with the white ones – it was bad. Tito decided he wanted Mongo and he didn't give a crap about what people would say or if it would hurt him."

Machito: "La orquesta nuestra siempre tuvo problemas por la situación racial de esa época."

Mario: "Eso es porque tu era muy negro…"

Laughter

Charlie: "We laugh about it now, but sometimes it got real scary. I used to play up in Buffalo and we had a 'brown skin' fellow playing bass. The owner of the club was a nice guy and let us play, but he told us to be careful when we left early in the morning. Shit – in Buffalo of all places. Traveling with a racially mixed band was always a hassle."

Tito: "I remember I had to cancel a few gigs in Florida. In those days the promoter and the owner would come around to see who they were hiring. When they saw Willie and Mongo they would cringe. Shit! The guy from the Casablanca Club in Miami told me 'the band is great but we can't take the percussion guys, you have to replace them." I told them no way. I cancelled the contract for the Casablanca and then later for another big hotel down there. So Charlie and I looked for work up north in Chicago and on the West Coast. There was no way I was going to trash my drummers. Bullshit!"

Machito: "I hate those racial divisions. I have hated them since I was a little boy in Cuba. I worked with Chano Pozo in New York and when he died I suffered for five days just thinking about how badly he was treated. I don't know why I'm thinking about it now. But racial problems were real in Cuba and they are real here too. I hate that people make a difference between blacks, black Cubans, white, Puerto Ricans – I hate it.

Tito: "Macho I think you have been drinking too much."

Miguelito: "He gets that way when we talk about the discrimination that existed in the 1940s and 1950s. Coño! La verdad es que era una jodienda. Creo que las cosas han mejorado mucho, pero todavía el camino hacia la justicia es larga."

Mario: "Macho se parece a Marlon Brando, no…"

Machito: "Mario estoy hablando en serio… But you are right there is a little bit of Brando in me. Brando se parece a mí."

Laughter

Miguelito: "Estoy contigo Macho. Yo siempre he querido ser un buen ser humano; ser un buen músico; y ser un buen cubano. Pero, coño, que mucho hijo de putas hay en este mundo."

Machito: "Amen."

Miguelito: "Some day it won't matter where people are born, what they look like and how they talk. That was the problem in Cuba. The blacks were nothing. They were mistreated, lied to and abused. I used to see dark skin musicians get turned away from nightclubs – not here – in Cuba. It was shameful. We are paying for it now. I hope that some day what we are talking about is nothing more than a distant memory."

Mario: "In the 1930s Panchito Rizet played at the El Morocco, Alberto Socarras played in a white club. There was a lot of segregation. I got a letter from someone to go up to 110th Street because some Latinos wanted to start a group. Juanito Sanabria was there. I said that I was not going to join because everyone was white. The black bands were organized and so were the white bands – this was in the 1930s. The Latinos had nothing and they were split apart. We still have the same shit. I remember I told Macho that I wanted to start my own band. He told me to wait, but finally we started it.

Machito: "He was nervous. It was hard in those days. Mario era negro."

Mario: "Pero hermoso, coño."

Some laughter

Charlie: "In those days it was hard, if not impossible for black orchestras to play south of 110th Street. Benny Goodman had Lionel Hampton and they gave him trouble."

Tito: "But he told them to go stick a finger in their respective assholes."

Laughter

Mario: "I wanted to play below 110th Street. We got a chance to be the substitute band. We go to play in a club and when our time comes to get on the bandstand we could not find our music. It was stolen. On December 7, 1941, we played – it was Pearl Harbor. Miguelito was at La Conga Club. He told me to come over to La Conga. We began to rehearse. The owner comes out of his office and we get into an argument. He wasn't sure about us because there were a lot of black cats. He agreed to let me do my thing and we were a smash. I remember in Florida, in Miami Beach we had the same problem. We had to sit at the back of the bus and go into the club through the back door. Shit!"

Charlie: "You told me about the mayor of Miami…"

Mario: "Oh yeah! The mayor of Miami Beach came to complain to the owner of the club. He was a real son of a bitch – un racista cabrón. 'You told me that there were no Negroes in the band,' he says to the owner. 'You said it was a Latin band. The drummer is black and so are some of the others.'

So the man tells the mayor if you think they are black then move them out. The mayor said he would let us play but that he would not ever let us return. Que hijo de la gran puta – racista. Un cabrón."

Tito: "I know, it was like that right through the 1960s. People were never sure how to categorize us – white, black or in between."

The King of the Rhumba-Cugat

Machito: "I remember when Miguelito was working with the Casino de la Playa in 1937. He came to the United States to work with Xavier Cugat. Él fue el que me convenció a venir a trabajar con Mario. I guess in a strange way we owe a lot to Mr. Cugat. He is a wonderful man. But in all honesty he is a terrible musician. He knows how to play a violin, but he knows nothing about clave, knows very little about mambo, and knows even less about Cuban music."

Mario: "Macho no tenga miedo de dejarnos saber lo que tu opinas de Xavier Cugat."

Laughter

Miguelito: "He was a nice man. He helped me a lot."

Machito: "Pero no sabia un carajo de música. El rey de la Rumba – Coño! Que paquete."

Miguelito: "El siempre dijo que lo del era ganar dinero y que con la música Afro-Cubana que era tocada genuinamente en los estados unidos ganar dinero no era posible. It was too African. But he did record some authentic style music, eh!"

Machito: "He is a great businessman. God Bless him. I remember I worked in the Paramount with him and I was getting paid $100 a night. Then I found out that I was supposed to be getting paid $1,000. He was a great businessman. Cugat era un ladrón y un mentiroso."

Charlie: "Maybe he didn't like the way you were singing?"

Tito: "Shit! I know he was stingy. He wasn't a bad guy – just tight."

Machito: "He was more than stingy and cheap. He was a con man."

Charlie: "I remember there was a dance in 1941 and it was advertised that Miguelito Valdés would be appearing with Xavier Cugat. Machito was the other band. Thousands of people showed up and Cugat never appeared.

Machito: "He told the promoter he would be there. I think he even got paid…"

Miguelito: "He never mentioned a word about appearing at the Palace – never, nunca."

Mario: "I told him about it in 1957 when we went to Cuba. I told him that if he wasn't careful he was going to get his toupee tossed in the trash."

Machito: "Él era un maricón."

Miguelito: "Cugat was always worried about his toupee. He was worse than Vicentico."

Laughter

Charlie: "But after people found out that Miguelito was not going to be there what followed was chaos. There was a big fight and the place was torn apart.

Mario: "I remember the other band – Orquesta Siboney – was there. We were watching the riot. I had the money from the promoter in a shopping bag. I made sure we got paid, shit. I looked at the leader of Siboney. 'What are we going to do. I have the money. Lets get the fuck out of here.' We left by the back door. Todos los músicos de las dos bands corriendo juntos. When we got outside I started taking the money out of the bag and paying everyone – our band and the other band. We were running down the street with our instruments and counting money. I can still hear the sirens."

Laughter

Miguelito: "Coño! Chico, he never said a word about me going to play up there – not once. You know I kept in touch with him forever. Y Tito siempre se comunicaba con él… a través de los años."

Tito: "Yeah, he never said shit about not showing up for that gig. He never said anything about collecting the money and not showing up. Doesn't sound like him. I mean I know he was a tightwad, but, not showing up…"

Charlie: "And, causing a riot."

Machito: "He was a mother fucker!"

Mario: "Shit, as we were running out of the place I saw the owner of the club, a Mr. Fisher. He yells to me: 'Who is going to fix up my place?' I looked at him. We were trying to get out of the place fast. So I took $50 out of the shopping bag gave it to him and we kept running."

Federico: "Did the promoter really contract with Cugat?"

Mario: "No. I ran into him one day and he said he never knew he was supposed to play there. No one ever talked to him… Eso es lo que hacían en cuba – anunciaban a un tal como Beny Moré y venía la gente. Lo que pasa es que Beny estaba por el carajo, en otro país."

Tito: "The Manhattan Center was a place that could get rough. People were always fighting, not over the bands, over women."

Miguelito: "And where were you? Estabas en el mismo centro de la riña. Coño, Tito."

Tito: "Shit! I was no where near any of that kind of shit."

Machito: "Jimmy was always taking care of you – making sure that you just played music and danced... He made sure that you got to where you were supposed to be."

Tito: "True."

(Laughter)

Salsa!

Miguelito: "Hablar del racismo me desanima. Shit! Let's talk about music... something else."

Charlie: "So what do you think about *salsa*?"

Tito: "That should get him going. You have been drinking too much. You know he (Miguelito)... for that matter all here get a little excited... We just love to talk about sauce – bullshit."

Laughter

Miguelito: "It is bullshit..."

Machito: "Salsa is what you put in food. It's not really music."

Miguelito: "Its like the rumba. In the 1930s everybody played rumba. It was a bolero-rumba, a guaracha-rumba, and a tango-rumba. Coño! Tocaban hasta valses con rumba. Sacaban la rumba hasta por el culo, coño."

Tito: "Like in the mambo era..."

Miguelito: "Algo así, pero esa música era distinta. Digo... Las orquestas eran sublime. The orchestra played with incredible precision. The musicians were good and they had a feeling for the music, for the dancers. Hoy, todos suenan igual. Me entienden?"

Machito: "*Salsa*, para mi no significa nada – algo que se le pone en la comida para darle gusto. Ese Pacheco y los jóvenes comerciantes de las disqueras Latina como la Fañia le pusieron un nombre a todo música Latina..."

Mario: "Y por ahí derrumbamos nuestra música... La música afro-cubana que nosotros tocamos se fue pa'l carajo – it went to shit!"

Miguelito: "Chico, estas con lo negativo..."

Mario: "So tell me what happened? Que es lo positivo, Shit."

Tito: "Pacheco did what that fuck Masucci told him to do. He wanted to make money, and screw all the young musicians just like the promoters did with the rock n' rollers in the 1950s. Charlie started all the shit with his record in 1963."

Laughter

Charlie: "It was only the title of a record, and a song, shit. It had nothing to do with a trend. Besides *'Salsa Na Ma'* was a charanga and I lost my shirt on it. By the time it came out everybody was listening to the boogaloo."

Tito: "What shit! Que mierda, coño."

Mario: "That is really bad. It was when we started losing our music."

Federico: "By that time the Palladium had lost its luster. Even the jazz clubs in the area were closing. Los blancos nunca le gusta que los negros y los Latinos tuvieran éxito en midtown. Siempre estaban jodiendo."

Miguelito: "Mira! Todos los países latino americano tienen un estilo de esa *Salsa.* The Dominicans play merengue. The Puerto Ricans play danza, bomba y plena. In Venezuela there is the joropo. In Argentina it is the tango. Everyone has something…"

Machito: "So the record companies tied it up into one package and everything is called salsa."

Tito: "It's a little more complicated. Today all that you hear is the bands playing the same beat, with the same tumbaos. The clave is there…"

Mario: "Just barely! Shit."

Laughter

Tito: "Shit! Its almost as if no one wants to try anything new, or take a chance. They just want to do what the other guy is doing."

Mario: "There is too much singing and not enough good arrangements."

Machito: "In the old days…"

Mario: "Coño! Macho tú eres el mas viejo aquí…"

Machito: "Y él más guapo."

Laughter

Tito: "We arranged for the orchestra. The orchestra was the showpiece. I know what you are saying, Macho."

Machito: "Can you imagine me singing a song from start to finish? Coño! Yo soy bueno, muy bueno pero me parece que él publico merece oírle a la orquesta. Miguelito tiene una voz increíble. He is probably the best singer here. But can you imagine him singing from start to finish without a break. Un sonero bueno busca donde meter sus poesías y la orquesta le abre el paso. Not like today…"

Mario: "Most modern singers, soneros are pretty bad."

Tito: "Sometimes it reminds me of the doo wop groups that used to sing on the street corners. Some of these guys were good."

Charlie: "Some were bad."

Laughter

Tito: "What I mean is that some were successful because of luck and some were real good – they had voices and quality. We are losing that with our singers. Every shit head thinks he can sing, the band leaders today don't know if he can or can't and what you have is the salsa crap."

Miguelito: "Salsa is what we started more than 30 years ago. Hay mucho bueno que ha ocurrido y también hay mucho que no es bueno."

Charlie: "Most young people today do not understand the roots of the music. The mambo was the son danzón. It was spicy and ignited spirits, but at the same time some of us toned it down and played a cool 4/4 beat, a little off key. Tito's mambos could be ferocious or they could also be easy going. The cha cha was a little more melodic, more difficult to dance. I think that's why it did not last so long – it was too difficult to dance. The rumba that was popular in the 1930s was really an American thing that incorporated light rhythm and just a little clave."

Machito: "Not that much until Mario started the band"

Laughter

Charlie: "The bolero was also Cuban in orgin. The guaracha is a vigorous Cuban dance beat that is generally played in a triple meter. It is either counted at 2/3 like a waltz or 2/4, which is the beat of the classic danza – not many people realize this. Its important to talk about the guaracha because it predates most of our contemporary music and even in the 1950s people got it confused with the mambo. It is a lively and highly danceable music with lyrics, which originated in Spain. It is distinguished mostly by its rhythm; it is generally played with a bolero section in 2/4 time and a clave section in either 6/8 or 3/4 time, although the order of these sections is sometimes reversed. It all depends on the arrangement. Typically, a guaracha ends with a sensual rumba section – not exactly what we think of rumba, you know. I remember listening to the radio and hearing *"Corneta"* sung by Daniel Santos. The guaracha came to Puerto Rico from Cuba in the mid-19th century, and developed into the island's so called jíbaro style that most closely approaches contemporary Latin dance rhythms. There was no room in the guaracha for improvisation – it was a straight set piece. Arcaño and Arsenio changed all that. Pérez Prado supposedly incorporated it into the big band format."

Mario: "Mierda! Shit!"

Tito: "Augh!"

Laughter

Machito: "Tienes razón Tito. Siempre sonaba como que se estaba cagando."

Laughter

Charlie: "But it was from the danzón, or French connection that the mambo came, not the guaracha. The guaracha is more like salsa that we hear today." And when Cuba turned to communism with Fidel, and we severed diplomatic and trade relations between Cuba and the United States, the ongoing flow and interaction of Cuban and New York musicians and dancers became limited. And as a result, Puerto Rico and New York have emerged since the 1960s as the primary sources and representatives of the contemporary salsa music that we dance to nowadays here in New York City. We still have a fascination about Cuban music and the statements by many that New York *Salsa* is Cuban, it is clear that we do not dance to Cuban music nor do we dance in a Cuban style. We dance a New York and Puerto Rican style. Even in Cuba things have changed. The old people frequent places where the classic Cuban music genres like danzón, cha cha and mambo, even guaracha are played – it is getting just like that here. Tito told me the other day that he gets the feeling that the dancers he plays for are getting older and older..."

Tito: "The other day I read some bullshit about salsa and that it continues ancient traditions of the Yorubá; cleansing your soul in dance and having your body lifted. Jesus Christ, who thinks up this shit? It is purely commercial crap. It may have some roots to African, European and I don't know what... But it is commercial music at its best. It is not jazz and has nothing to do with it. The ancient Yorubá must turn over in the heavens – what bullshit."

Mario: "Shit! Y sé esta poniendo peor, coño."

Tito: "It is danceable and that is why it doesn't go away quietly. The shingaling, boogaloo died a quick death in the early 1960s because there was no real dance for this crap. Bossa Nova, cha cha chá and even mambo are always going to be around – they are self-sustaining truer and purer Afro-Cuban percussive rhythms that are also danceable."

Charlie: "I was listening to a piece the other day and it almost sounded like every 12 bars there was a repetition. I mean like you know, when the saxes blow a riff, after several repetitions they drop a note or half tone just to give it a different feeling..."

Tito: "Those mother fuckers at Fañia could not orchestrate for one saxophone – most of the Masucci ass kissers think it is a bathroom utensil. I like to bring in the trombones – to state the same theme, maybe, but with a different pattern – sometimes you can even switch a half tone. Sometimes you can do it with the piano, the trumpets or even the saxes."

Mario: "Los violines de las charangas generan ese sentir. Two violins play one guajeo while another one plays something slightly different, como en las orquestas de metal."

Charlie: "Some charangas use cellos playing a low extended montuno or ostinato. The violins play something else."

Machito: "You did that in your pachanga album."

Charlie: "Yeah! I used cello to get depth of sound, just to be a little different."

Tito: " He did not want to sound like Pacheco. That's the whole point here. The contemporary groups don't explore, they don't have options. They don't care to find out what is underneath the main texture of our music. Shit there is so much."

Miguelito: Oye, yo no se mucho de esa corporación disquera, Fañia, pero algunos músicos son bueno. Tito me dijo eso en varias ocasiones, no."

Tito: "Yo creo que sí. Pero yo no quiero tener nada que ver con ellos. They are the Funny All-Stars and if the executives did not dish out cash to have the recordings these shits make you would not hear them. The music business is all fucked up."

Miguelito: "Si, si eso es correcto, pero hay algunos Buenos – Harlow tiene una buena orquesta. Tu hermano Eddie tiene una gran orquesta, Pacheco suena bien aunque no toca nada novedoso. Estoy seguro que hay otros, no."

Charlie: "Si hay buenos. There are good bands, no kidding. One young bandleader came up to me the other day and asked me to help him learn about harmony. 'Its not something you learn in a couple of minutes,' I said. I tried to explain the concept, briefly."

Mario: "Briefly, shit."

Charlie: "I told him how in past periods of music, a composer devised many ways to elaborate harmonies in order to create various rhythmic and sonorous effects, you know, patterns."

Tito: "I remember when I was at Juilliard we studied how harmonic support for melody has to enhance the rise and decline of melody lines. A cadence represents arrival of a complete part of the piece of music with no need to move further. The other harmonic cadence is on going – eventually they play off of each other."

Charlie: "I didn't even go there. I just tried to explain simple things."

Miguelito: "Our music can go so far if only people that make it take time and care to learn the fundamentals. Podemos llegar a la luna gozando guaguancó…"

Mario: "Y el "Babalú!"

Laughter

Miguelito: "I would just like to see our young people continue to progress, to keep studying. I don't know if what they are doing is good or bad. I do know that a lot of them are in a hurry and that a lot of them – los jóvenes – no toman el tiempo para educarse – no solo la música, pero las tradiciones. We all have history – of how we got here, where we came from, and what has happened. Look at Cuba. Ahí la cagamos. You have to study the past so you can improve the future. Tito is always telling me that our history is important. So what we do today is going to be manifested in some future. He is right. I would like to see our young people study – learn from Charlie and Tito. They are up the block. Let's not be in such a hurry. Que es lo que estábamos hablando? Necesito otro trago… I am tired of hearing singers that all they do are yell, jump up and down and disguise their shortcomings with flashing lights. I want to hear chords that roll and bass lines that excite me and make me want to listen. Ask Federico how it was in the Palladium. People who could not dance stood in front of the bandstand watched the band and felt the music – there was musicianship and inspiration. Tito could dance and it fit in with the band. Tito también toca el piano y el saxofón. Una noche veo a Tito, coño, sentado con Jimmy y los italianos tocando el clarinete. Que coño! Tito Rodríguez tocaba timbales y vibráfono y bailaba, coño! Could he dance and so did his percussion guys. It was different. Now people don't even dress sharply."

Tito: "Tu no baila tan mal…"

Mario: "They look like bums! They play like shit."

Miguelito: "No, no! Coño, Mario! Everything is casual. Salsa is not social, musical, cultural, or hybrid force that has embraced jazz. No me jodas. I don't like it. I just don't like it."

Laughter

Charangeas and Tipicas!

Mario: "When I came to the United States in 1927, I was playing clarinet for the best charanga orchestra in Cuba – Orquesta Antonio Ma. Romeu. It was not very easy to travel with a full band and when we got here there was not a Latin band in New York – none. A few Latinos that lived here asked him to play for them. We had no timbales because in those days the noise of the percussion made the needle bounce. So Romeu got somebody, a Puerto Rican fellow, and after he played the first number Mr. Romeu told the fellow 'don't play no more.' It was a very small community – mostly Puerto Ricans, a few Cubans and a lot of Gallegos. I went back to Cuba and returned in 1930, and I discovered a group called Santo Domingo Serenade. It was a mixed group of Cubans, Puerto Ricans, Dominicans and a fellow from the West Indies. They played one Latino song at night.

It was awful. Charanga music was the most popular in Cuba. There were conjuntos and sextetos. The son was just starting to be heard in Havana. It came from the mountains. The white people liked this music because they thought it had nothing to do with the Afro-Cubans. But Romeu and the other charangas quickly adopted it into the danzón format."

Charlie: "It was called danzonete."

Machito: "There was the Sexteto Habanero. I was working with María Teresa. In the 1930s it was charanga and sextetos that were popular. In Cuba the big bands were playing popular music. They did not play Cuban music. A los negros no se le permitía tocar en publico, recuerdas."

Mario: "Vicente Sigler es uno de los cubanos que viene a nueva york en los años treinta. He starts a band with Puerto Ricans and Dominicans and Cubans. Don Azpiazu comes next and his band featured the great Antonio Machín. That was the first big Latin Band in the United States. That is where it all started. I played trumpet in people's houses for 50 cents."

Charlie: "He was lucky if he got paid."

Mario: "The Happy Boys was organized by Federico."

Federico: "I had three bands: The Happy Boys, the Swing Boys and Snow White."

Machito: "Mario tú era el que estaba aquí. Estaba Antóbal.

Federico: "In 1930 there were other groups. Machin was already here."

Mario: "I was here playing before Machin started on his own."

Federico: "No..."

Mario: "Coño! There were some Latin bands that were organized in the 1940s – they were white bands that played the American style rumba. There were a number of clubs that opened up, but they were segregated."

Federico: "There were a lot of clubs that opened in Harlem and in East Harlem."

Tito: "I visited all of them."

Mario: "I started playing for Chick Webb and on one occasion I heard from Romeu. He asked me how I was doing. He was a great musician. In the 1930s, during the swing era, the time of the big bands, he was always experimenting. He used trumpets, trombones and clarinets with his violins. He had a lot of ideas. He is the father of the modern charanga. Arcaño is the father of the mambo, with Arsenio. Romeu had a flute player that was an incredible musician – Francisco Delabart. Le decían *"Flauta Mágica."* Era increíble. Se me paraban los pellos cuando lo escuchaba tocar. The Cuban charangas have always been popular for dancing. They were the main dance bands. You know that before the charangas they were called orquestas tipicas – military bands that started playing syncopated music. Just like the Dixieland jazz bands came from military bands that played ragtime – syncopated music."

Mario: ¿Oye Conzo, estas grabando todo esto?

Joe: Yeah.

Mario: Charlie es el historiador aquí. Al igual que lo es Miguelito cuando no esta hablando shit."

Miguelito: Deja que lo expliqué Charlie. Él es el que sabe de la danza y el danzón.

Charlie: "The danzón orchestra or charangas have a long history in Cuba. With them came a lot of the innovations in Afro-Cuban music. We forget that. The big bands that existed in the 1940s and early 1950s were about 10 pieces. First Tito Rodríguez started with a sextet. Tito came in with the conjunto, and both of them quickly expanded their sound following in the footsteps of Machito and the Afro-Cubans who had a big band that mirrored the swing era style orchestras."

Tito - In Cuba the big bands did not really play what we now call Afro-Cuban music. They played in hotels for the white crowds, very little or no percussion – it wasn't permitted."

Mario: "It was the tipicas that really were the movers of change, you know. Yeah, they played danzones but they played everything else. They sounded like Dixieland jazz bands. I played clarinet in one. Coño! It was hard to be heard. These guys blasted away on the horns while the timbalero hit the danzón beat, sometimes on the skins, and sometimes on the cowbell that usually hung on the side. The trumpet and cornet players used to cut the shafts so they could sound louder – louder was better. Coño! This is where it all started. Later the son came along and the white people said that it was the real Cuban music. Shit! The same thing happened in New Orleans. Ahí es donde el jazz toma vigor con las típicas de Dixieland. The big band grew from the American típicas…"

Charlie: "Those were ragtime orchestras – military bands with banjos and violins."

Mario: That's where the big bands come from. In Cuba they heard what was happening here – in New York. First the sextets expanded to conjuntos, and Arsenio added a full percussion section. Arcaño added a full percussion section. He was sticking his nose out at the authorities. Then…"

Tito: "Casino de la Playa came along and that changed everything. They adopted some of the American swing band styles, put an emphasis on Afro-Cuban and the big bands were on their way."

Mario: "But it was you and Tito Rodríguez that really excited them

– the Cubans. There are people in Cuba that think Tito Puente is Cuban. Machito's Afro-Cubans…"

Miguelito: "Es la misma mierda, no!"

Federico: "Y Machito y los Afro-Cubanos - muy progresivo..."

Tito: "Yes and no… I think the three of us together helped bring about an exciting type fusion. At the time none of us ever gave it a thought. We were too busy here fighting to make a living."

Laughter

Mario: "Pero mi punto es que las charangas siempre han estado al frente de todo. Es un punto interesante, no."

Big Bands

Miguelito: "¿Que es lo que constituye una orquesta, un big band genuino? I heard Tito play "Picadillo" when he used to play with his pick up group. There were two trumpets, sometimes three, percussion and him playing vibes. Esto no es una orquesta."

Machito: "An orchestra – a real one – is when you have a lead singer and at least three saxophones and two trumpets. You also have a full Afro-Cuban percussion section – tumbadora, timbales, maracas o güiro y un bongosero."

Charlie: "Before Arsenio expanded the conjunto it usually consisted of two to three trumpets, a tumbadora, bongo and güiro. There was a piano and one singer, sometimes two. Arsenio added several more trumpets and a timbalero. Roberto Faz had a similar style. If you look at La Sonora Matancera, they were really only a sextet. These types of groups were popular in Cuba among the upper crust. The big bands in Cuba, that played Afro-Cuban music, were organized in the 1950s – Riverside, Beny Moré' Bebo Valdés and Chico O'Farrill come to mind. From there the Afro-Cuban jam session evolved.

Mario: "O'Farrill era un genio. He used to like to try new things and was always looking for a big sound – but a refined big sound. Tito me hace recordar a Stan Kenton – un sonido pero muy controlado, with a big powerful build up. Tito Rodríguez era swinging pero muy táctil. Coño como el ponía sus músicos a bailar. Shit, que jodienda."

Miguelito: "Y la orquesta de Machito…"

Mario: "An orchestra that could be pleasing and exciting."

Tito: "Bullshit! He's being modest. They were the best, the teacher, the educators and innovators. But I am the best!"

Mario: "El rey… Shit!"

Charlie: "Todos – los dos Titos y Machito, para me son los reyes."
Loud laughter
Miguelito: "Charlie siempre el diplomático."

The Future

Tito: "Ever since I have been in this business I have always strived to expand its acceptance. Right now as a genre we – those of us who play Afro-Cuban music – are a miniscule part of the picture. The industry is in turmoil…"

Miguelito: "It has been like that forever."

Tito: "I don't think we can fix what is wrong with the music industry, but it would be a good thing if our music was listened to by a wider audience. I don't think the Grammy Awards organization is a viable course. This is all show and no substance. Maybe if they make some changes, I am not sure about that. But I believe that we who play Afro-Cuban music, Latin jazz, or whatever need to work hard to learn the core subjects – culture, classics, history and the elements of music theory, harmony, and all that."

Miguelito: "I think it is important that we learn our culture, learn about who we are and then study music. And, when I say study music, I agree with Tito and Mario and Charlie. You have to study the classics so that you can build on it, build on the ideas and expand the structures. Yes, Tito is right.

Charlie: "I see us appearing on major network shows, performing major frontline concerts, being in the forefront of American society.

Tito the Prankster

Charlie: "One night Machito showed up at the Birdland; his piano player had been in an accident. I was playing at the Palladium with Tito. Mario sends the band boy to find someone to fill in. But it was only me who was around.

Tito: "What a pair of balls, Mario."
Laughter

Charlie: "I'm running back and forth between the Palladium and the Birdland. I play a full set for each band and then Tito tells me to tell Mario that he should pay me for the night – this is at 3:00 A.M. I run back to the Birdland and Mario says that Tito should pay me because I played for him. Later that night – morning I find Mario, Machito and Tito in a bar down the block laughing their heads off. 'Where is my money,' I cried out. 'Sit down and have a drink, you look tired," Tito yelled."

Mario: "Esa fue idea de Tito. He sent someone over to me during the night and to tell me that he wanted to scare Charlie…"

Tito: "I figured Charlie would figure it out right away, but running back and forth tired him out. He also had too much to drink…"

Charlie: "My friends…"

Machito: "Tito likes to play pranks on people. Since I know him he is doing that."

Monotonus Montuno

Mario: "Mira que cosa… El otro día Macho y yo estábamos ensayando cuando, aparentemente un periodista, me pregunta: 'Porque la música que ustedes tocan es tan monótona y repetida. Coño! Que jodienda!"

Machito: "He really got mad. Federico estaba ahí."

Federico: "Es obvio que el tipo no sabia un carajo de música."

Miguelito: "Espero que tomaron el tiempo para ponerlo rehecho – tu sabes, educación: Music 101…"

Charlie: "Afro-Cuban music 101."

(Laughter)

Tito: "The problem today is that people, especially the younger generation, doesn't listen – they have to see it on a fucking video. There is so much going on in an orchestra…"

Mario: "Federico was trying to explain it, but he is too nice…"

Federico: "Coño! No me dejaste hablar."

Mario: "Bullshit! Tu sabes que el que te hizo la pregunta es un pendejo, coño."

Federico: "You know that you have to speak softly. Everybody thinks they know how to make music. Es increíble lo poco que saben hoy."

Mario: "But you kept on letting this shit tell you about something he doesn't know."

Machito: "Mario, tu sabes que el lo hizo bien, le explicó lo de los ritmos, las variantes y la harmonización…"

Mario: "He confused the shit out of the guy. He confused me… Shit!"

(Laughter)

Federico: "You wanted to kick him out the door. Eso no esta bien tampoco."

Charlie: "Who was it?"

Mario: "Somebody that writes about music in the magazines – un come mierda que se cree que lo sabe todo…"

Tito: "Who was it? Who was this person?'

Miguelito: "What were you rehearsing?"

Mario: "Macho estaba cantando un improvisado. Estábamos relajando, tu sabes. We were making it up as we went along. We were doing a lot of shit."

Tito: "Who the fuck was it?"

Federico: "Mario se puso rojo."

Tito: "That's hard to do, for him. I thought maybe, Mario was trying to sing."

(Laughter)

Federico: "If that was the case, we would have all run out the door, me, Macho and the guys in the band."

Mario: "Shit!"

Miguelito: "Coño¡ Eso es Verdad – Mario cantando, wow!"

Tito: "Mario, you probably scared the shit out of him, that is if you were trying to sing."

Ray Barretto – A Nervous Soul

Mario: I remember one day Ray Barretto called me, and said he was going down to Florida to play. He needed some guys – musicians. I was shocked. He had a nice sounding conjunto in those days. I mean, I didn't follow him, and the truth was that when he left Tito I never gave him a second thought."

Tito: He had the charanga, then the charanga with trumpets and then… Shit! Charlie what did he do then?"

Charlie: "He got rid of the trumpets and brought in trombones and then he had trombones, trumpets and violins and no flute… he was always nervous, always searching."

Tito: "Sounds like you…"

Laughter

Charlie: "He made a few good recordings before he dropped his charanga – damn good – I even liked his crossover album – *'American Hits Latin Style,'* I think that is what it was called."

Mario: "I made some suggestions. He came back and called to thank me and said he was going to just play jazz for a while… he was tired of the way Afro-Cuban music was going. I told him to stick with something, anything for a few days."

Tito: "He was a very nervous soul. I guess he is like us – always looking beyond, whatever works. Remember he was sitting here with us last week. He wanted to talk to Miguelito."

Miguelito: "He is a very nervous soul. Me parece que eso es algo bueno porque una persona como Ray siempre quiere tratar cosas nuevas."

Charlie: "Ray is never satisfied with just sounding good. He reminds me of someone...(Tito). He has to have it right. If a piano player can't read the music and feel it at the same time – he is tossed out on the street. If the percussion is out of whack – he will change the drummer in a heartbeat."

Miguelito: "Coño¡ Ese suena a Tito, no! I'm glad I could keep time."

Tito: "He is confused – just like the rest of us. We are trying to figure out what the fuck is happening to our music!"

Ideals

Miguelito: "One day when I went to see Pupi Campo and his show I got there early and he was arguing about the way to play a piece with Joe Loco. Joe got pissed off and I saw him leave. Then Charlie sat in. By the end of the night Joe was back. But Charlie told me that Pupi wanted the piece not to sound too Afro-Cuban or jazzy. There were a lot of white and Jewish people in the audience. Joe said for him to go and fuck himself."

Charlie: "I sat in, but I was getting ready to leave with Tito... Pupi was careful not to get me too pissed off. He did go out and apologize to Joe."

Mario: "That's what I mean. We are always too willing to give up our values and beliefs just to appease others. Shit!"

Dancers

Machito: "I always get a kick out of how the people – the young people dance now, today. The young man stands in one corner and the girl stands in another corner. The music is playing – talk about repetitious – a salsa band can be repetitious, and the dancers are jumping up and down. I am astonished at what I see – they never touch each other. There is no harmony. The two people just jump up and down. I am dumbfounded. Its almost like they are fighting."

Mario: "Someone asked me how can I stand what is going on today. I get it going because I separate the two things."

Charlie: "The music has a lot of directions and the dancers go where it leads them. My music is still a little more on the traditional style. I don't know what is going to happen a year from now. I don't think that real Afro-Cuban styles have penetrated the American market.

Tito: "We have to keep reinventing ourselves and we have to promote what is good about music. It is Afro-Cuban music – the real thing. To have real Afro-Cuban music you have to have good musicians."

Miguelito: "And you are not going to let the bad ones play for you. They have to be able to have clave."

Tito: "And be able to read music."

Mario: "Chico, ese es uno de los problemas. Tocan música como bailan. No hay harmonías."

Tito: "Macho cuéntale a Miguelito y Charlie lo que ocurrió en el Corso's hace unas semanas."

Machito: "I am singing and playing maracas. Everybody is having a good time; at least it looks that way. I see this guy walk up to a young lady and he slaps her across the face. The bouncers saw it too. She slaps him back. He walks away and starts dancing with another woman. She starts dancing with two other women. I don't really know what was going on. But its what I am saying there is no connection."

Miguelito: "No se baila como antes – suave y con movimiento sensual – nothing fancy..."

Federico: "Cuando se tocaba un bolero en el Palladium no se veía las parejas moverse."

Charlie: "Everybody was trying to get telephone numbers..."

Laughter

Machito: "Anyway, when I'm leaving with the band after the dance is over; the woman and man who slapped each other come up to me. They are husband and wife. Shit! All night they are dancing with other people. I am getting too old for this."

Hearty laughter

Percussionists

Mario: "Do you remember when there were a lot of good – great drummers – timbaleros? The other day someone was asking me if I could recommend a timbalero. I thought for a while and then said: 'call Tito. He is the only one alive that can keep good time, the rest stink."

Miguelito: "Or they are too high."

Charlie: "No one wants to just sit back and keep time today... Everyone wants to be a star."

Tito: "There are still some good drummers –timbales, conga, bongo – out there."

Mario: "Estos tipos de hoy se pretenden estrellas. No saben marcar tiempo como antes. I remember a long time ago there was a lot of good, solid drummers – Moncho Muñoz – the son of the Puerto Rican bandleader. He was one of those old bands we used to like to hear. There was Federico's son, Papi Pagani. He was solid. Uba Nieto was one of the best."

Machito: "Él era boricua."

Mario: "Yes. He was always breaking the sticks because he would strike the bell so hard. Shit! One night we had to send someone in the band out on Broadway to look for sticks because Uba broke them all. He sat there for about an hour tapping the skins with his hands. No one realized that he was using the claves to strike the sides. Thank God he knew enough not to strike the damn cowbell with the clave sticks. He was incredible for his sense of timing. These guys today all they think about is that they can play better than Tito. They don't know half of what he knows. I saw a guy one night come out with three congas. Shit! He couldn't play one. Punteaba todo fuera de tiempo y fuera de clave."

Tito: "Maybe he was trying something new… a new beat. Uba was a steady guy on timbales. He knew how to fit his playing to what was being played – a lost art."

Mario: "First you have to learn how to keep basic time. Some of these guys are all over the place. I don't see you do that, not when you are playing serious."

Tito: I remember when I watched Gene Krupa play. He was damn good. He had a knack for knowing when to break it up, a knack for sitting in the background and just keeping time. Buddy Rich – as big a pain in the ass as he was – could be soft and mellow and very precise. Good percussionists are hard to come by – even rare. It is not easy to keep time for everyone. It looks easy, but it's not."

Miguelito: "The idea that anyone can keep time is garbage. Hay que practicar muchas horas – especialmente marcando tiempo."

Mario: "Tito no toca así. Él sabe como tocar aunque a veces le gusta repicar."

Miguelito: "You have just fed his ego and he is going to be unbearable for the rest of the year."

We had spent a number of hours in the Asia Restaurant. When we left Tito, Charlie and I walked back to the office. It was dark. "Just save the tape, Joe. There is a lot of history in there. Maybe someday someone will be interested in it. Of course, I was going to save the recordings. I had sat through more than 10 hours of listening to my heroes. I was still feeling a little bit in awe.

Charlie laughed. “There is a lot of bullshit too.”

Tito laughed. “I still think we are an important part of the history of our music.”

“I agree,” Charlie responded. “ What do you think Joe?”

I nodded in the affirmative. The damn tape recorder was a little heavy. I had had a little too much to drink too.

Tito and Charlie were going to catch up with Miguelito later. The Machito Orchestra was going to be appearing in some hotel in Manhattan. Federico was taking the subway to go home.

Tito On the Bridge

Theolonus Monk and Tito hugged each other in the middle of the hectic commotion backstage at the Apollo Theater.

"Hey, man that was good, Tito," Monk said as the two musicians clinched as I looked on.

"They're waiting for you," Tito panted in a loud voice struggling to be heard in the tedious turmoil of the afternoon jazz show at the Apollo Theater. Monk smiled in my direction. His eyes were red and hazy. Then he walked off in the direction of several other people who were preparing to perform. "Come on Joe," shouted Tito, "we can catch the rest of the show from upstairs." Neither of us was feeling any pain – lunch, over indulging in drinks and even candy. We were floating as we searched for empty seats.

We managed to find seats on the upper balcony as the Master of Ceremonies announced: "And now ladies and gentlemen lets give this master of jazz a rousing welcome to yet another return to his roots." The lights dimmed. The spotlight was aimed at the end of the stage. The large auditorium was quiet. "Theolonus Monk!" The packed theater crowd went wild. Out onto the edge of the stage came Monk.

Tito taught me to really appreciate a wider range of music. Monk, according to Tito, was one of the mainstays of modern jazz. Monk was a master of the "effective pause and space and time." In Afro-Cuban music the pause and silence between notes and musical phrasing is sometimes called syncopation or playing between the beat. Tito thought of Monk as "an eccentric jazzman."

Tito's orchestra had played six numbers that pleased the mixed matinee crowd. Jimmy was paying the band, and making sure the music was packed up, and the instruments accounted for. Tito figured Jimmy was not going to hang around. It was early and Jimmy had a date with the racetrack. We waited with the rest of the audience for Monk to make his appearance.

The emcee shouted Monk's name again. Monk walked onto the stage from behind the black curtains. He started to walk to the center – slowly, almost feeling his way. The large room was silent. The spotlight beamed on him as he sat at the grand piano in the middle of the historic stage. Like everyone else in the room we waited in anticipation. Tito kept nudging at my side with an elbow. He whispered: "Shit, watch this." The orchestra in the pit waited too, for him to deliver his piano etude before joining in.

Monk looked down at the keyboard. He lifted his hands. One finger came down. The note exploded – at least it seemed that way – throughout the old theater.

Tito said later Monk hit a C-sharp. Who am I to question him? The single note rang out through the theater. The place went crazy. The fans were standing, cheering, gasping – it was a wild scene. Monk, the master jazzman, after striking the note, stood up, smiled and walked off the stage. The audience was energized, even breathless. "Shit!" shouted Tito. "Did you see that?"

"See what? He hit one fucking note and left. He is drunker than we are," I shouted trying to be heard in the midst of the pandemonium."

"The man is great," gasped Tito.

"The hell," I responded. "He didn't do anything."

A few minutes later we were on 125th Street walking towards the car. We stopped in the middle of the crowded sidewalk, looked at each other and burst out in laughter. "He was more shit faced than the two of us," Tito laughed. This was just one of those bizarre moments we shared.

A few days later when I related the story to Jimmy he smiled. "This is what happens. Everybody in the place was probably shit faced. "So is he going to score Monk's One Note as a mambo?" He shrugged and kept on paying the bills. A second later he looked, smiled. "I hope you don't expect to be reimbursed for that crap…"

A few weeks later Tito and his orchestra opened the Latin Tinge of the Newport Jazz Festival[106] that was staged at Carnegie Hall. *"Mambo Inn," "Ran Kan Kan,"* and *"Tito Timbero,"* had the large crowd on its feet. *"Mambo Diablo"* with Tito's prolonged vibe solo that slipped masterfully from the mild major key tones into the somber exotic chromatic scale impressed even Duke Ellington, who was waiting in the wings with his orchestra. Ellington shook hands with Jimmy as he walked off the stage. "Wow!" Ellington gasped with a wide smile. "Terrific!" He continued to smile and walk to the front of the stage.

The trumpet man graciously accepted the accolades of one of the masters of sophisticated jazz. "It took everything I had to remain cool," Jimmy informed me when he caught up with me on the other side of the backstage area. "Where the fuck is Tito?" Jimmy gasped.

"I don't know," I responded. We set off to look for him and tracked him down outside.

"Duke Ellington was mesmerized by our work here today," Jimmy told his partner and friend. "'It was anticlimactic,' Ellington said to Felipe Luciano. 'Don't you ever let Tito open for me again.'"

Tito smiled. "Well, of course, he should be – we are the best." After a few moments of silence in a serious tone Tito added: "That is quite a compliment, eh!"

A few months later Ellington passed away. To Tito he was one of the best. "He had that sophistication that tears away barriers. He had his own unique style." Tito never forgot how impressed Ellington was when he heard the orchestra that day at the New Port Jazz Festival. But then again, Tito and Ellington were old school. They were fiercely competitive and yet they recognized good music wherever it came from. From this point on Tito and the Orchestra and eventually the jazz ensemble played at the Newport Jazz Festival each summer.

Tibiri Tabara

The 1970s were upon us and Tito's hair was getting white. His energy was that of a young man. But he privately admitted that his creative juices had moderated. The reason, he said, was little competition. He did not consider the music of the small salsa ensembles coming out of El Barrio and the Bronx to be on a footing with the sound of a sophisticated, working band. The radio stations relentlessly pushed the small groups and it was popular among the younger generation. There was no room for the big bands on the airwaves even as they struggled to adopt. The music that was promoted in Tito's view for the most part was forgettable. "It is repetitive and does not explore the depths of Afro-Cuban rhythms," he maintained. Some of the conjuntos and ensembles were indeed good, but for the most part he felt that the many bands that existed "were being exploited by scavenging promoters and ambitious record company executives."

However, Tito was in great demand. Over the years he had acquired a strong following from where he least expected – the Anglo population. His orchestra was busy; and he was still eager to find an edge whenever and wherever. But it was important to remain pleasing to his audiences – young and old, new and established. I called him Pops – my way of reminding him that time was moving ever forward. Tito and Margie were together, living in Manhattan. It was a romance he maintained very private. One day he announced he was going to be a father again. It caught the members of his orchestra by surprise. Jimmy and I were stunned. He was 47-years-old and being a parent to two children (Ronnie from his earlier marriage, and now Audrey) many people that were close to Tito expected that he would slow down – he didn't. In 1970 Audrey was born. A year later, in June 1971 Tito Puente, Jr. was born. Tito maintained a hot and cold relationship with his oldest son Ronnie, who like his father studied music. However, Ronnie was more inclined to follow a general business career path.

During 1970 and 1971, Tito and his orchestra were in the studio for recording sessions that resulted in the release of six long play albums that featured for the most part the singers familiar to the current generation of dancers. The albums had mixed results. The album *"Etc. Etc. Etc."* teamed Tito with one of his favorite singers, Celia Cruz. As far as he was concerned his work with her had not been as successful as he would have liked. "She is one terrific lady. I have not been able to come up with the formula that could give us success we are seeking." He considered *"Eleguá,"* an okay tune – nothing like his orchestral masterpiece of 1956, and *"Sugar, Sugar,"* a popular tune gives us another look at both Tito and Celia.

In a turn around, Santos Colón featured his former boss and orchestra in a Fañia recording. It gave Tito an opportunity to explore the romantic genre and also to generate pleasure with the traditional Afro-Cuban flavors. The long play album, *"Santitos,"* uses strings mixed in with the brass and was something Tito enjoyed doing. For several nights he worked on the arrangements. On one of those nights he wandered over to my apartment on 92nd Street.

"Have you got time for a lost soul," he said over the intercom.

"Tito?"

"Shit, yeah! Let me in. Its cold and its raining..."

A few minutes later – 3:00 a.m. – we were sitting in the living room sipping drinks. I was listening to Tito. In the background was the music of Stan Kenton, Duke Ellington and Machito and his Afro-Cubans. "They are struggling too," he jibed. I offered to play his latest recordings. "No!" he said emphatically. "Absolutely not." I waited for him to offer an explanation. "I was working with the arrangements on the Santitos album. I think it's going to be nice."

Tico issued a compilation of Tito's work with Santos in 1970 just to counter the Fañia Records marketing effort. The compilation was titled *"Imágenes."* It featured a lot of boleros, some traditional Afro-Cuban moods – what is generally called typical Tito Puente was on the menu. Santos Colón, according to Tito, indicated to him that he wanted to do a "big album." Tito laughed. "He (Santitos) was not sure that the people at Fañia were up to the task – a big sound. All they do is small shit and spend money to have their shit played over the radio." He sipped his drink. Kenton was coming into the coda – a big buildup before the climax. "He does concerts. That is where his fans and followers are. I will probably be doing the same thing soon. If they keep on closing the dancehalls and clubs it will be hard to keep the band going."

This was always a concern, not only for Tito but also for the Machito organization, for most bands that managed to keep working long after the swing era ended in 1947. "It was us – me, Tito (Rodríguez) and Machito that kept the big band phenomenon going – Kenton, Basie, Ellington and a few others are also responsible, but it was the three of us that really pushed the envelope all the way." He shrugged. By the time he left the sun was out, it had stopped raining.

The album backing his former singer Santitos Colón *"Santitos Featuring Santos Colón"* was released with little or no fanfare. The lack of marketing by Fañia Records and it owner, Jerry Masucci, and partner, vice president Johnny Pacheco, were ominous signs for Tito. But despite the lack of enthusiasm on the part of the Fañia bosses the combination of Santitos Colón and the Tito Puente Orchestra would be well received by a mixed public – the adults of the Palladium era and a sprinkling of adolescents who preferred what Tito now called "sophisticated Afro-Cuban music." He was convinced that given the proper marketing push the music he loved to play was still palatable and with first-rate innovations the fan base could expand and could even become a significant part of the ever-changing American music scene. He was going to die trying – that was his conviction.

Tito, Jimmy and Morris Levy held a strategy meeting. It was agreed to feature Tito and his orchestra showcasing popular vocal singers – whether he liked them or not. *"El Sol Brilla Para Todo,"* featuring La Lloroncita was a bomb. Quetcy Alma "La Lloroncita" Martínez was a native of Arroyo, Puerto Rico, who had performed as a youngster on New York Spanish radio and local Spanish language theater venues. She got her nickname: "Lloroncita" (Crybaby) because of the tears that flowed from her eyes when she belted out a romantic song. She was popular in the late 1960s and into the mid 1970s when she simply disappeared. Tito, who normally did not admit failure, shrugged whenever the album was mentioned. "Maybe the album cover had some redeeming qualities," he supposed. On the heels of that disappointment Tito followed with *"Imágenes,"* and then he recorded *"Alma Con Alma"* that reunited him with Celia. Tito called *"P'alante!"* a sort of sleeper album that somehow managed to get recorded in an era that was totally going berserk in terms of the recording industry. The orchestra is the centerpiece here and Tito is at his best arranging "a la Kenton" – his description – such selections as *"P'alante," "No Voy A La Luna," "Lindo Palomar," and "Mi Jevita." "Cuero," "Hit The Bongo"* and *"Aragüita"* are in the contemporary jam session range, while *"No Puedo Ser Feliz," "Nuestra Canción,"* and *"Obsérvalo"* are designed to feature Santos. The Venezuelan singer Meñique is the other featured vocalist.

The introduction of Meñique to do vocals did not please Santitos. One afternoon during the recording session he approached me. He was almost embarrassed. "¿Oye Joe, que es lo que Tito esta pensando, con el nuevo cantante?"

"Yo no sé, Santos. I don't know," I responded cautiously. Santitos was a quiet type of guy. He usually went along with the flow. "He just wants to experiment."

Santos added, "Habla con él - Tito. ¿Mira ver que es lo que el estas pensando, si es que va hacer cambios?"

"You ask him," I responded. Santitos walked away, not in a very happy mood. When I spoke to Tito later about Santitos' concern he laughed it off. Meñique was just one of Tito's gimmicks. Santos Colón had nothing to worry about.

When the Fañia label was organized in 1964 it functioned out of the back of a truck, by former police officer and attorney Jerry Masucci[107] and Johnny Pacheco. By the 1970s Fañia Records literally controlled the radio airwaves and was squeezing Tico Records into oblivion. It was in the middle of the burgeoning salsa explosion. Masucci and Pacheco pushed the young and less experienced bands that included musicians like Willie Colón, Héctor Lavoe, Rubén Blades and Pete "El Conde" Rodríguez. In 1969, Afro-Cuban music pioneer Arsenio Rodríguez died. His final album for Tico was *"Arsenio Dice."* By 1972 the Machito Orchestra, Ray Barretto and Eddie Palmieri bands departed Tico Records. Pancho Cristal did so as well, leaving Art Kapper, Miguel Estivíl, and Fred Weinberg to conduct production duties. Twenty-four long play albums had been released in 1968, but album output would diminish in subsequent years.

As early as 1964 Masucci and Pacheco were taking advantage of Spanish language radio with the new salsa music, effectively pushing from sight and sound the older, experienced venues that played the more traditional tropical flavored music. Tito realized what was happening to the music he loved, and the music he loved to play. He did not like Masucci. He maintained a cordial relationship with his former musician Pacheco but was extremely careful not to discuss business of any sort with him. Masucci and Pacheco met in 1962. Pacheco used Masucci for his divorce and Masucci saw a business potential in the Latin music scene. In the early 1970s, Pacheco sold off his interest in Fañia to his partner but remained as the musical director.

Tito felt that the tiny Afro-Cuban music genre had missed an opportunity to reach beyond its small fan base and really make an impact on American music and beyond. It was a view that was shared by Charlie Palmieri and Mario Bauzá. The three of them often spoke about "the missed opportunity." But Tito was resolved to press on with his brand of Afro-Cuban music. "There is always a way, you know. There is opportunity lurking with every breath." He was searching for the attention-grabber to keep him on top.

Tito first encountered Masucci when he appeared as a guest with many of the Fañia musicians at the Red Garter Club in Greenwich Village. Tito participated in several jam sessions that featured Eddie Palmieri, Pacheco, Larry Harlow, Willie Colón, and Ray Barretto. He viewed the meeting as uneventful, but from that point on he decided to keep his distance. Word came to Tito from various sources that Masucci was "a little nervous about Tito because he was a hothead." Tito shrugged it off. "These are the turbulent times we live in," he commented. "There is war, upheaval, and trouble everywhere. I want to make music not exploit young people like that son of a bitch (Masucci)," Tito told Charlie one day.

The turbulence Tito spoke of was the war in Vietnam that continued to rage and would persist until 1975. President Richard M. Nixon, who opened relations with China, was coming under closer scrutiny over the way he managed the country. He resigned in disgrace in 1974 as a result of the Watergate scandal. The My Lai court-martial resulted in convictions; and, four students were killed by national guardsmen at Kent State University in Ohio; and, Spiro Agnew, who had a meteoric rise to the vice presidency of the United States – a former Governor of Maryland - came under investigation by the Justice Department for corruption extending back to his days as a County Executive. Specifically, he was charged with taking kickbacks from contractors seeking construction work. Agnew vehemently denied all charges but resigned the Vice Presidency on October 10, 1973.

Trouble was in the air. The Vietnam War, court-ordered busing of students to integrate schools racially, and student protests had shaken the country. Prisons were seeing a surge in the pressure — both from within and from outside prison walls. Inmates sought better conditions, fueled in part by racial unrest. In the imposing Attica State Penitentiary, a maximum-security facility 30 miles south of Buffalo, New York, the tension had been particularly conspicuous for months. Inmates, who were predominantly African-American and Puerto Rican, were incensed and exploded in riot. Nine Israeli athletes kidnapped from the Olympic Village in Munich were killed in a gun battle at an airport.

In the world of entertainment the big news was the breakup of the Beatles. Simon and Garfunkel were the unsung heroes of rock music and the thumping sound of disco was the fad. The disco movement that began in the United States and spread its influence worldwide, was originally regarded by many as a poor substitute for genuine soul music, nothing had been more capable of filling a dance floor. After Vietnam, Watergate and long afternoons on a gas line, kids didn't want to deal with issues any more. They just wanted to dance. The disco boom would peak in 1978 with the enormously successful "*Saturday Night Fever*."

At the start of 1976 there was little warning that the world of popular music would be turned upside down by the New Wave Music also known as Punk Rock. The use of various types of social drugs took hold – the most popular being cocaine – it would get many names over the years – coke, powder, dust, and many more. Tito joined the disco fry – his orchestra was one of the earliest to experiment with the new exaggerated thumping sound. His album in 1974, *"Tito Puente Unlimited"* laid a big fat egg. He shrugged it off. "If you don't try it, you can't know what will work," he replied to the media critics. "The music was ahead of its time," maintained Pops.

The challenges were apparent to Tito and he was going to take them on in his accustomed way – head on. He had been drawn to Kenton's work from an early age and now the bandleader's new "The Neophonic Orchestra" that was formed in late 1964 and held a series of concerts at the Los Angeles Music Center intrigued him. Kenton[108] attracted some of the finest players and composers in Los Angeles, many of them seeing the venture as a refreshing break from the studio grind. The list of composers who contributed original pieces to the orchestra's 1966 season is amazing: Marty Paich, Oliver Nelson, Pete Rugolo, Hugo Montenegro, Lalo Schifrin, Bill Holman, Russ García, Nelson Riddle, Dizzy Gillespie, Claus Ogerman, Shorty Rogers, Gerald Wilson, Ralph Carmichael, Bob Florence, Van Alexander, Gil Melle, Mel Tormé, George Shearing, Frank Comstock, Lennie Neihaus, and Bob Cooper. In the 1970s Kenton's orchestra was in concert mode. Tito read a lot about how Kenton and his musicians were promoting big band jazz in college campuses.

It seemed that Tito and Kenton had much in common – more than they realized. Both musicians were constantly exploring new directions in music, and the focus or centerpiece was the big band. Tito, as early at the

1960s, wanted his style exposed to the young. Kenton began collaborating with schools, attending workshops at which he and his musicians would tutor younger musicians in the late 1960s and continued doing it until he was weakened by poor health. While the popular recording world had left the big band structure behind, school ensembles and workshops developed hundreds of performers, arrangers, and composers who would go on to become professional musicians. Some of the biggest names in jazz today came out of this association.

Kenton continued to keep a touring band going until the mid-1970s, when his health failed. He released four new albums a year on Creative World, often recordings of concerts at schools such as Redlands University. Kenton's last public appearance, at California State University at Northridge, was a reunion of many of his former band members, including Milt Bernhart, Laurindo Almeida, Lennie Neihaus, and Maltby. He suffered a massive stroke in August 1979 and died a week later. Tito considered Kenton a true pioneer of big band music and American jazz. Kenton was not afraid to be innovative within the framework of the big band, according to Tito. "He was a musician who was not afraid to experiment, a musician who insisted on hard work, study and practice."

Tito started talking more and more about working with young people. Whenever he could manage it he would stage concerts in schools. Charlie was also on hand to play the piano and to talk about the music. "Charlie is the scholar, the historian," maintained Pops.

Another musician that Tito focused on was vibraphonist Roy Ayers.[109] I used to spend days pounding the Manhattan pavement searching for his recordings – old and new. Once one of the most visible and winning jazz vibraphonists of the 1960s, then an R&B bandleader in the 1970s and 1980s, Roy Ayers achieved a reputation as one of the prophets of acid jazz. A tune like *"Move to Groove"* by Roy Ayers has a crackling backbeat that serves as the prototype for the shuffling hip-hop groove that became ever-present in acid jazz records; and his relaxed 1976 song *"Everybody Loves the Sunshine"* has been frequently played. Yet Ayers' own playing has always been rooted in hard bop: crisp, lyrical, and rhythmically resilient. His own reaction to being canonized by the hip-hop crowd as the "Icon Man" is tempered with the detachment of a survivor in a rough business. As a vibraphonist he had an energetic style that allowed him flexibility to adapt – from the more bop style of Herbie Mann to the repetitive danceable disco, according to Tito.

"I'm off," cried Tito one night after we had listened to Ayers and Kenton selections in my apartment. "I have to practice..." When he practiced, which was often and for long periods of time, he was alone and in a world separated from the hectic commotion of people. Whether it was the timbales, the vibraphone, the piano, and even on occasion the saxophone – Tito practiced long arduous hours to sustain his proficiency, his focus was to sustain, even improve his ability. His long hours of practice also centered on training himself to be able to adapt to any new situation, and to progress.

There has always been a buzz around the music industry that revolved around whether Tito was or was not linked or even knew anyone in the crime syndicates. If asked in a public setting his response was a smile and a shrug. But one night in Brooklyn around 1971, the band was making a hasty departure to get to the next dance from the Hotel St. George in Brooklyn Heights. Once the music books, miscellaneous instruments and equipment were loaded onto the transport carts, Jimmy Frisaura and I left the crowded ballroom. Jimmy reflected as we walked to the elevators that this was once the place where the Brooklyn Dodgers stayed when they played over at Ebbets Field. In the lobby we caught up to Tito who was talking with several fans – mostly young ladies. He smiled when he saw us approach.

"Do you have everything?" inquired Tito.

"Yeah! He (Johnny Pacheco) was just setting up when I left," Jimmy responded. Tito had left the dance at the Hotel St. George before the last number. He was avoiding Pacheco, who was now not only the leader of a successful traditional style conjunto – two or three trumpets, percussion, piano, bass and a tres (traditional Cuban style guitar) but also the senior vice president of Fañia Records. It wasn't that he was angry with Pacheco; Tito did not want to talk about any kind of business tonight. The Tito Puente Orchestra had performed in Arizona the night before. The trip included a brief stopover in Chicago. So everyone was tired - that is except Tito.

Tito smiled at his several fans as they strolled away to join the festivities. "No one dresses up any more," Tito nonchalantly pointed out.

"What!" responded Jimmy in a surprised tone?

"We have lost our class too… You know… You remember everybody dressed to kill, not so long ago. Shit! I'm getting old…"

Jimmy laughed. "Well while you worry about what we should or should not be wearing I am just going to leave you and make sure we get to our next gig – up near Castle Hill. You will be on time?"

Tito responded: "Of course."

"…And don't forget your jacket and tie," quipped the trumpet player.

The lobby was quieter. It was about 1:00 a.m. "I will be there."

"No stops…"

"Jesus Christ…" groaned Tito in a perturbed way. Tito was pissed.

Jimmy was firm. "No fucking stops. The people want to see you. Oh and by the way we have to be at the studio by 10:00 a.m. according to Morris.

"When did you talk to him?" asked Tito surprised.

"Just before we left Chicago. He did not sound too good."

Tito observed: "He has not been feeling too good lately and he has a lot of legal crap going on. I'll see you in a little while," Jimmy said.

"Do you think he will hang on – I mean keep the record company?"

"I don't know. I just don't know. A lot of people tell me he may not. You know who I mean – they are friends of yours too. They are very close to Morris. But we have to be ready for anything. The business is all fucked up." Tito smiled at a passerby. "Anyway, Morris can take care of himself."

"We're doing okay with bookings even though we have to move the guys around two and three times a night. I always worry about the deadbeat promoters – there are plenty around too," Jimmy said.

Tito looked at Jimmy. "That is one thing I don't worry about. We will always get paid. You know no one will fuck with our money. You know this too, eh!"

The two musicians smiled.

As Jimmy and I walked toward the Henry Street exit he turned and shouted to Tito: "We have more of this tomorrow – two gigs in two different boroughs and then again on Sunday.

"Did you get the money from the promoters?" asked Tito.

"I have it and will deposit it in the morning before I go to the studio."

The next night we were all up at Corso's Ballroom and as Tito led the band a fight broke out. I was standing on the side, watching the band, holding a drink when I noticed a glass whiz by and splatter broken on the next table. A woman jumped up and literally climbed over two tables and landed on top of - I found out later – the woman who threw the glass. Someone bellowed: "It's a cat fight." The Puente Orchestra kept on playing; Tito kept perfect time striking the cowbell, and kept his eye on the fight. A third woman joined the wrestling match; bouncers were trying to separate them. It was all going on in front of the bandstand.

"He's with me," cried one of the women.

"Eres una puta," cried the other women.

The grappling continued. Jimmy came down from his usual spot in the horn section. He stood next to Tito. Later he told me that some of the musicians were concerned about Pops. The three women were fighting over him, each one claiming that Tito was with them. Tito was unconcerned.

"Yeah! I know them," he groaned when we talked about the incident. "Man did you see that woman fly over the table?"

Jimmy and I could only shrug. He never did tell us which of the three combatants, who were all tossed, he was with.

The next obvious step was to put into action a concert orchestra. He had discussed it with Morris Levy on several occasions, starting in 1972. Morris Levy and Tito dubbed the proposed album *"Tito Puente and his Concert Orchestra."* Tito on various occasions at the office overlooking Broadway and at the Asia Restaurant had expressed his thoughts openly to Charlie Palmieri and Joe Loco. Jimmy and Tito talked about it. It was time to make the move in that direction.

The nuances of a concert orchestra versus a dance band did not escape Tito when he embarked on the project. To him the dance ensemble of 15 to 20 musicians represented a specific style of playing. The musicians worked together frequently, understood the repertoire that was before them and were able to take special liberties – allowed by the leader – that conformed to the particular dancers, location and overall ambiance. Tito's style of orchestration was tight, replete with various types of breaks that included the so-called "off-time" Cuban pause, riff or ostinato modifications and a general buildup. The driving rhythm within the syncopation that Tito orchestrated had to be felt more than played directly from the music sheet. "Without clave," he would gasp, "we have shit!" The musicians that worked for him on a steady basis understood this cardinal rule. No one wanted to stir up his temper or run awry of Tito's sharp ear. It was well known that he would not hesitate to physically toss a musician or a performer out on the street. He was not about to change his methods.

Tito had already gained some experience in directing a large orchestra – his 18-piece band on stage with musicians of the Metropolitan Opera Company. The event was in 1967, at the Amphitheater of City College of New York Campus on 138th Street, during a special tribute to Puerto Rico. He had the occasion to introduce Celia Cruz, who at the time had not achieved the status of a vocal diva, and Ruth Fernández. Ms. Fernández was a noted vocalist from Puerto Rico and had recorded the album *"Es de Borinquen"* with Machito and his orchestra. His repertoire included selections from his long play album with Celia, *"Cuba y Puerto Rico Son,"* and several classic melodies composed by Rafael Hernández.

A concert orchestra was generally larger and as a rule needed to accomplish a number of objectives that went beyond pleasing dancers. The studio could be a perilous place for an unsuspecting bandleader. Tito wanted his concert orchestra work to be notable. He wanted to prove that the big band was not a relic. Among the concerns he had to overcome was the fact that he did not have top-notch percussionists – Willie and Mongo were working on their own and flourishing. Ray Barretto was a successful bandleader. Tito's style of music required steady and experienced musicians. The studio was another issue. Broadway Recording Studios was not Webster Hall where he had played, conducted and recorded many of his most memorable albums to date. However, new recording technology would permit him to try out some new ideas.

One option that was not available to him was inclusion of a string ensemble. Morris Levy would not hear it. "It is too fucking expensive," he exclaimed to Tito. "You can make it work without the Goddamn strings," he insisted. Tito did not go into one of his tirades. He sensed he would not win the argument. He knew his friend was under pressure from on-going federal investigations into his alleged mob activities. He would make do without the strings. For the studio orchestra he recruited additional musicians that enlarged his orchestra to about 28 pieces, including four veteran vocalists. The enlarged orchestra was versatile and multi-talented and as Frisaura often emphasized "capable of playing "clave."

There were five trumpets: Tony Cofresí, Dave Tucker, Paul Bogosian, Manuel Santos and Jimmy, who also doubled on the valve trombone. Tucker was a veteran of the 1961 Eddie Palmieri band, and Cofresí played often with many of the popular Latin ensembles. Featured on trombone were Lewis Kahn, who also played violin and was a veteran of various bands that included Larry Harlow and several charangas, and David Taylor. A veteran, Taylor preferred jazz and often played with Maynard Ferguson, Wynton Marsalis and Gato Barberi. He also enjoyed playing classical music, and in a Broadway theater pit. The sax section was deep with talent: Pete Fanelli (alto, flute and piccolo), Don Palmer (alto and soprano), Sal Nistico (tenor and flute), Dick "Taco" Meza (tenor and flute) and Rene McLean (baritone). Dave Kurtzer played the bass sax. Sal Nistico was a veteran of the Buddy Rich and Woody Herman orchestras and McLean drew his experience from Europe and South Africa. Veteran Mike Collazo was recruited to play the drums, Luis "Madamo Masso " Díaz was on tumbadora and the multitalented and experienced Little "Ray" Romero on bongo and other small percussion. Filling in on the bass was Izzy Feliu. The chorus featured veteran Vitin Avilés, Adalberto Santiago and Yayo El Indio, along with Frankie Figueroa.

The array of keyboards – piano, organ, electric piano, and keyboard was played by Tito's friend and associate: the adaptable and resilient Charlie. Vinnie Bell, a pioneer of electric guitar formats, who dabbled in jazz, classical and fusion music, was recruited by Tito to round out the concert orchestra.

Tito's musical program was as varied and textured as he had ever attempted. "I guess you could say there was something in this album to please a varied audience – dancers, big band aficionados, multi ethnic people, and young people." *"Mambo Diablo,"* his masterpiece composed and performed and recorded in the early 1950s, was given a contemporary arrangement designed for a big band. Some diehard fans still preferred his original version – Jimmy was one of those. The new arrangement had been discussed and argued over by Tito, Jimmy and Charlie for days leading up to the studio sessions, and right up to the moment the orchestra prepared to play it for a wrap. "I guess I won the argument," Tito groaned. "We went back and forth and I almost caved. Jimmy wanted it one-way – more of the original way; Charlie wanted to try out something else. He was always experimenting with the fucking keyboards and organ. I told them both 'bullshit!'"

Insistence on striking a balance between what some historians[110] / [111] perceived as old style Cuban music and what was now called salsa, Tito reworked not only *"Mambo Diablo,"* but also *"Picadillo."* In his discussion with his two collaborators he reinforced again that the "boogaloo collapsed because it was crap and not danceable." Only a handful of the popular bands and ensembles were capable of providing positive results with real fusion of American and Afro-Cuban music. "The kiddy bands did not have the depth to explore real changes, and the shrinking recording industry was pushing the inexperienced youths, much like the record producers exploited the doo wop groups in the 1950s," underlined Tito.

An important selection included in his concert recording was Manuel de Fallas's *"Ritual of Fire."* Here Tito briefly explores the 12-tone musical approach that he had studied at Juilliard decades before. The condensed selection is part of de Fallas's *"El Amor Brujo"* ballet. It was composed for an eight-piece ensemble and the Spanish composer expanded it into a full orchestral composition that consisted of a series of dances - The spicy *"Dance of Terror"* and the forceful *"Ritual Fire Dance"* has become famous as orchestral excerpts and piano transcriptions. *"In the Cave"* reminds one of a quest of eternal mystery. *"The Magic Circle"* summons timeless astonishment with a pre-tonal medieval sound that commands an evocative reverie in 7/8 meter, graced with a sharp countermelody. de

Falla was one of classical composers that Tito considered influential in conveying a feeling and sense spirit for people who speak Spanish.

Tito even considered a contemporary arrangement but was overruled by Levy and others who maintained that such an album would not sell. de Falla in his orchestration technique developed effects of great beauty and originality, and even borrowed traditional sounds related to traditional music. He was a contemporary of Debussy and Ravel, who like de Falla developed harmonic schemes that today are still considered thoroughly modern.[112] The percussion, including trap drums, introduces the selection. The horns and reeds follow in a tight precise melody. Quickly the orchestra switches to 6/8-time and then into an exhilarating cha cha chá or slow mambo beat. The orchestra goes back and fourth several times and concludes with a double mambo beat and blasting trumpets. The arrangement is tight – in fact the entire album is tightly scored – on purpose.

Noro Morales' *"110th Street and 5th Avenue"* is full; typically tight arrangement that features Charlie Palmieri playing an electric piano that is followed by intermixing saxophones. There is something for everyone here – trumpet solo, saxophone solo and Tito on timbal. *"Prepárate Para Bañarte"* was a popular cha cha chá charanga piece recorded by Belisario López in Havana in 1955, and then again in 1961 as a pachanga with Belisario's New York based ensemble. Tito's twist is slightly less melodious, played in a speedy 4/4-mambo beat and features a flute. *"Black Brothers,"* composed by Tito and Mario is a rocking contemporary piece that pays tribute to the neighbors on the west side of Lenox Avenue. *"Picadillo"* is yet again given a new look with Tito using marimba rather than the vibraphone. The album was conceived by Tito to accomplish a number of objectives – showcase the orchestra at a concert level, permit the musicians to be expressive, and incorporate a big sound with the contemporary harmonies. The technology in place permitted Tito to experiment with overdubbing, playing several instruments on several selections.

Royalty, Celebrities and Saints

Tito did not realize it but to the people that were close to him it was apparent that he was becoming something of an icon. His orchestra was in demand. Everywhere he went and performed fans swamped him, simply wanting to say hello. One evening as Tito and I were leaving Patsy's Restaurant on West 56th Street, a voice called out "Hey Tito." I turned and I have to admit I was surprised. From the corner of the room Frank Sinatra was standing and smiling. Tito turned, smiled and walked over to the singer. Tito introduced me to Sinatra. He clasped my hand firmly and smiled. Then he clasped Tito's extended hand. "It has been a long time," Tito said.

"Was it in Cuba or before that?" Frank said with a huge grin.

"Oh! Man… My memory is not that good," replied Tito. "It certainly has been a while. Loved your last album. Let me leave you and your guests. We will catch up later, soon."

Frank clasped his hand, firmly again. "Yeah! Very soon. And, don't forget when you go west, to Vegas, look me up."

"We have a lot of catching up to do."

Sinatra laughed. "Do you get to Cuba, ever, anymore."

"Damn, no… Too much trouble."

"Too bad. There was a lot of great music coming from there… One can only imagine what could have been." Sinatra smiled. The two men were still holding the handclasp. "You should go, no."

"Then the Cubans in Miami would string me up. No. Too much trouble."

Tito and Sinatra released the handshake.

We turned to leave. As we turned to leave a gentleman sitting next to Frank stood up. He joined up with us. He was Jilly Rizzo, Sinatra's best friend and bodyguard. He also was the proprietor of Jilly's, a dark 120-seat saloon at Eighth Avenue and 52nd Street. Its hey days were between 1952 and the mid-1970s.[113] It was one of Tito's late night watering holes, a place where he was well know and yet be out of the limelight. "You know Frank wants to do that recording with your orchestra."

"I know, we can't seem to get our schedules down in order to set up the dates," Tito said as we walked out to the street.

Jilly placed his arm over Tito's shoulder. "Well Frank wants me to keep trying. So why don't I have Don Costa[114] give you a call. Or he can call someone you tell him to. Okay?"

"I'll be traveling for the next few weeks. I will have someone get a hold of him." Tito looked at me. He smiled.

"Stay in touch and don't forget that you're always welcome at Jilly's." We all laughed. Jilly and Tito embraced. I shook his hand and we headed toward Seventh Avenue.

As we walked up the street Tito said that he would get Al Santiago to help coordinate the recording session. "It would be nice if it happens. He is a hell of a singer…"

A few days later Al took the subway down to midtown and came into the King Karol Record Store where I was working. He just wanted to let me know that he was on the quest – getting Frank and Tito together. Tito insisted on keeping the task as quiet as possible. He did not want people speculating and conjuring up "ridiculous half-ass stories." Al and Don went back and forth trying to get the two men together, and they came close several times, but it never happened. It is interesting to note that in an unauthorized biography of Frank Sinatra written by Earl Wilson,[115] the vocalist lists two goals he would like to achieve – recording a duet album with Ella Fitzgerald, and recording an album with the Tito Puente Orchestra.[116]

One day in 1976 Al called me asking that I have Tito call him. I found Tito at the Asia Restaurant. "Al is excited. He needs to talk to you about the Sinatra stuff." Tito showed no excitement but he did leave the table and hastily walked to a telephone. A few minutes later he returned. "Frank Sinatra is scheduled to open at the Westchester Premier Theater in April. Al and Costa think he might be able to fit a recording date in." The next day Tito found out he was traveling with the band and one of the stops would be in Mexico City. Al Santiago and Don Costa would keep on trying to get the two entertainers together.

The Mafia, at a cost of seven million dollars, built the 3,500-seat Westchester Premier Theater.[117] The FBI was watching Sinatra at the time because of his alleged connections with the mob. Among the goodfellas and friends in the picture taken with Sinatra backstage at the Theater in Tarrytown on April 11, 1976, were *capo di tutti capi* Carlo Gambino, head of the crime family that bore his name; Gambino's brother-in-law Paul Castellano, who later succeeded Gambino as head of the family, only to be killed in a coup orchestrated by his successor, John Gotti; and West Coast boss Jimmy "the Weasel" Fratianno who would later turn witness against the Mafia.[118]

When Frank Sinatra played the theater again in September Tito and the orchestra were in California, traveling there from Puerto Rico. Al and Don continued trying to connect the two artists for nearly two years, probably more, to no avail.

The theater in Tarrytown featured shows with some of the biggest names of the era. In addition to Sinatra, Dean Martin, and Steve Lawrence and Eydie Gorme played to packed houses. The promoters also contracted the Tito Puente Orchestra. Jimmy had something to do with the scheduling of the first performance. Jimmy was always tight lipped about arrangements to have Tito and his orchestra play at the controversial theater. Tito always deferred to Jimmy and simply shrugged and smiled – never providing details.

"No one in the audience spoke Spanish," laughed Tito. It was a packed house and the audience was not in the least bit timid. For the performance

Tito and Jimmy reviewed the orchestra book of more than 1,500 songs. It was a mixed repertoire of songs that was presented – *"That Old Devil Moon,"* (Burton Lane and E.Y. Harburg), *"The Continental,"* (Herbert Magidson and Con Conrad) and *"What is This Thing Called Love"* (Cole Porter). *"Tito Timbero"* He brought the audience to its feet many times.. There was a thunderous ovation. Many of those that came to see Tito perform had been at the Sinatra show. A lot of people came backstage afterwards to say hello to Tito and Jimmy. They were rubbing shoulders with a lot of Frank Sinatra's friends and acquaintances.

When the two men were discussing the repertoire Jimmy suggested to Tito that maybe "the Italian National Anthem would fit in."

"Shit, Jimmy don't get carried away," retorted Tito.

The orchestra was dressed to kill – in dark evening suits, and Tito had on a white jacket. When he appeared on stage the crowd greeted him as one of their own – for decades he had cultivated a fan base that went beyond the Latino aficionados. Later that night when things quieted down and we were alone he sat back and looked around. "You know Jimmy, maybe we should have played that anthem." We all laughed.

Tito and his orchestra also played *"Oye Como Va"* – not the rock version, but one along the traditional Afro-Cuban lines. He had the audience in the palm of his hand. He was enjoying the renown, the public interest and the popularity. It was what he lived for.

As far as Tito was concerned Afro-Cuban music was taking a beating in 1972, even in Cuba. The pure sounds that he loved had drifted into yet another realm – Latin Rock. The music coming out of Cuba was disappointing. The traditional stuff – if it existed was being buried – and Cuban officials were pushing the new wave of electronics into the world market. To Tito it was inexplicable. "If I didn't know better I would tell you that the corporate types from the old record companies defected to Havana," was his humorous attempt at explaining what was going on.

Carlos Santana, who was born in Mexico, in 1947, the son of a mariachi violinist, played violin as a young student apprentice, was at the forefront of the Latin Rock popularity explosion. He organized a rock group and performed in 1968 at New York's Anti-Vietnam War Rock Festival scheduled for Woodstock, New York, but at the last minute was moved to Bethel, New York. In 1969 he recorded the album *"Santana,"* that was a big hit and in 1972 he released *"Abraxas"* that included a psychedelic rock version of Tito's 1962 tune, *"Oye Como Va."* To Tito's surprise it was a hit. In fact, he was stunned by its success in a rock format, and by what subsequently occurred.

Charlie Palmieri had just finished one of the jingles he had been working on. He addressed a manila envelope, stuffed the music sheets into it and sealed it. "I have to get this over to the advertising people later this afternoon," he said almost speaking to himself. Joe Loco, back from Puerto Rico was doing something - reading. The door opened.

"Holy shit!" Tito exclaimed as he entered the cluttered office. "You'll never believe what just happened to me this morning."

"Neither can I," offered Joe with a large grin. "You didn't get run over by a car because you are here. No, maybe you rode on the subway all night long." We laughed.

Tito threw his jacket over a chair and sat. "I just came from the bank. I deposited some money. Man, shit its good to know that not everyone is a crook. I almost pissed away $30,000."

There was silence. "Did you?" Charlie prompted in a surprised voice.

"Well, you know that shit we recorded, what 10 years ago, *"Oye Como Va,"* was picked up by this guy from California – Carlos Santana, and it has been playing all over the radio. So I get a royalty check yesterday and head over to the bank." He waited for someone to prompt him.

I laughed. "So, what happened?"

"I just came from the bank. I went to deposit the royalties – the checks and all that. So I hand over the deposit slip and I'm standing there – I must have looked like a jerk. 'You didn't add this right,' the woman tells me. She glides the deposit slip back. I look at it and shit I don't see anything 'you're missing three zeros on this check…'"

"Holy Shit!" gasped Joe from his desk. "It was for what…"

"It was the royalty money for *"Oye Como Va."* The amount of the check was $35,000. I'm telling you I'm getting old…"

The room was silent. The royalties would continue to flow.

There were two subjects that Tito did not talk about – religion and politics. That is why it was something of a surprise when he mentions Nilo Tandrón one night when we were leaving Jilly's and bumped into Frank Sinatra. It had only been about two weeks since Tito almost mishandled a $35,000 check. Tito met Tandron during one of his early visits to Havana. Tandrón had been a professional dancer, and moreover a "babalao." A babalao or guru is the priest in the Santería religion that is practiced in Cuba and many nations in South, Central America and the Caribbean.

Things were going pretty good in terms of bookings for the orchestra.

The biggest concern Tito and Jimmy had was paying the ever-increasing cost of air transportation to the Far East, and even the West Coast. There was a gasoline shortage brewing and the prices were exploding. The other major concern was that even though Tito and his orchestra had produced 15 long play albums from 1970 through 1973, success of the recordings varied from album to album. Tito, Jimmy and even Morris Levy agreed that not being able to get playing time on the radio was impacting sales. There was not much that could be done. It was apparent to Tito that Levy was consumed with other matters.

Tito and Celia collaborated on two albums: *"Algo Especial Para Recordar/Something Special to Remember"* and *"Celia Cruz y Tito Puente en España."* The releases did not generate much interest and sales were mild. Two long play albums were recorded with Noraida, the widow of Cuban vocalist Beny Moré – *"La Bárbara Del Mundo Latino"* and *"Me Voy A Desquitar."* For Cotique Records, Tito's orchestra backed up vocalist Meñique – *"Meñique."* Also, I coordinated the 20-tune RCA Victor compilation of Tito's music from the 1950s – *"The Many Moods of Tito Puente."*

Despite what Tito and other bandleaders considered to be a tightening market for the Afro-Cuban music genre, Tito and his orchestra were busy. The unexpected royalties from *"Oye Como Va"* permitted him to move his family to Tappan in the suburbs of New York. José Curbelo, who had moved to Florida and was slowing his work pace considerably, was still finding bookings for the orchestra across the continent, the bills were being paid promptly for a change and even pending Internal Revenue Service issues were being attended to. Everywhere Tito showed up – fans embraced him. Female fans clamored to meet him. Politicians sought him out for endorsements, or just to have their picture taken with him. Celebrities wanted to meet him at functions. He did not realize it – but he had transcended beyond his music. Tito achieved what many prominent Latinos had sought – recognition for accomplishments beyond the narrow Latino fan base. He was enjoying every moment.

This was not the work of Santería, Tito insisted. His success was a result of his music, of how he played it, and mostly because it was "Good music that was genuinely Afro-Cuban through and through." However, from his youthful days in El Barrio he had developed a profound respect for the Yorubá based religion. He felt it was time to make a 100 percent commitment. He had relied on Tandrón for spiritual support and advice from his earliest contacts. Tandron would be his sponsor. It was going to take Tito about a year to achieve the status of practitioner of Santería.

Tito had to adhere to rules and standards that had been developed over hundreds of years; they answer only to Olorun[119] and the orishas or deities for their actions. Before a person can even be considered for initiation they must have an intricate knowledge of the rites and myths, not unlike Catholic confirmation. Initiation of a new santero is very structured and well defined.

Each stage has it's own rules and requirements for advancement and Tito threw himself into the process wholeheartedly. For the first year and seven days of his initiation he dressed in white. Wherever he showed up to perform he wore a white suit. Tito refrained from touching or being touched by anyone. There are many rules and processes he had to follow. The secretive nature of the initiation into Santería has many reasons – it is a process that has been handed off from one generation to another for hundreds of years. The members of many sects will not allow just anyone to join. The details of his personal journey into Santería, Tito maintained close to his heart.

"The music I play and the music I love is in no small part embedded in the Yorubá traditions. It is spiritually comforting. I only focus on the positive aspects of my association with the practice of Santería," was his take. He was interviewed often about his involvement with the practice and his response was always pretty much the same.

In 1974 Harry Sepulveda was working at Record Mart, located at the 42nd Street subway station. He had been there for many years. The tiny shop at the busy station was the Mecca for authentic Afro-Cuban music and other genres from South of the Border. Harry was an institution and he was one of the main reasons that people came from far to buy music. He was knowledgeable and provided his opinion with every purchase. Whether you liked it or not he was going to tell you about your purchase. He made a discovery one morning while unpacking a shipment. Packed with a recent delivery of records were several titles that would be stacked in the budget section of the small shop. While he was placing them in order he noticed the album *"Revolving Bandstands,"* recorded by Tito and the Buddy Morrow orchestras in 1960, and finally released as a budget LP.

Harry called Domingo Echevarria, who was a music aficionado and worked for the haberdasher Hart, Schaffner and Marx. Domingo called me. I called Tito. After listening to his verbal outburst – I held the telephone far from my ear but the voice exploded over the hand piece – everyone in the room heard him. When he finally calmed down he urged me to run to the Record Mart and purchase as many of the long lost albums as I could lay my hands on. It was a brief walk from the Broadway office to the subway station. Harry had set them aside.

The album cover had new photos of Tito with his white hair and Morrow that were taken two years earlier. At Tito's request I had been in contact with the powers that be at RCA Victor trying, with no success, to get demonstration copies of the long awaited album. They offered me copies of everything – Tito Puente recordings, recordings by other artists, just about anything – but not *"Revolving Bandstand."* Tito had never heard the finished product and neither had Morrow as far as he knew. The RCA Victor executives never gave a reason for keeping the album from being released.

The record was released with two of the tunes missing, and with zero publicity, almost as an afterthought. When Tito came to the office he looked at the albums and smiled. "Well, I guess it could be worse – they (RCA Victor) could have dumped the tapes in the fucking East River." However, he sensed that this was a positive omen, in a strange way.

Several possibilities were provided for the delay in releasing the album – most likely some executive decided the album would not sell, and so pushed it onto a storage shelf. I was told by an executive that it might have had something to do with RCA Victor being unable to obtain the rights for release, or maybe even a conflict between warring corporate divisions. When Morris Levy departed it was common knowledge that a lot of people in the big record company were happy to see him go. *"Revolving Bandstands"* was one of his projects.

The release of his *"Tito Puente Unlimited"* album on the Tico Record label that year was a bust and it was taking a severe beating from the Spanish language reviewers. Tito's exploration into disco music was not well received. "Just another experiment that turned to shit," he laughed. The positive side of this was that *"Revolving Bandstands"* was finally available. "A great buy for a buck," he laughed.

Domingo was recruited as a consultant for BMG years later. BMG purchased control of RCA Victor and in 1993 with help from Harry and me, Domingo managed to reissue a digitally processed CD that included the full session of the historic recording made by Tito and Morrow. He worked as a researcher in the BMG/RCA Victor and eventually was able to discover other gems in the vaults and helped have them reissued under the Tropical Series.

Distractions

Every one of Tito's close friends had a name for her. Charlie could not stand the sight of her; Joe Loco politely left the office when she walked in; I called her the "vampire." The musicians were as nervous as a teakettle coming to a boil. We knew that his tempestuous association with this woman was causing serious problems. There had been other interludes, other distractions, but for the most part Tito kept them away from his music. His personal life was private. In a strange way Tito led three lives– his music, his flamboyant outgoing lifestyle, and his family. Family matters were absolutely private – he made the decisions, solved the big problems and sternly disciplined the offspring, when needed. His wife took care of day-to-day household matters. Tito maintained his associations with the people in the music business. This included Julio Gutiérrez, the Cuban pianist, Myrta Silva, the Puerto Rican vocalist, TV personality and former vocalist of La Sonora Matancera, dancer Nilo Tandrón, who sponsored Tito's entry into the Santería rituals, and Bobby Collazo, Cuban vocalist and bandleader. This was an openly gay group of entertainers who were still active and prominent.

Tito enjoyed their company mostly because they talked about the "old days in Cuba," reminders of his travels to the island. "It was the Golden Era of music," he liked to remind me. This small group and others often gathered at Victor's Restaurant on 52nd Street. The number of people depended on who was in town.

His music was possibly his greatest love. Very few people – very few – got close to him. It was his way. But this was a situation that reverberated. The orchestra was impacted and the distraction was interfering with his business associates. Just how long it would last none of us could even guess. It started around 1973 and for about two years she followed Tito around like glue stuck to paper. He did not seem to mind. Jimmy and Tito argued often and loudly about his failure to make appearances at a number of scheduled engagements. Those arguments were ugly. I tried to approach him several times but he gave me one of his cold looks and turned away. He did not want to hear anything about it.

But things were coming to a head. Charlie had serious words with the woman. His vocabulary was out of character. Joe (Loco), who was usually mild mannered and enjoyed a good laugh had to tell her to "shut the fuck up" one afternoon when she was hanging around the office. He had had enough.

The woman demanded to know where Tito was, what he was doing, but she was asking the wrong guy - Joe Loco. Jimmy had related to us that a recent rehearsal and several recording dates ended in dismal failures because she was present. This was out of character for Tito–a woman messing with the music. It had never happened before. Jimmy tried his best to keep the musicians calm. It was bad.

And, a few days after Joe lay into her, the "vampire." Joe's verbal outburst took place in the office in front of Charlie and me. It got back to Tito that same afternoon. The stew had finally boiled over.

Joe and Charlie had had enough. An unsuspecting Tito arrived at the office this particular afternoon. Charlie looked at Joe. They both looked at me. I knew what was coming. Tito realized something was up. His two old friends circled around his cluttered desk and cornered a gullible Tito. Tito jumped ready to fight. They sat him down and told him "this is a fucked up situation." Only a few people could confront Tito in this manner. He was facing two of them. Charlie was usually the easygoing guy, but he was furious, annoyed and exasperated. Joe was more prone to be in your face, and this afternoon the two of them were in his face. Tito had no place to go.

Tito tried to argue, almost meekly. Apparently he realized that his behavior was way out of line. He was not going to win a shouting match. He sat at his desk and pouted quietly. About a week later she was out of the picture. Just what he said to the vampire none of us knew. But by the night we were heading to the Westchester Premier Theatre he was – musically speaking – his "old self again," as Jimmy described him. Joe Loco departed for Puerto Rico again and this time he remained on the island.

Morris Levy, who had cultivated the Tito Puente Orchestra style for more than 25 years up until 1975, was now beset with more legal problems. Investigations of his connections with the Mafia, and severe tax delinquencies, finally forced him to make a decision. Levy was also dealing with his poor health. He began to sell off parts of his record empire. Because of their long relationship he called Tito into his office one afternoon, and told him that Jerry Masucci was getting control of Tico.

"He (Masucci) is a fucking shit head," gasped Tito.

"For all I know he is probably a cock sucker too. But there is nothing I can do. You know all the problems that are going on," answered the impresario. "I know he doesn't like your kind of music. He thinks you and the others of your generation are over the hill. But that's the way this cock sucker is."

Tito calmly gazed at his old friend. "I know I have a contract, but I'm not going to just sit back and let this prick do whatever he wants."

Levy laughed. "I know. He doesn't really know what a fucking hothead you are – not like those of us who are still around."

Soon after the sale of Tico and Alegre record holdings was completed the operation shifted to the Fañia offices at 888 Seventh Avenue. Tito figured that not much would be happening – this was fine with him. Joe Cain, who had been Tico's A&R executive, recruited Louie Ramirez, a protégé of Tito to handle the production function. However, as Tito surmised, Masucci basically diminished the activities of both Tico and Alegre. This was fine with Tito. Masucci was now in control of promoting the younger bandleaders. He had eliminated the competition. Tito understood the change and accepted the legalities, however, he was prepared to hold out making any recordings for the new Tico owners until it suited him. Right now he was too busy.

Around this time Tito had received a telephone call from Franc Peri.[120] Tito was never forthcoming about his conversation. All he would say is: "Fuck Masucci and his funny music coke stars." The name, Fañia, would send Tito into incensed rage. It took Jimmy, Charlie and me a lot to calm him down.

Peri was a small businessman. He had been an admirer of Tito and his music from the days when he danced at the Palladium Ballroom. Peri wanted to use Tito's band to record instrumental big band music for dance studios and schools. Tito, Charlie and Jimmy would not tell me more than that. The way the three of them acted made me think something was not right. But as it turned out Tito and Peri came to terms on making the recordings. Since Tito expected a long feud with the Fañia executives, he did not want anyone to know what he was up to.

Levy mentioned to me that Tito and Jimmy had talked to him about making the recordings. "It sounds like a good thing, Joe. But Tito was a little concerned about the Fañia people. I told him they could not touch him – don't worry."

Tito and Charlie worked together on 95 percent of the arrangements. Tito and Charlie are listed as consultants on more than a dozen long play albums, numerous 45 R.P.M. records, and more than 100 selections that were released through 1980. Also recruited, as a consultant for the recordings, was Alfredito Levi. Several days each week, over an extended period of time, Tito and Charlie traveled with the band to an obscure recording studio in New Jersey.

The musicians that took part in the recordings were mostly those that participated in Tito's concert album. Peri contracted strings for many of the selections. Almost every kind of dance music was incorporated into the recording repertoire. Tito plays timbales, trap drums, vibraphones and marimbas or piano on just about every song. Charlie is heard on the piano throughout. In one-way or another the Tito Puente style is captured in these forgotten recordings. Tito plays trap drums or piano in an album that features authentic tango music: *"Amor y Tango"* – including Palmieri imitating the German Bandoneon (accordion) with a melodica, also known as the "blow-organ" or "key-flute." The melodica was probably first used as a serious musical instrument by jazz musician Phil Moore, Jr. on his album *"Right On,"* recorded in 1969. Melodicas are unusual because unlike most conventional woodwind instruments, they make use of a piano keyboard rather than a specialized fingering system using holes and/or buttons. When Charlie blew on the wind melodica Tito played the piano. If Mike Collazo was not available to play the traps either Tito or Alfredito performed the task. The percussion ensemble featured José Madera, Jr. and Louis Bauzó. The flute assignments were handled by Dick "Taco" Mesa, a veteran of Tipica 73 and Tito's band. Jimmy coordinated the brass and wind arrangements.

Tito played vibes on foxtrots and swing music. He and Charlie arranged – *"In the Mood"* and *"String of Pearls,"* Glenn Miller standards. The string section is added to the Cuban standard *"Ay Mama Inez."* First Charlie improvises over the violins, and then Tito sets down his gentle vibe solo.

Viennese waltzes such as *"Skaters Waltz,"* and *"Artists Life,"* composed by Johann Strauss include a violin choir, Charlie's piano and Tito's gentle percussive support. For the sessions Charlie and Tito composed several merengues. Tito reworked many of his hits, measured them down a notch and presented them with a surprisingly fresh feeling. The recordings were released listing the performers as "The Latin All-Stars," "Roper Dance Orchestra," and "The Dancing Strings." Tito and Charlie are acknowledged as musical directors. The music was not released to major markets. It was distributed to dance studios for the most part.

In 1976 the Tito Puente Orchestra was booked solid, at least three or four nights a week and usually at two different dances. When he was in town, on Monday nights he was the "house band" at the Pan American Lounge in Queens. It was a popular venue for a non-Latino crowd, especially when Tito and his band were playing. He had been playing in the intimate club for several years. "This is where the boys hang out," Jimmy liked to kid. "They are big fans of Tito, you know," he often repeated. Another Queens locale that the orchestra played was Strattan's, on Northern Boulevard. The lounge was a hangout for reputed crime syndicate associates.

One night at the Pan American Lounge the orchestra was playing *"Mambo Inn,"* and Tito was in the middle of what fans had come to expect – a prolonged musical exchange between a saxophone and a trumpet. Suddenly, onto the stage walked a heavyset man – one of the boys, I guessed. I was sitting at a table with friends of Jimmy. "I wonder what that guy wants?" someone in the group said.

Tito did not as a rule permit interruptions but to my surprise he turned toward the big man, and smiled. The man leaned over Tito, whispered in his ear and then turned and slowly walked off the bandstand. Tito looked over to Jimmy, and then placed the sticks on the top of the timbales. Jimmy casually signaled to the other two percussionists to pick up the slack for Tito, who was now walking off the bandstand with an obviously well connected gentleman toward Jilly Rizzo's table.

When the two of them appeared again it was at a table with a group of notable "family" friends that included Jilly Rizzo. Tito, Jilly and the others remained at the table. They laughed and at times it seemed everyone was talking at the same time. When the set was over Jimmy came and got me. We joined Tito.

"We are still trying to get the two stars together," Jilly said over the noise looking at Jimmy.

"Any luck?"

"We'll keep on trying. Frank wanted me to let Tito know, if I ran into him." Jilly smiled. "You know he still remembers bumping into you in Havana. That was a long time ago. He also remembers the young kid that sat in for Buddy Rich..."

"Man!" groaned Tito, "That was a hundred years ago" There was a lot of laughter.

The conversations continued for a little while longer. Tito stood up. Jimmy and I stood up. "We will keep trying," Tito said politely. There was a firm handshake between him and Jilly.

Jimmy was grabbed from behind. Someone I did not know embraced him. "Don't lose touch with your friends," he said. Jimmy smiled. We walked to the bandstand. I left and took a taxi home. It was obvious that Tito and Jimmy would be out very late. I had to go to work in the morning.

The Tito Puente Orchestra was always prepared for unforeseen events. Tito believed that he had to be ready to out-perform any competition, no matter who or what or where. "I was not always sure what surroundings we were going to be in, and who would be facing off against me. Jimmy knew that when he put the material in for whatever trip we were scheduled to take. It happened a lot, you know. The band gets to a place and the promoter says 'play this kind of music.' After a while we realize the people are not dancing. Oh shit! Switch… and off we go. You have to be ready for anything in this business."

Contracted by promoter Ralph Mercado to be the band that would introduce the Fañia All-Stars at the Tribute for Tito Rodríguez, held in 1976 at Madison Square Garden was one of those events. The Tito Puente Orchestra mesmerized the huge vociferous Garden fans – 22,000 strong. He played tunes from his book and when he came to the end he brought the people to their feet with his rendition of *"Salsa Y Sabor."* The timbal solo was one of Tito's best. His showmanship was extraordinary and the band was in top form.

"If Masucci thinks the old cats are going to lay down and die," Jimmy said in an excited voice after the orchestra completed the opening, "he is dead wrong."

Tito calmly walked to where Masucci and Mercado were standing, by a tunnel that led to the stage area in the center of the arena. He grabbed their attention with a cold look. "This is the last time I will open for the Funny All-Stars." Both men looked surprised, shocked. Pops was true to his word. Tito turned and walked to where Jimmy was with a group of fans. "Its time to blow this place," he told Jimmy.

We did stay for a while. "They sound like shit," Tito moaned. "I knew it was going to be like this. No one is in control; everybody is doing what the fuck they please. Tito Rodríguez must be turning over in his grave." Finally, we left. Normally, Tito and some of the band liked to linger for the jam session that generally capped a performance. "We are out of here," he insisted.

Once on the street Tito opened up again. "If that shit head thought for a moment that I was going to fumble the opening – boy was he wrong. Did you ever see such a bunch of bullshit? I know, I know some of these guys are good, but Christ they are all over the fucking place – it's like no one is in charge. Everybody wants to be the star. It like an Abbott and Costello comedy – no arrangements, just get on stage and make fucking noise."

Its what people want, I told him.

"Yeah! Everything is loose…" chimed Jimmy. "No formality. Funny a few weeks ago we were at the Westchester Premier Theater and just like tonight we won over the crowd – with good music."

"This Masucci guy wouldn't know good music if it hit him in the fucking face."

Jimmy laughed. "No depth."

We kept walking. "I know. That's why I tell you we are not going to lay down and die for that prick. Tito (Rodríguez) was probably right – he got out just in time – before pricks like this got into the business. I don't think he would have trusted this new piece of work – Masucci. We were better in the old days (laugh). Listen to us."

"The competition was brutal, not like now..." Jimmy groaned.

"Me, Tito and Macho...There were other great bands too," exclaimed Tito.

"The bands, I guess were bigger and tighter," I noted.

Tito responded: "Damn right. Better musicians for the most part – at least they took the time out to learn. Today, this new shit is all about protests and patria... Half of these guys don't even know about their heritage... Coño! What shit."

We crossed Seventh Avenue and walked into a bar for a nightcap.

Pérez Prado - On The Road

The flight into Mexico City was always scary. Up to the top of the sleeping volcano and into the valley below could be turbulent. Tito had no idea what to expect. José Curbelo had booked a 10-day tour of the Mexican capital city and points south – Vera Cruz. His old boss and booking agent failed to inform him that he would be playing against his old archrival – Damaso Pérez Prado. In 1977, perhaps Pérez Prado, was no longer the king of the mambo, but he was still something of an icon in Mexico. When the jetliner was approaching the busy airport, Tito related, "José decides to mention: 'Oh by the way, the orchestra will be playing in the same club where Pérez Prado is engaged."

"Shit," Tito said. "Okay." It was funny he thought. The band had been on the road – South America, Puerto Rico, into New York City, out to the West coast. It was a roller coaster.

The Latin Roots Exhibition[121] was held at Lincoln Center Library, and in the middle of the events was Tito sharing his stories of music with Jacqueline Onassis, Harry Belafonte, Billy Taylor, Dizzy Gillespie and Geoffrey Holder among others. Lucy and Desi Arnaz, Jr. were among the guests. They called their father, Desi Arnaz, Sr. to tell him he had to make the trip east to see the large mural of him playing the conga drum. He was at the exhibit a few days later. Newsman and author Pete Hamill took an interest in Tito and his music and was among the visitors to the exhibit. Machito, Mario, Miguelito, and Tito often greeted guests and walked them through the paintings and photos, explaining and talking about the history of the music. In California the orchestra traveled from San Francisco to Los Angeles. Briefly he renewed his acquaintance with Abbe Lane, Olga San Juan and many others.

Tito thought back – just a few years earlier he was given the keys to New York City in 1969 by Mayor John V. Lindsay; Tito was a guest of Dave Garroway on the NBC-TV Today Show; and he even hosted his own TV show, though it was a flop it had been fun. It seemed as though he and his orchestra were either packing or unpacking, never remaining in one location too long. The jetliner was rolling down the runway. He looked out the small window of the aircraft. He was ready for his nemesis.

Before the bus could whisk the band away Tito and Jimmy strolled off to the side and engaged in an intense conversation. In actuality the two men were simply making sure that everyone in the band was ready – of course, he knew they would be. Tito came back to the group beaming with a big smile. Jimmy joined the band members who were headed to another hotel. "I'm ready for the son of a bitch." He laughed again. At the hotel located on Paseo Reforma[122] near Chapultepec Park,[123] Tito grabbed Curbelo long enough to tell him: "You know that for so many years he (Pérez Prado) was a thorn in my side. Everyone thinks that Tito (Rodríguez) and I were bitter rivals. Bullshit! This is the guy that was pissing me off..."

Before heading to the California Ballroom Tito tracked me down in New York and gave me a rundown of what was happening. He was not excited, nor was he nervous. Tito was looking forward to performing with his orchestra. "Start slow – a la Kenton – and then go in for the kill," he quipped during the long-distance conversation. "Don't forget to call – at whatever time," I said. "Call before you and Jimmy and the band go celebrate."

One shrewd observer – bass player Bobby Rodríguez – almost smiled inwardly as he and the orchestra played the music Tito and Jimmy had picked for the opening set of the Prado/Puente duel – both orchestras were equally billed on the marquee and as the guest the Puente organization went first. There was nothing to overwhelm the packed house, Rodríguez later recalled. A few mambos, a few cha cha chás right out of the book. Tito was viewing the audience, observing the dancers – there were not many who were out on the floor, obviously waiting for the Prado Orchestra. The age of the patrons was mixed.

Pérez Prado had not seen Tito since he had played the Waldorf Astoria. Tito was in the audience and he was not impressed. In fact, recalling those days reminded him how RCA Victor promoted Prado's music rather than his – he was not a happy camper. His intention was to stomp the competition – tonight it just happened to be Pérez Prado. The orchestra was attired in dark tuxedos and Tito wore the typical white jacket, the color required by the santero religion. In the wings, watching was Pérez Prado, who like his rival, had every intention of making mincemeat of him.

When Tito finished out strolled the Cuban mambo king. The crowd roared. He still had a strong following and it was ever so apparent. Tito was not shaken, annoyed or bewildered. He expected it. "I told you," he said to several members of the band who were with him. "He is big here. We did it right…" Tito smiled.

In his dark tailored suit and wearing a cape he walked onto the bandstand to wild adulation. He smiled. His hands moved. The orchestra broke into "Mambo Jambo." The dance floor filled to capacity. The orchestra followed with *"Mambo No. 5,"* and then *"Patricia."* Tito watched, almost amused, claimed Jimmy who was standing by his side.

"Cherry Pink and Apple Blossom White," followed. Tito's smirk widened.

The repertoire was Pérez Prado's million sellers both in Mexico and the United States – in New York they were hits but not with the predominantly Puerto Rican followers of Afro-Cuban music, not in the 1950s. In fact, Tito was aware that Pérez Prado was never booked to play the Palladium. It almost made him laugh openly – but he controlled himself.

When the noise died down and the Tito Puente Orchestra was in place Tito once again strolled to the front. He looked at the people, smiled and then "1,2,3 Augh!" Only his musicians, and perhaps José Curbelo noticed Tito's imitation of his rival. He could not resist imitating Pérez Prado. The orchestra snapped into *"Cua Cua."* The trumpets blared, the saxophone section came in smoothly and the percussion provided a pulsating beat that proved irresistible to the dancing crowd. *"Hong Kong Mambo,"* a 1950s classic and *"Ran Kan Kan,"* completely placed the crowd under Tito's control. The contemporary arrangements – swift and clear-cut, the robust New York – Afro-Cuban style percussion, the deep excursions into jazz were all served up to the dancers. There was no question that Tito still was capable of taking control with his style of music.

"He kicked ass," Jimmy yelled in the background from the hotel room he was occupying with Tito.

Tito yelled, "The whole fucking band is in here. Joe, it was a massacre. Everyone thought I was going down after the first set. I knew what he was going to do – all the mediocre crap is all he played. After that it was easy.

We even played that shit – *"Oye Como Va."* It came out great, better than I thought."

A few months later Tito, in one of his mellow moments recalled the night he faced off with his musical nemesis. "He (Pérez Prado) always had good musicians. He even had good ideas. Our meeting probably did not prove a fucking thing – except that I was pushing hard – you know full steam, while he had been in semi retirement. He put that band together just for the concert. Even with the sharp Mexican trumpets of the band was not as cohesive and polished as mine – we play together all the time." Then he added, "Shit! I still don't see what all the commotion was about this guy – yeah, it was syncopated, but very light nothing like the Arcaño-Rodríguez approach – potent, African and powerful."

Generations

In March 1977, Tito was booked to face off with Carlos Santana at New York's Roseland Ballroom. Well, he said, why not. It was the obvious move to be made by the promoters. Puente and Santana had the capability to draw fans that would fill up the 5,000 capacity ballroom, several promoters concurred, including Ralph Mercado[124] and his partner Ray Avilés. The California based promoter Bill Graham was all for turning the idea into action. He had long been a fan of the Tito Puente Orchestra from the days when he was a bus boy in the hotels of the Borscht Belt. Graham had befriended Tito and now he was a promoter of big musical spectacles. Graham was absolutely sure the meeting of Tito Puente and Carlos Santana would be a success.

There were a few detractors among the media that felt Tito was over the hill.[125] In actuality, the Tito Puente Orchestra was at its busiest, playing up and down the East Coast, in South America and the Caribbean, and across the United States. For the most part the venues were filled. "Sometimes we would show up and the place was empty," admitted Jimmy. "It is the nature of the business. But usually people young and old came to see Tito and the band."

Tito had already decided that he was going to use Ralph Mercado as a promoter. "He is aggressive and hungry." However, Tito would keep him at arm's length – he was never going have a close affiliation with Mercado. It was not that he did not like him; he was just not like Curbelo. Mercado was into everything – he was signing up the Fañia stars, he in effect controlled what kind of music was played on the airwaves with Jerry Masucci, and this effectively impacted if the Tito Puente Orchestra was successful. Mercado teamed with Graham and for Tito that was a positive.

To Tito meeting Carlos Santana was a "no brainer!" Besides he considered it would be another step in the evolutionary process. "Let's see what happens," he muttered to Charlie as he and Jimmy went over the menu of music they would perform. It was the routine meeting that had been repeated so many times over the many years that the two men had worked together and interestingly enough neither Jimmy or Tito mentioned Carlos Santana. "We'll do this number this way," barked Tito. "...And do this one this way."

Santana was a rock star, nothing more and nothing less, to Tito. Latin Rock did not generate enthusiasm for Tito. He was playing at the Roseland and he wanted to make sure that the band was ready.

"There will probably be a big crowd of his fans," Charlie said."

"So!" responded Tito.

I put my two cents in: "Maybe you should play *"Oye Como Va,"* the way he plays it..."

"Bullshit!"

Charlie laughed. "I know Santana plays small music – a rock ensemble – a lot of echoes and electric guitars. Anyway he is on your turf."

Tito laughed. "Just one more fish to fry, but I don't think we are even compatible – musically speaking. He is in another bag."

There were two groups of fans at the Roseland that night. The young were awed by the Santana's raw electrical sound as he played his music. The Puente Orchestra's rendition of *"Pa Los Rumberos,"* roused the dancers. *"Salsa Y Sabor,"* that included Tito's slick timbal solo was the icing on the cake. The two men met on the stage at the end of the concert and played yet another rendition of *"Oye Como Va."* This was not confrontation, no decisive battle of music genres and no power play. Both Santana and Tito played what they knew and what they liked to play. They joined together as expected. The rock followers were not swayed. The mambo dancers were encroached.

In 1979 Tito and Santana faced off again in a jam session at the Piers on 79th Street in Manhattan. The concert was to highlight Carlos Santana and his music but along the way Tito, Eddie Palmieri, David Valentín, Papo Vázquez, Rubén Blades, Jerry González, Orestes Vilató, and Armando Péraza stopped by and joined the rock group on stage. The spiced up New York style Afro-Cuban jam session went on for 20 minutes. Several thousand fans got to enjoy the friendly encounter.[126]

Tito and I drove his mother from his house in Tappan to her apartment in the Bronx one afternoon. She did not like to stay at her son's home more than a few days at a time. Whenever she visited the house to spend time with her grandchildren Margie had to cover the large bust of Tito that was given to him by a well-intentioned civic organization. "Ay! Dios mío, que cosa más fea!" Doña Ercilia exclaimed the first time she ever saw it. "Ese no es mi hijo." Latin Times Magazine gave the bust to Tito in 1978.

"It's me, your son," retorted Tito. "Ese soy yo..." Tito made sure that he kept his sometimes-expletive words in check.

"Oh no," she responded.

There was no point in arguing. After that a large cloth cover was draped over the bust.

Tito always tried to get his mother to spend a few days a month at the house. On Thanksgiving Day, all the Puente children and the family gathered at Ronnie's house – it was the tradition. Once or twice a month Tito would bring his mother to Tappan. Whenever we visited her in the Bronx she would inquire about the bust. "Lo bote'" lied Tito. Her mind was sharp, and at her advanced age she still moved around the apartment with ease. When we got to the apartment Tito's mother insisted that we go up to her apartment so she could whip up a quick dinner – rice, red beans, chicken and everything that goes with a traditional Puerto Rican meal. It did not matter if we had had dinner an hour before. Tito would shrug. "We better go up if we know what's good for us." If Tito had plans this evening he had to delay them. He rarely won an argument with his mother. She was a great cook.

While she served up the tasty rice and beans she complained that her son was getting too fat. "Estas demasiado gordito, Tito," she observed.

Tito shrugged. It would be fruitless to argue with her. We attacked the delicious food Doña Ercilia placed before us.

When we got to the Asia Restaurant the dining room was almost empty. Charlie Palmieri and Ray Barretto were at a table. We were supposed to meet up with Jimmy. But at the Asia Restaurant you never knew whom you were going to see. All the way down from the Bronx Tito was talking about making a second recording for the new owners of Tico Records, and about shifting promoters. He had not recorded an album for nearly three years. He had been rather busy – the number of public appearances was mind-boggling. For more years than he could remember Tito had been connected to Alpha Artists that was owned by his former boss, José Curbelo. But the former popular bandleader was getting tired and was now less involved. The business now in the hands of partner Landy Soba and Curbelo's son-in-law, Chet Holland. Tito did not like Soba and he did not care for the son-in-law.

Once Curbelo indicated that he was moving to Florida and was going to be less involved in the business Tito started looking for a replacement. Up and coming entrepreneurs like Ralph Mercado, a New York born Dominican, and Ray Avilés, a New York Puerto Rican, saw an opening to expand their fledgling booking agency. The two men were forceful and seemed willing and able to spend cash – that Tito viewed as a positive. Tito had an insatiable appetite for extra curricular activities and he did not carry a credit card. Tito started to use the services of Mercado and Avilés for a number of bookings. Tito said. "I have been talking with José (Curbelo) since before Mexico City. He understands my situation," Tito explained.

A few weeks earlier Mercado and Tito had talked about possibly recording a big band tribute to the late Cuban vocalist Beny Moré. We saw a documentary about the life of the singer at the Neorican Poets Café located on the lower East Side of Manhattan. The way Moré bellowed out pulsating Afro-Cuban songs, or inspired when he sang boleros had always interested Tito. I had to track down a copy of the documentary. Tito studied every aspect of the entertainer – recordings, videos, researching the man's life. Tito wanted to follow up with a tribute to the singer.

Sitting in traffic Tito quipped: "Its funny how now that Fañia is on its way out that Masucci contacts Ralph to do some big band records… You know Joe, there is no one in Fañia that has ever arranged for a big band."

"What about Louie (Ramirez)?" I inquired. "He's pretty damn good and knows how to get the horns and reeds working together. He learned from you. They could use him."

Tito turned his head from side to side and then he looked at me: "He has never done this kind of shit – 16 and 17 piece band type of arranging."

"Masucci has to know you think of him as a shit head, no."

Tito responded with a smirk. "Yeah! That's true, but he is trying to keep his funny stars in first place. The difference between him and me is that I accept change and move on. He and Pacheco had a great gimmick but they fucked it up – they never changed. You know – this business is always changing."

I always marveled at how Tito could find parking with little or no effort. The average guy or woman could quite possibly spend hours looking for a parking spot in a place like midtown. "Shit! I fit in here," he laughed. "The Puente touch!"

I groaned.

Tito and I slid into the empty seats at the table occupied by Charlie and Ray. "So tell me Ray," Tito said, "have you decided what you want to do – in terms of your approach?" Tito asked his former percussionist in a jovial tone.

"You are in a good mood," Ray Barretto smiled.

"We've been talking about a lot of things," Charlie said clasping his drink with both hands and twisting it around and around."

Ray looked over to Tito. "You know me… Jazz is my true love. But for the time being I will stick with this sound – the enlarged conjunto. You know – not a big band, but bigger than a conjunto." He smiled. "You know Charlie wants to go down to Puerto Rico to live and work."

"Bullshit!" gasped Tito. "Why do that?"

Charlie laughed. "The weather. There is probably a lot of work, and if not I can walk on the beach…"

"Until your dick falls off," laughed Tito. "The other day I heard you playing with Cachao on the recordings of the 1976 concert. Incredible! It was Charlie at his best. Now you want to go and sleep it off in Puerto Rico."[127]

Ray was smiling. "The euphoria of the moment is still making him glow."

I jumped in. "Cachao and his Descarga, and before that he had the big charanga orchestra…"

"Just like the old days – Arcaño y su Radiofonica. It was a lot of fun," Charlie chimed in almost blushing.

Tito laughed. "You looked sharp in your tuxedo. It reminded me of the old days."

"The Palladium!" Ray Barretto said easily.

"Oh yeah! Shit!" huffed Tito. "But think about it, Cachao in that concert offered a glimpse of the past and hopefully, maybe the future. The jazz and jam sessions that are designed with the purpose of making good music, being entertaining, and being progressive is the future." Tito was thoughtful for a moment. Charlie was huffing and puffing on his cigarette. Ray fixed his glasses. "You know what a real progressive step in our music is…"

"No," groaned Ray.

"But you are going to tell us," exclaimed Charlie.

"Chamber orchestras with big band musicians fitting in. You know, like you just did with Cachao," Tito said in an excited tone. "Shit! It's the way to go."

Ray smiled. "You know that a company like Fañia is not going to take a chance."

Charlie released more smoke and watched it float into the air. "It is something to consider. It is not really very far-fetched. It would give you an opportunity to score for more than 16 or 17 pieces. Some of these new musicians would not make it."

"The funny all-stars?" laughed Tito.

"You always liked the control aspects of the music, no?" asked Ray.

Tito responded: "You have to have some sort of control or you end up with this salsa bullshit. I like – no I love jazz. I think that is where all this is going. I was in Monterey and it was a blast. I worked with Cal Tjader – a very nice guy. He reminds me of you (Ray Barretto). He's been all over the place trying to find his niche, I guess that's what we are all trying to find, a place where we fit in."

"Well, I'm prone to jazz – with that Afro-Cuban swing. I think that all the potential has not been explored. There are a lot of things that we can do. And now with Machito going it alone; did you hear any more about it?" pressed Ray.

Tito shrugged. "You know a lot of shit. Mario announced he was retiring. Machito did not want to say much about it – family squabbles. I don't know. Mario was pissed. Machito wanted to have his daughter in the band… one big mess. I guess its just another indication that the big bands are just about done."

"Harmonies on the horizon," Charlie chuckled. "Machito will keep it going, maybe not like the old band, but he is a fighter."

The room was silent for a moment. The shadow lifted from Tito's face. "Hey, you got to do what you like and you have to hope that you can hit on something that people like. It's nice to get up there and belt out songs about your heritage, and to promote the land of your fathers… But it's all bullshit if you don't really know about your country, your fathers… I guess its one way of learning. That's what has been going on for the last few years – very rigid sounding groups with very little depth. That is what that shit head has been pushing for so long, but now it seems people want to hear good music, and good music played well. You know Ray, you got to do what you want, not what the record companies want. Me, I'm going to explore jazz again."

Ray laughed. "Just like you did 100 years ago." Everybody laughed

"That seems to be a natural extension, no!" Charlie said

Tito added, "In Monterey we had the crowd into it. Cal and me did a nice give and take. I've been invited to go back for the festival next year. Don't get me wrong, I'll keep the band, but I'm doing more jazz."

"No salsa!" quipped Charlie.

"Augh!"

We all laughed.

Puente's Night Beat

There were a lot of celebrities in Studio 54 this night. He played mostly disco music from his failed album and as far as Tito was concerned, he was laying a big fat egg – music wise. After the first set that lasted approximately 20 minutes Tito, Jimmy and the band gathered in an out of the way dressing room. Tito Puente and his Orchestra was the first Latin band invited to perform at Studio 54. "What the fuck is happening?" Tito asked in a flustered tone. Most everyone shrugged. "It seems everybody is getting off on coke, rather than listening to the shit we are playing."

Someone in the back groaned: "Maybe they don't like Latin music..."

"Bullshit!" screeched Pops. He looked at me.

"I don't know... The music sounded okay. This is a fucking disco. It all sounds the same," I replied. The small room erupted with laughter. Tito was stone cold serious. His mood was dark, very dark.

"Well if we can't get them to dance we may never be back..." Tito looked around the room. He shrugged. "We go on in 10 minutes. Lets see how we fix this shit." Tito dashed out of the room. He, like most of us was headed to the bathroom. As Tito and I were coming out of the rest room - clearly marked "MEN" – several women were going in.

"Man!" gasped Tito. We were both a little shocked. Like most everyone else in the nightclub we indulged in sniff, the popular white candy. It was everywhere. Even strangers walked up and calmly offered to share it with you. "There is enough dust in the air in the bathroom to make anyone dizzy, shit!" exclaimed Tito. Tito and I looked on, somewhat shocked, as the well-dressed ladies entered the separate stalls... Once inside, they sat down and they began sniffing away.

"Shit!" exclaimed Tito. "Let's get the fuck out of here." We left before anything else happened.

Tito was nervous and in a hurry to get to the bandstand, and to attend to his special guest, Cesar Chávez, whom he had left in the hands of the club operator Steve Rubell, who was already feeling no pain. On the way into the main room I suggested Tito play Latin. He shrugged. Tito was concerned about leaving Chávez alone for too long. The Mexican-American activist, who founded the United Farm Workers Movement in 1962, befriended Tito while the orchestra was touring California years earlier. He was a big fan of Tito's music. They kept in touch until Chávez's death in 1993.

Studio 54 was a New York City discothèque located at 254 West 54th Street in Manhattan. It opened on April 26, 1977, and closed in March 1986. From the 1950s to the mid-1970s, CBS used the location as a radio and TV stage that housed such shows as What's My Line?, The $64,000 Question, Password, To Tell the Truth, Beat the Clock, The Jack Benny Show, I've Got a Secret, Ted Mack's Original Amateur Hour, Captain Kangaroo, and the ill-fated CBS version of the Johnny Carson Show. The soap opera Love of Life was produced there until 1975.

"54", as it came to be called, was notorious for the pleasure seeking that went on within; the balconies were known for sexual encounters, and drug use was rampant and out of control. Its dance fl oor was decorated with a depiction of a Man-in-the-Moon that included an animated cocaine spoon.

Studio 54[128] was the favorite disco for celebrities, including Michael Jackson, Elton John, Truman Capote, Margaret Trudeau, John Travolta,

Tito Puente and Jaqueline Kennedy Onassis, June 23, 1978.
(Joe Conzo Jr. Archive)

Jackie Onassis, Elizabeth Taylor, Barbra Streisand, Gloria Swanson, Mae West, Martha Graham, Rod Stewart, Alice Cooper, Bette Davis, Freddie Mercury, the Gabor sisters – Eva and Zsa Zsa, Bette Midler, and Lillian Carter, President Jimmy Carter's mother. The music world's top performers also graced the club's stages to perform their new songs: Donna Summer, Grace Jones, Gloria Gaynor, Chic, Sylvester and The Village People all sang their signature tunes during the never-ending nights of partying. The flashy, publicly visible Steve Rubell and Ian Schrager operated Studio 54. In December 1978, Rubell was quoted in the New York newspapers as saying that Studio 54 earned $7 million in its first year and that "only the Mafia made more money." Shortly afterward the club was raided and Rubell and Schrager were arrested for skimming $2.5 million. After the arrests Rubell blamed President Jimmy Carter's White House Chief of Staff Hamilton Jordan of sniffing cocaine in the basement. A grand jury met 19 times and interviewed dozens of witnesses before concluding that Rubell's testimony was not reliable enough to file charges.

Tito was well aware of the celebrities in the nightclub. As he prepared to start the late set Liza Minelli walked up to him to say hello. There was always a never-ending line of celebrity well wishers; Tom Jones, and Margo Hemingway (she sat in on the final set), who begged him to let her work out on the timbales. Also in the audience that night was Myrta Silva. The orchestra started the second set with popular disco tunes of the period. But just like the first time around, things were quickly going downhill. Tito looked around to Jimmy. He was as perplexed and agitated as Tito. People were standing around, drinking and talking and sniffing white powder – in public. I stood near the bandstand holding a drink and chatting with Chávez and Myrta.

"The good stuff – play the book..." Jimmy finally yelled to Tito. Later Jimmy told me: "What could happen – they (the patrons) would just continue to ignore us."

Tito shrugged, I could see him even smile. Without hesitation Tito raised his hand and almost without missing a beat the orchestra shifted into a percussive swing. African percussion went into high gear. Tito struck the cowbell crisply – there was no more fooling around. Jimmy and the trumpet section followed the driving rhythm. Tito and his singers belted out "*Babaratiri*," and within minutes the mood of the club changed – everyone was out on the floor dancing. "*Pa' Los Rumberos*," followed.

Needless to say the engagement at the popular venue was a resounding success. Tito and the band were booked frequently to perform while the nightclub existed.

Everyone had a buzz. We were probably in slightly better shape than most of the patrons. Jimmy watched over the musicians as they packed during the wee hours. Tito made sure that Cesar Chávez was escorted to his hotel. He was feeling no pain. Myrta left on her own. She was feeling no pain either. "Joe, did you see where I put the check?" A few moments before one of "54's" managers handed him a check and he stuffed it in his jacket pocket.

"You put it in your jacket," I responded.

Tito called back "No, I looked there. It's not there."

"It is there."

Back and forth we went. Jimmy tried to jump in but thought better of it. Most of the musicians had drifted out. There were only a few customers left in the place and they were four sheets to the wind. "Bullshit!" exclaimed Tito in an irritated tone. "It has to be somewhere else. We faced off in the middle of the room and began shouting profanities at each other – neither of us would back down. Finally Jimmy jumped in. "Cool off you guys, we'll look for it later." I turned and left Tito standing in the middle of the room, still shouting and still cursing. I grabbed a taxi and went home.

Two weeks later on a Saturday morning Jimmy called my home. I was surprised to hear from him – especially so early. I knew that the band had played at the Pan American Lounge the night before. "He's been asking for you," Jimmy said gently.

"Yeah! Did he find the fucking check?"

"It was where you told him to look. He will be at the office most of the day – you know that Charlie's send off is at Beau's tonight."

A few hours later I met up with Tito at the office. As I walked into the office he looked up. "Where have you been?" he asked with a frown.

"Jimmy called me."

Tito said, "Yeah! I told him to call you."

We made up – neither of us apologizing to the other. Tito never brought up the subject of the check – it was his way. Charlie's farewell party up in the Bronx was a resounding success. Many, including Machito, Joe Quijano, Ray Barretto, and Johnny Pacheco, attended. Tito seemed a little down – the Machito Orchestra as it had existed since he was a young man no longer was led by his friend and mentor Mario Bauzá; Joe Loco was living in Puerto Rico, playing piano bar music in some hotel; Charlie Palmieri was heading for Puerto Rico. Toward the end of the night he told me he planned to close the office as soon as Charlie was gone.

It was one of those moments that Pops got pensive and considered how much had changed in the world of music. The big bands he loved were gone; Machito would keep the Afro-Cubans going, probably never to sound like it once did. It was the same for him. He was maintaining his orchestra, but sometimes, in one of his candid moments he would tell me: "Joe our time is passing." Then in the same breath he reverted to his Cagney-like swagger. "But not yet!"

One Success At A Time

It was true, of course, that during the 1970s Tito Puente and his Orchestra had faded from the radio waves. But the orchestra continued to be persistent and unrelenting in performing and brandishing the Tito Puente style of music. "Salsa and small music," as he referred to it ruled the Spanish language radio stations. This did not bother him in the least. He received award after award in recognition of his accomplishments – many of the honors and tributes coming from a varied non-Latino community. He understood that his followers, perhaps slightly older were solidly in his camp. It was during this period that he took particular interest in National Public Radio (NPR). As more talk shows hit the commercial radio waves jazz had significantly expanded its presence in NPR and along with it came the big bands sounds, and this included the music of the Palladium-era big three – the two Titos and Machito.

In 1978 he was contemplating just how to use this to his advantage. But first things first – he wanted to complete the tribute album to Cuban icon Beny Moré.

Louie Ramirez had been on the telephone with Tito over a period of several weeks. It was early summer 1978 and Tito was picking out his favorite Beny Moré tunes for the record album that Ralph Mercado suggested he do for Tico. It was not a smooth process. Tito wanted nothing to do with Jerry Masucci, and it was obvious that the Fañia owner was keeping his distance from Tito. So it was left up to Mercado to convince all the parties involved that an album paying tribute to the Cuban bandleader and vocalist was in everybody's best interests. I made a tape for Tito of Beny Moré tunes from several albums I had in my collection.

Fañia Records was on a downhill turn and Tito was reluctant to help it cling to life. "The small music sound is on the way out," he said looking over to Charlie

Charlie Palmieri was huffing and puffing on a cigarette as he packed his things, cleared out his desk and prepared to leave once and for all. "Yeah! But you always wanted to do this album. So what if it is for your pal…" There was a mischievous smirk on Charlie's face. "What do you think Joe?" he asked me.

"Tito has Ralph running back and forth. Ralph Mercado smells money," I responded in a sarcastic tone.

Tito laughed. "Well anyway Louie and I have a head start." Tito stood up, walked to the back where the piano was located, played the basic melody of *"Encantado de la Vida,"* a ballad that he was going to include in the recording.

"Not too many people around these days that can do that tune justice," quipped Charlie as he lit another cigarette.

"Damn Charlie," Tito said in an agitated voice, "those fucking things are going to kill you."

Charlie blew smoke in Tito and my direction. I was smoking too. "Shit! Look who's talking?" We all started laughing.

The telephone started ringing. "Who the fuck is that?" asked Tito.

"Hello," I said.

"Well!" Pops inquired, still annoyed.

"Its Congressman Robert García," I said. "He wants to talk to you." Tito grabbed for the telephone. Charlie was still huffing and puffing and he still had a wide grin. "Wait. George Mora is getting him."

Finally Tito and Robert García were talking. I helped Charlie carry out some of the boxes to a car he had parked a few blocks away and we decided to go to the Asia Restaurant. About an hour later Tito swaggered into the restaurant. "Don't you ever stop smoking," he said teasingly to Charlie. Then he announced in a matter of fact tone: "We are going to Washington D.C. to play for the President."

"The President of what," asked Charlie.

"Of the United States." Tito sat down and ordered a drink.

Congressman García had been elected to the House of Representative in 1978 in a special election. Herman Badillo had long been the sole elected voting Puerto Rican Congressman but decided to give up his seat and sought the Democratic nomination for mayor of New York, unsuccessfully in 1969, 1973, 1977, 1981 and 1985, coming closest on his second try, when he was defeated by then-New York City comptroller Abe Beame[129] in a runoff primary. In 2001, Badillo also unsuccessfully sought the Republican mayoral nomination, losing badly to billionaire businessman and political neophyte Michael Bloomberg, who would go on to prevail in the general election. In 1978, García was elected as the first Chairperson of the fledging Congressional Hispanic Caucus. He was one of two Puerto Ricans that formed the Caucus. The other was Baltasar Corrada who was the Resident Commissioner of Puerto Rico, and as such had no voting rights in Congress.

García convinced the five Mexican American elected representatives that the Tito Puente Orchestra should be the one to perform at the first annual event. He also had the support of Congressman Charlie Rangel. Both García and Rangel had served in the New York State Assembly and State Senate. Both had served in Korea, and both had danced to the music of Tito Puente at the Palladium.

"The only thing that I can't play," explained Tito, "is *'The Peanut Vendor*" – El Manicero. He rolled his eyes. Bob had made the request because President Jimmy Carter was a peanut farmer in his home state of Georgia, and it might appear disrespectful. "I said of course." He rolled his eyes again. "Bullshit!"

Jeremy Marre[130] a film producer arrived in New York in 1978. I was contracted by him to assist in the production of the award-winning documentary *"Salsa."* The film chronicles salsa music in New York City for starters and features a concert in a Bronx school staged by Tito Puente and his orchestra with help from his friend Charlie Palmieri. I called my ex-wife, Lorraine Montenegro. With her support we were able to use the facilities at 156th in the Bronx for the jam session. In the documentary Tito and Ray Barretto are jamming together, Felipe Luciano talks about his life in the "Young Lords," a pro-active political gang that he led in the 1960s. Celia Cruz and Rubén Blades are heard singing. The film also gives an overview of the complexities of "Afro Latin" music.

The film was released in 1979. "I'm not sure he understood the difference between Afro-Cuban music and salsa," squawked Tito to Charlie. "But you look good teaching music history to the kids," he laughed. "We need to teach the history of our music to the kids. Some day, maybe we can start some kind of scholarship for it – you know, Charlie."

Charlie smiled and nodded in agreement. He responded: "I think it was okay. There were some things that could have been better explained in the film."

I added that the segment of my wedding reception – when I married my second wife, Laura, and Tito was the best man, was pretty good. This part of the documentary features the Tito Puente Orchestra with Charlie Palmieri on piano and Ray Barretto on congas – pretty powerful I noted. This was a terrific version of *"Picadillo."*

"Yeah! But there was too much politics," Tito said. "I hate it when the two things get muddled. Felipe talks too much bullshit – I mean about politics. He is not a musician. He's a smart guy. I guess you need people that are looking out for social issues." We laughed.

Charlie looked at me and then looked at Tito. "But he tries. And who cares what he thinks… He seems to be fair about promoting the Latino point of view." Charlie laughed. "He should sit down here and try to figure out these notes. Man, whoever composed this must have been crazy."

I looked at the sheet on Charlie's desk. "That's your handwriting, your style, isn't it? It looks very complicated, a lot of fucking notes to play, no. Maybe it is good." Of course, Charlie knew I did not read music.

Charlie laughed out loud. "Oh shit. Its my arrangement of *'Lullaby of Birdland.'*" He turned the sheet around. "Well I'll be damned, it was upside down!"

"Coño, me cogiste de pendejo," I blurted.

"I have been wanting to pull that on someone for the longest time. Victor Borge used to do that on the Jack Paar Show," Charlie said. Both he and Tito were gasping for air from their childish prank. I looked at Tito. He could see I was not a happy camper. He and Charlie kept laughing.

Tito was gagging. "Hey, I didn't do it. He did it."

It was just another day at the office. "You're leaving this to go to Puerto Rico!" I said. They kept on laughing.

A few weeks after the departure of Charlie, Tito focused on closing down the office and getting the musicians for the Beny Moré venture gathered up and scheduled into the recording studio. There was no point in keeping the office since it was Charlie and Joe who had used it to bang out their music for the advertising companies. Tito was balancing his time between Strattan's and the Pan American Lounge, and taking a strong interest in jazz. He was constantly on the telephone with Louie, who had lined up arrangers for the album. The arrangers included pianist Eddie Martínez for *"Bonito y Sabroso,"* Jorge Milet for "*Dolor y Perdón"* and *"Santa Isabel de Las Lajas,"* Tito's original percussionist Frankie Colón arranged *"Se Me Cayo el Tabaco,"* and Marty Sheller provided the scoring for *"Encantado de la Vida"* and *" Baila Mi Son."* Pianist Sonny Bravo worked on "*Camarera del Amor"* and Louie Cruz arranged *"Francisco Guayabal."* Tito completed the arrangements for *"Que Bueno Baila Usted,"* and *"Yiri Yiri Bon."* Louie insured that every score was received, reviewed and approved by Tito, who tailored each to his own taste. Ralph Mercado insisted on using all these people, and Tito agreed. But he told Louie Ramirez: "I will redo them all if I don't fucking like what I see."

He told me during the recording session that the arrangements from Sonny and Frankie, his first conga player, "were pretty good."

While he was working on the details I received a call from George

Simon, a percussionist and historian of the Glenn Miller Orchestra. He asked if I wanted to be a member of the selection committee that was reviewing Grammy Award[131] entries for 1978. This was the year that the Grammy organization was reaching out to incorporate Latin music. He had contacted among others, music historian Max Salazar and journalist Pablo Guzmán to participate in the selection process.

Tito had a dim view of the Grammy Awards. But he openly admitted that it was an important trophy, and he wanted one, especially since Eddie Palmieri had been awarded a Grammy prize in 1977 for his album *"Son of Latin Music."* Tito was congratulatory and bestowed accolades on the younger brother of one of his closet friends – Charlie Palmieri. But he brooded over his music never having achieved this recognition. His album *"Legends"* was also nominated for a Grammy, but that is as far as it went. Whenever the topic of the Grammy Awards came up, he gave his crass description of the process while precise, is for the most part unprintable. "Tito is like Dr. Jekyll and Mr. Hyde about the award," Jimmy chided his friend. "The doctor character would politely explain why he wanted such an award. Mr. Hyde would kill to get it."

Certainly that was Tito, in a way.

As early as 1957, Tito had been recognized for his musical contributions by important jazz societies. The Grammy group had long overlooked Afro-Cuban music and Latin music in general, was Tito's opinion. He had a clear view: "I think the Grammys are nothing more than some gigantic promotional apparatus for the music industry. There is no attempt to really find or discover or even consider good music. It is a big joke. It is a gimmick. It caters to a low intellect and it feeds the masses. It has overlooked Latin music since its conception. And, I guess it does not have to because it doesn't need to. It does not honor the art or the artist for what he or she has created. It's the music business celebrating itself. That's basically what it's all about." That stated he went about the business of completing his work.

Tito did not deny that he would have liked to have his old singers join him on what he considered a historic long play recording – Vicentico Valdés, Gilberto Monroig and even Bobby Escoto. But to battle with the Fañia owner would be a futile effort. Ralph Mercado conveyed this to Tito in no uncertain terms. He had to use the vocalist under contract to Fañia. Celia Cruz, José "Cheo" Feliciano, Ismael "Pat" Quintana, and Santitos Colón, according to Tito would provide the strength he sought.

In La Tierra Studio located on Broadway, Tito was his old self – focused, tyrannical and ruthless in terms of how he wanted his music performed. The studio was a far cry from what he was used to working in.

To him there would never be another Webster Hall. But the equipment was state of the art and after he set about arranging the places for his musicians he was ready. The younger musicians were somewhat taken by his all business and no nonsense attitude. The veterans were comfortable. "I think they (the older musicians) took a little joy in watching Tito work over an unseasoned musician, especially one that was not accustomed to the routine of the big band," I heard Jimmy telling Santos. They both laughed.

" Coño! That's how you learn," replied Santos. "This is what it used to be like. No missing notes. Si fallas estas frito."

Before settling into the recording session he reminded a group of musicians that were nearby: "Remember we are paying tribute to one of the greats of our music. He (Beny Moré') is the guy that put Pérez Prado on the map. Without that voice Pérez Prado would still be farting in eastern Cuba."

"Who is Pérez Prado?" someone asked.

Tito looked around to see who made the remark. No one came forward. "Will someone take the shit head that said that outside and kick his ass? Jesus Christ. I'll bet you don't even know who the fuck Beny Moré' was."

Mistakes by the musicians were quickly pointed out – in Tito's accustomed punitive manner. Slip-ups were quickly addressed and the session continued. One episode occurred when Junior González was behind the microphone singing *"Se Me Cayo El Tabaco."* Tito raised his hands for the orchestra to stop. You could here a pin drop from the silence in the studio. "Quien lo cago?" someone whispered not wanting to be heard. Tito was looking down at the music. I looked at him first then turned to see who had made the comment. Everyone was standing still, or sitting and in total silence.

"Get me some blank score sheets – some paper, some pencils – plenty of pencils," he screeched at Louie Ramírez, who had a look of anguish. Louie quickly scooped up the music paper and pencils and handed them to Tito.

"I'm going into the room. I don't want to be bothered – no one in Joe, okay. If my mother wants to come in you tell her no." I nodded in the affirmative. The studio was quiet.

Louie came over to me. "What the fuck happened?"

I shrugged my shoulders. "I don't know. He is in the room writing some music parts. He must have heard something that was wrong or he did not like."

"Frankie Colón arranged the piece, and I know Tito gave it the once over before he gave it back to me. Shit… I know it was right. I went over it," Louie said nervously.

I looked at Louie and told him that we would learn soon enough if someone had screwed up. Louie's face was haggard. His tongue was stuck into the inside of his cheek. He paced back and forth for nearly an hour. The band sat quietly. Jimmy had been through this before. I believe he was the only calm one in the studio. He kept the musicians together. "Hang tight all – probably something was missing. We will know soon enough."

After about an hour Tito came out of the room. The sight of Tito looking stern heightened the tension in the room. He climbed onto the bandstand and handed out music sheets to the reed section. He turned away and took his place. "Okay lets do it." A few seconds later he bellowed: "One, two, three…" The music shattered the silence and the session continued.

It was a few days after the mixing was completed that Tito mentioned to me in a matter of fact manner that he did not like the sound of the saxophones. "It sounded weak. I needed to beef up the saxophones to balance them with the rest of the orchestra." He never talked about it again. The recording was completed in a day. To spend more time in the studio would cost money, and would be deducted from Tito's share. During the years that the orchestra worked at Webster Hall, Tito and the orchestra spent an average of three days putting together all the music, and making sure that there was sufficient material. Times had changed. Even the modern technology could not make up for the mistakes made in the rush to get the album recorded. But this was a different Tito.

Even though Tito was cognizant that time was money he was still a disciplinarian and a ruthless band director. He required musicians who could sight read, and who also had at least a minimal understanding of the recording process – even though this time it was rushed. Tito's arrangements were complex and required thoroughly trained, skilled and practiced musicians. His percussionists included Mike Collazo, José Madera, Jr. and John "Dandy" Rodríguez. This was a solid percussion ensemble, unmatched in the period of the recording. Sonny Bravo was on piano. He replaced Rubén Rivera because he was not a solid sight-reader. Tito was in an experimental mode at this time and Rivera opted to keep a steady job with Orquesta Broadway. John "Dandy" Rodríguez recommended Bravo to Tito. The tall pianist came from a musically inclined family and had played with Fajardo's charanga orchestras in Miami and New York during the early 1960s, and several other ensembles. He was one of the original musicians of Tipica 73. Fajardo had warned Tito that Bravo was not an easy person to get along with. But Tito was willing to put up with his "constant complaining and bellyaching."

The packaging and release of the album was set for September 1, 1978. Ralph Mercado and Jerry Masucci were planning a live concert to be held at Radio City Music Hall in the late winter of 1979 – it depended on the success of the album and if its entry into the Grammys in the Tropical Music Category was successful. Tito completed the mixing and put the project out of his mind, or so he thought. *"Homenaje A Beny Moré"* was a success that reached a younger audience while pleasing his mature followers. The tone of the music was typical of the 1970s – more energetic and brash than the original music recorded in the 1950s by Beny Moré and his orchestra.

"Que Bueno Baila Usted" is less exotic than the original selection but is robust and daring. The brass is taut and syncopated. The saxophones are mellow and light. The use of five vocalists gives the popular tune a different feel. Tito arranged it specifically to fit in the wide range of vocalists. He was concerned about the brass overpowering the singers. He accomplished his goal and the selection was one of the most popular. *"Encantado de La Vida"* is a light and airy approach to the Beny Moré classic. Celia and Cheo provide a provocative and sensual give and take atmosphere that made this one of Tito's favorites.

"Homenaje A Beny Moré, Vol. 2" would follow in 1979, and volume three that featured Celia Cruz was recorded in 1985. The first album was the one that Tito liked the most. Overall his peers and critics did not rate any of the albums as being among Tito's best efforts.[132] One critic wrote in a Spanish language newspaper that the "music was too fast and lacked the romance of the genuine article." Tito laughed at the critics. "Fast is what people want now a days. I don't disagree that the hip feeling is gone, but overall it is a good album." Prior to its release, Tito made sure that he promoted it.

He did not expect Masucci and Fañia to push his LP, but he planted a seed in Ralph Mercado's head. "Tell what's his name that if he doesn't want his record company to go into the crapper he might want to consider promoting the album." Tito was well aware that what he called "small music," or conjuntos were losing their popularity and that the market was changing, shifting toward visuals, cassettes, etc. He was his own best promotion force. Tito appeared on Spanish radio and the English language jazz and Latin programs whenever he had an opportunity. Mercado was well suited for the task of energizing the Fañia executives. Every day until the album was released, Tito made it a point to have me call Ralph. "It will be out on time," groaned Ralph to me. "I'll call Tito and let him know I am working on it."

"It's not about the Grammy," Tito told me. "It's about busting Ralph's chops, and bugging that shit head Masucci."

The album garnered Tito's first Grammy Award. As much as he cherished the award, he felt the album could have been better. "Shit! I'll take it because it was a long time in coming."

One afternoon about week after Tito finished work on the album, we were in the Asia Restaurant when Louie literally stumbled through the entrance. Tito looked at me. "Look his tongue is stuck to the side of his cheek. Something must have happened." Tito had the highest esteem for Louie Ramírez who was a successful bandleader in his own right. Many of his peers concurred that he followed the Tito Puente music philosophy in terms of tight straightforward orchestration. He was one of the few in 1970s era that could lead, compose and score music for a big band. He had worked with Tito Rodríguez and sat in with Tito Puente.

Ramírez was staff producer and arranger for the Fañia Records through the1980s. In the 1950s, he played with Joe Loco, and in the 1960s he played for Joe Cuba's sextet. He was a major contributor to Johnny Pacheco's first charanga album in 1960. Al Santiago sold Alegre to Tico in 1966, and subsequently it became part of Fañia. Louie arranged and produced countless LPs for Fañia, Vaya, Tico, Alegre and others. He was the only arranger working for Fañia Records that understood "the big band concept," according to Tito.

Louie loved people and they appreciated him. At any hang out session, Louie was at the center of the gathering, telling jokes, impersonating people, making up and embellishing stories. His imitation of Ray Barretto was a classic. Tito and Ray both laughed whenever he did it – speaking slowly, breathing deeply and taking forever to make a point. Louie could have been a professional comedian but music was his love, according to Tito. And Tito should know. Sometimes they would sit in the office, at a bar, in an after-hours club and trade tales, barbs, insult each other and laugh until they were dizzy. "Something must have happened with that fucking recording we just finished." Louie was walking toward our table. Suddenly, Tito laughed out loud. "Louie must be having trouble with La Lupe." La Lupe was making a comeback and had been signed to record an album for Tico, and Louie was the musical director and producer. "He looks like shit," quipped Tito who by now was roaring with laughter.

"Oh shit!" I said. He gasped for air. "Man I have been looking for you everywhere. I swear that bitch is out of control. The fucking is woman is possessed," huffed Louie. He was sweating and the tongue clung to his cheek. He looked pathetically funny and at the same time sad.

"If you stick that tongue any deeper into the side of your mouth," Tito laughed, "it will break through your fucking skin."

Louie plunged into the open seat. "Kick a man when he's down," gasped Louie. "I need help. She is out of control. I don't know what you two have, had, and I don't care. But you are the only one that can control that bitch." Louie later told me he had a plan – it was based on begging, pleading, cowering and crying if need be. After a number of drinks he finally convinced Pops to help him.

"I'll help," Tito announced. "But keep those pricks away from me. You know how I feel about that squeaky shit head."

Louie nodded fighting to contain his glee. "Masucci and the others won't interfere. I swear they don't even want to make this fucking recording. It seems she (La Lupe) had a second wind – making a comeback, I guess. But man she is fucking nuts."

When La Lupe saw me, Louie Ramírez and Tito enter the studio she nearly fainted. "¿Que es lo que tu hace aquí?" She squawked in a shaken voice. The musicians in the midtown Manhattan studio were as surprised as La Lupe to see Tito Puente. Many of them had worked with him. Most of them had a look of relief – maybe now we can get this recording moving – I guessed was on the minds of the musicians.

Tito walked to the center of the room. He gazed coldly at the singer. "Se terminaron los juegos y el relajito. ¿Entiendes? Do you understand? No more bullshit." Tito gazed coldly at the woman. La Lupe was silent.

Tito had not seen La Lupe for more than a year. He made a guest appearance at her show billed as "La Lupe Returns" at the Bronx Theater. It was sold out despite the frigid January weather. Also on the bill was Machito and his orchestra. Toward the end of the show Tito made an unannounced appearance and brought the spectators to their feet with a thunderous ovation. La Lupe, with a surprised look on her face, began crying uncontrollably when Tito embraced her in a bear hug, looked at her and said a few words to her. Tito then took over the timbales from Mario Grillo, Jr. and the orchestra played Cheo Marquette's *"Oriente"* with La Lupe singing a sturdy lead vocal and improvising the phrase: *"Ay ay ay Tito Puente me Botó."* The words reminded the audience of the tumultuous relationship the two entertainers had, and that Tito had unceremoniously tossed her from his band.

A few weeks after the reunion Tito and La Lupe met up again at the Chez Sensual nightclub on Westchester Avenue in the Bronx. This meeting was not pleasant. She was scantly dressed in a provocative white satin dress that resembled a slip. First she started in on me – "Oye Joe…" and rubbing up against me.

I groaned. "You better straighten out." She was feeling no pain as she stumbled toward one of the tables. Tito finished playing a set and was approaching her, I intercepted him and told him what had happened and how she was attired. As much as Tito relished the limelight, and even enjoyed controversy, he looked at the "white see-through outfit" and shrugged. He was going to walk away, but then changed his mind. He confronted her and said: "Jesus Christ! You are making a Goddamn spectacle of yourself. Put on your coat or get out of here." She was furious. But she decided to walk away from the crowd who was staring at her. Soon after, she left. They did not meet again until Louie Ramírez escorted Tito into the studio.

Louie was glowing watching the woman cower. After so many days of turmoil her silence was refreshing. Louie did not hide his pleasure when he saw her shock when her old boss walked into the studio. Tito looked stern and cold, waiting to see if she was going to erupt in one of her temper tantrums – she stood still and waited for Tito's next set of instructions. Louie and Tito looked over the music, ignoring her. Tito made a few notations, instructed the musicians and for the next several hours the flamboyant La Lupe, gave a sparkling performance. The album was released soon after. Much to the chagrin of the Fañia owners, and at the behest of Louie the recording was titled: *"La Pareja – Tito Puente and La Lupe."* It was considered a successful enterprise.

"There was a love-hate relationship between La Lupe and Tito," Madera[133] pointed out. "Some of Tito's best work in the 1960s and 1970s, in terms of his arrangements and presentations occurred when he teamed up with her." As puzzling as this might sound it is a fairly accurate observation. Her comeback in the 1970s was brief. She was banned from television in Puerto Rico after she tore her clothes off during a ceremony on island television. Masucci at Tico Records decided to dump her even after her success with Tito. He wanted to focus on the less controversial Celia Cruz. He also did not want Tito Puente around too much – he considered the bandleader a relic whose time had passed.

Later that night we went to Elaine's, located between 88th and 89th Streets. Elaine's had been made famous by its regulars who came for conversation and the homey, old-Italian-neighborhood feel. Sparkling lights set the mood as the crowd dined on mediocre food. Elaine made a fuss over people she recognized. The cozy tavern feel of Elaine's, was due to the worn wood, black ceiling and bustling bar. People squeezed around tables, carrying on conversations with one another as if they were at a party. Whenever she was around, Elaine Kaufman always saluted Tito as one of her regulars. Those who had rubbed shoulders in the saloon included Frank Sinatra, Jacqueline Kennedy Onassis, Woody Allen, Mikhail Baryshnikov, Danny Aielo and Leonard Bernstein,. There were writers such as Tennessee Williams, Norman Mailer, William Styron, George Plimpton and Pete Hamill who frequented the East Side tavern. This was a quiet night. It was late and the place was dark. We walked in. "Hey Tito!" The voice was easily recognized. It was Tony Bennett. "How's it going?"

"You know, just keeping busy and staying out of trouble." Tito did not talk about the recording session. The drinks were served by one of the cleaning staff. Tony and Tito relaxed and the two men began to reminisce about the 1950s when the big bands were popular, ballads were in vogue, and there live performances were the norm. Tito recalled Tony Bennett's performance at Carnegie Hall. Also featured that night with Bennett, was Cuban percussionist Candido Camero, who also played with Tito.

Tony Bennett laughed when he remembered visiting the Palladium. "Those were certainly great times." They talked for about an hour. The lights were going out, and the workers were closing. "Remember seeing you one night playing the sax," recalled Bennett with a smile.

As we walked to get a taxi after saying our goodbyes Tito laughed: "Shit he remembers things I had forgotten. But they really were great times."

The Jazz Scene

Just before Tito departed for the West Coast with the Latin Percussion Ensemble in the summer of 1978, Jilly Rizzo contacted him. The telephone call from Rizzo distracted him. It helped him calm down and to give the band some peace and quiet. He was not concerned about playing at the Monterey Jazz Festival for a second year in a row. Tito was in one of his nervous moods. There were nearly a dozen performance contracts and he was going to be on the West Coast and he was worried about getting back to meet contractual obligations.

Rizzo was still pursuing teaming Tito and Frank Sinatra for a recording. "He (Frank Sinatra) wants to do this, but because all that is happening he figures that he should wait." Tito understood. He was not in the least dismayed. In fact he was satisfied that when the time was right the two entertainers would get together. There were grand jury investigations and indictments surrounding the bankruptcy fraud of the Westchester Premier Theater, and Sinatra's name was swirling around it. Neither Sinatra nor Rizzo were ever implicated in the sordid matter. As far as Tito was concerned he had other fish to fry – traveling to Monterey first and then going to Washington, D.C. to play for the President of the United States.

The flight to the San Francisco area was uneventful. Tito reflected: "There was no music. I just met Jorge (Dalto). He made a few suggestions. Patato would do whatever I wanted. We agreed that we should keep it simple. We would make it up as we went along. The only one of the musicians I wasn't sure about was Alfredo. He was dealing with personal problems – he was being investigated for using and selling drugs. It was his problem."

The ensemble that Martin Cohen, LP Instruments, gathered for Tito Puente to lead featured: Cuban violinist Alfredo de la Fe, Patato, Argentine jazz pianist Jorge Dalto and bassist Salvador Cuevas, and saxophonist Mario Rivera rounded out the group. The principal function of the LP Jazz Ensemble was to promote the company and who better to lead the showcase ensemble than Tito. He was a successful bandleader, a percussionist, composer, arranger, and instrumentalist. He was quietly excited about the transition to a small venue, but he would be leading veterans.

Cohen had been a long time fan of Tito Puente, going back to the days of the Palladium. Latin Percussion was established in 1956 when Cohen saw Cal Tjader's ensemble performing at the Birdland. Working out of a basement constructing Afro-Cuban style percussion instruments, Cohen also became a steady patron of the Palladium, and in particular Tito Puente.[134]

The second visit to the Monterey was more subdued than his first when he had the 17-member big band and he and Cal Tjader played together on the stage for the first time. Tito told me before he left he was not sure how it would be with a small ensemble. He enjoyed the big sound. He had performed at the Newport Jazz Festival a few days earlier and the fans that turned out to see him still enjoyed his big band Afro-Cuban music. If Tito had any misgivings or doubts, these dissipated when he arrived at the hotel where most of the participants were housed. While he was checking in, Dexter Gordon, who was on the program, came over to say hello. Gordon had recorded with Machito and was appearing at the jazz festival with his quartet. Dizzy Gillespie greeted Tito in the lounge. During the evening Cal Tjader came by to say hello and it was he who recommended that Tito include "Philadelphia Mambo," which they would play as a duet.

In the morning as the musicians headed to the festival, Dalto complained that his room had been switched. When he tried to get into the room he was locked out. Dandy gazed at Tito with a grin. Whatever had happened Jorge Dalto had it straightened out, after losing a few hours of sleep. It was left to me to explain to Jorge that it was Tito's prank – having him locked out of his room. Jorge took it rather well.

Also performing at the annual summer event was Kenny Burrell, The Hi-Lo's, Billy Cobham, Bob Dorough and Ruth Brown. The first jazz festival was held in 1958[135], and featured Louis Armstrong and vocalist Billie Holiday, who would die nine months later.

There was a loud roar from the crowd when Tito and the LP group were announced.[136] Tito opened with an ad-lib mambo that "Jorge made up as we went along," according to Tito. The tune featured Jorge's piano, Mario's sax, and Tito's timbales. Alfredo de la Fe showed off his violin virtuosity. Using reverb and echo enhancing sound plug-ins, it took him about three minutes to introduce *"My Favorite Things."* It also took a stern look from Tito to get him on track. After a 4/4 time straight jazz interlude, Tito, Patato and Dandy switched to a 6/8 Afro-Cuban beat. Dandy played the chekere.

If anyone thought Afro-Cuban music had died it was firmly reestablished by the sextet in *"Montuno."* The violin provided several intricate four to six note ostinatos or repeated montuno phrases a la charanga style, while Patato and Tito conversed in back and forth percussive responses. "We made it up as we went along. Alfredo and Jorge were exceedingly adept at not only following along, but by also lending their musical proficiency without hesitation," explained Tito. The tempo changed several times and Patato also provided some vocals along with his magical percussive skills. The group brought the audience to its feet with a surprise ending – Tito and the men in chorus singing *"Oye Como Va."* The classic *"Cuban Fantasy"* featured Jorge on piano and Tito on vibes. The final number was *"Philadelphia Mambo"* that reunited Cal and Tito in a duo that was a wild crowd pleaser.

New York was humming this spring. Miguelito Valdés blew into town and made several appearances with the Tito Puente Orchestra. One of the most memorable was at the Roseland Ballroom, but it almost did not happen. Miguelito always had an impact on the way Tito played. "I make him work harder," Miguelito often told me. But a few weeks before the engagement that was publicized as a "Tribute to Miguelito Valdés" a copy of one of the promotional brochures was sent to Tito. He blew his stack when he saw it. "La Sonora Matancera, The Machito Orchestra and special guest Tito Puente and his Orchestra" – this precise order – would be performing at the Roseland. It took him about a week to calm down. One afternoon while journalist and music aficionado Felipe Luciano was conducting an interview with Miguelito, Tito and several others stepped aside and talked.

"I can't do this," he told Miguelito.

A surprised Miguelito with wide eyes gasped: "What?"

Calmly, Pops explained that he could not perform at the event if the promotional material and the billing were not changed. "I live here and you live in California. If I let it go by I will never hear the end of it – especially the way things are around here with all the negative bullshit and the radio stations pushing the small music."

Miguelito smiled. He put his hand on Tito's shoulder. "Coño, Tito…" The two performers were laughing. "No te preocupes, esto lo arreglo yo."

There was brief conversation. Then Miguelito contacted the independent promoter of the event, Phil Peters. A few days later Miguelito called Tito and told him that changes to the billing he suggested would be made.

At the Roseland we all met up. It was packed with dancers. "He sweats and makes his band just burst with energy," Miguelito said to me toward the end of the night. It was just before the final set of the night.

"What, is he giving you a line of shit?" exclaimed Pops when he saw the two of us chatting at a table. "I have to work hard because he misses a lot of notes," Tito laughed joining us at the table.

"Ay coño, Tito deja esa mierda. Tu sabes que cuando yo canto, tu tocas mejor," Miguelito laughed. It was great just to sit back and watch the two friends.

"Oh yeah," Tito blurted. "Bueno en este ultimo set te voy a enseñar quien es el verdadero rey…" There was laughter.

Miguelito placed his large cigar – a Cuban, he only smoked Cuban cigars – in the ashtray. He stood up. "Bueno vamos a tocar un duo de timbales," he said winking at me and with a big smile on his face he turned to Tito. "¿Bueno, que?" Miguelito turned back to me and blurted, "¿Qué tu crees Conzo? ¿El viejo puede conmigo?"

I only shrugged and laughed.

Tito jumped up and the two entertainers dashed off toward the bandstand. "Try and keep up," Tito bellowed as the two men scrambled to the bandstand.

"El Cumbanchero," composed by Rafael Hernández in the 1930s is a rumba, which Miguelito insisted the orchestra play. [137/138] Once on the bandstand Tito shouted and off went the orchestra – for about 16 bars then

Miguelito took over the timbales. There were two distinct styles of timbal improvising. Miguelito, a versatile self taught percussionist struck the heads Cuban style – almost laid back, sharply syncopated and off-beat. Tito, always more energetic, interwove his Krupa and Rich brashness within the clave. The two men complemented each other. The horns, reeds and everyone and the supporting percussion kept pace with the two stars. Tito nudged his friend to the side and played his solo. Miguelito pushed him to the side gently and struck the drumhead. Back and forth they went until at one point the two were belting out their rolls, slaps and syncopated drumbeats together. It was as if they had rehearsed and played it dozens of times. Each was not trying to show the other one up – no, not at all. It was just musical inventiveness by two maestros that had been friends for a long time.

Suddenly in the midst of what seemed chaotic and astonishing percussive mayhem, Miguelito looked at Tito and yelled, "¿Cual es la clave? What is the key?"

Tito laughed, continued to strike away at the two heads of the timbales – in the center of the small drum for a sharper ringing sound, at the sides of the big head for a more robust and deep sound. Without hesitation he looked at Miguelito and shouted as loud as he could, "Mi bemol (E flat)." A moment later Jimmy brought in the sax section followed by the trumpets. In his strong and unmistakable style Miguelito first improvised a set of lines a la Cuban sonero and then filled in Rafael Hernández' libretto:

Cumbanchero
A cumba cumba cumba
cumbanchero...
A bongo bongo bongo
bongocero...
Riquitique va sonando
el cumbanchero, bongocero que se va...
Bongocero que se va...

A cumba cumba cumba
cumbanchero...
A bongo bongo bongo
bongocero...
Riquitique va sonando
el cumbanchero, bongocero que se va...
Bongocero que se va...

Y suena así en tambor veriquití
bom bom bom bom Ba...
y vuelve a repicar veriquití
bom bom bom bom Ba...

A cumba cumba cumba
cumbanchero...
A bongo bongo bongo
bongocero...
Riquitique va sonado
el cumbanchero, bongocero que se va...
Bongocero que se va...

Miguelito left New York a few days later. It was the last time Tito would see his dear friend.

Tito and his orchestra journeyed down to Washington, D.C., and in his own right, made history – more than he realized at the time. He was scheduled to perform at the Hispanic Congressional Caucus Dinner during the first week in September 1978, and would become the first authentic Latin American orchestra to play for the President of the United States. Tito was cool. But we all knew he was as excited as the rest of us were. "He is like a big baby," growled his trumpet player/partner in laughter the morning we were packing to head to the airport. "Did you ever see anyone pace so much? He thinks we are going to screw up and make him look bad."

"Its just another gig," he groaned looking around the room. "Its no big deal," he insisted to us in a nervous tone.

Jimmy, who had been his partner and friend for more than 30 years laughed. "Bullshit! You are worried. You always worry."

"Well, these guys (the musicians) could fuck up."

"Don't be so damn mistrustful of your guys," I said in an effort to soothe both Tito and Jimmy.

Tito looked at me. "Well, its bullshit. Just another gig…" The noise of the bags and instruments being carried to the bus was steady. Tito was silent.

Jimmy turned to me and smiled. "It will be fine. We'll get down there; Tito will pull one of his pranks on some unsuspecting guy. We'll get drunk and the next day we will knock them dead." He laughed. "Hey Tito don't forget we are playing for the President." Jimmy started to walk away. He nudged me expecting a response.

"Fuck you, Frisaura."

Jimmy and I laughed as we headed for the street.

The Hispanic Congressional Caucus Dinner has become the culminating event of the annual National Hispanic Heritage month. In 1978, the dinner was held at the Washington Hilton Hotel. It was organized by Congressmen Ed Roybal (D-California), Kika de la Garza (D-Texas), Henry B. González (D-Texas), Robert García (D-New York) and Resident Commissioner Baltasar Corrada (D-Puerto Rico). This was the second event and the organizers were not quite sure how it would turn out. "The room was filled with Hispanics from every corner of the United States," recalled García, who was also the chairman of the caucus.

Mexican-Americans, Puerto Ricans, Cuban-Americans, dominated the guest list, but Latinos were not the only ones that were well represented. The guest list included prominent actors, politicians, and business people. Charlie Rangel (D-New York) the representative from Harlem was among the many members of the Congressional Black Caucus in attendance. And in this mix was Tito Puente and his orchestra.

"Ladies and gentlemen," the voice came over the sound system in the large ballroom, "the President of the United States." Usually what would follow is *"Hail to the Chief,"* but the orchestra surprised everyone.

The orchestra began softly – the introduction of Moisés Simon's *"Peanut Vendor"* (El Manicero). President Jimmy Carter and his wife, followed by Secret Service personnel, came into the room. The crowd stood up, applauded and the music built up. Clearly, the President was amused by his entrance music. At the time Carter was popular with the Latino community. especially because of his community-based programs. A few years later he pardoned Lolita Lebrón, who was a Puerto Rican Nationalist, serving a life term for her part in the short lived uprising in the 1950s. Carter would also have to deal with a fuel crisis and the siege of the U.S. Embassy in Iran. But this night he was in a room that he would address partially in Spanish and talk about the advances that Latinos in the United States were making.

García and Tito talked briefly afterward. Pete Hamill,[139] the author and columnist of the New York Post and a fan and friend of Tito Puente, was sitting at the table assigned to the musicians. "Well, it went over well, don't you think," laughed Tito.

"He (Carter) thought it was a highlight of the night." Laughed Hamill.

"So he knew the tune," asked Tito.

Bob García laughed. "Who doesn't know that song. You made history tonight, Tito."

"Of course," Tito said with a sheepish grin. He was not going to admit it, but he was incredibly honored to have played for the President of the United States.

Another Wave

The dinner crowd had just about cleared out. Bill Beauchamp, the owner of Beau's in the Bronx, had sent over a complimentary round of his best brandy. The cold rain this November night had not let up. Jimmy, Vicentico, Pops and I sat at a table that was in the corner of the dining room. We were all feeling gloomy. We had just come from the memorial funeral service,[140] and Tito was recalling his friend Miguelito who had passed away suddenly on November 8, 1978, in the Hotel Tequendama in Bogotá, Colombia. He was stricken by a heart attack. At the time Tito and the orchestra were working on the West Coast.

Vicentico pushed back from the table and was feeling his pockets for a cigar.

In the morning, before going to the church to attend the service for his old friend, Tito had visited several radio stations to promote his *"Homenaje a Beny Moré"* album. On his own Tito had been pushing the album, visiting the various radio shows. He started doing this during the summer. The orchestra was in and out of New York City, playing in Chicago, Dallas, San Francisco, several places in South America, and of course Puerto Rico. Surprisingly the recording was getting plenty of play on the radio. Tito figured that his manager Ralph Mercado had something to do with the marketing aspect of the recording. The Fañia organization, according to Mercado, was planning to do a live concert at Radio City Music Hall toward the end of winter, around the time of the Grammy Awards ceremony. Ralph was good that way, according to Tito. "He can smell a dollar and that is a good thing."

But the shock of his friend's sudden death was still heavy on him. He internalized his pain – but you could sense his sadness. He felt gloomy. I knew that he was not feeling good; we were too close for me not to see it. I don't recall him ever being so down. "Miguelito was so full of energy, so full of life. He was one of the pioneers. Slowly we are going down for the count. Who is next?"

"Hey, is that something," Jimmy offered, "Charlie Palmieri is back." Jimmy winked toward me. He was trying to change the subject.

Tito shrugged. "It is a great place, Puerto Rico; but there is no work for someone like Charlie – not permanently."

"Eddie Palmieri tried living and working in Puerto Rico. It was a disaster," I added to the conversation. "Joe Loco is still there, and working."

Tito laughed: "Shit, he's some kind of monument or something."

"A national treasure," is what he told me and Joe," Jimmy added.

"Ha! Well, at least he is playing music..." Tito said.

"I used to like going to Puerto Rico," Vicentico said in his heavy Spanish accent. He was still searching his pockets. "I never worked there for a long time. Everyone tells me that there is not enough work. It's like the Cubans who work in the music business in New York. They all want to go to Miami to work. They get there and a few weeks later they are back here – no work. You have to be in New York to survive in this business."

Tito looked at Vicentico. "Shit! ¿Que estas buscando – perico?"

Vicentico looked shocked. "Coño, Tito," he replied almost embarrassed and red faced.

By now we were all looking at Vicentico. "Fajardo lo trato y fracaso. Algunos muchachos de la Orquesta Broadway lo trataron – fue un fracaso."

Jimmy raised his voice. "Someone at the church today asked me if we are going to go on a hiatus to honor Miguelito's memory." Tito looked at Jimmy and said: "Who the fuck is going to take care of the band? They need to work. We'll honor my friend – shit yeah, we'll honor him. We will drink all night and play music. That's how we honor him."

Jimmy nodded in agreement.

Something fell out of Vicentico's pocket and fell to the floor. He started to lean over.

Jimmy squawked, "There is something under the table, it just hit my foot. Instinctively we were all kicking the floor under the table.

Tito was watching Vicentico as he leaned down trying to get his hand to the floor. "What happened? Did you drop your blow?" Tito rolled his head back in laughter.

Vicentico was flushed and red faced. "Be careful or your damn rug will fall off your head." Jimmy gasped. We all started laughing

"Coño!" exclaimed the singer. "El tabaco se me cayo."

"Bullshit," Tito laughed. "That's not your fucking cigar. What is that white stuff – candy?"

Vicentico rose up. He had a look of satisfaction. "You see my fucking cigar." He dusted it off and put it in his mouth. "No white powder. Coño no hable esa mierda aquí," Vicentico groaned. Now we were all laughing. When the laughter died down and he had lit his dark Cuban cigar Vicentico said: "You know they say that the white stuff – I don't do that – but they tell me it is good for the digestion."

The laughter was deafening. "Long live Miguelito," Tito said raising his glass.

We sat there drinking and smoking until Beau's closed. We talked about Joe Quijano and his plan to produce a "Roast for the King." Tito and I met Quijano in September soon after Tito returned from Washington, D.C. The meeting was held at Separate Tables, a restaurant frequented by mob notables – a location where Tito was well known along with Jimmy. Tito agreed to help out his fellow musician.

The orchestra traveled to Panama for a three-day engagement at an old swanky nightclub in Panama City. Tito's mentor and former promotion manager José Curbelo had arranged it.

The orchestra played a number of selections made popular by Miguelito. Tito announced that he would close out the last night – New Year's Eve – with *"El Cumbanchero,"* the selection he and Miguelito had performed the last time they were on the stage together in New York.

In 1979, while performing on the West Coast, Tito and I visited Miguelito's home in Palm Springs. His widow, Diane, gave Tito and me a lot of memorabilia and music, which was donated to Boys Harbor. Occasionally, Tito signed out some of his friend's music to work on new arrangements. Tito recalled some of charts were used by Miguelito's band when he visited the Palladium in the early 1950s. "He had a great band. I sat in with him one night. Eddie Cano was his piano player."

Madera and I were in the control room observing the recording session that was organized by Al Santiago for his independent Gaucho Records label. He called Tito and told him he wanted to do a tribute to Miguelito. Tito and Jimmy were in Latin Sound Studios two days later. The featured artists included Fajardo, Charlie, Luis "Perico" Ortiz and Machito.

Madera made a special arrangement of *"A Luz Babalu,"* designed to incorporate the solos of Tito, Charlie and Fajardo in just over five minutes. It was a straightforward variation of the popular tune. Madera and I watched Machito sing the lyrics. Fajardo followed with a crisp flute solo. It was a resonating and inspiring improvisation the Cuban flautist is known for. The transitions from percussion to brass were flawless. Charlie easily glided his montuno variations into the piece. Tito sashayed into his timbal solo. The selection ran about six minutes and then it was over.

Joe looked at me quietly. He did not say a word.

"It sucks," I said.

"Should I tell him," José asked.

"Of course, tell him. It was shit."

José turned on the microphone. "Tito," he called into the studio. Tito looked at us. "Joe says to tell you that the timbal solo sucks." Charlie gazed toward Tito with a hint of a grin. Machito had a similar look. Everyone else in the studio was still.

Tito rolled his eyes and grunted. "Tell Joe Conzo to go fuck himself." This sort of lightened up a tense moment.

A few minutes later Tito, Joe, Charlie, Fajardo and Machito listened to the recording playback. He turned around to Charlie. "Let's do it again." He looked at me with a glare – I could tell what was on his mind – so could Madera. He knew that musically speaking he was off – not very good. He would never admit it. The only admission of fault was in the fact that he gathered up the musicians again and returned them to the studio. "Ready," he shouted. "1-2 –3…" and the ensemble was off. Charlie and Fajardo matched their previous inspirations on piano and flute. Machito was right on and this time Tito's solo was sparkling.

"Really nice," José said to me.

"Oh yeah!" I looked through the glass. "But I'm not going to tell him… Anyway, not until later. He is still fuming about fucking up, about you catching the mistakes, and then telling me. Shit. He knows I don't know shit about music. So he is going to be pissed. But he'll get over it." We laughed.

A few minutes later Louie Ramírez took over the sound stage with a 20 piece all-star orchestra. They recorded a selection: *"Don Alfredo,"* composed by Al and dedicated to his father. The Gaucho 45 R.P.M. was released a few weeks later, but did not get much radio airtime. Eventually it was lost. Tito figured that Al, known to be somewhat eccentric, did not push it too forcefully that even had the powers that be at Fañia were not about to let it become a hit. "It was nice to do a favor for Al" was all he ever said about it.

C'est Magnifique

Simply stated I was in awe. Leonard Bernstein walked up to Tito. "Hey Tito, I have wanted to talk with you for the longest time," he said as he placed his arm over Tito's shoulder. We had just walked into Sardi's, in the Broadway Theatre District. The room was packed. It was a party for the opening of "Zoot Suit."[141] The place was overflowing with the who's who of the theater and the entertainment world. As Bernstein and Tito drifted into the crammed room Bernstein continued: "You know that piece you did a few years ago – de Fallas's music – "The Ritual of Fire..."

Tito was cool as a cucumber and strolled in step with Bernstein toward the center of the large crowded dining room. "That was years ago..."

"Well I always thought your approach was rather unique. Did you consider using violins?" Bernstein said as they made their way through the room.

"Actually, we did talk about that with the producers," Tito replied.

"I liked the jazz album you did years ago – *"My Fair Lady."* It was an intriguing..." Bernstein and Tito disappeared.

A few weeks before the musical opened in New York, the Schubert Organization authorized Ralph Espada, the principal producer of the New York show, to contact Tito to help promote the New York venture. "Zoot Suit" had opened in the Los Angeles area in 1978, and sold out every performance. The backers were hoping for similar success on the Great White Way. Tito had a large fan base in California; a substantial portion was Mexican. He wanted to be helpful. But he suspected that there would be difficulties in conveying Mexican-American problems to a mostly Puerto Rican population – especially one that was not theater oriented.

But there were distinct similarities. Zoot suit styles were worn in Harlem in the 1940s. "I remember in the early years of the Palladium," he told Olmos, "a lot of Puerto Ricans who had recently migrated dressed in the peg pants, large shoulders and narrow waist jackets – we called them 'Marine Tigers.'"[142] Zoot suiters most often were not affiliated with gangs or violence, and even exploded into mainstream style when worn by figures such as Frank Sinatra. Tito sensed that nothing he could do could help the production be successful.

By the end of the night the crowd at Sardi's started to sense that New York critics were much less enthusiastic about the show than their counterparts on the West Coast.[143] Edward James Olmos was among the young actors at Sardi's that night. He was one of the many Mexican-Americans that traveled to Broadway, and who Tito hosted at several functions. Many of them went up to Corso's a few nights before the opening to get a taste of what Tito called "Afro-Cuban music." He reminded Olmos: "I don't play salsa. I play Afro-Cuban music."

"Okay, okay carnal," laughed Olmos.

Tito and Machito And Dizzy

Dizzy Gillespie was getting off the stage after playing with the Machito Orchestra. Tito's band was setting up almost directly opposite the musicians of his rival's band. Tito was taking in the sight of the large audience gathered inside Avery Fisher Hall for the New York City segment of the 1978 Newport Jazz Festival – Jazz Latino. "Hey Tito, I warmed them up for you," Dizzy laughed as he approached us in the backstage area. "The acoustics are just right and the crowd is up for you." He was teasing, of course.

"Shit!" puffed Tito. "This is a piece of cake. Machito and I will be calling you out in a few minutes so don't mess up those pretty little lips."

Gillespie laughed. "Little!" After the laughing subsided he added, "and remember cool Afro-Cuban with jazz."

"The Afro-Cuban is easy. I'm just a small fish in that big jazz pond of yours," replied Pops.

"Oh that's bullshit. You're always trying to snow me," Dizzy laughed again.

Tito grinned. "Now we will warm up the crowd up for you."

Dizzy smiled. "The Afro-Cuban beats. I'm ready."

Tito strolled out with his accustomed Jimmy Cagney style swagger as the audience roared. He looked back at Dizzy and gave him thumbs up.

"Who says the big bands are dead," Dizzy said turning to me. I laughed.

It was another of those rousing music moments. Machito and Tito were introduced together by emcee Felipe Luciano. In his heavy accent Machito announced to the audience: "He has been working hard for the last 25 years, without a break."

With his hand around his mentor's shoulder Tito informed the audience that at the *"Newport Jazz Latino 1978"* he was commissioned to compose *"Mambo Adonis"* (which later Tito re-titled *"Machito Forever,")* and would be played by the two orchestras. "I will direct the Machito Orchestra, and Machito will lead the Tito Puente Orchestra."[144] There was a roar.

The two bands started precisely on the beat. Back and forth the two big bands dueled for nearly 15 minutes. The Puente trumpets got it started, followed by the Machito saxophones. The two percussion ensembles made it look easy. They not only blended but also complemented one another. "It's like being in the Palladium," gasped an excited Dizzy who was watching with delight. It was, exciting, reverberating and arousing.

First the Machito saxophones glide in their solos, followed by the Puente musicians. The percussion was dazzling and steady. All this culminated about 10 minutes into the performance with Tito brandishing his sticks and with precision slapping and whacking the timbales as only the King could do. Fittingly, Dizzy and the Machito Orchestra completed the performance with *"Manteca,"* as it was orchestrated in 1948.

New Sounds From Cuba

The Spanish language media and the hand full of self-styled salsa experts of the period continued to list Tito Puente and his orchestra as terminally ill, this despite the orchestra working almost every night in the New York City area, extended engagements on the West Coast, performances on radio and television throughout South America and the Caribbean. Tito often played school venues where he and Charlie Palmieri provided more than just music. Charlie had a gift, Tito often noted. "He could provide interesting historical facts about the music we play. He had a gift of gab, you know."

Eddie Rodríguez and his wife always enjoyed when Tito and his friends dropped in for dinner or just a few drinks. The owners of Lord Jim's Restaurant on Broadway, across the street from where Tito had his office, even created a special dish for Pops – arroz con picadillo. It was not a stylish and elegant place. It was clean, the service was good and the food was great. It was a place that was accessible and the host and hostess were terrific. Tito loved eating there.

Saturday night we were sitting in the restaurant and Tito was talking to me about bandleader Larry Harlow[145] claiming "foul," and accusing the Fañia bosses headed by Jerry Masucci, of submitting Tito's album *"Homenaje A Beny Moré"* after the Grammy Awards deadline. "Isn't he a pain in the ass," exclaimed Tito in an amusing tone. The awards were announced in March, and followed by a concert based on the music of the album at Radio City Music Hall. It was a success for Masucci and company, thanks to Mercado's aggressive promotion that reaped the benefits for the failing Fañia label.

The concert was not without a problem. At the last minute, Tito and Jimmy discovered that pianist Sonny Bravo approached Ralph Mercado for a higher rate of pay. This pissed off both Pops and Jimmy. They powwowed during the afternoon and Tito called me at home. "Jimmy says we can get another piano player," Tito told me.

"He's right," I retorted quickly. "You said yourself that good musicians can be found anywhere. Shit! You don't even need a piano – not for this gig."

There was a brief pause. "Fuck him…"

"Fire his ass." I said.

Tito then looked at Jimmy. "I should have listened to Ray (Barretto) and Fajardo. They told me Sonny was a great piano player. They also told me he was a pain in the ass. What a pair of balls. Shit!" After that we finished eating our arroz con picadillo.

Just what Tito and Jimmy told Sonny I don't know for sure. But by the time the concert at Radio City was set to start, Sonny was back at the piano.

"He pleaded and begged," quipped Jimmy. That was all he would say. Sonny, a veteran of many of New York's top Latin bands had the reputation of being "a whiner," according to the musicians' gossip circle – the stories about Bravo are confirmed by Madera. Tito liked the way Sonny played which is why he put up with his crap.

The entire stable of popular Fañia singers were on hand and Tito and the orchestra did them justice. "Did anyone expect anything different," exclaimed Jimmy.

I was listening to Tito recall Larry Harlow's challenge to Tito winning his first Grammy. Palmieri was back from his short stopover in Puerto Rico. He was happy to be back in New York. As soon as he tossed off his coat and sat down he lit a cigarette. "Damn its cold outside."

"To think you gave up the tropical breezes of Puerto Rico for this …" I chimed.

The smoke cloud rolled into the air. "Shit! Couldn't find work – maybe a small party here and there, but nothing steady. Joe (Loco) is doing good, you know. He is playing at one of the big hotels, in a lounge. He says it is very relaxing, sometimes boring, but very relaxing. And, the way things are going with music…" Charlie rolled his eyes.

"I know, I know. Joe is happy. If he heard some of the shit coming out of Cuba he would throw up," moaned Tito. "I mean some of it is good, but most of it is shit. That fucking Fidel really fucked things up, I mean musically speaking."

"Don't hold back," I said. "He was just telling me about the bullshit with Larry Harlow claiming foul about Tito's Beny Moré recording. It was submitted on time. I know. I was involved with the Grammy selection process."

Charlie laughed. "Does that mean that he did not really win?" We all laughed. "I always liked Larry's style. He is a pretty good musician and a stand up guy. So who is busting chops, the Fañia people?"

More amusement. "I think that we should have Jimmy get some of the boys to break a few knees," I proposed.

"It's Ralph's problem now. Larry and Ralph can duke it out. He told me that everything was done on time - no fucking screw ups. But maybe he did fuck up the submission. You know Ralph, he is always running around." Tito looked at me with a deep stare. "You did get the material, the LP in on time. Shit! That would be a pisser if the Fañia boys fucked this up too. Anything is possible with that shit head Masucci." Tito looked around the room. "Anyway Mercado and Masucci will deal with it. The concert at Radio City was a smash – never a doubt."

"You mean you still are drifting toward your end," laughed Charlie.

Tito smiled. "You know what I say. There are three sides to every story – what might have happened, what we say happened, and the truth. I hope Larry sorts this shit out. I don't trust anybody in that company. They make the guys at RCA Victor look like angels." We laughed.

"They need this success – your Grammy – especially after the Fañia Cuban fiasco. It must have cost him (Masucci) a lot of money for his excursion down to Havana. Dexter Gordon, Hubert Laws and Stan Getz were part of the mix. Did you hear Irakere, they are supposed to be pretty good," Charlie added.

Many of Columbia's top recording artists made the visit to Cuba where they performed (and recorded) at a series of concerts with some of the top Cuban bands. The Weather Report, the CBS Jazz All-Stars (an all star ensemble that featured Dexter Gordon, Stan Getz and Woody Shaw) and The Trio of Doom (John McLaughlin, Jaco Pastorious and Tony Williams), Stephen Stills, Kris Kristofferson and Rita Coolidge mixed it up with the popular Grupo Irakere. The Fañia All-Stars performed alongside artists the rock and pop stars and with Cuba's Grupo Irakere and Orquesta Aragón.

Tito stated: "The Fañia All-Stars are dysfunctional and lack direction. They are not bad musicians – not all of them. There is no fucking direction. They all want to be stars. It's a good thing that some of the Cuban pros helped them out." He laughed.

"So what do you think of Irakere?" Charlie insisted, almost ignoring Tito's previous comment."

Tito looked at me and smiled. He looked at Charlie through the smoke. "Damn those things are a killer."

"So what you sniff is healthy?" Charlie retorted with a cynical laugh. "So what do you think?"

Irakere[146] was an ensemble that is torn between Afro-Cuban music and jazz, according to Tito. "What I have heard tells me that they all seem to be terrific musicians… trumpets, reeds, you know. I would like to meet the piano player. He is Bebo Valdés' son. He sounds good. But overall it's a hodgepodge of shit. There certainly is some inventiveness. Does that cover it?"

Charlie shrugged. "So I guess you don't like them. Well, they seem to have a wide range – repertoire – promising. I heard a recording of this band – Los Van Van…"

"What shit," interrupted Tito. "I mean that stuff is bad – like listening to a charanga that has lost its driving moves… That fucking electric bass guitar…" Tito was acutely aware that charanga music – violins, flute and rhythm – was, if not the most enjoyed by Charlie, it was high on his list. The charangas had made something of a comeback starting around 1976. Fajardo had a locally popular charanga orchestra; Charanga 76, Orquesta Ideal and Orquesta Tipica Novel were some of the more popular ensembles in the New York area during the early 1980s. "It seems a lot of guys are giving this music another shot. They sound a little less sophisticated than the ones that were around when you and Pacheco and Ray were involved… But this music that these guys play – the Van Van… We are scraping the bottom now."

Charlie laughed. "I agree. They are really bad. When Ray switched from a full charanga to violins and brass I thought it innovative. You know Fajardo used to include trumpets. Jorrín used them in Mexico."

"But Ray and Jorrín kept control of the music. There was melody, there was a driving syncopated rhythm, there was an idea that they were experimenting with. I liked his excursion with the pop stuff in one of his albums *(Hits Latin Style).*

"Yeah!" I added. "Some of it was okay."

Tito laughed. "I like to kid him. 'You know Ray, I own you,' I tell him. The company Morris (Levy) and I own published his hit *"Watussi."* Ray always gets nervous when I talk like that."

"He knows you are kidding him?" I said.

"But that Van Van stuff - that stuff is pure crap," Tito noted sipping on his drink. "Sometimes I wonder if the music I really love will make a comeback. Shit! Probably not."

"It never goes away – it evolves," chided Charlie. "It's always evolving."

Tito smiled, sipped his drink and added, "but into what?"

The Scholarship is Born

"We are here tonight to honor TP, Tito Puente," exclaimed Charlie Palmieri decked out in his evening tuxedo. "He is El Rey del Timbal. And let me tell you he has banged a lot of cueros in his lifetime," he continued to the roar of laughter. Across the dominions of what is known in the Spanish-speaking world, the word "cuero," which means skin also has another meaning (woman of low reputation). And so started the "Tito Puente Roast,"[147] produced in 1979 by bandleader Joe Quijano. It was designed to follow the successful and popular Dean Martin hosted television roasts of Hollywood stars. It was staged and filmed at a midtown Manhattan studio.

Felipe Luciano followed Charlie. Luciano borrowed his opening from words generally associated with Baptist ministers. In a sharp bright tone – emulating the pointed sound of a preacher – he bellowed: "We come here tonight to honor a good man." From this point on it was down hill. After describing Tito as a man who gave "platform shoes" considerable stature Luciano continued: "It is rumored that President Dwight Eisenhower heard Tito play and caught up with him backstage at the Palladium. Tito thought he was a groupie. You know how dumb musicians can be. Tito thought the man named Ike was a groupie so he looked at him and said 'So you want some blow?'" There was a roar. "Ike was surprised. No he told Tito. I never tried that stuff."

Next Luciano said: "Tito has turned to religion. He was taught that if he bathes with a certain white powder he could become invisible. Some people tell me that when they go to see the Tito Puente Orchestra he is never there."

The program also featured Myrta Silva, the Puerto Rican singer gravely gazed at Pops and then said: "They wanted me to share a room with you. I looked at him and said: 'Oh no honey, you are not my type.'" Next, Raul Marrero the popular romantic vocalist of the period was introduced. Joe Quijano had to nudge him off the stage because he started to undress. He was bombed, announced Joe to a laughing audience. Cindy Rodríguez, the daughter of Tito Rodríguez, was eloquent in her recognition of her late father's rival and friend.

It was Joe's plan to market the event to various media outlets, but he was not quite successful. But unexpectedly a number of participants, some corporations included, donated money. "What do we do with this," I asked after Tito cleaned himself off. Margie Puente ended the "Roast" by dunking her husband's face into a large cake. "Getting even," she said as she pushed Tito's head into the cake, "for all those wonderful years." The Tito Puente Orchestra also performed three numbers, including a version of the classic *"El Rey del Timbal."* The timbal solo is classic Tito. Another number, *"No Puedo Ser Feliz,"* features Pops on the vibes — a rarity on film. Finally, Puente and his band play a contemporary version of his popular *"Oye Como Va"* that features a young Mitch Frohman on flute. Jimmy plays the valve trombone and Madera, who would become his musical director, is featured on percussion.

Tito had often talked about starting a scholarship fund to help young people in the entertainment field. "Whatever you have," he said hold on to it. Tomorrow we will talk to the lawyers to get the fund started.

No one in Tito's small group of friends really had any idea of how to establish or organize a not-for-profit-fund that would be used to benefit young Latino musicians. It was an idea, an objective and a goal that Tito had long desired to achieve. A few days after the roast Tito called me – I remember it clearly – it was dark, it was raining and it was 5:00 A.M.

"Shit! Don't you ever sleep?" I groaned still trying to open my eyes. "I just got home." He knew that we were at the Roseland Ballroom.

Tito was excited. "I want you to call Bobby Rodríguez and I want you guys to get together and talk. Then the three of us will meet."

"What do we talk about?"

"Don't ask so many fucking questions." Tito hung up the telephone.

It must be important and he must have just thought about it because at the Roseland he was busy entertaining a packed house of mostly Italian-Americans – some of them may not have been American. There was very little English, or for that matter Spanish spoken. The event was highlighted by the arrival of Todo Marino, a Gambino family mobster.[148] I was standing with Jimmy when the portly man entered the packed ballroom with his protective entourage. Tito and the orchestra were getting ready to play. But the room suddenly became silent. It was eerie. You could feel all eyes were on Todo Marino. Jimmy leaned over to me and whispered: "They are not looking at us." Sometimes Jimmy liked to be sarcastic.

Todo walked to where Jimmy and I were standing. The two men embraced. "Where is Tito," Todo asked softly. He looked at me and smiled.

We clasped hands." Joe, Joe Conzo," he said. "Jimmy told me about you. Nice to meet you."

A moment later Tito was standing between Jimmy and me. Tito and Todo embraced. "Thanks for coming to play," Todo said.

"You know that I am always available to help out," Tito responded. He turned to Jimmy and added, "Jimmy said you needed the band here tonight. It is always a pleasure."

Todo and his entourage slipped past us and as the group made their way through the ballroom he turned and said with a wide grin, "Some of those old mambos from the 1950s would make this place shake." He smiled and waved to us. Jimmy and Tito left me standing with my drink in hand and headed to the bandstand. I was never quite sure of the purpose of the event and neither Tito nor Jimmy gave me any details. Tito was the headliner and the program also featured disco queen Gloria Gaynor.

Bobby Rodríguez and I met up a few days later and we talked, mostly about the music we loved – the big bands. Two days later we met Tito at a midtown watering hole. Tito wanted to organize the "Tito Puente Scholarship Fund." He looked at us and said, "I don't know just how to do it, so you two guys will be my point men on this." It was typical Tito – go do this as soon as possible. He handed us several checks that he received at the "Roast." The rest is history. The fund was organized as a non profit (C5013); $300 were deposited in the bank. Tito established a connection to the Juilliard School of Music, and in February 1980 the organization officially hosted its first fundraiser at Lehman College in the Bronx. Tito described the first event as "stumbling and fumbling." But he was positive that we were on the right track, and that what Bobby and I had started would get bigger and better.

Tito was upbeat after the first event. He wanted to do a second event quickly. We started planning for the scholarship's second event but the death of Tito's mother on June 2, 1980, dampened our spirits. Tito was in Puerto Rico visiting his friend Joe Loco. At the time Joe was fronting a piano and percussion ensemble at La Concha Hotel in the heart of San Juan's Condado section. Tito called me from the island after he spoke with Margie. "Cancel all engagements for the next week," he said. He and Charlie Palmieri were scheduled to play at an outdoor concert in the Bronx. "I will do that one," he said.

It was one of the few times in our association that I asked him about his father. "Should I try to see if your father…"

He shut me down and growled, "No, no. Leave it alone." If his father was alive or dead I would never know. He did not speak about him.

The viewing was held at Walter B. Cooke Funeral Home in the Bronx. Tito and his family quietly gathered for one day of observance. It was a low-key family matter. I was there for a little while and at Tito's request I traveled to Manhattan to accept an award on Tito's behalf from the State of New York from Governor Hugh Carey. Whatever pain or grief Tito was feeling he kept well hidden – it was his way. He was silent while at the funeral home. On the day of the viewing he quietly departed. The orchestra played the outdoor event in Manhattan, 117th Street, in the late afternoon. Jimmy kept the band working around the city while Tito was in mourning during a 10-day period.

Morris Levy had been trying to contact Tito for a number of days after he heard about the death of Tito's mother. He tracked me down at Boys Harbor on 104th Street and 5th Avenue; a few days after Tito's mother had been laid to rest. Tito and Morris continued to sustain a close relationship. They were partners in the music publishing business. The two men shared ownership of Little Dipper, Planetary and Patricia publishing companies. Levy was still at Roulette located in Manhattan. "Hey Conzo," he said brusquely in his accustomed manner. "I have a check for Tito. Can you come and get it?"

The afternoon I saw him he looked frail. "How are you doing?" I asked.

"Same old shit," he said with a smile. "Fighting the fights. Please give my condolences to Tito and the family." He handed me a check for $10,000.

I nodded. The next day I gave Tito the check that Levy had entrusted to me.

Author and journalist Pete Hamill was the emcee for our first Scholarship Fund event held at Lehman College. It was not extravagant, but one of the first things Tito did was to pay a musical tribute to his late friend and competitor, Tito Rodríguez. The second Tito Puente Scholarship fund raising experience was more successful, better attended and memorable. It was not without its own unique set of problems. Spanish Raymond Marquez, Harlem's infamous illegal numbers operator, was among the consistent contributors to the Scholarship Fund. He had purchased a slew of tickets for the second event to be staged at Lehman College. There were other notables and leaders of several notorious gangs in and around El Barrio who also purchased tickets for the fundraiser. When the members of these gangs discovered that they might be seated in proximity to each other, the calls started coming in.

"Tell Tito that I can't sit near you know who," Spanish Raymond moaned to me over the telephone on the afternoon before the event.

"Jesus Christ, if I tell Tito that this is a problem… You know he will be pissed." I responded defensively. Actually, I was a little nervous talking to Spanish Raymond. "Why can't you all sit together for one night and listen to the music." Spanish Raymond grumbled a half dozen words and hung up.

When I told Tito about the hassle with the seating he found it rather amusing. "Shit! I hope that none of these guys are packing. It would be something if they get into a tangle – cops, who knows what." He laughed. They all sat together.

The Tito Puente Orchestra opened the scholarship fund event with a stinging rendition of *"Sopa de Pichon,"* that featured Tito's mentor Machito. Celia Cruz was also on hand. Mongo Santamaría, who besides taking a prolonged conga solo, also featured a haunting cello played by Enrique Orengo. It was quite a night. The scholarship fund turned over about $3,000 to the Juilliard School. But because of a legal restriction, the school could not allocate the funds specifically for assisting Latino music students. However, the school did recruit several students of Latin extraction. By 1982, the affiliation with Juilliard was amicably terminated and the Fund was set up to distribute the money to various organizations and Hispanic students.

In 1983 we hosted a fundraising event at Avery Fisher Hall in Lincoln Center. The program included Cheo Feliciano and the reunion of Mario Bauzá and Machito. They had not spoken to each other in more than five years. The Machito Orchestra drew from its robust musical library and with Machito singing and playing marcas and Mario directing and playing the saxophone, the audience came to its feet. Bobby and I devised the reunion. We discussed it with Tito and he said: "Damn that is a great idea I just had."

And I responded: "Fuck you."

Another memorable moment came when the Tito Puente Orchestra played the Rafael Hernández tune, *"Canta,"* and Machito sang a duet with Cheo Feliciano who had recorded a full orchestra version of it that was beautifully arranged by Louie Ramírez.

Over the next nearly 20 years, the Tito Puente Scholarship Fund contributed nearly $100,000 to organizations that worked with young aspiring Latino entertainers. The Fund was abolished after his death.

Over a period of about 10 years many notable entertainers performed at the various money raising venues that Tito hosted. Machito, who in 1982 won the first Grammy for the album *"Machito and his Salsa Big Band"*

and opened the doors to Europe for Tito and his orchestra with his success throughout the continent, was a frequent supporter. Celia Cruz was another artist who helped out in those early years of the scholarship effort. The late jazz violinist Noel Pointer and jazz percussionist Art Blakely joined with Paquito D'Rivera, David Valentín and Ray Barretto in a wild jam session at the Apollo Theater in 1986. Santos Colón and Vicentico Valdés appeared with Tito at Lincoln Center in 1986. Johnny Pacheco played his flute with the Puente Orchestra several times during this period. A memorable fundraiser was held at the Lincoln Center Library, which included an extraordinary solo piano performance by Charlie Palmieri. Tito performed with his jazz ensemble and with the big band. He was determined to keep them both fully functional. Max Roach, Eddie Palmieri, Miriam Makeba, Graciela and many others participated.

The success of the scholarship endeavor resulted in a number of prominent musicians that included Johnny Pacheco and Ray Barretto, to attempt to institute a similar organization. However, these attempts were short lived. The Urban Coalition in New York also presented a formal proposal to the Tito Puente Scholarship Fund to assume control and maintain it. Tito and I were vehement in our rejection of the offer. "This is not what I want. I don't want anyone except me and the people I have picked to operate the Fund to have anything to do with it – not even my family. And that is final," he stated.

The legal advisor recommended that we set up a board of directors. Tito suggested that we start with two board members. We talked about it – briefly. "I want Bob Sancho and Charlie Candelario to be on the board," insisted Tito. Sancho had been a long time fan of Tito. He is Vice President, External Affairs at Bronx Lebanon Hospital, and Candelario is the head of the 111th Street Boys in El Barrio.

"Yeah! And what will be their responsibilities?" I asked Tito one night when we were driving from a gig somewhere in Brooklyn. Tito was in an irritated mood. We were lost, and had taken our second trip around Prospect Park. He was looking for the Brooklyn Bridge – any bridge that would get him back to familiar territory – Manhattan. "Where the fuck are we?" he snarled.

"You're asking me?"

He snapped, "Who else is in the fucking car."

"I told you we should wait for Jimmy and follow him out," I responded.

"He is probably lost too."

Fortunately we spotted a sign: "To Manhattan," and that calmed Pops. I pressed him about the Tito Puente Scholarship Fund Board of Directors."

"They will do what you tell them to do. You and Bobby run the thing."

I laughed. "And you have the final say."

He laughed. "That's the way it is."

The list of contributors grew and included prestigious friends and firms. But sometimes Tito himself would have to get on the telephone and convince a potential donor that it was for a good cause. Sometimes he had to be devious. "Joe call Ralph Mercado," he growled, when told that his chief booking agent had not as yet stepped up. "Tell him that Curbelo has two tables. Make him feel like shit." Ralph hated to part with money as Tito had discovered many years ago.

"Okay." Ralph sent his check over the next day. We kept our fingers crossed that it would not bounce.

One afternoon several weeks after Tito's mom passed away, he called and asked me to meet him at Victor's Café on 52nd Street in Manhattan. He had been home all day practicing. He was coming into Manhattan via limousine for an interview with Pat O'Hare of the New York Daily News. In the evening we were heading to New Jersey to catch up with Jimmy and the band. Roberto "Manos de Piedra" Duran was feeling no pain this afternoon when we ran into him at Victor's Café. A few weeks earlier he scored an unexpected victory in the ring over favorite Sugar Ray Leonard, in what has become known as the "Brawl in Montreal."

Tito was not a big sports fan. In the 1960s the band often appeared at the former Lightweight Champion Carlos Ortiz's[149] Tropicoro Club on Longwood Avenue in the Bronx. It eventually became the property of the New York Police Department. Pops liked to taunt restaurant owner Victor de Coral about the huge painting of Duran beating Leonard that he placed on the wall of the dining room between hundreds of photos of celebrities. That was about his only comment on the fight. Duran came over to Tito, embraced and we hung out together. He followed us to the Daily News headquarters on 42nd Street and then back to the restaurant where we had a few more drinks.

As we were waiting to be picked up by a limousine – Duran wanted to tag along to the gig in New Jersey - on the street we heard: "Tito, Tito." it was the police officer who usually walked a beat in the area.

"Hey, Angelo," called Tito. "What's up?"

Angelo walked briskly to us and said: "The chairman (Frank Sinatra) is in Jilly's and he was wondering if Mr. Duran could drop by so he could congratulate him on his victory over Leonard?"

In impeccable Spanish Tito conveyed the request to Duran. "El señor Sinatra le pide, que si por favor Ud. puede pasar por el restaurante que esta a dos cuadras de aquí para que pueda felicitarlo."

Duran snarled. "Dile a ese maricón que le parto la cara..." It was common knowledge – even to us – that there were heavy bets placed on the fight in favor of Leonard.

Tito looked at the officer, who seemed to understand that Duran was not at all flattered by the request. Then he looked at Duran with a stern glare. He placed an arm around the fighter's shoulder. "Déjame decirte algo – un consejo – si tu té aproxima al señor Sinatra con esa actitud, Ud. deja de existir. ¿Comprende? Let's get into the limo." Duran climbed in quietly. Tito turned to the policeman. "Please convey to Jilly and Frank that maybe next time. We are late for our appointment in New Jersey." We left late that night and the champ was still swamped by well wishers and fans. I don't know how he got back to New York.

The officer smiled. "I certainly will. Have a nice night Tito."

A while later Tito and I were back at Victor's Café. The painting was gone.

Fajardo was at the bar with several friends. Victor came over. "Hey Victor. You want to hang a picture of Joe to fill the big hole in the wall."

"Que bomba," laughed Fajardo. Leonard had defeated Duran in the rematch.

"¿Oye, Conzo, te mete en al cuadrilátero con Duran 'No Mas?"[150] someone in the crowd shouted.

Tito looked at me. "You look just like him – Duran."

"Fuck you." Everyone was laughing.

"I'm still in the 1960s when Carlos Ortiz was the champ. A very nice guy," Tito said tasting his drink.

They Just Fade Away...

The contentious relationship Tito had with the powers that be at Fañia did not improve even after winning a Grammy. The successful display of the Fañia all-star singers at Radio City Music Hall backed up by the Tito Puente Orchestra irritated Fañia owner Masucci, while filling the pockets of co-producer Ralph Mercado. As Tito's booking agent the burden of keeping the peace was Ralph's responsibility. "You go and keep him happy," Tito often told his agent. "Just make sure me and the boys get paid. And, if he has something to say about my work with the jazz group tell him to have the balls to say it to me. For my part I will live up to the terms of my contract." Tito thought that the people who operated Fañia were not happy about Tito's success with the Latin Percussion Ensemble. But he was determined to work with both the orchestra and the jazz group.

Ralph sort of kept the peace and worked with the Fañia executives to convince them that it was in the recording company's interest to make sure that Tito lived up to the terms of his contract with the subsidiary Tico Records. Ralph knew that the small West Coast jazz recording company Concord had approached Tito. It was Cal Tjader who suggested to Concord that it recruit Tito. Tito and Jimmy and John Burk, who represented Concord, came to the East Coast early in 1980, met briefly at Lincoln Center during a concert that featured Cachao. After the brief meeting Tito turned to me and said: "This is perfect. He and his boss (Carl Jefferson) are great guys."

Jimmy added, "So we can start recording for Concord with the jazz group."

"Yeah!" groaned Tito. "Fuck Fañia. Que se vayan pa'l carajo los cabrónes."

Jimmy rolled his eyes. He spoke very good Spanish. "Ralph can handle the shit heads."

I put in my two cents: "Go for it 'Pops.'"

"Fañia has not helped us with shit," Jimmy said.

"Ralph gives them all the ideas," Tito said. Then imitating Masucci's unique voice and exaggerating the feminine tone Tito added: "'Oh Ralph you are so smart…'" Tito rolled his eyes. "Anyway I want to do this jazz thing especially now because all the nightclubs are closing up, or getting smaller. They don't even have a real piano in a lot of these clubs – what shit. Now you have to carry around a toy piano."

He was ready to make the leap but he was not going to give up keeping the big band alive. In 1980 he recorded "*Dance Mania '80.*" It was a bomb. Tito went into the studio. "Everything was hurried," Madera recalled. "It was like the clock was ticking. The album was contemporary and everything was recorded in overdrive. Tito didn't think it was all that bad.

"Just ask your musicians," I told Tito after it was released. "It stinks…"

He gave me that patented cold look and bellowed: "Bullshit!"

Jimmy was heading to the racetrack that day. "He's right," Jimmy called out to Tito as he left the room.

"Bullshit to you too." He turned around and gave me one of those chilling gazes.

During this period he also started conversations with Cohen over at

Latin Percussion. Eventually there would be an agreement that LP would make and distribute Tito Puente model percussion instruments and that Tito would receive commissions or royalties. Tito was never clear what the final agreement was, but he said it was fair.

In 1981, he hastily gathered the band once again to record *"C'est Magnifique,"* an album that featured singer Azuquita. It was his brainchild. He sold the idea to Ralph, and Ralph convinced Fañia that it was a great idea. Journeyman vocalist Camilo Luis "Azuquita" Arguméde who was born in 1945 in Colón, Panama was a veteran of the successful Tipica 73, Roberto Roena y su Apollo Sound and Cortijo y su Combo. Ralph sold the idea to Masucci. This was the last album Tito recorded for Tico. "Good riddance," he said.

The highlight of the album is *"Guaguanco Arsenio,"* which is dedicated to the memory of the great Cuban musician. Tito composed it and it features Tito playing the piano. The four plus minute number features a Noro Morales style piano solo by Pops, who also is featured on timbales. During his improvisational piano solo Tito gives a feeling of quasi baroque, something he learned when he was a young student under the tutelage of his childhood piano teacher, Doña Victoria Hernández.

The orchestra included Mark Friedman and Bobby Porcelli, alto saxophone; Mitch Frohman, tenor saxophone, Mario Rivera, baritone saxophone and flute; Jimmy Frisaura (concert master), Richard Caruso and Larry Farrell, trombone; Lionel Sánchez, Paulo Di Paula and Hector Zarzuela, trumpet; Sonny Bravo, piano; Andy González, bass; John "Dandy" Rodríguez, Jr., José Madera, Jr., and Patato, percussion. The repertoire included *"Azúcar Pa' Un Amargao"* and *"Negro de Sociedad,"* two contemporized standards that are nothing like the originals. Azuquita composed the other five selections. The orchestra is outstanding in terms of musicianship, but lacks feeling. Madera who formed an integral part of the band at this time, bemoans the weakness of the album. So do I. However, the piano solo by Tito is worth the price of the album. "He was focused and concentrated on this piece," according to Madera Jr.

The fact that he played the piano did not surprise me, Madera or Jimmy because we had seen him at the piano on a number of occasions. It was generally an impulsive act, as if he thought about something in his past. An example of his piano virtuosity occurred one night when we visited a nightclub in Manhattan, where Eddie Palmieri and his band were playing. Tito suddenly disappeared through the crowd and was walking toward the small bandstand. I was standing with New York Daily News reporter, Enrique Fernández. A few minutes later the sound of the orchestra changed. The piano montunos, the hard pounding that is generally associated with

Eddie was different. And, when I looked up I saw Eddie taking a timbal solo. Tito was comfortably sitting at the keyboard wailing away. Slowly the packed room began to realize the switch and seemed pleased with the different sound.

Desi Arnaz blew into New York City unexpectedly in the spring of 1982. At first Tito was inclined to brush him off but later thought that for old times sake, maybe he should spend some time with the Cuban entertainer, who he had once rubbed shoulders with in the old Conga Club way back when. Maybe his change of heart was due to the fact that Charlie Palmieri told Tito that Desi had spent considerable effort to locate Tito, so he could meet up with him, or maybe it was that I reminded him that Desi had come East a few years earlier to view the exhibit at Lincoln Center. Whatever the reason he agreed to meet up with him. But he left it up to me to connect with Desi Arnaz and attend to his needs while in New York.

It was not easy locating Tito to let him know that Desi was scheduled to arrive. It started with a call to Jimmy, who was out of town with Tito and the band traveling somewhere in Europe taking advantage of the resurging popularity of big band Afro-Cuban music that resulted from Machito and his Afro-Cubans' success. The word got to Al Santiago who called Ralph Mercado, who called the house in Tappan, New York. Finally, Charlie Palmieri got a hold of me and I managed to catch up with Tito.

"Oh shit, what does he (Arnaz) want," squawked Tito on the telephone.

I handed the telephone to Charlie and a few minutes later I was on my way to meet Desi. "I'll catch up with you later." I suspected that Tito would not show.

I was surprised to see how old Desi Arnaz[152] looked. In the 1970s, Arnaz appeared on television with Mike Douglas. He also headlined a Kraft Music Hall special to promote his autobiography, "*A Book.*" In 1976 he served as a guest host on Saturday Night Live, with his son, Desi, Jr. The program contained spoofs of *I Love Lucy* and *The Untouchables*. Arnaz, Jr. played the drums with the Saturday Night Live band. Desi sang both *"Babalu"* and another favorite from his dance band days, *"Cuban Pete."* He ended the broadcast by leading the entire cast in a raucous conga line through the Saturday Night Live studio. I ran into Desi in midtown. He was bombed. He wanted to see "action." So our first stop was up in the Bronx – Beau's. With Charlie's assistance we gathered up some of the people that Desi wanted to see – Machito, Mario, Charlie and a few others. Desi, Machito, Beau and I made our way, barely, to the Chateau Madrid where Candido and his ensemble were playing. Desi Arnaz spent his time slipping, sliding, groping women and drinking. At one point he grabbed a woman from the rear. All hell broke loose. I stepped in between Desi, the woman and the man she was with. Machito came running down off the bandstand to help calm things down. Desi focused his anger on me. "Eres un maricón," he accused me. "You are making out with my woman." Several bouncers were ready to escort him out but Machito convinced them that Desi would be leaving on his own. I managed to get him to his limousine.

A few days later Machito told Tito about the altercation at the Chateau Madrid. "I know, I know," said Tito to Machito. "Joe dragged his ass out of there before someone busted him in the face. It would be funny, but that could be one of us."

"Yo no creo eso," Machito said pleasantly. "Hemos vistos muchas cosas, pero el señor Desi estaba un poco mas allá. You know – on his way to meet his maker, I guess. Coño, le dijo a Joe… He told Joe… que era un maricón. Que desgraciado."

Tito laughed. "I know, I know. But Joe told him to go fuck himself. That's what he would tell me."

I nodded in agreement.

Tito looked at his old friend, smiled. "I hope we get to the promise land in better shape." We smiled.

The death of Afro-Cuban music icon Frank "Machito" Grillo[153] in 1984, shocked everyone in and around the Latin music industry. It had a profound impact on Tito. Machito was waiting to go on stage at Ronny Scott's nightclub in London when he suffered a fatal heart attack. Tito was shaken to the core.

Ramón Rodríguez, who oversees the Boys Harbor program located on Fifth Avenue in El Barrio, contacted me in Florida where I was living with Nancy Castro – wife number three. I was stunned by the news of Machito's death. I went out and got drunk to help fight off my depression. Later that afternoon, Ralph Mercado called. "He (Tito) is in bad shape," he gasped over the telephone. "We don't know what to do. He is locked in his bedroom and will not talk to anyone."

I called Tito at his home. "Tito is locked in the room. He doesn't want to speak to anyone… We are concerned about him. He has never been this way before," Margie explained in an anxious voice. Tito's health was now a concern. She managed to connect me with Tito.

"Joe," I could barely hear him. "Macho is dead." He was incoherent. His breathing was irregular. We went back and forth for a few minutes.

Worried I shouted: "I'll be there as soon as I can." An hour later I was on a flight heading into New York.

Tito and I met outside of the Walter B. Cooke Funeral Home in the morning. There were dozens of black limousines parked in front of the funeral home. The pavement on 85th Street and Third Avenue was packed solid with people waiting to pay their last respects. Passersby could be heard commenting – it must be some gangland member. There were musicians, neighbors, politicians and government officials. It looked like a gathering of the United Nations membership – people from every ethnic group waited patiently to pay their respects to the Grillo family.

"I know him," someone commented walking down 85th Street. "It's Tito Puente. I heard Bill Murray talk about how he will 'be famous some day.'" The remark was made in the movie "Stripes" where Murray defends maintaining his Tito Puente record collection when his girlfriend starts complaining. Another passerby gasped: "Some big mobster must have just died." The funeral home was like this for three days. New York City Mayor Edward Koch was among the many who slipped in quietly.

Tony Ramone, the owner of Corso's Ballroom came over to us. Tito was still trembling, but he somehow managed to take a deep breath and regain some of his composure. Ramone embraced him. "You're the last one."

Tito pushed Ramone away and gave him a fiery gaze. Tito knew what he meant. Tito Rodríguez had died many years ago, and now Machito was gone. Tito was the last of the big three. He knew it and he understood it. Tito had been dealing with it since he learned his mentor had passed away. Tito took Margie by the hand. Ramone stepped aside. The limousines continued to line up on 84th Street. The crowd grew. Several ushers opened a path into the building for Tito, Margie and me.

We walked into the room. Tito broke down again. I had never seen him like this. He walked up to the coffin sobbing. He knelt before his friend. His hands reached into the coffin and he pulled Machito up. "Macho, Macho," Tito moaned. Margie, who was standing next to him leaned over and tried to console her husband. He pushed her off. He just cried.

"Tito, Tito," I said to him softly. I was standing on his other side. "Let him go. It's over. Machito is gone." I managed to get Tito to release his late friend. Finally Tito stood up. He wiped his eyes and face with a handkerchief

"I'm okay." He turned and went to pay our respects to the family. Tito was present during the three days of the wake.

A few doors down from the funeral home was an Irish pub. On each day of the viewing, from opening to closing in the wee hours of the morning the bar was packed with dozens of notable people in New York City, and other points. The list of musicians was long – starting with Machito's old friend Mario Bauzá. Others included Joe Cuba, Johnny Pacheco, Eddie Palmieri, Larry Harlow, José A. Fajardo, Vicentico Valdés and Louie Ramírez. There were dozens of musicians that had been influenced by Machito, worked with him, or just knew him, that came to pay their last respects. Everyone from Tito's band was present and Jimmy Frisaura was among those who remained for the three days of observance.

The most prominent leaders of El Barrio's various crime factions and civic groups and their representatives were present and accounted for. Spanish Raymond was a prominent figure, who along with several of the wiseguys from the Italian sector tried to out do one another in ordering rounds of drinks for those who gathered. The bar was packed solid – three and four deep and every table was occupied. The large entourage of Harlem's west side lords was not going to be out done either. If there was ill will among the many different gangs it was put on hold. Everyone was there to say goodbye to a wonderful man, Machito.

"It's hard to believe that he is gone," yelled Charlie Palmieri over the crowded bar. He was smoking, slugging the Scotches down like water. Charlie was standing in the crowded pub trying to have a conversation with a group of us.

Cuban vocalist Rudy Calzado and Fajardo were standing together, shoulder to shoulder looking at Charlie and Mario, who was puffing on a long dark Cuban cigar. "Hay muchos recuerdos buenos," The smoke filled the room and the noise was deafening.

"He helped me when I needed it," I shouted.

"Oye Conzo, él asistió a muchos," growled Mario. The sudden passing of Machito took it's toll on Mario. He puffed on his strong cigar. "Coño, estamos cayendo como palo. El otro día murió Willie (Bobo)."[154] Tito had been with Willie for a few hours during a West Coast engagement that took the jazz ensemble into the San Francisco area.

There was a murmur. Tito joined the gathering. "Spanish Raymond just paid for this round…" He looked around. He was calmer now. "Shit! The old guys are dropping," was his only reference to Willie's death.

Charlie smiled and changed the subject. "So now you have two Grammys," he said looking at Tito.

Tito won his second Grammy in 1984, for his recording *"Tito Puente*

On Broadway," that was released by Concord Picante Jazz in 1983. It was recorded with the Latin Jazz Ensemble and featured among others Jorge Dalto, piano; Jimmy Frisaura, trumpet and trombone; Alfredo de la Fe, violin; Bobby Rodríguez, bass; John "Dandy" Rodríguez, percussion, and Mario Rivera, soprano and tenor saxophone and flute. "It was okay," shrugged Tito. He had calmed down somewhat. "Joe says that I complain too much about the fucking Grammy awards."

"Son necesarios," laughed Fajardo.

"Coño que sí," yelled Mario. "Lo que pasa es que cuando teníamos las grandes orquestas nadie le importaba pinga..."

"Pero ahora están dándoles el reconocimiento," exclaimed Charlie.

"Oh bullshit," yelled Tito. He looked at me. "Joe, tell him how these things are awarded."

"By a lot of people all over the country. Most of the people know very little about our music, or who the fuck you are, and they don't give a shit."

Tito groaned. "Look how long it took your brother to get noticed," he said looking at Charlie. I still think you should have kicked his ass when he started with that boogaloo crap..." Laughter erupted.

"Oye Charlie, tu estas fumando mucho. Esas cosas matan," Mario growled as he puffed on his cigar.

Charlie blew smoke into the air. "Ese habano no es bueno para la salud tampoco."

Mario blew smoke into the already cloudy room. "Shit!! This is safe compared to what the people are huffing and sniffing around here. Have you been into the bathroom?"

Rudy Calzado laughed. "Una nube de polvo..." Everyone was laughing now.

Fajardo groaned at the comment. "Coño, chico no bromeé así... Tu sabes. Alguien oye esta conversación y se van a creer que..."

"Coño, Fajardo... como que tu eres un angel," Mario retorted.

Rudy added, "Somos todos angelitos."

"Shit!" laughed Mario.

Someone walked by. "Where is the bathroom?"

"He probably wants to get high," Tito said.

Long after the funeral home closed for the evening the hundreds of people that went to pay their respects to Machito remained in the pub. The stories, memories and recollections of Machito were told and retold by those of us who knew him, and with each retelling the story grew.

In 1978 the Machito Orchestra, the one led by Mario Grillo with his father Machito, was energized by renewed popularity, but as far as Tito was concerned his old rival, his mentor, his friend had burst open the European floodgates. The big band Afro-Cuban sound was in vogue. Machito and Mario had sort of reconciled their issues. Tito felt he had something to do with this. But Mario remained in semi-retirement. Tito shrugged and accepted that now it was called "salsa," but it was Machito and his Afro-Cubans that paved the way.

In 1980 the Grammy Award for the best Latin recording was given to Grupo Irakere. It irritated Tito to no end that a "Johnny come lately group with a lot of great musicians, of course, but with little or no vision, could win the Grammy." He would slide into a fuming irritable mood where every other word out of his mouth was a gross blasphemy, insensitive and in shockingly poor taste. Tito graciously accepted the Grammy Award for Machito in the Best Latin Recording category for *"Machito & His Salsa Big Band '82."* Right after that Tito and the band were off and running to gigs all over Europe.

He was somewhat calmed when he and Lionel Hampton connected. Hampton, a lifelong Republican Party follower, contacted Tito to invite him to one of the inaugural balls being held in honor of President Ronald Reagan. From that point on the Tito Puente Orchestra was one of the featured performers at presidential inaugural festivities. After Reagan left office the orchestra played for President George Bush Sr., and President William Clinton, twice. He never played for President George W. Bush.

Hampton and Tito had established their friendship during the heydays of the New York Palladium and Jazz Alley era. During a break while performing at the Palladium it was Tito's quiet habit to walk up to Birdland or one of the many clubs that featured the Hampton ensemble. He would sit quietly in the shadows and observe his childhood idol. The visits by Tito were not unnoticed. One night, just before closing Lionel Hampton invited Tito to sit in with him. Tito was not shy, at all. Lionel Hampton enjoyed walking up to the Palladium and on occasion would take a vibe solo. "Mongo, Willie and me just kept time. The band would sit back and listen to Lionel," Tito recalled. When he reminisced about it he could not recall if the patrons realized that Hampton occasionally sat in with the orchestra. "There were a lot of musicians that used to sit in – especially late at night, just before closing."

Sixty-year-old Tito was also busy with the jazz ensemble. The jazz ensemble won a second Grammy in 1983 for *"Tito Puente and the Latin Ensemble on Broadway."* The ensemble included experienced and diverse musicians. This was Tito's dilemma – how to mold "eccentric and individualistic performers to – follow the leader." Tito's music style and arrangement format, from his earliest days, had been dependent on his control. This was how he achieved the effect and impact he desired. "It was the Puente sound," according to his percussionist and music director Madera, "that he was not going to sacrifice his full-bodied style just to play jazz." Tito was glad to take the Grammy – it was recognition of his work. But he was not entirely satisfied with the effort, after all his first love was the big band.

The small jazz group recorded *"El Rey"* live at the Great American Music Hall in San Francisco in May 1984. The popular and controversial *"Oye Como Va"* was reworked and given a contemporary flavor that features Mario Rivera on flute and the exceptional piano styling of Jorge Dalto. Critics in the Latin media continued to harp on the similarity of *"Oye Como Va,"* to the Cachao" composition *"Chanchullo."* Tito shrugged it off. "The problem with most critics is they don't know a fucking thing about music. All you have to do is listen to the baseline. Montuno baselines are similar – not the same – similar. Arcaño's piano player, Jesús Lopez, developed a basic format. But everybody plays it different. It is a simple baseline montuno – nothing more and nothing less." The fact remains that Tito enjoyed reaping the financial residues of the popular tune. But it was not one of his favorite compositions. Tito recorded *"Chanchullo,"* in 1959 that featured Johnny Pacheco. His favorite version of the Cachao classic can be heard in an obscure Gema Records 45 R.P.M. release in which the Cuban bass player leads Antonio Arcaño's orchestra. The flute player is Eulogio Ortiz, who had an exotic style that Tito liked. Mario Rivera's flute embellishments are superb and modern. On side B of the 45 R.P.M. was *"El Que Sabe Sabe,"* composed by Ernesto Duarte. Tito included his version of this tune in *"Dance Mania 80's."*

What Tito considered unique about his controversial tune was that the harmonic articulation is created in the A-minor key. "What Tito did heed, as he had done early in his career," Madera reflected, "is intricately unite African black notes with European white notes. That was his mastery. *'Oye Como Va'* is a simple set of phrases that caught on." Tito commented on a number of occasions thathe could not understand the fuss over such a simple phrase that was the basic melody of the tune. Tito laughed when people realized that it was he who composed the tune, and not Carlos Santana, who made it a hit.

The classic *"Autumn Leaves"* (Jacques Prevert, Johnny Mercer and Joseph Kazma)) and the medley *"Stella By Starlight* (Ned Washington and Victor Young) */ Deliró* (Cesar Portillo de la Luz)*"* features Tito on vibe. He is relaxed and straightforward in his playing. "At this time in his career," according to Madera "he (Tito) really seemed to enjoy playing the soft and intricate melodies. He was more than just a percussionist. The other notable selections of the album are John Coltrane's *"Giant Steps,"* and *"Equinox."* These are strictly contemporary pieces and are used by Puente and the ensemble to experiment in an up-tempo beat with the Afro-Cuban clave embedded into the work. "Did it work?" Madera asked. "Some say it did, some say it was not very good. But what is for sure is that the Tito methodology and style of orchestra is evident – complete control."

"It was a suburb outing," re-enforced Madera, who had become a permanent fixture in the Puente organization. Actually, José said that of all the Concord sessions of the 1980s and 1990s, this may have been the best one. "There was a little of the old Tito, a little of the new and the ambience was just right. We all thought it would win something." Everyone expected that the album was a sure pick for the Grammy - number three for Tito – at the awards in 1984, but Eddie Palmieri was picked for his album *"Palo pa' Rumba."* We were all disappointed but Tito did call Eddie to congratulate him. Tito won the next year, in 1985, for the album: *"Mambo Diablo."* This endeavor won in the new Latin Tropical category. Special guest playing his own composition, "Lullaby of Birdland," is legendary British born pianist George Shearing.

Tito was among the many Latino musicians and entertainers of this period that lobbied extensively for a Latin jazz category, which was finally included for the 1993 Grammy Awards. During the period of his emersion into jazz Tito was doing a balancing act moving from his big band to the jazz ensemble and back again. He was comfortable in the jazz format, but among his concerns was making sure that his band did not disintegrate. His relationship with his musicians, especially those who had been with him for a long time began to change. "He trusted them more – Mario, Madera, Dandy and Bobby," according to Jimmy. "He had a contentious relationship with Sonny Bravo. To Tito the piano player was a "stuffed shirt who was always complaining about something, anything, but he could really play piano."

By the end of the 1980s José was his main go to guy for arrangements and keeping a handle on the management part of the Tito Puente Jazz Ensemble and Orchestra. One afternoon Tito admitted in his unique way that he was getting tired. But then he added unabashedly: "But I didn't say that and if you say something I'll kick your ass."

I shrugged and never said a word.

Soon after taking over the LP Jazz Ensemble, it was renamed the Tito Puente Latin Jazz Ensemble. But Tito was not about to close his lifelong love affair with the big band. Over a period of a just a few years the ensemble's sound would change considerably as did the personnel. Violinist Alfredo de la Fe was gone – to Colombia to avoid federal prosecution for drug problems. Jorge Dalto[155] left around 1983 to pursue other endeavors.

Shortly after Machito's death Tito and a small ensemble went out to Los Angeles, then back to New York and then on to Europe. The popularity of the orchestra even surprised Tito. The orchestra played in Spain, France, and Finland and blew into London for an engagement at Ronnie Scott's, where he opened his engagement by playing *"Mambo Adonis"* in memory of his mentor, Machito.

Through 1989 four more commercially successful Latin jazz albums or compact discs would be recorded: *"Sensación," "Un Poco Loco,"* which takes its name from the title song that features the orchestra and ensemble that is a combination of bop and Afro-Cuban harmonies. Bud Powell composed it. Incorporated into the recording session are West Coast musician Pete Escovedo (congas) and Rebecca Mauleon (synthesizer) on *"Prelude to a Kiss."* Juan Ceballos and John Santos join in on the chorus in a modern salsa selection titled: *"El Timbalon."* Once again Tito remembers Machito in the modern arrangement of *"Machito Forever."* The 1988 recording of *" Salsa Meets Jazz,"* features the extraordinary alto saxophonist Phil Woods.

In 1988 Tito once again had to deal with the death of a close friend and colleague. Tito was saddened by the death Joe Loco on March 7, 1988. They were childhood friends. The two of them were rivals for the pretty women in the neighborhood; they played pranks on each other and they played music together. It had been years since Joe gave in to the hustle and bustle of making a living in the competitive New York music market. "My music is dead," he told Tito and me one afternoon in San Juan a few months before his death. "I give you credit for hanging in there," he said talking directly to his old friend while we strolled down Ashford Avenue headed toward the La Concha Hotel. Joe was still the leader of a small lounge ensemble – piano, bass and light percussion. He had been at it for a number of years.

"You know something," Tito quipped, "at least you still get to play a real piano. All the clubs in New York now require us to bring toy pianos. I get a kick out of watching the old timers lugging a keyboard into the small area of a bandstand."

"You mean guys like Sonny," I added in.

"Shit, he's just one of a lot of guys," Tito laughed.

Joe joined in the laughter as we approached the hotel. "Look I'm something of a celebrity here – you know, a national treasure, so I'm told."

Tito started laughing loudly. "Shit Joe! Every time I see you I hear the same shit. The only treasure about you is that you had keen eyes for the babes. So you have retired?"

There was silence. "Not from music, shit, from chasing women…" They both laughed. We entered the club and stayed around to listen to Joe play the piano – all his old hits, his favorites, what Tito called "Latin jazz – the good stuff." We left about 3:00 a.m. Tito would not see Joe again.

A month after Joe Loco passed away, Charlie Palmieri suffered a heart attack. Tito kept in touch with his friend and was happy to see Charlie back on his feet by the time Tito left New York for a series of concerts and engagements in the Far East. Charlie was in good spirits the night we got together for dinner – nothing special – just to talk about "the old days," Tito said.

A few weeks later, on September 12, 1988, Charlie Palmieri suffered another heart attack. José Encarnación called me at work to tell me that Charlie had died. Once again I had to call Tito the bad news. He had been at Lionel Hampton's home in Harlem and had just left headed for Lord Jim's in midtown. Encarnación and I met up with Tito outside the restaurant. "The big guy is dead," I said hastily before the Spanish language media could reach him – there were several reporters waiting inside. Tito gazed at us. Ralph Mercado was walking up the street. Tito repeated my words softly. It was not a shock, but I knew Tito well enough to know that he was sad. The passing of his colleagues, peers and friends over the past few years, I believe, were taking a toll on him.

Several reporters gathered around Tito. He answered their questions and then looked at us. "Come on let's go. We walked down the street, Tito, Joe, Ralph and me. When he was far enough away from the inquisitive reporters he looked at me and then at Ralph. "Does anyone have some candy?" After a while we circled back to Lord Jim's and spent several hours reminiscing.

The following three days Tito and I sat with Eddie Palmieri and the Palmieri family at the Castle Hill Funeral Home. His friend was laid to rest at St. Raymond's Cemetery in the Bronx.

Tito garnered a fourth Grammy Award winner, *"Goza Mi Timbal"* that was recorded on Concord. But just before getting ready to record it, to travel to San Francisco for the session, Jimmy suffered a hemorrhagic stroke. It was July 1989. Tito was in Miami with the band.

Bob Sancho met Tito at the airport and explained to him what had happened to Jimmy. "Jimmy is down, but not out," Tito expressed to me the next morning. Bob explained that would require by-pass surgery. Jimmy had to recuperate for nearly two months before returning to work. But a few weeks after returning to work, he slumped over in his car and had to be rushed to a hospital. According to Bob, the Jimmy had suffered a blood clot in his brain that resulted in aphasia – the loss of motor skills. He would have to be retrained in all basic skills. The business leadership of the band was temporarily turned over to Dandy– it was not a job that he enjoyed. So Tito told Jack Hooke to help out Dandy, especially with payroll.

While recovering in the hospital Jimmy was paid a visit one afternoon - Tito and Bill Cosby. "Hey, hurry up and get better. You know he (Tito) can't live with out you," Cosby told Jimmy. "That made me feel good," Jimmy remembered.

"I'm going to California to do the recording." Tito was in a good mood. Jimmy was recovering and was expected to return to the band soon. Jimmy's absence from the band was taking a toll on Pops. He had to deal with the day-to-day operation of the band. It suddenly hit him just how important Jimmy Frisaura was. " Damn, Joe, these fucking guys are always complaining. There is always something that has to be done. Shit. I know he is a good trumpet man, but man he is a lot more, you know." I nodded in agreement. "You know Joe, I had a dream."

He was always having dreams. "Okay, what did you dream."

"That this recording is going to win a Grammy. I told Jimmy and he agreed with me. He was having trouble talking, but Sancho said that therapy would get him back to normal. I got José working on the arrangements. It will be terrific." Let me note that most all of Tito's dreams did not correctly predict future events.

Madera described that recording session as "turbulent, to say the least. The musicians –Bravo, piano; Sam Burtis, trombone; Mitch Frohman, soprano saxophone; Madera, percussion, Bobby Rodríguez, bass; Dandy, percussion and David "Piro" Rodríguez, trumpet were the regulars. To this core ensemble was added Mary Fettig, soprano saxophone, flute; Rebecca Mauleon, synthesizer and chorus; and, John Santos, chekere, bongos. "In a way, not surprising, it was an enlarged ensemble," Madera explained. "Tito loved the big sound. He never gave in to the ensemble although he was at his best in his approach to the vibes."

The musicians complained among themselves that "too many corners were cut," and "it was not vintage Puente." What is apparent is that Tito had become closer to his musicians. There was a comfort factor developed that had started during the previous five years. No one could really explain it or pinpoint it. "Maybe Tito was getting old and soft," Bobby Rodríguez told me. "Maybe it's because we're were all getting older. Whatever the reason the Puente efficiency is apparent in delivery, even if it was a commercial endeavor."

José concurred. "No matter what, we were going to make him sound good," he laughed. "We all had Jimmy on our minds." The recording was completed in two days and dedicated to Jimmy Frisaura.

The compact disc included a typical Tito menu of Latin jazz, pure Afro-Cuban selections and fusion. *"All Blues,"* composed by Miles Davis features a kaleidoscope of rhythm that does justice to the Davis fusion tune. Tito composed *"Ode to Cachao"* which features the heavy thumping bass lines, played by Bobby Rodríguez, that were the centerpiece of the mambo. *"Cha Cha Chá,"* composed by Chucho Valdés is subtle in its approach and *"Picadillo a lo Puente,"* is yet another approach to what has become a timeless classic. The group also tackles jazz classics such as *"Straight, No Chaser,"* (Thelonious Monk), and *"Pent Up House"* and *"Airegin"* (Nigeria backwards) composed by Sonny Rollins.

Tito was happy that the recording was successful. He had other fish to fry – Europe, the Far East were waiting for the Tito Puente style of Afro-Cuban music to stream in – delight, excite and provide pleasure. In 1991 Tito was 68-years-old. But there was still a lot to do.

Un Poco Loco

Bill Cosby's eyes were wide open. His eyeballs rolled around and around. He looked down at Tito who was striking the center of the larger timbal head with his left hand – actually using the index finger with controlled wrist action, marking time while striking the large cowbell using several driving variations of the four-beat mambo. Bill opened his mouth and gasped, "Wow!" He turned to his right. Arturo Sandoval was blowing a high F on his trumpet. Bill gasped again, "Wow!"

The Village Gate in New York City's Greenwich Village was jumping, and Tito and his jazz ensemble were at the center of it. The ensemble was playing one of those improvised melodies that professional musicians often put together on the spot – especially when the audience is in the mood. This night Bill jumped up on the small bandstand hugged Tito, hugged Sandoval and then hurriedly went to each of the musicians and clasped hands. He had been a long time fan of Tito Puente. Bill Cosby always made it a point to get to the Village Gate whenever Tito was playing there.

As Sandoval, the Cuban trumpet player and former member of Grupo Irakere, performed his horn cadences the well tuned percussion of the Tito Puente ensemble – José and Dandy - along with Tito kept sharp pace. As Sandoval hit his high F from the rear of the bandstand, another trumpet bellowed an E and then an F note. Sandoval looked back. He smiled. Bill Cosby issued another, "Wow!" Roberto "Piro" Rodríguez was giving Arturo Sandoval a run for his money.

For the next 15 minutes the tightly packed Village Gate vibrated with the venerable sounds of what Tito insisted was "Afro-Cuban jazz that had been played by me for a 100 years, or more." Tito was in an exceptional mood this night. Jimmy was back, albeit a little slower, but as rambunctious as ever and able to play. The West Coast trip had been a success, and as far as Tito was concerned, Italy had been conquered – musically speaking.

"The first time I met Tito," exclaimed Bill speaking at a crowded table in the overflowing lounge, "was when he came and knocked at my door."

Someone dared to ask: "Why did he come and knock on your door and where were you living?"

"Just like that he knocked on my door and when I opened it there he was – just standing there…" There was laughter and Bill never did answer the question. For that matter Tito was never clear how the two met.

"Bill is a big jazz music fan," was Tito's response. "He is one of those people who has made it and continues to push for those that are coming up from behind. That is a hell of a quality – not to forget your roots."

Up On The Strip

Tito's induction into the Hollywood Walk of Fame developed a life cycle of its own. Pops wanted this. He felt that it was a good thing for him especially at this juncture in his career. His name was synonymous with the music he had helped to shape and make popular throughout his long illustrious career. He guest starred on several television shows including The Cosby Show, and The Simpsons. In 1990, Tito was awarded the "James Smithson Bicentennial Medal." The body of work produced by him continued to grow. At this point in his life there was no real musical competition.

Tito's close circle of friends was diminishing. Charlie Palmieri had passed away – Tito requested that a portion of funds collected by the Tito Puente Scholarship Fund be set aside and used to assist rising Latino musicians who specialized in the piano; Machito was gone – salsa was popular but the sophistication produced by the big bands had virtually disappeared. Tito did not compose music – not much anyway and he religated most of the arranging to his musical director. Tito and the band was still in much demand but he had come to realize that the atmosphere and ambiance of the 1990s – for that matter of the future was much different.

The release of *"Tito Puente Presents Millie P"* on the RMM label that was owned by Ralph Mercado was typical of the period. Millie Puente, according to Tito was his niece on some days and on other days his cousin. No one was sure if they were even related. "She was something," Jimmy liked to instigate. Millie Puente was an attractive woman who was described as a vocalist and played percussion. The album was with the big band. Needless to say the recording went nowhere. There were two noteworthy selections on the CD: a ballad, *" Si Usted Me Quiere"* that was composed by Dionrah Riva, in which Millie P sings and Tito lifts the song with his brief vibe improvisation, and a contemporary mambo, *"Tito and Millie"* composed by Tito that features a percusive give and take by the two artists. For the most part the CD was panned.

A few months after the release Ralph asked Millie to fill in for an ailing Celia Cruz at a New York concert. She refused. "I don't fill in for anyone," she told Ralph who relayed the message to Tito. She quickly faded from the New York salsa scene. Tito did not seem disappointed, he was concentrating on getting his star in Hollywood. He did mention to Ralph that he should push a little harder on the recently released recording. Ralph ignored his request. When I asked Tito about it he shrugged and said that the album was not that bad.

"Most people in the business feel it was a piece of crap."

Strange, I thought he did not argue. "So maybe it was not a terrific album, so what. Bullshit."

I responded: "Maybe it is a little too fast…"

"What does Ralph know about music. Everything is fast now. That's the way you have to play. I may be the only romantic left in the Latin music field – you know someone who is concerned with the totality of the song, the delivery, the efficiency of a certain feeling. All the young people want now is fast, faster and fastest," he reflected one afternoon as we prepared for the ceremony in Los Angeles. He continued to record but his detractors, musical purists and aficionados maintained that his best work was behind him. But he shrugged them off.

In order to get a star on the Hollywood Walk of Fame, the interested entertainer must agree to attend a presentation ceremony within five years of selection, and pay a $5,000 fee to the Trust for costs such as security at the star ceremony[156]. Although a lot of people claim controversy and mystery regarding the way the stars are nominated and approved, the nomination process is very straight forward. An application is necessary to be submitted during the nomination process before the annual Hollywood Walk of Fame selection meetings in June every year. Anyone can nominate a talent with their permission in writing. Tito paid most the front money but managed to convince Ralph Mercado that it was in the best interest of all that RMM and Ralph foot the majority of the investment for the Walk of Fame star. At first Ralph balked but Tito was convincing.

Getting Tito what he wanted was a lengthy process. A committee was organized that included Los Angeles Disc Jockey Carmen Rosario, Actor Dennis Cole, Steven Loza (Tito Puente and the Making of Latin Music, 1999), and Josephine Powell (When the Drums are Dreaming, 2007). It was my job to supply the information, letters from New York Mayor David Dinkins, Governor Mario Cuomo, and Bill Cosby, and to make sure the documents were properly dated and correct. The day the announcement was made Tito and the ensemble were performing at the Playboy Jazz Festival at the Hollywood Bowl – it was a brief excursion to the West Coast. On stage with him was Miles Davis and Doc Severinson – a participant in Tito's 1950s recordings, along with Joe Williams. Bill Cosby made the announcement at the packed outdoor theater. We were all excited.

It was a busy several weeks leading up to the ceremony. There were several groups associated with the nomination, and at times, things got a little confusing. There were luncheons, cocktail parties, late night parties and impromptu parties where people just gathered to eat, drink and be merry. Tito did not know most of the people but he indulged himself in the frolicking and merrymaking without hesitation.

One morning we found ourselves in Tito's suite with a group of people that Tito started out by describing "rather cool and standoffish." The guests were invited by Josie Powell. Tito was gracious but bored. "You know most of these people are Born Again Christians," he whispered to me.

"Oh shit!" I stared at him intently. "So! I'm going to go into the other room with my candy."

Tito laughed. "Watch! Does anybody want blow?"

"Can I join you," one of the guests said without any hesitation – none whatsoever.

A moment later there was a chorus of people that wanted to join me and Tito. I was a little surprised. So was Tito. "Hey," one of Josie Powell's friends said, "Once in a while is not bad, if you get my drift."

Tito was wrapped in wild laughter. "So much for abstenance," he laughed.

Among those who attended the ceremony was Celia Cruz, who already had her star on the famous walk. Tito's family went west –Margie, Audrey Puente, Tito, Jr., as well as Ronnie's wife with the grandchildren, Janeen and Julianne. The big band was gathered up and when Ralph realized he was paying for it he called me to complain. "I'll be glad to tell Tito that you don't want to pay for this."

"That's not what I said. I just think that the expense… Well, you know."

"Yeah."

I could sense Ralph was sweating. "Okay, okay… But look I hope Tito is not thinking of moving to the fucking West Coast."

"Where did you get that stupid idea."

"Me and Jack (Hooke) were talking and I told him Tito is not available for local concerts."

"What did Jack say?"

Ralph responded. "Like you, that I'm nuts. But look at the cost of this fucking Star of whatever shit."

I wanted to laugh. Ralph was squirming again. He had to dish out money. "Look I will tell Tito."

"No, no," Ralph hung up. A few minutes later Tito arrived at my room. I told him, in detail about my conversation with Ralph.

"What is he doing, losing his fucking mind. Live out here. He is nuts. He's just worried that he is spending a lot of money – good for him. By the way where is he?" Tito did not wait for a response. He turned to leave and as the door closed he said, "I'll find him in the lobby or lounge. I need some cash." I could hear Tito laughing as he left my room. Mercado hated to part with his money. He was late with payments, his checks bounced, and he had a hundred excuses for hanging you out to dry, but he always had a wad of cash and because Tito was always up to mischief, Ralph was good to have around.

"He is not a musician. He doesn't know jack shit about music. But he knows how to stage big shows and he always has cash," is how Tito explained it.

Rita Moreno[157] was one of the many guests at his induction. Rita tossed back her head and laughed when I asked her why she did not have a star.

The winner of an Oscar, a Tony Award and an Emmy, stopped laughing. "It is a fabulous honor for Tito. He wanted it. But I'm not sure that the cost of it is worth it. I mean if they want to honor me then they should pay for it." Rita has always been outspoken about the organization of the Hollywood Walk of Fame.

Tito entered the cluster of people in the lobby. He placed an arm around Rita's shoulder. "Is she complaining about this again?" he laughed.

Actor/comedian Frank Gorshin,[158] who was in the hotel, joined the group. "Hey can I get my picture taken with the King?" he said laughingly.

"Anytime," quipped Tito.

"Wow!" said the Brooklyn born entertainer. "A Jew surrounded by Puerto Ricans and in of all places California. This is big." Everyone laughed.

It was not one of the best-organized events but in the end Tito got his star near the Chinese Theater. He was surrounded by hundreds of well wishers- famous and not so famous. He was a little tipsy – the excitement, attending parties, drinking. But when it came time to play on cue he climbed onto the bandstand. Fittingly the orchestra played Marcelino Guerra's popular *"Pare Cochero."*

The Mambo Kings

"It was the best of times. It was the worst of times…" Jimmy moaned one afternoon a few weeks after the filming of the movie *"The Mambo Kings – Play Songs of Love"* was completed and we had returned to New York. He really looked good and his recovery was proceeding rapidly. He laughed, "There are more stories that could be told about making the movie than I could ever imagine. The stories about you being a very bad boy are things legends are made of."

Tito barked, "Fuck you Jimmy Frisaura." Then he laughed. Tito looked at him. "Hey, if I used the amount of candy people claim I do, I'd be a white ghost. If I had as many women as all of you think I had in California…"

Jimmy laughed. "Shit California. What about… Well you know."

"Fuck you again. If I had affairs with half the women you guys think I had I would be enshrined in some fucking sex palace surrounded by all virgins. And, if I drank as much as all of you think I do…"

"Bullshit!" Jimmy said as we gathered at Lord Jim's. "I'm told that you behaved like a wild man." Jimmy looked at me and with a smile added, "Actually he was untamed and set the movie industry back a hundred years."

"Kiss my ass Frisaura," Tito exclaimed with gusto.

"But hey, I don't know. This is what the guys tell me."

Tito frowned. "Kiss my ass. I see you are feeling better," he laughed. "Joe was there. Tell him how I helped make that movie great. It should have been filmed here, in New York. Man what shitty dancers!"

I responded, "Oh yeah! These dancers were pretty bad – you can't imitate the New York style."

"I hear you were in all sorts of trouble too, Joe," laughed Jimmy.

"Oh, kiss my ass. Tito was the star."

Jimmy smiled. "It doesn't matter, you two cover for each other. But I know Tito is the real wild one, always on the prowl."

"Fuck you," grunted Tito. "Joe is right. They do dance funny out there."

The filming of the movie was memorable and the stories Jimmy heard were pretty much true and not exaggerated as Tito claimed. Arnold Glimcher was the executive director and producer. He was a New York art dealer who managed the Pace Gallery in upper Manhattan. He was known in the art world as a vendor of art works by painters like Picasso,

Julian Schnabel and others. Glimcher was among those present at the gala party a few weeks earlier when Tito got his Hollywood Star. His efforts to work out a deal to film his movie in New York City were a dismal failure. He convinced Tito to play himself in the film. He failed to get Cuban born actor Andy García, but was able to recruit Armand Assante, an actor from Cornwall, New York. Glimcher convinced Spanish actor Antonio Banderas to appear in his first major American motion picture. He was unable to control Tito, and his choreographer Michael Peters, to figure out just how the root of Afro-Cuban dance music – clave – fits into four beats to the bar.

Even though his hair was white, Tito played himself and thoroughly enjoyed reliving those great Palladium memories but he was always of the opinion that the film would have been more successful if it was filmed on the East Coast. "The kind of dancers he (Glimcher) was looking for are all over the place in New York. I'm not putting the West Coast down, but let's face it – the real mambo comes from Cuba, and then New York."

Celia Cruz tried to resolve a discussion among the extras one day when she informed the debaters – a group of extras from the two sides of the country. "Pérez Prado invented the mambo," she said.

"Is she losing her mind," Tito panted when he heard about her attempt to be informative. "Pérez Prado did not invent shit. Augh!" He dashed across the set. He was growling talking in a loud voice. "Jesus Christ everyone knows that it was Arcaño that did the fucking inventing – the López boys. It was Aresenio who did the inventing. They are the ones that did all the fucking work not that jerk. Shit, he couldn't even play at the Palladium." He kept walking straight off the set. I don't know if he ever found Celia, or if she even heard about his outburst.

Tito managed somehow to convince Glimcher to use as much talent from the East Coast as possible. Among those that appear in the movie is Desi Arnaz, Jr., who plays his father and uses clips from the original "I Love Lucy" television show, Johnny Pacheco was recruited to help with the music selection. José "El Canario" Alberto, who is cast in the role of Cuban icon Beny Moré, and Frank Grillo, who portrays his father, Machito, were among those that represented New York. Pacheco and Tito had gone their separate ways since the 1960s. Tito was still stewing over his participation with Masucci and the Fañia Record Company. It was common knowledge in the industry that Masucci and Pacheco had attempted to push Tito into extinction during the 1960s and early 1970s – they failed.

One thing that Tito credited Pacheco with was his ability to make "Celia Cruz a successful, super star singer." Tito was never able to push Celia's style of singing with his big band. None of many dozen recorded attempts where Tito and Celia teamed up had been really successful. "Celia can belt out a song. She is in her environment in a small band – a conjunto with trumpets and percussion. Not every diva can sing in a big band environment. Pacheco was able to give her the room within his conjunto framework."

The Grand Ballroom at the Ambassador Hotel, a famous West Coast location, was converted into the New York Palladium. Tito did not think that the set captured the essence or atmosphere of the dancehall in Midtown Manhattan, neither did Glimcher. It became more apparent as the filming evolved. Tito's take: The music was too fast, the dancers danced out of clave, and the feeling of the historic moments that were being recreated was not there."

The movie *The Mambo Kings Sing the Songs of Love,* an adaptation of Oscar Hijuelos' Pulitzer Prize-winning novel, is the story of two brothers who leave Cuba and settle in New York to seek fame and fortune. During one of the filming sequences, Tito and the band are playing a torrid version of *"Pa' Los Rumberos"* that also features Armand Assante dueling on timbales with Tito. The dance floor is packed. I am about to have my big scene. I'm supposed to kill someone in the middle of the dancehall. Tito and Armand are going at it. Everything is building up.

My big scene is about to emerge. The crescendo is escalating. My girlfriend in the scene was Millie Puente. Carlos Gomez, the actor, came over to her and we start arguing – I'm defending her honor. We argue. The break in the scorching mambo is coming. Gomez whips out a knife. I pull out a gun. I am waiting to hear Tito and his percussion unit do the "bang, bang, bang," in the syncopated offbeat Cuban percussive style.

Suddenly there is a shriek. "Stop, stop," yells Tito at the top of his lungs to everyone's surprise. The music stops abruptly. The dancers stop and there is a look of dismay on most – even I was stunned. There is a look of alarm in the filled room. Glimcher has a look of shock. "What is the matter?" he stammers.

"Están fuera de clave. The dancers are not dancing to clave – they are out of time."

"What the fuck is clave?" he says.

An example of what Tito was talking about

Tito walked to Glimcher. “Look I’m sorry but everybody is out of step.”

The problem is the majority of the extras – the dancers – were not familiar with the Afro-Cuban 3-2 count within the four-beat, the essential ingredient of Latin music. For the next hour choreographer Michael Peters worked with the dancers. It seemed a lot easier to work in dance patterns and sequence for Michael Jackson and those dancers that worked in his 1980s award winning *“Thriller.”* On the set he could be heard screaming: “What the fuck is clave? Does anybody here know about it?” Tito attempted to explain. Peters listened intently. He then began to redo the dance number.

Over and over they attempted to fit the dance patterns, the moves, the steps into the mambo. It was a dismal failure each time. The scene was attempted a dozen times, maybe more.

“Watch Dandy’s wife, Dolores dance with Ralph Garay,” suggested Tito to the director. Garay was Tito’s friend and driver when he visited California. Garay was a New York bred Puerto Rican, and a pretty good dancer. When he was not dancing he drove Tito around Los Angeles. Peters and Glimcher watched, made adjustments, changes and tried just about everything they could think of. Nothing worked.

Eventually on the 15th attempt, Peters came up with the solution. In the movie the scorching musical dance scene culminates in a conga line – similar to those seen in the 1930s, that did not require cohesive moves and tight dance sequences required for the mambo. I finally got to defend Millie’s honor. Later, Tito apologized for throwing the shooting schedule off. In fact, on several occasions Tito and I, and several of the musicians who remembered what the real Palladium Ballroom was like tried to explain to producers “This sort of thing – killing someone - could never happen at the New York Palladium.”

Tito exclaimed to Glimcher: “Look if anybody ever tried a stupid stunt like this one – I mean killing someone, the bouncers would be on you in a second and you would find your mauled body being shoved out a back door and then you would be tossed head first down the stairs and out the door.” Glimcher shrugged. “Ask Joe, or anybody from New York.”

At this point Tito stared at a few of the musicians that were there and me. He shrugged and started to walk away. “I wish we were at the Palladium now. This really sucks.” He walked away.

Glimcher said to me: “But this is Hollywood.”

Another humorous episode that occurred during the filming of the movie involved Armand Assante. He is of Irish/Italian decent and a native of Cornwall, New York. He had been a fan of Tito’s since he could remember. He enjoys playing trap drums so it was assumed that learning to play basic timbal rhythms would not be overly difficult.

"Fuck this shit," he howled one night, throwing two sticks into the air. He screamed at Glimcher during the rehearsal in a house that was being used during the filming of the movie. According to Dandy, the actor was so frustrated with the tempos that were required that he just blew his stack. "It was one of those things that surprised the shit out of everyone," he recounted.

A few days after the incident Assante came over to Tito and me while we were on the set. "I just want to apologize for my frustration," he said sheepishly.

"Hey, don't worry about it. Tito has been playing forever and even he makes mistakes," I said.

"Bullshit!" Tito bellowed.

Everyone laughed – nothing like levity to ease tension.

There were no academy awards for any of the actors and Tito's behavior at times was well beyond mischievous, but we had a blast.

It was about this time that we started gathering at Willie's Steakhouse on Westchester Avenue in the Bronx. The restaurant had been in several locations along the long avenue. Kenny Giordano is well known and an enterprising businessman. Willie's was host to many of the top local Latino and Cuban celebrities and musicians. This became one of Tito's favorite hangouts. Among the many notable musicians who visited the establishment were Bill Cosby, Al Pacino, Judge Edwin Torres, Sandra Santiago (Miami Vice), Armand Assante and Marc Anthony. The musicians' list is also formidable. It includes Eddie Palmieri, Chucho Valdés, Joaquin Oliveros, Johnny Pacheco, Jimmy Sabater, José A. Fajardo, and Chocolate Armenteros. Tito participated in many of the jam sessions that lasted well into the morning – they are memorable.

When Willie moved to 1832 Westchester Avenue in 2000, Kenny asked Tito play at the grand opening. On the guest list was Bill Cosby and Celia Cruz.

Mixing With The Stars

In his wildest dreams Tito never imagined that he would be a guest performer – or even a distinguished guest – playing his music for the world's most famous puppets on Sesame Street.[159] Yet here he was. "One, two…"

"Wait, wait who are you?" posed an angry puppet, Oscar the Grouch.

Tito lowered his hands. "My name is Tito Puente."

"Well I was about to start a meeting here," he says. "So I suggest you and your band go play somewhere else."

Tito responded: "Hey don't you like my music?'

"Well, is your music lively?" Oscar inquires. The other puppets cheer for Oscar. The children on the set are quiet. This is building into a major confrontation between Tito and Oscar (all part of the script, of course). "And, does it have a nice catchy rhythm that people love to dance to?"

"It sure does," Tito answered with a wide smile.

The puppets are dismayed. "Well we don't like," growls Oscar.

"Wait a minute," Pops pleads. "I have a feeling we can even get grouches like you to like my music and dance to it."

Oscar dares Tito, who grabs up his sticks. "Arriba muchachos." His sticks click together and for the next several minutes the band, the puppets and Tito blast away with the classic *"Ran Kan Kan."* Oscar the Grouch is totally into it.

Tito appeared as a guest on the popular children's show on numerous occasions. He also appeared on "The Simpsons" where he portrays himself in the episode "Who Shot Mr. Burns?" It was televised in 1995.

Just before a tour to Spain and several other European countries in 1992, Tito appeared with Bill Cosby on the David Letterman Show. Both Cosby and Tito show their agility by climbing up a ladder to the second tier of the Ed Sullivan Theater. A few weeks before this appearance I received a call from a Bill Cosby agent to see if Tito would be interested in making a commercial for Coca Cola. I asked Tito if he would do it and he was happy to help out, and of course work with Bill.

We got into one of our back and forth verbal battles soon after the "Did you feel it?" commercial was released. Tito got a check for $10,000 and wanted to give his manager and agent Mercado a 15 percent commission. Jimmy was agitated. I can't remember when he was so annoyed. "Will you try to reason with your pal," Jimmy groaned one afternoon when we were in Lord Jim's. "He is being a shit head."

I sat down at the table. "Don't tell me what I should do," shouted Tito to Jimmy. "Ralph should get a commission."

"For what?" I asked. "He had nothing to do with the Coca Cola commercial."

Tito was firm. "He is the agent."

"He is a shit head. His boy Jack Hooke almost lost you a gig because he wanted $30,000 for you to appear with the band. You had to intercede or the band would have lost the job. I got the call from Bill Cosby's agent about this commercial. Ralph did not do jack shit." Hooke was a former partner of Tito's friend Morris Levy. He ventured into the rock n' roll realm with Alan Freed in the 1950s. Jack Hooke also was Mongo Santamaría's manager. He eventually teamed up with Mercado, who told him to handle the Tito Puente account. He was a tough negotiator and even battled with Mercado over money that was due me for my editorial work on *"Live at Birdland,"* and *"Mambo Birdland."*

Tito did not like to get brow beaten. He leaned back. He pushed the table away, knocking over a few glasses. Some of the patrons looked up. "I'm telling you both it is my decision. Fuck you both."

Ralph Mercado was in the throws of some business problems. His reputation for paying his performers on time was at best questionable, and when he did issue a check the joke was – "get it to the bank, and fast, and then pray." Several of his clients, many of them the vocalists from Fañia were abandoning his representation. Celia Cruz had signed with Sony. I guess Tito was just trying to be loyal – he was pigheaded that way. "Maybe we should wait until the check he sent you clears the bank," I said trying to soothe a situation that was getting out of hand.

Robert Sancho, the music enthusiast, community activist and businessman, confirmed Mercado's financial woes. Sancho was a long time friend of Tito, and while a member of the Tito Puente Scholarship Fund Board of Directors, recalls how the musicians complained about Ralph's bad paying habits. "He was a tremendous negotiator and he was always looking for new venues to expose the talent he had in his stable. But he overextended his organization. He was known as 'mala paga.'"

Jimmy was gazing straight at him. "You know he bounces checks like rubber. You want to make sure the boys are paid."

Tito relaxed. He crossed his arms. There was a faint smile. "Well, I know that if he bounces a check you will take care of it," Tito said looking straight at Jimmy.

"So we wait," I said.

"Okay, okay, we wait. Ralph would look funny in a wheelchair." We laughed. As it turned out Tito did not fork over any commission to Mercado. Jimmy did not have Ralph injured when several checks bounced, including one for the Tito Puente Scholarship Fund. Tito had to get on the telephone and remind Ralph that the funds were for a good cause, for the young people who aspired to be performers, Tito was eloquent and sincere

– Ralph eventually made good on the bounced check. It was always that way with Mercado.

Tito knew that Celia Cruz was angry with him. But before getting on the flight to Madrid in 1994, he had already made up his mind. If she wanted to stay in a different hotel, then so be it. Tito recalled that on the flight over to Madrid, Celia sat by his side for a little while. "I was listening to her and really she was bugging the shit out of me. But you would be proud of me, Joe. I kept quiet."

Celia said to him that she would not be staying at the same hotel as the rest of the group because she had learned that there were Cuban musicians "from Cuba" that were staying there. For nearly an hour she complained about Fidel Castro, about the Cuban communists, about everything that was wrong with Cuba. Tito listened attentively, but managed not to show his disinterest. He had heard it all before. He was already half bombed anyway. Through her rampaging epitaph he nodded politely and sipped whatever alcoholic beverage the flight attendant served him.

Finally, he announced to the ordained diva of salsa music "I am playing with the band and you will be singing with the band. When we finish I am going to hang out with the musicians from Cuba. If they are jamming, and if they invite me, I am going to play with them. And, I don't really care if you are a registered Republican, or whatever party member. That is your business."

After a concert performance Tito joined up with the members of Orquesta Aragón and Los Papines. He did not tell them about his confrontation on the flight from New York to Madrid. He remembered that years ago Celia had to be taken out one door because Richard Egües and other members of the famous Cuban charanga were joining him in a club in New York. Interestingly enough, Rafael Lay, Jr. the director and violinist - son of one of the founding members of the famous orchestra - always had kind words for Celia and for the many Cuban entertainers that were living abroad – no matter what reason they had for departing Cuba.

When the Fidel Castro regime closed entry into Cuba and the United States initiated its embargo, Tito decided he would not travel to Cuba. This was a decision based on appeasing the Cuban exiles, most of who lived in the Miami area. However, he also was determined not to forsake his cherished pastime of jamming with Cuban musicians no matter where he ran into them. He stood by his conviction.

A few days later the orchestra was bound for Venice, Italy. The flight was delayed, and for a while it looked like Tito and his men were not going to arrive in time to perform at a scheduled sold out concert. It was a tired, physically drained, stressed out collection of musicians who climbed on the huge stage in an auditorium filled with screaming fanatical enthusiasts, Madera acknowledged.

Tito laughed when he remembered the occasion. "We were delayed coming out of Madrid so we partied – you know – no holds barred. Then we went to the airport and had to wait so we partied more. Shit it was scary when we got to that big fucking auditorium in Venice."

Despite the harried appearances the issue was settled on the first note. Lifting his sticks in his usual manner Tito smacked them together and counted: "One, two, three…" The sound of the trumpets blared, the saxophones filled in along the lower register and the trombones erupted. The percussion was precise and strong. *"Mambo Adonis,"* was re-titled, *"Machito Forever,"* a tribute to his mentor Machito, and the audience was awestruck. The Tito Puente Orchestra assembled on the bandstand with shirts hanging out, ties undone, jackets wrinkled and some sporting a 5:00 o'clock shadow, but if they looked tired, they did not sound tired. By the time the concert ended the people were standing on their seats, dancing in the isles. "I don't remember seeing something so wild and wonderful as that," recalled Dandy. The men played their hearts out for Tito and he knew it.

Chucho Valdés was a big fellow. Tito had met his father in the 1950s when he visited Cuba. In fact Tito had met Bebo Valdés several times, according to the stories told by Vicentico and Miguelito. Bebo, in Tito's view, had formidable arranging skills and a distinctive manner in handling the big band sound. Since he was not an admirer of the once popular Cuban ensemble Irakere, Tito did not delve into such details as who were its members. When Tito heard him playing piano on one of his many albums he let it be known that the next time Chucho Valdés was in town he would he would like to meet him.

Out of the blue one afternoon as we crawled up the FDR Drive, Tito broached the subject of the 6"4" pianist. "I don't care about Irakere," he told me. "But this guy is good." Arturo Sandoval, he knew was an incredible horn man. He met him and they had jammed at the Village Gate. Paquito D'Rivera was a terrific jazzman. Paquito's specialty was the soprano saxophone.

"Well, we can do that if you make a U turn and we head back to the city." By this time we were on the Palisades Parkway, heading to his home in Tappan. I was being sarcastic, of course.

"Don't give me any of your shit," he laughed. "I would like to meet this guy."

Sancho made the initial connection in the summer of 1995. As fate would have it, his call came to the Tito Puente Restaurant where several Venezuelan newsmen were interviewing Tito and Celia Cruz about the new movie *"Yo Soy El Son Cubano"* that had been produced by Ralph Mercado. The interview in the recently opened eatery was going well. Tito opened the restaurant in partnership with the owners of the Shrimp Box and several other popular City Island restaurants. The ambiance of the restaurant was strictly Latino and the eye catcher was the wall-to-wall mural of the Afro-Cuban music greats – Machito, Mario, Tito Rodríguez and many others. Celia was in a good mood. Tito was talkative. Ralph sat quietly as the gentlemen from Venezuela asked their questions.

A waiter informed that there was a telephone call for me. "Hello," I said. It was Sancho.

"We're are on our way over to City Island. Chucho is with me."

"Shit!" I gasped. "Celia is ..."

"Well, maybe you should get rid of her... I'm kidding," Sancho teased.

I told Bob that I would page him once I spoke to Ralph and Tito (there were no cell phones). I walked and pulled Ralph away. "Bob Sancho and Chucho Valdés are on their way here. You know..."

Before I finished a shocked Ralph wheezed: "Shit!"

"Cut the interview short. Do something. You know how Celia hates Cubans from Cuba." Even as I uttered the phrase it sounded stupid. But we all knew how she felt and none of use wanted to upset her or hurt her feelings.

Ralph was a little nervous. "How the fuck do I tell her to leave?" He was muttering to himself.

"Whatever you do you better be fast and you better be cool." I picked up the telephone and paged Sancho. I stood by the telephone. A few minutes later it rang. "Sancho, I told Ralph to get Celia out of here. I'll call you when the coast is clear."

"You better hurry," he said. "We're not too far away – Pelham Parkway."

Ralph managed to have the Venezuelan journalists speed up their questions, he whispered to Tito what was happening and then he flat out lied: "Celia I think your transportation is ready to take you back to Manhattan." He said it with a straight face, in perfect Spanish and in a soft casual tone. His brow was moist. Tito looked at him. I could tell that Pops was enjoying watching Ralph squirm. Finally, Celia and Tito hugged one another and Ralph quickly escorted her out the side door because I told him that Sancho and Chucho were just pulling into the parking lot.

"What a pain in the ass," I gasped as Celia, Ralph and the two Venezuelans departed through the side entrance.

Tito started laughing. "Hey that is who she is. She is a great lady. But she has a bug up her ass about Cubans that live in Cuba." He closed his eyes and shrugged. As the door closed on one side of the room the front door of the restaurant opened and in walked Sancho with Chucho. He had a big grin. Tito and him embraced.

"¿Donde esta Celia?" he asked in a gentle tone.

Surprised Tito said: "Ella acaba de salir." Then he looked at Chucho and realized that he, the big piano player, was pulling his leg. "Shit!" We all laughed. The two musicians talked for hours and late, before closing, they improvised Afro-Cuban jazz – Tito switching from the vibes to the timbales, and Chucho easily mastering spontaneous piano ostinatos to go along with the subdued mood – it was as if they had been matched before. They felt comfortable playing together, talking and reminiscing.

The next night Tito, Chucho and Carlos Emilio, a guitarist, another veteran of Grupo Irakere, met up and entertained the patrons of the Tito Puente Restaurant.

A few months later Tito and his ensemble were in France. Chucho joined the ensemble for several improvised jams that dazzled the French public. They teamed up again several more times through the 1990s.

Tito told me a few days later that he had talked to Ralph and that Celia did not have any idea what was going on that afternoon. Tito laughed: "He told me, 'I don't know how she did not know what we were doing, pushing her out one door so that this Chucho guy could walk in. Shit, that was really stupid – grown ups acting like a bunch of idiots.'"

Tito's recordings and music catalogue continued to grow. He was traveling around the world playing his music – a mixture of contemporary Latin Jazz, big band Afro-Cuban music, and even salsa to young and old audiences. "This is a salsa tune," he would announce. But we have been playing it for a hundred years," he would announce. What followed was one of his hundreds of classics, followed by another, and another. He was no longer concerned that his composition, *"Oye Como Va,"* was not attributed to him. "I get the royalties," he informed the surprised public.

But there were ominous signs that he was getting tired. He walked a little slower. Margie started to accompany him on his overseas trips around 1997. She could do this now because the children – Audrey and

Tito Jr. – were grown up. He was still rambunctious, mischievous and his eye for good-looking women did not fade. But when she was with him he was straight as an arrow. He still liked to party and enjoyed playing childish pranks on the band. Tito even got me one night when the ensemble appeared with the Hollywood Bowl orchestra – he piled about two feet of ice at my door, had someone call me so when I opened the door I found myself knee deep in slush. When he saw me the next morning he asked how I was. He knew I was pissed, but he would not admit he was behind the prank.

Physically he just moved slower. But the work schedule did not diminish. From California the ensemble traveled to Japan and then back to San Francisco. Venezuela was a frequent stop as was the Dominican Republic and Panama. In between these excursions there were recording sessions.

The jazz ensemble and the band were recording an average of two albums per year through the 1990s – *"The Mambo King"* on the RMM label was his heralded album number 100 and was released in 1992. It was followed by *"Out of This World,"* (Concord Picante), 1992; *"Mambo of the Times,"* (Concord Picante), 1992, *"Live at The Village Gate,"* (RMM), 1992; *"Royal T,"* (Concord Picante), 1993; *"Master Timbalero,"* (Concord Picante), 1994; and *"In Session,"* (Concord Picante), 1994.

In 1996 President Bill Clinton was reelected and in October 1997, Tito was invited to the White House to be presented with the "Medal of Honor and Lifetime Achievement Award." As Tito and Sancho waited on line to meet and greet President Clinton and First Lady Hillary Clinton, Tito turned to Sancho and said: "Does he know who I am?"

Sancho recalled that the President stopped briefly to chat with each of the guests in the line. When he reached us he extended his hand. Tito and the President clasped hands firmly. "Hi, my name is Tito Puente."

The President smiled. "Tito! I know who you are. I have listened to your music for a long time. It is really nice to finally meet you." Sancho recalled that for a brief moment Tito was stunned. But he quickly gathered his composure.

"It is a pleasure to meet you and the First Lady," responded Tito with a wide sincere smile, according to Bob. At this ceremony Tito donated the timbales that he used at the 1996 Summer Olympics to be displayed with the collection of cultural history.

There was little room on the bandstand. The brass section had very little elbowroom behind their music stands, and six-foot five-inch piano player

Sonny Bravo[160] (who grew up in Miami) sat hunched over an electronic keyboard instead of a real piano. The musicians looked exhausted. Tito and the orchestra flew into Miami from Berlin, Germany a few hours before and dashed over to the Yuca Restaurant on Lincoln Road. The tiny nightclub was on the second floor and it was packed with patrons and news media eagerly awaiting Tito and his band. The event had been booked by Jack Hooke as a party to release *"Tito Puente: 50 Years of Swing,"* a three-disc collection on RMM Records that was produced by me and Nelson Rodríguez, an A&R man assigned by Ralph.

Beads of sweat were streaming from the musicians' brows, the uniforms were wrinkled – there was no time to change so the shirts did not match. Tito lifted his sticks looked around then began to play the saucy *"Complicación,"* with Tito's characteristic big sound and precise percussive, electricity was shaking the room. Flashes from the cameras popped, the video technicians rolled. The people took to the floor. It surprised everyone to learn that the orchestra had just arrived from a 12-hour flight from across the Atlantic Ocean.

Celia Cruz and Oscar DeLeón joined Tito and the band. Laughingly and lightly they improvised a montuno laid down by the orchestra. Tito, as usual, stood up front, wildly hammering the skins and clicking the metal sides of his timbales, circling his head with the sticks then crashing them down on the cymbals. The trumpets rode over the saxophones and the trombone and the piano hummed. It was hard to keep from dancing. While playing, he reminded some old Borscht Belt fans of his comic, eyes popping, tongue lolling out of his open mouth.

"Hey Tito," an elderly fan called out.

Tito looked up, smiled and tossed his sticks over his head while the percussion came to a dead stop. The bass and piano continued to thump. On the back end of the 4/4 count the trumpets and reeds rolled in. In the middle of the next four beat count Tito slapped the head of the skin, created a trembling roll and the entire percussion came back in – it was taut and clear-cut. You could hardly move on the tiny dance floor. Some of the dancers were having trouble keeping time – the younger ones. The older dancers simply moved in the tiny space provided, much like the old Cubans did. "The Cubans had a knack for just gliding within a small square. The old soneros (singers) would sing something like 'y baila en un solo ladrillito," he informed one of the young Latino journalists present.

Later after the event was winding down Tito spoke openly to the media and anyone else who would listen. In the midst of it he signed autographs, smiled for the cameras of the amateurs who wanted to have their picture taken with him, and shook hands with well wishers.

"Them people aren't so hip to my music," he said referring to the younger people in the crowd. "They didn't feel it." Surrounded by cameras and lights, "I'm not afraid to tell them anymore now -- I don't care," Puente asserted. "If you're out there in the audience, you better educate yourself to my music. When you listen to me, you've got to feel the rhythm and the beat, the rhythm and the excitement of the Palladium era. My music still has that excitement. I couldn't change now; it's too late."

And in no uncertain terms, he reminds the media, "salsa is sauce. It is not music. It is not the music I play, do you dig." He smiled and turned away.

"How do you feel about the situation that exists with local Cuban residents not wanting to listen to music from Cuba..."

Tito did not wait for the question to end. He reeled around. Tito looked straight into the swarm of people. "I play Cuban music. I love Cuban music. I do not play politics."

The next day was not a day off, but Tito telephoned Hooke to say that the band was exhausted and it seemed that he and Mercado had overbooked them. "You fucking guys are behind desks. We have to run from airport to airport, nightclub to nightclub while you mother fuckers ring up your hefty commissions."

"Hey Tito... Is everything all right?" growled Hooke in his customary gruff voice. They went back and forth for a few minutes. Tito looked at me. He smiled. Obviously Jack Hooke had caved in to some of Tito's requests.

But the next day the orchestra appeared live on the local TV show "Sábado Gigante." Tito managed to have the orchestra perform live rather than mimic recorded background music.

Back in New York a few days later, Tito was relaxing at Victor's Café. "You should be proud of me. I did not say what was really on my mind."

"Bullshit!" I said with a grin.

"Yeah! Bullshit!" he laughed.

The Hollywood Bowl is a gigantic amphitheater. The Hollywood Bowl Symphony Orchestra is among the world's most prestigious music organizations. The first incarnation of the orchestra was in 1945 as the "Hollywood Bowl Symphony Orchestra" under the direction of Leopold Stokowski. In 1990 the orchestra was reorganized and focused its program on seeking out new talent and developing a pops format. John Mauceri, a transplanted New Yorker, who attended high school with my wife Linda, led the orchestra from its founding in 1990 until he stepped down after the 2006 Hollywood Bowl season. During this time, his titles included Conductor, Principal Conductor, and finally, Director. He now holds the title of Founding Director. The Hollywood Bowl is a famous modern amphitheatre in the Hollywood area of Los Angeles, California that is used primarily for music performances. It has a seating capacity of 17,376. It is the home of the Hollywood Bowl Orchestra, the summer home of the Los Angeles Philharmonic and the host of hundreds of musical events each year. Among the many artists that appeared at the amphitheatre was Cuban composer Ernesto Lecuona in 1931, when Tito was eight-years-old.

Tito and his orchestra were ready to tackle the semi-classical venue. He arrived in Los Angeles three days ahead of the schedule for the 1999 summer concert that had been arranged by Mauceri. It was a typical sweltering summer day. Mauceri had met Tito several months earlier while on a visit to New York. He stopped in at the Blue Note in Greenwich Village. Mauceri knew Tito was the headliner and wanted to meet him. It was a brief meeting. But Mauceri must have been impressed with the ensemble and especially the enthusiasm of the audience packed into the tiny popular New York club. For some time Tito had his eye on playing in a large venue with his orchestra at the center of a symphony orchestra. He had been trained for this. And, he knew that big symphony orchestras like the one in Los Angeles were looking to expand its repertoire.

"It's a perfect fit," Tito told the director of the Hollywood Bowl Orchestra. Mauceri and no one noticed, except perhaps the musicians. indicated he would get back to Tito, and he did a few months later.

During the abbreviated rehearsals, the symphony orchestra had a problem playing Tito's original *"Mambo Gozón"* that was going to introduce Pops and his men. The night of the performance Mauceri and his symphony orchestra played the music as it was written. It just did not sound right. "It is awful," gasped Tito. "I know this is a great orchestra but the percussion is way out in fucking left field." As the orchestra played the Tito Puente composition it struggled through the inter changing trumpet and reed ostinatos, and when the Cuban style breaks were called for – well the percussion was all over the place. "You have to follow the music, yes," explained Tito. "And you have to feel it too." The Hollywood Bowl Orcherstra was "out of clave" but it did not seem to matter. The concert went on. It did not seem to matter to the audience. The spectators were enthralled with Tito's performance. He played a standard tribute to Orquesta Aragón and the Cuban charangas, and then the Duke Ellington classic *"Going Fishin'."*

When the orchestra started the Marcelino Guerra classic *"Pare Cochero,"* Tito screamed to the audience "Dance, dance!" It was definitely a crowd pleaser. The fans, young and old jumped up and began dancing in the aisle and on top of the seats. But the big number of the night was *"Fofi,"* an original Cuban style descarga that featured all of his muscians taking individual solos. As played by the Tito Puente Orchestra even the Hollywood Bowl Orchestra was able to figure out how to fit the 4-4 time signature into the 3-2 clave framework. The crowd was pleased, energized and even mezmerized as the Hollywod Bowl musicians streamed through the five and six note ostinatos so familiar in Cuban charangas. When it ended the crowd seemed dismayed. But Tito, his orchestra and the musicians from the Hollywood Bowl Orchestra smoothly shifted into the next number quickly. *"Oye Como Va,"* kept everyone on their feet. It was quite a night. Tito and his band had successfully opened a new door, albeit with a few slips – integration of Afro-Cuban Rhythms and an Afro-Cuban big band interwoven with the classical symphonic orchestral system.

Exploring and experimenting with a symphonic approach to jazz had been going on for sometime – George Gershwin, Aaron Copland, Leonard Bernstein and others. Tito always believed the Afro-Cuban music and Latin jazz were treated as orphans simply because the musical directors and policy makers were clueless about how to bring the two forms together. From the moment he assumed leadership of the jazz ensemble he talked about finding a way to expand Afro-Cuban jazz into a symphonic realm. Just think about it – a super big band."

Madera confirms "the boss was using the ensemble as a vehicle to keep the big band fully functional. He was looking for a gimmick, as he always said to keep moving forward." Tito maintained that contemporary salsa would eventually fade – it was uninspiring, lacked innovation and was " musically lackluster and repetitive." The next step in the evolution of Afro-Cuban music in the United States was in the classical direction. The Hollywood Bowl concert served as an important learning experience. It taught him that the musicians of a classical orchestra have to be provided with the music arrangement and materials in advance.

During this period he selected flautist David Valentín as the music director of the Tito Puente Jazz Ensemble. "I think he can handle that. José will still be my go to guy, just like he is for the big band."

For the concert in San Antonio, Texas several months later, Tito and José forwarded the musical material several weeks in advance. An important personnel change occurred during this period of transition. Veteran bass player Bobby Rodríguez was not only losing his eyesight but heavy drinking resulted in his failure to show up for rehearsals and scheduled performances. Tito had to let him go. There was a tug of war for the position. Gerardo Madera, the brother of José Madera, Jr., was supposed to get the job but at the last minute Mercado and Hooke pushed for Tito to recruit Bernardo Minoso, a veteran of the Mongo Santamaría Ensemble. Mongo was in ill health and retiring from the business. Tito acquiesced to Hooke. But from the start Tito was not overwhelmed by Minoso's ability to play the straightforward style of the Tito Puente Orchestra. "Minoso is good, but he is too fucking funky. That is the shit that Mongo used to play."

Some reports claim that among the guests who came to the celebritity room to greet the musicians was Marlon Brando.[161] He was not among the well-wishers. Tito would have remembered him – the former New York Palladium fan who sat in with the big bands and played bongo. Brando played the part of Sky Masterson, who whisks Jean Simmons to Havana for a night of fun and dance. He displays many of his mambo skills learned at the the Palladium during the 1956 movie. By this time he was in semi retirement and a recluse.

Tito told Mercado and Hooke in 1998, that he would like his oldest son Ronnie Puente be being more involved in the management of his orchestra. This was probably because on February 23, 1998, Tito's friend, colleague and partner of nearly 50 years passed away. Jimmy Frisuara had suffered a fourth heart attack a few days before. We all knew that he was not doing well Everyone around him could see that he was not taking it well. In his quiet macho way he was now coming to terms with the fact that he was not going to live forever. He had mentioned to me that there was "some kind of problem with the heart." But what it was – he would not talk any further about. "Its bullshit, that's all," he insisted. Tito was terrified of doctors.

Tito called me at home the afternoon of Jimmy's passing. "Hey Joe," he said in his accustomed gruffy manner – the tone I had come to recognize when he was attempting to disguise his feelings.

"Yeah."

In a cold voice he announced: "Joe, you know Jimmy died."

"Jesus Christ, Tito," stammered. I was shocked.

A minute later he added: "Oh yeah, by the way Santitos died too."

It was now a double shock to the system. I finally responded, "Are you going to Puerto Rico for the funeral?."

He offered a cool response. "No. I'm going to be here for Jimmy. I will send flowers to the funeral in Puerto Rico."

There was a moment of silence. "Joe, you know you and me go back… You know what I mean. There are fewer and fewer of us left." There was silence. "Thanks, Joe…" His voice trailed off.

"For what?" I responded.

Tito responded: "Shit! Just thanks." He hung up. In his strange way he was reaching out. We had shared many adventures.

At the funeral Tito quietly. Jimmy and Tito had been connected at the hip for nearly a half century dating back to when they played for the Pupi Campo Orchestra. They had traveled the world together. Jimmy covered for Tito, and Pops covered for Jimmy. The funeral procession included many of Jimmy's Italian connections – the wiseguys that Jimmy and Tito often talked about. Jimmy was gone and I was just wondering why Tito would not permit himself to breakdown the way he did when his mentor, Machito, died. Maybe it was because the entire band was in the funeral parlor, maybe it was because it was not the manly thing to do. I do believe he was feeling the strain of the two passings. Jimmy had been in retirement for a number of years. They often talked. Jimmy was one of his closest and dearest friends. He was going to miss him.

Tito missed Jimmy. He was the buffer between Tito and the musicians. Jimmy paid the bills, listened to the complaints, resolved issues, planned travel, prepared the music and was the housekeeper. Rarely did Tito get into the day-to-day operation and management. Jack Hooke and Tito promoted Dandy to the position of band administrator. "It was a disaster," exclaimed Tito. Almost in the same breath he said: "Would you be interested in the administration?"

"What! Are you nuts," I gasped. "You need me on the outside looking in, Tito. Paying the bills is not my cup of tea. You know that."

He calmed down. "Jack and I have to look around. Jack doesn't want to do it and I don't trust Ralph."

A few days later he brought the subject up again. He told me about bringing on Ronnie. Tito told me he had discussed it with his wife, Margie. She agreed with him that bringing Ronnie into the band would be a good idea.

"Do you think, Ronnie wants to do this?" I asked.

"Oh, I think so. He has knowledge of running a business. He knows music." My feeling at this time was that Tito was still dealing with Jimmy's departure, his death. In his own way he was looking to the future. Tito wanted the band working after he was gone.

Soon after, Ronnie Puente came on board. A few weeks later Tito and I spoke briefly when we met at Willie's Steakhouse. I had been on vacation. I asked him how it was going with the changes he had made in the band. I guessed that things were not right by the way he shrugged. He was evasive and cranky – just like he got when he did not want to deal with something.

Finally, after a few drinks he grumbled: "Jack Hooke is running the band again and Ronnie is no longer in the picture."

We had a few more drinks. The musicians were setting up for one of those jam sessions. I was going to ask him what happened, but thought better of it. He glared at me. He could see I was not ready to drop the subject.

Tito growled: "Forget about it. NEXT!"

During this period the band was still playing around New York, in New Jersey, out in Long Island, and north in the Boston area. Tito realized that his friend and partner Jimmy Frisaura, had been more than just a good musician. The actual management of a band requires a good deal of skill and intuition. Tito was not a good manager. Audiences are different, and a leader has to quickly get a sense of what each particular one wants – cool jazz, a mixture of standards to go with Latin, fast music. Jimmy was responsible for this. As early as the 1970s, Jimmy had approached Tito and told him he needed to start thinking about "the future of the Tito Puente Orchestra."

Tito admitted he brushed him off. Now with his band in turmoil – his own doing – he realized just how much he missed his band manager. Jimmy knew when to vary tempos, modify key signatures, and change the character of the piece for dancers, listeners and guest artist. A band manager is the go-to-guy. Jimmy listened to the problems of the musicians, resolved them quietly and moved on.

Tito continued to record: *"Jazzin': Tito Puente & India (Plus The Count Basie Orchestra),"* 1996 (RMM); *"Special Delivery: Tito Puente & Maynard Ferguson,"* 1996 (Concord Picante); "*Dancemania '99 – Live At Birdland,"* 1998 (RMD) and *"Mambo Birdland," 1999*" (RMM). That year Concord Records approached Tito to participate in a jam session with its stable of Latin Jazz musicians that included David Valentín on flute, Sheila E (daughter of Pete Escovedo), percussion, her father, Poncho Sanchez, and others. Mercado had agreed to let Tito do the recording but failed to give a firm commitment. In between Tito slipped into Wisconsin to perform with the Milwaukee Symphony Orchestra.

"I think they (the orchestras) enjoy this type of thing. It gives us all a chance to try something different, something new. You know it is a gimmick. You have to have a gimmick – try something out, stay ahead of the curve. And besides, you know me, I love the big band – and what is bigger than a symphony orchestra that has the best musicians in the world."

That summer the Scholarship Fund held its major fundraiser aboard the Circle Line Dinner Yacht. Bob Sancho and Marcos F. Pérez arranged to have Joaquin Oliveros flown in from Havana, Cuba as the guest flautist. Oliveros was well known for his incredible abilities as a muscian playing the conical unadorned wooden six-hole, five-key flute. He had been to New York in 1996 to participate in a concert at Hostos College, and to conduct several workshops at various colleges in the North East.

The yacht was packed with contributors and supporters of the Fund. As the boat sailed around Manhattan Island Oliveros slipped to the front of the bandstand. "Okay! A gozar," yelled Tito after the orchestra completed the introduction to *"Juventud del Presente."* Oliveros did not know the tune, but Tito yelled to him "Mi bemol" – E flat. The flute took off and Tito and the band followed. "Okay, ahora si vamos a gozar."

For the next 10 minutes Oliveros stood in the middle of the packed dance floor blowing his heart out. The dancers simply moved to the side to keep from bumping into him.

Afterward he asked Tito: "¿Como salió?. No estoy seguro si estaba en clave."

Tito laughed. "¿No te diste cuenta que todo el mundo lo estaba gozando?"

This was the last time Tito played at the Tito Puente Scholarship Fund gala. It was the 21st anniversary of the Fund.

The flight out to California was not an easy one. The weather was lousy and Tito was not even sure it was worth his while to go out for the Grammy Awards. "What difference does it make." The Latin segment of the Grammy Awards was not televised. This always annoyed Pops.

All was not well with the Mercado organization. Hooke had passed away a few months earlier. Celia Cruz left the crumbling Mercado music empire. The son of Gilberto Monroig, Glen, successfully sued Ralph for plagiarism. Tito and the band continued to deal with being paid late, bounced checks, and dozens of other excuses. Yet, Tito decided that he would hang in with Ralph, who was was now planning to unite Pops and Eddie Palmieri in an album to be titled: *"Masterpiece."*

In the midst of all his turmoil, Ralph told Tito that Eddie Rodríguez would be the person in charge of the Tito Puente Orchestra account. Tito had met Rodríguez in California on one of his trips to the West Coast. "Okay, okay, no problem," he told Ralph one afternoon over the telephone.

When he finished his brief conversation he turned to me and grinned. "What the fuck does Ralph think. This Eddie guy is a nice guy, I guess. But he is no fucking Jack Hooke. I don't want him sticking his nose into my band. José and you, and the rest of the guys know what to do. Fuck this shit."

Rodríguez had a tough time keeping up with Tito, mostly because he was kept at a far distance. Tito did not trust him like he did Hooke, whom he had known from the days when Morris Levy was in the picture.

Of course Tito knew what Ralph was up to. He was attempting to recoup some of his lost glory, mostly get cash, and be able to reorganize his floundering organization; and, he (Ralph) was planning a large concert that would incorporate all the artists that were still in his stable. The headliners would be Tito Puente and Eddie Palmieri.

"He always has a something up his sleeve," Tito said on the flight into Los Angeles.

"It does sound like a tipical Ralph production – a lot of singers…"

"All bullshit," exclaimed Tito. "Anyway we'll see."

The Grammy for the tropical category went to Tito for his 1999 recording *"Mambo Birdland"* on the RMM label – it was Tito's fifth Grammy Award.

During a reception after the awards at the Biltmore Hotel, Tito, Tony Bennett and B.B. King huddled together and talked about – what else – music. "We'll make sure that we get together," King said toward the end of the night.

Bennett smiled. "Oh yes. It's a great idea, to do a few shows together."

Tito smiled. "We'll stay in touch and make sure we do this.

On the way to our rooms late that night Tito turned to me and said "This is the last time I'm going to one of these things." He shrugged and walked to his room.

"You know you need to take care of your ticker."

Tito groaned. "I knew I should not have told you about the hole in my heart. Shit! I'll take care of it when I can, not now." A while back Tito told me he had been diagnosed with a leaking heart valve – in 1992. He refused to talk about it. According to him he said the doctors said there was no urgency.

"You've been fucking around with this heart stuff for years. You need to get it taken care of."

"You are not my fucking wife."

We were yelling at each other. I decided not to press him further. "Okay, whatever…"

He smiled. "Goodnight mother."
"Kiss my ass."

April in Paris

Tito, Eddie Palmieri, Ray Barretto, Louie Ramírez, Nicky Marrero, and others played a 20-minute jam session of *"Picadillo"* at the Latin New York Awards in 1977.[162] When Tito returned from California he listened to my personal recording and decided that he would try to convince Ralph to use something like it. "Eddie is at the top of his game," Tito said while we listened to the tape. "Ray is right on the money. Not bad, not bad at all."

"Your solo is okay," I chided him.

"Bullshit! It's great," he laughed.

Tito tried to convince Ralph on several occassions. The only concession he got from his manager was that he would accept a "Tito arrangement." So Tito provided him with two original arrangements – the second one was for *"Ti Mon Bo"* just as it was played in the original 1958 recording. Ralph balked, but accepted the two pieces. On the CD *"Ti Mon Bo"* is retitled: *"El Puente Mundial."*

The musicians in Tito's band, like Tito were not excited about the new recording. "It was pure salsa," they said to me. Madera shrugged it off. "Just another day at the office. Tito was thinking about other things – Dallas, Puerto Rico and down the road. He knew everyone would have preferred more jazz style numbers." The guest artists included Michael Stuart, Oscar D'León, Pete "El Conde" Rodríguez, Frankie Morales, Milton Cardona and Herman Olivera. Tito was not excited, not in the least.

During one of the studio recording sessions recalled Madera Jr. "we played and played and played *'El Bochinche'* for about 20 minutes. It had no end. I jumped up and yelled, 'Stop, damn it.' I offered some changes, re-arranged some of the middle parts to make it tighter. It was a little better." Overall, according to Madera it was mostly Eddie Palmieri's musicians that worked on the album. "We sat around for several days waiting."

He laughed when he remembered his last disagreement with Tito "It was the last time I argued with Tito, and it was over a selection *'Itutu Ache'* that called for a changeover from 6/8 time to the 4/4 time signature and Tito insisted that the actual band change came in on the back end of clave. His transition was not working. 'We come in on the the first 3 of the 3/2 clave,' I told him. He growled and we went at it for a few minutes. When he saw I was right he gritted his teeth in his usual way."

Tito mentioned the incident to me. I couldn't help but laugh. "So José was right."

Tito gritted his teeth and huffed about. "Anyway it worked out."

Nothing about the album recording session that reunited Tito and Eddie could qualify it as a masterpiece, Tito said. "Musically speaking everybody is there, we all did what we were supposed to do – but no one was inspired." For the most part Tito left the decision making to Ralph. Tito got the impression from Eddie that the piano player was not completely focused on the new album. Before leaving for Texas we heard the unedited takes in the studio. Tito looked at me. I shrugged. "This is Ralph's baby now. It really isn't worth a shit."

He added, "I figured you would think it was shit."

I laughed. "I didn't say that."

Tito gazed at me. "I can see your body language. Anyway, we have other things to do." We left the studio.

On April 22, the orchestra performed in a concert with the Dallas Symphony Orchestra. The orchestra traces its origins to a concert given by a group of forty musicians in 1900, with conductor Hans Kreissig. It continued to perform and grow in stature. In 1945, it appointed Antal Doráti as music director. Under Doráti, the orchestra became fully professional. Several times during the history of the orchestra it has suspended operations, including periods during the First and Second World Wars from 1914 to 1918, and from 1942 to 1945, and more recently in 1974 due to fiscal restraints. Subsequent music directors have included Georg Solti and Eduardo Mata. Andrew Litton was music director from 1992 to 2006.

The expansive modern performing arts facilty seats just over 2,000 patrons and it was packed for the concert that featured an overture that included the music of George Gershwin. The music of Tito Puente included *"Machito Forever,"* and followed with the music of Duke Ellington, Rafael Hernández, a Cuban medley, and *"Fofi,"* the symphonic Afro-Cuban jam that combines the two orchestras in a musical free-for-all.

"It was just a set of Afro-Cuban montuno riffs or guajeos that were developed in the 1930s, by the fathers of the mambo in Cuba," Tito explained to an inquisitive Dallas journalist the night of the concert. "At first we did not have a formal arrangement. The horns or reeds introduced it with a syncopated, almost layed back approach. Then the horns come in and everybody gets involved. Cuban orchestras play this type of stuff all the time."

The reporter was still not sure. "How does everybody know what to do?"

Tito laughed. "When you play with the same guys all the time, there is a feeling that fits into the music. A simple look at the guys, the wave of a stick, a signal means that a break is coming, the riff has to change, or someone will take a solo. It could mean the the saxophone section continues to state the theme while the trumpets or trombones rise above and produce a new harmony – this is done in classical music. The main difference is we have Afro-Cuban percussion and it all has to fit into clave."

"What is clave?" asked the perplexed journalist.

"That would take a lifetime to explain. Just think of it as African root rhythms and feeling, melding with European root rhythms – not an easy thing to explain, and not an easy thing to do – but that is Afro-Cuban music."

The journalist smiled. "Salsa!"

Tito shrugged.

On April 20, 2000, Tito celebrated his 77th birthday. He never dreamed he could have achieved so much. The next stop was Puerto Rico. Tito had plans and goals – he was not going to slow down.

Right after the concert the orchestra flew into Washington, D.C. for the Lifetime Legends Awards.

Tito returned to New York City. Tito, Bobby Rodríguez and me met up in a pizzeria on Sixth Avenue in Manhattan to talk about the Schorlaship Fund summer event. We talked for a while and then Tito and I headed to Town Hall where Tito, producer Gary Marshall and actor Hector Elizondo were being honored. Tito performed with the house band. It was the last time he performed in New York City.

110th Street and Fifth Avenue (Epilogue)

Though Mercado was staging a salsa concert in Hato Rey, a few miles from the performing arts center, it did not phase Tito in the slightest. Following each of the concerts with the various symphony orchestras Tito requested and was given a recording of the performance for his personal use. He requested the same courtesy from the Centro de Bellas Artes Luis A. Ferre administration, speaking personally with the director on several occassions. In 2000 Puerto Rico had just elected a new governor – Sila Calderón, the former mayor of San Juan.

"You know Joe," Tito told me as we walked around San Juan the Thursday afternoon of the inaugural concert, "I keep getting the run around with the people at the arts center. You need to stay on top of it."

I shrugged. "It's Puerto Rico."

"Yeah but this Muñiz fellow, he looks a little shady too. He promises you a lot of shit. I don't know. Just keep your eye on them. All we can do is keep trying," Tito said.

The concert was a success. My dear friend passed away on May 31, 2000, at 11:05 a.m., a few hours after undergoing a complicated quadruple heart by-pass surgery and a valve replacement. Tito had waited too long. He never heard his last performance. Neither the performing arts center, nor the promoter delivered the recording as had been promised.

It was an incredible sendoff. The procession of dignitaries, government officials, entertainers and musicians and just fans was endless. The rain did not deter the multitude of people who gathered around the Riverside Memorial Funeral Home on 76th Street and Amsterdam Avenue in Manhattan. My friend layed in a shiny white casket. He was dressed in the white of the santero religion that he followed. The timbal sticks lay clasped in his hands. There was a clear plexi glass cover over him. I could almost detect an ever so slight smile on his lips – the one I knew so well.

The last presentation of the Tito Puente Orchestra was at Lehman College in the Bronx where it performed for the final fundraising event of the Tito Puente Scholarship Fund. The Tito Puente estate, unsure of what Tito's desire at the time of his death, decided to discontinue the charitable efforts of its founding benefactor. The last album recorded by Tito, *"Masterpiece"* was released in September 2000. I remembered our conversation about the unedited cuts that RMM provided Tito shortly before his death – the day we talked. "What a piece of shit," he groaned. I laughed to myself.

Today, the Mambo Legends Orchestra is led by Madera and Dandy. Its home base is in Denver, Colorado. It is often described as one of the most exciting, colorful and authentic orchestras currently on the music scene. It is no surprise that radiating trumpets, swinging saxophones, piercing trombones, harmonious vocals and an electrifying percussion section comes from the veterans of The Tito Puente Orchestra. They include: Lewis Kahn, trombone; Mitch Frohman, Bobby Porcelli, Peter Yellin, alto saxophone; Pedro Miranda, baritone saxophone; Kevin Bryan, trumpet; and, Sonny Bravo, piano.

Located in Hostos Community College is the Tito Puente Legacy Project," which includes memorabilia of Tito Puente's career that was produced by me.

A few others carry on the legacy. Arturo O'Farrill, the son of prolific arranger and composer Chico O'Farrill, teaches music, leads a concert orchestra based at Lincoln Center for the Performing Arts.

"Tito Puente was our ambassador," he maintains. "He represents what Latin music is all about. The hard work, the dedication, the commitment to excellence, but infused with deep passion, unbridled joy and hard-core swing." O'Farrill was born in Mexico and educated at the Manhattan School of Music where once Tito walked the hallways when it was known as the Juilliard School of Music.

Bobby Sanabria is an exceptional percussionist, arranger, composer and educator. In addition to leading his own Latin jazz oriented orchestra he is the Director of the Manhattan School of Music Afro-Cuban Jazz Orchestra. Each year he exposes the students to the complexities, the intricacies and spectrum of Afro-Cuban music. "Do you know that Tito Puente would toss you out on the street," he admonishes a trumpet player during intense rehearsals. The student cringes. A few minutes later, after taking the student members of the band to task, he stands in front of the orchestra and passionately offers them a history on the various aspects of the music they are learning.

"Two words immediately come to mind when I think of Maestro Tito Puente, excellence and virtuosity. His command of all the various aspects of music – arranging, composition, band leading, conducting and his mastery of percussion (drums, vibes, marimba, and timbales), let alone the little known fact that he was a dancer, played piano, alto sax, clarinet, can be considered – super human." By now he has the students gazing at him with deep interest. They are learning about the masters of Afro-Cuban music in New York. Each year the orchestra, appropriately attired – much like they were a half-century ago – perform at various venues. Bobby and the MSM orchestra have been nominated for a Grammy for the "Kenya Revisited" album in 2008. In 2009 the orchestra paid tribute to the music of Tito Puente in several concerts and workshops.

Tito Puente Jr. leads his own band in Florida and plays some of his father's music.

In 2007, the U.S. Post Office located at 124th Street, between Lexington and Third avenues was named after Tito Puente.

One hundred tenth (110th) Street and Fifth (5th) Avenue is known as "Tito Puente Way."

*****

Discography

Years after Tito Puente's death the discography has grown with the release of previously unpublished music. This list includes recordings by Tito Puente and his orchestra for which it was not credited. For example, during the 1970s, more than a dozen long play albums were released by Roper Records, Inc. Because Tito and Charlie Palmieri were under contract to other record companies, these were credited to The Latin All-Stars, Roper Dance Orchestra, The Dancing Strings, etc. This list does not include more than 40 tunes that were produced for Roper on 45 rpm discs, or early recordings Tito Puente made for such labels as Verne, Decca and others. There are countless live performances that are not included in this discography.

#	RECORDING TITLE	DATE	LABEL / ID
1	Tito Puente & Friends	1950	Tropical 5138
2	Mambos (Volume 1)	1952	Tico 101
3	Mambos	1952	Tico 103
4	Mambos	1952	Tico 107
5	Mambos	1952	Tico 114
6	Mambos	1952	Tico 116
7	King Of The Mambos	1953	Tico 120
8	Tito Puente at the Vibes	1953	Tico 124
9	King Of The Cha Cha Chá	1954	Tico 128
10	Cha Cha Chá	1954	Tico 130
11	Mambos	1954	Tico 131
12	Mamborama	1955	Tico 1001
13	Mambo with Me	1955	Tico 1003
14	Cha Cha Chá for Lovers	1955	Tico 1005
15	Dance the Cha Cha Chá	1955	Tico 1010
16	Puente in Percussion	1955	Tico 1011

17	Cha Cha Cha At The El Morocco	1955	Tico 1025
18	Cha Cha Chá	1955	Tico 134
19	Cuban Carnival	1956	RCA Victor 1251
20	Puente Goes Jazz	1956	RCA Victor 1312
21	Mambo On Broadway	1956	RCA Victor 1354
22	Let's Cha Chá with Puente	1956	RCA Victor 1392
23	Night Beat	1957	RCA Victor 1447
24	Mucho Puente	1957	RCA Victor 1479
25	Be Mine Tonight (with Abbe Lane)	1957	RCA Victor 1554
26	Puente Swings, Vicentico Sings	1957	Tico 1049
27	Puente in Love	1957	Tico 1058
28	Herman's Heat, Puente's Beat (with Woody Herman)	1958	Everest 5010
29	Top Percussion	1958	RCA Victor 1617
30	Dance Mania	1958	RCA Victor 1692
31	Dancing Under Latin Skies	1959	RCA Victor 1874
32	Mucho Cha Cha	1959	RCA Victor 2113
33	Puente At Grossingers	1959	RCA Victor 2187
34	Tambo	1960	RCA Victor 2257

35	Pachanga in New York (with Rolando Laserie)	1961	Gema 1145
36	Puente In Hollywood (with Jose "Rolando" Lozano)	1961	GNP 70
37	Pachanga Con Puente	1961	Tico 1083
38	Y Parece Bobo	1962	Alegre 842
39	Bossa Nova By Puente	1962	Roulette 25193
40	Vaya Puente	1962	Tico 1085
41	El Rey Bravo	1962	Tico 1086
42	Perfect Combination / Gilberto Monroig	1963	Alegre 853
43	More Dance Mania	1963	RCA Victor 7147
44	Tito Puente In Puerto Rico	1963	Tico 1088
45	Tito Puente Bailables	1963	Tico 1093
46	Excitante Ritmo de Tito Puente	1963	Tico 1106
47	The World Of Tito Puente	1963	Tico 1109
48	Ahora Si / Celio Gonzalez	1964	Alegre 8490
49	Mucho Mucho Puente	1964	Tico 1115
50	De Mi Para Ti (Featuring Santitos Colon)	1964	Tico 1116
51	The Best of Tito Puente & Gilberto Monroig	1964	Tico 1117
52	Otro Descubrimiento (with Noraida)	1965	Millie Latino
53	Llamada de Amor - Tito Puente y Los Hispanos	1965	Musicor 3137
54	Una Tarde De Julio - Fabrizzo Y Tito Puente	1965	Rhino 501
55	My Fair Lady Goes Latin	1965	Roulette 25276

56	Nuevo Triunfo / Alberto Beltran (TeePee Vibes & Orchestra)	1965	Seeco 9214
57	En Su Momento (with Celio González)	1965	Teca 555
58	Puente Swings, La Lupe Sings	1965	Tico 1121
59	Tu y Yo - Tito Puente & La Lupe	1965	Tico 1125
60	Carnival in Harlem	1965	Tico 1127
61	Cuba y Puerto Rico Son (with Celia Cruz)	1966	Tico 1130
62	Homenaje A Rafael Hernández - Tito Puente y La Lupe	1966	Tico 1131
63	Puerto Rico Canta y Baila (with Myrta Silva)	1966	WS 4264
64	Bienvenido! / Welcome! a Ismael Rivera y Rafael Cortijo	1966	Tico 1140
65	Eras! (with Manny Roman)	1967	Decca 4879
66	Basilla Nueva	1967	Decca 74910
67	Stop & Listen - Santitos Colon	1967	Tico 1147
68	20th Anniversary of Tito Puente	1967	Tico 1151
69	El Rey y Yo - La Lupe	1967	Tico 1154
70	What Now My Love - Shawn Elliot	1967	Tico 1156
71	Invitation to Love (with Bobby Capó)	1968	Musicor 4035
72	Two Sides of La Lupe	1968	Tico 1162
73	El Rey Tito Puente	1968	Tico 1172
74	El Sonido Moderno (with: Al Escobar)	1968	Tico 1184
75	El Fantástico El Lupo	1969	Cotique 1028

76	Puente on the Bridge	1969	Tico 1191
77	Quimbo, Quimbamba / Celia Cruz	1969	Tico 1193
78	Con Orgullo - Tito Puente y Sophy	1969	Tico 1198
79	Santitos - Santos Colon	1970	Fania 387
80	Cuba Linda / Rolando Laserie	1970	Musart 14510
81	Social Security Administration Presents the Tito Puente Show	1970	SSA 70-10733
82	El Sol Brilla Para Todos (with: La Lloroncita)	1970	Tico 1206
83	Etc., Etc., Etc. (with Celia Cruz)	1970	Tico 1207
84	Social Security Administration Presents the Tito Puente Show	1971	SSA 71-10733
85	Imágenes / Santitos Colon	1971	Tico 1213
86	Pa'lante	1971	Tico 1214
87	Alma con Alma / Tito Puente y Celia Cruz	1971	Tico 1221
88	Te Reto (with Sophy)	1971	Tico 1222
89	La Bárbara del Mundo Latino (with: Noraida)	1971	Tico 1223
90	Yo Me Voy A Desquitar (with: Noraida)	1971	Tico 1226
91	Celia Cruz & Tito Puente in Spain	1971	Tico 1227
92	Meñique / Meñique	1972	Cotique 1068
93	Many Moods Of Tito Puente	1972	RCA Victor 3012
94	Social Security Administration Presents the Tito Puente Show	1972	SSA 72-10733

95	Pa' Los Rumberos	1972	Tico 1301
96	Algo Especial Pa' Recordar (with Celia Cruz)	1972	Tico 1304
97	Lenni Sesar	1973	Fania 368
98	Social Security Administration Presents the Tito Puente Show	1973	SSA 73-10733
99	Tito Puente & his Concert Orchestra	1973	Tico 1308
100	Long Live the Kings / Santitos Colon & Meñique	1974	Cotique 1072
101	Mr. Estilo - Frankie Figueroa	1974	Marylou 1025
102	Revolving Bandstand (with Buddy Morrow Orchestra / 1960)	1974	RCA Victor 2299
103	Latin Holiday (with Charlie Palmieri)	1974	Roper 1005
104	American & Latin Swinging Happy (with Charlie Palmieri)	1974	Roper 1006
105	Cha Cha Chá (with Charlie Palmieri)	1974	Roper 1009
106	Social Security Administration Presents the Tito Puente Show	1974	SSA 74-10733
107	Tito Puente Unlimited	1974	Tico 1322
108	Dancing in Love (with Charlie Palmieri)	1975	Roper 1010
109	Music for Lovers (with Charlie Palmieri)	1975	Roper 1012
110	Merengue & Cha Cha Chá (with Charlie Palmieri)	1975	Roper 1016
111	Social Security Administration Presents the Tito Puente Show	1975	SSA 75-10733

112	Latin Jamboree (with Charlie Palmieri)	1976	Roper 1021
113	Latin Gold (with Charlie Palmieri)	1976	Roper 1028
114	Social Security Administration Presents The Tito Puente Show	1976	SSA 76-10733
115	Amor y Tango (with Charlie Palmieri)	1977	Roper 1032
116	Artistry in Motion (with Charlie Palmieri)	1977	Roper 1033
117	Tropical Adventure (with Charlie Palmieri)	1978	Roper 1039
118	A Latin Happening (with Charlie Palmieri)	1978	Roper 1040
119	Homenaje A Beny Moré (Volume 1)	1978	Tico 14 25
120	The Legend	1978	Tico 1413
121	La Pareja / Tito Puente y La Lupe	1978	Tico 1430
122	Just Like Magic / Latin Percussion Jazz Ensemble	1979	Latin Percussion LPV 102
123	More Cha Cha Chá & Merengue (with Charlie Palmieri)	1979	Roper 1041
124	Homenaje A Beny More (Volume 2)	1979	Tico 1436
125	Tito Puente Live At Montreux Jazz Festival	1980	Latin Percussion LPV-100
126	Dance Mania 80's	1980	Tico 1439
127	C'est Magnifique (with Azuquita)	1981	Tico 1440
128	On Broadway	1983	Concord 207
129	El Rey	1984	Concord 250

130	Mambo Diablo	1985	Concord 283
131	Homenaje A Beny Moré (Volume 3)	1985	Vaya 105
132	Sensación	1986	Concord 301
133	Un Poco Loco	1987	Concord 329
134	Salsa Meets Jazz	1988	Concord 354
135	Goza Mi Timbal	1989	Concord 399
136	Tito Puente Presents Millie P	1990	RMM 80375
137	Out of this World	1991	Concord 448
138	The Mambo King	1991	RMM 80680
139	Mambo of the Times	1992	Concord 4499
140	Live At The Village Gate	1992	Tropijazz / RMM 80879
141	Royal T	1993	Concord 4453
142	Unreleased Out Takes - Dance Mania (recorded:1957)	1994	BMG/RCA Victor 74321-21009-2
143	Master Timbalero	1994	Concord 4594
144	In Session	1994	Tropijazz / RMM 81208
145	Tito's Idea	1995	Tropijazz / RMM 81571
146	Special Delivery	1996	Concord 4732
147	Jazzin' - Tito Puente & India, Count Basie Orchestra	1996	RMM 82032
148	50 Years Of Swing (3CD Box Set)	1997	RMM 82050
149	Hong Kong Mambo / Out Takes	1998	BMG/RCA Victor 74321-63749-2
150	Dancemaina 99: Live At Birdland	1998	RMM 82270
151	Mambo Birdland	1999	RMM 02828-404472

152	Masterpiece - Tito Puente & Eddie Palmieri	2000	RMM 84033
153	*The Complete RCA Recordings (6-CD Box Set / Volume 1)	2001	BMG 743288474-2
154	*The Complete RCA Recordings (6-CD Box Set / Volume 2)	2001	BMG 743288422-2
155	Tito Puente The Early Years - Live Mambo Music	2007	Mambo Music 34479-62667-6
156	*The Complete Tico 78 RPM Recordings Vol 1	2008	Emusica 773130389-2
157	*The Complete Tico 78 RPM Recordings Vol 2	2008	Emusica 773130416-2
158	*The Complete Tico 78 RPM Recordings Vol 3	2008	Emusica 773130416-2
159	*The Complete Tico 78 RPM Recordings Vol 4	2008	Emusica 773130480-2
160	Live At Monterrey Jazz Festival (recorded: 1977)	2009	MJFR 30700
161	Live At The Playboy Jazz Festival (Recorded: 1994)	2009	PBD 7504
162	Dance Mania - The Legacy Edition	2009	RCA Victor 88697 447102
163	Mambos	1950s	TICO 113
164	Rumbas And Tangos	1950s	TICO 117
165	Sambas	1950s	TICO 118
166	Rumbas	1950s	TICO 119
167	Mambos By Tito Puente	1950s	Seeco 23
168	Mambo Medly	1950s	Seeco 52
169	Music For Romancing	1950s	TICO 1009
170	Rumba Picturesque	1950s	TICO 1026
171	The Best Of the Borsht Belt Shows	1950s	WTG
172	Vicentico Valdes Sings	1954-55	Seeco 9081

173	Piano Espanol Lalo Schfrin	1962	TICO 1070
174	Giberto Monroig Saludo Carino Mericana	1970	xmx141
175	Tito Puente Live From Soundscape	1980	DIW B-000007t04
176	Tito Puente Plus	1983	Bear 15686
177	Tito Puente Plus	1983	Bear 15687
178	Salsa-Salsa Wallbank-Warwick	1984	5004
179	Tito Puente Concord Jazz Heritage Series	1998	41142
180	Latin Beats	2000	MRBL 17

*Contains previously unreleased selections

End Notes

1. Mambo with Me

1.The history of the Puerto Rico Symphony Orchestra (PRSO) dates back to **1956** when cellist Pablo Casals visited the iPuerto Rico to see his family and to discover the land where his mother was born. Soon after, he would dedicate most of his work to foster classical music in Puerto Rico. In 1957, he organized the first annual Casals Festival, where he invited internationally renowned classical musicians to perform several concerts to Puerto Ricans and tourists alike. It was during this multi-week festival that state legislator Ernesto Ramos Antonini presented a bill which would create the Puerto Rico Symphony Orchestra, receiving much praise and support from both the public and other state legislators. After the law was signed by then Gov. Luis Muñoz Marin the task of organizing the orchestra was given to the same group which organized the Casals Festival. The first live concert was performed on November 6, 1958 in Mayagüez, hometown of Casals' mother.The orchestra has hosted various internationally renowned artists, including Plácido Domingo, Luciano Pavarotti, Justino Díaz, Kiri Te Kanawa, and Alicia de Larrocha, among others, and has performed in Central and South American countries as well as in the U.S. mainland. In addition to its 48 week regular season, the symphony orchestra also organizes concerts and activities for the purpose of fulfilling Casals' dream of fostering classical music in Puerto Rico. These activities include: *Conoce tu Orquesta* ("Know Your Orchestra"), *La Sinfónica en tu Pueblo* ("The Orchestra In Your Town"), *La Sinfónica en las Universidades* ("The Orchestra in Universities"), and *La Sinfónica en los Residenciales* ("The Orchestra In The Projects"; i.e. public housing,), as well as performing in the annual Casals Festival. The orchestra is currently managed by the Musical Arts Corporation of the government of Puerto Rico, who also organizes the annual Casals Festival. The PRSO regularly performs at the Luis A. Ferré Performing Arts Center. Its current roster includes 80 regular musicians from different nationalities, including **Puerto Rico**, **Spain**, **Cuba**, the **Dominican Republic**, **Argentina**, **Colombia**, **Great Britain**, **Germany**, **Russia**, **Romania**, and the **United States**. **(Puerto Rico Symphony Orchestra Website**)

2.**Roselín Pabón**, born in Mayaguez, Puerto Rico, May 7 1958, commenced his musical studies at the Mayaguez Free School of Music. He obtained a B.A. degree at the Baltimore Peabody Music Conservatory in 1968, a master's degree in musical direction and a doctorate degree at the University of Indiana. Pabón is a pianist, trombonist and a composer of danzas. He studied classical piano with Jesús María Sanromá and has been an invited guest director in South America, the United States and Europe. **Toro Vargas, Cirilo**. *Diccionario Biográfico de Compositores Puertorriqueños,* Ediciones Guayacán, Ponce, Puerto Rico, 2003

2. Dancing Under Latin Skies

3.The music store now known as Casa Amadeo opened as Casa Hernández in the Bronx, New York, just prior to the large post-World War II Puerto Rican migration to New York City. When the United States directed all its investment in Puerto Rico's sugar sector, the divestment in Puerto Rico's labor-intensive coffee and tobacco sectors left many workers unemployed. Between 1950 and 1960, 500,000 individuals (about 20% of Puerto Rico's population) migrated off the island. The primary destination was New York due to existing shipping routes, and later, the frequent air travel that operated between San Juan and New York. Earlier, East Harlem had become New York's largest Puerto Rican community by the 1930s. El Barrio (the neighborhood) as it came to be known, was usually the first stop for migrants arriving from the island. By the late 1940s and early 1950s many Puerto Ricans moved northward to the southern portion of the Bronx, relatively close to el Barrio and made accessible by the many subway lines that traversed it. Soon the South Bronx was to become the largest Puerto Rican community in the city. Against this backdrop, the story of Casa Amadeo begins in East Harlem. Victoria and Rafael Hernández migrated to New York City and were to become key players in the burgeoning Latin music scene. Born in Aguadilla to poor Afro-Puerto Rican tobacco workers, Rafael, Victoria and their brother Jesús all became accomplished musicians. Rafael became part of James Reese Europe's 369th Infantry "Hellfighters" military band (the famous African-American regimental band that toured throughout Europe and is credited with introducing jazz there). In 1919, he, Victoria, and other family members moved to New York City., Victoria opened Almacenes Hernández, in 1927possibly the first Puerto Rican-owned music store in New York City. Located on 1724 Madison Avenue between 113th and 114th St., the store supported her family and gave Rafael time to write music--he would become one of the most prolific and well-known composers in Latin America. In November 1939 Victoria and Rafael sold Almacenes Hernández to Luis Cuevas, a record producer from Puerto Rico. In 1941, they opened their second music store, Casa Hernández, in the Bronx at 786 Prospect Avenue. The storefront is located in a ground floor commercial space in the Manhanset apartment building, where Victoria resided and where Rafael stayed when he was living in New York City. Victoria gave piano lessons to budding musicians in the neighborhood. Rafael, though he moved to Mexico, spent periods of time residing at the Manhanset with his sister, so the store continued to be a gathering place for musicians. Music stores were integral elements of the burgeoning Latin music scene in the 1920s, 30s and 40s, continuing through the 1950s "mambo era" and the later development of salsa. Musicians went to the record stores looking for orchestras and conjuntos (musical groups) that were in need of instrumentalists. Music stores such as Casa Amadeo also became gathering places for musicians, knowing they could find work either from record companies looking for session players or from bandleaders looking for instrumentalists. The major record companies, such as Victor and Columbia, depended on store owners to act as "middlemen" in obtaining musicians for recordings and to gauge the community's musical tastes as to what might sell: and some record stores produced records right on the premises. To help ease the difficulties of being transplanted from Puerto Rico, record stores, along with institutions such as hometown social clubs, were places where new migrants flocked to hear and buy the sounds of home. In today's world of impersonal mega-music stores, Casa Amadeo retains many of the original features from its humble beginnings and continues in the tradition of providing music for the community, acting as an unofficial "archive" for musicians searching for the best selections of songs for their albums, and providing a gathering place for musicians and fans from around the city. Casa Amadeo is one of the few physically in tact spaces that remain representing the heyday of the Bronx Latin music scene. Architecturally, the Manhanset Building in which Casa Amadeo is located is a significant representative example of early 20th century residential and commercial architecture in New York City. Built in 1905, the Manhanset is notable as an example of Neo-Renaissance style architecture. The design of the building reflects a predominant use of Renaissance forms and details including a rusticated stone base at the first and second stories, accentuated main entrance porch with Corinthian columns, three-dimensional stone carving, and prominent sheet metal cornice with paired scroll brackets. The popularity of this style was influenced by the principles of the French Ecole des Beaux-Arts and the architecture of the 1893 World's Colombian Exposition in Chicago. Casa Amadeo is significant because it embodies the history of the development of Latin music in New York City and its role in the Puerto Rican migration experience. Victoria Hernández, the store's founder and sister of one of Latin America's greatest composers, Rafael Hernández, sold the store in 1969 to musician and composer Mike Amadeo, the son of popular Puerto Rican composer Titi Amadeo. The store is recognized by musicians and music historians as a site significant in the history of Latin music in the City: and as the oldest Latin music store in New York City, Casa Amadeo's story is a microcosm of the Puerto Rican experience in New York. (**New York Daily News,** 2010)

4.The Great Depression in the United States was the worst and longest economic collapse in the history of the modern industrial world, lasting from the end of 1929 until the early 1940s. Beginning in the United States, the depression spread to most of the world's industrial countries, which in the 20th century had become economically dependent on one another. The Great Depression saw rapid declines in the production and sale of goods and a sudden, severe rise in unemployment. Businesses and banks closed their doors, people lost their jobs, homes, and savings, and many depended on charity to survive. In 1933, at the worst point in the depression, more than 15 million Americans—one-quarter of the nation's workforce—were unemployed. The depression was caused by a number of serious weaknesses in the economy. Although the 1920s appeared on the surface to be a prosperous time, income was unevenly distributed. The wealthy made large profits, but more and more Americans spent more than they earned, and farmers faced low prices and heavy debt. The lingering effects of **World War I** (1914-1918) caused economic problems in many countries, as Europe struggled to pay war debts and reparations. These problems contributed to the crisis that began the Great Depression: the disastrous U.S. stock market crash of 1929, which ruined thousands of investors and destroyed confidence in the economy. Continuing throughout the 1930s, the depression ended in the United States only when massive spending for **World War II** began. (Galbraith, John Kenneth. *The Great Crash: 1929.* Houghton Mifflin, 1955.)

5.With the outbreak of the Cuban revolution, numerous Puerto Ricans in New York became active in the cause of Caribbean liberty. At a meeting held December 22, 1895, in Manhattan's Chimney Hall, Seventh Avenue and 25rh Street, the zealous expatriates organized the Puerto Rican Section of the Cuban Revolutionary Party. (**Liden, Harold**. *The History of the Puerto Rican Independence Movement, Volume I, 1981,* Master Typesetting of Puerto Rico, Inc.)

6. In 1917 James Reese Europe traveled to San Juan, Puerto Rico, in search of reed players. So it was that eighteen leading Puerto Rican musicians found themselves recruited into the band. That this was a seminal moment cannot be emphasized enough; the point when highly skilled Latin musicians came into contact with Black American music and learned to play jazz over the course of the Great War. This was a combination of musicians from Harlem and Puerto Rico: James Reese Europe - Director, Conductor, Arranger Eugene Mikell - Assistant Conductor Felix Weir Assistant Conductor; Dope Andrews, Herb Fleming, Amos Gillard, Rafael Hernández -Trombones - Arturo B. Ayala, Gregorio Felix Delgado, Rafael Duchesne, Antonio González, Jesus Hernández, Elige Rijos, Genaro Torres –Clarinets; Sixto Benitez, Alex Jackson, Lee Perry, José Rivera Rosas - Tubas; Frank DeBroit, Pops Foster, Jake Porter, Russell Smith – Cornets; Pablo Fuentes – Bassoon; Calvin "Piccolo" Jones,Piccolo – Flutes; Ceferino Hernández, Pinkhead Parker – Saxophones; Froilan Jimenez, Nicholas Vazquez, Baritone Horns; Eleuterio Melendez, Francisco Melendez – Mellophones; Noble Sissle, C. Creighton Thompson – Vocals; Hurbert Wright, Steven Wright, Karl Kenny, and Whitney Viney – Drums (**Nadal, James**. *James Reese Europe*, All About Jazz)

7.The cause was the competition for housing, employment and political identity. The musical battle, a conflict between Cuba and Puerto Rico, was promoted at El Campo Amor Theater, located at 116th Street and 5th Avenue. It occurred during the spring of 1935 when a message flashed across the screen: 'FLASH! FLASH! FLASH!' then: "WAR! WAR! WAR! - Between Cuba and Puerto Rico...at the Park Palace between the orchestras of Alberto Socarras of Cuba and Augusto Coen of Puerto Rico." (**Max Salazar** – Latin Beat Magazine).

8.**Hughes, Langston & Lincoln, L. Eric.** *A Pictorial History of Black Americans*, Crown Publishers, N.Y., 1956. Noble Sissle was born on this date in 1889. He was an African-American musician and lyricist. Sissle and Eubie Blake became songwriting partners that same year after they met as members of Joe Porter's Serenaders. Their first song was *"It's All Your Fault."* They got some help in writing it from their friend Eddie Nelson and showed it to Sophie Tucker. Tucker had arrangements made and used it the night after she heard it. In 1916, Sissle worked for James Reese Europe in his Clef Club, and soon was leading his own group within the organization. The summer of that year, Blake rejoined him. Sissle and Blake, who billed themselves as "The Dixie Duo," were eventually highly successful. Patterned after their Clef Club presentations, their act was performed without blackface and with an on-stage piano as their only prop. Their many hit songs in vaudeville included Gee; I'm Glad I'm From Dixie. Sissle and Blake met the men with whom they were to make history at a NAACP benefit in Philadelphia in 1920. Flournoy E. Miller and Aubrey Lyles were veterans in black show business that believed that the only way African-American performers would make it back into white theaters with any dignity was through musical comedy. So the four men put together their resources and set about to write, direct, manage and star in their own musical comedy. Shuffle Along was patterned after the African-American shows presented during the first few years of the century, and when a casting call was issued, a number of performers from those early shows turned out. The partners found a backer, and after a shaky road show tour, Shuffle Along opened in New York on May 23, 1921.

9.**Powell, Josephine**. *"When Drums are Dreaming,"* Authorhouse, 2007

10.**Olga San Juan** (March 16, 1927 – January 3, 2009) was a Brooklyn-born dancer and **comedian** of **Puerto Rican** heritage who was active in films primarily in the 1940s. She was married to late actor **Edmond O'Brien** in 1948, divorcing him in 1976, with whom she had three children, including television producer Bridget O'Brien and Maria O'Brien and **Brendan O'Brien**, both of whom became actors. In 1951, she starred on Broadway in the Lerner & Loewe musical, Paint Your Wagon. El Nuevo

Dia, San Juan, Puerto Rico, 2009

11.**Noro Morales** (1911 - 1964) was one of the most popular Latin bandleaders of the 1940s and 1950s, in New York. He grew up in a musical family, which was invited in 1924 to become the official orchestra of the president of Venezuela. Noro took over as conductor after his father died, eventually moving the band back to Puerto Rico. He moved to New York City in 1935 and within two years was leading his own rumba band. Installed as the house band at the legendary club El Morocco. **Toro Vargas, Cirilo**. *Diccionario Biográfico de Compositores Puertorriqueños*, Ediciones Guayacán, Ponce, Puerto Rico, 2003

3. Carnaval In Harlem

12.**Malavet Vega, Pedro.** *Historia de la Canción Popular en Puerto Rico –1493-1998*, Editora Corripio, Juan Morel Campo, Composer and conductor, born in Ponce, Puerto Rico, May 16, 1857, died April 26, 1896. He was the most important figure in Puerto Rican music of the 19th Century. He composed countless *danzas*, the dance (along with the *bomba* and *plena*) most closely associated with Puerto Rico. He conducted concerts, operas, and operettas throughout Puerto Rico and South America, and died conducting one of his own *zarzuelas* at his beloved La Perla theatre in Ponce.

13.**Klauber, Bruce H.** *World of Gene Krupa That Legendary Drummin' Man*, Pathfinder Pub of California, 1990

14.**Lincoln Collier, James.** *Benny Goodman and the Swing Era*, Oxford University Press, 1989

15.**Scanlan, Tom**. *The Joy of Jazz – Swing Era 1935-1947*, Fulcrum Publishing, Golden, Colorado, 1996

16.**Orovio, Helio.** *Diccionario de la Música Cubano-Biográfico y técnico*, Letras Cubanas, 1992

17.The origin of Puerto Rico's big bands originates in the old military, municipal and school bands of the 19th century. During Spanish rule, military bands in Cuba and Puerto Rico were the only large musical organizations active in the country. As early as 1812 the Asturias Regiment Band was performing at public functions in San Juan. The popular music of the period was the contradanzas that came from Havana. During those years, the "retreat" or outdoor band concert became popular. On weekends, the military ensembles would play free concerts at city parks and public squares. Eventually the military bands added violins for indoor performances and became known as "orquesta tipicas." The custom did not change much after the United States defeated Spain in 1898. One of the first "orquesta tipicas" was organized in Puerto Rico in 1883 - the Ponce Firemen's Band - directed by composer Juan Morel Campos. In 1900, Francisco Verar Mercado organized the first Band of the Police Force of Puerto Rico. One year later, Luis R. Miranda – a U.S. Army officer and prolific composer of danzas - was conducting the Puerto Rico Infantry Regiment Band. Soon after, Manuel Tizol organized the Aguadilla Firemen's Band and Jesús Muñoz formed the Juana Díaz Band. There were more than 20 tipicas or bands working on the island by 1911. The influence of Cuba was apparent even as the two islands drifted apart politically because of the Spanish-American War. The percussion of the tipicas, like their counterparts in Cuba, existed of a snare drum. The Cubans developed the pailas from the cavalry kettledrum. This would become known as timbales. The influence of American band styles was also prevalent and apparent to many. **Toro Vargas, Cirilo**. *Diccionario Biográfico de Compositores Puertorriqueños,* Ediciones Guayacán, Ponce, Puerto Rico, 2003

18.**Toro Vargas, Cirilo.** *Diccionario Biográfico de Compositores Puertorriqueños*, Ediciones Guayacán, Ponce Puerto Rico, 2003

19.**Giro, Radames**. *El Mambo*, Editorial Letras Cubanas, Habana, Cuba, 1993

20.**Lincoln Collier, James.** *Benny Goodman and the Swing Era,* Oxford University Press, 1989

21.An Afro-Cuban recreational event, dance, and accompanying music. The rumba, of which there are several named subtypes (e.g., *guaguancó, yambú, columbia*), is secular but contains elements from African-derived sacred traditions. It is accompaniment of two or three drums of the conga type (low-pitched *tumba*, often a *segundo*, and a higher-pitched *quinto*), a pair of wooden sticks (*palitos, cascara*) beaten on a wooden surface, and sometimes *claves*. The rumba begins with a short introduction (Diana or *llorado*) followed by improvised verses, both sections for solo singer with choral refrain passages; a third and concluding section is one of *call-and-response exchanges between soloist and chorus. Adopted and transformed by Cuban urban popular ensembles, the rumba became known internationally in the 1930s. Although the term has been loosely applied, the popular rumba is most typically dance music in rapid duple meter, with the energetic character, emphasis on call-and-response patterns and intricate percussion playing of its traditional counterpart. In the United States it was called "*Rhumba*". (**Randel, Don,** editor. *The Harvard Dictionary of Music*, The Belknap Press of Harvard University Press, Cambridge, Massachusetts; London, England, 1986)

22.**O'Meally, Robert G**., editor. *The Jazz Cadence of American Cultural*, Columbia University Press, New York, 1998

23.**Malavet Vega, Pedro**. *Historia de la Canción Popular en Puerto Rico, 1493-1898*, Editora Corripio, 1999

24.**Starr, S. Frederick,** *Bamboula! The Life and Times of Louis Moreau Gottschalk*, Oxford University Press, New York, 1995

25.**Orovio, Helio**. *Diccionario De La Música Cubano-Biográfico Y Técnico*, Letras Cubanas, 1992 (Valdés b. Sept. 6, 1910, Belén, Habana, Cuba – d. Nov. 9, 1978, Bogotá, Colombia)

26.**Orovio, Helio**. *Diccionario De La Música Cubano-Biográfico Y Técnico*, Letras Cubanas, 1992

27.**Pérez, Marcos "Sonny".** *Conversations with Antonio Arcaño*, 1991.

28.**Acosta, Leonardo**. *From The Drum To The Synthesizer*, 1984

29.**Giro, Radames**. *El Mambo – Todo Lo Que Usted Quiso Saber Sobre El Mambo*, Editorial Letras Cubanas, Habana, Cuba, 1993

30.**Oliveros, Joaquin**. Cuban flautist (discussions, 1999-2001)

31.**Cagney, Jimmy.** *Cagney By Cagney*, Doubleday & Company, Garden City, New Jersey, 1976

32.**Yablonsky, Lewis.** *George Raft*, 1990

33.Well-known dancer, Diosa Costello had appeared opposite Desi Arnaz, Van Johnson, and Eddie Bracken in the hit 1939 Broadway musical Too Many Girls. All four were eventually picked up by Hollywood but Costello was too much a specialty for stardom. She briefly decorated the "Good Neighbor Policy" musical They Met in Argentina (1941) and later popped up in Laurel and Hardy's "The Bullfighters" (1945), once again mainly providing local color. Always better known on-stage, Costello returned to Broadway in the original 1949 production of South Pacific and later decorated numerous nightclub acts. (**Wollstein, Hans J.,** All Movie Guide)

34."History doesn't always repeat itself in the self same way. That is, as far as nightclub, entertainers are concerned. It was about nine years ago at La Conga that Desi Arnaz and Diosa Costello stirred up a tempest of rhythm before a cafe society looking for new thrills and getting it. George Abbott, a great rumba fan, was a nightly visitor. How could the kids lose? Thanks to Abbott, they didn't (**Craigs Big Bands and Big Names**)

35.**Toro Vargas, Cirilo**. *Diccionario Biográfico de Compositores Puertorriqueños*, Ediciones Guayacán, Ponce, Puerto Rico, 2003. (Ladislao Martínez Otero (1898-1979).

36.**Hajdu, David**. *Lush Life – A Biography of Billy Strayhorn*, Grant Books, London, England, 1996

37.**Kelley, Kitty**. *His Way – The Unauthorized Biography of Frank Sinatra*, Bantam Books, New York, 1986

38.**Conzo, Joe.** Archive. (Asia Restaurant conversations - 1970).

39.**Friedman, Norman.** *U.S. Aircraft Carriers*., Naval Institute, Press, 1983
Department of the Navy, Historical Center. *Dictionary of American Naval Fighting Ship*

40.**Morison Samuel Eliot**, *the Battle of the Atlantic*, 1984)

41.**Loza, Steven.** *Tito Puente and the Making of Latin Music*, University of Illinois Press,1999; and, **Powell, Josephine**. *Tito Puente – When the Drums Are Drumming*, AuthorHouse, 2007 - refer to the pilot in quotation marks as "He." Tito never recalled the young lieutenant's name.

42.Sanabria and Socolov - 1990

43.The encyclopedia of big band, lounge, classic jazz and space-age sounds, Internet, 2007

44.**Salazar, Max**, 1984

45.**Morison Samuel Eliot**, *the Battle of the Atlantic*, 1984

4. Mucho Puente

46.1) **Orovio, Helio**. *Diccionario De La Música Cubano-Biográfico Y Técnico*, Letras Cubanas, 1992
2) **Giro, Radames**. *El Mambo*, Editorial Letras Cubanas, Cubanas, La Habana, Cuba, 1993
3) **Acosta, Leonardo**. *Elige Tu, Que Canto Yo*, Editorial Letras, Cubanas, La Habana, Cuba, 1993

47.**Arganian, Lillian**. *Stan Kenton: The Man and His Music*, Artistry Press, 1989
48.**Minahan, John.** *The Torment of Buddy Rich – A Biography*, Universe, Incorporated, 20001)
49.1) **Frankl, Ron & Huggins, Nathan I.** Charlie Parker, Chelsea House Publisher, 1989
2) O'Meally, Robert G., editor. The Jazz Cadence of American Cultural, Columbia University Press, New York, 1998
50. **Williams, Martin.** *The Jazz Tradition – Modern Jazz in Search of Maturity*, Oxford, New York, 1983
51.**Berendt, Joachim.** *The New Jazz Book – A History and Guide*, Peter Owen Ltd., London, 1964
52.**Berendt, Joachim.** *The New Jazz Book – A History and Guide*, Peter Owen Ltd., London, 1964 Feather, Leonard (editor). Encyclopedia Of Jazz, 1960 Edition, Bonanza Books, New York, 1960
53.**Cal Tjader** Profile, **All About Jazz**, Internet, 2007
54.Teadoro Moscoso led a project Operation Bootstrap that realized that agriculture alone would not be able to employ the burgeoning island population, and sought to use the advantages of free access to the mainland United States market and ready, inexpensive, but trained labor to rapidly industrialize the society. The rapid economic progress of Puerto Rico during the decades of 1950-1970 made the island the "miracle of the Caribbean". The ambitious Fomento (Puerto Rico Development) project stimulated various industries through federal and local tax exemption and government assistance. Moscoso succeeded in attracting worldwide capital investment to Puerto Rico, which in turn helped transform the island into a modern bustling industrial society. The publication, The Economist later reported: "one century of economic development . . . achieved in a decade." An example of the success shows the change from agricultural to manufacturing employment (extracted from Fernando Pico, Historia General de Puerto Rico)
55. **Schillinger, Joseph.** The Schillinger System of Music, Da Capo Press, 1978\

5. On The Way To Broadway

56.**Cuellar Vizcaíno,** Manuel. *La Revolución del Mambo / Con Arcaño y sus Maravillas*, Editorial Letras Cubanas, 1993
57.**Orovio, Helio.** *Diccionario De La Música Cubano-Biográfico Y Técnico*, Editorial Letras Cubanas, 1992
58.**Owen, Frank.** *Clubland: The Fabulous Rise and Murderous Fall of Club Cultural*, St. Martin's Press, 2003
59.**Geyer, Georgie Anne**. *Guerrilla Prince – Untold Story of Fidel Castro*, Little Brown & Company, 1991
60.**Orovio, Helio**. *Diccionario de la Música Cubana – Biográfico Y Técnico*, Editorial Letras Cubanas, Habana, Cuba, 1991
61.**Powell, Josephine**. *When the Drums Are Dreaming*, Authorhouse, 2007

6. Mambo Diablo

62.**Toro Vargas, Cirilo**. *Diccionario Biográfico de Compositores Puertorriqueños*, Ediciones Guayacán, Ponce, P.R., 2003
63.**Ricci, Michael**. *Mongo Santamaria Biography Profile*, All About Jazz, Internet Service
64.**Nadal, James & Ricci, Michael**. *Willie Bobo Biography Profile*, All About Jazz Music Center, Internet Service
65.**Richman, Irwin**. *Borscht Belt Bungalows: Memories of Catskill Summers*, Temple University Press, 2003
66."To make an impression on Ellington, Strayhorn decided that not only would he find Ellington in New York by following the bandleader's subway directions but he would write a new composition using the directions as the theme. Ralph Koger, a reporter for the Pittsburgh Courier remembered meeting with Duke and his plans to see him, and he played me the song he was writing to give Duke in New York. He said, 'Listen – Duke gave me directions and I turned them into something. So he played me the tune, and sure enough, it told you how to get to Harlem: 'Take the "A" Train.'" (**Hajdu, David.** *Lush Life – A Biography of Billy Strayhorn*, Granta Books, London, 1996)

67.All of the Tico records have since be released as the *"Complete Tito Puente Orchestra Tico Recordings,"*
68.**Dawson, Jim & Propes, Steve.** *45 RPM: The History, Heroes & Villains of a Pop Music Revolution,* Backbeat Books, San Francisco 2003
Betz, Frederick *Strategic Technology Management,* McGraw-Hill, New York, 1994

7. Palladium Nights

69.**Pérez, Marcos.** *Reminisces of the Palladium-1954*, San Juan Star
70.**Salazar, Max**. *Mambo Kingdom*, Schirmer Trade Books, 2002 "Very little has been written about the Palladium. I decided to change that situation but I could not have done this article without the help of Vernon Boggs, sociologist, and David Carp, radio show host, Latin music historian, journalist, and investigator. Both unearthed information this is at the heart of the Palladium.
71.**Ettinger, Roseann**. *Fifties Forever: Popular Fashions for men, Women, Boys & Girls*, Schiffer Publishing, Ltd. 1999
72.**WEDNESDAY WAS SHOWCASE NIGHT**. They held different contests, from pie eating to skirt-raising showdowns and Mambo dancing eliminations. The Palladium became the place to be seen at. Different jazz musicians and celebrities would sit in and play with the Latin bands – Dizzy Gillespie, George Shearing, Cal Tjader, Marlon Brando and Sammy Davis Jr. The area was a musician's paradise, with the Palladium on West 53rd Street and Broadway, and the jazz clubs on West 52nd Street – Birdland, The Onyx and Cubop City. You never knew what nuances would be occurring on any given night or who was going to show. The Palladium also became a showcase for many new dance rhythms such as the cha-cha, the merengue and the pachanga. They became just as popular with the masses as the mambo. The Palladium also succeeded in attracting famous musicians from Cuba and Puerto Rico – José Fajardo, Orchestra Aragon, and Cuba's great Beny Moré; and from Puerto Rico: Cortijo and Ismael Rivera, Cesar Concepción and many others (Conzo, Joe. *The Palladium*, Times Herald Record article, 2004)
73.**Gilberto Valdés**, a multi-talented Cuban instrumentalist and composer had introduced the "Cuban flute" (six hole-five key unadorned wooden flute to the jazz scene in 1949 recordings he made with Dizzy Gillespie and Machito y sus Afro-Cubanos, organized what is the first charanga style orchestra on the U.S. mainland in 1954, and in 1956 produced and directed a 64-piece Cuban All Star orchestra (Gran Orquesta de 64 profesores) in a **Puchito** Album commemorating the 75th Anniversary of the danzón. The orchestra featured Antonio Arcaño, José A. Fajardo, Cheo Belén Puig, Pedro Hernández, Israel "Cachao" López, Richard Egues and many others.
74.**Esposito, Tony.** Editor, *Giants of Jazz Piano*, Alfred Publishing Co. Inc., 2004
**DeCastro Sister Biography*, Primarily A Cappella,, Internet, 2007
75.**Joe Conzo** Archive-open reel tape
76.**Caridad Ayala, Caridad.** Historian, *Club TropiCaliente History - Excerpts of Internet Article Club,* May 2010
77.Live recording of Sammy Davis Jr. singing with the Tito Puente Orchestra. **Joe Conzo** Archive

8. Tito's Cuban Carnaval

78.*Arthur Murray Dance Studio History,*; **Arthur Murray** Website, Internet 2010
79.**All About Jazz; "**Richard Puente, second son of the Late Latin jazz legend Tito Puente and percussionist with famed disco group Foxy, died in his sleep Sunday morning. (2004 - 7 - 18) In the prime of a richly rewarding career that has included two Grammy nominations and two gold records, the accomplished 51-year-old multi-instrumentalist was hospitalized after suffering from viral encephoplopathy due to a prior brain injury that was the result of a mugging over 10 years ago. In 1974, Richie and fellow musician Ish Ledesma formed the band Foxy, playing rock and underground disco covers and originals. By 1975, they had a recording contract with Henry Stone's T.K. label out of Florida and recorded five albums, one f which went gold. In 1979, Richie toured with the Jacksons (featuring Michael Jackson) on the Destiny Tour, where Foxy was the opening act for Sister Sledge. Since his departure from Foxy, Richie became a session musician for Criteria Studios, recording with such renowned artists as Peter Frampton, Eddie Money, George and Gwen McRae, Blowfly (Clarence

Reed) and Abba. In 2000, Richie returned to the stage with renewed vigor, playing percussion for Edward Villela's Miami City Ballet production Mambo No. 2 a.m. and appearing as a guest artist at Roseland Ballroom in New York City for the Linda McCartney Breast Awareness Garland Foundation in the Latin Segment tribute to his father, Tito Puente."

80.**Carlini, Ari**. Son's comment posted on Internet, 2005

81.**Knoedelseder, William.** *Stiffed: A True Story of MCA, The Music Business, and the Mafia*, Harper/ Collins Publishers, 1993

Kurutz, Steve. *Morris Levy Biographical Essay*, Yahoo! Music, Internet, 2007

82.When executives of the Columbia company announced the long-playing record to the press in 1948, they portrayed it as a revolutionary new technology that would take "the musical world by storm." This was more a marketing ploy than an accurate depiction of the development of the technology--most of the innovations in the new product had been made years before, even the playing speed of 33-1/3 rpm dated from the 1930s when it was used in long-playing transcriptions of radio programs. Nevertheless, the Columbia company touted its long-playing record as a major event in the history of sound recording and eagerly expected the rest of the recording industry to adopt it. Columbia miscalculated the reaction of RCA, long its rival in the record business and a company that prided itself on being the leader in new technology. RCA had developed a long-playing disc in the 1930s, but it had failed to catch on. When RCA heard of the Columbia research project it hurriedly introduced its own microgroove, 45 rpm, seven-inch disc, and the "Battle of the Speeds" was on. This delayed the introduction of microgrooved discs because the customer had to choose from four speeds of revolving disc: 78, 33-1/3, 45, and 16 rpm. It was not until the mid-1950s that the 12-inch disc established itself as the format for long-playing records, and the introduction of the Westrex stereophonic sound system in 1957 made it the format for high fidelity recordings. As had been expected, lovers of classical music and audiophiles embraced the new long-playing disc. The record companies were kept busy transferring their recordings of orchestral music from piles of 78 rpm shellac discs to one long player. A new source of music for the long player was found in the Broadway play; the sound track for *My Fair Lady* was the best-selling long-playing recording of the 1950s, and it was followed by soundtracks from other plays and films. Artists like Frank Sinatra moved into the long-playing format in the 1950s, producing thematic albums such as *Come Fly with Me,* which contained songs about travel. Yet pop music--music for teenagers--stayed on the 45 rpm single format. The single was cheap (less than a dollar), easily carried around, and the three-minute playing time was perfect for AM radio, which wanted lots of time between songs for commercials. (**Millard, Andre.** *Long-Playing Record "excerpts"*, St. James Encyclopedia of Pop Cultural, 2007)

83.**Dannen, Fredric.** *Hitmen-Power Brokers and Fast Money Inside the Music Business,* Helter Skelter Publishing, 2003. Originally published: Times Books, a division of Random House, 1990. "Much harder to qualify was another source of Morris Levy's wealth and power: a lifelong association with the Mafia. A Sephardic Jew (or "Turk," in his words) from the poorest section of the Bronx, Morris was never a member, but he did business with several crime families. The Genovese family of New York cast the longest shadow over his career. Morris always disavowed mob involvement; when the subject of his well-known gangster friends came up, he was fond of pointing to a framed portrait of himself with Cardinal Spellman remarking: "That don't make me a Catholic." (page 33).

84.**Shanok, Sarah**. *The Bowery's up and Clear Channel's down*, New York Press, Internet, 2008
Webster Hall History, Webster Hall Website

85.**Lachatañere, Romulo**. *El Sistema Religioso de los Afrocubanos* (author's translation), Editorial de Ciencias Sociales, Habana, Cuba-1992

* **Hughes, Rupert** (Editor). *Music Lovers' Encyclopedia*, Doubleday, Doran and Company, Inc., New York, 1939

9. It's A Puente

86.**Russo, Peter D., Esperian, John, & Esperian, John H. Offshore Vegas** – How the Mob Brought Revolution to Cuba, Universe Incorporated, 2007

87.**Collazo, Bobby**. La Ultima Noche Que Pase Contigo – 40 anos de farándula cubana, Editorial Cubanacan, P.R., 1987

88.**Ortiz, Fernando**. *La Africania de la Música Folklórica de Cuba*, Editorial Letras Cubanas, Habana, Cuba, 1993

89.**Ray Santos** (born, December 28, 1928, New York City). graduated from Juilliard School of Music. He played for Machito, Tito Rodriguez and Tito Puente at various times during the 1950s and 1960s. he is four time Grammy® Award winner for Latin music, and Academy Award nominee for Best Song in a Motion Picture - "The Mambo Kings." He has collaborated with artists such as Linda Ronstadt, Julio Iglesias, Dizzie Gillespie and Noro Morales to name a few. "I wasn't into music at the time; however, of the young guys playing at the time the one I remember the most was Charlie Palmieri. Charlie lived over on 108th Street between 3rd and Lexington. He lived in the same building my father's Army buddy, Esteban Rodriguez, lived in. Esteban was Charlie's godfather. I got to know Charlie through Esteban. I didn't get to know Tito Puente or Joe Loco, who were from the neighborhood, until the 50's when I got involved in music. As a young kid, the only professional musician I knew personally was Charlie. (Jazz Con Clave.com, 2009)

90.**Bobby Sanabria** conducts the Manhattan School of Music Jazz Orchestra in "Kenya Revisited", a compact disc that pays tribute to Mario Bauzá and the Machito Orchestra 50 years after the historical recording. Manhattan School plans the release of the soundtrack of "A Tribute to Tito Puente and his Music," that was staged in 2009 at Borden Auditorium, MSM, New York.

91.**Feather, Leonard** (editor). *Encyclopedia Of Jazz – 1960*, Bonanza Books, New York, 1960

92.**Quirk, Robert E**. *Fidel Castro*, W.W. Norton & Company, 1993

10. El Rey Bravo

93.**Joe Conzo**, **David A. Perez** Archives – A 15-minute live recording made at the New York Palladium

94.Charlie Palmieri was born November 21, 1926 in New York City. He died September 12, 1988. His friendship with Tito Puente dates back to their childhood in El Barrio. Taught piano at Schuylerville Music Center in the Bronx.

Biography in: "*The Scribner Encyclopedia of American Lives*". Volume Two, 1986-1990, pages 681-683. New York: Charles Scribner's Sons, 1999.

95.**José Luis Feliciano Vega**, better known as Cheo Feliciano (b. July 3, 1935 in Ponce, Puerto Rico) is a vocalist and a composer. He settled in Spanish Harlem with his parents in 1952. Bandleader, Tito Rodríguez, recommended him to Joe Cuba for his sextet in 1955. (SalsaClasica.com, biography)

96.**Kurutz, Steve**. *Morris Levy Biographical Essay*, Yahoo! Music, Internet, 2007

The Story of Tico Records, Spectropop Presents, Internet Document Eliot, Marc. *Rockonomics: The Money Behind the Music,* Scholastic Library Publishing, 1989

97.The pachanga dance craze had a tremendous impact on the sound of Latin New York, as evidenced by the large number of pachanga albums released during the early '60s, both on major and independent labels. The dance was a high-energy mix of merengue and cha-cha-chá rhythms. Flute-and-violin *charanga* bands dominated the scene, and none were more popular than those led by pianist Charlie Palmieri and percussionist-turned-flautist Johnny Pacheco. Both Palmieri and Pacheco recorded for Al Santiago's Alegre label, which would later be bought out by Roulette. However, for the time being, Alegre's artists were competition, and Teddy Reig had to keep his artists viable in the marketplace. Soon, he had signed charangas led by Rosendo Rosell, Pupi Legarreta, and Alfredito Valdés, Jr. Though Alfredito chose to abandon his solo career in order to join Machito's Afro-Cubans, his George Goldner-supervised album was so popular, it rated a reissue in 1969. Reig also revamped the orchestras of Machito, Pete Terrace, and Arsenio Rodríguez to fit the pachanga mould. (**Patrick, Mick & Chapman, Phil**. *George Goldner Profile*, Spectropop Internet Service)

98.**Quirk, Robert E**. *Fidel Castro*, W.W. Norton & Co., New York, 1993

99.**Moyar, Mar**. *Triumph Forsaken: The Vietnam War, 1954-1965,* Cambridge University Press, 2006

100.**Jonnes, Jill**. *South Bronx Rising – The Rise, Fall and Resurrection of An American City*, Fordham University Press, 2002

101.**Ray, Ricardo**. *Excerpts of "Se Solto" Album Analysis* . Internet Service Technically speaking, "Danzón Bugaloo" is probably the first song *labeled* as a boogaloo but that doesn't mean that it's the first boogaloo song in terms of style. As Flores also notes, there's no shortage of antecedents to the boogaloo from the worlds of cha cha and guajiras and other proto-Latin soul styles. However, Ray was the first artist - it seems - to have consciously labeled what he was doing as a new Latin dance/rhythm known as "bugaloo" (interestingly, some people would go on to spell it "bugalu" or "boogaloo" but Ray's contraction of the two seems relatively unique. What's interesting about "Danzón Bugaloo" is how it doesn't quite conform to the músical "norms" we associate with boogaloo but perhaps that's the "danzón" influence. It may also be the fact that the song is a cover of "Whipped Cream" by Herb Alpert and the Tijuana Brass. You have to admit there is a deep, rich web of connections when a White musician trying to capture the sound of Mexico at the border would get covered by a Nuyorican, fusing Cuban dance with Black R&B lyrics and rhythms. However, though "Danzón Bugaloo" has its own eccentricities, there's no denying that "Lookie Lookie" lays down what would become a classic template for the boogaloo: a repeating piano muntono riff, English lyrics, an anchored, measured sense of percussion plus an added bonus of having the song swing into a higher tempo mid-way through. It's not the most scintillating boogaloo ever recorded but for the first attempt, it's more than laudable.

102."The Tito Puente Orchestra and his invited guest, Celia Cruz and the Count Basie Orchestra shared the Carnegie Hall marquee on June 18 1962. The concert orchestra at the packed concert hall on West 57th Street was classical Tito Puente. The orchestra was forceful and evocative. In typical fashion the orchestra built momentum and drive until the concert hall shock and the patrons were left in awe. Celia Cruz was up to the task of keeping up with Tito's New York style of Cuban music. It would be the first of many engagements he would share with the Cuban diva." (**Powell, Joséphine.** *When the Drums are Drumming*, Authorhouse, 2007)

103.**Tito Rodríguez, Jr.,** (born on February 20, c. 1955), is an arranger, composer, percussionist and bandleader. as an arranger, composer, producer, and bandleader. At age 21, Tito released his debut tropical music album *Curious?* for TR Records, a label owned by his father. He has composed and arranged for the many Latin artists including the Sally Jessy Raphael Show. In 2002, Tito combined forces with Mario Grillo (Machito Jr.) to perform original charts from the era of their fathers. The resulting album, "*The Big 3 Palladium Orchestra: Live at the Blue Note*," was released. Tito Jr. decided to create the *Tito Rodríguez Orchestra with Tito Rodríguez Jr* early in 2008. The orchestra plays his father's original charts creating an updated version of his father's original Mambo beats. A multi-faceted artist, Tito experienced successes offstage including raising two children and competing as a tennis professional, ranking 150th in the world. His father's music is a continual source of inspiration, and Tito honors this legacy while infusing originality and 'swing' that is his very own. Tito is a living embodiment of Latin Jazz heritage and creative artistry for American audiences, and for the world. (Tito Rodríguez Website, 2010)

104.**Rivera, George**. *The King of Latin Music, Video Documentary*, George Rivera Productions, 2000

11. A Meeting Of Masters

105.**Conzo, Joe.** Archive, Tape recordings made at Asia Restaurant, New York City, 1974 (Transcription: **David A. Perez**)

12. Tito On The Bridge

106.**George Wein**, **Nate Chinen**, **Bill Cosby**, **Nate Chinen**. *A Memoir* - Da Capo Press , April 2004. The Newport Jazz Festival was established in 1954 by the jazz impresario **George Wein**, prompted by socialite **Elaine Lorillard**, whose wealthy husband helped finance the festival's startup. The Newport Jazz Festival moved to **New York City** in 1972 and became a two site festival in 1981 when it returned to Newport and also continued in New York. The festival has been known as the JVC Jazz Festival since 1986. Two of the most famous performances in the festival's history include **Miles Davis**'s 1955 solo on "'**Round Midnight**" and the **Duke Ellington** Orchestra's lengthy 1956 performance of "**Diminuendo and Crescendo in Blue**".

107.Jerry Masucci would eventually become sole owner of Fañia Records and the numerous other labels and umbrella labels in South America that he acquired and created. Jerry recognised the talents of his stars, he signed and owned them. His money and business acumen launched unknowns to stardom. He put together all his artist's and invited others outside of his label to sing with Fañia artists. Masucci a clever man, from lawyer to record producer, to promoter, to feature film Maker. Jerry Masucci had Johnny Pacheco to direct stage productions and Larry Harlow directing the artist in the studio. The history of Fañia is the man behind the scenes. Jerry Masucci served in the U.S. Navy during the

Korean War. He became a member of the New York City Police Department. After attending college at night; he took a leave of absence and attended Mexico City College where he played halfback with their football team while earned a degree in Business Administration, Majoring in foreign Trade, and graduating first in his class with cum laude honors. He then returned to the Police Department as a plain clothes policeman and attended New York Law School during the day he graduated from the New York Law School in 1960. He thereafter received a Doctor of Law Degree. Jerry then resigned from the Police Department and worked in Havana, Cuba, as assistant to the Director of Public Relations in the Department of Tourism. A lawyer with Pariser and Masucci, in 1962 Johnny Pacheco used Masucci for his divorce and Masucci saw a business potential in the Latin music scene. In 1975 "Live at Yankee Stadium" was included in the second set of 50 recordings in the List of recordings preserved in the United States National Recording Registry. **Internet**; Wikiipedia Free Encyclopedia)

108.**Easton, Carol**. *Straight Ahead: The Story of Stan Kenton, DaCapo Press, 1981*

109.**Roy E. Ayers** was born on October 9, 1940 in Los Angeles, CA. He grew up in a musical family were his father played trombone and his mother piano. At the age of five he got his first piano lesson by his mother and by that, a first introduction to the wonderful world of music. He started to play the piano and before young Ayers could spell his name, he was jamming hot bogie-woogie riffs. At the age of five he received a vibes set as a gift from the famous vibes player Lionel Hampton. It would, however, take 12 years, till he was 17, before he started using the instrument on a more serious level. As his interest for the vibraphone grew, he got more and more involved in the west coast's lively jazz-scene. He started playing with artists like Curtis Amy (1962), Jack Wilson (1963-67), Chico Hamilton and Gerald Wilson Orchestra (1965-66). In 1966 bass player Reggie Workman persuaded Roy into a jam with flute player Herbie Mann at the club Lighthouse at Hermosa Beach, CA. The jam session evolved into becoming a steady four-year gig with Mann at the Lighthouse. It also brought Ayers into the direct limelight, which attracted him enormous attention. During this period he also got a wider músical perspective and got interested in other kinds of music forms than the be-bop he grew up with. After contributing on Mann's hit album," Memphis Underground", and after recording three own solo recordings on Atlantic with Mann as producer, Ayers left Mann's group in 1970 and moved to Manhattan, New York. In New York he formed his own group, nowadays a quite famous constellation by the name of Roy Ayers Ubiquity. (**Roy Ayers Internet Web Site**)

110.**Storm Roberts, John.** *The Latin Tinge*, *Original Music*, 1979 "In many respects, Latin music during the 1960s and 1970s mirrored the 1920s and 1930s. In each case, the first decade emphasized a growth that would take full effect in the second. The 1930s saw the introduction of Latin music as a sub-style within U. S. popular music as a whole; the late 1970s saw its clear emergence as a more ingredient in the sound of almost all American popular idioms. Yet, paradoxically, Latin music had not for a long time seemed so irrelevant to the mainstream as it did in the early 1970s, despite occasional Latin-influenced hits – Paul Simon's El Condor Pasa" was one, Gato Barbieri's "Last Tango in Paris," film theme another."

111.**Storm Roberts**, **John**. *The Latin Tinge, Original Music*, 1979 "New York Latin musicians themselves were depressed about the state of their music on two grounds. On the one hand, they were acutely conscious that it was generally ignored. On the other, many were perturbed by developments within the hardcore style. The return to Cuban orthodoxy continued unabated after the collapse of the bugalu movement. The most successful bands were firmly committed, at least in theory, to the tipico Cuban sound."

112.**Nichols, Roger**. *Ravel Remembered*, W-W-Norton & Company, London, 1987)

113.Frank Sinatra mentions Jilly in a number of his recordings: Jilly's Restaurant is mentioned twice in his and **Sammy Davis Jr.**'s song "*Me and My Shadow*"**.** At the beginning of the album "Sinatra at the Sands." Frank jokingly welcomes his **Las Vegas** audience to "Jilly's West." In his cover version of "*Mrs. Robinson*"**,** he changes the name "Jesus" to "Jilly." Actor/comedian **Brad Garrett** told some funny stories about being **Frank Sinatra**'s opening act, and how Jilly temporarily fired him for allegedly making a bad joke about Frank. Jilly allegedly sent him, as a punishment, to open for **Liza Minnelli**. Jilly appears as a bartender in *The Manchurian Candidate* where one of his stories sets off **Laurence Harvey** into a hypnotic trance.(Triva, Internet Service)

114.**Don Costa** (July 10 1925 – January 19 1983) was an American pop music arranger and record producer best known for his work with Frank Sinatra. Costa was born Dominick P. Costa in Boston, Massachusetts to an Italian American family He became a member of the CBS Radio Orchestra by the time he was in his teens. In the late 1940s, Costa moved to New York to further his career by becoming a session musician. He played guitar along with Bucky Pizzarelli on Vaughn Monroe's hit recording "Ghost Riders in the Sky." It was around this time that Costa started experimenting with combinations of instruments, producing musical arrangements, and peddling them to a few notable big bands (Artistopia, Internet Service)

115.**Earl Wilson** (b. **May 3, 1907** in **Rockford, Ohio** – d. **January 16, 1987** in **Yonkers, New York**) was an journalist, gossip columnist and author, best known for his nationally syndicated column, "It Happened Last Night." Wilson's column publsihed from the New York Post from 1942 until **1983**. He chronicled of the "Golden Age" of Broadway and **show business** and published a book in **1971**, "The Show usiness Nobody Knows."He signed his columns with the **tag line,** "That's Earl, brother." His nickname was "Midnight Earl." In later years, the name of his column was changed to Last Night with Earl Wilson.

116.**Wilson, Earl**. *Sinatra: The Unauthorized Biography*, Penguin Group (USA) Incorporated, 1977

117.**Kelley, Kitty**. *His Way – The Unauthorized Biography of Frank Sinatra*, Bantam Books, 1987

118.The photo was taken backstage at the Westchester Premier Theater in Tarrytown, New York, on April 11, 1976. According to Fratianno in his authorized biography The Last Mafioso, it was Gambino's idea to go backstage and pay a visit on the Frank Sinatra.

119.**Ortiz, Fernando**. *La Africania de la Música Folklórica de Cuba*, Letras Cubanas, 1993. Olorun - Is represented as the "Father" or God of the sky he is viewed as a God of tranquility, purity and harmony. He is normally and strongly linked with the color white and has power and control over all white elements such as the brain, bones, teeth, clouds and much more. He is known to be the spiritual father of Obatala and Odudua.

120.**Franc Peri** established Roper Records, Inc in 1960. to produce high quality dance records for national and international distribution. The company distributes quality music recordings to dance studios, ballroom competitions, instructors, and professional dance associations. In addition to its classic ballroom catalogue, Roper Records catalogue includes music for the performing arts, with an extensive collection of ballet, tap, and jazz compilations. These are produced with many of the finest pianists and music supervisors in the industry. (Roper Records, Inc. Website)

121.**Joe Conzo, Felipe Luciano** and **Charlie Palmieri** organized Latin Roots Exhibition. The exhibit lasted about seven months and was staged at the Lincoln Center Library. Schlitz Beer produced it. It paid tribute to the founders of the Afro-Cuban music genre in the United States – Machito and his Afro-Cubans, Tito Rodríguez, and many others.

122.One of Mexico City's most outstanding avenues is Paseo de la Reforma. Along its central extension are examples of architecture, numerous banks and offices, ancient residential areas now transformed into fashionable venues, embassies, luxury hotels, exclusive art galleries and spectacular monuments. During the mid-19th Century, Mexico City experienced painful encounters with the outside world as it suffered invasions by both North American and French forces. During the French intervention, a new urban model was proposed by the administration of emperor Maximilian of Hapsburg: the construction of an avenue which would communicate Mexico City, starting from the Bucareli roundabout, with Chapultepec Castle. Originally named The Emperor's Avenue, it was a 12-kilometer long boulevard.

123.At the end of **Paseo de la Reforma** looms Chapultepec hill, a centuries-old forest encircles it, and a castle crowns its summit. For hundreds of years it has been a focal point in this city. It is complemented by important cultural centers including world-class museums (Museum of Anthropology), amusement parks, a zoo and lakes, and is crisscrossed by access routes. These routes are most used by hordes of visitors; many of them making up typical extended Mexican families, with their far-reaching family ties.

124.**Mercado Jr., Ralph** (September 29, 1941 – March 10, 2009). Born in Brooklyn, New York to a Dominican father, who was a dockworker, and a Puerto Rican mother.

125.**Powell, Josephine**. *When the Drums Are Drumming*, Authorhouse, 2007 "Low points in his career have been the rise of in the early 1970s of Fañia Records, whose artists have received 10 times more airplay than Puente: and the unfavorable critique of Tito Puente's 1974 Tico LP Tito Unlimited by two DJs and writer John Storm Roberts."

Salazar, Max. *Mambo Kingdom*, Schirmer Trade Books, New York, 2002 "Tito was now at the very bottom of the space he created. Most of his former engagements at upscale ballrooms, clubs, and hotels were now closed. His current bookings were no longer held at smart clubs."

126.Jam Session Video and soundtrack, **Joe Conzo** collection

127.Salsoul Records released Cachao y sus Descarga, Volumes 1 and 2 in 1977. The original concert featured two distinct styles of Afro-Cuban music: the Danzón-mambo as developed by Antonio Arcaño and the López brothers in the 1930s and the Afro-Cuban Descarga (Jam Sessions) that was developed in the 1950s. Charlie Palmieri is the pianist on the enlarged all-star orchestra his piano solos on "Adelante," "Se va el Matancero" and "Jovenes Del Ritmo," composed by Israel "Cachao" López in the 1930s is considered to be passionate and evocative. (**David A. Pérez**) "

13. Puente's Night Beat

128.**Haden-Guest, Anthony**. *The Last Party: Studio 54, Disco, and the Culture of the Night,* HarperCollins Publishers, 1997 - Packed with stars, models, socialites, and everyone else who could sneak past the fabled velvet ropes, Studio 54 defined disco and launched the celebrity-driven culture of today. Writer Haden-Guest takes readers behind the scenes and tells the whole story -- the glory days, the drugs, the deaths, and the corruption. There was a place where virtually all the themes and energies of the 1970s -- disco, the cult of celebrity, the coke and the Quaaludes, the glam and the glitter, the pre-AIDS sexual abandon, the emergence of gay culture, uninhibited women, and the general air of debauchery -- were played out with maximum flamboyance. Studio 54 was the quintessential midtown Manhattan nightspot of the late 1970s and early '80s, where the gay and straight worlds intersected; where celebrities and wannabes crowded in to disco, drug and who knows what else; in front of which people waited for hours in hopes of being admitted (two women arrived naked on horseback as Lady Godivas; the horses were let in, but the women weren't). Haden-Guest, a regular writer for New York magazine and Vanity Fair, reports on his beloved 'Night world' -- the life of New York clubs -- with an enthusiasm that assumes all were swept away by disco-mania. The club closed with one final party called "The End of Modern-day **Gomorrah**," on February 4, 1980. Tito and his orchestra appeared a few weeks before for the last time. **Diana Ross**, **Janice Dickinson**, **Jocelyne Wildenstein**, **Richard Gere**, **Gia Carangi**, **Reggie Jackson**, and **Sylvester Stallone** (who, legend has it, bought the last drink) were among the guests that last night. New York lawyer **Gary Naftalis** successfully represented Schrager in the ensuing tax-evasion prosecution. After the club's closing, cocaine and money were found in its walls. Schrager and Rubell were found guilty and would spend 13 months in prison.
129. **Chris McNickle_Kenneth T. (Ed.) Jackson, K**enneth T. Jackson (Ed.). To Be Mayor of New York: Ethnic Politics in the City. Columbia University Press, 1993Abraham David "Abe" Beame (March 20, 1906 – February 10, 2001) was mayor of New York City from 1974 to 1977. He presided over the city during the fiscal crisis of the mid-1970s, during which the city was almost forced to declare bankruptcy. He was also distinguished for being New York City's first Jewish mayor. He was born in London, and grew up on New York's Lower East Side, and became city budget director from 1952 to 1961. He was a Democrat and was elected to two terms as city comptroller in 1961 and 1969. In 1965 he was the Democratic nominee for Mayor, but was defeated by the Republican candidate, John V. Lindsay. Beame was a "clubhouse" or machine politician, a product of the Brooklyn wing of the regular Democratic organization (that borough's equivalent of Manhattan's Tammany Hall) as opposed to the "reform" Democrats who entered New York politics in the 1950s. After defeating State Senator John Marchi in the 1973 mayoral election, Beame faced the worst fiscal crisis in the city's history and spent the bulk of his term attempting to ward off bankruptcy. He slashed the city workforce, froze wages, and restructured the budget, which proved insufficient until reinforced by actions from newly created state-sponsored entities and the granting of federal funds. He also served during the blackout crisis. After a tumultuous four years as mayor, he ran for a second term in 1977 (shortly after the New York City blackout of 1977, one of the low points in NYC's history) and finished third in the Democratic primary to U.S. Representative Edward I. Koch and New York Secretary of State Mario M. Cuomo. Beame outpolled former Congresswoman Bella Abzug, Congressman Herman Badillo and Manhattan Borough President **Percy Sutton** in the 1977 primary. When he left office in 1977, the city budget had changed from a $1.5 billion deficit to a surplus of $200 million.
130. Director, Writer and **Producer Jeremy Marre** has made a wide variety of television programs. Many have won major international awards, including a Grammy and two Emmys. He also produced and directed the film *FORBIDDEN IMAGE*, about the Indian erotic arts, with an original score by Ravi Shankar, for ITV. *BEATS OF THE HEART* a 14 hour, multi-award-winning series on world music that was networked several times on British television, accompanied by Marre's book of the same name and 14 videos/DVDs. The films include *"Roots, Rock, Reggae"*"(Jamaican music) and

"*Rhythm of Resistance*"' on black music as resistance to apartheid in South Africa and *"Salsa"*. These are now digitally re-mastered. With writer Gerald Durrell, he produced and directed the 12-part animal communication series *OURSELVES AND OTHER ANIMALS* (for Channel 4 and CBC). Jeremy has also made several South Bank Shows for ITV, including the Golden Harp winner on *SALSA MUSIC*, profiles of *HERBERT VON KARAJAN* and *CLAUDIO ABBADO* (for ITV/Granada International). (**Jeremy Marre Web Site**, 2008)

131.**Wild, David.** *And the Grammy Goes to... The Official Story of Music's Most Coveted Award.* Publisher: State Street Press Pub. Date: October 2007 - The Grammy Awards were originally called the Gramophone Awards—or Grammys. They are presented annually by the **National Academy of Recording Arts and Sciences** of the United States for outstanding achievements in the record industry. The awards ceremony features performances by prominent artists, and some of the more prominent Grammy Awards are presented in a widely-viewed televised ceremony. The awards were established in 1958. Prior to the first live Grammys telecast in 1971 on ABC, a series of taped annual specials in the 1960s called The Best on Record were broadcast on NBC. The first Grammy Award telecast took place on the night of November 29, 1959, as an episode of the NBC anthology series *Sunday Showcase*, which was normally devoted to plays, original TV dramas, and variety shows. Until 1971, awards ceremonies were held in both New York and Los Angeles, with winners accepting at one of the two. The Recording Academy and record companies are responsible for entering into nomination the works that they deem most deserving. Once a work is entered, reviewing sessions are held by over 150 experts from the recording industry. This is only to determine whether or not a work is eligible or entered into the proper category for official nomination. The nomination process requires that members vote only in their fields of expertise. They may nominate in the four general categories (Record of the Year, Album of the Year, Song of the Year and Best New Artist) and in no more than nine out of 31 fields on their ballots. Once the nominations are secured, Recording Academy members may then vote in the four general categories and in no more than eight of the 31 fields. Ballots are tabulated secretly by the major independent accounting firm Deloitte Touche Tohmatsu. As of 2006, the eligibility period for the Grammy Awards begins October 1. In 2000 the Latin Grammys were established.

132.One of numerous conversations with **José Madera Jr.**, the musical director of the Tito Puente Orchestra during that 1990s, and son of Machito saxophonist "Ping" Madera, explained, "at the time Tito was struggling to figure out how to maintain a successful musical organization knowing full well that the market forces were constantly changing. He would have much preferred to dig into his Afro-Cuban roots that combined the intricacies of two flavors – black and European, and intertwine them in his established syncopated manner, but the resources were not available." (2008)

133.**Madera, Jr., José.** He is the son of saxophonist José "Pin Madera who was one of the original members of Machito y sus Afro-Cubanos.

134.The company's first endorser was Afro-Cuban and jazz drummer Willie Bobo. LP has over 500 **endorsers**, a list which reads as a veritable "who's who" of the music world. Musicians like **Tito Puente**, **"Patato" Valdez**, Carlos Santana, **Giovanni Hildago**, **Armando Peraza** and many more all use **LP products**. Because they are the best, their equipment must be the best as well. The company that started in the Cohen garage now has a staff of research, design and product developers that keep an ongoing stream of new products coming out. In addition, over 250 people are employed at the manufacturing facility in Thailand. What started as a small family operation has grown to become Latin Percussion, the world's largest producer of hand percussion instruments. (**Latin Percussion Web Site**, 2008)

135.**Minor, William and Wishner, Bill**. *Monterey Jazz Festival: Forty Legendary Years* -The opening night of the first Monterey Jazz Festival in 1958 featured performances by Gerry Mulligan, Max Roach, Dave Brubeck, Cal Tjader, the Modern Jazz Quartet, Harry James, and, just nine months before her death, Billie Holiday. The evening's highlight, however, came when Dizzy Gillespie, acting as the program's emcee, welcomed his hero, and occasional rival, Louis Armstrong to the stage. As thousands of fans gasped, Dizzy dropped to his knees and kissed Pops' hand in homage. This great moment, bringing together two generations of jazz, and two of the most important and beloved personalities in the music's history, is but only one of the many jazz memories recalled. Calling itself, he "world's oldest ongoing jazz festival" — the peripatetic Newport Jazz Festival is actually four years older — Monterey has firmly established itself as one of the premier jazz events in the world, annually drawing tens of thousands of fans each autumn weekend. The festival welcomes musicians from all over the world playing all kinds of jazz-related music: blues, bebop, Dixieland, Latin, mainstream, avant-garde. It also sponsors an outstanding education program that has helped many young musicians.

136.The description of the music is based on a live recording of the performance. (**Joe Conzo** collection)

137.The description of the session at the Chateau Madrid is based on a live recording. (**Joe Conzo** collection) Rafael Hernández did not care much for the rumba he composed, *"El Cumbanchero,"* but it became so popular that when he was invited to the White House in 1961 for a ceremony honoring the Governor of Puerto Rico, President Kennedy said to him, "How are you, Mr. Cumbanchero?" (Peerless Web Site, 2008)

138.**Pete Hamill** is a journalist and author and has written about Tito Puente and Latinos for many years. ''A long time ago, Pete Hamill told me that it was the responsibility of any American intellectual to speak Spanish, to be aware of how Hispanic this country is," said John Rockwell, director of the Lincoln Center Festival. (**Peter Watrous,** *Latin Music Is Getting A Spotlight Of Its Own*, New York Times, 1997)

139.**Miguelito Valdés** was cremated.

14. C'est Magnifique

140.Zoot Suit. The drama's narrative revolves around the Sleepy Lagoon Murder Trial but Zoot Suit is not entirely built on facts. Rather, the characters are loosely built composites of the real 38th Street Gang that became entangled in the World War II system of chaotic and circus-like structures of legal, governmental and media institutions. Twenty-two Chicano youths were arrested after the unexplainable murder of José Diaz on August 2, 1942 near the popular barrio swimming hole, the "Sleepy Lagoon." Twelve of them were sentenced to San Quentin before being release on appeal in October1944 - three found guilty of first-degree murder and nine for second-degree murder. The East Los Angeles community created the Sleepy Lagoon Defense Committee to appeal the conviction based on the injustices that occurred throughout the mass trial. As a result of the tensions and anti-Mexican sentiment created from the trial skirmishes and fights broke out in June 1943 between soldiers stationed in the city and the barrio youth. The musical, instead of becoming a docu-drama, focuses on the social relations and symbolic historical events around the trial and the riots. The main character Henry Reyna (built on the real leader of the 38th Street Gang, Henry Leyva) interacts with his environment and his psyche, the narrator El Pachuco, to build a myriad of symbolic meanings about the identity of a Chicano at this moment in time. Henry is the core of the piece and he was very difficult to trace. Zoot Suit launched the career of Edward James Olmos, and ran for over a year in a transfer to the Aquarius Theatre on Sunset Boulevard. But it quickly and dismally failed on Broadway in 1979, possibly because the New York Latino community largely is Puerto Rican and not Mexican. This important and memorable show then disappeared, perhaps regarded as difficult to produce because of its requirement for Latino actors, or the feeling that it would not appeal to a broad audience (even though the Taper production disproved that). A film version produced in 1981 starring and Daniel Valdéz (the playwright's brother, who had played Henry in the stage production as well) and Olmos brought this vivid portrayal of social injustice to movie theaters. (Joséph Tovares. Zoot Suit Riots. A Visual Production, WGBH Boston, 2001)

141.The SS Marine Tiger was a decommissioned Merchant Marine cargo vessel that transported thousands of Puerto Ricans to New York City from the late 1940s through 1955. (Websites hosted by **William Swegle** (U.S. Merchant Marines), 2008; **Victor González**, a passenger, 2008; Ariel Blondet, 2008)

142.The Shubert organization picked up the option for the play in New York and Zoot Suit opened in the Winter Garden Theater on Broadway on March 25, 1979. Critics, however, met opening night, with overwhelming negative reviews. It closed in April 29th, after 17 performances at an $800,000 loss. (Various published news reports)

143.Newport Jazz Latino 1978" live recording. (**Joe Conzo** Archive)

144.Larry Harlow, known as "el Judio Maravilloso," born Lawrence Ira Kahn comes from a family of musicians with roots in Brooklyn, New York. He is 71. Johnny Pacheco signed him to a contract at Fañia Records in 1964. He recorded more than 40 albums and is listed as producer of about 200 more for other artists that were signed to Fañia. He composed a salsa opera, *"Hommy"* and *"La Raza*

Latina-Salsa Suite." He also led campaigns for musicians' rights, paid for audit of Fañia accounting records that he claimed hid royalties, and worked to get Latin music greater recognition within the Grammy Awards structure. (**New York Times**, August 2010)

145. North American jazz aficionados first heard **Grupo Irakere** when Gold Promo Records released an album with the music of this ensemble. It had been out of Cuba briefly and Columbia taped them live at New York's Newport Festival and at Switzerland's Montreux Jazz Festival. The result was a noisy, ambitious, frenzied mixture of everything.

146.Personnel: In 1979, members included Jesús "Chucho" Valdés, piano; Enrique Plá, drums; Carlos Emilio Morales, guitar; Paquito D'Rivera, clarinet and sax; Arturo Sandoval, trumpet; Carlos Del Puerto, bass; Oscar Valdés, vocals and percussion; Carlos Averhoff, flute and sax; Jorge Varona, trumpet; Jorge Alfonso and Armando Cuervo, percussion. D'Rivera and Sandoval left 1980; (**Gold Promo Stamp Records**)

147.**Joe Quijano** produced the Tito Puente Roast. It was recorded for distribution April 30, 1979. The show was filmed at MTI Studios in NYC. Among the participants were Ray Barretto, John Edward Olmos, Raul Marrero, Ralph Mercado, Al Santiago, Roger Dawson, Federico Pagani, Catalino Rolon, José Curbelo, Cindy Rodríguez (daughter of Tito Rodríguez), Myrta Silva, Bobby Capó and many others. Joe Conzo was the co-producer. (**Tito Puente notes, Cesta Records, Inc.)**

148.**Drury, Bob & Eppolito, Lou**. *Mafia Cop*: *The Story of an Honest Cop Whose Family Was the Mob*; Simon & Schuster Adult Publishing Group; June 1992

149.**Carlos Ortiz**, born September 9, 1936, in Ponce, Puerto Rico, was a three time world boxing champion, twice in the lightweight division and once in the Jr. Welterweights.He defeated Kenny Lane, this time Ortiz retaining his world Lightweight title with a 15 round decision in San Juan. But in 1965 he went to Panama and fought yet another member of the International Boxing Hall Of Fame, Ismael Laguna who defeated him in 15 rounds to claim Ortiz's world Lightweight title. A rematch in San Juan followed, and Ortiz regained the world Lightweight title beating Laguna by a 15 round decision. On June 29, 1968 his world lightweight title to Dominican Carlos Cruz on a 15 round decision in the Dominican Republic. The rematch was schduled to be held in San Juan, but Cruz died in the Dominicana De Aviacion DC-9 crash off the Dominican Republic's Atlantic Ocean coast when he was flying to meet Ortiz, in the same plane crash that also killed most members of the Puerto Rican Women's National Volleyball team, as well as the rest of the passengers on the plane (Dominicana DC-9 air disaster). Ortiz is a member of the International Boxing Hall Of Fame. (Ring Magazine, 1980)

150.In the November 1980 re-match Durán shockingly quit. Leonard claimed that his strategy was to use speed and agility to taunt and frustrate Durán, believing it was his best chance of winning the fight. In the eighth round, Durán turned around, walked to his corner and gave up, supposedly saying the now famous words, "no más" (no more). However he claims to have actually said, "No quiero pelear con el payaso." In 2002, he was chosen by The **Ring Magazine** to be the 5th greatest fighter of the last 80 years. He held world titles at four different weights - **lightweight** (1972-79), **welterweight** (1980), **junior middleweight** (1983-84) and **middleweight** (1989). He was the second boxer to have fought in five different decades. (**Boxingfanatics.com** – 2008)

151.Concord Records was established in 1980 by **Carl Jefferson** created the **Concord Picante** imprint to provide a much-needed home for such seminal Latin jazz musicians as Cal Tjader, who released the label's first album, the GRAMMY-winning La Onda Va Bien. A quarter of a century later, the label boasts an all-star roster of Latin music legends that includes Tito Puente. (**Concord Records** Official Web Site, 2008)

152.**Desi Arnaz**, a lifelong smoker, was diagnosed with **lung cancer** in early 1986. He died several months later on **December 2, 1986,** at age 69. Two days earlier, on what would have been his and Lucille's 46th wedding anniversary (November 30), she telephoned him. They shared a few words, mostly "I love you's." She said "All right, honey. I'll talk to you later." She was, in fact, the last person to ever speak with Desi Arnaz. His death came just five days before Lucille Ball received the **Kennedy Center Honors. (Wikipedia, the free encyclopedia)**

153."*Machito: A Latin Jazz Legacy*" was released in **1987** A documentary film was produced by **Carlo Ortiz**

154.**Willie Bobo** played on innumerable sessions in New York, recording with artists like **Miles Davis, Cannonball Adderley, Herbie Hancock, Wes Montgomery, Chico Hamilton** and Sonny Stitt**.** In 1969, he moved to Los Angeles where he led jazz and Latin jazz combos, appeared on **Bill Cosby's** first comedy series (1969-1971) and short-lived 1976 variety show, and recorded on his own for Sussex, Blue Note and Columbia. One of his last appearances, only three months before his death from cancer, was at the 1983 Playboy Jazz Festival where he reunited with Mongo Santamaría for the first time in 15 years. (**All Music Guide,** Internet Service, 2009)

155.**Jorge Dalto** (1948 - 1987) was an Argentine-born jazz pianist whose version of *''This Masquerade"* with the guitarist George Benson won a Grammy Award in 1976. He was the pianist arranger on Benson's mega album *"Breezin.'"* He was one of the principal keyboardists in the fusion movement of the era. He studied piano in his home country and came to the United States in 1969. In 1973, he settled in New York, playing with Latin jazz groups such as Tito Puente's and the Machito Orchestra. He was the featured pianist on Dizzy Gillespie's *"Afro-Cuban Moods,"* in 1975. He appeared on albums of the period with artists as; Flora Purim, Spyro Gyra, Paquito D' Rivera, Djaban, Eddie Daniels, Carmen McRae, Rubén Blades among others. (**All About Jazz**, 2008)

15. Un Poco Loco

156.FOX News reported in 2003 that the fee is currently $25,000 and is often paid by sponsors such as film studios and record companies, as part of the publicity for a release with which the honoree is involved. On other occasions, the fee is paid by a fan club. Often, it is paid by the nominating person himself or herself.

157.Energetic dancer, singer, and actress Rita Moreno was born Rosa Dolores Alverio in Puerto Rico to a family of independent farmers. She moved to New York City with her mother at age five and went on to become one of the few people to win an Oscar, a Tony, an Emmy, and a Grammy throughout her long career. At age 13, she took her vibrant stage presence and star quality to Broadway, and by the next year she had made it to Hollywood, where MGM studio executives suggested she change her name to Rita. Her big breakthrough came in 1961 with her role as the spitfire Anita in "West Side Story," winning her an Oscar and a Golden Globe for Best Supporting Actress. During the 1960s, she took her talents back to the stage and got married, but she did appear in the films "Carnal Knowledge" with Jack Nicholson and "Popi" with Alan Arkin. As a mother during the '70s, she turned to television and got involved with the PBS children's series The Electric Company, which led to a Grammy award for her recording contribution to the soundtrack album. She also won Emmy awards for her work on The Rockford Files and The Muppet Show. Meanwhile, she reprised her Tony-winning Broadway role of entertainer Googie Gomez for the 1976 film version of **The Ritz**. (Answers.com – Internet)

158.**Frank John Gorshin, Jr**. (**April 5, 1933 - May 17, 2005**) was an **American actor** and **comedian**. He was perhaps best known as an **impressionist**, with many guest appearances on the *Ed Sullivan Show* and on *The Tonight Show* with host **Steve Allen**. His most famous acting role was as **The Riddler** in the "*Batman*" **live action television series**. Gorshin also played the role of New York's famous 1920s Mayor Jimmy Walker in the 1960s Broadway musical: *"Jimmy"*. **(Frank Gorshin – Official Website** – 2008**)**

159.**Sesame Street** is a copyrighted television show. Various Video clips are presented on You Tube - Internet

160.**Bravo, Sonny.** (October 7, 1936), Born Elio Osacar in New York City. Was considered an outstanding baseball prosepect but an injury in 1956 resulted in his seeking a career in music. He performed with many Afro-Cuban style orchestras most notable among them José A. Fajardo (circa 1963) and Tipica 73. He joined the Tito Puente Jazz Ensemble and Orchestra in the late 1970s.

161.**Powell, Josephine**. *When the Drums are Dreaming* – Authorhouse, 2007

162.**Joe Conzo** Archive – 2009

Index

Symbols

A

B

C

D

E

F

G

H

I

J

K

L

M

N

O

P

Q

R

S

T

U

V

W

Y

Z